BUSINESS DATA COMMUNICATIONS

BUSINESS DATA COMMUNICATIONS
Basic Concepts, Security, and Design

Fourth Edition

JERRY FITZGERALD
Jerry FitzGerald & Associates

JOHN WILEY & SONS, INC.
New York   Chichester   Brisbane   Toronto   Singapore

Wiley Series in Computers and Information Processing Systems for Business

Cover art by Marjorie Dressler

Acquisitions Editor	Beth Lang Golub
Marketing Manager	Carolyn Henderson
Production Supervisor	Marcia Craig
Designer	Laura Nicholls
Manufacturing Manager	Lorraine Fumoso
Copy Editing Supervisor	Richard Blander
Illustration	Anna Melhorn

This book was set in 10/12 pt Times Roman by Achorn Graphic Services and printed and bound by R. R. Donnelley & Sons. The cover was printed by Lehigh Press.

Recognizing the importance of preserving what has been written, it is a policy of John Wiley & Sons, Inc. to have books of enduring value published in the United States printed on acid-free paper, and we exert our best efforts to that end.

Library of Congress Cataloging in Publication Data:

FitzGerald, Jerry.
    Business data communications : basic concepts, security, and design / Jerry FitzGerald.—4th ed.
        p.   cm.
    Includes indexes.
    ISBN 0-471-54845-6 (cloth)
    1. Data transmission systems.   2. Computer networks.
3. Office practice—Automation.   I. Title.
TK5105.F577   1993
004.6—dc20
                                           92-26478
                                             CIP

10 9 8 7 6 5 4 3 2

ABOUT THE AUTHOR

Dr. Jerry FitzGerald is the principal in Jerry FitzGerald & Associates (JFA). He has extensive experience in risk analysis, computer security, audit and control of computerized systems, data communications, networks, and systems analysis. He has been active in risk assessment studies, computer security, EDP audit reviews, designing controls into applications during the new system development process, data communication networks, bank wire transfer systems, and electronic data interchange (EDI) systems. He conducts training seminars on risk analysis, control and security, and data communication networks.

Prior to starting his own firm in 1977, Dr. FitzGerald's employers were the following:

- SRI International (formerly Stanford Research Institute): Senior Management Systems Consultant
- California State Colleges and Universities: Associate Professor at both California State Polytechnic University at Pomona, California, and California State University at Hayward, California, where he taught Information Systems
- University of California: Instructor in the business school at the University of California at Berkeley and a Computer Systems Analyst at the University of California Medical Center at San Francisco
- Singer (formerly Friden): Computer Systems Analyst
- Lockheed Missiles & Space Company: Programmer

Dr. FitzGerald's education includes a Ph.D. in Business Economics and a Master's Degree in Business Economics from the Claremont Graduate School, a Master's Degree in Business Administration from the University of Santa Clara, and a Bachelor's Degree in Industrial Engineering from Michigan State University. He is a Certified Information Systems Auditor (CISA) and holds a Certificate in Data Processing (CDP). He belongs to the EDP Auditors Association (EDPAA), the Institute of Internal Auditors (IIA), and the Information Systems Security Association (ISSA).

Dr. FitzGerald's publications and software include the following: *Business Data Communications: Basic Concepts, Security and Design*, 4th edition © 1993; *Designing Controls into Computerized Systems*, 2nd edition © 1990; RANK-IT® A Risk Assessment Tool for Microcomputers; CONTROL-IT® A Control Spreadsheet Methodology for Microcomputers; *Fundamentals of Systems Analysis: Using Structured Analysis and Design*, 3rd edition; *Online Auditing Using Microcomputers* (a book and diskette containing 28 utility programs for the audit and control of PCs); *Internal Controls for Computerized Systems* (a book containing nine completed Control Spreadsheets); and over 60 articles in various publications.

ACKNOWLEDGMENTS

My thanks to the many people who contributed to the preparation of this fourth edition. First, I am indebted to the staff at John Wiley & Sons for their strong support on this project. The list of staff members includes: Beth Lang Golub, Information Systems editor; Laura Nicholls, designer; Katharine Rubin, production manager; Marcia Craig, production supervisor; Anna Melhorn, illustration coordinator; Richard Blander, editing supervisor, and Betty Pessagno, book copy editor.

Boris Starosta, an independent technical illustrator, did an excellent job of interpreting my drawings and improving on them. Achorn Graphic Services also did an excellent job of typesetting this book. Robert Orr of Purdue University spent many hours developing the Next Day Air Service cumulative case study.

Next, my special thanks to Ardra FitzGerald, who edited the original book manuscript, rewrote many areas to simplify the technical descriptions, worked on some of the original art, read the copy-edited manuscript, and developed the extensive index.

Finally, my thanks to the following companies for supplying the communication software. They include Network Dimensions for *GrafNet Plus*, SAV-NET USA for *Cost Analysis for Multiple Locations (CAML)*, Economics & Technology for *Private Line Pricer*, NMI Network Analysis Center for *MIND-Data/PC*, Network Design and Analysis for *AUTONET/MeshNet/Designer*, Triticom for the *LANVision Series*, and RSA Data Security for the RSAREF public key encryption software. Please see the last page of the Preface for the page numbers on which these software packages are discussed in the book.

Jerry FitzGerald

PREFACE

PURPOSE OF THIS BOOK

This book has two intended audiences. First and foremost, it is a university textbook with basic coverage of voice communications, data communications, and networking (see the Summary Contents on page x). There is now a chapter-by-chapter case study at the end of each chapter. Moreover, the text is accompanied by a 400-page *Instructor's Manual* and it is updated three times a year via a *newsletter*. Several software packages (mentioned at the end of this Preface) are available to educational institutions adopting this text. These packages are for drawing network configurations on a microcomputer, calculating and comparing the costs of different voice calls, calculating the price for voice grade leased circuits, optimizing and pricing a network, simulating the operation of a local area network with LAN management software, and public key encryption.

Second, this book is intended for the professional who already works in data communications and networking. The book has many detailed descriptions of the technical aspects of communications, along with illustrations where appropriate. Moreover, managerial, technical, and sales personnel can use this book because of its emphasis on technical details, individual pieces of hardware and software, and its coverage of wide area networks (WANs), metropolitan area networks (MANs), backbone networks (BNs), local area networks (LANs), and enterprise-wide networks. This book ties it all together, enabling you to begin to feel that you not only understand the individual pieces of hardware, software, and circuits, but that you also know how to configure them into the many networks we see worldwide.

The entire book is oriented toward business rather than electrical engineering and mathematics. It assumes the reader wants to learn about building and using networks, rather than designing circuit boards or other communication devices as would an electrical engineer. The mathematics of data communications has been replaced with simple English descriptions and illustrations that show technical details or how a concept works. As an example, examine Figure 6-17 on page 240 to see the difference between X.25 packet switching and frame relay.

WHAT'S NEW IN THIS EDITION

Although the basic chapter-by-chapter format has not changed, the fourth edition contains substantial changes because of new technical concepts, standards, and evolving network configurations. Throughout this edition we have defined terms carefully and used more explanatory boxes. As an example, see the boxes on pages 5 and 39. There also is a cumulative case study that begins in Chapter 1 and continues through Chapter 13.

Many changes and additions have been made to the existing sections in each chapter. Furthermore, new sections have been added on such subjects as frame relay, cell relay, fast packet multiplexing, T carriers, synchronous optical network (SONET), switched multimegabit data service (SMDS), Government Open Systems Interconnection Protocol (GOSIP), serial port (UART/USART), installing a LAN, Ethernet, 10Base-T, token-ring, token-bus, Arcnet, FDDI, LAN servers, LAN security, Simple Network Management Protocol (SNMP), Network Management System (NMS), SMT-station management for FDDI, V.32, V.42, digital channel banks and digital cross-connect switches, electronic data interchange (EDI), automatic number identification (ANI), interactive voice response (IVR), personal communication networks (PCNs), network configurations (WAN/MAN/BN/LAN), and several new software packages. These are just some of the new sections in the fourth edition. To see the entire scope and detail of this book, scan the Detailed Contents starting on page xii.

The Glossary and Acronyms section has been expanded. Moreover, a blue border has been added to the right edge of its pages to make the section easier to locate. The very extensive Index means it is easy to find anything in this book, making this a reference book as well. In addition to subject headings, the Index has numerous subheadings that will direct you more precisely to the item for which you are searching. These subheadings help you locate information quickly, without having to check numerous pages listed indiscriminately after only a main subject heading.

There are too many new illustrations to enumerate, but you might sample a couple by looking at Figure 9-2 (page 418) and 11-2 (page 510). As an example of the new *simplified technical descriptions*, read the first four paragraphs in the Bridges section beginning on page 538.

Chapter 11 on local area networks (LANs) has been almost completely rewritten. This chapter now contains enough material to teach an entire course on LANs. Moreover, if your goal is to design a LAN, Chapter 11 on LANs can be combined with Chapter 8 on network design.

Chapter 8 has been revised substantially to help teach how to design a network. It now has extensive cross references, by page number, to related technical topics. This cross referencing has been added to lead you directly to the required technical detail should a question arise during a design project. In addition, the description of each of the 13 design steps now includes a specific deliverable, more details have been added to the chapter, more circuit costs have been included, and more network drawing, pricing, and optimizing software is now available for use on microcomputers.

The following software packages are available for schools using this textbook. Each of them runs on a microcomputer.

GrafNet Plus®   This software requires Windows® to run. It is used for drawing network configurations. See the GrafNet Plus description starting on page 246 to obtain more information and to learn how to get a free copy.

Cost Analysis for Multiple Locations® (CAML)   This software is used for calculating and comparing the cost of voice calls among several types of calling plans. See the CAML description starting on page 368 to obtain more information and to learn how to get a free copy.

Private Line Pricer®   This software is used for calculating the cost of voice grade leased circuits and optimizing the circuit layout. See the Private Line Pricer description starting on page 374 to obtain more information and to learn how to get a free copy.

MIND-Data/PC®   This software is used for calculating the circuit cost of a network and optimizing the circuit layout. See the MIND-Data/PC description starting on page 381 to obtain more information and to learn how to get a free copy.

AUTONET/MeshNet® **and AUTONET/Designer**®   This software is used for calculating the circuit cost of a network and optimizing the circuit layout. See the AUTONET description starting on page 384 to obtain more information and to learn how to get a copy.

LANVision® **Series**   There actually are seven software packages in this series. They are used for managing workstations, monitoring performance, performing protocol analysis, and bridging between LANs. See the LANVision Series description starting on page 551 to obtain more information and to learn how to get a free copy.

Public Key Encryption   The RSA REFerence (RSAREF) Implementation software is available for message and digital signature authentication. See the RSA Digital Signature description beginning on page 646 to obtain more information and to learn how to get a free copy.

Jerry FitzGerald
Redwood City, California

SUMMARY CONTENTS

CONTENTS

Chapter One

INTRODUCTION TO
DATA COMMUNICATIONS

The purpose of this chapter is to introduce the concepts of data communications and to show how we have progressed from paper-based systems to modern networks. It begins by describing why it is important to study data communications and how the invention of the telephone and the computer have transformed the way we communicate. Next, a section on the purpose and scope of this book will help you adapt it to meet your specific needs. The chapter then continues with sections on the definition and uses of data communications, basic components of a data communication network, how systems evolved into today's networks, types of networks, examples of current and future networks, and telecommunication careers.

WHY STUDY DATA COMMUNICATIONS

It all started around 3300 B.C. with Sumerian clay tablets. They were the ideal way to communicate. Provided you didn't drop them! Next came Greek messengers. Your scroll would always get there—if your runner didn't collapse first. Today you can send and receive vital business information . . . in writing . . . in seconds.

The reasons for studying data communications are embodied in the occupational history of the United States. In the 1800s we were an agricultural society that was dominated by farmers. By the 1900s we had become an industrial society dominated by labor and management. Now, as we approach the twenty-first century, we clearly have moved into an information society dominated by computers, data communications, and highly skilled individuals who use brain power instead of physical power. The industrial society has reached its zenith, and the communication/computer era, dubbed the information society, is advancing rapidly.

In an industrial society, the strategic resource is *capital*. In an information society, the strategic resource is *information* that must flow on communication networks. This information society started in the mid-1950s.

Knowledge of data communications is even more important when you realize that satellites are transforming the earth into a "global village." In other words, the compression of time achieved through satellite communications allows us to be in immediate contact with all other companies or people and to use business information in a timely manner.

In an information society dominated by computers and communications, value is increased by knowledge, as well as by the speed of movement of that knowledge. This new information economy will completely destroy David Ricardo's labor theory of value[1] because in such a society information increases value, not the labor of individuals. Knowledge can be created, it can be destroyed, and it is synergetic because the whole usually is greater than the sum of the parts. In fact, the whole may be many times greater than the sum of the parts if you have the proper communication network to transmit the information. Knowledge that cannot be disseminated (transmitted) may be of zero value.

The main stream of the information age is communications. The value of a high speed data communication network that transmits information is that it brings the message sender and receiver closer together in time. As a result, we have collapsed the *information lag*, which is the time it takes for information to be disseminated throughout the world. For example, in the 1800s it might have taken several weeks for a message to reach the United States by ship from England. By the 1900s it could be transmitted within the hour. Today, with modern data communication networks, it can be transmitted within seconds. Collapsing the information lag speeds the incorporation of new technology into our daily lives. In fact, today's problem may be that we cannot handle the vast quantities of information we already have.

Finally, the transition from an industrial to an information society means you will have to learn many new technologically based skills. Instead of becoming a specialist in a certain subject and working in that area for a lifetime, you will have to adapt and possibly retrain yourself several times. For that reason, the study of data communications will become a basic tool that can be used during your entire lifetime. You will incorporate your data communication knowledge into several careers, such as circuit designer, programmer, business system application developer, communication specialist, and business manager. Even now, many of the basic job tasks of our society require technical knowledge in the use of data communications, such as citizens band radios in trucks, microcomputers in your home connected to national or international communication networks, and personal communication devices like mobile telephones (cellular radio).

In summary, collapsing the information lag may be the single most important reason for you to study communications. This is so because new communication technology is being incorporated into the fabric of the information society as fast as people can learn how to maintain and use this technology. Once you have learned

---

[1]Ricardo said it is a person's labor that adds value to goods and services.

the basics from this textbook, you will need to "keep up with communication technology" for the remainder of your life.

A BRIEF HISTORY OF COMMUNICATIONS IN THE UNITED STATES

Today we take data communications for granted, but it was early pioneers like Samuel Morse, Alexander Graham Bell, and Thomas Edison who developed the basic electrical and electronic systems that ultimately evolved into voice and data communication networks. In 1837 Samuel Morse exhibited a working telegraph system; today we might consider it the first electronic data communication system.

In 1841 a Scot by the name of Alexander Bain synchronized school clocks by using electromagnets. Two years later he patented a printing telegraph—the predecessor of today's facsimile. The earliest commercial facsimile network was established in France in 1865. Then in 1876 Alexander Graham Bell invented the first telephone capable of practical use, and it became the basis for our voice communication networks. The telephone was a remarkable improvement, for Morse's system required the operators at each end to use Morse code. This code, which became an auditory signal at the receiving end, could be interpreted into letters, which then became words, sentences, and paragraphs as the operator wrote them down on paper. Obviously, the telegraph was not going to be the most widely used method of communication.

When the telephone arrived, it was the communication device everyone wanted. In 1879 the first private manual telephone switchboard (PBX—private branch exchange) was installed. By 1880 the first pay telephone was in use, and the telephone became a way of life for Americans because they could call from public telephones.

The certificate of incorporation was registered for the American Telephone and Telegraph Company in 1885, and by 1889 AT&T had a recognized logo. This logo was in the shape of Philadelphia's Liberty Bell and had the words Long Distance Telephone written on it. By 1910 the Interstate Commerce Commission (ICC) had the authority to regulate interstate telephone business.

The first transcontinental telephone service and the first transatlantic voice connections were both established in 1915. By 1930 the cost of a three-minute telephone call from New York to London was reduced from $45 to $30. In 1934 President Roosevelt approved the Communication Act, which transferred regulation of interstate telephone traffic from the Interstate Commerce Commission to the Federal Communications Commission (FCC)

Although the transistor would seem to be more related to computers than to communications, it was invented at Bell Laboratories in 1947. The transistor is a major component in today's communication switching systems. In 1951 the first direct long distance customer dialing began. The first international satellite telephone call was sent over the Telstar satellite in 1962, and touchtone telephones were marketed in 1963. Their push buttons were easier to use than rotary dials, and they became quite popular. By 1965 there was widespread introduction of commercial international telephone service by satellite.

The famous Carterfone court decision in 1968 stated that non-Bell equipment could be connected to the Bell System network. This was an important milestone because for the first time independent modem manufacturers could connect their equipment to the Bell networks. Such connections were illegal prior to this decision.

Picturefone service, which allows users to see as well as talk with one another, began operating in 1969. All through the 1970s there were many arguments and court cases regarding the monopolistic position that AT&T held over other companies wanting to offer communication services. The litigation led to the January 1, 1984 deregulation of AT&T, which is described in Chapter 7.

During 1983 and 1984 traditional radio telephone calls were supplanted by the newer cellular telephone networks. By 1985 Bell Laboratories had invented the ballistic transistor that operates 1,000 times faster than the original transistor they invented in 1947. Digital networks began serving the public in the 1980s. These networks allow the simultaneous transmission of voice, data, and images.

By 1988 there was considerable competition in both the voice and data communication markets as a number of independent companies began selling communication services in a manner similar to automobile marketing. In the 1990s we can expect to carry smaller and less expensive portable telephones, just as we carry a calculator today. We also can expect decreasing charges for long distance calls, and the facsimile machine will continue to increase in importance.

Now that we have experienced the transition from very large computers to microcomputers, we are moving more deeply into a world composed of interconnected computers and networks. Microcomputers (also called personal computers or PCs) are ubiquitous little computers that seem to materialize in every aspect of our lives. They appear at retail stores, on the college campus, at business and governmental organizations, and in our homes. We truly are in the midst of the information revolution because we tend to computerize everything we can.

As we move closer to the end of this century, the most important area related to computers will be *networking*. This means we will be using more *wide area networks* (WANs) that span the globe, *metropolitan area networks* (MANs) that include a local metropolitan area like a city, *backbone networks* (BNs) that connect an organization's computers together, and especially *local area networks* (LANs) that interconnect the microcomputers located throughout an organization or on a college campus. See the box on Network Definitions to learn more about networks. The future of computers is very bright indeed, and it definitely includes networking. You do not have to be a computer specialist to need some knowledge about the interconnection of mainframe computers, minicomputers, and microcomputers.

This decade also is bringing forth a new employment speciality, that of the *Network Administrator*. Previously, a few people administered the organization's wide area or backbone networks. Today, and even more so in the future, the existence of local area networks means many network administrators will be required in organizations. (Incidentally, the last section in this chapter describes some universities that offer majors in data communications.) By the year 2000, it will be commonplace for individuals to have local area networks in their homes. These LANs will interconnect several computing devices (mostly personal computers), and they will be connected by telephone lines, by an optical fiber cable, or by direct satellite transmission to other networks elsewhere in the world.

NETWORK DEFINITIONS

Local Area Network (LAN)   A group of microcomputers or other workstation terminal devices located in the same general area and connected by a common cable (communication circuit) so they can exchange information. LANs are used within buildings or college campuses. They can be connected to larger backbone networks that allow message transmission around the world.

Backbone Network (BN)   A large central network in which everything within the organization is connected. It usually is a network that interconnects everything on a single company site. It also can be similar to a metropolitan area network, but for a single organization such as a company or university, in which all the terminals, microcomputers, mainframes, local area networks, and other communication equipment are connected.

Metropolitan Area Network (MAN)   A network spanning a geographical area that usually encompasses a city or county area. It interconnects various buildings or other facilities within this citywide area.

Wide Area Network (WAN)   A network spanning a large geographical area. Its nodes (microcomputers) can span cities, states, or national boundaries. This network interconnects data transmission facilities on a countrywide or worldwide basis.

PURPOSE AND SCOPE OF THIS BOOK

Data communications is a very complex subject, but this is not a complex book. Many books in this field are complex, and rightly so, because they are intended as reference sources for the experienced network designer. This book requires no prior experience in data communications, voice communications, or electronic engineering. Rather, it assumes a basic understanding of data processing and a desire to complement this background with a general knowledge of data communications. After completing a course of study based on this book, you should be able to

- Understand the available alternatives in hardware, software, and transmission facilities
- Put that understanding to work by making informed decisions among these alternatives
- Integrate these decisions into a cohesive data communication network design, and carry it forward into reality
- Understand today's technology, as well as how to remain informed
- Perform design activities for networks of increasingly greater scope and complexity as you build experience, judgment, and confidence
- Market or sell data communication products

As you read this book, you will encounter many new terms because the world of data communications has its own language. A comprehensive Glossary is included at the end of the book because it is not always possible to interrupt the presentation of complex subjects with a thorough definition of a new word. This Glossary contains both words and acronyms. The author has evaluated the text carefully to ensure that all the jargon of data communications has been included in the Glossary and that the technical details are described thoroughly. In addition, there is a very detailed Index so you can look up specific subjects you want to pursue. This Index contains both headings and subheadings to better direct you to the topic of interest.

There are many good books and periodicals on data communications. The Selected References at the end of each chapter provide a selected sample of current books, serial publications, and computerized literature resources. Before continuing, you may wish to browse through the Summary Contents in the frontmatter on page x, the Detailed Contents in the frontmatter beginning on page xii, the Glossary beginning on page 681, and the Index at the end of the book. If you spend five minutes familiarizing yourself with these four areas, it will help immensely as you read through the book.

DEFINITION OF DATA COMMUNICATIONS

Data communications is the movement of encoded information from one point to another by means of electrical or optical transmission systems. Such systems often are called *data communication networks*. This is in contrast to the broader term *telecommunications*, which includes the transmission of voice and image (graphical) as well as data. In general, these networks are established to collect data from remote points (usually terminals or microcomputers) and transmit that data to a central point equipped with a computer or another terminal, or to perform the reverse process, or some combination of the two. Data communication networks facilitate more efficient use of central computers and improve the day-to-day control of a business by providing faster information flow. They provide message switching services to allow terminals to talk to one another. In general, they offer better and more timely interchange of data among their users and bring the power of computers closer to more users. The objectives of most data communication networks are to

- Reduce the time and effort required to perform various business tasks
- Capture business data at its source
- Centralize control over business data
- Effect rapid dissemination of information
- Reduce current and future costs of doing business
- Support business expansion at reasonable incremental cost as the organization grows
- Support organizational objectives in centralizing or decentralizing computer systems
- Support improved management control of the organization

Figure 1-1 shows the flow of information in three different types of networks—those requiring real-time interaction between terminals, those designed for collecting data, and those used for retrieving information.

USES OF DATA COMMUNICATIONS

Although data communications can be used in many different situations, business operations that exhibit some of the following characteristics usually benefit the most from a data communication network.

- Widespread use of microcomputers
- Decentralized operations
- A high volume of mail, messenger service usage, or numerous telephone calls between its various sites (voice communication corridors, that is, telephone calls may be replaced by data transfer corridors)
- Repetitive paperwork operations, such as re-creating or copying information
- Inefficient and time-consuming retrieval of current business information
- Slow or untimely handling of the organization's business functions
- Inadequate control of the organization's assets
- Inadequate planning and forecasting

Figure 1-2 lists eight types of data communication systems. This figure also summarizes many important characteristics of these typical uses of data communications, giving specific application examples and typical transactions for each application. Consider the information given in the Typical Characteristics of Transactions column, and observe how these characteristics change from one usage to the next.

Also note that today's networks often combine several of the data communication usage modes shown in the left column of Figure 1-2. For example, a local area network interconnecting a firm's departments might be used for source data entry and collection, real-time interactive networking, information retrieval, conversational timesharing, and message switching. As this example demonstrates, networks today are more complex because they are used for multiple tasks.

BASIC COMPONENTS OF A COMMUNICATION NETWORK

The three basic components of a data communication network are the source, the medium, and the sink. The *source* is the originator of the message; the *medium* is the path through which the message flows; and the *sink* is the mechanism that accepts the message. In this definition, a terminal or microcomputer often alternates as both a source and a sink. The medium is nothing more than the communication

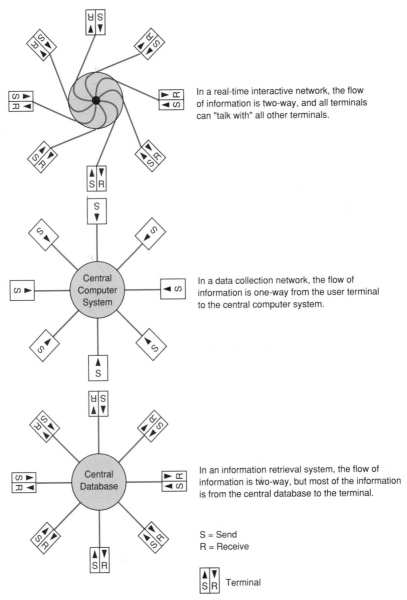

In a real-time interactive network, the flow of information is two-way, and all terminals can "talk with" all other terminals.

In a data collection network, the flow of information is one-way from the user terminal to the central computer system.

In an information retrieval system, the flow of information is two-way, but most of the information is from the central database to the terminal.

S = Send
R = Receive

Terminal

Figure 1-1 The flow of information.

line (or circuit) over which the information travels. Usually, the lines are leased from a "common carrier" such as the Bell Operating Companies, AT&T, MCI, or US Sprint, although an organization can install its own lines. A *common carrier* is a company recognized by the Federal Communications Commission (FCC) or an appropriate state licensing agency as having the right to furnish communication services to individual subscribers or business organizations.

Data Communication Usage Modes	Examples of Applications	Typical Characteristics of Transactions
Source data entry and collection	Sales status data Inventory control Payroll data gathering	Transactions collected several times per day or week; direct response message not issued for every transaction
Real-time interactive network	Point-of-sale system Airline reservations Electronic data interchange (EDI)	Transactions arrive frequently (every few seconds) and demand response within a few seconds
Remote job entry (RJE) data collection	Remote high speed reading and printing Local access to distant computer power	Transactions usually bunched and require processing times ranging from minutes to hours. Input and output for each transaction may take seconds or minutes.
Information retrieval	Credit checking Bank account status Insurance policy status Law enforcement Government social services Hospital information systems	Relatively low character volume per input transaction, response required within seconds. Output message lengths usually short but might vary widely with some types of applications.
Conversational timesharing	General problem solving Engineering design calculations Text editing	Conversational response required within a few seconds
Message switching	Company mail delivery and memo distribution	Delivery time requirements range from minutes to hours
Real-time data acquisition and process control	Numerical control of machine tools Remote meter and gauge reading	Remote sensors continuously sampled and monitored at widely varying time intervals
Interprocessor data exchange	Processor, program, and file-sharing applications of all types	Infrequent burst arrivals consisting of large data blocks requiring transmission to another CPU, usually within microseconds

Figure 1-2   Data communication usage modes.

Telecommunications and teleprocessing are other terms used to describe data transmission between a computing system and remotely located devices. The terms *data communications, telecommunications,* and *teleprocessing* can be used interchangeably. We will use data communications because of the combination of computing and communications, although the term *telecommunications* may be used for the integration of data communications, voice communications, and imaging systems, along with the use of host computers and microcomputers.

Figure 1-3 shows the basic components of a data communication network. You must have a sender, which usually is a terminal, but it also might be a microcom-

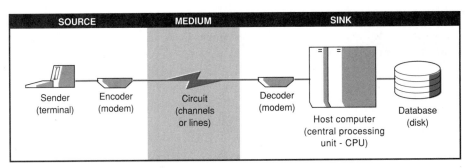

Figure 1-3 Basic components.

puter, video terminal, or other device. Once the user has entered a message, it goes to the encoder, which is called the *modem*. In this example, the modem converts the signal from its direct electrical pulses into a series of varying frequency tones. The electrical pulses that are converted are referred to as *digital*. A digital signal is discrete because it is either on or off, much like a radio on/off switch. The frequency tones into which these digital pulses are converted are referred to as *analog*. An analog signal can be likened to the volume control on a radio because it changes continuously. This encoding process puts the transmission into a mode that is compatible with the various transmission media, such as copper wire, microwave, satellite, fiber optic, or other facilities.

In Figure 1-3, these transmission media are referred to as a *circuit*. These are the telephone company circuits over which your message moves. When your message reaches the distant host computer, it first passes through the decoder, which is another modem. This modem converts the signal from analog (frequency tones) back to digital (electrical voltages). Finally, your signal (in reality your message) is passed on to the host computer for whatever processing might be required.

Figure 1-4 depicts a basic data communication network. Known as a *point-to-point network,* it connects a single microcomputer to a host mainframe computer. This simple network includes terminals, connector cables, modems, local loops, telephone company switching offices, interexchange channel (IXC) facilities, a front end processor, and a host computer.

The *terminals* or *microcomputers* are a human-to-machine interface device where people can enter and receive data or information. This device might have a video screen, printer, and keyboard. In the future this device may be voice actuated.

The *connector cable* in Figure 1-4 connects the modem to the terminal or microcomputer. The connector cable sometimes is called the *RS232 interface* because the standard that defines which signal is carried on which wire is the RS232 standard. These cables have anywhere from 9 to 25 wires in them, the number depending on their use. For example, microcomputer-to-modem cables usually have 9 wires.

The *modem* is a solid state electronic device that converts direct electrical signals (+ and − voltages of electricity) to modulated signals that can be sent over data communication circuits. The most common form of modulated signal is a frequency modulated signal where the direct electrical voltages are converted to frequency

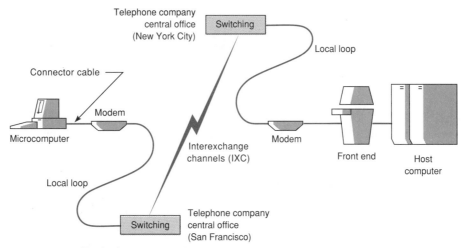

Figure 1-4   Basic data communication network.

tones. For example, a high-pitched tone might equal a binary 1 and a low-pitched tone a binary 0.

The *local loops* in Figure 1-4 are the connections or "last mile" that interconnects your home or office to the telephone company central office (switching office), or to the special common carrier network if you are using a common carrier other than the local telephone company.

The *central office* (sometimes called *end office* or *exchange office*) contains the switching and control facilities that are operated by the telephone company or other special common carrier. When you use dial-up communication circuits, your data transmission goes through these switching facilities. When you have a *private leased circuit*, however, the telephone company wires your circuit path around the switching facilities to provide a clear unbroken path from one modem to the other.

The *interexchange channels/circuits* (sometimes called *IXC circuits*) are the circuits that go from one telephone company central office to another central office. These circuits can be microwave circuits, copper wire pairs, coaxial cables, satellite circuits, optical fibers, or some other transmission medium.

The *front end processor* is a specialized minicomputer with very special software programs. These software programs, along with the front end hardware, control the entire data communication network. For example, a powerful front end processor may have 100 or more modems attached to it through its ports (circuit connect points).

Finally, the *host computer* is the central processing unit (CPU) that processes your request, performs database lookups, and carries out the data processing activities required for the business organization.

Three other definitions you should memorize are shown in the accompanying Three Important Definitions box. They will be defined in more detail in Chapter 5.

Another example of a data communication network is shown in Figure 1-5. Where Figure 1-4 showed a network that transmitted between New York City and San

THREE IMPORTANT DEFINITIONS

Asynchronous/Synchronous   In asynchronous transmission a message is sent one character at a time (character-by-character). In synchronous transmission the entire message is transmitted as one block (not character-by-character).

Full Duplex/Half Duplex/Simplex   Full duplex transmission is the sending of messages simultaneously in both directions. Half duplex transmission is the sending of messages in both directions, but in only one direction at a time. Simplex transmission is the sending of messages in one direction only.

Two-Wire/Four-Wire   Dial-up telephone lines (circuits) have two wires connecting the caller with whomever is being called. Two-wire circuits are used for half duplex transmissions. The telephone company provides a four-wire circuit when a telephone line is a private leased circuit for the exclusive use of one organization. These four-wire circuits are used for full duplex transmissions.

Francisco, this figure shows a local area network (LAN) like one that might be in a single building. This small local area network shows eight devices interconnected by a local area network cable. In this network, the messages move around the ring in one direction only. Chapter 6 (Network Configurations) contains many more pictures of various types of networks, and Chapter 11 (Local Area Networks) contains more detailed explanations on local area networks.

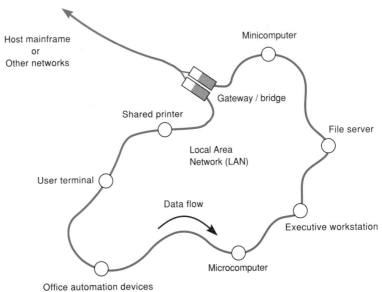

Figure 1-5   Example of a local area network (LAN).

SYSTEM PROGRESSION FROM THE 1950s TO TODAY

The natural evolution of business systems, governmental systems, and personal systems has forced the widespread use of data communication networks to interconnect these various systems.

In the 1950s we had batch systems with discrete files, and users carried their paper documents to the computer for processing. The data communications of that era involved human beings physically carrying paper documents (see Figure 1-6).

During the 1960s we added communication circuits (telephone lines) and gave online batch terminals to users who entered their own batches of data for processing. The data communication aspect involved the transmission of signals (messages) from these online batch terminals to the computer and back to the user.

During the late 1960s and into the 1970s we developed online real-time systems that moved the users from batch processing to single transaction-oriented processing where the response back to the user was required to be three seconds or less. It was during this time that data communications became a necessity.

As the 1970s progressed, we added database management systems that replaced the older discrete files. We also developed integrated systems whereby one business system automatically creates and passes transactions to some other business system. With integrated systems, the entry of an online real-time transaction might automatically trigger two or three other transactions. For example, when an online terminal user from a purchasing department enters data indicating the purchase of 100 execu-

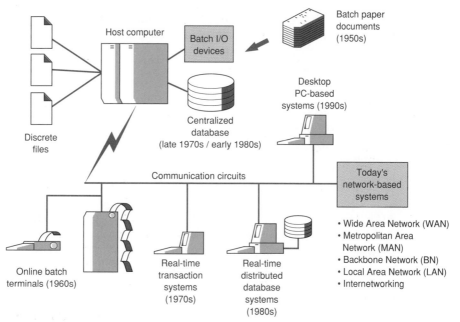

Figure 1-6 System progression.

tive desks, the system might initiate three related transactions. Transaction 1 might go to the Accounts Payable System. There it sets up the original matching file where the purchase order is matched to the invoice, which in turn is matched to the receiving dock ticket showing receipt of the goods. Transaction 2 might go to the receiving dock to prenotify them to expect 100 executive desks in two months. Transaction 3 might go to the Cash Flow Accounting System so preparations can be made to pay for (cash availability) these executive desks. As you can see, both data communications and data processing are interconnected in online real-time systems.

We are fast approaching completely distributed systems where user departments are given their own computers (microcomputers with disks) and the data communication network has to be even larger and more reliable. The office of the future that interconnects word processors, facsimile devices, copiers, teleconferencing equipment, microcomputers, mainframe host computers, and other equipment will put tremendous demands on data communication networks. In addition, local area networks will have to offer greater reliability and speed.

Finally, the ultimate in network reliability must be achieved before we move completely to distributed databases. High reliability is necessary because if one distributed site uses another distributed site's database and the communication circuit fails, it might lock up the database so no one can use it until the communication of the transaction is completed.

TYPES OF NETWORKS

The following is a reasonable application-oriented scheme for classifying networks, although you may choose to add other applications.

- Single application
- Multiple application
- Organization-wide
- Multiorganization
- Value added
- Common carriers
- International

The *single application* network is within a single corporation or government agency, and it is used for one specific purpose. For example, in banking it might be a network to handle bank balance inquiries for the automated teller machines, checking accounts, or passbook savings. An example might be a LAN.

The *multiple application* network is designed to handle many different applications that share the network and the common database and/or processing facilities. A multiple application network might be found in a manufacturing organization. This type of network might handle business systems involving raw materials inventory, production planning, the manufacturing process, finished goods inventory, sales and distribution, general ledger accounting, cash flow, accounts payable, accounts receivable, and so on. An example might be a LAN or a MAN. Refer again to the previous box on Network Definitions.

Organization-wide networks are developed by large corporations and government agencies that have many computer centers. The purpose of these networks is to interconnect the scattered centers. For example, a large government agency might have multiple computer centers around the country to keep track of agricultural data, farming patterns, crops, and acreage records. This organization-wide network would serve its users by allowing local and remote access to any of the data centers and transmission between these data centers. An example might be a MAN, WAN, or BN.

Multiorganization networks serve groups of similar corporations, such as airlines or universities. When you make airline reservations, if any leg of your trip is to be on another airline, the multiorganization reservation network handles transmission of the data to the other airline so proper reservations can be guaranteed. An example might be a WAN.

Value added networks are constructed with leased lines (circuits) and serve many customers in different geographical areas. Usually they are general purpose computer networks like the ones developed by public companies such as Telenet, Tymnet, US Sprint, or MCI. These value added carriers transmit either data or voice. Their objective is to allow large numbers of users to use their network for a fee, which is dependent on the amount of time spent on the network (voice calls) or the volume of data transmitted (data calls). In other words, they lease circuits from the telephone company and build a network. By doing so, they add value to the raw communication circuits because these circuits are now functioning networks. An example might be a WAN.

Common carriers (telephone companies) provide nationwide data networks that can be used for a set fee. You also can lease communication circuits from them to build your own network for single or multiple applications that may be either organization-wide or multiorganizational. These common carriers also offer value added networks. In addition, *special common carriers* lease communication circuits in competition with the telephone companies; therefore, the telephone company may or may not provide your circuits. An example might be a WAN or a MAN.

International networks may be single/multiple application or organization-wide/multiorganizational, and they span the globe. In other words, an international network passes over country borders. Special limitations related to the flow of information (transborder data flow controls) may be imposed on these international networks. These limitations are enacted by the government of each country. An example of an international network might be a WAN.

CURRENT AND FUTURE NETWORKS

Between now and the year 2000, data communications will grow faster and become more important than computer processing itself. Both go hand in hand, but we have moved from the computer era to the communication era.

Systems based on communications can be found in virtually every segment of industry. For example:

- Online passenger reservation systems like American Airlines' SABRE and United Airlines' APOLLO have revolutionized the travel industry. They have helped increase these carriers' market shares by as much as 20 percent. Large car rental and hotel chains could not function effectively without their reservation systems.

- Overnight delivery industry leader Federal Express Corporation has the COSMOS parcel tracking system. COSMOS enables online inquiry of parcel status from remote locations, locates delayed shipments, and sends invoices to customers automatically. The Federal Express delivery vans even carry onboard terminals.

- The American Hospital Supply Corporation became a networking pioneer when it installed the health care industry's first order-entry terminals in hospitals. The ASAP system's success is legendary, and competitors still are trying to catch up.

- The Cirrus banking network covers 46 states. Its 1,425 member banks process some 200 million transactions annually and provide such services as cash withdrawals and balance inquiries from checking, savings, and credit accounts. Other services include direct debit retail point-of-sale transactions and international currency conversions from Cirrus' automated teller machines.

Technological developments are primarily responsible for the enormous increase in the use of communication networks. The two primary technological factors are size and speed. First, the size of electronic components (microprocessor circuits) is decreasing dramatically as circuit density increases. For example, in 1959 one megabyte (1 million bytes) of memory required a space equal to the size of a room 7 feet square by 8 feet high. Today the same amount of memory requires only about one-quarter cubic inch of space. Moreover, in 1959 one megabyte of memory cost about $25,000. Today that same megabyte costs about $50.

Second, the speed of microprocessor chips used in data communications has increased by many magnitudes. We are on the threshold of using a totally new type of transistor. This *ballistic transistor* switches 1,000 times faster than the transistors used in today's communication switches and microcomputers. The fastest bipolar transistor switches on and off 140 billion times a second.

Superconductors will have a major impact on future data communication circuits. Experiments have shown that superconductors can transmit data at extremely high rates and have the potential to become the building blocks for a new generation of faster communications. Superconductors are materials that conduct elecricity without resistance. Based on an assumption that the temperature at which a material becomes a superconductor can continue to be raised, experiments have proven that superconductors will have the ability to transmit data as much as 100 times faster than optical fibers.

Advanced 16-megabit chip technology has resulted in dramatic performance enhancements and increased storage capacity. The high speed chip's dynamic random access memory (DRAM) takes only 80 nanoseconds (billionths of a second) to access stored data. At this speed, coupled with its fastest rate of data flow, this single chip can "read" a 2,200-page document in only one second.

With regard to speed, it was only about 15 years ago that we were first able to transmit at 9600 bits per second (bps) on a standard telephone circuit. Using various digital technologies, we now can transmit at 64,000 bits per second on the same telephone circuit, and with the use of fiber optics it is quite easy to transmit at millions of bits per second. In the future we will transmit at billions of bits per second with fiber optics.

There are many exciting prospects ahead with regard to communications. Some of these prospects will be discussed in the following paragraphs.

Electronic Data Interchange (EDI)   *Electronic data interchange* is the paperless transmission between companies of orders, invoices, and other business documents. It truly is the biggest step toward the paperless office. Companies using EDI have networks interconnecting their microcomputers and computer systems to those at other companies. These connections allow them to initiate transactions electronically and then transmit the transactions to another company where they can be viewed on a microcomputer's video screen or printed if necessary.

An EDI message has two parts called *envelopes*. First is an outside envelope, which contains the interchange control information for addressing the message. Like the paper envelope you use to mail a letter, this is the electronic envelope required to transmit the message. Second is an inside envelope, which contains header information, the actual data being transmitted (such as an order), signature authentication encryption, and error detection and correction information.

EDI improves efficiency and productivity, as well as reducing the number of times human operators have to handle and process documents. On the other hand, it creates a whole new set of legal problems. The biggest problem is the legal liability of an electronically transmitted document. Historically, a paper document with an official signature has been the primary piece of evidence with regard to the legal authority concerning an order or other business contract. According to historical precedent, the paper document with the proper authorized signature is the "authentication" that an order was placed. Today, business appears to be moving toward public key encryption for authenticating electronic data interchange documents. Public key encryption is discussed in Chapter 13 starting on page 643.

The networking technology is available today to implement EDI. The most difficult tasks in making EDI a reality are the agreements among different companies located in different countries as to how they will exchange and format the documents, and the legal questions over the authentication of signatures required on electronically transmitted documents. As with other complicated technologies, there must be standards for them to work effectively. In the United States, the EDI standard is known as ANSI X.12. An international standard called EDI for Administration, Commerce, and Transport (EDIFACT) is being developed.

Voice/Data   Equipment that combines voice transmission and data transmission over a single communication circuit is already available. Combining these would be very

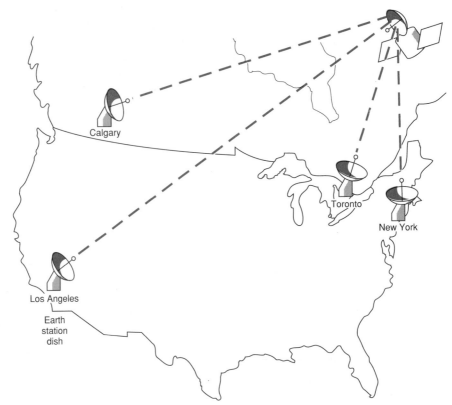

Figure 1-7   International information flow.

cost effective in most governmental and private business organizations because much higher circuit usage could be achieved at reduced costs. Approximately three quarters of today's communication costs are for voice, and one quarter are for data transmission.

The normal voice telephone systems can have *store and forward* capability for voice information. In other words, if you call someone who is not present, the telephone system accepts your voice message and forwards it later to the person when he or she calls in. The system can even try repeatedly to contact the person until the telephone is answered and your stored message is delivered.

Satellite   With *home satellite TV* you will be able to communicate directly with other people via the satellite dish located on the roof of your house. This satellite dish antenna might lead you to transmit either voice or data directly from your house in the United States to someone else's house in Canada or England (see Figure 1-7).

Such use of satellites by individuals leads to widespread possibilities with regard to the freedom and flow of information and ideas. Because the borders of a country may no longer be closed to the free flow of data, information, and ideas, people around the world may become more politically aware.

The world witnessed the reality of satellite communications during two recent events: Desert Storm and the failed coup in the Commonwealth of Independent States (formerly the USSR) when hard-line Communists tried to overthrow Mikhail Gorbachev. During both events news reporters used small portable satellite dishes to transmit their news stories from on-the-scene and in real time. In the first event, everyone saw a Cable News Network (CNN) reporter in Baghdad transmitting pictures of the incoming American missiles going by his hotel room window. Later they saw the U.N. inspection team try to obtain Iraqi nuclear, chemical, and biological weapon information as required by the cease-fire agreement. The world saw at first hand how this U.N. team was treated. In the second event, both individual Soviet citizens and other people worldwide were able to witness the fall of the Communist leaders and the rise of democracy. Earlier, the world witnessed the tearing down of the Berlin Wall and the merging of East and West Germany. These on-the-scene, real-time news reports have all been possible because of satellite technology.

Videotex   *Videotex* is the two-way transmission between a television set in your home and organizations outside your home. It allows you to carry on a two-way dialogue with a doctor, take courses in your home, provide security services for your house, review information retrieval databases, perform teleshopping from your local store, conduct teleconferences (picture and voice) from your home, play video games, have access to community meetings, view first-run movies, interconnect with satellite television programming, use electronic mail message networks, connect with your bank, review the most current news stories, or use voice store and forward message systems. Canada already has videotex (called Telidon there), as do England and France, but it has not been accepted by the public in the United States.

Audiotex   *Audiotex* is a service in which you dial a telephone number and get connected to a system that provides a voice recording. A simple example of audiotex is an answering machine. More complex systems consist of interactive audiotex services where, instead of just playing a recorded message, the interactive audiotex allows callers to pick a topic on which they want more information. Current area code 900 telephone numbers allow callers to pick topics, such as information about today's horoscope, the weather, or an update on current sporting events.

Smart Buildings   Today's intelligent buildings permit the tenants or managers to make various changes without making any physical changes to the physical components of the building. Older buildings have electrical wiring for 120-volt electric current. Newer buildings, on the other hand, contain wiring for all sorts of uses, such as electricity, data communications, voice communications, image processing, and the many control systems required in large office buildings. A *smart building* consists of many automated systems and their associated electrical and network wiring. Smart building systems that are interconnected by networks include basic controls such as those for heating, ventilation, and air conditioning. Furthermore, they also control lighting, fire, safety features, security, electrical power regulation, escalators, elevators, and any other information pathways used by microcomputers or other network computers. Today's smart buildings are already wired for local area networks by using either, or both, coaxial cable or fiber optic cables.

Transborder Data Flow   Many countries today restrict the flow or movement of data across their national boundaries. The United States is probably the most open with regard to the flow of information into and out of the country. Even the United States, however, limits *transborder data flow* by restricting the sale or delivery of some technological equipment or information to countries that are viewed as less than friendly.

Canada requires the initial processing of all bank transactions to be done in Canada, and foreign networks can cross the border only at one crossing point. Canada's Banking Act prevents the processing of bank transactions outside Canadian boundaries unless some processing also is performed within the country. Transmitting financial data outside the country, or subsequent manipulation of that data, requires government approval. Germany requires significant local processing of all data transmitted over communication circuits (private or public telephone facilities). Brazil requires corporations to maintain copies of most computer databases inside Brazil, rather than connecting with existing databases outside the country. Most offshore processing of Brazilian data is prohibited. When possible, companies must purchase Brazilian computer equipment and software rather than import it. France is considering taxing data. Sweden has a data inspection board that must approve the export of data files or the transmission of personal data out of Sweden. In England secret encryption keys must be shared with the postal and telegraph service. Belgium and France have imposed up to a $400,000 fine for transmitting data defined as sensitive. Spain requires that money be deposited in an escrow account before data files can be transmitted out of the country. Such data protection laws are a type of tariff or duty on the free flow of information.

A preliminary agreement between the United States and the European countries represented by the Organization for Economic Cooperation and Development (OECD) has led to a policy declaration on transborder data flow. This declaration states that it is the intent of the 24 OECD member countries and the United States to "promote access to data and information and related services, avoid the creation of unjustified barriers to the international exchange of data and information, and seek transparency in regulations and policies related to information, computer, and communication services affecting transborder data flow." This policy may help ease the free transfer of information between countries, although there still are political and economic barriers, and the licensed common carriers selling communication services sometimes look out for their own special interests first.

Data Monopoly   In addition to transborder data flow, it also is possible to have an intercompany data flow problem within a single country. In this situation the question is that of a *data monopoly* within a specific country. For example, the U.S. Department of Justice monitors computerized airline reservation systems as a form of data monopoly. The Department has stated that it may seek divestiture of the highly successful airline reservation systems from the airlines that own them. It claims that the United Airlines and American Airlines reservation systems are used to monopolize the sales of airline flights. It contends that these two air carriers tend to get most of the reservations because most travel agencies use one of these two reservation systems. If travel agents have to scroll or page through many different screens to locate competing carrier flights, then they may be more likely to select those flights that are easy to access.

On the international scene, three U.S. airlines filed a complaint with the Department of Transportation charging that the Lufthansa Airlines reservation system is biased. The complaint alleges that the flights of U.S. carriers are relegated to the third and fourth screens, if they are shown at all. The three U.S. airlines claim to be losing millions of dollars in annual revenues because of the bias built into the Lufthansa reservation system.

These may be the world's first legal issues involving a data monopoly in our information-based society. A monopoly usually involves goods or services, but in this situation it is claimed that basic information is monopolized to enhance one business to the detriment of others. This issue should be watched as a trend for the future. How many other industries or businesses can enhance their own economics through a data monopoly? Do we have the proper laws to address this issue?

As we enter the next century, we are moving from the manufacturing/management era to the information era in which information is the single most valuable resource of an enterprise. Information may become more important than management structure, manufacturing ability, or financial capabilities. Thus, a country that restricts information most likely will slow its economic growth, thereby lowering the standard of living for all its citizens.

Encryption More encryption will be used on data communication circuits. *Encryption* is the method of encoding data to make it secret during transmission. Encryption on public networks will become standard, as will Forward Error Correction (FEC). *Forward error correction* is the process of automatically correcting most circuit-originated transmission errors without retransmitting the message that contains the error.

Public Networks *Public networks* will have "standard interfaces" to connect almost any terminal to anything. In other words, any terminal or microcomputer will be able to communicate with any other terminal or microcomputer on the public network.

Along with more satellites to make better use of television news, we may even have citizens band radio via satellite. The laws will be changed to encourage satellites, and governments (for economic reasons) will create a good data communication environment within their countries.

More companies will purchase their own computer-based private telephone systems for internal use. They will interconnect with the rest of the world through rooftop antennas that transmit via satellite.

Another way these companies will transmit to the rest of the world may be through cellular radio local loops. With cellular radio, radio transmission towers are placed in strategic locations throughout a city. The messages from companies or private homes are transmitted over the airways as radio frequency transmissions to these towers. The towers then connect to land-based communication circuits, microwave circuits, or satellite transmission systems for the long haul (interexchange channel—IXC) transmission of voice and data. Cellular radio local loops would replace the copper wire local loops that you see now. In other words, cellular radio towers would both augment and replace telephone lines that currently use telephone poles or underground copper wire cables.

Optical Disks   One of the major requirements for adequate data communications in business systems is a large document storage and retrieval system for information contained in business documents and for archival storage of documents, market data, books, television shows, movies, local news, and the like. We are on the verge of mass data storage on *optical disks,* such as you see today for recorded movies. Forecasters predict that optical disks will cost about $10 each in the future.

If you stacked optical disks (similar to the way records are stacked in juke boxes), you could store the entire contents of the U.S. National Archives on only 1,000 12-inch disks. These disks are a "write-once" medium so you have security in the knowledge that no one can modify your data. Optical disks have approximately a ten-year life.

There are optical disks that can be erased and rewritten. Today's prototypes are very costly, but when the manufacturing bugs are worked out, they should become quite popular. One of the prototypes squeezes reams of data, sound, pictures, or computer information into a 5¼-inch optical disk. This erasable optical disk can hold as much data as 250 5¼-inch floppy diskettes. For recording, a high power writing laser quickly warms a tiny area on the disk's magnetic surface, causing the magnetized molecules to align with the magnet below. On playback, a filtered, low power laser beam strikes these molecules and is altered slightly as it bounces off the disk. The reflected light then is converted into an electronic signal that can be displayed on a computer screen or fed into a network. For erasing, the laser reheats the area more slowly so it has time to recrystallize gently and take on a neutral characteristic.

Teleports   One emerging concept is the *teleport.* This is a large, flexible satellite communication dish antenna that uses data transmission frequencies not used in terrestrial communications. This is a promising development because teleports can operate in microwave-congested metropolitan areas. These earth stations are connected with multiple fiber optic cables, coaxial cables, and microwave links to locations throughout the metropolitan area they serve. Teleports usually are constructed by companies that are independent of the telephone companies. The earth station dishes shown in Figure 1-7 are examples of teleports.

A teleport is an urban communication gateway that provides efficient and economical communication services to long distance users. By having these earth stations closer to urban areas, telecommunication customers receive reliable and economic service. Today's teleport earth station (major hub) ranges in size from 20 to 40 feet in diameter, but each year new technology provides smaller antennas with the same reliability as the older, larger antennas. Teleport transmission rates range from 56,000 bits per second to 2,048,000 bits per second or higher. Furthermore, all-digital bit streams avoid the need for analog-to-digital conversion and, consequently, ensure an almost error-free signal.

About two dozen teleports currently operate in the United States. Operating teleports are located in Atlanta, Chicago, Dallas/Ft. Worth, Houston, Washington, D.C., Ocala (Florida), Carteret (New Jersey), Raleigh (North Carolina), Seattle, Los Angeles, San Francisco, and New York City. In larger cities the distribution area from the teleport is sometimes as far as 250 miles. This means that there are high speed, terrestrial-based communication links from the teleport out to customers who may be as far as 250 miles away from the teleport itself. At the New York teleport, businesses are linked to the facility via a fiber optic cable network that has been placed throughout the metropolitan New York area. Communications Satellite Corporation (COMSAT) operates international earth station teleports in New York, Chicago, San Francisco, Houston, and Washington, D.C. These international earth stations offer business customers access to international satellites. Numerous other countries also are setting up international teleport earth stations.

Telecommuting Another emerging trend is *telecommuting* in which employees perform some or all of their work within the home instead of going to the office each day. If you were the telecommuter, some benefits might be less time wasted in commuting to work, improved quality of life, optimized scheduling of both your work and personal life, monetary savings on both clothes and travel, less stress, greater time flexibility, and a higher level of concentration at home because of fewer distractions.

One key area in which telecommuting helps is for "at-home" diagnoses of data processing or data communication problems. This is true especially for after-hours work. In an emergency in which a technician has to communicate with the mainframe, telecommuting is much quicker than a long drive by automobile.

CATV (Cable TV) The cable television companies will be increasing their role for two-way communications into and out of homes. They are in direct competition with rooftop satellite antennas and the major television networks. These cable TV companies and common carrier data communication businesses may merge into a business cable for the private, commercial, and government markets. This communication pipeline into your home, via both the telephone system and cable TV, is a critical issue because of privacy and security considerations. As an individual consumer, you will need to secure extra privacy for your data and your life. For example, if you use cable TV, someone might determine which television shows you watch in order to build a personality profile. In addition, the TV company could keep track of your purchases, financial transactions, and anything else that is received or transmitted on the cable hooked to your television. Personal privacy may be a concern here.

As the term implies, cable TV traditionally operates over a coaxial cable. This may change as cable television converts to optical fiber technology. The use of optical fiber will allow cable firms to offer more television channels, interactive television where the user interacts to do such things as play video games supplied by the cable company, and a large selection of movies from which the user chooses.

Teleconferencing Did you know that every day 20 million meetings are held in the United States and that more than three quarters of these meetings last less than 30 minutes? Over one half of all meetings can be handled by voice communications only, one third of all meetings are for the exchange of information only, and almost 90 percent of U.S. air travel is for business. For these reasons you will see a distinct increase in video *teleconferencing*. With teleconferencing, people from diverse geographic locations can "attend" a business meeting in both voice and picture format. In fact, even documents can be shown and copied at any of the remote locations.

Communications will be enhanced further with the availability of integrated circuit chips containing over 1 million components per chip. These chips will encourage hardware solutions (firmware) to current software problems. This capability will increase both the speed and reliability of data communication networks. The chips, which currently allow you to have a video screen, will give you an entire wall as your picture screen and some day an entire holographic wall for your data pictures. Early in the twenty-first century virtually no paper will be stored in business communications. Everything will be stored with microchips and large-scale memory devices or optical disks.

Digital Termination Systems (DTS) The use of a *digital termination system* provides a way to bypass the telephone company local loop or "last mile" between a user application and long haul digital transmission (IXC) facilities. Digital termination systems are sets of technology and service options that might include microwave, cable TV, telephone company wire pairs, infrared, digital radio broadcast (cellular radio), optical fiber, and rooftop antenna satellite services.

Electronic/Voice Mail Both electronic mail and voice mail will grow quite rapidly. *Electronic mail* will grow primarily in the business sector and between the homes of individuals owning microcomputers. *Voice mail* will grow as more special common carriers and telephone companies offer voice store and forward systems and as more organizations put voice mail software on their networks.

We are living in an era that is controlled, and soon will be dominated, by data communications. If you think the computer has had an impact on your life or your lifestyle, then you might be surprised, when you look back, to try to determine the changes that were brought about because of data communications. The ultimate in data communications has been a standard part of the television series "Star Trek," where they use a "transporter" to beam people down from space ships to various planets. While this is science fiction today, it might not be science fiction in the twenty-first century. Chapter 2 discusses voice mail and Chapter 7 discusses electronic mail (E-mail).

TELECOM CAREERS

In an isolated village far above the Arctic Circle, a young Eskimo intently studies a computer screen filled with data, generated as part of a University of Alaska business course delivered entirely by data communications. When she finishes the lesson, the student takes a test that is scored within seconds by a computer 1,000 miles away in Anchorage. When she needs to do library research, she turns to an electronic card catalog to find the books she needs.

In the remote Outback of Australia, a student has difficulty tuning out the static during a two-way radio transmission that is used for the Australian "School of the Air." The two Northern Territory schools at Alice Springs and Katherine provide correspondence course radio lessons with weekly problem solving and communications with the teacher. Once a year the teacher actually visits the students who live in these remote Outback cattle or sheep stations.

You have seen how communications have affected your own education, but these are two other examples of the widespread use of communications in education. Beyond the use of communications as an educational tool, numerous career opportunities are available in both corporations and government agencies. At a time when doctors, lawyers, dentists, accountants, and MBAs are in good supply, jobs for telecommunication managers abound. The need for qualified managers in the telecommunication industry is urgent and growing. It is estimated that the industry will create 100,000 new management jobs. The demand is acute for two reasons. First, technological innovations have created rapidly changing new products, and, second, deregulation has paved the way for new suppliers of communication hardware and software.

A selected example of some of the universities offering telecommunication degrees are

University of Colorado	Two-year Master of Science degree program for full-time students
Ohio University	Bachelor degree in Communication Systems Management aimed at the technical aspects of voice, data, and image communications
University of Pittsburgh	Master of Science in Telecommunications, including network concepts and legal and regulatory issues
Texas A&M University	Bachelor degree in Engineering Science emphasizing telecommunications slanted toward the technical aspects of communications
Golden Gate University	Bachelor of Science, Master of Science, and Master of Business Administration in Telecommunication Management

For a comprehensive list of telecommunication programs, contact the Manager of Education for the International Communications Association at 1-214-233-3889. Their list describes 54 graduate programs, 35 undergraduate programs, and 108 associate certificate and vocational-technical programs.

If you choose a career in telecommunications, remember that this function is a major support service for the way a company conducts its business operations. In other words, communications are changing the way both private companies and government agencies conduct their basic business functions. For this reason, it is desirable to have a basic background in general business subjects, such as finance, marketing, economics, and accounting, to go along with your data processing and communications knowledge. A career in telecommunications will be a very salable item at least through the year 2000. Today people with three or four years of experience make annual salaries of $45,000 to $75,000. Telecommunications is a stronger job market than general data processing.

KEY TERMS

Analog
Asynchronous
Backbone network (BN)
Cable television (CATV)
Central office
Circuit
Common carrier
Connector cable
Data communications
Data monopoly
Digital
Digital termination system (DTS)
Electronic data interchange (EDI)
Electronic mail (E-mail)
Encryption
End office
Exchange office
Four-wire
Front end processor (FEP)

Full duplex (FDX)
Half duplex (HDX)
Host computer
Interexchange channel (IXC)
International network
Local area network (LAN)
Local loop
Medium
Metropolitan area network (MAN)
Microcomputer
Modem
Multiorganization network
Multiple application network
Network Administrator
Networking
Organization-wide network
Point-to-point network

Private leased circuit
Satellite
Simplex
Single application network
Sink
Source
Synchronous
Telecommunications
Telecommuting
Teleconferencing
Teleport
Teleprocessing
Terminal
Transborder data flow
Two-wire
Value added network (VAN)
Voice mail
Wide area network (WAN)

SELECTED REFERENCES

1. Becker, Pat. "LANs Around the World," *LAN Magazine,* vol. 7, no. 4, April 1992, pp. 36–37, 39–40, 42. [Discusses the problems of worldwide networking.]

2. Heller, Martha. "Present and Future Perfect," *LAN Magazine,* vol. 6, no. 10, October 1991, pp. 155, 157, 159–160, 162, 164. [A case study describing the Yale University network.]

3. Herman, Barbara, and Tracey Tucker. "Telecomm People of '91," *Teleconnect,* vol. 9, no. 12, December 1991, pp. 58–59, 62–64, 66–68, 71, 74–77. [Gives insight as to why some telecommunication managers are successful.]

4. Johnson, Johna Till. "Videoconferencing," *Data Communications,* vol. 20, no. 15, November 1991, pp. 66–68, 70, 72, 80, 82, 84, 86, 88. [Discusses the present and future of videoconferencing.]

5. Martin, James. *Telecommunications and the Computer,* 3rd ed. Englewood Cliffs, N.J.: Prentice Hall, 1990.

6. Rowe, Stanford H., II. *Telecommunications,* 2nd ed. New York: Macmillan Publishing Co., 1991.

7. *Scientific American,* vol. 265, no. 3, September 1991. [Special issue devoted to communications, computers, and networks.]

8. Stallings, William. *Business Data Communications.* New York: Macmillan Publishing Co., 1990.

9. Stamper, David A. *Business Data Communications,* 3rd ed. Redwood City, Calif.: Benjamin/Cummings Publishing Co., 1991.

10. Wright, Benjamin. *Law of Electronic Commerce: EDI, Fax, and E-Mail: Technology, Proof, and Liability.* Boston: Little, Brown & Co., 1991.

COMPUTERIZED LITERATURE RESOURCES

Computers have had a major impact on libraries and methods of locating printed information. One approach to locating printed information is to use subject-oriented indexes, but many people feel that using these indexes is too time consuming and tedious. Because of advances in computerized database technology, many of the indexes that can be found in libraries or information centers can be accessed via terminals. In addition, some indexes are available *only* in a computerized format.

The following indexes are available in a number of systems, among them DIALOG (a Knight-Ridder company), ORBIT Information Technologies, and BRS (Bibliographic Retrieval Services). These systems may have just a few indexes, or they may have hundreds of indexes with millions of references. Examples of online databases that may be of interest to data communication educators and professionals are outlined below. Contact your librarian for assistance in using these valuable resources.

Abstracted Business Information.   Available only in computerized form. References articles related to the business aspects of data communications such as managing in a data communication environment. Provides bibliographic information and abstracts. 1971– .

Books in Print.   Lists books, symposia, and other monographs sold by U.S. publishers. Excellent for learning what books are available in a particular field. The paper version is indexed by author, title, and subject. The computerized version is useful because terms can be used for which adequate subject indexing is unavailable, as when a subject is either very narrow or an emerging topic. 1948– .

COMPENDEX (COMPuterized ENgineering InDEX).   Emphasizes the engineering aspects of data communications. It is useful for determining how others have applied data communications in an industrial or factory-type situation such as an industrial control application. Includes international journals, technical symposia, reports, government documents, and so on. Provides bibliographic citations and abstracts. 1970– .

INSPEC.   The printed counterparts of this computerized index are *Physics Abstracts, Electrical and Electronics Abstracts,* and *Computer and Control Abstracts.* Because computers are an integral part of data communications, the *Computer and Control Abstracts* portion of this database is an excellent resource. Includes the technical aspects of applications, techniques, hardware, software, technological developments, architectures, economics, and the practical aspects of implementing such systems. References are international in scope with abstracts. 1969– .

PROMT and *Funk and Scott Index.*   These complementary indexes share the same database. *PROMT* abstracts marketing-oriented articles that discuss products, processes, and services for sale. Indexing is by product, country or state, and "event" (for example, sales, new product/process, demand, profits, cost per unit, industry structure/members, regulatory actions). Citations are brief, but abstracts are informative. The *Funk and Scott Index* has no abstracts; it is an index to the same references cited in *PROMT,* plus others that are too short to abstract (for example, a one-line announcement that one firm has contracted with another for a specific product and a specified dollar amount). Items are international in scope and include journals, trade literature, government documents, and so forth. They focus on data communication equipment, networks, office automation, and telecommunications. 1972– .

Ulrich's International Periodicals Directory.   A guide to journals published in all countries. Provides the name of the journal, publisher information, publication frequency, price, and whether the journal includes such items as advertisements or illustrations. Arranged and indexed by subject. An excellent way to locate journals in a specific field such as computers. The computerized version enhances retrieval because one can obtain the titles of all journals with a specific word in the title. 1932– .

QUESTIONS/PROBLEMS

1. What agency of the U.S. government is responsible for regulating interstate telephone business?

2. What type of network allows the simultaneous transmission of voice, data, and video images?

3. In data communication systems a _____ is transmitted from the source to the sink.

4. What are the electrical pulses that are converted for transmission called?

5. The frequency tones that are transmitted are called _____ .

6. Define superconductor and state its importance.

7. A _____ is an urban communication gateway that provides cost-effective communication services to long distance users.

8. A _____ bypasses the telephone company local loop.

9. Can a microcomputer be both a source and a sink?

10. What is the value of information that cannot be transmitted?

11. In an information-based society, the _____ resource is knowledge that creates information.

12. Write your definition of the term *data communications* and compare it with the definition given in the Glossary.

13. Define four or five uses of data communications.

14. If the typical characteristics of a transaction are "relatively low character volume per input transaction, response required within seconds, output message lengths usually short but might vary widely with some types of applications," then identify some examples of business applications that might use an information retrieval type of network.

15. What is the difference between data communications and telecommunications or teleprocessing?

16. What is a circuit?

17. Compare the definition of local loop in Chapter 1 with that in the Glossary. Next, look at Figure 1-4 and be sure you understand the concepts of local loop and central office. Write down these definitions because you will use them repeatedly. Notice how the Glossary can help.

18. Define the progression of systems from the 1950s to the present.

19. Is it possible for a large business organization to have a combination of all seven categories of networks that were described in this chapter?

20. What types of companies can be classified as common carriers?

21. How might transborder data flow restrictions affect a university?

22. Present the issue of data monopoly to an economics instructor and relate his or her comments to your data communication class.

23. Identify the closest college or university offering a degree in telecommunications or data communications.

24. Why would transborder data flow restrictions hamper business?

25. Describe the most recent data communication development you have read about in a newspaper or other periodical.

26. In the business world there are many examples of the source/medium/sink relationship shown in Figure 1-3. Take at least one entry from the Examples of Applications column of Figure 1-2 for three usage modes and identify some of the source/medium/sink relationships that apply.

27. The Uses of Data Communications section in this chapter lists the characteristics of organizations that can benefit from data communication systems. Examine these characteristics and identify who or what function in the organization will benefit and describe how.

28. After completing a course of study based on this textbook, what should you be able to do?

29. Define information lag and discuss its importance.

30. As we approach the year 2000, what will be the most important area related to computers?

31. What is a new employment speciality necessitated by the introduction of LANs?

32. How do LANs differ from MANs, WANs, and BNs?

33. Describe a point-to-point network.

34. Describe electronic data interchange.

35. What makes it so difficult to implement EDI?

36. What is audiotex?

37. What is a smart building?

38. How does videotex differ from audiotex?

NEXT DAY AIR SERVICE CUMULATIVE CASE STUDY

This is the beginning of a cumulative case study about a fictitious firm we call Next Day Air Service. The case study begins here in Chapter 1 and continues through Chapter 13. It does not have one final "unique" solution because there are too many alternatives when dealing with WANs, MANs, BNs, and LANs and real-life network design can have several workable answers. Instead, it requires you to complete tasks that are related to topics covered in each chapter. If there is an ambiguous or unresolved question at any time, add your own assumptions. The end of each chapter contains the case narrative, related figures, and a set of questions/problems.

Introduction to Next Day Air Service

The Next Day Air Service (NDAS) firm was founded in 1985 to compete in the expanding market for overnight package deliveries. Next Day Air Service provides local pickup and delivery of these parcels, as well as other small freight items. The founders initially restricted their efforts to the rapidly growing Central Florida region.

To support its operation, Next Day Air Service purchased a facility near the Tampa International Airport. This facility consisted of a main building and a secondary building for dispatch and fleet maintenance. Because Next Day Air Service intended to expand its services throughout the Southeastern United States, this facility also served as NDAS's corporate headquarters.

From 1985 to 1990, Next Day Air Service experienced very rapid growth. As business volume increased and the company's reputation became firmly established, facility expansion became imperative. Consequently, NDAS purchased land adjacent to its corporate headquarters so it would have room to relocate both the maintenance shop and the company's vehicle parking lot. In addition, Next Day Air Service tripled the size of its building to accommodate its growing business. Finally, in 1992 Next Day Air Service completed the expansion of the office building to house its corporate operations.

With its business volume increasing, NDAS realized it would have to develop branch offices throughout its service region if it were to continue its current growth pattern. In addition to the corporate offices in Tampa, NDAS also purchased or leased facilities in several other Southeastern cities, including Orlando, Miami, Atlanta, New Orleans, Dallas, and Memphis. Figure 1-8 shows the Next Day Air Service map of operations.

Next Day Air Service also contracted with the Chicago-based firm of Overnight Delivery, Inc. (ODI) to provide overnight shipping service between Atlanta and the Greater Chicago Area. Moreover, NDAS also entered into agreements with other air carriers similar to the one it made with ODI. The purpose

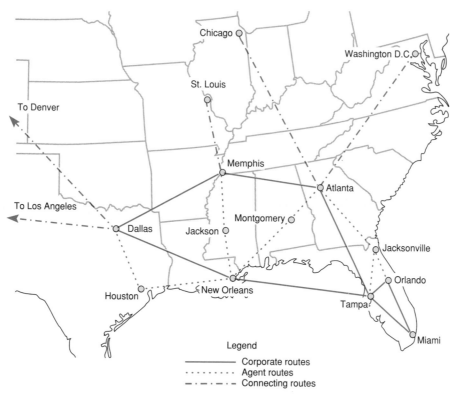

Figure 1-8   Next Day Air Service map of operations.

of these agreements was to enable NDAS to provide service throughout the United States. As Figure 1-8 shows, connecting routes established with other carriers lead from Memphis to St. Louis and from Atlanta to Chicago and Washington, D.C. These routes allow NDAS to deliver parcels to the Northeast and Midwest. There are flight links out of Dallas to both Denver and Los Angeles. These two routes have been added recently to provide delivery service to the Northwest and West Coast respectively. After extending its flight routes, NDAS added agents in the cities of Jacksonville, Montgomery, Jackson, and Houston. To date, this is the scope of NDAS's parcel delivery operation.

Initially, Next Day Air Service contracted with a computing services company to handle its billings. As the computing power of small computers increased, NDAS decided to purchase a minicomputer and take responsibility for its own data processing. The Payroll Department now runs the payroll twice monthly on this minicomputer. Employees submit their timecards and supporting documents on the first and third Mondays of the month. The Payroll Department then prepares the paychecks for both hourly and salaried employees. The paychecks are sent via overnight delivery on the following Thursdays. Although the Information Services/Data Processing Division performs all data

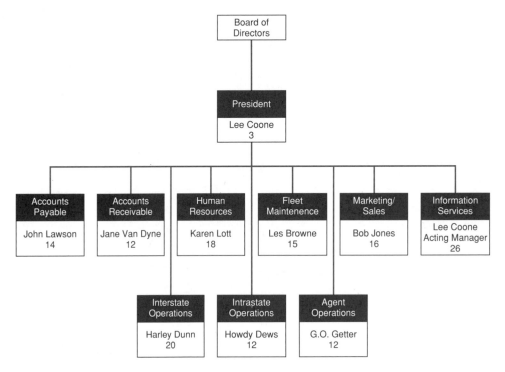

Figure 1-9   Next Day Air Service organization chart.

entry, processing, and check printing, John Lawson in Accounts Payable is the person who generates, reviews, and approves the reports and totals. Because so many new employees have been added at both the corporate and branch offices, a new full-time position has been added in Accounts Payable to handle the payroll and assist Mr. Lawson. Moreover, the subject of paying employees weekly has been discussed. Figure 1-9 shows the Next Day Air Service organization chart.

The branch offices currently batch all billing data by order date and send it daily to the corporate office when they send other interoffice correspondence by overnight delivery. When Information Services/Data Processing receives them, it enters the batches and processes them daily. The billing processing normally takes place from 48 to 96 hours after freight and parcel delivery. Once this processing has been completed, the database supports resolution of any questions or problems associated with the billings.

Because of an increasing volume of paperwork brought about by continued business expansion, the varying complexity of the billing process, and the preferred rates being given by competitors, Next Day Air Service's corporate management has decided to automate the billing process throughout its Florida offices. This is to be the first step in a series of strategic moves planned to provide online transaction processing and real-time customer information by using a data communication network. It is expected that online transaction processing will speed the billing process and improve turnaround time significantly. The online Query System will enable agents at remote offices to obtain instantly such information as credit status, correct delivery address, and package delivery status.

The current status of automation varies greatly among the various departments. The Sales and Marketing Division, headed by Bob Jones, has several microcomputers (one for each of his account representatives). All of these microcomputers are connected to a small local area network (LAN) that serves only the Sales and Marketing Division.

The Accounts Receivable Division, headed by Jayne Van Dyne, is responsible for all billing and collection activities. It recently acquired a small minicomputer to support databases for both customer billing and "bad debt" expenses.

The Accounts Payable Division, led by John Lawson, maintains its own vendor database that is stored on its minicomputer. This database also contains the other service carriers' billings, such as those from ODI to NDAS. This division also is responsible for the payroll.

The Fleet Maintenance Division has no computer capability. Its management has chosen to trace all necessary information manually. Les Browne, the maintenance foreman, prefers this mode of operation and in the past has steadfastly refused to automate his division's recordkeeping processes.

Dispatch, which is a part of the Fleet Maintenance Division, also processes its work manually. Dispatch currently bundles incoming packages twice daily according to their major destination point for overnight delivery. The bundles of packages are marked with the following information.

- **DEST:** City, State
- **DATE:** Current date
- **TIME:** Time package left dispatch
- **NPKG:** Number of individual packages in the bundle
- **INIT:** Initials of the person preparing the bundle

When the bundles arrive at their respective delivery points, the off-loaders mark the arrival time on the bundle's tags, write their own initials on the back of the tags, and return the tags to corporate headquarters. The packages are then delivered.

At this time, the various remote offices are not able to communicate with either the corporate headquarters or with one another, except by voice telephone, facsimile, mail, or interoffice mail sent on company aircraft along with the daily batched transactions.

Corporate management realizes that these islands of automation (minicomputers and microcomputers) represent the beginning of an integrated system.

It also sees the necessity for standardizing and streamlining systems and procedures before any serious networking can be accomplished. Its first step in this direction has been to create and staff a new Information Services Division that will be responsible for all computer and data communication operations. At present, Lee Coone, who is the corporate president, has assumed the role of manager until someone else can be chosen to fill this position permanently.

You have just been hired as a systems analyst and data communication consultant for this new division. Your first assignment is to assess the current level of automation, determine which functions are to be automated, make recommendations concerning the type of automation system to be installed, recommend appropriate organizational changes (if any), and most important, determine the type of data communication network that will be required to meet NDAS's current operations and future growth.

Moreover, corporate management has stated that both electronic mail and voice mail capabilities are to be a part of Next Day Air Service's network. The details of these two features may be omitted for the moment (voice mail is discussed in Chapter 2 and electronic mail in Chapter 7). While completing this assignment, you must remember to allow for expansion into other technological areas of networking, such as internetworking by connecting a WAN and a LAN. In addition, do not hesitate to use the Index to find related subject matter that supports your recommendations. Your instructor may provide additional guidelines regarding report formats, library resources, other assumptions, and the like. Be sure to provide adequate justification to support your recommendations.

Questions/Problems for the Next Day Air Service Case

1. Describe the current state of Next Day Air Service's office automation, integration, and networking. Begin by explaining how each department uses computer technology, what hardware they may use, and what functions currently are automated. Also assess which department is most in need of a network.

2. Based on the "types of networks" discussed in this chapter, what kind of network would appear to be the most beneficial to Next Day Air Service? Justify your answer.

3. What are the current characteristics or practices that identify NDAS as a possible candidate for its own data communication network?

4. Which two of the four networks described in the Network Definitions box might be appropriate for NDAS?

Chapter Two

VOICE COMMUNICATIONS

This chapter introduces the voice telephone communication network that originally was developed for voice telephone calls. It is this network that is used for most data communication traffic, especially when the transmission speed is 19,200 bits per second or less. Virtually all dial-up calls (direct distance dial or DDD) that transmit data use this network. A "voice grade" lease line, such as one from a corporate headquarters to a remote sales branch, also uses this network.

THE TELEPHONE

The purpose of a telephone network is to establish a voice communication path between any two telephones within the network. In order to accomplish this communication successfully, the network needs a device to convert the sound waves produced by the human voice at the sending end into electrical signals for the telephone. Then it must have another device to reconvert these electrical signals back into sound waves so they can be heard by the person at the telephone receiver. All this must be accomplished in a way that allows the receiver of the call to hear the original voice sounds of the sender with a minimum of distortion.

Telephone instruments contain devices for converting the audible sound signals we humans produce into electromagnetic signals that can be sent through the telephone. These devices, called *converters,* permit the passage of signals from one medium to another. Although it is theoretically possible, and somewhat possible in practice, to have only one device for converting sounds to electromagnetic impulses and back again, power limitations require two separate converters. Because of this limitation, telephones have two converters. The one that changes the audible sound to its corresponding electromagnetic signals is called a *transmitter* and the one that converts the electromagnetic signals back to their original sound is called a *receiver*. Figure 2-1 shows how these two converters are placed within the telephone handset.

The way this mechanism works is that a telephone transmitter converts mechani-

Figure 2-1 Telephone converters. The transmitter and receiver in the telephone handset convert audible sound signals to electromagnetic signals, and then back to audible sound.

cal vibrations in the air (the sound waves) into electrical "sound" vibrations for their transmission in an electrical circuit. At the other end, a telephone receiver changes the electrical voice signals back into an audible sound by magnetically vibrating a diaphragm that is in step with the incoming electric voice signals.

In order to call someone using the telephone, you must dial that person's telephone number. Dialing the telephone number is the same as entering the person's terminal address, except in this case the terminal is a telephone. There are two ways to accomplish this dialing. The left half of Figure 2-2 shows the older rotary dial type of telephone dialing mechanism, and the right half shows the newer touchtone type of telephone dialing mechanism. The rotary dial generates electrical pulses on the telephone line by opening and closing an electrical relay when the dial is turned and released. When you dial a 7, the telephone instrument generates seven electrical pulses, each approximately 1/20 of a second long. Rotary dial, *dial-pulsing* telephones are the dinosaur of the telephone industry.

The right half of Figure 2-2 shows the layout of a touchtone telephone keypad, which is typical of the newer, more sophisticated technique called *dual tone multifre-*

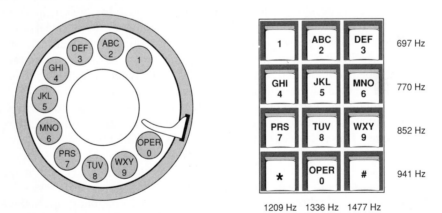

Figure 2-2 Rotary dial and touchtone keypad on a telephone. The rotary dial telephone produces a specific number of electrical pulses for each digit dialed. The tone dialing on a keypad produces frequencies, which are in hertz or cycles per second; therefore, Hz = Hertz = Cycles per second.

quency (DTMF) touchtone dialing. The keypad on a *tone-dialing* telephone has two sets of frequencies, as shown on the right and bottom borders of the figure. When you dial the number 7, the tone that is transmitted to the central office is a combination of 852 hertz and 1209 hertz. This is how cellular telephone calls make it possible for third parties to ''listen in'' and identify the number that is being dialed.

VOICE COMMUNICATION NETWORK

The basic voice communication telephone network is not only the largest, but also one of the oldest of our twentieth-century data communication networks. This network includes the telephone in your home that is used to call friends, relatives, or other people. In today's business communication cost structure, voice calls represent three quarters of the amount spent for communications, and only one quarter is spent on true data transfer.

This network is the one that connects your telephone to the telephone company *end office* (also called *central office* or *exchange office*) where switching is performed.

Switching includes identifying and connecting independent transmission circuits to form a continuous path from your telephone to the telephone you are calling. Figure 2-3 shows the interconnection of telephones through the end office in our basic voice network. Note that the local loop on this figure is nothing more than the copper wire pairs that go from your home to the telephone company end office where the electronic switching system equipment is located. The end office uses the telephone number you dialed as an ''address'' and searches out the other telephone so the two can be connected.

Calls made within the same end office or interoffice trunks are known as *local calls* (see Figure 2-4). Calls that use the tandem trunks and the tandem office are

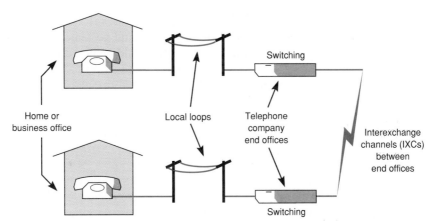

Figure 2-3 Telephone interconnection in the voice communication network.

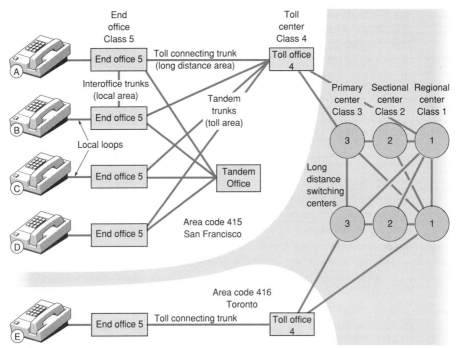

Figure 2-4 End office hierarchy. The end office (class 5), tandem office, and toll office (class 4) route calls throughout a city. Calls going outside a city use the class 3, 2, and 1 switching centers. Depending on the distance of the call and the traffic on the circuits, a call from Telephone A to Telephone E could be routed either by its most efficient route (5 — 4 — 3 — 3 — 4 — 5) or by its least efficient route (5 — 4 — 3 — 2 — 1 — 1 — 2 — 3 — 4 — 5).

known as *unit calls,* for which there may be an extra charge for each minute of time. The calls that use toll trunks are known as *long distance calls.*

The worldwide telephone network is so complicated that it would be difficult to present a single drawing showing its configuration. Department of Defense officials have indicated that the network in the United States is so integrated that it offers a unique emergency backup capability, for it would be almost impossible to destroy all communications in the United States. It should be noted that even though Figure 2-4 shows telephones at the end of the local loops, terminals or other data transmission equipment also might be attached to the dial-up telephone network.

Voice grade leased circuits are normal telephone circuits that have been taken out of dial-up telephone service by the common carrier (telephone company) and dedicated to one organization. These leased communication facilities sometimes are called *private circuits, private lines, leased circuits,* or *dedicated circuits.* The leasing organization makes them available for use on a 24-hour basis, seven days a week. It might be helpful to understand the distinction between a leased circuit and a dial-up circuit. If you have a leased circuit from New York to Atlanta, it is one continuous, unbroken circuit path between the two cities. This circuit is "wired around" any telephone switching equipment at the telephone company central offices; therefore, switching equipment cannot cause errors or distortion of messages. When not leased, the same dial-up circuit is wired through all the switching equipment required to locate the telephone numbers that are dialed. Dial-up circuits do not have one continuous, unbroken circuit path between these cities. Voice grade circuits are the most common form of leased communication channel or facility. Leased circuits used for voice calls often are called *trunk lines* by the people who manage the voice telephone systems.

Notice that we have used the words *circuit, line,* and *channel* when discussing the transmission of voice calls. Another similar term is *link*. People often use these terms interchangeably, but there are subtle differences between them. See the box on Transmission Circuit Terminology for five basic descriptions related to the paths over which both voice and data transmissions move. The proper usage of these terms will become more obvious in later chapters when you learn how to increase transmission capacity by changing from one communication *medium* to another or by using other techniques to "pack" more transmissions onto a single circuit.

TRANSMISSION CIRCUIT TERMINOLOGY

Medium   The medium is the matter or substance that carries a message from one point to another. The communication medium might be copper wires, a thin strand of glass in an optical fiber cable, or air in a satellite or microwave transmission because the electromagnetic signal travels through the air from a ground station to a satellite in space or between two ground-based microwave antennas.

Circuit   A circuit is simply the path over which data moves. It can be a copper wire, a through-the-air satellite link, or a combination of the two. Contrast circuit, which is a path, with medium, which is the material over which the message travels.

Line   Line frequently is used interchangeably with circuit; however, this usage is not completely accurate. Line implies a physical connection between two points, such as a copper wire. By contrast, circuit is more accurate when referring to satellite or microwave transmissions because there is no physical connection. Line, the older of the two terms, was used by those who worked with voice telephone systems that were in existence long before data communications existed. People who work with voice telephone services also use the term *trunk* or *trunk line,* which means an incoming communication circuit from the telephone company central or end office.

Link   A link is an unbroken circuit path between two points.

Channel   The term channel can be confusing because common usage allows for two definitions. In the first, channel is used interchangeably with circuit, such as when there is a communication channel or a communication circuit between two points. In the second, channel means the subdivision of a circuit. For example, a company that has a communication circuit between Los Angeles and New York subdivides it into four channels so four different messages can be transmitted simultaneously over the one circuit. Alternatively, you may read an article in which the writer refers to a channel (circuit) that has been divided into four subchannels. Sometimes the real world is not perfectly clear.

VOICE CALL CONTROL

To control voice calls, business organizations install *call management systems.* These systems monitor telephone call traffic, point out peak periods, identify the number of operators needed to handle different call volumes, and keep track of telephone operator efficiency and other factors relevant to voice telephone communications. Hardware boxes that perform these various functions can be installed to work with private branch exchange (PBX) switchboards. Call accounting software is a specialized database application. Most PBXs have a serial RS232 port, which is the same as COM1 on a microcomputer. The PBX uses this port to send out a specially formatted message every time a call is completed or other specific actions occur. This output usually is called the *station message detail recording* (SMDR), but some vendors use their own terminology.

Recording the SMDR records is the first task in call accounting, followed by processing the records, assessing the cost of calls made, and reporting and administration. Before widespread use of microcomputers, many companies connected a serial printer to the PBX's serial port to record the information on each call.

Today's systems send this output to a call recorder, which holds the SMDR data until it is transferred to a microcomputer for analysis. The software, called a *call accounting package,* can "cost" the calls and prepare a bill for each telephone extension.

Most call accounting packages come with a standard repertoire of call accounting reports. At the minimum, you can expect a report detailing the calls made from each extension, including the time, length, total cost, cost per minute, average call length, the number called, and so forth. Some packages can group the telephone extensions according to an organization's departments and divisions. The best programs produce ad hoc reports on demand.

Call monitoring systems monitor the levels of call activity by showing the current status of various trunk lines, the number of calls in progress, the number of calls waiting in queues, the wait time before incoming calls are answered, the length of calls, the number of calls lost because the caller hangs up, and the status of different operators. Such information helps manage telephone operator performance by measuring the number of calls handled, the length of each call, the percentage of time spent on the telephone, the average time on hold, and the time spent waiting to be connected.

Some of these systems actively control outgoing telephone circuits by not allowing certain area codes or the first three digits of certain telephone exchanges to be dialed, thereby restricting outgoing calls. These systems also can place the outgoing call on the lowest cost telephone circuit first and move to the more expensive telephone circuits only when the least cost ones are unavailable. For example, a system might first try to place a telephone call on the organization's leased communication circuits (trunk lines). If the trunk lines are busy, the system might try the outgoing 800 lines, and finally the regular direct distance dialing (DDD) network. Other features might be the accumulation of statistics about where calls are placed and their approximate cost for budgeting purposes, although cost figures can be obtained from the telephone company for each telephone in the organization or from the organization's SMDR call accounting software.

AREA CODES

Area codes for dial-up circuits will be changing. The middle digit of every area code in the United States currently is either a 1 or a 0. The telephone company set them up this way because the telephone company's central office switches were programmed to use the 1 or 0 in the area code as a signal to identify a long distance call. Beginning in July 1995, however, the numbers 2 through 9 also will be used as the middle digit in new area codes. Today there are 152 available area codes in the United States. The number of available area codes will be increased to 792 when this new capability for the middle digit is introduced.

Did you ever notice that area codes appear to be placed around the country in a helter-skelter fashion? One explanation of this anomaly is the fact that area codes were set up when everyone had rotary dial telephones. The lower numbers were assigned to the busiest locations, like 212 for New York City and 213 for Los Angeles. The same policy could not be followed as the telephone system continued to grow because all the lower numbers were used quickly. In reality, what once was a good plan designed so people would not have to dial the higher digits (such as 7, 8, or 9) stopped working as we quickly consumed all the area codes having lower digit numbers. This meant we could not continue with the philosophy of giving the lower numbers to the busiest telephone locations. Furthermore, with today's push-button telephones, it no longer makes a difference because it takes the same amount of time to dial either a 1 or a 9. In contrast, a 0 is the most time-consuming digit to dial with rotary dial telephones.

Area codes are used for dialing to other areas within a single country. For that reason, the 415 area code for San Francisco also might be used in another country. Consequently, a *country code* precedes the area code when you are calling another country. You can obtain a complete set of these country codes from the telephone company by calling 1-800-874-4000 and asking for extension 101. As an example of various country codes, the country code for Russia (formerly the USSR) is 7, the country code for Australia is 61, and the country code for the United Kingdom is 44. People who call the United States or Canada from other countries must dial 1 for our joint country code.

When dialing an international call from the United States, you first must dial 011, which provides direct access to an international telephone line. This is required because callers in a country like the United States can dial all the telephone numbers in their own area codes without dialing any other special numbers. To dial outside your area code, you must first dial a 1 before the area code to tell the system you want to dial a number in another area code. Furthermore, you must dial 011 to dial outside your country.

Putting all this together, if you were calling the city of Moscow in Russia, you would dial 011-7-095-555-2222. The 011 in this number directs the call to an international telephone line. The 7 tells the telephone switching equipment that you are calling Russia. The 095 is the city code (area code) for Moscow and its suburbs. The fictitious telephone number 555-2222 represents the telephone you are calling in Moscow. It is dismaying for Americans to learn that there are only 91 simultaneous telephone circuits between the United States and Russia, and only about 57 of these 91 circuits terminate in Moscow. To send a facsimile to Moscow may require dialing many times over several days before you can make a connection. Incidentally, whereas the United States has seven-digit telephone numbers throughout the country, this is not true in all other countries. In fact, some countries have a mixture—for example, seven-digit telephone numbers in metropolitan areas but only six-digit numbers in rural areas. These six-digit numbers usually indicate old switching equipment that is incompatible with the international dialing system. They can be used only for in-country calls, not international calls.

The best way for you to see the area codes for the area in which you live is to look in the front of your local telephone directory. Somewhere in the first 20 to 40 pages is a full-page map showing the United States with its time zones and all the area codes. Furthermore, the directory contains a list of the major cities, as well as other municipalities near you, so you can see their specific area codes. Finally, many telephone directories also list the international country codes and major foreign city codes within each country.

BANDWIDTH ON A VOICE CIRCUIT

Analog transmission takes place when the signal sent over the transmission media continuously varies from one state to another. This is analogous to having a dimmer switch on an electric light that allows the light to vary from very bright to very dim, but it is a continuous varying light as contrasted with a light that just turns on and off. (The on/off switch is digital.)

Most telephone circuits use analog transmission because they were developed for voice transmission, not data transmission. New networks today are built for *digital transmission*.

Figure 2-5 shows that most transmissions over voice grade circuits are within the human hearing range. This is because most of the telephone networks were built for human speech rather than for data. Human hearing is in the range of approximately 20 to 20,000 hertz,[1] although most people cannot hear above 14,000 hertz. Figure 2-5 also shows the frequency range for coaxial cable, microwave, satellite, and laser (optical fibers). *Bandwidth* refers to a range of frequencies. It is the difference between the highest and the lowest frequencies in a band. The bandwidth of a voice grade circuit is from 0 to 4000 hertz. The bandwidth is 4000 hertz, whether it is a leased or dial-up voice grade circuit.

---

[1] Hertz is the same as "cycles per second"; therefore, 20,000 hertz is equal to 20,000 cycles per second. One hertz (Hz) is the same as 1 cycle per second. One kilohertz (kHz) is 1,000 cycles per second (kilocycles); 1 megahertz (MHz) is 1 million cycles per second (megacycles); and 1 gigahertz (GHz) is 1 billion cycles per second.

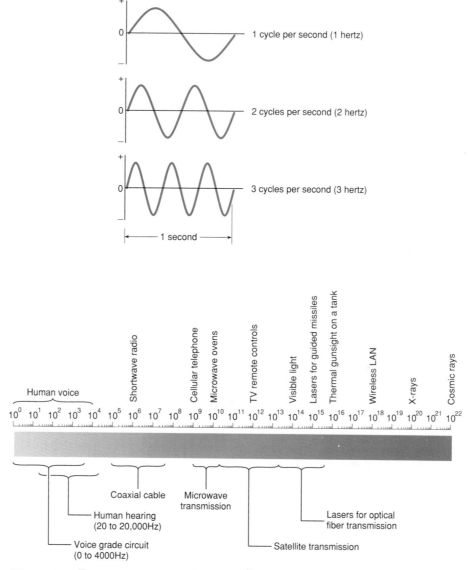

Figure 2-5 Frequency spectrum (zero to 10^{22} hertz). The top of this figure shows the concept of cycles per second. Hertz means cycles per second. 10^{10} can be written as a 1 with ten zeros to its right or 10,000,000,000; therefore, it represents 10 billion cycles per second or 10 gigahertz (GHz). The bottom part of this figure shows some typical uses of the frequency spectrum and the frequencies at which they apply.

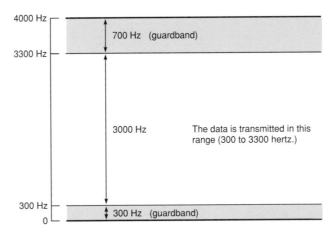

Figure 2-6 Voice grade circuit bandwidth (0 to 4000 hertz).

A voice grade communication channel or circuit is the most common communication circuit today. This circuit is used with dial telephones, and it typically is the circuit that is installed when organizations lease private or dedicated communication circuits. The bandwidth of this communication circuit is 4000 hertz.

Figure 2-6 shows how this 4000 hertz bandwidth is divided for data transmission usage. To start, there is a 300 hertz *guardband* at the bottom of the bandwidth and a 700 hertz guardband at the top. These prevent data transmissions from interfering with other transmissions when these circuits are stacked on a microwave or satellite link; thus, they prevent the frequencies used for your communications from overlapping with those of other communications. They can be compared to the plastic insulation that is put around a copper cable to keep it from short-circuiting with another copper cable.

Figure 2-7 demonstrates how the guardbands provide 1000 hertz of empty space between adjacent communication channels. Each voice grade circuit is stacked up using the available bandwidth. This leaves the bandwidth from 300 to 3300 hertz for your data transmission (see Figure 2-6). It is within this 3000 hertz usable bandwidth that the modem transmits the data signal.

Out-of-Band and In-Band Signaling All calls made on the voice network must be controlled so that switching and other operations can take place. This control is achieved by a process called *signaling* in which the transmitting end of a telephone network informs the receiving end that a message is to be transmitted. In other words, it is a two-way process that includes supervision to inform the caller when the called party is ready to talk, if the line is busy, or if the other party has hung up the telephone instrument. *Supervision* is the part of the signaling that holds the communication path together while the conversation (session) takes place. Put simply, signaling can be viewed as the command and control process. Two of the most widely used signaling techniques are out-of-band signaling and in-band signaling.

Out-of-band signaling uses one or more tone frequencies that lie within the pass-

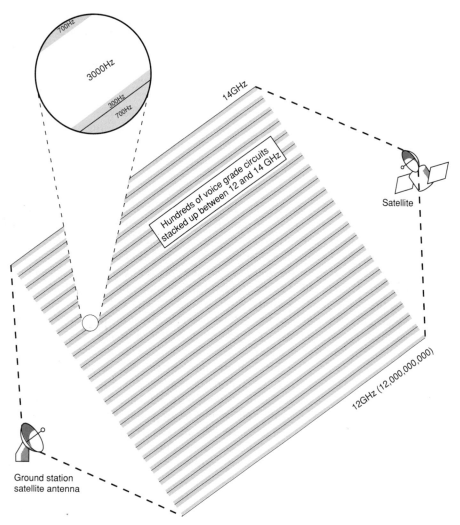

Figure 2-7   Guardbands.

band of the transmission facility, but just outside of the usable voice bandwidth. *Passband* is the complete range of frequencies being transmitted between the two devices. For example, examine Figure 2-6; there you will see that the passband for a voice grade circuit is 4000 hertz (0 to 4000 Hz). The out-of-band signaling tones usually are somewhere in the 700 hertz guardband that lies between 3300 and 4000 hertz. Placing the signaling tones in this part of the passband means they are less likely to interfere with transmitted speech or data signals. The tone sent back to a pay telephone to signal coin return, a signaling tone sent to a long distance operator in another city, and a tone sent to acknowledge that a telephone is busy are all examples of how out-of-band signaling is used in voice telephone networks.

With *in-band signaling,* tones are transmitted within the usable bandwidth of the passband. In our Figure 2-6 example, this is the 300 to 3300 hertz range. For voice telephones the in-band signaling tones are transmitted within the speech band, usually at 1600, 2400, or 2600 hertz, although 2600 hertz is used the most. In-band signaling is very flexible because speech and supervisory signals share the same transmission facility, but these signals are sent at different times. In-band systems are arranged so that supervisory signals are on the line only at initiation and termination of a call. As you might expect, in-band signaling is more complex than out-of-band signaling because it requires a more elaborate filtering system to separate the supervisory signals from the speech signals. An example of data communication in-band signaling is the high-pitched tone sent to disable echo suppressors when you first log on to a network.

Capacity of a Voice Grade Circuit   Bandwidth is what you examine when determining the capacity of a voice grade circuit. By capacity we mean the maximum speed at which signals can be transmitted. Having a wider bandwidth provides faster *transmission speeds*. This means more data can be transmitted in the same amount of time, that is, we have greater *throughput*. To see this relationship, refer again to Figures 2-6 and 2-7. It is the 3000 hertz bandwidth that limits maximum transmission speed. For example, the modem controls the speed at which data bits can be transmitted on voice grade circuits, but the 3000 hertz bandwidth limits the maximum speed. As an analogy, you control the speed at which your car travels by pressing the gas pedal, but the horsepower of the car's engine limits its maximum speed. In this analogy, you are like the modem and the car's horsepower is like the bandwidth.

Let us examine the relationship between bandwidth and bits per second. Assume a situation that uses a dial-up circuit, with 2600 hertz out of the 3000 hertz available to the modem. The remainder might be unusable because of noise and distortion, or it might be used for ringing operators, signaling the return of coins in a pay telephone, or other telephone company signaling functions.

The accompanying box on Calculating the Capacity of a Voice Grade Circuit relates capacity to the 3000 hertz usable bandwidth. (It assumes 400 hertz are used for signaling functions or other purposes, leaving 2600 hertz for the messages.) It also shows how the signal-to-noise ratio fits into the equation. The theoretical maximum of 25,900 bits per second can be exceeded by using data compression techniques.

Wider Bandwidths   There are many bandwidths wider than a voice grade communication circuit. Referring back to Figure 2-7, notice that the bandwidth for the satellite transmission in it is from 12 gigahertz to 14 gigahertz, which is a bandwidth of 2 billion cycles per second. If you divide 2 billion by 4,000, you can see that it is theoretically possible to have 500,000 voice grade telephone circuits on that one satellite transmission channel. In real life this is not possible because of various supervisory signals and other interfering electronic functions, although many thousands of telephone circuits can fit on one satellite link. Also note that the individual 4000 hertz voice grade circuits on the satellite link in Figure 2-7 are passbands within the larger 2-gigahertz satellite band.

As you read further into this book, you will see that many other communication facilities have a wider bandwidth. For example, in Chapter 7 the bandwidth for

CALCULATING THE CAPACITY OF A VOICE GRADE CIRCUIT

In 1928 H. Nyquist worked on time intervals between data samples. He showed that one cycle of a signal can contain a maximum of two baud. His work proved that the maximum theoretical signaling speed in baud is twice its bandwidth, or

$$\text{Baud} = 2 \times \text{Bandwidth}$$

This theoretical signaling speed became known as the *Nyquist rate,* and it is the maximum rate of transmitting pulse signals through a system. This work was significant because it showed that if a communication channel is sampled at a rate at least twice the highest baseband frequency at which the message transmission occurs, then the samples should contain all the information that was in the original message.

In 1948 Bell Laboratories engineer Claude Shannon, who created information theory, wanted to find out how much information could be delivered in a telephone call of a certain duration. He first looked at how well the signals used to convey the information could be distinguished from one another. To avoid garbled messages, the signals or code words used to convey information must keep their "distance" from one another.

First Nyquist, and then Shannon, proved that there is a theoretical maximum capacity, and it is based on bandwidth. A random stream of bits going across the 2600 hertz bandwidth has a maximum capacity of 25,900 bits per second. This is demonstrated by using *Shannon's law:*

$$\frac{\text{Maximum bits}}{\text{per second}} = \frac{\text{Available}}{\text{bandwidth}} \, \text{LOG}_2\left(1 + \frac{\text{Signal-to-noise}}{\text{ratio}}\right)$$

$$\text{Maximum} = 2600 \, \text{LOG}_2\left(1 + \frac{1000}{1}\right)$$

$$\text{Maximum} = 25{,}900 \text{ bits per second}$$

This calculation uses a 30-decibel signal-to-noise ratio. The *signal-to-noise ratio* is the strength of the transmit signal in decibels (dB) compared with the level of background white noise (Gaussian noise) on the channel/circuit. A signal-to-noise ratio of 30 dB is 1000/1, and a signal-to-noise ratio of 20 dB is 100/1. This means the signal is 1000 or 100 times more powerful than the background noise on the circuit.

Incidentally, if the signal-to-noise ratio is lowered to 20 decibels in the above example, then the maximum transmission capacity is only 17,300 bits per second. Therefore, the higher the signal-to-noise ratio, the greater the maximum capacity in the channel. Also, the greater the bandwidth, the greater the maximum capacity.

wideband services allows for transmission up to 230,400 bits per second, digital services have a bandwidth wide enough to allow 56,000 bits per second, and Integrated Services Digital Networks allow two 64,000 bits per second channels. There are many others, one of which uses what we call T-1 through T-4 circuits. The bandwidth for these circuits is wide enough that the speed can range from 1,540,000 to 274,176,000 bits per second.

As an analogy, think of bandwidth as being like a water pipe. A 1-inch diameter water pipe allows only a certain amount of water to pass through it. You can raise the water pressure and get a somewhat greater quantity of water through the pipe, but there is a physical limitation as to how many gallons per minute can pass through a 1-inch diameter pipe. If you need more gallons per minute, your only option is to install a larger 2-inch diameter pipe.

Bandwidth is the same. A voice grade circuit has a 4000 hertz bandwidth, just like the 1-inch water pipe. You can install very fast modems to push the data bits faster and you can use compression techniques to increase throughput, but you still are limited to the 4000 hertz bandwidth. If you need to transmit more data, your only option is to get more bandwidth, which means getting a circuit with a bandwidth greater than 4000 hertz. For example, instead of a voice grade circuit with only 4000 hertz bandwidth, you could use a Series 4000 wideband circuit having a 48,000 hertz bandwidth. This increased bandwidth allows you to move from a transmission speed of approximately 19,200 bits per second to approximately 50,000 bits per second. When people say, "I need more bandwidth," they actually are saying they need to increase their bits per second transmission speed.

SIGNALING ON A DIAL-UP CIRCUIT

There are two basic aspects to consider in the use of a telephone: the information that is conveyed during the conversation (the *session*), and the coded control signals that set up and terminate the call (*control signaling*). Data transmission also has session and control signaling. Some of these control signals convey information, such as the telephone number that might be passed from end office to end office, or the status of certain equipment, such as whether it is busy or whether a person has answered a call.

The control signals that are passed through the telephone network do some of the following.

- The dial tone indicates that dialing can begin.
- A busy signal indicates to the caller that the call cannot be completed. Sixty pulses per minute implies that the called person's telephone is in use or that the central office to which it is connected is overloaded.
- A high speed busy signal (120 pulses per minute) indicates that the long distance trunk lines (IXCs) are busy or overloaded.
- A ringing tone indicates that the called number is ringing.
- A loud pulsing noise indicates that something has gone wrong and the caller should restart the process.
- The tones heard when you are dialing a number using a touchtone keypad indicate that the numbers are being transmitted from your telephone to the telephone company central office.
- There are many other control signals for the telephone company, such as

signals for passing a number between central offices, recording billing information, giving the status of certain equipment, ringing long distance operators, diagnosing and isolating system failures, controlling special equipment such as echo suppressors, and indicating coin return in pay telephones.

AUTOMATIC NUMBER IDENTIFICATION (ANI)

Automatic number identification (ANI) is a process whereby the long distance carrier provides its customers with the telephone number of the incoming caller. Figure 2-8 shows how MCI handles ANI by using multifrequency in-band signaling. When the call comes in to the MCI switch, it sends the receiving telephone a signal to alert it that an incoming call is on its way. This process is called "seizing the line." Notice the top arrow in Figure 2-8, which is marked SEIZE. The receiving telephone sends back a signal that MCI refers to as a WINK. This signal is acknowledgment that it is operational and ready to receive an incoming call.

MCI then sends a start signal that it calls a key pulse (KP), the 10-digit ANI (calling party's number), and a stop bit called ST. MCI also might send a key pulse along with a *dialed number identification service* (DNIS) and another stop bit. DNIS is a service in which MCI provides its customers with the 800 telephone number the caller dialed. This allows the called telephone to receive either the regular telephone number (ANI) from which the call originated or the 800 number (DNIS) from which the call originated. After the telephone has received all the digits of either the ANI or the DNIS, it acknowledges their receipt by sending an ACK WINK signal. Then it goes *off-hook,* which means it lifts the handset and answers the incoming call if there is an automatic answering machine. If there is no answering machine, the telephone keeps ringing until someone lifts the receiver and puts it in an off-hook position so a conversation can begin. By contrast, hanging up the telephone at the end of a call is referred to as going *on-hook*.

There are various uses to which the ANI service might be put. For example, the calling telephone number can be displayed in a little window on your telephone. This allows the option of not answering the call, assuming you know it is from a telephone number you do not want to answer. Some companies use ANI to record

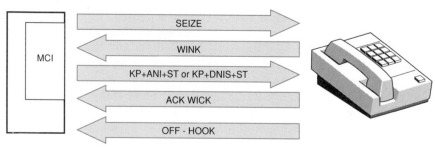

Figure 2-8   Automatic number identification (ANI).

the ANI number for future use, route the call to a specialized telephone sales agent or to a database for some automatic use, or send it to an interactive voice response (IVR) unit (discussed in the next section). In the last case, the IVR unit replaces the telephone shown in Figure 2-8. The interactive voice response unit can offer a variety of options so the caller can receive specific information automatically. This routing can be quite sophisticated. For example, if the DNIS shows that the call came in on a certain set of 800 numbers, it will route it to the IVR; but if it shows that the call came in from a normal area code (ANI) like 305 or 415, it will route the call to a telephone sales agent.

ANI has become tangled in the privacy debate because it is easily confused with its consumer-oriented counterpart, Caller ID. The end results of ANI, DNIS, and Caller ID are the same; that is, numbers for calls originating in an equal access central office are delivered to the person being called. The difference is that *Caller ID* operates within the service area of a particular group of central offices such as within a city, whereas ANI applies to long distance calls and DNIS applies to area code 800 calls between different service areas. Caller ID also incorporates the capability for calls to be transmitted with a *privacy blocking designator* in which the caller enters a code that blocks transmission of his or her telephone number. This prevents the person being called from seeing the telephone number of the person placing the call.

INTERACTIVE VOICE RESPONSE (IVR)

Interactive voice response is a voice processing application that gives callers specific information based on <u>unique</u> information the callers provide to the IVR system. IVR is interactive communications, and it is different from auto-attendant operation.

An *auto-attendant operation* simply <u>routes</u> callers based on information the callers provide by touchtone; it does not return information to the caller. Notice that the caller does not have to supply any unique information; the caller just presses the proper key on a touchtone telephone in order to be routed to another function or person. Another voice application is *audiotex,* which gives every caller the <u>same</u> information. If a system allows the caller to press certain keys on the touchtone telephone so it can determine what the caller wants to receive, that is auto-attendant. The part of the process that gives the caller the latest news, the current weather, or the lottery numbers is audiotex because it gives every caller the same information.

It is possible for a system to combine all three features. For example, assume Jane Smith wonders if the bank received her last bank-by-mail check and decides to call the bank to find out her current checking account balance. Upon receiving Ms. Smith's call, the auto-attendant feature allows her to press the proper keys to determine whether she wants to talk with an operator, receive information on banking hours, go directly to someone's extension telephone, or receive unique information on her bank account. If Ms. Smith presses the key to learn about banking hours, the information she hears is the audiotex portion of the system because every caller who presses that key hears the same message. On the other hand, once Ms. Smith presses the proper key to get to the portion of the system that allows her to receive unique financial information related to her bank account, then that is the interactive voice response part of the system. That part might instruct her to use the touchtone keypad to enter her checking account number. If the checking account number she provides is a valid one, the IVR then might instruct her to enter the last four digits of her Social Security Number. If that number matches the one stored with her checking account number, the system looks up the balance in Ms. Smith's checking account and, using a voice response system, supplies the current balance in her checking account. Notice that the auto-attendant feature routes calls to wherever they should go, whether it is a human operator, an audiotex system, or an interactive voice response system. The audiotex part provides each caller with the same message, in this example, the bank's operating hours. By contrast, the interactive voice response part extracts unique information from the system and delivers it to a specific customer. As you deal with voice telephone systems, it may be important to understand the subtle differences between auto-attendant, audiotex, and interactive voice response systems. See the box on Interactive Voice Response (IVR) for Car Dealers for an actual example of how such a system works.

INTERACTIVE VOICE RESPONSE (IVR) FOR CAR DEALERS

Car dealers can use interactive voice response (IVR) to great advantage. For example, a dealer can check the stock and order parts over the telephone without the benefit of a live, human telephone operator. To do this, the dealer calls an 800 number and uses a touchtone telephone to enter the appropriate dealer number and password. Then there are four choices: Check the price and availability of a part, enter an order, check the status of an order that already has been placed, or exit the system. When checking on prices and availability of a part, the dealer enters the 14-digit part number. The system responds in a digitized human voice whether the part is in stock, the current dealer price for the part, and the suggested retail price.

To place the order, the dealer enters the part number and the quantity required. The system reads the order back to the dealer in a digitized voice. Because the dealer places the order directly into a computer, order fulfillment begins immediately. If the order is placed before noon, it will be delivered the next day. If the dealer orders the entire stock of a part, the database is updated immediately so the next caller who asks for information on that part will hear that no stock is available. Should the dealer have difficulty using the IVR system, the appropriate touchtone codes can be touched for connection to a live human operator who can provide assistance. A system such as this, when combined with electronic data interchange (EDI), will someday be the ultimate in reducing paperwork and increasing the productivity and efficiency of ordering parts and billing. EDI would be used for invoicing the dealer and for handling payments, thereby automating the entire process.

DIAL-UP CIRCUITS

Dial-up (also called *direct distance dial—DDD*) is a network in which the organization uses the public telephone system, whereas private leased circuits are for your exclusive use. Dial-up networks are usually point to point, but you can build a three-point dial-up connection which is known as a *conference call.* In other words, the user might dial up two other telephones and simultaneously interconnect these three telephones. The basic configuration for dial-up circuits in a data communication network is the same as the one shown in Figure 2-3, except there is a terminal instead of a telephone.

When using the dial-up telephone network for voice communication only, the basic procedure is to

- Lift the telephone receiver to place the telephone in an off-hook position. This signals the central office that you want to make a call. The central office responds with a dial tone to indicate that you may dial the number.
- Dial the telephone number. Notice that after you dial the first digit, the dial tone breaks (stops). That is a control signal to indicate the number is being received at the end office.
- After dialing, you receive one of three signals: a busy signal, a ringing signal, or a loud pulsing signal that identifies a system malfunction.
- Begin your verbal conversation when someone answers the telephone. When two people or data terminals talk to one another, it is called a *session.*

When the device at the end of the line is not a standard telephone, but a data-type device such as a microcomputer, the procedures to sign on to the system and begin working might be to

- Lift the telephone receiver to place the telephone in an off-hook position. This signals the central office that you want to make a call. The central office responds with a dial tone to indicate that you may dial the number.
- Dial the telephone number.
- Wait for the tone; when you hear the tone, press the modem's ON button and replace the telephone receiver to an on-hook position.
- Depress the carriage return or Enter key on your terminal keyboard when the online light flashes on. (This step may vary in different systems.)

Note that the above four steps would be accomplished through the keyboard on a microcomputer using a communication software package.

- The other computer may ask for any of the following information. (This is the user sign-on procedure.)

    User ID   *Enter your ID and press the carriage return or Enter key.*

Password   *Enter your password and press the carriage return or Enter key.*

Account Number   *Enter your account number and press the carriage return or Enter key.*

*   *You must now tell the computer which programming language, system, or file you want to use.*

- The system responds, and you are ready to use the system through the dial-up network. This procedure varies with different systems; there may be fewer or more steps.

Even though the above example may not match perfectly the sign-on procedures for the dial-up network at your organization, it is typical of the procedures used when entering a computer-based dial-up network.

In some cases a dumb ASCII terminal must connect to a mainframe via a protocol converter (a device that makes message formats compatible). The ASCII terminal does not have the intelligence to dial, but there are intelligent modems on the market. With an intelligent modem, the user merely presses a preset series of keys that prompts the command sequence within the modem to request the telephone number from the ASCII terminal keyboard.

VOICE SYSTEM MISCELLANY

This section includes a variety of facts and miscellaneous information related to voice telephones. The information is a potpourri that jumps from topic to topic, but it all relates to voice telephones.

Telephone Plugs   *Modular jacks and plugs* were developed to make it easier to change or move telephones. The typical telephone connects to the connector on the wall by using a *RJ-11 plug* (RJ stands for remote jack or registered jack). This is the same plug that connects either the telephone instrument or a modem to the local loop voice grade circuit. Figure 2-9 shows the RJ-11 plug. If you unplug a telephone's RJ-11 plug, you will see four copper strips, one for each of the four wires that go between your telephone and the circuit.

Analog Versus Digital Telephones   Is your telephone analog or digital? This determines what kind of equipment is compatible with your telephone. All telephones used to be analog; however, digital PBXs are ushering in many digital telephones. To tell the difference, look at the telephone dial. If it is a rotary dial, it is analog. If the telephone has a touchtone keypad, it may or may not be digital. Turn the telephone over to see if it says, "Complies with Part 68, FCC Rules." If it does, you also should see a *Ringer Equivalence Number* (REN). Analog telephones have a REN; digital telephones do not. A Ringer Equivalence Number indicates how many accessories (ringers) can be connected to your analog telephone line and still allow it to ring. A REN of 1.0B means you can attach one accessory with a REN of 1.0 or two

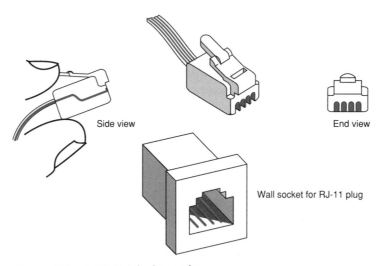

Figure 2-9   A RJ-11 telephone plug.

accessories with a REN of 0.5 each. Furthermore, some touchtone telephones have a switch on the bottom to convert to a rotary dial telephone even though they have push buttons. When you push the buttons on touchtone telephones, you hear musical tones. For rotary dial telephones, you hear a series of clicks instead of musical tones.

Recording Telephone Conversations   Can you legally record telephone conversations? The Federal Communications Commission (FCC) says yes, as long as you let the other party know you are recording (FCC Rule 64, Part E). The beep tone every 15 seconds is not necessary, as long as you give a verbal notification at the beginning of the taped conversation. You also may be subject to state-imposed regulations in the form of state laws or state-mandated Public Utilities Commission (PUC) rules governing the recording of telephone conversations.

Decibel Levels   Voice communication circuits, sometimes called analog or broadband networks, cannot be tested or designed without reference to something called a *decibel* (dB). The decibel is a fundamental unit for measuring differences between two different signal levels. For example, if someone cuts a "tap" into a telephone line to listen, there might be a 0.5 dB loss in signal strength. Similarly, the signal loss over 100 feet of a certain type of telephone wire might be described as a 5 dB loss in power. To us, this means the signal is weaker. It loses power and we cannot hear it as well. The decibel is a ratio between two levels of power, and it is used only to express gain or loss in signal strength. In your home, the decibel gain might describe the power increase between the input of a music signal into your amplifier and the output of the same signal after it is amplified and sent to the speaker system.

It is not necessary to get into the logarithmic calculation of decibels unless you are going to be a telephone or network engineer. Some practical examples of the loudness of varying decibel levels are the following.

- A firecracker is about 160 decibels.
- A portable tape player at full volume is about 125 decibels.
- A jet airplane at takeoff is about 120 decibels.
- A live rock concert is from 105 to 114 decibels.
- An automobile horn at 3 feet is about 110 decibels.
- Heavy traffic is about 80 decibels.
- A freight train at 100 feet is about 75 decibels.
- A vacuum cleaner at 10 feet is about 70 decibels.
- A whisper is about 30 decibels.
- Rustling leaves are about 20 decibels.

For your purposes, it is quite adequate to remember that decibels tell you the gain or loss in signal strength. You can hear the difference in a 10 dB gain or loss of a signal. You might review the last two paragraphs of the Calculating the Capacity of a Voice Grade Circuit box presented earlier in this chapter to gain a better understanding of how signal strength relates to transmission capacity.

Famous Firsts of Dial-Up Telephones   Before we proceed to the next section, here are five famous ''firsts'' related to the dial-up telephone system.

1. The first telephone directory, a single sheet listing of 50 names, was published in February 1878 in New Haven, Connecticut. There were no telephone numbers or addresses. You had to ring the operator to ask for the person or business by name. This was in the days of the old hand-cranked telephone.

2. The first telephone numbers appeared in the Lowell, Massachusetts, telephone book in 1880. Numbers were listed along with names during the measles epidemic. The purpose was to help inexperienced operators make connections when they did not know all the subscribers.

3. The first yellow pages directory appeared in 1883 in Cheyenne, Wyoming. It was not a business directory, but merely the result of a printer running out of white paper.

4. The first yellow pages directory with business listings and advertisements was printed in Detroit, Michigan, in 1906.

5. Herbert Hoover was the first president to have a telephone on his desk. Prior to 1929, the president had to use a telephone booth outside his office.

ECHO SUPPRESSION/CANCELLATION

Two-wire circuits (dial-up circuits) have a problem with echoes. When people talk on a two-wire circuit, echoes may occur under some conditions. *Echoes* arise in telephone circuits for the same reason that acoustic echoes occur: there is a reflection of the electrical wave from the far end of the circuit.

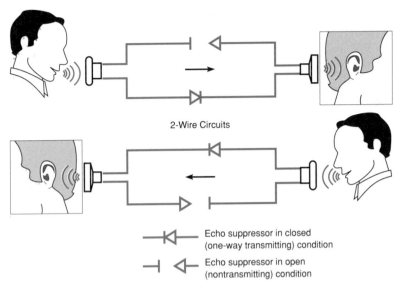

2-Wire Circuits

Echo suppressor in closed
(one-way transmitting) condition

Echo suppressor in open
(nontransmitting) condition

Figure 2-10   Echo suppressors.

Telephone companies install *echo suppressors* on two-wire circuits to prevent the echoing back of your voice when you are talking to someone. The echo suppressor permits transmission in one direction only. When you talk, your voice closes the echo suppressor. When the other person starts talking, his or her voice closes the echo suppressor in his or her direction; because you have stopped talking, your echo suppressor opens. Obviously, if you are both talking, the power of your voices so overwhelms the echoes that you do not hear them. This is because the echo suppressors close in both directions when you both talk. Figure 2-10 depicts the operation of echo suppressors.

Lease data circuits (private dedicated lines) do not have echo suppressors; therefore, echo suppressors are not present on lease circuits used for data transmission. Echo suppressors are present only in dial-up circuits.

When a computer is dialed using a modem, there is a loud ringing tone as the computer answers. The purpose of this tone is to disable the echo suppressors. The tone is held on the line for approximately 200 to 400 milliseconds in order to disable or close the echo suppressors in both directions. Immediately after the tone ceases, the carrier wave signal comes up, perhaps a 1700 hertz tone, and it is this carrier wave signal that keeps the echo suppressors closed in both directions. If the carrier wave is lost (perhaps because of an electrical failure) for approximately 150 to 300 milliseconds, the echo suppressors reopen. This reopening causes the dial-up data transmission to have many garbled or destroyed characters. The only choice at this point may be to redial the call and start over in order to close the echo suppressors in both directions.

Many garbled characters occur after the echo suppressors reopen because echo suppressors take approximately 150 to 200 milliseconds to open and close. To illustrate this effect, assume we are transmitting when such a lapse occurs. We lose the first 150 milliseconds of the next transmission because the echo suppressor is not fully closed and the data bits cannot get through. If we change directions, the first 150 milliseconds of our data transmission also are lost while the echo suppressor closes. It is for this reason that dial-up modems disable the echo suppressors before transmission.

One approach to controlling echo is to reduce the propagation time. *Propagation time* is the time it takes a signal to travel from one end of a pair of wires to the other end. If two speakers are 1,000 miles apart, the propagation delay is about 10 milliseconds so the round-trip echo delay is 20 milliseconds. When the echo delay is 20 milliseconds or less, anything the speaker hears is simultaneous with his or her own speech, and it is not interpreted as an echo; therefore, no problem exists. As the echo delay approaches 45 milliseconds, however, the echo sounds like an echo and it interferes with the conversation. Longer echo delays may make conversation almost impossible because the returning echo is a mimic of the original spoken words.

To meet today's high speed data communication needs, a different type of echo control equipment is used on many circuits. These devices, called *echo cancellers,* do not just suppress the echo; they subtract it. They are placed at PBX connections, public switched network gateways, and in private networks. An echo canceller contains an internal model of the echo delay for the circuit on which it is being used. The echo canceller subtracts the amount of propagation time from the original signal on the circuit. This internal model of the echo delay adjusts automatically, thereby allowing the canceller to handle a wide variety of different circuit conditions to minimize echoes. Many private line leased networks install their own echo cancellers. The basic difference between the two devices is that an echo suppressor suppresses the return of the echo, whereas the echo canceller subtracts the echo timing from the original signal.

TASI (VOICE CALLS)

The *Time Assignment Speech Interpolation* (TASI) technique is used on some of today's long distance, frequency division multiplexed voice lines. It allows for the packing of extra voice conversations into a fixed number of circuits.

Usually when two people conduct a telephone conversation, both parties do not speak at the very same moment, and for a small portion of the time neither speaks. Most long distance voice circuits are four-wire circuits. When each person speaks, only one pair of the four wires is used. Thus, two of the four wires always are empty, unless both people speak simultaneously, which cannot last a very long period of time.

TASI electronic switching equipment detects a user's first word, and within a few milliseconds the equipment assigns a communication circuit to that speaker. Actually, an almost undetectable portion of the first syllable may be lost, but it is seldom noticed in voice communications. When a person ceases talking, the circuit is switched away and given to someone else. When the person speaks again, the TASI equipment assigns a new circuit path. Occasionally, if the circuits are over-

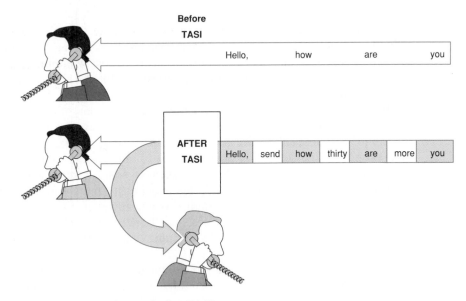

Figure 2-11   Before and after TASI.

loaded, the TASI equipment may be unable to find a free path. Even though it is for a very brief period of time, several words might be lost when this occurs (see Figure 2-11).

The benefit of TASI equipment is that, if there are 100 circuits, more than 100 voice calls can be handled simultaneously.

VOICE CALL MULTIPLEXING

To *multiplex* is to simultaneously place two or more calls on one circuit. The telephone company multiplexes received signals, whether they are voice or data. This is called *group multiplexing,* even though technically it may be data that is being multiplexed.

Name	Number of Voice Grade Circuits
Group	12
Supergroup	60
Master Group	600
Jumbo Group	3,600
Jumbo Group Multiplex	10,800

Figure 2-12   Group multiplexing.

AT&T Communications has devised a group multiplexing function. The telephone company takes groups of calls that are destined for the same area and multiplexes them together. This permits groups of calls to travel on a single coaxial cable, microwave system, satellite transmission, or optical fiber transmission media. Figure 2-12 shows the names given to these groupings and the number of voice grade circuits in each group.

For example, assume your company already has multiplexed 16 conversations onto one outgoing circuit. The telephone company may further multiplex this one circuit into a "group" for transmission to its destination. This means your 16 conversations are transmitted as only one of the 12 calls in the group (see Figure 2-12). In addition, the telephone company may again multiplex it into a jumbo group of circuits. Multiplexing done by the telephone company is *pure multiplexing* (not statistical), and it is totally transparent to users. In pure multiplexing there is no holdup or delay of messages.

If you want to look ahead and learn more about multiplexing now, look at Figure 4-2 on page 124. It shows a four-level multiplexed data transmission on a single 3000 hertz bandwidth telephone line. This figure shows a data connection where 0s and 1s are being transmitted over four separate channels on a single telephone circuit. If this were a voice call, the four separate channels transmitting the 0s and 1s would be replaced by four separate voice transmissions. Do not be concerned about how this is accomplished now because you will learn more about multiplexing in Chapter 4.

SWITCHES (VOICE AND DATA)

When data is to be sent over a network with many terminal locations, some arrangement must be made to enable different terminals to communicate with one another. Early communication networks used permanent connections between each pair of terminals. When the number of terminals exceeds two or three, however, this system gets increasingly expensive. Figure 2-13 depicts this situation; it shows six terminals with every station individually connected to every other station. Fifteen lines are needed in this case. The number of lines needed for a network of this type may be calculated as

$$\binom{N}{2} \quad \text{Number of lines} = \frac{N^2 - N}{2}$$

where N = the number of terminals or stations.

A more economical and flexible interconnection arrangement is to allow for temporary connections between any two stations that wish to communicate with each other. This process is called *switching,* a methodology that eliminates the need for direct wire connection between all station pairs in a network. If Station D has the ability to connect any two stations temporarily, then the 15-line configuration of

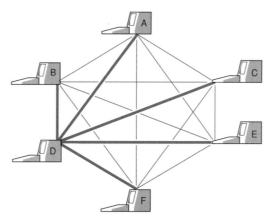

Figure 2-13   Direct wire connection for six terminals requires 15 circuits, but if a switch is placed at D, only 5 circuits are required. This is a MESH network because A through F can all interconnect with each other.

Figure 2-13 can be reduced to a 5-line configuration, consisting of one line from each station going into the central switching station (D).

The basic functions of a switch are to

- Interconnect the *stations* (or *nodes*) to provide a communication path between them
- Store and forward messages
- Control the establishment and release of the various connections
- Check network equipment to determine whether it is busy or inoperative

Circuit Switching   Circuit switching is the most common type of switched network. Your telephone at home uses circuit switched connections. In *circuit switching,* the central switch site (usually the telephone company's central office) establishes a connection between two stations, and a message goes directly from one telephone to another. Picture this as a voice message going from one telephone to another after the two communication circuits are switched together at the telephone company central office. If the two telephones cannot be switched together (connected), you get a busy signal and have to try again (redial) at a later time. The major disadvantage of circuit switching is that you cannot get a message through the network if the two circuits cannot be connected together. For this reason, store and forward networks are more popular.

Store and Forward   *Store and forward* switching systems may first try circuit switching. If one of the circuits is busy, the central switching site stores the incoming message from the sending terminal or telephone by copying it onto a storage medium such as a disk and retransmits that message to the destination telephone or terminal at a later time.

With modern high speed computers, data communication networks are able to combine the store and forward concept with the circuit or line switching concept. This combination offers data communication network users the highest level of throughput. A modern communication switching network offers circuit or line switching so the originator of a message can be connected immediately to the station to which the message is addressed; if that station is busy, the computer center accepts the message, stores it on a magnetic device (generally a disk), and automatically transmits the message to the proper addressee as soon as the line is free.

A sophisticated telephone system at a business or modern data communication network operates by combining circuit switching with store and forward. Voice mail systems allow you to call someone and, if there is no answer, leave a voice message that will be forwarded at a later time. This is a perfect example of circuit switching with store and forward. Electronic mail (E-mail) is also a store and forward system.

End Office Switches   There are many very large, high speed switches within telephone company end or central offices. Figure 2-4 showed the five classes of these switches. They are used to search out telephone numbers and switch circuits so two telephones can be connected together, even though one of the telephones may be in San Francisco and the other in London. One of the most popular *end office switches* is the AT&T 5ESS® switch. This is an extremely reliable high speed switch used for circuit switching and even store and forward in some cases. In addition to the high speed switching of calls, it can automatically route calls to alternate circuits when the original circuit is overloaded or temporarily out of service, queue calls with an automatic call-back option for better utilization of facilities, connect multiple location switching systems together, and the like.

Newer switching schemes (software and hardware) are being implemented throughout the United States. In the past, your telephone call went to a switch in a local end office that telephoned ahead to the next end office so your call could be routed. Although this whole process was automatic, it used not only some of the voice grade circuit capacity between cities for routing calls but also some of the capacity for turning one of the circuits over to you when the call was routed and the person at the other end picked up the telephone.

A new switching scheme is called *Common Channel Signaling System 7* or simply SS7. This method uses an entirely separate computer network for the purpose of setting up and routing calls. It does not use the regular voice telephone network for the mechanics of routing calls. SS7 uses a second network for call routing because the switching computers of the regular voice telephone network are nearly overloaded with data relating to traffic and other signaling required to handle millions of voice and data calls.

A network node in SS7 is called a *signaling point*. There are three types of signaling points. First, a *service control point* (SCP) supports applications providing services such as 800 numbers. Second, a *service switching point* (SSP) is the point of origin of a request for services. Third, a *signaling transfer point* (STP) is like a packet switch because it accepts a packet (usually a 128-character message block) on an incoming channel and transmits it on the appropriate outgoing channel.

The term in SS7 that is most closely associated with a communication circuit is

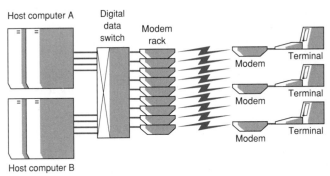

Figure 2-14   Digital data switch. A modem rack is a cabinet at the central site that holds many modems. Sometimes only the modem circuit cards are in the rack, and sometimes the entire modem box is in the rack. The digital data switch can connect any modem in the modem rack to any of the four ports in either host computer A or host computer B.

a *signaling link*. A signaling link is a communication line that can exchange messages reliably between two adjacent signaling points. By contrast, a *signaling data link* refers to the physical properties of the communication circuit.

The SS7 switch specifies the protocols that allow telephone companies to use the databases in public data networks. Calls placed in a SS7-based network contain information on both calling and called numbers. This data is sent to a host computer (a service control point) that interprets the message for routing. Regional and local toll-free dialing are now available because the called and calling numbers can be linked in a database on a host computer. SS7 allows the telephone companies to link their own databases to those of other vendors.

Digital Switches   There are several types of *digital switches*. *Digital data switches* (also called *digital cross-connect switches*) provide users with a way of switching between different host mainframe computers without having to access back through the modems (as shown in Figure 2-14). A digital data switch can manage traffic and set up inbound and outbound queues of messages during periods of peak usage; this maximizes the available resources. Digital data switches offer port contention, which is a sharing of the ports on a front end processor. This sharing can be done on a first-come, first-served basis, or some incoming messages can be given priority over others. Some digital data switches provide security restriction through the use of passwords.

A *digital matrix switch* combines technologies found in T-1 multiplexers, PBXs (switchboards), time division multiplexers (TDMs), statistical time division multiplexers (STDMs), and circuit switches. Digital matrix switches are used to change connections between ports, such as on a front end processor. When a front end fails, the network control center operator can type a command on the switch's console to change the terminal and modem port connections. This effectively moves each modem and circuit combination to the spare front end processor. Although very similar, this is different from a data PBX switch in which users initiate the switching; with digital matrix switches, the network control center operator initiates the switching of the ports. In Chapter 4 the section on Multiplexers discusses both digital channel banks and digital cross-connects.

Another type of digital switch is a *data PBX switch,* which is used only for switching data (no voice transmission) during digital transmission. A typical data PBX might connect up to 144 asynchronous 9600 bits per second circuits. It automatically switches among all the circuits, depending on the address to which a message is destined. Other features of data PBXs include

- Allowing terminal users to select different computers or destinations from their keyboard without moving any cables.
- Providing port contention so that users can be connected to the first available port, or they can "camp-on." (To *camp-on* is to be held in a waiting queue until a port is freed.)
- Offering many other features of voice PBXs, such as call forwarding and security restriction.

Network Switches   Even though switching can be built into the front end processor, statistical multiplexer/concentrator, PBX, or host computer, there are many standalone message switching systems. A typical message switching system might be run by a minicomputer or microcomputer. It functions as both a message switch and a store and forward system. Sophisticated message switches use stored program techniques and highly reliable third generation solid state circuitry.

A typical standalone switch might have 12 or more communication circuits that operate at different speeds. The system should be able to support various code structures and be expandable to handle more communication circuits.

A standalone switch should be able to dial and receive calls automatically, as well as switch messages between any of its circuits. Another feature should be a delivery/verification/confirmation response, with the message sender knowing when the message was delivered by receiving a positive delivery acknowledgment. Sophisticated switches allow various addressing schemes such as 3, 5, or 7 addressing characters to address a multitude of circuits, individual terminals, and individual devices attached to a microcomputer. Finally, a good switch should provide for in-transit storage of an adequate number of messages (at least 500). It should have the ability to retrieve messages that were sent during the day, possibly during previous days, and message logging for transaction trails or historical purposes. Some switches also provide alarms in case of circuitry failure and self-diagnostics to locate the failure. The telephone company central office is a network switch.

Uses of Switches   To many people, switches are an obscure piece of hardware, so we wish to expand on their usage. Most switches today are located in the telephone company's central office where they are used for the important function of switching calls (circuit/line switching) between the calling and called parties. For example, when you dial a telephone number, the switch finds the other telephone instrument,

SOME USES OF SWITCHES

- **Town Hall Meetings** The public can interact and talk directly with the U.S. President to help formulate domestic and foreign policy.

- **Opinion Polling** Viewers can register opinions on subjects ranging from politics to personalities with results tabulated and made available during the broadcast.

- **Financial Services** Brokerage houses can offer sales leads, stock tips, and instant stock quotations.

- **Banking** Banks can provide information on budgeting, investments, loans, insurance, and estate planning. Banks already use switches to route messages through their automated teller machine (ATM) networks.

- **Catalog Shopping** Department stores or mail order companies can invite customers to purchase goods by telephone without operator assistance.

- **Computer Security** Businesses wanting tighter control over access to their database can furnish a list of approved users and passwords to the telecommunication company (common carrier) for insertion into the switch. Unauthorized attempts to gain access can be routed to a busy signal or a rejection announcement.

- **Network Services** Remote meter reading and diagnostics on various home systems can be automated at far less cost than with existing methods.

- **Lottery by Telephone** In states that have lotteries, this service could help lottery commissions avoid the expense of furnishing and maintaining lottery terminals operated by humans.

whether it is located across town, across the state, across the country, or in another country.

Switches also may be used in connection with a "pay-per-view" television service in which you dial in appropriate identification numbers and a special movie or television show is directed to your home, with billing at a later time. Cellular telephone companies are major users of switches. Many other types of businesses can use switches. See the accompanying box on Some Uses of Switches to learn more about these business applications.

PBX (SWITCHBOARDS)

A *private branch exchange* (PBX) is a switchboard within which all the telephone lines of an organization terminate. Usually, several circuits go from this switchboard to the telephone company's end office. These circuits generally are referred to as trunk lines when they are devoted primarily to voice transmissions from a switchboard. In data transmission we refer to these same circuits as leased circuits, private circuits, or dedicated circuits.

First generation manual PBX systems started in the late 1800s. In those days you had to ring the operator to ask for the business or person by name. There were no telephone numbers. You may recall from an earlier section that the very first telephone directory was published in 1878, and the first telephone numbers did not appear until 1880. These first generation switchboards were totally manual. An operator manually connected the wires coming from a home or place of business to the other set of wires that led to whomever was being called. In this case the operator acted as the switch.

A business organization could have from one to dozens of incoming trunk lines (local loops) going to the PBX. From the PBX there were inexpensive wire pair connections to numerous telephones located throughout a building. When a call arrived at the PBX switchboard, an operator determined the extension of the called party, manually plugged the call into the correct extension, and pushed a toggle switch to ring that telephone. When the called person answered, a busy light turned on at the switchboard, signifying that the line was in use. This busy light turned off as soon as either party hung up, at which time the PBX operator removed the plug, making the extension and trunk available for other calls.

Second generation PBX systems appeared on the scene in 1929 with the Bell System 701 family of switchboards. The major difference between the two generations was that an operator was no longer required to handle outgoing calls or intra-office calls. These switchboards sometimes were referred to as *private automatic branch exchange* (PABX). We will discuss the automating of switchboards later in this section, but first we wish to introduce key systems.

The *key system* was one of the first telephone systems the telephone company installed on a customer's premises. It would be more correct technically to call the PBX we described earlier a key system because this switchboard had clear lighted buttons, thick connecting cables, and a telephone switchboard operator who would plug in a cable and use a toggle switch to connect and ring voice telephone instruments. Figure 2-15 shows one of these cord-style switchboards.

With modernization, the original cable-connected key systems/PBXs became more automated. In the next stage outgoing calls did not require operator intervention, and an incoming call could be switched automatically to an extension within an organization, also without operator intervention. The term *PABX* was popular for many years, but today people refer to these automated switchboards as PBXs, key systems, and sometimes CBXs (computer branch exchanges).

The 1970s saw the development of a category of PBXs that now is termed the second and a half generation. This is not quite a full-generation jump. These systems used a computer to control the switch, and they offered such functions as programmable telephone moves between various locations and least cost routing of telephone calls. *Least cost routing* requires a switchboard that can choose between a telephone trunk line the organization already leases, different common carriers, or dial-up. In this case, the lease line would have the lowest cost, with varying common carriers next, and dial-up the highest cost. Because the earlier second generation PBXs did away with most of the operators, they lost the intelligence necessary to

Figure 2-15 Cord-style switchboard operated by three people. Photograph courtesy of AT&T Archives.

call a person back when a line was free. The stored programs inherent in the second and a half generation systems restored such functions because the program could call the person back when a line was free.

The first of the third generation systems began to appear in about 1979. Since then many vendors have announced third generation products, such as the American Telephone & Telegraph ATTIS System 85 and the Rolm CBX II. Third and fourth generation PBXs have three main characteristics: distributed architecture, non-blocking operation, and integrated voice and data.

Fourth generation digital systems, like the AT&T DEFINITY® (Generic 1 and Generic 2), can perform switching for very large voice and data networks (see Figure 2-16). For example, they can handle up to 30,000 telephones in a building and 6,000 outgoing trunk lines. These systems may be misnamed switchboards or PBXs because they can switch and route all the voice or data messages for an organization.

This fourth generation is the all-digital switchboard, sometimes referred to as a *digital PBX*. Digital PBXs are popular because the switching is so fast and so error free that it allows data transmissions to go through the same switchboard as the one used for voice communications. In fact, if you are using a digital switchboard, your voice transmissions must be digitized prior to going through the switchboard. With digital switchboards, therefore, everything is transmitted in a digital format.

Digital PBXs use a *distributed architecture* that is either hierarchical or fully distributed. *Hierarchical systems* distribute routine functions to the switching module, but real control resides in the central processor. In *fully distributed systems,* the switch module processes its calls independent of any other system component. Fully distributed systems are said to be inherently more reliable because failure of

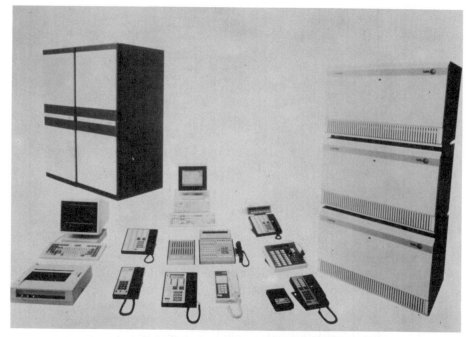

Figure 2-16 American Telephone and Telegraph's DEFINITY® digital switchboard. The large boxes on the left and right contain the solid state circuits, software, and the incoming/outgoing trunk lines. The telephone instruments in the foreground are various DEFINITY operator interface units. Three of these smaller units replace the entire cord-style switchboard in Figure 2-15. Photograph courtesy of AT&T Archives.

a single control module, no matter how catastrophic, cannot produce overall system outages. Those in the hierarchical system camp counter that fully distributed PBXs cannot perform under high load conditions because of internode control and synchronization problems.

In a *nonblocking operation* intraoffice calls *always* can be placed between any two telephones within an organization. For example, if the switchboard carries lines for 2,000 telephones within the organization, then 1,000 people always can be talking with people at the other 1,000 extensions. *Integrated voice and data* means both voice and data can be transmitted over the same communication circuit and through the same PBX.

Today's PBXs have features such as inherent broadband architecture and integrated packet switching. *Inherent broadband architecture* is the ability of a PBX to transmit at extremely high data rates, usually 56,000 bits per second or greater, whereas *integrated packet switching* adds the capability of handling packet switching services (discussed in Chapter 6).

These newer digital PBXs can use digital transmission and switching techniques because they are designed with 32-bit microprocessor chips that act as the central controller/central intelligence. A typical digital PBX uses a star architecture so that

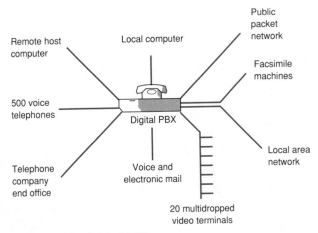

Figure 2-17   Digital PBX.

individual telephones or microcomputers can be connected directly to the central digital switchboard (see Figure 2-17). Some features of these new digital switchboards are

- Simultaneous transmission of voice and data.
- Format and protocol conversion that allows the interconnection of different vendors' word processors, host mainframes, microcomputers, and terminals.
- A local area network controlled from within the switchboard. Microcomputer workstations on the local area network connect to the switchboard in a star configuration, and the PBX digital switch redirects messages among microcomputers connected to the local area network.
- Both voice mail and electronic mail.
- Modemless switching for digital transmission.
- Asynchronous and synchronous data transmission.
- Both circuit switching and store and forward capabilities.
- Nonblocking switching.
- Automatic alternate routing to ensure that calls are routed over the least cost communication facility.
- Authorization codes to restrict access for security purposes.
- Connection to high speed outgoing circuits, such as T-1 or ISDN.

Now there are even wireless PBXs. One wireless PBX is capable of supporting 2,000 lines and 400 simultaneous telephone calls. This system does not have a nonblocking switch. A *wireless PBX* uses spread spectrum (see the Glossary) radio technology in frequencies just above 900 megahertz. The obvious major benefit of a wireless PBX is that twisted pair telephone wires do not have to be installed throughout the building for connecting the telephones to the PBX. Once a telephone message leaves the PBX, it is on regular telephone cabling for the trunk lines to the local loop between the business and the telephone company. The wireless part of the PBX is within the building, not between the building and the telephone company's central office.

CENTREX

Another widely used switching technology is *CENTREX*, the Bell Operating Companies' tradename for an automatic system that can route incoming or outgoing calls directly to the person being called without intervention by a PBX switchboard operator. With CENTREX, the PBX switch is located at the telephone company's central office. Each telephone station has its own telephone number, the last four or five digits of which are an internal organization telephone extension number. With CENTREX, incoming telephone calls go directly to the telephone being called. People within the organization can dial inside extensions (four or five digits) or outside telephone calls to other organizations, also bypassing the telephone switchboard operator. Any central telephone numbers still can be routed to an information switchboard operator if the organization so desires. With CENTREX, all the switching equipment can be housed and maintained at the central office of the local telephone company. This feature makes switching equipment more reliable, allows faster maintenance, and eliminates the need to manage or test the equipment yourself. Modern-day CENTREX offers many of the features of a digital PBX, such as

- Automatic call-back where a calling party encountering a busy station can be called back automatically when the called station becomes available
- Call forwarding
- Call holding/transfer
- Conference calling
- Ability to change a telephone number through software rather than rewiring to a new telephone instrument
- Ability to connect to dictation equipment
- Paging people throughout a facility
- Speed calling in which often-used numbers are stored in the system
- Station message detail recording (SMDR)

CENTREX Customer Premises Equipment (CPE) includes all the extra telecommunication equipment that can be purchased from vendors other than the telephone company. This equipment is built specifically to enhance CENTREX systems, although consideration must be given to the extra floor space and backup electrical power required to run the extra equipment. This equipment might include call tracking devices, message tracking devices, or any other PBX operator attendant-related equipment.

DATA-OVER-VOICE (DOV)

Data-over-voice systems operate with "in-place" telephone wires, so data and voice share the same transmission medium. This is accomplished by superimposing the data transmission on top of the voice bandwidth and allowing a private branch exchange (PBX) or CENTREX system to separate the data and voice signals for routing to their proper destinations.

A data-over-voice system that uses a building's existing twisted pair telephone circuits consists of a programmable hardware device for interfacing the data and voice inputs onto the telephone circuits and a hardware box for separating the voice and data. The purpose of the separation box is to route voice signals to the PBX and data signals to the microcomputer to which they are addressed. As these products gain in popularity, they may become gateways for connecting local data-over-voice telephone circuits to local area networks. Products such as these cost approximately $400 to $500 per port, which is comparable to local area network costs. Data-over-voice hardware sometimes has an additional advantage. It may eliminate the cost of pulling new wires or cables throughout a facility because it can use existing twisted pair telephone wires.

Data-over-voice (DOV) is an analog transmission technology that soon will be replaced by *digital data-over-voice* (DDOV). Digital data-over-voice is the digital transmission of both voice and data signals. It allows a user to run a 19,200 bits per second dedicated data transmission session and a voice conversation. These two transmissions are concurrent and they take place over a standard two-wire telephone connection. The latest systems let voice and data share a single twisted pair telephone wire, and they also support data switching without the use of a PBX. Such systems can transmit data at 19,200 bits per second (asynchronous) or 64,000 bits per second (synchronous). If a special adapter board is added to the microcomputer, these digital data-over-voice systems can support micro-to-micro communications, file transfers, and interconnection to various file servers. The advantage of digital transmission is that it has fewer errors than analog: digital transmission guarantees that 99.95 percent of all data transmission seconds are error free. This circuit is much more reliable and higher in quality than a normal analog transmission circuit.

VOICE MAIL

The public telephone network that handles voice messages has been around for over 100 years. Because this network is primarily a circuit switching system, it has one tremendous disadvantage. When the remote telephone is already in use or no one is present to answer calls, the telephone call (the message) cannot be completed. Both voice mail and electronic mail overcome this disadvantage.

With regard to voice mail, great technical advances have occurred to make the telephone more accessible, easier to use, more attractive, and a true message switching system. In other words, *voice mail* is a store and forward switching system as opposed to a circuit switching system. Voice mail is a flexible means of sending a spoken message to someone, even when the person is not at the telephone. The sender speaks into the telephone, and the message is stored for later forwarding to its recipient. In effect, this turns the telephone system into a message switching system.

Actually, voice mail is the transmission of a voice message to a recipient's voice mailbox. Using a touchtone telephone with its standard 12-key dialing pad, the caller can record a message, listen to the message before transmitting it, and even change it if necessary. The message then can be sent to one or more recipients or even to a predefined group, such as a department within a corporation or government agency. When it is convenient, the recipients check their voice mailboxes, scan to see who sent incoming messages, and choose to listen to some now while saving others for later. Recipients can listen to the message, stop playing it if they are interrupted, skip ahead or back, or replay the message at will. After hearing the message, the recipient can generate a voice reply immediately and send it to the person who sent the original message. Other options might be to forward the message to a third party and, of course, to discard the original message.

Voice mail has five major advantages over the traditional telephone. With voice mail it is no longer necessary to

- Place several calls to a person to find that person near the telephone
- Move meeting schedules to match time zone differences around the world
- Place a number of calls to send a similar message to many different people
- Know where a person is located geographically to complete a call to the person (all you need to know is the voice mailbox address, which he or she checks each day)
- Type your messages
- Wait at your telephone to receive an important message

With voice mail, the sender can place a call without interrupting the recipient, without having to know whether the recipient is in the office, and without regard to the time of day or night.

If a two-way information exchange is necessary because complex points must be discussed, then voice mail has a nice feature that can be used to set up a precise time, date, and telephone number to ensure the connection can be made the first time. It is here that the newer telephones will have the most advantage because of their ability to transmit both voice and picture simultaneously. Video display telephones allow users to see the person with whom they are speaking (possibly for security reasons) and actually to show documents over the system.

In general, public telephone users more readily accept voice mail than electronic mail. This is because electronic mail requires, first, the ability to type and, second, access to a keyboard in order to type the text of a message. Psychologically, human beings were built to accept and transmit voice messages, whereas the ability to enter text messages must be learned as a special skill. More people can speak than can write a complete sentence correctly, let alone type a message.

As voice mail gains in popularity, it will be the glue that holds together and controls the business office because different people will need to converse with or leave messages for various other people. Whereas typists will have no problem with electronic mail, nontypist managers and executives may rely more on voice mail because the spoken word can be entered faster than the typed word.

When you purchase a voice mail system, some important application features to consider are

- Password control for security and privacy.
- Type of hardware to be used such as 12-key touchtone telephones or video telephones.
- Training aids such as booklets, audio prompting, or, if you have a video display telephone, a help key that provides pictorial representations of how to use the system.
- Keypad templates to aid users in remembering how to use the 12 keys.
- System designed to direct messages to any telephone, to only company telephones, or directly to a user's address message queue without regard to the telephone.
- Other message addressing schemes such as to individuals, to a unique telephone, to groups of individuals, to preorganized numeric codes, to system directories, or custom methods used by an individual organization.
- Type of system data that might accompany the message, such as date of call and time, address of sender and receiver, time of message, or other system data.
- Provision for priorities or different message categories as might be used in a large corporation.
- Ability of users to give answers to requests or to request information. Someone may call in wanting information about a publisher's books or software packages. By asking callers which product they want, and telling them to press 1 for books or 2 for software information, you can disseminate information on your products without operator assistance. (See the Interactive Voice Response box earlier in this Chapter.)
- Depending on size and cost considerations, systems starting with one port and going up to 256 ports. Ports are used for incoming telephone circuits (trunk lines).
- Ability of the voice mail system to run on a microcomputer.
- Capability of interfacing with PBX (switchboards) systems using either analog or digital communication technology.
- Generation of valuable reports, including accounting functions and various other business reports that a system administrator can use for maintenance and billing.
- Message desk option, with which an operator attendant can transfer a voice

mail message from a nonuser, or an outside user can enter a voice mail message into the system.

- A message log for security and message receipt authentication purposes.
- Outdialing, or the ability to dial an outside call (local or long distance) automatically in order to deliver a user's voice mail message to another user or nonuser of the system. This function is helpful for contacting someone during nonbusiness hours or weekends when people are less likely to call into their voice mailboxes.
- Future delivery, which lets a user create a message and send it to another user at a predetermined future time, either by dropping it into a voice mailbox or by outdialing it.
- Edit functions, including stop, start, skip forward, skip backward, delete, reply, add, and subtract. The edit function is important for users who want to replay and edit their messages.
- Broadcast abilities, allowing one message to be directed to multiple users.
- Time stamp and date stamp, allowing users to embed a time and date, which a user can call up to determine when a message was directed to him or her.
- Receipt acknowledgment, whereby the system notifies a sender that a user has responded to a sent message and offers proof of delivery. It may show how long messages are in the system.
- Message forwarding, whereby a user who has received a message can send it to another system user and also can add dialogue to the first message. This is similar to memo passing.
- Help keys or audio prompting.
- Speed control, so the user can slow down or speed up the received message, and also adjustable volume.
- Various security levels that restrict access to the system by requiring an access code and a follow-up security code.
- Messages ranging from 30 seconds to almost indefinite lengths, depending on disk storage capabilities.

Finally, the number one advantage for voice mail is that everyone who currently has a touchtone telephone already has the terminal required to use this system and basically understands how this terminal (the telephone instrument) works. To see how one of the voice mail systems works, use your telephone and dial 1-800-6WATSON.

KEY TERMS

Analog transmission	Audiotex	Automatic number
Area code	Auto-attendant operation	identification (ANI)

Bandwidth
Call accounting package
Call management system
Call monitoring system
Caller ID
Camp-on
Central office
CENTREX
Channel
Circuit
Circuit switching
Common Channel
  Signaling System 7
Conference call
Control signaling
Country code
Data-over-voice (DOV)
Decibel (dB)
Dedicated circuit
Dial-up call
Dial-up circuit
Dialed number
  identification service
  (DNIS)
Digital cross-connect
  switch
Digital data-over-voice
  (DDOV)
Digital data switch
Digital matrix switch

Digital PBX
Digital transmission
Direct distance dial
  (DDD)
Dual tone multifrequency
  (DTMF)
Echo
Echo canceller
Echo suppressor
End office
End office switch
Exchange office
Guardband
Hertz (Hz)
In-band signaling
Interactive voice response
  (IVR)
Key system
Leased circuit
Line
Link
Local call
Long distance call
Medium
Multiplex
Node
Nonblocking operation
Off-hook
On-hook

Out-of-band signaling
Passband
Privacy blocking
  designator
Private automatic branch
  exchange (PABX)
Private branch exchange
  (PBX)
Propagation time
RJ-11 plug
Session
Signal-to-noise ratio
Signaling
Spread spectrum
Station
Station message detail
  recording (SMDR)
Store and forward switch
Supervision (signaling)
Switching
Time Assignment Speech
  Interpolation (TASI)
Transmission speed
Trunk line
Unit call
Voice grade leased circuit
Voice mail
Wireless PBX

SELECTED REFERENCES

1. Fermazin, Tom. "How to Prevent the Misuse and Abuse of Your Voice Mail System," *Voice Processing Magazine,* vol. 4, no. 2, February 1992, pp. 34–37.

2. Gilder, George. "What Spectrum Shortage?" *Forbes,* vol. 147, no. 11, May 27, 1991, pp. 324–325, 328, 330, 332.

3. Leibowitz, Ed. "ANI Phenomenon," *Teleconnect,* vol. 9, no. 11, November 1991, pp. 136, 138–141.

4. ———. "PBX Technology Advances," *Teleconnect,* vol. 9, no. 7, July 1991, pp. 98, 100.

5. Newton, Harry. *Newton's Telecom Dictionary: The Official Glossary of Telecommunications and Computer Acronyms, Terms and Jargon,* 4th ed. New York: Telecom Library, Inc., 1991.

6. Oppedahl, Carl, et al. *The Phone Book: How to Get the Telephone Equipment and Service You Want—and Pay Less for It.* Mt. Vernon, N.Y.: Consumer Reports Books, 1991.

7. Padgett, Kim Wilson, ed. "Accounting for Your Company's Calls," *Voice Processing Magazine,* vol. 3, no. 11, November 1991, pp. 30–31, 33.

8. Tedesco, Eleanor H. *Telecommunications for Business.* Boston: PWS-Kent Division of Wadsworth Publishing Co., 1990.

QUESTIONS/PROBLEMS

1. The basic voice telephone system commands _____ of the amount spent for data transfer.

2. Name the three basic types of telephone calls.

3. Why are leased circuits more free of errors than other dial-up circuits?

4. What are the functions of a call management system?

5. What is the significance of the 1 or 0 in an area code?

6. What is bandwidth?

7. What is a guardband?

8. What is signal-to-noise ratio?

9. There are two factors in all telephone calls, whether voice or data messages. What are they?

10. How do echo suppressors differ from echo cancellers?

11. TASI is a means of packing more conversations into a fixed number of circuits. How does it do this?

12. What is multiplexing?

13. Why are switches needed?

14. What is the important feature that makes store and forward systems attractive?

15. What is it called when intraoffice calls always can be placed between two telephones in an organization (e.g., no busy signals)?

16. What makes digital transmission and switching possible in the newer digital switchboards?

17. When are data PBX switches used?

18. With _____, incoming or outgoing calls are routed directly to the person being called without intervention by the operator. (This hardware is located at the telephone company central office.)

19. How is data-over-voice accomplished?

20. In a data-over-voice system, what does the separator box do and what may it do in the future?

21. Can circuit switching and store and forward switching be combined in the same system? If so, describe how it would work.

22. If you have 11 microcomputers to interconnect without switching, how many lines (circuits) are required?

23. What is the difference between a private circuit, a leased circuit, and a dedicated circuit?

24. When you dial a call, sometimes you get a 60 pulses per minute busy signal and sometimes a 120 pulses per minute busy signal. What is the difference?

25. When you dial into a computer, the first thing you hear is a loud tone. What does that tone do?

26. If there is a dial-up computer system at your organization, compare the steps for gaining access to this computer system with the steps that are listed in this chapter.

27. Define the difference between circuit switching and message switching.

28. If the total bandwidth of a satellite channel is 360,000 hertz, how many voice grade channels are supported? *HINT:* See Figure 2-7.

29. What is a PBX? Define it.

30. How does voice mail differ from electronic mail (E-mail)?

31. If the signal-to-noise ratio is 10 dB, how much more powerful is your signal than the background noise?

32. Describe briefly how out-of-band signaling and in-band signaling differ.

33. What is the purpose of a telephone system?

34. What two devices change human voice sounds into electrical signals that can be transmitted over wires and then back into the original human sounds?

35. How do dial-pulsing telephones differ from tone-dialing telephones?

36. What is a voice grade leased circuit called?

37. How do you dial from the United States to another country?

38. How does 20,000 cycles per second differ from 20,000 hertz?

39. What is a passband?

40. Describe automatic number identification.

41. How does the automatic number identification service differ from the caller ID service?

42. How does interactive voice response differ from auto-attendant operation?

43. Describe audiotex.

44. What is the function of the RJ-11 plug?

45. How can you distinguish a digital telephone from an analog telephone?

46. What is a decibel?

47. How is AT&T's 5ESS switch used?

48. How does a digital data switch differ from a digital matrix switch?

49. Why is digital data-over-voice replacing data-over-voice transmission technology?

50. Looking at Figure 2-4, what is the least efficient and most efficient routing of a call from Telephone D to Telephone E?

NEXT DAY AIR SERVICE CUMULATIVE CASE STUDY

Background on Next Day Air Service

Assume you have presented to President Coone your preliminary report on the steps required to bring Next Day Air Service to a competitive position with respect to data processing and data communications. He supports your recommendation that Next Day Air Service would benefit from an organization-wide multiapplication network that would integrate word processing, electronic and voice mail, document and package tracking, billing, and payroll. He also supports your position that the first priority should be improved voice and facsimile communications. Consequently, he has directed you to gather certain data that will help you determine the extent to which the voice communication system will have to be overhauled.

At the minimum, Mr. Coone wants to know the number of telephone calls made to all offices, the number of voice and facsimile messages sent and received, the number of FAX transmissions, the cost of all telephone equipment, and the average monthly percentage of local and long distance calls and other telephone services. After a brief discussion, you agree that three months of itemized charges should be adequate to support your analysis. In addition, you agree to survey the branch offices concerning the type and quality of telecommunication equipment already in place. The purpose of obtaining this information is to determine whether it will be easy to integrate such equipment into a future communication network.

Figure 2-18 contains a list of the Next Day Air Service offices, their current staffing levels, and the average number of calls made per day from each office. Figure 2-19 provides a detailed breakdown of the daily calls made between offices and customers. In Figure 2-19, the boxes in which similar cities intersect (that is, Miami–Miami) reflect the number of local calls made from the office to customers concerning their inquiries.

Each office receives both local and long distance calls throughout the day. These calls relate to the status of packages, pickups, deliveries, payroll, and personnel inquiries. At present, telephone messages are carried by hand and placed on the appropriate person's desk. These handwritten messages sometimes are difficult to read and often get lost.

Most offices have one or two telephone circuits from which to make and receive calls. Only the large offices like Tampa, Miami, Orlando, Atlanta, Dallas, Memphis, and New Orleans have more than two circuits for voice calls. Each office has a facsimile machine with its own circuit. These FAX machines have been acquired over a period of several years, which has resulted in a "hodgepodge" of makes and models. Local telephone companies like Southern Bell and Bell South provide the local telephone service; a variety of common carriers like AT&T, MCI, and US Sprint provide long distance services.

With regard to network control, you should include recommendations for

Office	Current Staffing	Average Number of Calls per Day
Atlanta	25	282
Chicago	2	124
Dallas	17	177
Denver	1	50
Houston	4	163
Jackson	4	114
Jacksonville	6	196
Los Angeles	1	41
Memphis	12	216
Miami	19	216
Montgomery	4	94
New Orleans	16	206
Orlando	21	214
St. Louis	2	58
Tampa	148	361
Washington, D.C.	3	33

Figure 2-18   Office list for Next Day Air Service.

using either centralized or decentralized switching. Evaluate whether one large centralized PBX should be used as a control center for the network or whether several small PBXs would create a more durable system in case of a general network failure. Be sure to include a location for any recommended PBX.

Mr. Coone also needs a recommendation on whether to switch both voice and data through one switch or whether to use both a voice PBX and a data PBX/data switch. (*HINT:* You may want to look at Chapter 12 to read about combining voice and data.) You also must consider store and forward switching, as well as integrating facsimile processing into the network. If considering a voice mail system, you must discuss the various functions that should be included, as well as how the NDAS personnel are to be trained in its use. Again, be prepared to document your information sources and be able to defend your recommended plan.

Questions/Problems for the Next Day Air Service Case

1. What information is needed to begin planning a voice communication network? What basic communication facilities and features should you include in a plan for an integrated data and voice communication network? Recommend a particular type of PBX to serve as the network's control center, and explain the reasoning behind your choice. Consider integrating both store and forward switching and facsimile processing.

2. Evaluate whether one large centralized PBX should be used as a control center for the network or whether several small PBXs would create a more durable system in case of general network failure. Include a recommended location for any suggested PBXs.

Origin / Destination	Atlanta	Chicago	Dallas	Denver	Houston	Jackson	Jacksonville	Los Angeles	Memphis	Miami	Montgomery	New Orleans	Orlando	St. Louis	Tampa	Washington
Atlanta	55	13	16	4	12	11	21	3	18	30	8	21	27	4	35	4
Chicago	13	12	6	–	4	2	12	–	21	11	2	8	13	–	20	–
Dallas	16	6	25	7	35	7	11	9	17	3	2	16	4	2	16	1
Denver	4	–	7	8	6	1	3	–	7	2	1	3	2	–	6	–
Houston	12	4	35	6	21	4	7	3	11	4	2	18	7	5	21	2
Jackson	11	2	7	1	4	15	3	1	18	2	7	21	4	1	16	1
Jacksonville	21	12	11	3	7	3	28	2	4	26	3	7	33	2	31	3
Los Angeles	3	–	9	–	3	1	2	4	1	4	1	2	4	–	7	–
Memphis	18	21	17	7	11	18	4	1	31	12	9	17	8	18	21	3
Miami	30	11	3	2	4	2	26	4	12	42	7	13	21	6	31	2
Montgomery	8	2	2	1	2	7	3	1	9	7	17	12	7	2	13	1
New Orleans	21	8	16	3	18	21	7	2	17	13	12	32	8	6	21	1
Orlando	27	13	4	2	7	4	33	4	8	21	7	8	37	2	35	2
St. Louis	4	–	2	–	5	1	2	–	8	6	2	6	2	9	11	–
Tampa	35	20	16	6	21	16	31	7	21	31	13	21	35	11	70	7
Washington	4	–	1	–	2	1	3	–	3	2	1	1	2	–	7	6

Figure 2-19 Average number of calls per day between Next Day Air Service offices. Assume that 10 percent of the total calls by city are facsimile transmissions. Note that this chart reflects the average number of incoming *and* outgoing calls per office per day. To keep calculations simple, assume the number of inbound and outbound calls per office per day are equal. For example, the Atlanta–Miami connection experiences 30 long distance calls per day. Half of these calls are from Atlanta to Miami, and the other half are from Miami to Atlanta.

3. Recommend whether to switch voice and data through the same PBX or to have separate voice and data PBX switches.

4. How might audiotex, IVR, automated attendant, and voice mail be used at Next Day Air Service? Provide specific examples.

5. Compute the approximate number of trunk lines (circuits) needed at each location to accommodate the average number of daily calls (see Figure 2-18). Assume that the average time to complete either an inbound or an outbound call takes five minutes. Round up to the nearest whole number and assume an eight-hour day (480 minutes). Add one circuit to accommodate the FAX machine.

6. Based on Figure 2-19, calculate the percentage of calls made between Next Day Air Service locations (long distance) and local calls within the same city (Atlanta to Atlanta).

Chapter Three

DATA COMMUNICATION HARDWARE (PART 1)

This chapter describes only the basic mandatory hardware that is required to configure a data communication network. Local area network (LAN) hardware is described in Chapter 11. The next chapter covers other pieces of hardware that make networks more efficient, faster, more secure, easier to use, able to transmit several simultaneous messages, and able to interconnect with other networks.

INTRODUCTION

This chapter describes only the basic hardware that is required for data communications. The basic hardware needed for a functioning network includes the host mainframe computer, the front end processor, modems, and terminals. The communication media (circuits/channels/lines) are not hardware; they are described in Chapter 5 starting on page 190, and local area networks (LANs) are described in Chapter 11.

Figure 3-1 shows the basic hardware configuration for a data communication network. This chapter discusses each major type of network hardware, starting at the host computer end and working out to the remote end. The next chapter builds on this figure by adding other hardware, such as multiplexers, intelligent controllers, protocol converters, and line adapters.

HOST MAINFRAME COMPUTER

The *host mainframe computer* generally is considered to be the central computer or central processing function for a large-scale data communication application processing system. In distributed processing, several host computers may be tied to-

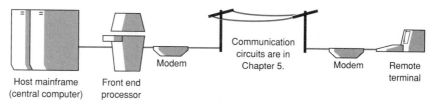

Figure 3-1   The basic hardware needed for a data communication network.

gether by the data communication network. Although the host computer is not truly a part of the network, it performs many network functions because these functions may be shared by the host computer and front end processor.

The suitability of a computer to serve as the host computer for an online, real-time data communication network depends on both its own capabilities and the capabilities of other hardware attached to it. Many computers today can be used for online, real-time data communication networks, provided the attached hardware can handle the tasks for which the host computer is inefficient. In other words, the characteristics that make a computer suitable for data communications do not necessarily make it good for "number crunching." In particular, data communication work involves many short periods of activity to service a single arriving or departing character or message. A computer whose hardware or software makes this kind of operation clumsy or time consuming does not perform well in the data communication environment. For such a machine to be effective, auxiliary hardware is required.

The interface between the data communication network and the processing functions of the host computer falls into three categories: minicomputers, microcomputers, and mainframe computers.

Minicomputer   The first of these categories is a *standalone minicomputer* configuration. In this configuration, the minicomputer handles a specific set of communication facilities and terminals. The circuitry to handle data communications is built directly into the minicomputer. In other words, the minicomputer's architecture is designed so it can interact in a real-time mode. Figure 3-2 shows a standalone communication configuration in which the minicomputer is able to handle all communication tasks. This type of computer is a stored program computer with communication as well as computing capabilities. It typically is used in a mode where the emphasis is on communication rather than data processing. It often is found in the manufacturing environment for process control, and in areas where the user queries a database on the status of a certain product, inventory level, or the like. This field is dominated by minicomputers that have been developed and programmed for special purpose processing and communication functions. This configuration is being replaced by local area networks.

Microcomputer   The second category is a network that uses microcomputers, micro-to-mainframe connections, and local area networks. Although some people may think of this configuration as just a small network, many are large local area networks handling several hundred terminals or microcomputers. Usually, this type of

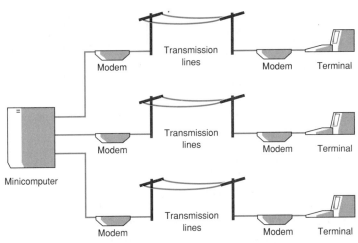

Figure 3-2   Standalone communication configuration.

network is totally within the corporate/government business office or facility/campus area. It does not require long distance communication circuits, and, when users want to transmit outside of this local network, they must address their messages so the messages can be transferred to other networks through the gateway. Because these networks are so important in today's business and scientific environment, two other chapters in this book are devoted to them: Chapter 10, which discusses micro-to-mainframe connections, and Chapter 11, which discusses local area networks (LANs). Figure 3-3 shows both a LAN and a micro-to-mainframe configuration.

Mainframe   The third category is a general purpose computer, and it usually is a wide area network (WAN) encompassing a large geographical area. Large general purpose computers are used for both data communications and application processing, but with greater emphasis on the online, real-time data communication portion of the system. In this configuration, there is a distinct division of labor between the front end and the general purpose computer (see Figure 3-4).

As our networks have grown, so too have their demands on the host mainframe. These demands have outpaced the mainframe's ability to handle both its own processing tasks and those required to control network communications. As a result, the front end processor has taken over many of the mainframe's communication control tasks.

FRONT END PROCESSOR (FEP)

The *front end processor* can take two forms. The first is a nonprogrammable, hardwired, communication control unit designed by the computer manufacturer to adapt specific line and terminal characteristics to the computer. The second form is a front

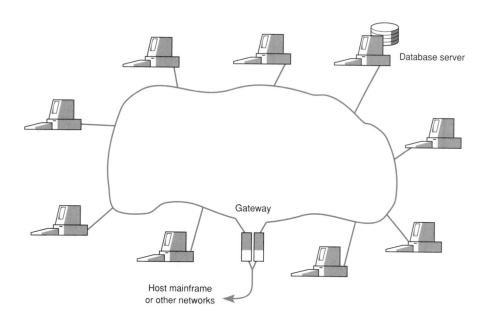

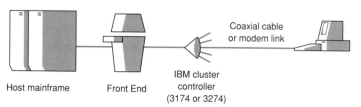

Figure 3-3 Local area network (top) and a micro-to-mainframe connection (bottom).

end processor that is programmable and can handle some or all the communication input/output activity as well as perform some processing.

Such a configuration is employed primarily in situations where the input/output and computing processing requirements are very large and where rapid response time is of the essence. This type of configuration is used in large data communication networks such as wide area networks (WANs).

The general trend today is to remove every data communication task you can from the host computer and move it further out into the network. Figure 3-5 shows the downline movement of some of the communication functions that can be moved out of the host computer. This movement increases the efficiency of each piece of hardware because it offloads some of its duties to the next piece of hardware.

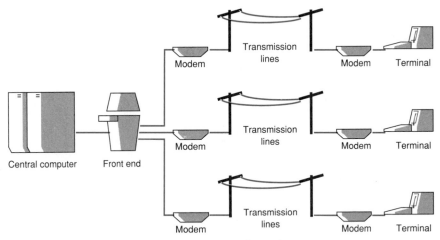

Figure 3-4   Front end/central computer configuration.

For example, the *data channel* (a part of the host computer) handles the movement of all data into the host computer memory and the movement of completed processing out of the host computer memory. The front end processor now handles most, if not all, of the control functions related to data communications. Modems perform modulation to enable the flow of data on communication circuits and specific diagnostic checks. Next, some of these control functions are passed off to other devices such as switches, statistical multiplexers, and remote intelligent controllers that might be located hundreds or even thousands of miles away from the host computer. This also implies that the massive quantities of software that used to

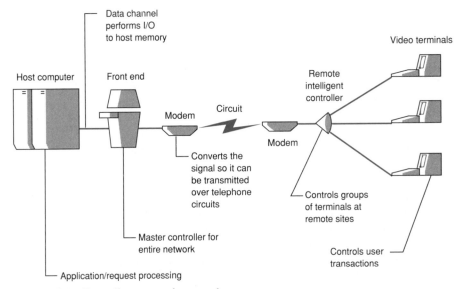

Figure 3-5   Downline network control.

reside solely in the host computer are removed and located downline in other pieces of hardware such as front ends and remote intelligent controllers.

Finally, the ultimate proof of this movement of software and hardware functions out of the host computer is exemplified by distributed data processing where application user departments now have microcomputers to perform their own data processing functions. The result is that user application departments have their own distributed databases so they can store their own files. As this happens, each business function has its own data processing host computer, even though it might be a small microcomputer, and its own distributed database files. Therefore, data communication networks become the fabric or glue that holds the business organization together because there are multiple host computers, ranging in size from a mainframe down to a microcomputer.

Functions of the Front End Processor   A front end processor is a computer that has been programmed specifically to perform many different control and/or processing functions required for the proper operation of a data communication network. This computer might be a mainframe, a minicomputer, or, as is becoming the case more often today, a microprocessor-based computer.

As mentioned in the preceding section, the primary purpose of a front end is to offload some of the processing and control functions of the data communication network from the host computer to a specially designed and programmed communication processor. These devices are programmable, and they are equipped with extensive software packages. The software defines the architecture of the network; it determines which of the various protocols and software programs are used for communicating with this communication processor device.

The primary application of the front end is to serve as the interface between the central data processing system (host computer) and the data communication network with its hundreds or even thousands of input/output terminals or nodes. Many of the newer and more powerful front end processors can perform *message processing* because they have enough storage capacity, processing power, and disk units. For example, the processor might receive inquiry messages from remote terminals, process the messages to determine the specific information required, retrieve the information from an online random access storage unit, and send it back to the inquiring terminals without involving the host computer. In networks of this type, application-oriented processing is as important as message receipt and transmission.

Another function related to processing is *message switching*. This function occurs when the front end receives a message, determines that it only needs to be switched to some other terminal or node, and performs the circuit switch or message switch. It also can use a store and forward process to hold the message and forward it at a later time.

The basic component parts of a front end processor are as follows (see Figure 3-6).

- *Channel interface* is the hardware interface that permits the communication processor to connect directly to the standard data channel of a host computer.
- *Software* is the highly specialized set of stored programs that define the specific

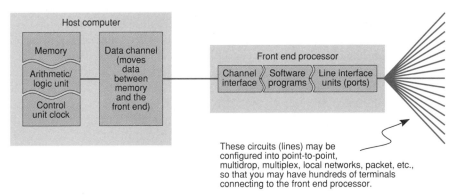

Figure 3-6   Front end processor.

architecture/protocols of the front end. The software determines which standard protocol should be used for a given front end. Some of this software now is being built into *firmware*. That is, the programs themselves are coded into circuit chips instead of being programmed logic. Some sophisticated front end processors have firmware (a circuit card with built-in program code) that serves as a protocol converter so you can interconnect a computer using one protocol to a host mainframe computer using another protocol. *Protocols* are the rules (techniques) that enable two machines to talk with one another.

• *Line interface units* (also called *ports*) are hardware devices used to link the communication processor with the modems that terminate each communication circuit. A specific front end may have the capacity for 10 or 200 ports (circuits).

There are over two dozen vendors of front end processors, including each of the major host mainframe manufacturers.

The general functions of front end processors are discussed next. Not all communication processors perform all these functions; therefore, you must check an individual model to be sure it performs the functions necessary for your network.

Communication Line Control

Polling/selecting of individual terminals, intelligent terminal controllers, or network nodes. *Polling* is asking each terminal whether it has a message to send, and *selecting* is asking each terminal whether it is in a condition to receive a message.

Automatic answering, acknowledgment, and dialing for outgoing calls.

Port selection, which allows several circuits to share a single port. The *port* is the plug or connection point where the individual lines enter the front end processor. You can control which group of terminals can have access to the host computer.

Ability to address messages to specific circuits or terminals. Examples are a broadcast address that goes to all terminals, a multiple address that goes to a select group of several terminals, or a single address that goes to a specific communication circuit or specific terminal.

Circuit switching, which allows one incoming circuit to be switched directly to another when it is available. This creates a straight-through transmission path for the movement of messages from one terminal location to another. Associated with circuit switching is a store and forward capability similar to that in voice mail or electronic mail systems. When the second half of the circuit path is unavailable, the communication processor records the incoming text and transmits it to the other terminal when the circuit is free.

Automatic routing of messages to a backup terminal when a specific terminal or circuit is out of order.

Addition or deletion of communication line control codes. Line control codes (the grammar of data communications), such as END OF BLOCK, BEGINNING OF BLOCK, or START OF MESSAGE, must be deleted before the message is passed to the host computer or must be added before the message is passed to the outgoing communication circuits.

Protocol/Code Conversion

Code conversion, that is, the software or hardware conversion from one code format to another such as ASCII to EBCDIC.

Conversion from one protocol to another, which allows different machines to talk to each other if they all use different protocols such as HDLC, SDLC, and X.25.

Assembly of Characters/Messages

Assembly and disassembly of bits into characters. Bits are transmitted in serial fashion on a communication circuit. The front end assembles these serial bits into parallel characters for the host computer to accept.

Assembly/disassembly to handle synchronous or asynchronous modes of transmission.

Handling of transmission speed differences where different communication circuits transmit at different bits per second rates, such as 2400 bits per second versus 56,000 bits per second.

Data and Message Editing

Control editing, which consists of adding items to a message, rerouting messages, rearranging data for further transmission, or looking for nonexistent addresses.

Message compression or compaction, which is a methodology for transmitting meaningful data messages but through the transmission of fewer data bits.

Signaling of abnormal occurrences to the host computer.

Assignment of consecutive serial numbers to each message and, possibly, time stamping and date stamping of each individual message.

Message Queuing/Buffering

Slowing the flow of messages when the host computer or the remote terminal station (node) is overburdened by traffic.

Queuing messages into distinct input queues and output queues between the front end processor and host computer or between the front end processor and outgoing communication circuits.

Giving priorities to different communication circuits or automatically assigning priorities to various types of messages to speed throughput of various message types.

Handling the timeout facility, such as when a specific terminal station does not respond or when a circuit ceases to respond. The system times-it-out and, in the future, skips it so normal operation can be continued.

Error Control

Error detection and automatic transmission for parity checks on message blocks (cyclical redundancy checks and others).

Forward error correction techniques to reduce errors flowing through the communication circuits.

Message Recording

Logging all inbound and outbound messages on magnetic tape for a historical transaction trail.

Logging the most recent 20 minutes on a magnetic disk for immediate restart and recovery purposes.

Other Functions

Multiplexing.

Dynamic allocation of task management queues.

Automatic switchover to a backup host computer in the event of a primary host failure.

Circuit concentration where a number of low speed communication circuits might interface to one higher speed communication circuit.

Performance of some functions of the Packet Assembly/Disassembly (PAD), if the front end also is serving as a Switching Node (SN) in a packet switching network. In this situation the front end contains the multiple databases required for alternate routing and packetizing of messages. (Packet networks will be discussed in Chapter 6.)

Network Control   Networks can operate in a *central control mode* or an *interrupt mode*. The central control mode involves the centralized polling of each station device (terminal or node) on the network. *Polling* is the process of individually giving each of the terminals permission to send data one at a time.

The interrupt philosophy implies that when a terminal sends data, the incoming data stream interrupts the host computer and the host stops processing so it can handle the incoming data. Because this mode of operation is wasteful of processing capacity, it generally is not used on host computers except for some minicomputer systems that have very few terminals and on local area networks.

The host computer contains software that provides the interface so the data communication network can process requests. For example, teleprocessing monitor programs control the routing, scheduling, and movement of data within the host computer. Telecommunication access programs handle the routing, scheduling, and polling of terminals in the network, although today these telecommunication access programs usually are offloaded to a front end processor. Chapter 9 (Protocols and Software) has a Teleprocessing Monitors section and a Telecommunication Access Programs section.

MODEMS

Another essential piece of equipment is the modem at the host end of the network. A modem also is the first piece of equipment encountered at the remote end. Review Figure 3-5 to see where these two modems are located. *Modem* is an acronym for *MO*dulator/*DEM*odulator. A modem takes digital electrical pulses received from a computer, terminal, or microcomputer and converts them into a continuous analog signal that is acceptable for transmission over an analog voice grade circuit. Until recently, all of these devices were *analog modems* because the signals were sent over analog communication circuits. The introduction of all-digital circuits required digital modems, which will be discussed in a later section of this chapter.

The modem that transmits the signal is the modulator because it modulates, or puts some form of intelligence on the carrier wave, whereas the receiving modem is the demodulator because it demodulates or interprets that signal upon its receipt. A modem has both a digital side and an analog side. The *digital side* is the one toward the business machine (terminal or computer), whereas the *analog side* is the one toward the communication circuit.

To *modulate* is to adapt a signal so it can be transmitted over the type of transmission circuits in use. The modem performs this adaptation. In addition, even though some communication circuits have a theoretical maximum transmission capacity in bits per second, you do not always use this full capacity. It is the modem that drives the line. In other words, it is the modem that sends the signal at whatever speed you wish to transmit. Modems operate at speeds of 300, 1200, 2400, 4800, 9600, and much higher in bits per second.

To demonstrate how an analog modem operates, our examples use *frequency modulation*. More specifically, they use the *frequency shift keying* (FSK) technique that switches between two frequencies (tones). To our ears, the change in frequency results in a change in the pitch of the tone. A high-pitched tone is a higher frequency and therefore has a greater number of cycles per second (hertz), whereas a low-pitched tone has a fewer number of cycles per second.

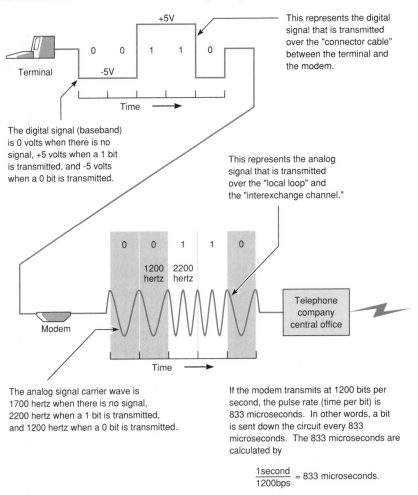

Figure 3-7   Operation of a modem.

To learn about the operation of a modem, examine Figure 3-7. Starting in the upper left corner, this figure shows the data stream of 0s and 1s that might be coming from a terminal, going into a modem, and going on to the communication circuit. Notice how the 0s and 1s from the terminal are represented as +5 volts of electricity for a 1 and −5 volts of electricity for a 0. Next, the modem modulates or changes the voltages of electricity into two different frequency tones represented as 2200 cycles per second for 1s and 1200 cycles per second for 0s. In other words, when the modem receives −5 volts of electricity, it converts that to a signal of 1200 cycles per second. If you were listening during the transmission, you could hear the 2200 and 1200 hertz tones because they are within the range of human hearing frequencies.

If the modem operates at a speed of 1200 bits per second, then the timing between changes from the higher to the lower frequency is 833 microseconds (1/1200 = 833

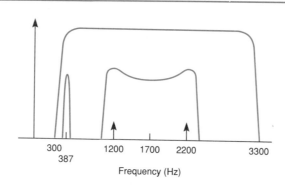

A significant factor to consider when using a 202 modem is line turnaround time required for switching from transmit mode to receive mode. Echo suppressors in the telephone equipment that are required for voice transmission on long distance calls must be turned off by the modem to transmit digital data. The modem must provide a 200-millisecond tone to the line to turn off the echo suppressors every time it goes from transmit to receive mode; hence, if short records are being transmitted, the turnaround time can slow throughput considerably.

SPECIFICATIONS

Data:

Serial, binary, asynchronous, half duplex on 2-wire lines

Data Transfer Rate:

0 to 1200 bits per second—switched network

0 to 1800 bits per second—leased lines with C2 conditioning

Optional 5 bits per second AM reverse channel transmitter and receiver available for switched-network units (387 Hz).

Figure 3-8   Bell 202 modem (half duplex/1200 bits per second).

microseconds). On the other hand, if there are two 1 bits in a sequence, then the higher frequency is held on the circuit for a period equal to 1666 microseconds (2 × 833 microseconds).

In reality, a much more complicated sine waveform is sent down the communication circuit; it contains the combination of all the frequencies (2200 and 1200). The oversimplified description above suits our purpose because we are trying to show how a modem converts electrical signals to frequency tones. Frequency tones (frequency shift keying—FSK) are the most popular method of transmitting data across telephone lines, although other modulation techniques are used at higher bits per second rates.

Figure 3-8 shows the frequency assignments for a Bell 202 modem. Notice the usable bandwidth of the voice grade circuit (300 to 3300 hertz) and the 1200 and 2200 signal frequencies. Compare this figure with the 300 to 3300 bandwidth shown in Figure 2-6 in Chapter 2.

Modems are classified by the speed at which they operate. The less expensive modems used with microcomputers usually operate at 300, 1200, and 2400 bits per second, although microcomputers easily can handle greater speeds. With larger and more centralized networks, modems traditionally operate at speeds of 4800, 9600, 14,400, 19,200, 38,400, 50,000, 56,000, 1,544,000 bits per second, and higher. An example of a fast modem for use with microcomputers might be one that can send data over ordinary telephone lines at speeds of 38,400 bits per second. Such a modem uses a data compression technique to achieve four times the throughput on a 9600 bits per second communication circuit. At lower line speeds of 300, 1200, and 2400, most modems can talk to any Hayes-compatible modem. (That is, they have the ability to communicate with a modem manufactured by Hayes.)

Even with progress toward all-digital networks, we still need analog modems to pass data over the thousands of currently installed analog circuits, most of which will not be able to operate digitally for many years. In fact, both dial-up and leased line modems continue evolving with such features as improved error correction, data compression, echo cancellation, and increasingly sophisticated management and diagnostic features.

Modem Speed Versus File Transfer Time   High speed modems save on line charges. For example, at 1200 bits per second it takes approximately one hour to transmit a 120-page file, but at 19,200 bits per second transmission time drops to approximately four minutes.

To illustrate the dramatic effect of higher transmission speeds, here is an example of some theoretical times for sending files of different lengths at different speeds. First, let us define some of the files. A 1,000-byte file (10,000 bits using start-stop asynchronous transmission) is about one half a video screen in terms of output. A 10,000-byte file might be a four- to five-page document. A 50,000-byte file might be several complex graphic pictures. A 100,000-byte file might be a good-sized spreadsheet or a 45-page document. Figure 3-9 illustrates the comparative transfer times for these file sizes.

The mathematics in Figure 3-9 were calculated as described here. First, the number of bytes in the file are multiplied by 10 bits per byte (8 bits per character plus 1 start and 1 stop bit). The result equals the number of bits to be transmitted. Then the number of bits to be transmitted is divided by the bits per second transmission speed of the modem, which gives the theoretical transfer speed in seconds. Remem-

File size	Bits per second			
	300	1200	2400	9600
1,000 bytes	33 sec	8 sec	4 sec	1 sec
10,000 bytes	5 min 30 sec	1 min 20 sec	40 sec	10 sec
50,000 bytes	27 min 36 sec	6 min 40 sec	3 min 10 sec	1 min 5 sec
100,000 bytes	55 min 33 sec	13 min 53 sec	6 min 56 sec	1 min 35 sec

Figure 3-9   File transfer time.

ber that this is a general calculation; it does not account for any control characters or the possibility of errors that might cause retransmission of some parts of the message.

Before transmitting data between two microcomputers or over a local area network, you may want to calculate how long the process is going to take. *File transfer time* can be estimated easily by using the following formula.

$$\text{File transfer time} = \frac{\text{Number of records} \times \text{Number of bytes per record} \times \text{Number of bits per byte}}{\text{Bits per second transmission speed}}$$

This formula will provide a close estimation, but it will not be accurate to the second. This is so because it does not take into account control characters that may be transmitted to control the transmission flow, nor does it take into account retransmissions caused by errors and other data transmission delays. The following equation shows a typical time for transmitting 2,000 records when using a 1200 bits per second modem.

$$\frac{2000 \text{ records} \times 85 \text{ bytes} \times 7 \text{ bits}}{1200 \text{ bits per second}} = 991.67 \text{ seconds or 17 minutes}$$

As you can see, the formula shows an approximate time of 17 minutes. As a rule of thumb, you might add 10 percent to this figure to account for transmission errors and the required control characters. When you add 10 percent of 17 minutes to itself, your estimate for the time required to transmit this file is approximately 19 minutes.

When you purchase modems, it is important to recognize that this piece of equipment is what governs transmission speed. If a slower 300 bits per second modem were used to transmit the same 2,000 records, it would take approximately 73 minutes. By increasing the speed to 19,200 bits per second, it would take only 62 seconds to transmit these 2,000 records.

Optical Modems   Transmitting on an optical fiber requires the use of an *optical modem*. This type of modem converts the electrical signals from a terminal or microcomputer to pulses of light that are transmitted down the optical fiber. Optical modems connect to the RS232 connector cable that connects to the front end or terminal/microcomputer. They operate using asynchronous or synchronous transmission at speeds up to 10 million bits per second. Current models can transmit up to 5 kilometers (1 kilometer is equal to 0.6 mile) without using amplifiers/repeaters to increase the power of the signal strength, but that certainly will be increased in the future, as will the 10 million bits per second speed. Optical modems contain a laser or light-emitting diode that originates the light pulses, along with the electronics needed to convert the electrical signal coming from the computer or terminal prior to transmitting the digital pulses of light.

A specific example of a fiber optic modem is one that operates over distances of up to 2.2 miles in full duplex mode and transmits at speeds up to 19,200 bits per second. This fiber optic modem is plug-compatible with RS232 connector cables between the modem and the terminal, and it was designed to link microcomputers with central host computer systems. Electronic data signals from a microcomputer enter the device and are converted to light sources. A light-emitting diode transmits the data over fiber optic cable to the remote modem, which reconverts the light signals back to electronic signals.

Short Haul Modems   Another type of modem is a *short haul modem* in which you use your own wire pair cable to transmit direct electrical signals. Sometimes this is called a 20-milliamp circuit (also called *current loop* signaling). Inexpensive (costing as little as $40) devices can serve as the interface for any RS232 port (COM1 port on a microcomputer) from a modem to a standard 20-milliamp loop system. Typically, these systems transmit at 19,200 bits per second over a distance of up to several miles. This type of modem also is called a *line driver*. When you put more electrical power (amperage) onto the communication circuit, you can drive your signal for a distance greater than several miles. Such short haul modems are used within buildings, a plant, college campus, or university facility. An example of a line driver is one that operates asynchronously over full duplex, four-wire circuits at speeds up to 19,200 bits per second for a distance of more than 1 mile. When this same line driver is used at lower speeds, transmission distance increases to 18 miles at 110 bits per second.

Microcomputer users often need short haul modems. For example, if you want to connect two microcomputers together and they are several thousand feet apart, a short haul modem may be the answer. One such device consists of a box approximately the size of a package of cigarettes. The standard RS232 connector plug for your COM1 port on a microcomputer is on one side of the box, and the cable going between the buildings attaches to the other side. You attach these small modems first to each end of your cable and then to the serial COM1 ports of the microcomputers. They get their power through the serial ports. Because short haul modems do not require an external power source, they sometimes are referred to as *modem eliminators*. These tiny modems are able to send data down the cable for distances of approximately 3,000 feet at 9600 bits per second, or up to 6 miles at 1200 bits per second. This type of short haul modem is analogous to increasing your RS232 connector cable beyond its 50-foot maximum length.

These modems are ideally suited for interconnecting microcomputers between two different offices in the same building. Typically, a pair of these modems with 500 feet of cable costs approximately $150. You should use a shielded wire, although two wires (twisted wire pair) with the standard RJ-11 telephone connector also works. To transmit data between microcomputers using these short haul modems, you need to call up your communication software package and transmit as the package instructs.

Another form of short haul modem is a *null modem*. Null modems also are modem eliminators. Because null modems are used exclusively for copying files between two microcomputers that are from 5 to 10 feet apart, they are described in Chapter 10, Microcomputers and Communications.

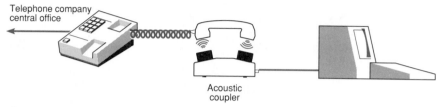

Figure 3-10   Acoustic coupler.

Acoustic Couplers   An older type of modem is an *acoustic coupler* (see Figure 3-10). This modem is used primarily for dial-up because it can interface with any basic telephone handset. All you do is call the computer and place the telephone handset into the acoustic coupler. The coupler performs the typical modem functions of converting direct electrical signals from the terminal to frequency modulated tones (frequency shift keying) that can be sent over any telephone communication circuit.

Dumb Modems   Modems typically have been differentiated as either smart or dumb. This differentiation is based on their varying abilities to respond to a command language through which a user's communication software package instructs the modem to perform various tasks, such as dialing calls, answering incoming calls, and redialing calls. *Dumb modems* must be set manually for parameters of speed, originate or answer mode, and so forth. The user sets these parameters with switches and then dials the call by using a telephone.

Smart Modems   By contrast, *smart modems* are commanded to perform their functions through the use of a command syntax language entered from the keyboard of a microcomputer. This language controls their functions, such as changing speed and dialing calls. For example, if a Hayes™ modem is used with your microcomputer, then you might type the letters AT. These letters instruct the modem to pay attention to the next set of letters because they constitute a command or parameter change. Therefore, typing the sequence ATD tells the modem to pay attention, and the D tells it to dial a number. The complete command might be ATD555-1212, which tells the modem to pay attention, prepare to dial a number, and to dial 555-1212. Selected examples from the Hayes modem command set are

A	Answer the call without waiting for telephone to ring
A/	Repeat last command
B	Put modem into the Bell 212A or V.22 protocol
C	Turn transmit carrier off/on
D	Instruct modem to dial the telephone number
E	Instruct modem to echo or not echo characters
F	Switch between half duplex and full duplex
H	Cause modem to be on-hook or off-hook
L	Set the modem's speaker volume
O	Use for digital loopback testing

Figure 3-11   Hayes Smartmodem® 2400. Reproduced by permission of Hayes Microcomputer Products, Inc.

Did you ever wonder what all those modem lights mean? While their significance might vary from modem to modem, here is an explanation of the eight lights on a Hayes Smartmodem® 2400 (see Figure 3-11).

MR—Modem Ready. This light is on when your 110-volt ac electrical power is turned on.

TR—Terminal Ready. This light shows that the modem has received a signal from the microcomputer to which it is connected, telling it that the microcomputer is now ready to do something, such as send data.

SD—Send Data. This light is on when data is being sent from the RS232 serial port (usually COM1) of your microcomputer to the modem.

RD—Receive Data. This light is on when the modem is receiving data from the distant computer and the modem in turn is sending it to the RS232 serial port (usually COM1) of your microcomputer.

OH—Off-Hook. This light is on when the modem is off-hook with regard to the telephone line. If the light is on, you probably are connected to the telephone company and using the circuit.

CD—Carrier Detect. This light turns on when the modem detects a carrier wave tone from a distant modem.

AA—Auto Answer. This light is on if the modem is set to answer incoming calls automatically.

HS—High Speed. This light is on when the modem is set to work at 2400 bits per second. It is not on when the modem is operating at 1200 bits per second.

Figure 3-12   Hayes Smartmodem® 9600B/SCIII on a circuit card. Reproduced by permission of Hayes Microcomputer Products, Inc.

Figure 3-12 shows an *internal modem* that is on a circuit card for a microcomputer. It functions exactly like the *external modem* in Figure 3-11, except it is installed inside the microcomputer.

Beyond smart modems is a classification that might be called intelligent or advanced modem features. These more expensive modems contain microprocessor chips and internal read only memory (ROM) coding to provide sophisticated communication protocols and diagnostic checking that run within the modem itself.

This is where you begin moving into a classification of equipment that overlaps with other equipment because some of the newer, more sophisticated pieces of communication hardware cross over the boundaries that define other pieces of hardware. For example, some modems not only perform digital-to-analog conversion but also operate as multiplexers, security restrictor devices, encryption devices, error detection and retransmission devices, and so forth. The problem is that there are many types of hybrid equipment on the market. As a result, it is no longer possible to say that a device is solely a modem because it might be a combination modem, multiplexer, and encryption device.

When a microcomputer uses a modem to dial a host mainframe computer, a lot more happens than meets the eye. In an ideal situation, you only have to know how to operate the communication software, which provides the communication capabilities. If you have a modem with a command syntax language, the software uses the microcomputer's operating system to set up a communication circuit to the modem via the microcomputer's serial port. It sets the requested speed and then issues any other commands required to set up the modem's dialing or answering capabilities.

Digital Modems   If the communication circuits use digital transmission for their entire length, instead of analog transmission as is done with normal telephone circuits, you need a *digital modem*. This modem shapes the digital pulses and performs all auxiliary functions, such as loopback testing and checking the circuit diagnostics. Its special function is to convert a digital signal from a computer or terminal to a more precise and more accurate digital signal. For example, a digital modem can take a weak electrical signal, put very precise timing characteristics between the pulses, put it out at a certain strength, and control its electrical characteristics. This is done to reduce noise, distortion, and errors. Digital modems are much simpler than analog modems.

Digital transmission (discrete on and off pulses) is the sending of digital pulses between your premises and the telephone company's central office and then transmitting the digital pulses over the long distance communication circuits between cities. When using digital transmission, a digital modem is necessary to shape the digital pulses. The correct name for this modem is either a channel service unit (CSU) or a data service unit (DSU). Sometimes it is referred to as a *DSU/CSU.*

The *channel service unit* performs transmit and receive filtering, signal shaping, longitudinal balancing, voltage isolation, and equalization functions, and it handles remote loopback testing. The *data service unit* is a channel service unit that, in addition, provides bipolar conversion functions. These bipolar conversion functions ensure proper signal shaping and signal strength for transmission that is almost error free.

Furthermore, the CSU terminates the circuit and performs signal regeneration. It also monitors the incoming signal to detect bipolar return to zero violations, ensures that the data stream does not contain 16 consecutive 0s, and ensures that at least three 1s are in every 24 bits transmitted. A bipolar violation might occur if a bipolar nonreturn to zero signal is transmitted (see Figure 5-18 in Chapter 5) when the receiving modem expected a bipolar return to zero signal. The 16 consecutive 0s and three 1 bits in 24 are signaling rules that must be met to transmit over an AT&T ACCUNET T-1 circuit. A DSU/CSU combination is needed for the digital data system circuits, but only a CSU is needed on ACCUNET because the AT&T ACCUNET T-1 circuit handles the DSU signal conversion function. The primary purpose of a DSU is to convert the data stream generated by the transmitting equipment into the bipolar return to zero format required for transmission over the digital network. Obviously, it is possible to obtain either a DSU or a CSU separately, or a box that is a combination DSU/CSU. The data rates at which DSU/CSUs operate must adhere to the AT&T specifications, such as 56,000 bits per second, 9600 bits per second, 4800 bits per second, and 2400 bits per second.

In the early days of digital transmission, you had to use both a DSU to manage the interface to the communicating computer and a CSU to manage the connection over the digital communication circuit. Today's digital modems incorporate both the DSU and the CSU into what some people call a DSU. In other words, most DSUs now incorporate the CSU, which used to manage the electrical characteristics on the circuit.

DSU/CSUs fall into three general speed rate categories: digital data service (DDS), T-1 circuits, and T-3 circuits. These three categories reflect the type of communication service that is available from the common carriers (telephone companies), and their names are derived from the speed of the circuit with which they operate. A DSU/CSU for *digital data service* communication circuits operates at a speed ranging from 1200 bits per second to 56,000 bits per second. A *T-1 DSU/CSU* operates at 1,544,000 bits per second over a T-1 circuit. The *T-3 DSU/CSU* operates at 44,376,000 bits per second over a T-3 circuit.

Some DSU/CSUs are able to handle something called *fractional T-1* services. This means that a T-1 circuit with a transmission speed of 1,544,000 bits per second can be divided into twenty-four 56,000 or 64,000 bits per second channels. The 56,000 bits per second channel is used for digital data transmission, and the 64,000 bits per second channel is used for digitized voice transmission. The DSU/CSU is then able to transmit data over one or more of these 56,000 bits per second channels. When a user who is transmitting over one of the 56,000 bits per second channels needs more transmission capacity (requires more bandwidth), a second 56,000 bits per second channel is immediately made available to the user. These twenty-four 56,000 bits per second channels are the individual fractional T-1 communication circuits.

V.32 Modems   The *V.32* modem provides full duplex transmission at 9600 bits per second over dial-up telephone circuits. In addition to offering this fast transmission over dial-up circuits, V.32 modems also are used for backing up leased telephone circuits.

The next improvement in V.32 modems was to have them encode the data to be transmitted into patterns called *constellations*. The addition of this feature turns the V.32 standard into the *V.32bis* standard. Thus, the V.32bis modem using constellation pattern encoding has a 50 percent gain in speed over a normal V.32 modem. This allows a V.32bis modem to transmit over dial-up analog circuits at speeds of 14,400 bits per second. Some modems to be marketed in the future use what is called the *V.fast* design. These V.fast modems should be able to transmit very close to 24,000 bits per second, which is near the theoretical maximum of 25,900 bits per second demonstrated by using Shannon's Law (see the box Calculating the Capacity of a Voice Grade Circuit in Chapter 2).

One problem you may encounter when using V.32 modems with networks is that some telephone companies use TASI to interleave many different calls onto one high speed communication circuit. TASI's constant switching between circuits causes breaks large enough that the V.32 modem cannot maintain the 9600 bits per second speed. When this happens, it has to drop to a lower speed.

Some telephone companies design their TASI dial-up circuits to disengage automatically when a data call is detected instead of a voice call. One way in which TASI circuits detect data calls is by the in-band signaling tone sent to disable the echo suppressors.

V.42bis Data Compression   A modem's transmission rate is the primary factor that determines the throughput rate of data, but it is not the only factor. The *V.42bis* standard governs the data compression that is executed in the modem. Before the V.42bis recommendation was developed, several other data compression techniques were implemented.

V.42 is the Consultative Committee on International Telegraph and Telephone (CCITT) standard for error correction in modems. We generally find it in modems transmitting at 2400 bits per second or faster. V.42 incorporates the Microcom Networking Protocol *MNP 4*; therefore, modems that have V.42 error correction are compatible with modems that use MNP 4.

V.42bis is the CCITT standard for data compression. It improves the transfer rate by a factor of four. *MNP 5* is Microcom's data compression protocol, which a number of other modem manufacturers also use. MNP 5 incorporates the features of MNP 4. Although MNP 5 is more established than V.42bis, it is less efficient than V.42bis and the two are not compatible.

The V.42bis compression function increases data throughput by stripping out the unnecessary bits in a transmission. As an example, many data transfers entail the sending of numerous columns of numbers. With ASCII code, a number is transmitted by using an 8-bit byte even though only four bits are required to represent the number. The V.42bis data compression technique recognizes the four unused bits and eliminates them from the transmission. This has the effect of doubling the throughput for numeric data. The actual gain in throughput provided by data compression depends on the relationship between how much numeric data and how much alphabetic data is being transmitted. The higher the amount of numeric data, the higher is the rate of throughput.

Dial-Up Backup   The possibility of a circuit failure always exists when you use either an analog modem or a digital modem (DSU/CSU) on a leased circuit. In case there is a leased circuit failure, you should have the ability to use the same modem to call a central computer site telephone number in order to reestablish the communication circuit, but with a *dial-up backup circuit* instead of the leased circuit that just failed. Depending on the quality of the dial-up circuit, you may be able to transmit at the same data rate as the leased circuit. On the other hand, you may have to transmit at a slightly lower data rate, such as moving down from 19,200 to 9600 bits per second.

Modems used on leased line circuits often do not have the ability to operate as dial-up modems. For digital circuits, the procedure used to be so complicated that a DSU/CSU had to be used for the leased circuit and a separate analog modem had to be used for the dial-up circuit. The dual capability was accomplished by purchasing an A/B switch and hooking the two modems together so the user could turn immediately from the A modem to the B modem and dial with the analog dial-up modem. Today combination units are available that usually cost less than the total of the components. The components in this situation would be a DSU/CSU, an analog modem, and an A/B switch. A typical DSU/CSU with built-in dial-up backup is a DSU/CSU that operates on the digital data service circuits and has a V.32 analog modem that can be used on a dial-up analog circuit.

If an analog circuit fails, you probably can use an analog modem in a dial-up backup configuration. The question you have to settle is whether you want to transmit in half duplex mode over a two-wire dial-up circuit or in full duplex mode over a four-wire circuit. When establishing a backup connection over a two-wire circuit, the central site modem calls the remote user's modem to establish a dial-up circuit. After establishing the link, the transmission begins in half duplex mode where one end sends a message and then waits until it receives a response from the other end before sending a second message. (Half duplex is two-way transmission, but only in one direction at a time.) Establishing a four-wire backup procedure requires the placing of two calls over two separate dial-up telephone circuits. One of these circuits transmits and one receives. This approach is somewhat more complex because the modem must be able to be connected quickly to two different telephone circuits to establish the full duplex four-wire transmission. (Full duplex is simultaneous two-way transmission.)

Features of Modems   Now that we have examined the types of modems and discussed their basic functions (to modulate a signal), let us discuss some of their optional features. The features listed below may not be in all modems; rather, this is a comprehensive list of the many features that may be built into modems.

- *Wireless modems* transmit the data signals through the air instead of by using a cable. They sometimes are called a *radio frequency modem*. This type of modem may work well with pen-based microcomputers and wireless networks.

- *Loopback* functions (see Figure 3-13) for diagnostic purposes probably are the single most important feature built into modems. Automatic loopback allows the user to set a remote modem on loopback and send a message to that modem. The message is looped back to the original sender, where it can be checked for accuracy to help diagnose where a fault might be in the network. Loopback switches help diagnose whether the problem is in the connector cable between the terminal and modem, on the digital or analog side of the modem, or in the local loop communication circuit. The digital side of the modem plugs into the terminal; the analog side plugs into the telephone circuits, unless you are on a completely digital network. In that case, a DSU/CSU is used instead of a standard modem.

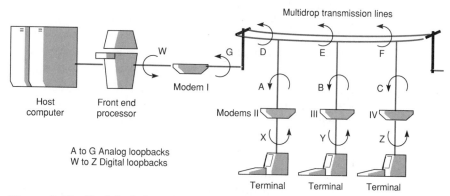

Figure 3-13   Fault isolation with loopback tests.

- Some modems can be turned on or off from a remote station. These contain automatic answering and calling capabilities, so a remote terminal can be started from thousands of miles away.

- Some modems allow the simultaneous transmission of both voice and data. One model allows a voice conversation to go over the circuit while simultaneously transmitting a data stream of 19,200 bits per second.

- Some modems allow a *reverse channel* capability for message acknowledgments. The purpose of a reverse channel is to avoid interruption of the ongoing message stream but still provide for a path over which message acknowledgments can be sent. For example, the modem could receive messages at 2400 bits per second but simultaneously send back, in the reverse direction, one character acknowledgment for each received message. This tells the original transmitter whether the message was received correctly. While this resembles full duplex transmission, it is different technically because of the vast differences of speed in each direction. The reverse channel may be transmitting at only 10 to 75 bits per second (see the 387 Hz channel in Figure 3-8).

- Multiplexing is built into some modems.

- Microprocessor circuits are built into some modems for automatic equalization to compensate for electronic instabilities on the transmission line. This equalization compensates for attenuation or delay distortion that causes errors, requiring retransmission of messages.

- Many modems today have built-in diagnostic routines for self-checking of their own circuits to determine where a fault might lie.

- Some modems have alternate speed switches so you can switch up or down in speeds, let us say from 9600 to 4800 bits per second.

- Some modems have *split streaming* by which the modem transmits four message streams at different speeds. One message stream is transmitted at 4800 bits per second, one at 2400 bits per second, and the other two at 1200 bits per second. This also is referred to as a *multiport modem.*

- Some modems are more efficient because they have a lower clocking or retrain time. *Retrain time* is the *turnaround time* when the message direction changes. For example, when you are transmitting in half duplex mode (one direction at a time), the modem is in the transmit mode, but when you receive a message, it must switch its electronic circuits to be in a receive mode.

- For efficiency, some modems have a longer flywheel effect for brief drops of the *carrier wave* (the 1700 hertz signal). When the carrier wave drops for a couple of microseconds, you technically have lost the circuit. With a built-in flywheel effect, however, the modem can remain connected to the circuit and pick up where it left off after the carrier wave returns. This assumes the drop is not for too long a period of time.

- Certification of modems involves AT&T and the Bell Operating Companies. For modems to operate over the dial-up telephone network without data access arrangements (DAA), they must be registered and certified with the Federal

Communications Commission. Certification is required only for dial-up and not for modems operating over lease circuits. When using the dial-up networks, it is wise to select certified modems because data access arrangements add extra cost to your circuits. The purpose of a data access arrangement is to limit the amplitude (power) of the signal presented to the telephone circuit.

- Some modems can perform network analysis, monitoring such features as the RS232 interface and circuit characteristics (analog), although usually this is performed by other test equipment. Tests are carried out during normal data transmission using out-of-band signaling (unused portions of the bandwidth).

- Modems provide status indication lights on the modem's front panel, such as MODEM READY (MR) or CARRIER DETECT (CD). These indicators are helpful but do not constitute comprehensive diagnostics, although at a remote site they may be the only form of diagnostics. When problems develop at a remote site, look at the modem status lights to see whether they are on. If not, one of them is working improperly.

TERMINALS/MICROCOMPUTERS

The *terminal,* which is the input/output hardware device at the remote end of a communication circuit, probably is the one piece of equipment with which you are most familiar. Obviously, both terminals and microcomputers can be used as input/output devices.

Shopping for a terminal can be a real problem if it is not done correctly. For example, a bargain terminal may have the wrong code format or an incompatible protocol, which requires the additional purchase of a protocol converter. A decision on which interface cable can be used with the selected terminal also must be made. This cable connects the terminal and the modem. Some systems use a RS232, others a RS449, and still others fiber optic cable. The selected terminal or microcomputer workstation must be compatible with the communication protocols used by the host mainframe computer, and its general characteristics and uses must meet the user's specific day-to-day business requirements.

There are several major categories of terminals, each of which is discussed in the following sections.

Microcomputers and Workstations   These devices are either general purpose microcomputers or specially designed input/output workstations that have custom-designed microprocessor chips. Many vendors have developed customized workstations for use in graphics, the factory, banking, and a whole host of other special situations. The basic input/output device is a microcomputer. Its functions include editing data, storing data, mathematical calculations, and prompting for information or forms design (handled on the video screen); all can be handled locally without assistance from the host mainframe computer.

Technically, there is a difference between a workstation and a microcomputer. A *workstation* usually provides all the tools professionals need for their daily work.

Figure 3-14 Microcomputer with keyboard and video display monitor.

Among these tools are specialized applications like mathematical modeling, computer-assisted design (CAD), intensive programming, and networking. Today's workstation has much more computing power than the average microcomputer. Workstations must offer true multitasking capability so the user does not spend a large amount of time waiting for the computer to finish one job before starting the next one. On the other hand, a *microcomputer* may not have the ability to handle all the specialized applications, and its multitasking ability may be significantly less. Most microcomputer users may be satisfied with printer sharing and telecommunications as a replacement for true multitasking capability. The primary use of a microcomputer is for such functions as word processing, accounting, and spreadsheet modeling. As microcomputers get more powerful microprocessor chips (80586 chips), they may become as powerful as contemporary workstations. Therefore, today you may be able to see the difference between a workstation and a microcomputer, but tomorrow they may be the same thing.

A microcomputer is shown in Figure 3-14. A complete description of microcomputers and how they operate in networks is presented in Chapter 10, Microcomputers and Communications.

Video Terminals   Video terminals typically have a television screen and a typewriter keyboard. These *video display units* (VDU) sometimes are referred to as video display terminals (VDT) or cathode ray tubes (CRT). Microcomputers have a VDU as their visual output device. Alphanumeric video terminals are used in the business office, whereas graphic video terminals are used by graphic designers. Airlines are

COMMUNICATIONS FOR THE AIRLINES

Almost everyone is familiar with data communications in the airline industry. American Airlines' SABRE system was the first automated airline reservation system.

Today the major air carriers have developed individual communication networks for reservations, flight planning, inventory, control, flight scheduling, and all the other applications required to run a major airline. The major systems have been developed by American Airlines, United Airlines, and Lufthansa in Europe.

An interlinking network is used by all the airlines to transfer messages among these various systems. The interlinking network is maintained by Aeronautical Radio Incorporated (ARINC). American Airlines and United Airlines have the largest base of terminals installed in travel agents' offices as well as for their own use.

Airline networks are built using dial-up and leased circuits and combining front ends and terminals to get an efficient network layout. In today's world the application of data communications to the airline business is not so much in the network itself, but more in the installed base of terminals located in travel agents' offices. This is because there is a correlation between the number of airline booking terminals in travel agents' offices and the number of flights booked on that airline.

As an example of the importance of these reservation systems, the American Airlines' SABRE system books an average of 470,000 airline reservations a day. They are handled by over 8,000 reservation operators located at five regional sites and through 68,000 terminals located in 14,000 travel agencies.

Several years ago this network was spread inefficiently over 1,100 separate voice and data lines. In a major overhaul, the network was consolidated onto 45 high capacity digital lines carrying both voice and data. Multiplexers channel the messages to 14 connection sites and split them out to their destinations. Traffic on the SABRE network has doubled, while operating costs have increased by only 30 percent.

major users of video terminals (see the accompanying box on Communications for the Airlines).

In addition to a standard keyboard, the video terminal has a marker on the screen called a *cursor*. It moves about the screen to show the terminal operator the next position in which a character will be printed.

When selecting a video terminal, you should consider what the transmitting line speed is, if users can rotate or tilt the screen for easy viewing, if split-screen mode is available so two or more screens can display simultaneously, whether the character matrix size is large enough for easy viewing, if a detachable keyboard would be advantageous, if a self-test mode is available, how many characters can be displayed horizontally and how many lines vertically, whether it can accommodate a separate printer that can be turned on and off as needed, whether it can handle multicolor applications, and which editing functions are available such as character insertion/deletion, line insertion/deletion, erasing, and paging.

With regard to the individual terminal operator, some specific items must be taken into account when ordering a video terminal or VDU for a microcomputer. Because eyestrain and fatigue are the two most common complaints of video terminal operators, the following features increase productivity.

- A video tube screen filter should be obtained to protect against electromagnetic radiation, which can emanate as microwaves, infrared waves, and ultraviolet waves. You want to block all three. Operators who wear eyeglasses with plastic lenses can have an ultraviolet filter coating applied to protect against ultraviolet radiation.
- An antiglare screen should be used to eliminate glare from the front face of the video tube. Glare is the number one complaint of people who use video terminals or microcomputers.
- Cursors should be visible from 8 feet away, and they should be seen easily at 3 feet. Sometimes it is advantageous to have the option of either a blinking cursor, an extra large cursor, or a cursor that is on as a steady light.
- Detachable keyboards or a sloped keyboard may be desirable.
- Reverse video may ease eyestrain. With this feature, the operator can change from a dark background with light characters to a light background with dark characters.
- Multiple colors also may reduce eyestrain.
- Adjustments for tube brightness, focus, and contrast are desirable to accommodate the variety of operators who might use a video terminal.
- Glare and eyestrain can be reduced with the use of window shades, proper lighting, and movable screens that cut reflective glare.
- To prevent muscular aches and fatigue, VDUs should have movable keyboards, document holders, and screens that tilt to a comfortable viewing angle for the user. The height of the video screen and its ability to tilt might be critical to the terminal operator who wears bifocal lenses. Today's computer furniture often requires that video screens be placed above eye level. This consideration should be borne in mind when purchasing such furniture because operators (especially those who wear bifocals) should be able to look *down* onto the screen to prevent neck strain.
- The characters on the video monitor tube should not jitter or flicker because this movement causes eyestrain. By using a magnifying glass to look at the characters, you should be able to determine whether they jitter or shake. *Jitter* is caused by an insufficient video reflection voltage that makes the electron beam inaccurate when refreshing the character. *Flicker* is caused by a fast decay of the phosphor and a slow refresh rate. Technically, you should accept nothing below 65 hertz (frequency). Many video data terminals are 45, 50, or 55 hertz, which does not provide a fast enough refresh rate to avoid noticeable or even subliminal flicker.
- On the controversial subject of screen color, displays with black characters on white screens provide the most legibility. Many users, however, feel that yellow/green tube color is the easiest to see and tends to reduce eyestrain.

You should seriously consider purchasing video monitors that have multicolor capabilities because color tends to reduce eyestrain and enhances productivity. Color also makes it easier to understand an application.

- Always obtain the highest possible video monitor tube resolution. For example, some video monitors have resolution of 800 (horizontal) by 560 (vertical) pixels. The higher the resolution (a greater number of pixels), the clearer the picture and the less eyestrain. (*Pixels* are "picture elements"; each one is a small dot on a video tube.) Also get the smallest dots (pixels) for higher resolution (0.28 dot size is good).

- Users should obtain a dot matrix printer with the greatest density of pins. For example, a dot matrix printer with a 24-pin print head is preferred. LaserJet printers should get 300 dots per inch.

Teleprinter Terminals   These older terminals lack a video screen, produce a paper printout, and have a typewriterlike keyboard. In this discussion, *teleprinter terminals* have no programmable capacity. (Intelligent terminals are a separate category.) This type of terminal performs its printing through an impact, a dot matrix, or even an electronic ink jet. Its characters can print at a speed ranging from 10 to 300 or more characters per second. In the past this was the most common terminal, but the video terminal replaced it because it was less expensive to produce.

A teleprinter terminal has a typical typewriter keyboard, except it may contain several special function keys for data communication networks. In this case, a third function might be assigned to a single key such as start, stop, delete, or end of transmission. The first two functions of the key are its normal lower case and upper case for an alphabetic character, and the third function enables data transmission.

Some of the features to look for in a teleprinter terminal are size of the dot matrix, maximum print speed, bidirectional printing, size of the printable character set, number of character positions across the paper, form feed mechanism or individual sheet insertion, and graphics printing capability. Some teleprinter terminals offer a self-test answer-back mode whereby the terminal circuitry can be tested for problems.

Remote Job Entry Terminals   Usually, *remote job entry terminals* are nodes of a network or terminal stations where several types of devices are connected. Data often is transmitted from a host computer to a remote job entry terminal that might have a variety of terminal devices such as a video terminal, a high speed printing terminal, several data entry devices (such as disk or tape), and perhaps a microcomputer. Terminals in such an area operate at higher speeds, such as 9600 bits per second or greater, because large quantities of data are transmitted from this terminal station to the central host computer.

Transaction Terminals   These terminals are used by individuals in their homes or place of business. The most common *transaction terminal* is the automated teller machine (ATM) used by banking institutions for cash dispensing and related functions. Your telephone is a type of transaction terminal that accepts voice or data transactions for transmission by using the touchtone keypad.

Other transaction terminals are point-of-sale terminals in a supermarket; these enter charges directly from the supermarket to your bank account, or they can be used for verifying credit or verifying checks. These terminals can be built into electronic cash registers. For an example of how transaction terminals are used, see the accompanying box on Communications in the Rental Car Industry.

Facsimile (FAX) Terminals   Transmission of an exact picture of a hard copy document, including legal signatures, is one of the most important features in today's business office. This is especially so in areas such as legal contracts, medical records and authorizations, and for the control of business records.

Facsimile machines (see Figure 3-15) have evolved through four generations (Groups 1, 2, 3, and 4). Groups 1 and 2 are older analog machines, whereas Group 3 is a newer analog machine. Group 4 machines transmit digitally. Most of today's FAX machines are Group 3. The older analog machine can take six minutes to

---

COMMUNICATIONS IN THE RENTAL CAR INDUSTRY

Another major application for large national and international communication networks is the rental of automobiles. Avis Rent-A-Car was the first major company to develop an online real-time rental car network. This network interconnects the major locations where automobiles are rented, picked up, and returned.

The networks used by rental car companies have multiplexed circuits. These circuits are leased from the major telephone companies or special common carriers selling communication circuits.

A rental car network is quite similar to an airline network because it keeps track of dates when cars have to be returned to their lessor, makes rental agreements with people who rent the cars, calculates the cost and mileage used, and performs other general accounting functions.

Both Hertz and Avis, in their latest round of technological one-upmanship, introduced handheld computer terminals that allow service representatives to completely check in returning cars almost before customers can unbuckle their seat belts. The Avis service, called Roving Rapid Return, allows customers to get a receipt immediately without having to enter the rental agency building, stand in line, and wait while someone processes the rental contract.

When a car enters the Avis lot, for example, a service representative enters the Avis registration number that appears in the car's rear window into one of the handheld terminals. The terminal, which is linked locally to the Avis worldwide "Wizard" network by FM radio, retrieves the driver's name and rental information from a central mainframe database. It displays the customer's name so the service representative can use it while obtaining the car's odometer reading and gas tank level. Once that information has been entered, the mainframe totals the customer's bill and instructs the terminal's printer to produce a final receipt if the credit card number was given earlier. The customer can leave as soon as the receipt is printed. The Hertz express check-in service operates in a similar manner.

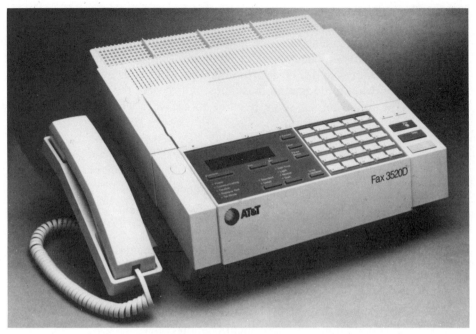

Figure 3-15   Facsimile machine. Photograph courtesy of AT&T Archives.

transmit one 8½ by 11 page. The Group 3 machines take less than one minute per page. Group 4 machines are just entering the marketplace. They will improve copy quality dramatically and reduce the actual transmission time for a standard Group 3 business letter from its current 20-second average to only 3 seconds. The Group 3 machines can transmit a page in 20 seconds, but by the time the FAX handles the call setup, transmits the page for 20 seconds, and disconnects the call, the total time to transmit the one page is about one minute. The top speed for Group 3 is 9600 bits per second, but it is 64,000 bits per second for Group 4 FAX machines.

A technological breakthrough for FAX is in the use of microcomputers. A "FAX card" or "FAX board" can be added to transform a microcomputer into a transmitting or receiving facsimile machine. This is not necessarily an inexpensive alternative, however, because FAX boards range from $300 to $500.

Did you ever wonder how a *FAX/VOICE switch* works? These switches allow you to connect both a facsimile machine and a voice telephone to the same telephone circuit. The reason, of course, is to save the monthly cost of a second telephone circuit. When a call comes in, the switch automatically connects to the facsimile machine or rings the voice telephone, depending on which is the correct action. If the incoming call is a facsimile, most Group 3 FAX machines transmit an 1100 hertz tone every three seconds. This is called the CNG (Calli*NG*) tone. When the switch hears the tone, it automatically switches to the facsimile machine. If the switch does not hear the tone, it allows the voice telephone to ring. In fact, the telephone can be an answering machine rather than a "plain vanilla" telephone! If you need a facsimile machine, a FAX/VOICE switch may be a better option than a microcomputer FAX card because microcomputer-based FAX cards may not always be online to receive incoming facsimiles. Moreover, if you leave your microcomputer online all the time so it can receive incoming dial-up calls, you may find either data being stolen from your PC or a virus. FAX cards in your microcomputer are best when all you want to do is send facsimiles, not receive them.

The following are some features to consider when you are purchasing a FAX machine.

- Ability to receive messages 24 hours per day
- Automatic speed selection at 2400, 4800, or 9600 bits per second
- Automatic feeding of multipage documents
- Automatic page cutting for received documents
- Selectable contrast and resolution
- Copy reduction to reduce oversize documents
- Automatic calling during evening hours
- Ability to serve as a backup copier
- Voice request to signal the caller's wish to speak with the distant operator
- Encryption and secret identification codes
- Sender's name and FAX telephone number, which are printed automatically at the top margin
- Time, date, and page number stamp
- Acknowledgment of all sent and received documents
- Automatic protocol conversion so a Group 3 machine can communicate with a Group 1 or 2 machine
- Fine and superfine switches. Group 3 FAX machines transmit in pixels (dots). The standard FAX is 203 by 98 pixels. By pressing the fine button, you improve resolution to 203 by 196. Superfine improves resolution still more to 203 by 391.

Facsimile transmission can be threatening to post office authorities because you can FAX a letter from one area to another for anywhere from $0.30 to $0.90, depending on the volume of traffic per month and the cost of communication circuits. For this reason, facsimile transmission is in direct competition with both electronic mail and post office letters.

Once a facsimile device is connected to a communication circuit, the following basic steps take place during transmission.

- You establish the call either by manually dialing your telephone or by having an automatic call placed (physical circuit connection).
- The FAX machine handles the premessage procedure, or *handshaking*, which consists of identifying the called station (facsimile machine) and any other procedures that might be required to set up the session.

- The FAX machine transmits the message (the *session*), which involves synchronization between the two devices, any error detection and correction methodologies, and movement of the message from one facsimile device to the other.

- The FAX machine completes the postmessage procedure, which includes END OF MESSAGE signaling at the conclusion of the page, any signaling that signifies more than one page, end of transmission, and anything else required to end the session (physical circuit disconnected).

Facsimile devices are connected by using either a standard interface cable to a telephone or a direct connection to the telephone circuit. Microcomputer-to-facsimile terminal links allow microcomputer users to create a file on their microcomputer and send it directly to a remote FAX machine without having to go through the process of printing it, physically carrying it to a facsimile machine that scans it, and then transmitting it. Users also can receive a FAX file, display it, manipulate it on a microcomputer screen, and then print it or send it to another FAX terminal.

The international Group 3 facsimile standard provides for transmission of any text or graphics image over ordinary telephone circuits. A scanner in the facsimile device breaks the original document into pixels (dots) at 203 dots per inch horizontally and 98 dots per inch vertically. Then it converts the pixels into a bit stream to feed into a modem. The receiving device takes the bit stream and prints the image. The most sophisticated devices use laser printers.

Because facsimile images always are pictures, a page can occupy a considerable amount of storage. Typically, it is 30 to 60 kilobytes for a page of text or 120 kilobytes in fine mode. This is true even when using Group 3's data compression scheme. A 20-megabyte hard disk devoted to facsimile images can store only 170 fine-mode pages. As a standard ASCII computer file, a page takes up only 2 to 4 kilobytes; thus, an ASCII page transmitted at 1200 bits per second is faster than a facsimile page transmitted at 9600 bits per second.

The Group 4 standard resolution is 400 by 400 dots per inch and requires an improved compression scheme. It also is designed for all-digital telephone circuits instead of analog dial-up telephone circuits; therefore, Group 4 facsimiles are not yet able to operate on standard dial-up voice grade telephone circuits. Finally, FAX machines have been so reduced in size that they now can be used in your automobile or carried in your briefcase.

Dumb/Intelligent Terminals   Whether a terminal is considered dumb or intelligent does not depend on whether it has a video monitor or hard copy printer, or on whether it is used for data entry or as a transaction terminal. Any of these previously mentioned terminals might be either dumb or intelligent. A *dumb terminal* does not participate in control or processing tasks. It usually does not have any internal storage for memory, nor does it have any microprocessor chips; it has the bare minimum required to operate as an input and output device. The older, really dumb terminals transmitted asynchronously, and when a character was typed, the terminal transmitted the character immediately. Thus, central computer systems had to have receiving buffers for each of these terminals so they could assemble the entire message before acting on it.

An *intelligent terminal* is one that has a built-in microprocessor chip with the capability of being programmed, and it has internal stored memory. The specific market for intelligent terminals has been superseded by microcomputers. In today's world, microcomputers and specialized microcomputer workstations constitute the bulk of intelligent terminals. Many intelligent terminals also have external disk storage capability or their own internal software-driven communication programs. Today, you should regard an intelligent terminal as a microcomputer (see Chapter 10).

Attributes of Terminals Many attributes might be considered when evaluating a terminal. The most popular method of entering data is through use of a typewriterlike keyboard, but there are other more technologically advanced methods. For example,

- *Light pens* are used to touch the screen. The light activates whatever it is you are selecting from the screen.
- A *touch screen* works the same way as light pens, except you touch a portion of the screen with your finger to make a selection.
- A *mouse* (not the furry kind, but a device with push buttons) is moved around the surface of a table, controlling the cursor as it moves around the video monitor screen to various selection features. When you find what you want to select (the cursor is at that location), you press a button on the mouse.
- *Direct voice entry* is starting to become feasible, but it still is in the early stages of technological development.
- *Page scanners* automatically read a printed page and enter it into the computer. Some scanners only have the ability to scan graphics, some can scan only text, and others have special software that enables the scanner to handle both graphics and text. Special software packages interpret the ASCII characters so they can be recognized by the application programs.
- *Numeric keypads* are used for entering numbers.
- Small cameras are available for the *direct digital entry* of graphics or pictorial data.

The speed at which the terminal operates (characters per second) and its ability to transmit asynchronously or synchronously are important attributes.

Output attributes include monochrome or color or the type of hard copy printer utilized. A color display certainly is superior to a monochrome display because it enhances productivity and reduces eyestrain. As mentioned previously, the higher the resolution of the video monitor, the lower the eyestrain and fatigue. With regard to printers, the higher the resolution of the print mechanism, the more acceptable the printer, although the speed at which the printing is performed might be the overriding feature. Speed may be especially important for those who share one printer with several users. For example, a typical dot matrix printer might print 100 to 300 characters per second, but a laser printer might be able to print 8 to 10 full pages per minute.

Other miscellaneous attributes to consider are the interface the terminal will use with its modem (RS232 or other), the compatibility of the data transmission protocol with that of the central host computer, the code that is used (ASCII), whether any applications require a portable terminal, the adequacy and availability of maintenance and support from the terminal's vendor, and so forth.

COMMUNICATIONS IN BANKING/FINANCE

This chapter has discussed the basic hardware needed to have a communication network. With this understanding, it is possible to discuss a specific application.

One of the major applications for data communications is in the banking industry. The increased pace and mobility of our society have placed a tremendous demand on our financial institutions. Customers require around-the-clock service, multiple banking locations, and virtually instantaneous response to their transactions. To meet these demands, financial institutions have implemented massive data communication networks, automated teller machines (ATMs), and automated funds management systems not only for individuals, but also for business organizations and government agencies.

The three main applications in banking are demand deposits (checking), loans, and savings. One customer may have several savings, checking, and loan accounts scattered across several bank branches. All activities of this customer are cross-referenced and transmitted through the data communication network. This cross referencing provides standardization of procedures and customer service across all branches, as well as the ability to extend banking services for easier customer access at any time of the day or night. Such networks also increase marketing opportunities for the bank to sell additional services to customers, such as stock sales, and to provide more timely and comprehensive customer information for management analysis.

Once a bank or group of banks develops a data communication network and interconnects it with one or more host computer processing locations, then any or all of these services can be offered. Some of the financial services offered over such networks include

- Automated teller machines where users can deposit or withdraw money, make transfers between different bank accounts such as savings to checking, pay various bills, and the like.
- At-home banking and telephone-based bill paying. These are being tested for use with the public telephone system and cable television.
- Point-of-sale (POS) terminals tied directly to a customer's bank account from the retail store in which the POS terminal is located.
- Automated clearing houses (ACHs) that facilitate the paperless dispensing and collection of thousands of financial transactions on a real-time basis.
- National and international electronic funds transfer networks, check verification, check guarantees, credit authorizations, and the like.

Many of the networks developed by banks are private networks that combine point-to-point leased circuits, dial-up circuits, multidrop, multiplex, and packet switching. As we move into home banking, they also will include any of the combinations of private home networks. It should be noted that banking networks that used to be located within a city are now operated over both state and country borders.

Many banks now participate in shared networks where a bank network system in one area of the country interconnects to another bank network in another area.

Banks also have to talk between themselves. Some of the networks that have been developed for interbank communication are

- SWIFT (Society for Worldwide Interbank Financial Telecommunications)
- CHIPS (Clearing House Interbank Payments System)
- MINTS (Mutual Institution National Transfer System)
- FED WIRE (Federal Reserve Bank Telecommunications Network)
- BANK WIRE (Interbank Network)

These networks are used solely for transferring information and payments between banks. Banks also create private networks and interconnect them for use with the general public. You might view the preceding list of networks as involving *wholesale* electronic funds transfer between banks. By contrast, private bank networks involve *retail* electronic funds transfer for use by the general public or customers of individual banks. A bank's network for its checking/savings branch offices, ATMs, POS terminals, home banking, and the like would be its retail network. Figure 3-16 shows a typical bank's retail network and its interconnection with the SWIFT wholesale network.

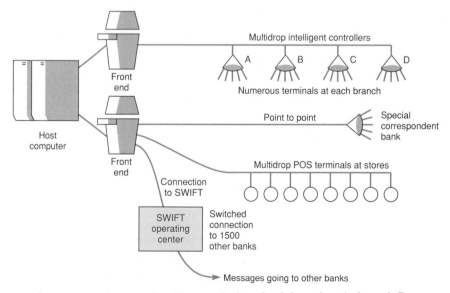

Figure 3-16 Bank networks. The terminals at bank branches A through D may be video terminals for tellers, ATMs for customers, or microcomputers.

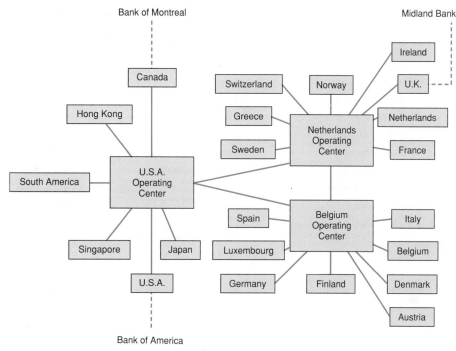

Figure 3-17   SWIFT banking network.

One of the most complex networks that has been developed on a worldwide basis is the Society for Worldwide Interbank Financial Telecommunications (SWIFT) network, which interconnects 1,500 banks in over 50 different countries. When the network started in 1977, it had an average volume of 60,000 messages per day. Now the average volume is over 400,000 messages per day.

Figure 3-17 shows the basic diagram of the SWIFT communication network with its three operating switching centers. From the switching centers, communication circuits go to a regional concentrator located in each country. The banks in the individual country interconnect with their regional concentrator. A regional concentrator in any country has a connection to its normal switching center and a backup connection to an alternate switching center.

If the Bank of Montreal (Canada) had a funds transfer for either Midland Bank (England) or Bank of America (United States), it would take the most direct path through the U.S.A. Operating Center in Figure 3-17.

KEY TERMS

Acoustic coupler
Analog modem
Analog side of modem

Carrier wave
Central control mode
Channel interface

Channel service unit (CSU)
Current loop

Cursor	Intelligent terminal	Protocol
Data channel	Internal modem	Remote job entry terminal
Data service unit (DSU)	Interrupt mode	Retrain time
Dial-up backup circuit	Line control	Reverse channel
Digital data service	Line driver	Selecting
Digital modem	Line interface unit	Session
Digital side of modem	Loopback	Short haul modem
DSU/CSU	Message queuing	Smart modem
Dumb modem	Message switching	Split streaming
Dumb terminal	Microcomputer	Teleprinter terminal
External modem	MNP 4	Terminal
Facsimile	MNP 5	Transaction terminal
FAX/voice switch	Modem	Turnaround time
File transfer time	Modem eliminator	V.32
Firmware	Modulate	V.32bis
Fractional T-1	Mouse	V.42
Frequency modulation	Multiport modem	V.42bis
Frequency shift keying (FSK)	Null modem	V.fast modem
	Numeric keypad	Video display unit (VDU)
Front end processor	Optical modem	Wireless modem
Handshaking	Polling	Workstation
Host mainframe computer	Port	

SELECTED REFERENCES

1. *Auerbach Data Communications Reports.* Published monthly by Auerbach Publishers, 6560 N. Park Drive, Pennsauken, N.J. 08109, 1965– .

2. *Black Box Catalog of Data Communications and Computer Devices.* Published monthly by the Black Box Corp., P.O. Box 12800, Pittsburgh, Pa. 15241.

3. *Communications Products & Systems.* Published bimonthly by Gordon Publications, 13 Emory Avenue, Randolph, N.J. 07869–1380.

4. *Datacomm Catalog.* Published by Glasgal Communications, 151 Veterans Drive, Northvale, N.J. 07647.

5. *Datapro Reports on Data Communications.* Published monthly by Datapro Research Corp., 1805 Underwood Boulevard, Delran, N.J. 08075.

6. Lewallen, Dale. "High Speed Modem," *PC/Computing,* vol. 5, no. 1, January 1992, pp. 206–208.

7. *Telecom Gear: The Market Place to Buy and Sell Telecommunications Equipment.* Published monthly by Telecom Gear/Telecom Jobs, 12 West 21st Street, New York, N.Y. 10010.

8. Tucker, Tracey. "Did You Get My FAX?" *Teleconnect,* July 1990, vol. 8, no. 7, pp. 38, 40–41.

QUESTIONS/PROBLEMS

1. What are the three categories for the interface between the processing functions of the central computer and the data communication network?
2. State the two forms a front end processor can take.
3. Where does the data channel reside and what is its function?
4. State the two control modes in which communication networks can operate and explain how they differ.
5. Is the host computer a part of the communication network? Explain why or why not.
6. What is the function of a front end processor?
7. What is the function of a modem?
8. What is a modem?
9. What governs transmission speed?
10. How are modems classified?
11. What is the purpose of loopback?
12. Define retrain time.
13. The input/output hardware device at the remote end of a communication circuit is called a _____ or a _____.
14. How do workstations differ from microcomputers?
15. What are the two most common complaints of video terminal operators?
16. How does a video terminal differ from a teleprinter terminal?
17. What single factor distinguishes transaction terminals from other types of terminals?
18. With what does facsimile compete?
19. What is the primary function of a facsimile?
20. What distinguishes a dumb terminal from other types of terminals?
21. Name at least four ways data can be entered into a terminal.
22. What is the difference between a front end processor and a modem?
23. List some systems applications in which an automatic answer capability is necessary; similarly, list some systems applications in which an automatic calling capability is necessary.
24. Review the list of functions of a front end processor. Identify what you consider to be the four most important functions of a front end.
25. Identify and describe the three basic components of a front end.
26. If your modem transmits at 2400 bits per second and also uses a 4 to 1 compression ratio data compression/compaction device, what is your data transmission in bits per second?
27. If you had to transmit a 10-page term paper of 20,000 bytes to your professor, approximately how long would it take (file transfer time) if your modem speed was 2400 bits per second using asynchronous transmission?
28. One of the modem lights is OH. What does that mean?
29. Can you identify the major categories of terminals discussed in this chapter?

30. Suppose you want to transmit a file of information to your corporate headquarters. How long will it take if there are 10,500 records of 95 bytes each, with 8 bits per byte? Assume you have a modem that transmits at 9600 bits per second.

31. Explain the problem that high speed full duplex modems have when transmitting data over dial-up circuits.

32. Do you need an analog modem with an all-digital network?

33. Which is the more complicated device for data transmission, a digital modem or an analog modem?

34. Name three types of DSU/CSUs.

35. Describe fractional T-1 services.

36. Describe the importance of constellation pattern encoding.

37. Why is V.42bis data compression so useful?

38. Why is dial-up backup desirable on a leased circuit?

39. What is the basic premise on which a FAX/voice switch works?

40. What are the advantages and disadvantages of FAX cards?

NEXT DAY AIR SERVICE CUMULATIVE CASE STUDY

Background on Next Day Air Service

Having completed the voice communication network study, Mr. Coone now has asked you to plan for the first phase of a bona fide corporatewide network. Ultimately, this network will integrate all the offices with Tampa and it will become the foundation on which to build a more sophisticated data communication network that includes a local area network (LAN).

Initially, the scope of the network will be limited to providing a simple voice grade dial-up capability from the company's remote offices and a local area network for the headquarters. Figure 3-18 shows the movement of invoice information. In reality, it shows the number of packages that are transferred between offices, but each package also requires one invoice to be sent. These averages were compiled from a two-week survey of each office. The average length of each invoice is 750 characters. Use this statistic as the basis for your computations.

Each number in the figure represents the number of packages, each of which requires an invoice, that moves from the city of origin to a destination city for delivery in the latter's delivery zone. Local deliveries are indicated in situations in which the origins and destinations are the same; for example, the intersection of Atlanta with Atlanta shows 50 deliveries.

Invoice information is to be transmitted from the origin to the destination. In addition, a copy of all invoice information must be transmitted to the home office in Tampa for billing purposes. For example, every day Los Angeles ships 15 packages to Memphis and each one requires an invoice. This means that Los Angeles will transmit fifteen 750-character invoices to *both* Memphis and Tampa every day.

In providing planning guidance, Mr. Coone has directed that your proposal be based on the following criteria.

- Next Day Air Service's financial position is such that it cannot afford to change to another hardware vendor. In other words, sweeping hardware changes are not an option. You may, however, consider dedicating one of the company's minicomputers as a network server. Alternatively, you may consider upgrading the minicomputer to a standalone mainframe from the same vendor. The computer should be capable of handling all the communication tasks. Should you decide on the upgrade, you must ensure that all terminals and microcomputers are hardware compatible.

- Although the dial-up circuits require a maximum transmission speed of 2400 bits per second, Next Day Air Service anticipates upgrading to either dedicated circuits or WATS dial-up circuits. Therefore, any leased or purchased communication equipment needs to be upwardly compati-

Origin \ Destination	Atlanta	Chicago	Dallas	Denver	Houston	Jackson	Jacksonville	Los Angeles	Memphis	Miami	Montgomery	New Orleans	Orlando	St. Louis	Tampa	Washington	Avg total pakgs/Day
Atlanta	50	40	35	15	32	10	25	10	20	30	12	25	20	12	45	40	421
Chicago	30	N/A	40	N/A	10	5	10	N/A	20	40	7	25	30	N/A	35	N/A	252
Dallas	25	30	80	35	45	5	15	70	30	25	5	30	15	25	30	25	490
Denver	20	N/A	30	N/A	15	3	2	N/A	3	15	2	13	4	N/A	8	N/A	115
Houston	15	7	45	7	N/A	2	8	7	13	12	2	23	17	12	30	1	201
Jackson	11	N/A	12	6	12	N/A	3	N/A	22	4	3	34	11	7	21	N/A	146
Jacksonville	13	7	13	1	8	2	N/A	3	7	20	3	5	20	1	35	3	141
Los Angeles	15	N/A	7	N/A	8	N/A	2	N/A	15	15	N/A	3	1	N/A	11	N/A	77
Memphis	16	4	13	2	7	9	3	8	70	11	4	9	2	21	6	2	187
Miami	33	5	7	2	3	1	16	2	4	110	2	21	26	1	45	3	281
Montgomery	8	1	6	N/A	4	3	2	N/A	2	3	N/A	9	2	1	3	1	45
New Orleans	12	7	16	1	12	6	3	2	7	3	6	100	8	2	25	2	212
Orlando	27	7	12	3	6	2	23	1	3	31	4	11	95	2	45	3	275
St. Louis	14	N/A	7	N/A	6	2	2	N/A	31	4	2	21	4	N/A	6	N/A	99
Tampa	55	11	13	4	8	3	22	3	7	31	3	17	43	6	90	3	319
Washington	21	N/A	2	N/A	3	N/A	7	N/A	2	4	1	3	2	N/A	4	N/A	49

Total   3310

Figure 3-18   Daily invoice (package) traffic for Next Day Air Service.

ble, and devices like modems should be capable of handling speeds up to 9600 bits per second.

Do not address any network configurations at this point. Be sure to allow for network growth. Because Next Day Air Service's financial position is somewhat tight, the president insists on a carefully thought-out proposal that justifies technological benefits, as well as overall costs.

Questions/Problems for the Next Day Air Service Case

1. Compute each office's number of bits sent per day (origin to destination) based on the data provided in Figure 3-18. Use 10 bits per character to keep computations simple, and assume all transmissions are error free. *HINT:* BPD = Packages $\times$ 750 $\times$ 10 $\times$ 2.
2. How many minutes will it take for the modem in each city to transmit

its invoices? Use the bits per day calculated in Question 1 and assume the modems transmit at 2400 bits per second.

3. Assume there is only one inbound circuit leading to Atlanta. Determine the appropriate minimum modem transmission speed in bits per second based on the inbound traffic to Atlanta. In this problem, assume the following conditions.

   - The peak load is twice the bits per day average transmission load.
   - Ten percent of the transmissions require retransmission because of errors.
   - There is a need for 50 percent growth.
   - All transmissions are to be accomplished in a 6-hour workday.

4. In Question 2, you calculated the transmission time in minutes per day based on a 2400 bits per second modem and 10 bits per character. Now calculate the "file transfer time" for Atlanta to transmit all its invoices to Tampa at the end of the workday. Why is this answer different from the time calculated for Altanta in Question 2?

5. Could all the NDAS offices transmit their invoices to Tampa between 5:00 P.M. and 6:00 P.M. each evening? Justify your answer.

Chapter Four

DATA COMMUNICATION HARDWARE (PART 2)

This chapter discusses the other hardware that makes a network run faster, more efficiently, and more securely. The pieces of hardware include multiplexers, controllers, protocol converters, encryption devices, and line adapters. The basic or mandatory hardware required to make a network run is discussed in Chapter 3. The hardware for local area networks (such as servers, repeaters, bridges, routers, gateways, MAUs, and cabling) is specialized; therefore, it is covered in Chapter 11 along with the other material on LANs.

INTRODUCTION

This chapter describes the additional hardware that helps the network to run more efficiently and faster, to be more secure and easier to use, to interconnect to other networks, and so forth.

We presented the basic network hardware in Chapter 3 (see Figure 3-1). The additional equipment presented here includes multiplexers, intelligent controllers, protocol converters, hardware encryption devices, and line adapters. Hardware that is specific to local area networks (LANs) is discussed in Chapter 11. Because hardware switches were used first in voice communications, they were discussed in Chapter 2 starting on page 59. Finally, as we move into the world of multiplexers, the somewhat subtle differences between a channel and a circuit become important.

MULTIPLEXERS

To *multiplex* is to place two or more simultaneous transmissions on a single communication circuit. Multiplexing a voice telephone call means that two or more separate

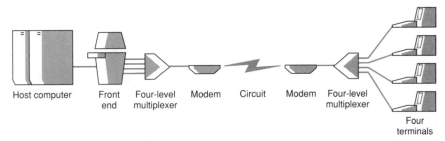

Figure 4-1   Multiplexed circuit (TDM). Compare with Figure 3-1 to see the effect of placing a multiplexer between the front end and the modem.

conversations are sent simultaneously over one communication circuit (line) between two different cities. On the other hand, multiplexing on a data communication network means that two or more messages are sent simultaneously over one communication circuit.

An important aspect of multiplexing is transparency. *Transparent* means the hardware multiplexer box does not in any way interrupt the flow of data. Neither the computer, nor the modem, nor the terminal/microcomputer using the modem knows the multiplexer is being used regardless of whether the transmission is on leased or dial-up circuits. When the circuit is multiplexed at one end and demultiplexed at the other, each user's terminal thinks it has its own connection to the host mainframe computer. Multiplexing usually is done in multiples of 4, 8, 16, and 32 simultaneous transmissions over a single communication circuit. Figure 4-1 shows a typical four-level multiplexed circuit. Multiplexers can be separated into major categories, such as frequency division multiplexers (FDM), time division multiplexers (TDM), and statistical time division multiplexers (STDM).

Frequency Division Multiplexing (FDM)   *Frequency division multiplexing* can be described as having a stack of four or more modems that operate at different frequencies so their signals can travel down a single communication circuit. Another way of looking at frequency division multiplexing is to imagine a group of people singing. There might be a bass, a baritone, an alto, and a soprano. What you hear is the combination of the four people singing, but sometimes you can identify clearly one or more of the individual singers.

With FDM, the frequency division multiplexer and the modem usually are combined into a single piece of hardware. For example, multiport modems are frequency division multiplexers. Compare Figures 4-2 and 4-3 to see that the FDM has only one piece of hardware (multiplexer/modem), whereas the TDM has two separate pieces of hardware (a time division multiplexer and a modem).

In FDM, the frequency division multiplexer uses the 3,000 cycles of available bandwidth of a voice grade circuit, dividing it into multiple subchannels. When we discussed modems for analog transmission in Chapter 3 (you might review Figure 3-7), the modem modulated the signal into only one pair of frequencies (two frequencies) that were used to transmit the binary 1s and 0s. In that case the frequencies were 2200 hertz and 1200 hertz. Now, our multiplexer in Figure 4-2 is subdividing

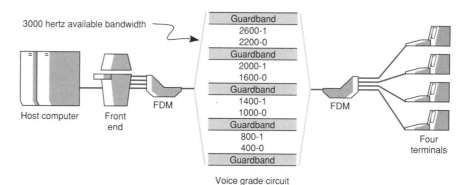

Figure 4-2 Frequency division multiplexed circuit (FDM).

the bandwidth of the voice grade circuit into four pairs of frequencies to allow four simultaneous transmissions of 0s and 1s.

The guardbands in Figure 4-2 are the unused portions of bandwidth that separate each pair of frequencies from the others. They keep the signals in each of the four *subchannels* from interfering with the adjacent subchannels and allow space for frequency drift. The guardband serves the same purpose as does a plastic insulator surrounding a copper wire; it keeps adjacent copper wires or subchannels from interfering with the others' transmission.

Another characteristic of FDM is that the subchannels need not all terminate at the same location as they do in Figure 4-2. Multidrop means the four terminals in Figure 4-2 can be at separate locations, such as on different floors in a building or even at different locations in a city. Therefore, frequency division multiplexing can be used in a multidrop network where each dropoff to a terminal operates at a different frequency and each terminal is in a different physical location.

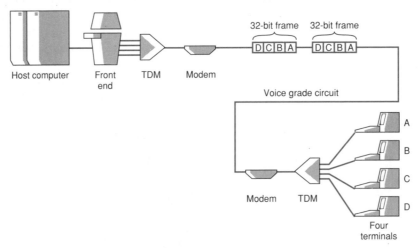

Figure 4-3 Time division multiplexed circuit (TDM).

Frequency division multiplexers are somewhat inflexible because, once you determine how many subchannels are required, it may be difficult to add more subchannels without purchasing an entirely new frequency division multiplexer that is divided into a greater number of subchannels. In addition, maintenance cost usually is greater for frequency division multiplexing equipment than for time division multiplexing equipment.

Time Division Multiplexing (TDM)   *Time division multiplexing* is really a type of time slicing or sharing use of a communication circuit among two or more terminals. Each terminal takes its turn. In TDM, the multiplexer takes a character from each transmitting terminal and puts them together into a frame. The frames are put onto a high speed data stream for transmission to the other end of the circuit. In Figure 4-3 we show a four-character frame for a four-level multiplexer. This is *pure multiplexing* because it is totally transparent to everyone on the network, including the system programmers. In pure multiplexing your messages are never held back or slowed by the multiplexer, as happens with statistical time division multiplexing which is discussed in the next section. Pure multiplexing is the same as *transparent multiplexing*.

In Figure 4-3 a character is taken from each terminal, placed in its frame, sent down the circuit, and delivered to the appropriate device at the far end of the circuit. If each of the four terminals transmits at 1200 bits per second, then the time division multiplex bit stream has to transmit at 4800 bits per second. Notice that there is no terminal addressing here. Each position of the four-position frame gives its character to the appropriate terminal at the other end, even if that character is a blank. If only three terminals were transmitting, then one position of the frame would contain a blank (nothing) when transmitted. When you start addressing each character position of a frame, then you are moving into statistical time division multiplexing.

Time division multiplexing generally is more efficient than frequency division multiplexing, but it does require a separate modem. (Frequency division multiplexing is in reality a special modem.) It is not uncommon to have time division multiplexers that share a line among 32 different low speed terminals, although these might be replaced with statistical time division multiplexers that can hold 32 higher speed terminals. It is easy to expand a time division multiplexer from, let us say, 8 to 12 channels. All TDM channels usually originate at one location and all terminate at another location. Time division multiplexers generally are less costly to maintain than frequency division multiplexers.

Statistical Time Division Multiplexing (STDM)   *Statistical time division multiplexing* allows the connection of more terminals to the circuit than the capacity of the circuit. In its simplest context, if you have 12 terminals connected to a statistical time division multiplexer and each terminal can transmit at 1200 bits per second, then your total is 14,400 bits per second transmitted in a given instant of time. However, if the STDM/modem/circuit combination has a maximum speed of only 9600 bits per second, then there might be a period of time when the system is loaded above its capacity.

The technique of statistical time division multiplexing takes into account the fact that there is some downtime because all terminals do not transmit at their maximum

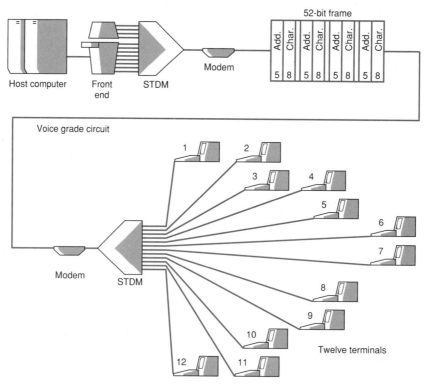

Figure 4-4   Statistical time division multiplexing (STDM).

rated capacity for every possible available microsecond. With this in mind, you start by addressing each character in a frame or message and time division multiplex on a statistical basis.

For example, assume we have a statistical time division multiplexer that multiplexes individual characters from 12 terminals. In this case, a terminal address is picked up in addition to the character and is inserted into the frame. Using the same four-character frame as in the previous figure, look at Figure 4-4. Notice that, in addition to the eight bits for each individual character, we have added five bits of address space (Add.). These five bits of address allow you to address 32 different terminals using binary counting ($32 = 2^5$). Now the multiplexer takes a character from each terminal only when the terminal has a character to send. The technique used is to scan through the 12 terminals and take characters from, let us say, terminals 1, 4, 5, and 12. These are sent immediately. Then all 12 are scanned again to determine which terminals need servicing. This process is repeated indefinitely. At the other end of the communication circuit, the character is given to the proper device because the 5-bit address included with each 8-bit character identifies the terminal device. Remember, with regular time division multiplexing, the frame size and the number of terminals connected to the circuit have to be equal so there is always an open frame position in which the sending terminal's character is placed.

Another type of statistical time division multiplexer involves multiplexing entire messages from terminals. With this type of multiplexer you *interleave* entire messages rather than characters. For example, when terminal 1 has a message to send, the multiplexer picks up the entire message (all of its characters) and puts it in a frame, after which the multiplexer immediately scans for the next terminal that has an entire message to send, and continues this process until the frame is full. The primary difference is that the first statistical scheme is for character-by-character transmission, whereas the second scheme is for block transmission.

Stat muxes, as they are called, use software and a microprocessor chip built into the multiplexer. They can support a number of devices at different speeds, without the modem having to equal the total combined speed of all the attached devices. An important aspect of statistical multiplexing is *flow control*. Because the statistical multiplexer allocates usage of the communication link based on the statistical demand of each attached device, the multiplexer must have a way to stop and start transmission from any of its attached terminals when the terminals try to communicate too much data. Without flow control and internal data buffers, statistical multiplexers would lose almost as much data as they send on a busy link.

Although STDM may be very efficient, you should be aware that it can cause time delays. When traffic is particularly heavy, you can have anywhere from a 1- to 30-second delay. Some data is held back by buffers when too many terminals transmit at maximum capacity for too long a period of time. A side effect of statistical multiplexing is the overhead. Software provides the benefits of statistical multiplexing, but it also reduces throughput efficiency on a circuit by 8 to 30 percent. One technique that improves the throughput of statistical time division multiplexers is to compress the data, thus reducing the number of bits transmitted per character or per message. Again, notice that several pieces of hardware are combined into a single piece of hardware. In this case, statistical time division multiplexing and data compression are combined.

Fast Packet Multiplexing   A *packet* is a block of data with 128 characters. *Fast packet multiplexing* is an improvement over time division multiplexing. A fast packet multiplexer is similar to a statistical time division multiplexer; therefore, it might be called an intelligent fast packet multiplexer. A fast packet multiplexer examines each incoming channel to determine whether, at that specific moment, it is idle or if there is an incoming packet. It then multiplexes 128-character packets just like the STDM in Figure 4-4 multiplexed characters.

The multiplexer's microprocessor chip uses fast packet multiplexing to divide the various data or voice conversations into packets. It then transmits them and, at the other end of the circuit, reassembles them into their original messages, whether they are data or voice transmissions. One difference between a fast packet multiplexer and a STDM is that the STDM multiplexes on a character-by-character basis, whereas the fast packet multiplexer multiplexes on a packet-by-packet basis and then transmits the packets to the distant node where they are reassembled into a meaningful data message or voice transmission. A more detailed explanation of packets and packet multiplexing is presented in the Packet Switching Networks section of Chapter 6.

Fiber Optic Multiplexing   A fiber optic multiplexer might take 16 channels of data, with each channel transmitting at 64,000 bits per second per channel, and multiplex them onto a fiber optic link. *Fiber optic multiplexers* operate similarly to time division multiplexers, but with much higher data transmission capacities. The transmission distances usually are limited to one to three miles unless amplifiers are used somewhere along the fiber optic cable. Fiber optic multiplexers are ideal for multiplexing T-1 circuits (1,544,000 bits per second). Fiber optic T-1 multiplexers can multiplex up to eight T-1 streams of data on a single fiber pair at a composite data rate of 14 million bits per second over 3 kilometers without amplifiers and, therefore, without cable splices.

WHAT IS A T-1 CIRCUIT?

A T-1 communication circuit is used for transmitting data messages, voice conversations, and images at high speed. It usually consists of four copper wires. T-1 circuits have enough bandwidth that the transmission speed can be up to 1,544,000 bits per second.

T-1 Multiplexing   (See the box on What Is a T-1 Circuit?) T-1 multiplexing requires a special kind of multiplexer combined with a high capacity data service unit (DSU) made especially for managing the ends of the T-1 circuit. A *T-1 circuit* is one that can transmit at 1,544,000 bits per second and be subdivided into 24, 48, or 96 voice grade circuits. These circuits are described more fully in the T-1 Circuits section of Chapter 7.

T-1 multiplexers are expensive and typically are sold based on the "port" capacity or maximum number of devices that can be connected to the T-1 multiplexer. Because T-1 circuits can carry digitized voice, data, and image signals, it is important to differentiate *T-1 multiplexers* by their ability to provide each of these three services.

One typical T-1 multiplexer can take a T-1 communication circuit that operates at 1,544,000 bits per second and multiplex it into 48 voice and data communication circuits. These 48 communication circuits can operate in either synchronous or asynchronous mode. Another T-1 multiplexer can subdivide the 1,544,000 bits per second circuit into 96 channels that can transmit at 9600 bits per second or even 200 channels that support 4800 bits per second. Other T-1 multiplexers can accept very high speeds (up to 768,000 bits per second for compressed image transmission) and, at the same time, multiplex lower speed (such as 4800 bits per second) data transmission paths through the multiplexer.

Digital Channel Banks and Digital Cross-Connect   In addition to T-1 multiplexers, there is a similar device called a *digital channel bank*. A digital channel bank multiplexes high speed T-1 circuits (1,544,000 bits per second) into 24 lower speed communication channels (64,000 bits per second). These 24 subchannels can be used to transmit data or voice. Because a channel bank's standard input rate is 64,000 bits per second, it typically cannot divide a T-1 channel into more than 24 subchannels.

Channel banks are more suitable than T-1 multiplexers for moving voice calls between PBXs (switchboards). The fact that channel banks cannot divide a T-1 communication link into more than 24 subchannels can result in inefficient handling of multiple data circuits. It takes eight channel bank termination devices (four at each end of the link) and four T-1 circuits to transmit 96 data streams at 9600 bits per second from Point A to Point B. Each of the four T-1 circuits carries 24 channels, each of which is capable of transmitting at 64,000 bits per second, but actually carrying only 9600 bits per second of data. By contrast, it takes only two T-1 multiplexers and one T-1 communication circuit subdivided into 96 channels to carry the same 96 data streams at 9600 bits per second from Point A to Point B.

For users of T-1 circuits, *digital cross-connect switches* are used to reconfigure the channels within the T-1 communication circuit. Remember that T-1 channels operate at 1,544,000 bits per second and typically are segmented into 24 individual channels, each of which operates at 64,000 bits per second. Traditionally, when using digital channel banks, if any one of these 24 different circuits within a T-1 link had to be routed to a different location, then the digital signal would have to be broken into 24 individual analog signals, put through a type of distribution patch panel, and returned to the digital signal state. This technique requires that two multiplexing devices (the digital channel banks) be configured back to back. One channel bank demultiplexes the digital T-1 signal into 24 channels, which then are patched to a port on the other channel bank and remultiplexed.

Digital cross-connects are used to switch multiplexed channels within the T-1's 1,544,000 bits per second digital facilities, without demultiplexing the signal as you would with channel banks. For example, a cross-connect switch that is connected to a T-1 circuit can route one of the 24 channels operating at 64,000 bits per second from an incoming T-1 to any of the other 24 channels on the outgoing T-1 circuit. Digital cross-connects are replacing channel banks, which provided the same switching function only when two of them were configured back to back. Some people refer to digital channel banks and digital cross-connects as *digital matrix switches*.

Multiport Modem Multiplexing   Multiport modems are high speed synchronous modems in the range of 9600 bits per second. Typical 4800 bits per second modems may be channelized (subdivided) 2×2400. Typical multiport 9600 bits per second modems may be channelized using any of these combinations: 2×4800, 4×2400, or 2×2400 with 1×4800 (see Figure 4-5 for another typical combination). The *multiport modem* may be regarded as a frequency division multiplexer.

Concentrators   In today's terminology, *concentrators* are special forms of statistical multiplexers. Concentrators are used for the same purposes as multiplexers. In fact, they originally were intelligent multiplexers (stat muxes).

The primary use for a concentrator is to combine circuits because you can have 16 low or medium speed circuits that are concentrated into one or two high speed circuits. For example, you might concentrate approximately twelve 4800 bits per

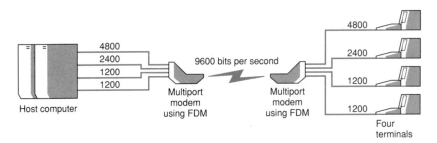

Figure 4-5   Multiport modem.

second communication circuits into one 56,000 bits per second digital communication circuit. Even though this does not work out in a perfectly equal way (12 ×
4800 = 57,600), the statistical intelligence takes care of the small difference. Like
statistical multiplexers, concentrators can buffer or hold back data. Some concentrators even can switch messages to different communication circuits.

To avoid confusion, you can assume that when you have pure or transparent
multiplexing, there is no basic programmed intelligence in the device, but when you
have intelligence and programming capability, it might be a statistical multiplexer
or a concentrator. In addition, the newer STDMs perform other functions, such as
switching and concentrating data. Multiplexers generally have end user terminals
attached to them, whereas concentrators do not. Figure 4-6 shows this point. For
example, the hardware devices located in San Diego, Los Angeles, Santa Barbara,
San Francisco, San Jose, and Reno probably are true multiplexers because they are
attached to end user terminals. On the other hand, the hardware devices in Phoenix,
Denver, Chicago, and New York probably are true concentrators because they do
not have end user terminals attached to them. The data communication hardware

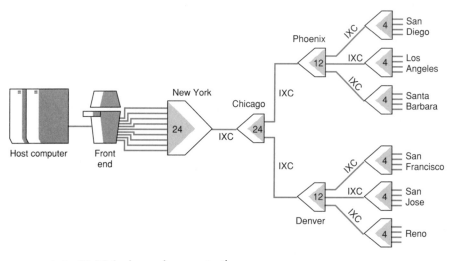

Figure 4-6   Multiplexing and concentrating.

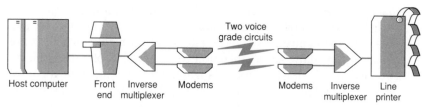

Figure 4-7   Inverse multiplexer.

industry is very changeable; this is not a hard differentiation, then, but only a guideline on how to tell a multiplexer from a concentrator.

Inverse Multiplexers   Sometimes called a *biplexer,* an *inverse multiplexer* can take a 19,200 bits per second transmission and divide it into two incoming or outgoing 9600 bits per second streams of data as shown in Figure 4-7. The two voice grade circuits in Figure 4-7 also could be two 56,000 or 64,000 bits per second digital circuits. Moreover, the modems sometimes are built into the inverse multiplexer so you do not see them as a separate piece of hardware.

In summary, the principles of multiplexing predate the invention of the telephone. Alexander Graham Bell experimented with a type of multiplexing for telegraph systems, but the technology needed to apply his technique did not exist in his day. Today's multiplexers are used on voice, data, image, and optical pulses of light. To do this engineers must find a way to divide the circuit or channel into subchannels so signals can travel together without interfering with one another.

INTELLIGENT CONTROLLERS

Remote Intelligent Controllers   Remote intelligent controllers, sometimes called *intelligent terminal controllers,* usually reside at the distant or far end of a communication circuit (see Figure 4-8). A *remote intelligent controller* is simply a scaled-down front end processor. In fact, you can have a remotely located front end processor for an area of the country where hundreds of terminals are located. In this case the remotely located front end is connected to the host computer front end by high speed data circuits.

Remote intelligent controllers control 4 to 16 local terminals, although some are

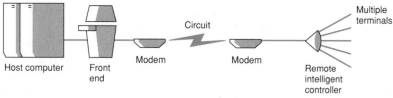

Figure 4-8   Remote intelligent controller.

much more powerful. There is a unique address for each controller and, therefore, a further address or unique memory space in the controller for each terminal connected to the controller. Remote intelligent terminal controllers are used primarily because they allow an organization to have full duplex transmissions between the two devices (the host computer's front end and remote local controller).

A remote intelligent controller might perform any or all of the functions performed by a front end, but as noted above, usually it is scaled down and not as powerful, although each vendor's terminal controller has its own set of functions. These controllers started out as simple devices to control 4 or 8 video terminals. Their power has been increasing ever since so that today one device might control 16 multifunctional terminals in a branch bank. The terminals in a branch bank might be entirely different from each other, say, 4 video terminals, 4 simple teller inquiry terminals, 2 high speed printers, 1 sophisticated wire transfer data entry terminal, 1 facsimile machine, and so on. This variety makes a remote intelligent controller especially desirable.

Today, microcomputers, especially the 386 or 486 versions, are replacing many of the intelligent control devices. Microcomputers serve as intelligent controllers when interfacing on micro-to-mainframe communication links.

Newer versions of the older controllers now possess even more power. For example, some of them can perform protocol conversion, allow direct connection to local area networks, handle 32 terminals instead of 16, perform multiplexing, and handle file transfer more easily than can be done through individual transactions.

LAN Gateways, Bridges, and Routers as Controllers   A *gateway* is a device that connects two dissimilar networks. Specifically, gateways are associated with local area networks. When you want to connect a local area network to some other network, a mainframe computer, or other devices, a gateway device must be connected to the local area network. A gateway can be viewed as being very similar to a remote intelligent controller. Like its cousin the remote intelligent controller, a gateway identifies the terminal addresses and handles the movement of messages from the local area network to the other network to which they are addressed. It also handles incoming messages from the outside network that are directed to a specific local area network terminal. *Bridges* and *routers* are two other devices that connect local area networks either to other local area networks or to wide area networks. Gateways, bridges, and routers are discussed in more detail in Chapter 11 on Local Area Networks.

Central Site Intelligent Controllers   In addition to remote intelligent terminal controllers, hardware controllers located at the central site connect directly to the front end processor. An example is shown in Figure 4-9. A *central site intelligent controller* can handle up to 32 outgoing lines. By connecting the central site controller to a single port on the front end, the front end port controls 32 circuits. The 32 circuits leaving the central site controller can be connected either to a modem or to a coaxial cable. Modems can be used if the connection goes to a remote site, whereas coaxial cable can be used if the terminal is in the same building (approximately 2,000 feet from the controller). A typical IBM central site intelligent controller is a ''3274 cluster controller.''

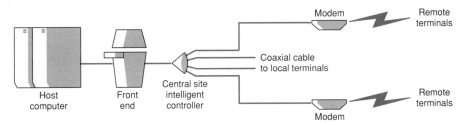

Figure 4-9   Central site intelligent controller.

The use of microcomputers as terminals is causing a problem with regard to intelligent controllers. For example, the long-standing mainstays, the IBM 3174 and 3274 controllers, are being overwhelmed with transmissions of data from microcomputers. This development can be attributed to our movement from a batch environment, through single transaction processing, to our present file transfer environment.

We used to send batches of data to the data center for key entry. This occurred entirely outside the communication links. Then we sent batches of data over communication links, but immediate processing was not required. Next we sent most of our business transactions over the communication circuits on a transaction-by-transaction basis. These individual, short transactions were processed and immediately returned to the sending microcomputer.

Now we are transmitting entire files of data (thousands of characters) by using microcomputers. This file transfer is overloading controllers that were built to handle many short transactions of 100 or less characters. For example, if one microcomputer, which is connected to a controller that has 16 microcomputers attached to it, starts transmitting a file, then the response time might be slowed by one or two seconds. If a second microcomputer starts transmitting a file at the same time, the response time might degrade by a few more seconds. But if a third microcomputer starts transmitting a file simultaneously with the first two, it can bring down (cause a crash) the intelligent control device. Thus, the people at the central site would have to restart the controller, which would delay everyone's data processing needs for 5 to 20 minutes.

PROTOCOL CONVERTERS

Protocols are a formal set of conventions governing the format and control of inputs and outputs between two communicating devices. In other words, protocols are the rules that allow two machines to communicate. As you already know, when you use the English language to communicate with someone, there are various rules (protocols) you must observe. For example, when you write to someone, you must observe the rules of English grammar and use proper sentence construction and punctuation.

Protocol converters are hardware or software used to interconnect two dissimilar computer systems or terminals so they can talk to each other. As an analogy, if an

American who speaks only English wants to speak with a French person who speaks only French, they need to have an interpreter to carry on a conversation. This language interpreter serves the same purpose as a protocol converter.

Protocol conversion is one of today's hottest topics, particularly when you consider its application to the problem of micro-to-mainframe communications. Because of IBM's dominant position in the computer industry, most protocol conversion allows non-IBM equipment to communicate with IBM equipment. In general, the basic approaches to protocol conversion can be divided into four categories: hardware protocol converter boxes, add-on circuit boards for microcomputers, software that resides in host mainframe computers, and local area network gateways.

Hardware Protocol Converter Boxes   *Hardware protocol converter boxes* convert the communication protocol used by one computer vendor to that required for another computer vendor's equipment. For example, some protocol converters allow an asynchronous terminal to communicate with IBM host computers that use Synchronous Data Link Control (SDLC) or Binary Synchronous Communications (BSC) protocols. Other protocol converters allow asynchronous terminals to interconnect with public packet switching protocols, such as X.25. These three protocols (SDLC, BSC, and X.25) are discussed in Chapter 9, Protocols and Software.

In today's networks, protocol converters might be located at either the host or remote terminal end of the circuit. Figure 4-10 shows the location of a protocol converter at the host computer end of a communication link, whereas Figure 4-11 shows one at the remote terminal end. Some protocol converters, similar to the one shown in Figure 4-11, offer 1 to 16 ports for the connection of individual terminals. Incoming information from the terminals have their protocols converted to the host computer's protocol before being transmitted.

Add-On Circuit Boards   *Add-on circuit boards* convert the microcomputers' protocols (transmission methodologies) to the protocol of the host computer to which they are transmitting. For example, there are two distinct types of add-on protocol conversion boards for IBM microcomputers. The first converts the microcomputer into a 3278 terminal that plugs directly into a 3270 terminal controller via a coaxial cable. The second makes the IBM microcomputer function as a 3278 terminal, but with an already built-in terminal controller. These add-on circuit boards are used for protocol conversion, which offers the user a direct micro-to-mainframe link with IBM host mainframe computers. In this chapter we simply define conversion hardware; for a complete description of micro-to-mainframe communications, see Chapter 10 (Microcomputers and Communications).

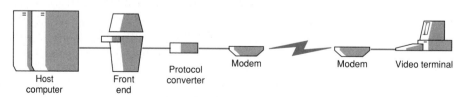

Host computer   Front end   Protocol converter   Modem   Modem   Video terminal

Figure 4-10   Protocol converter at the host end.

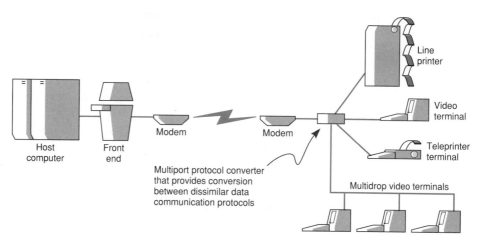

Figure 4-11   Protocol converter at the remote terminal end.

Software Protocol Conversion Packages   In addition to these first two hardware approaches to protocol conversion, host mainframe *software protocol conversion packages* are available. These software packages can support almost any ASCII terminal or microcomputer. If an organization has a very large number of terminals or microcomputers to connect to its host mainframe computer, software protocol conversion may be the most cost-effective method because the software package at the host mainframe can support hundreds of remotely located terminals or microcomputers. The user, however, must remember that the host mainframe computer software uses some of the computer cycles, which may slow processing or overload the host mainframe central computer. A hardware protocol converter, such as the one shown in Figure 4-10, does not use or interfere with host mainframe computer cycles.

LAN Gateways as Protocol Converters   *Gateways* are hardware devices that connect local area networks to other dissimilar networks. They accomplish this connection by translating one network protocol into another, thereby overcoming both hardware and software incompatibilities. For example, if an organization were to connect a 40-microcomputer local area network to its IBM mainframe, the connection probably would be made through a gateway if the protocols were dissimilar. In this case, local area network users would address their messages to the mainframe. Each message would contain the gateway address, along with the mainframe address (assuming there were several mainframes) and some sort of final destination address in the mainframe, such as a database, an E-mail system, or another terminal connected to the mainframe. Gateways are covered in more detail in Chapter 11.

Protocol Converter Selection Criteria   Now that we have described the four categories of protocol conversion, the following selection criteria should be considered when comparing protocol conversion techniques.

- Will it work with our local area network?
- How many terminals can the product support concurrently?
- Which types of terminals are supported?
- How easy is it to add new types?
- Does the organization specifically require either hardware or software protocol conversion?
- What is the increment of expansion if it is necessary to add more terminals?
- Does the quality of emulation meet user needs?
- What additional features and functions are available on each of the protocol converters being evaluated?
- Is the system adaptable for future enhancement, or will it rapidly become obsolete?
- Is this protocol converter reliable?
- What diagnostic capabilities does the product have?
- Are references from other users available?
- What is the quality of support and maintenance?
- Is it easy to install?
- Is it easy to use?
- Can it be customized?
- Is it cost effective?
- Does its use entail additional or hidden costs?

HARDWARE ENCRYPTION

Some data communication networks require very secure communications. In such cases, the techniques of *encryption* are employed. Encryption devices or encryption software encode and decode the messages in such a way that others cannot decipher the content of the messages. A much more detailed description of what encryption is and how it works appears in Chapter 13, Security and Control. In this section we want to focus on software encryption versus hardware encryption as it applies to network hardware.

Software encryption uses stored programs to do the encryption. This technique makes the network vulnerable to anyone who can copy the contents of the computer's memory. In data communications, software encryption generally is not used. Instead, software encryption is used for the storage of data on disks/tapes or for other types of programming security problems.

In data communications, *hardware encryption* devices are employed. They are located most often as shown in Figure 4-12. Data from the host computer's front end or the terminal enters the encryption device, where it is secretly encoded. Most hardware encryption devices have standard RS232 interfaces. These devices expect

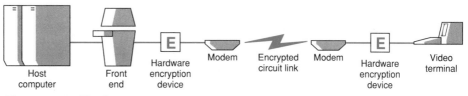

Figure 4-12   Hardware encryption.

digital information as input; their output also is digital. This is one reason why the encryption device usually is placed between the terminal and the modem. After encryption, the data is modulated or demodulated by the modem. Figure 4-12 is a "link" encryption setup because the data is encrypted over one link of a network. Remember that a link is one unbroken circuit path between two points.

Hardware encryption entails the use of a lockable box about the size of a modem. When this box is opened, the secret *encryption key* (which is stored electronically) is destroyed. Most encryption today is done on a link-by-link basis, except for military encryption, which is done on an end-to-end basis. For practical purposes, you can assume that *link-to-link* encryption is encryption of the data from modem to modem, and *end-to-end* encryption is encryption from user to user.

Many hardware encryption devices today employ the *Data Encryption Standard* (DES) that was verified and authorized by the U.S. National Institute of Standards and Technology (formerly the National Bureau of Standards). Most encryption devices also allow the insertion of several secret keys at one time to reduce the cost of key management. *Key management cost* is the cost incurred when you have to go to the remote end of a communication circuit to change the key. By having several keys, you can have a master key that is changed, for example, every two years; by transmitting new keys under the encryption of the master key, you can change the key daily if that is necessary.

Public key encryption is the other popular encryption methodology. This technique does not use a secret key, but it does use a public key and a private key. For this reason, the key management cost is extremely low when compared with the DES methodology that uses a secret key. The concept of public and private keys and the RSA Public Key Encryption methodology are described in Chapter 13.

LINE ADAPTERS

Rather than being one specific piece of hardware, *line adapters* are a class of communication hardware. The line adapter performs a specific task or allows interconnection of terminals or microcomputers to host mainframe computers in many types of configurations. Examples of this hardware are channel extenders, line interface modules, port sharing devices, intelligent port selectors, line splitters, digital line expanders, port/line security devices, data compressors, line protectors, bridges/gateways, network test equipment, and so forth. All these devices are discussed in

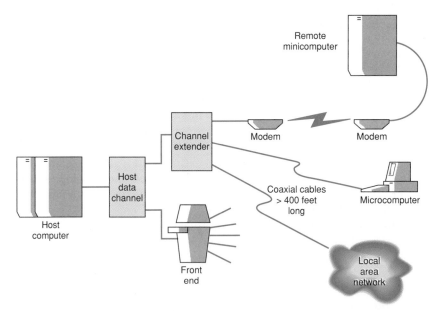

Figure 4-13   Channel extender.

this section, with the exception of bridges/gateways and network test equipment. Specifically, bridges and gateways are covered in Chapter 11, Local Area Networks, and network test equipment is discussed in Chapter 12, Network Management.

Channel Extender   A *channel extender* is a scaled-down front end (see Figure 4-13). It can link remote host computers or minicomputers to the central host facilities. Channel extenders attach directly to the host mainframe (the same place where a front end processor connects), and they can operate at 24 million bits per second or higher. In addition to interconnecting a remote minicomputer or mainframe to the central host mainframe, they can support disk drives, high speed printers, and microcomputers. Although channel extenders may be slower and less powerful than front end processors, they provide a less expensive way to improve response time for users at remote locations, offload some of the front end data communication traffic from local area networks or micro-to-mainframe connections within a building, or handle data processing requirements if the central site has problems. As their software becomes more powerful, the generation of channel extenders now in use will begin to compete directly with front end processors.

Distributed processing now can be expanded beyond the normal host mainframe data channel interconnection limits of approximately 400 feet. To extend the mainframe channel to another mainframe channel or to a remote data communication network, an organization might use channel extenders to allow connection of terminal equipment, channel couplers to allow connection to another mainframe channel, or connect the channel to a local area network (LAN). Some vendors use the terms *channel coupler* and *channel extender* interchangeably.

As an example of channel extension, IBM's 3737 channel-to-channel unit connects two host mainframe computers through their channels by using a T-1 circuit (1,540,000 bits per second). The benefit is that two host mainframes can be located hundreds of miles apart, thereby breaking the traditional 400-foot limit for channel-to-channel data transmission.

Line Interface Module   *Line interface modules* enable terminal users to connect to more than one network and switch between them, without plugging or unplugging any connector cables. For example, this device enables a terminal user to connect both to a central host computer and a local minicomputer, alternately accessing screens from either computer by using simple keyboard instructions. An extremely simplistic line interface module used with microcomputer printers is the two-position switch box that allows users to connect two printers to one microcomputer. In this case, users have to switch to whichever printer they want to use for printing a particular job.

Port Sharing Device   A *port sharing device* allows several incoming communication circuits to use a single port on a front end processor. All front end processors have a fixed capacity of ports. For example, if such a processor is designed to handle 50 ports, up to 50 incoming circuits can be connected to it. When users want to exceed the design capacity of a front end processor, a port sharing device may be used. Look at Figure 4-14 where you will observe that four incoming communication circuits employ only one port on the front end processor because a port sharing device is used. A channel extender is a more sophisticated port sharing device.

Although use of a port sharing device may not be a long-term solution, it can be a short-term holding action until a new network can be configured or new hardware purchased.

Intelligent Port Selector (Rotary Switch)   An intelligent port selector replaces the older telephone rotary switch. It provides the same connection facility as a rotary and

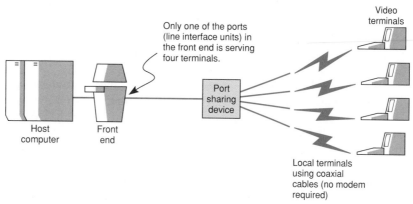

Figure 4-14   Port sharing device.

gives a response equivalent to a busy signal if no ports are available. This device is useful when there are many incoming dial-up communication circuits but not enough ports to allow all the terminals to connect at the same time. It is configured into the network at the same physical position as the port sharing device of Figure 4-14, but it may be connected to five or ten ports on the front end instead of one port as shown in Figure 4-14. On the incoming side (terminal side of Figure 4-14), 20 to 25 incoming lines may be connected to more than one port on the front end. This means the 25 terminals might be sharing five ports.

Intelligent port selectors (also called *rotary switches*) are nothing more than devices that answer incoming telephone calls and connect to the front end if one of the ports is available. For example, if there were ten ports, it would try port 1, then port 2, port 3, and so on. If any one of the ten was free, you would be connected. If all ten were busy, you would get a busy signal and would have to dial back at a later time. Intelligent port selectors can handle different speeds of transmission (bits per second) and different communication codes (ASCII or EBCDIC), be the interface between dial-up or dedicated (lease line) ports, offer a busy signal or the opportunity to stay on the line to be placed in a queue for future connection, and collect network utilization statistics.

Another piece of hardware that is similar to an intelligent port selector (rotary switch) is a *facsimile switch* (also called a FAX switch), which was described in the Facsimile (FAX) Terminals section of Chapter 3. Hardware is now available for voice telephones that combine the features of both a rotary switch and a FAX switch into a single hardware box.

For example, suppose we have four telephone numbers ranging from 555-1200 to 555-1203 and they are hooked onto a rotary switch. Our organization would advertise only the 555-1200 number on the firm's stationary. If someone were to call the 555-1200 number and two calls were already in progress, the rotary switch would switch over the calls in progress (that is, it would skip over the numbers 555-1200 and 555-1201) and ring the telephone with the 555-1202 number.

Now let us assume further that our firm does a lot of work using both voice telephones and facsimile machines. In this assumption, we also might have four facsimile machines connected with the voice telephones on our four incoming telephone circuits. Now when someone calls, the rotary switch "rings down" or skips over the circuits that are busy. On reaching the first free circuit, it determines whether the incoming call is a voice telephone call or an incoming facsimile message and routes the incoming call to the appropriate device.

Line Splitter   Line splitters are similar to port sharing devices except in the matter of location. Line splitters are located at the remote end of the communication circuit, whereas port sharing devices are at the central site close to the host mainframe computer. A *line splitter* is a "switch" that allows several terminals to be connected to a single modem. The three terminals in Figure 4-15 share the total capacity of the communication circuit, but the line splitter ensures that only one terminal at a time uses the circuit. In other words, these three terminals are treated as though they were on a multidrop circuit. A *multidrop circuit* is one in which two or more terminals or terminal controllers share the communication circuit, although only one

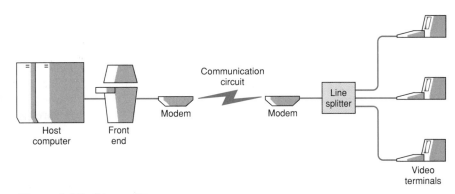

Figure 4-15   Line splitter.

terminal at a time is allowed to transmit its data. With a line splitter, costs are reduced to whatever it costs for a single communication circuit and a single modem pair. Otherwise (see Figure 4-15) your network would require three communication circuits, three modem pairs, and three ports on the front end.

Digital Line Expander   *Digital line expanders* enable customers to squeeze a greater number of voice or data channels into the bandwidth of a given communication facility. Companies with three or more analog leased circuits that run between two points might be able to save money by using a line expander because one such device provides up to eight voice communication circuits over a single 56,000 bits per second digital communication circuit. To use the digital line expander, the organization would cease to use its three analog circuits and, in their place, would lease one 56,000 bits per second digital circuit. The eight voice communication circuits provided by the digital line expander also can be intermixed with digital transmissions. An example of intermixing might be if you were to have six voice channels and one 9600 bits per second data channel, or four voice channels and one 19,200 bits per second data channel.

Port/Line Security Device   *Port/line security devices* provide *dial-back security* and are configured as shown in Figure 4-16. The procedure for using one such device is as follows.

1.   The user calls the host mainframe computer from the remote terminal.

2.   The dial-back security device at the central site intercepts the call and asks

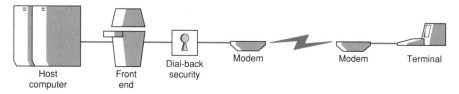

Figure 4-16   Port/line dial-back security.

for the user's ID and password. Some of these devices have circuitry for automatic *ring blocking*. This inhibits the modem from answering the caller by detecting a ring as it occurs and absorbing the ringing energy. In this case, the caller must enter an ID/password immediately because the dial-back security device waits only a short time before disconnecting the caller. The purpose of this ring blocking is to prevent a caller from hearing the carrier wave tone that modems use to disable the echo suppressors. In this case, computer hackers may not even realize they have called a dial-up modem device connected to a computer.

3. The user at the remote terminal enters his or her user ID and password.

4. After receiving the user ID and password, the dial-back security device instructs its modem to disconnect the circuit (hang up).

5. The dial-back security device verifies the user and, through the use of the password, obtains that user's preestablished telephone number from the central system.

6. If the user is a valid one, the dial-back security device then instructs its central site modem to dial the remote modem.

7. The remote modem answers, and the session between the terminal user and host computer begins.

Port/line devices provide security by allowing computer system access only to individuals who have proper passwords and by restricting these users to "registered" telephone numbers. Thus, a hacker who is searching for entry into a computer system cannot break through the dial-back mechanism. Even if the hacker has the correct password and user ID, the system is prevented from calling back to the hacker's telephone. If the hacker can find a way to "call forward" the "registered" telephone number, however, it might be possible to break through this security.

Data Compression/Compaction Devices *Data compression/compaction devices* are controlled by microprocessors and can increase throughput of data over a communication link literally by compressing the data. One simple way to do so is to look at the data being moved over the communication circuit and send an instruction that provides a count of any characters that repeat themselves in sequence. This basic technique is called *run length encoding,* and it normally is used in combination with other techniques. Another technique, called *code book compression,* uses specific codes to indicate a pattern of characters and phrases stored in each data compressor's memory. Thus, one character can be sent over a link to indicate many other characters.

A more complex method of encoding actually replaces standard ASCII and EBCDIC code. This technique, called *Huffman encoding,* uses tables of typically sent characters within a language and adjusts the number of bits it takes to send each character based on the relative frequency of that character in the language. Different Huffman tables optimize this technique for different applications or languages. A more flexible method, *adaptive Huffman encoding,* uses a mathematical algorithm to update the tables in real time to optimize the compression capability.

Data compression hardware devices are located in two places: between the terminal and the modem at the remote end of the communication circuit, and between the modem and host mainframe computer at the central site. Data compressors can be used on either dial-up or leased private circuits. Data compression also is achieved in the microcomputer or mainframe. An example is data compression before storing the data on a disk.

One specific example of a data compressor is a standalone device that compresses data in half duplex mode for synchronous communication. During operation, this device accepts data from the terminal at 14,400 (9600 × 1.5) bits per second, and compresses the data so it can be sent to the modem for transmission at 9600 bits per second. Obviously, the reverse process occurs at the other end of the circuit where the data is decompressed and transferred to the front end processor. This type of unit can accept input speeds of 4800, 9600, and 14,400 bits per second. Another compression unit can compact a data stream of 2400 bits per second from a terminal into a modem's 1200 bits per second operating speed. This unit has a 2:1 compression ratio. Some manufacturers are predicting an 8:1 compression ratio in the not too distant future.

Line Protectors   When non-AT&T devices are connected to the standard direct distance dial (DDD) telephone circuits, the devices can be registered in one of three ways: permissive, programmable, and fixed loss loop. The type of registration determines how the terminal, node, or telephone connects to the telephone line.

A *permissive* connection is used to connect a standard telephone to the telephone line or a data terminal to a switchboard. Permissive devices limit the amplitude (power) of the signal presented to the telephone line and use a RJ-11 plug. They limit both the voltage and current.

A *programmable* device has two main advantages. First, the modem always transmits at its maximum allowable level, and second, the telephone company installs a "data-quality" circuit. It uses an RJ-45 plug (see Glossary).

The *fixed loss loop* connection or *universal* connection has a switch on the jack to prevent installation of the wrong connector cable. When the fixed loss loop mode is used, the telephone company installs an attenuation pad to ensure that signals arriving at the telephone company central office do not damage their equipment.

These three devices protect the telephone company's circuits from extraneous signals that might damage the switching facilities at the central office.

KEY TERMS

Biplexer	Data compression	Fast packet multiplexing
Bridge	Dial-back security	Fiber optic multiplexing
Central site intelligent controller	Digital channel bank	Flow control
Channel coupler	Digital cross-connect	Frequency division multiplexing (FDM)
Channel extender	Digital line expander	Gateway
Code book compression	Digital matrix switch	Hardware encryption
Concentrator	Encryption	Huffman encoding
	End-to-end encryption	

Intelligent port selector
Intelligent terminal
   controller
Interleave
Inverse multiplexer
Line adapter
Line interface module
Line protector
Line splitter
Link-to-link encryption
Multidrop circuit

Multiplex
Multiport modem
Packet
Port/line security device
Port sharing device
Protocol
Protocol converter
Pure multiplexing
Remote intelligent
   controller
Rotary switch

Router
Run length encoding
Software encryption
Stat mux
Statistical time division
   multiplexing (STDM)
Subchannel
T-1 circuit
T-1 multiplexing
Time division multiplexing
   (TDM)
Transparent multiplexing

SELECTED REFERENCES

1. *Black Box Catalog of Data Communications and Computer Devices*. Published monthly by the Black Box Corp., P.O. Box 12800, Pittsburgh, Pa. 15241, 1-412-746-5530.

2. *Data Communications Catalog*. Published by Misco, One Misco Plaza, Holmdel, N.J. 07733, 1-800-333-5640.

3. *Data Communications Product Catalog*. Published by South Hills Datacomm/Cord Cable Co., 760 Beechnut Drive, Pittsburgh, Pa. 15205, 1-800-245-6215.

4. Minoli, Dan. "Channel Extension: Stretching the Corporate Network," *Network Computing*, vol. 2, no. 11, November 1991, pp. 102–103, 106–107.

5. *Network Products Directory*. Published annually by Glasgal Communications, Inc., 151 Veterans Drive, Northvale, N.J. 07647, 1-201-768-8082.

QUESTIONS/PROBLEMS

1. What is the purpose of multiplexing?
2. Multiplexing usually is done in multiples of _____, _____, _____, and _____.
3. Why is transparency important?
4. Of the different types of multiplexing, what distinguishes
   a. Frequency division multiplexing (FDM)?
   b. Time division multiplexing (TDM)?
   c. Statistical time division multiplexing (STDM)?
   d. Fiber optic multiplexing?
   e. T-1 multiplexing?
   f. Multiport modem multiplexing?
   g. Concentrators?
   h. Biplexers?

5. What does flow control accomplish and when is it important?

6. For what purpose are channel banks used?

7. What function do remote intelligent controllers serve?

8. What function do central site intelligent controllers serve?

9. Discuss the role of controllers in file transfer.

10. What is a protocol?

11. What is the purpose of a protocol converter?

12. Where are hardware protocol converters located?

13. How are microcomputer protocols to its host handled?

14. What is the primary disadvantage of software protocol converters?

15. Other than the obvious difference, how does hardware encryption differ from software encryption?

16. What is the difference between link-to-link encryption and end-to-end encryption?

17. How can you reduce key management costs in encrypted circuits?

18. How does a channel extender differ from a front end?

19. Line adapters are a _____ of communication hardware.

20. What is the function of a line interface module?

21. In what situation are port sharing devices used?

22. How do intelligent port selectors differ from port sharing devices?

23. How do line splitters differ from port sharing devices?

24. What is a multidrop circuit?

25. What is the purpose of a digital line expander?

26. How do dial-back security devices prevent unauthorized entry into a computer system?

27. What device increases throughput over a data communication link?

28. What is the purpose of a line protector?

29. What is the term used to describe the placing of two or more signals on a single channel?

30. If you were buying a multiplexer, why would you choose either TDM or FDM?

31. For data communication transmissions, which would you use, hardware encryption or software encryption?

32. Three terminals (T_1, T_2, T_3) are to be connected to three computers (C_1, C_2, C_3) so that T_1 is connected to C_1, T_2, to C_2, and T_3 to C_3. All are in different cities. T_1 and C_1 are 1,500 miles apart, as are T_2, C_2 and T_3 and C_3. The points T_1, T_2, and T_3 are 25 miles apart, and the points C_1, C_2, and C_3 also are 25 miles apart.

25 miles { T_1——1,500 miles——C_1
          T_2——1,500 miles——C_2 } 25 miles

25 miles { T_2 ...
          T_3——1,500 miles——C_3 } 25 miles

If telephone lines cost $1 per mile, what is the line cost for three independent lines? If a multiplexer/demultiplexer pair costs $2,000, can you save money by another arrangement of the lines? If so, how much?

33. How would you keep "hackers" out of your dial-up system?

34. How does fast packet multiplexing improve upon statistical time division multiplexing?

35. What is the guideline for differentiating a multiplexer from a concentrator?

36. What is the function of an inverse multiplexer?

37. How does a local area network gateway function as a remote intelligent controller?

38. How does a local area network gateway function as a protocol converter?

39. Which encryption method has the lowest key management cost, the data encryption standard or public key encryption?

40. How does a rotary switch work with a facsimile switch?

NEXT DAY AIR SERVICE CUMULATIVE CASE STUDY

Background on Next Day Air Service

At this point in the case, let us assume the portion of the network you developed earlier has been operational for about three months. The board of directors was pleased with the whole network concept. There was a noticeable increase in business, which presumably was brought about by an increase in customer satisfaction, which, in turn, was attributed to Next Day Air Service's newly established ability to process customer inquiries, improved package tracking, and billings.

Unfortunately, it is possible to have too much of a good thing. It appears that implementing the network has improved Next Day Air Service's efficiency so much that new business has resulted in overburdening the network hardware that is located at the corporate headquarters. Consequently, you have been asked to examine the possibility of improving the network further. The goals of such a reconfiguration are to achieve a 20 percent growth in traffic volume and reduce the total circuit cost of the network.

To reduce circuit costs, you are considering the possibility of acquiring either multiplexers or a concentrator. Multiplexer pairs offer the advantage of sending multiple transactions over a single circuit. On the other hand, a concentrator is a standalone device that can support line consolidation and provide auxiliary storage for store and forward transmissions.

Questions/Problems for the Next Day Air Service Case

1. What two cities appear to be the best locations for multiplexers? Use the map in Figure 1-8.
2. What offices would you link to the multiplexers in the two cities identified in Question 1?
3. How would you link the cities if there were four multiplexers located in Orlando, New Orleans, Dallas, and Atlanta?
4. Assume that Atlanta, Chicago, Memphis, Montgomery, St. Louis, and Washington, D.C. all use a multiplexer located in Atlanta. How long will it take to transmit their invoices (file transfer time) to Tampa at the end of the day? *HINT:* Look at Question 5 in Chapter 3 for additional details.
5. What type of multiplexer would you use (statistical or time division)? Support your answer.

Chapter Five

FUNDAMENTAL COMMUNICATION CONCEPTS

This chapter defines and describes the basic technical concepts of data communications. These concepts are approached from the nonmathematical viewpoint of what happens to the flow of data as a message moves from a remote terminal through the connector cable, modem, local loop, and telephone company central office, over the circuits, and into the front end and host computer. Each technical aspect of how the message moves is discussed. You do not need an engineering-level understanding of the topics in order to be an effective manager of data communication applications. It is important, however, that you understand these basic concepts and make intelligent use of them. Mastering the content of this chapter is a prerequisite to your competence in this field.

INTRODUCTION

This chapter concentrates on what happens when data moves from point to point. Although it requires covering some topics that may verge on electrical engineering, the discussions are phrased in lay terms. To begin our discussion of the basic technical concepts of data communications, examine Figure 5-1 which depicts a typical point-to-point network between a microcomputer or remote terminal and a central site computer. For simplicity, this configuration omits more complex design configurations such as multidrop, multiplex, and local area networks because such complexities would obscure the basic explanation of how data is transmitted. Instead we will present a simple, straightforward approach to the data transmission concepts as data flows from the microcomputer to the host mainframe computer.

As you can see in Figure 5-1, each component of the network is identified across the top of the figure, starting with the microcomputer or terminal and going through

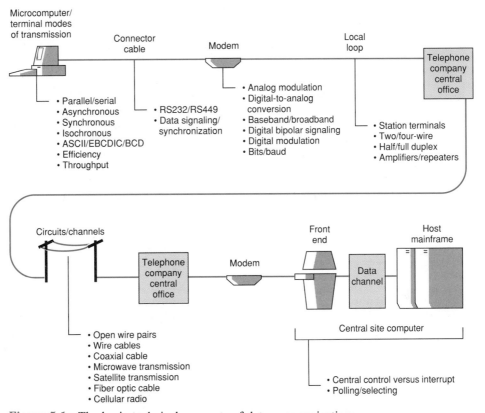

Figure 5-1   The basic technical concepts of data communications.

the connector cable, modem, local loop, telephone company central office, transmission circuits, and ultimately to the host mainframe computer. The technical concepts related to moving data from a remote miocrocomputer to a host mainframe are identified and described in this chapter.

As the discussion moves through the components shown in Figure 5-1, you can follow the movement of a data signal (message) and learn the basic technical concepts that enable the message to move across the communication network.

MICROCOMPUTER/TERMINAL

The first component in our network is the basic input/output device, which is shown as a microcomputer or terminal in Figure 5-1. Obviously, besides a microcomputer or terminal, this device could be a teleprinter, minicomputer, facsimile device, or any other terminal device that allows for input and output of data. At this point we will not describe the microcomputer itself because we are looking at the modes of transmission. Microcomputers, their internal architecture, operations, and commu-

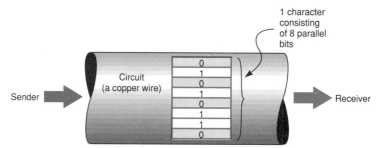

Figure 5-2   Parallel transmission of an 8-bit code.

nications, are covered thoroughly in Chapter 10, Microcomputers and Communications.

MODES OF TRANSMISSION

Look at the seven items listed below the microcomputer in Figure 5-1. Each one will be described in this section. As data leaves the microcomputer and begins traveling through the network, it requires consistent methods of transmission over the communication circuits or channels. All systems in our discussion transmit binary data, or data forms that are intrinsically binary. Binary data can be sent over communication circuits in either parallel or serial modes by use of asynchronous, synchronous, or isochronous transmission methodologies.

Parallel Mode   *Parallel mode* describes the way the internal transfer of binary data takes place within a computer. In other words, if the internal structure of the computer uses an 8-bit element, then all eight bits of the element are transferred between the main memory and any operational register within the same computer cycle. The same is true of the more powerful computers that use a 32-bit element or word length; all 32 bits are transferred between the main memory and any operational register in the same computer cycle. Although parallel transmission is seldom used outside computers, it is illustrated in Figure 5-2.[1] This figure shows how all eight bits of the USASCII[2] code (commonly called ASCII) travel down a channel simultaneously, followed a short time later by eight more bits of the next character. Normally, this parallel transfer is not used in data communications.

Inside computers, data typically travels around in parallel. The bits that form a character move between computer components at extremely high speeds along parallel paths, and arrive "together" at the different chips. Most printers use parallel communication, but this is possible only when the printer is very close to the com-

---

[1] Figure 5-2 and several subsequent figures used to depict transmission are conceptual pictures only; they are not representative of the electrical engineering facts of data transmission. Use them only to help in your understanding of the concepts.

[2] United States of America Standard Code for Information Interchange.

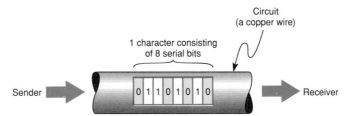

Figure 5-3   Serial transmission of an 8-bit code.

puter because parallel cables require many wires (one for each bit) and may not work reliably in lengths over about 25 feet.

Serial Mode   *Serial mode* is the predominant method of transferring information in data communications. Serial transmission implies that a stream of data is sent over a communication circuit in a bit-by-bit fashion. For example, the bits of information in an 8-bit ASCII code may be sent down a transmission circuit (channel) as shown in Figure 5-3. The ASCII code is used as an example in the following figures; it will be discussed later in this chapter, under Coding.

Serial transmission is distinguished from parallel because the transmitting device sends a single bit, then a second bit, and so on, until all the bits are transmitted. It takes *n* time cycles[3] to transmit *n* bits (eight in the case of ASCII). In parallel transmission, *n* bits of a character are sent, followed by a time interval, then *n* more bits are sent, and so on. In other words, with parallel transmission, the *n* bits of a character are sent in one time cycle, whereas with serial transmission, the same *n* bits of a character require *n* time cycles.

Thus, most data communication functions are performed by serial transmission. Three types of transmission are commonly used: asynchronous, synchronous, and isochronous. Note that all three of these transmission types are serial in nature.

Asynchronous Transmission   Asynchronous transmission often is referred to as start-stop transmission because the transmitting device can transmit a character at any time it is convenient, and the receiving device will accept that character.

With *asynchronous transmission,* each character is transmitted independently of all other characters. In order to separate the characters and synchronize transmission, a start bit and a stop bit are put on each end of the individual 8-bit character, so the total transmission is 10 bits per character, as shown in Figure 5-4. There is no fixed distance between characters because, if the terminal is one that transmits the character as soon as it is typed, then the distance between characters varies with the speed of the typist. If the asynchronous terminal holds the entire message in buffers and transmits the message when the operator presses the "send" key, then there is a fixed distance between characters because the terminal unloads its buffer on a character-by-character basis in a fixed timing sequence. Asynchronous

---

[3]If the *n* time cycles are not clear, look at the "bit pulse" timing factor of 833 microseconds in Figure 5-4 or Figure 3-7.

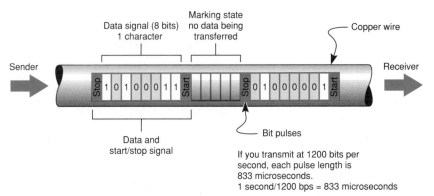

Figure 5-4   Asynchronous transmission.

transmission has a start bit and a stop bit to separate characters from each other and to allow for orderly reception of the message. Some older terminals may have multiple stop bits. The use of both a start bit and a stop bit is changing. With modern microcomputers and communications, many protocols have eliminated start bits and use only one stop bit.

In summary, the synchronization or timing takes place for an individual character because the *start bit* is a signal that tells the receiving terminal to start sampling the incoming bits of a character at a fixed rate so the eight data bits can be interpreted into their proper character structure. A *stop bit* informs the receiving terminal that the character has been received and resets the terminal for recognition of the next start bit. Synchronization of the character (timing between bits) is reestablished upon reception of each character.

Synchronous Transmission   *Synchronous transmission* (see Figure 5-5) is used for the high speed transmission of a block of characters, sometimes called a *frame* or *packet*. In this method of transmission, both the sending and receiving devices operate simultaneously, and they resynchronize for each block of data. Start and stop bits for each character are *not* required. In other words, if you had 100 charac-

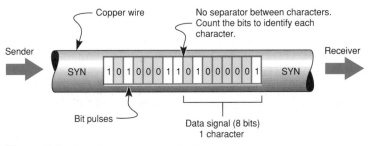

Figure 5-5   Synchronous transmission.

ters using an 8-bit ASCII code structure, the message part of the block of data would be 800 bits long.

Synchronization is established and maintained either when the line is idle (no data signals being transmitted) or just prior to the transmission of a data signal. This synchronization is established by passing a predetermined group of "sync" (usually written *SYN*) characters between the sending and the receiving devices. Figure 5-5 shows how the data signals are continuous and how one long stream of data bits is transmitted from the sending to the receiving device. In other words, the sending device sends a couple of 8-bit synchronization characters to the receiving device so the receiving device can determine the time between each of the bits.

After the SYN characters, the transmitting device sends a long stream of data bits that may have thousands of bits. The receiving device, knowing what code is being used, counts off the appropriate number of bits for the first character, assumes this is the first character, and passes it to the computer. It then counts off the bits for the second character and so on. If ASCII code is used, the receiving device counts off the first eight bits and sends them to the computer as a character; it then counts off the second eight bits and sends them as a character, and so on.

Synchronous transmission is more efficient than asynchronous because there are fewer control bits in proportion to the total number of bits transmitted. The synchronization takes only 16 to 32 bits (2 to 4 characters), whereas the stream of bits for the data block may be several thousand bits long.

In summary, we differentiate synchronous and asynchronous data transmissions by the fact that in asynchronous data transmission each character is transmitted as a totally independent entity with its own start and stop bits to inform the receiving device that the character is beginning and ending. By contrast, in synchronous transmission whole blocks of data are transmitted as units after the transmitter and the receiver have been synchronized. In Greek, the letters "asyn" mean not; therefore, asynchronous is not synchronous.

Isochronous Transmission   A third technique, *isochronous transmission,* combines the elements of both synchronous and asynchronous data transmission. In isochronous transmission, as in asynchronous, each character is required to have both a start bit and a stop bit. However, as in synchronous data transmission, the transmitter and receiver are synchronized. The synchronization time interval between successive bits is specified to be an even multiple of the length of one code bit. That is, all periods of no transmission consist of one or more 1-character time intervals. This common timing provides greater precision between the transmitting and receiving equipment than can be achieved with asynchronous techniques only. As a result, data can be transmitted at higher speeds.

Figure 5-6 illustrates the relationships and differences between asynchronous, synchronous, and isochronous transmission. In asynchronous transmission, there is no determination of the spacing between individual characters (indefinite time). Thus, both the sending and receiving equipment must have clocks to determine the time length of a bit, and the receiver must have special recognition circuitry to determine the beginning and end of a character. With synchronous transmission, the clocking signal synchronizes the receiver to the sender before a long, multichar-

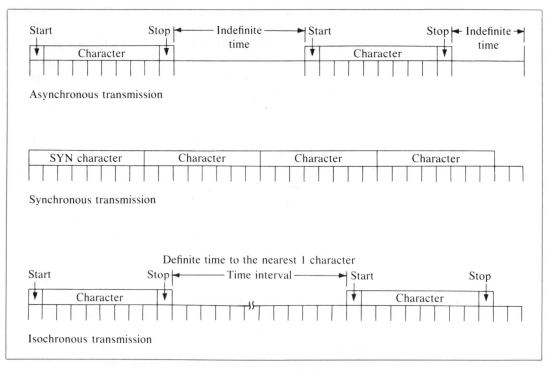

Figure 5-6 Comparison of serial transmission methods (asynchronous, synchronous, isochronous).

acter block of data is transmitted. In isochronous transmission, the clocking is supplied by the sending modem, and the receiving modem synchronizes to it for short periods. Each character begins on some multiple of the length of the bit element.

The primary reason for using isochronous transmission in preference to asynchronous transmission is speed. In practice, asynchronous data transmission generally is limited to 2400 bits per second by the timing precision of the sending and receiving modems. By contrast, isochronous data transmission can achieve data transmission rates of 19,200 bits per second.

In summary, the modes of transmission are parallel (all bits of a character sent simultaneously) and serial (bit by bit down the line). Furthermore, serial transmission, which is most prevalent, can be divided into three types.

- Asynchronous transmission, in which the data bits of a character are sent independent of the timing of any other character and are preceded by a start bit and followed by a stop bit.

- Synchronous transmission, in which the sending and receiving units are synchronized, and then a stream of many thousands of bits (a block) is sent.

- Isochronous transmission, in which each character still has a start and stop bit, but the sending and receiving equipment are synchronized for the length of each timing unit.

Coding (ASCII/EBCDIC/BCD/Baudot)   As mentioned earlier, data sent over communication circuits is binary. For this data to be received in a meaningful way at the other end of the circuit, it must be transmitted and received by a standard methodology. A very precise set of terminology has come to be associated with such transmission, and it is essential to your understanding of message movement.

A *character* is a symbol that has a common, constant meaning for some group of people. A character might be the letter A or B, or it might be a number such as 1 or 2. Characters also may be special symbols such as ? or &. Characters in data communications, as in computer systems, are represented by groups of *bits* that are binary zeros (0) and ones (1). The groups of bits representing the set of characters that are the "alphabet" of any given system are called a *coding scheme,* or simply a *code.* This section will discuss some of the codes used in data communication.

A *byte* is a group of consecutive bits that are treated as a unit or character. One byte normally is comprised of 8 bits and usually represents one character. However, in data communications some codes use 5, 6, 7, 8, or 9 bits to represent a character. These differences in the number of bits per character arise because the codes have different numbers of characters to represent and different provisions for error checking.

Coding is the representation of one set of symbols by another set of symbols. For example, representation of the character A by a group of 7 bits (say, 1000001) is an example of coding. We do not usually see characters at the bit level. Microcomputers and network diagnostic equipment do not show the character A as 1000001, although they might decipher a capital A as either a hexadecimal number 41 or a decimal number 65.

As we have seen, information in data communications normally is transmitted serially over a circuit. Codes for representing the information vary both in the number of bits used to define a single character and in the assignment of bit patterns to each particular character. For example, the bit group 1000001 may represent the character A in one coding scheme (ASCII), but the bit group 11000 may represent the character A in some other code configuration (Baudot).

United States of America Standard Code for Information Interchange (USAS-CII), or more commonly *ASCII,* is the most popular code for data communications. It is the standard code available on most terminals and microcomputers. This is an 8-bit code that has 128 valid character combinations. The number of combinations can be determined by taking the number 2 and raising it to the power equal to the number of information bits in the code. In this case $2^7 = 128$ characters. The eighth bit is the *parity bit* for error checking on individual characters; therefore, the code uses only seven bits to represent characters.

Figure 5-7 shows the 128-character ASCII code. It shows the ASCII printable character, its decimal number (Dec) equivalent, and its hexadecimal (Hex) equivalent. The bottom of the figure shows the data communication control characters and their decimal (Dec) equivalent, mnemonic, and meaning. Most microcomputer and printer documentation manuals depict ASCII as in Figure 5-7. Some writers depict the ASCII code chart as shown in the box ASCII Bits per Character Versus the Decimal Equivalent.

Rather than present the 7-bit configuration for each character, Figure 5-7 shows

ASCII	Dec	Hex	ASCII	Dec	Hex	ASCII	Dec	Hex	ASCII	Dec	Hex
	0	00	\<space>	32	20	@	64	40	`	96	60
☺	1	01	!	33	21	A	65	41	a	97	61
☻	2	02	"	34	22	B	66	42	b	98	62
♥	3	03	#	35	23	C	67	43	c	99	63
♦	4	04	$	36	24	D	68	44	d	100	64
♣	5	05	%	37	25	E	69	45	e	101	65
♠	6	06	&	38	26	F	70	46	f	102	66
•	7	07	'	39	27	G	71	47	g	103	67
◘	8	08	(	40	28	H	72	48	h	104	68
○	9	09	)	41	29	I	73	49	i	105	69
◎	10	0A	*	42	2A	J	74	4A	j	106	6A
♂	11	0B	+	43	2B	K	75	4B	k	107	6B
♀	12	0C	,	44	2C	L	76	4C	l	108	6C
♪	13	0D	–	45	2D	M	77	4D	m	109	6D
♫	14	0E	.	46	2E	N	78	4E	n	110	6E
☼	15	0F	/	47	2F	O	79	4F	o	111	6F
►	16	10	0	48	30	P	80	50	p	112	70
◄	17	11	1	49	31	Q	81	51	q	113	71
↕	18	12	2	50	32	R	82	52	r	114	72
‼	19	13	3	51	33	S	83	53	s	115	73
¶	20	14	4	52	34	T	84	54	t	116	74
§	21	15	5	53	35	U	85	55	u	117	75
▬	22	16	6	54	36	V	86	56	v	118	76
↨	23	17	7	55	37	W	87	57	w	119	77
↑	24	18	8	56	38	X	88	58	x	120	78
↓	25	19	9	57	39	Y	89	59	y	121	79
→	26	1A	:	58	3A	Z	90	5A	z	122	7A
←	27	1B	;	59	3B	[	91	5B	{	123	7B
∟	28	1C	<	60	3C	\	92	5C	|	124	7C
↔	29	1D	=	61	3D	]	93	5D	}	125	7D
▲	30	1E	>	62	3E	^	94	5E	~	126	7E
▼	31	1F	?	63	3F	_	95	5F	Δ	127	7F

Dec	Mnemonic and Meaning		Dec	Mnemonic and Meaning	
0	NUL	Null	16	DLE	Data Link Escape
1	SOH	Start of Heading	17	DC1	Device Control 1
2	STX	Start of Text	18	DC2	Device Control 2
3	ETX	End of Text	19	DC3	Device Control 3
4	EOT	End of Transmission	20	DC4	Device Control 4
5	ENQ	Enquiry	21	NAK	Negative Acknowledge
6	ACK	Acknowledge	22	SYN	Synchronous Idle
7	BEL	Bell	23	ETB	End of Transmission Block
8	BS	Backspace	24	CAN	Cancel
9	HT	Horizontal Tabulation	25	EM	End of Medium
10	LF	Line Feed	26	SUB	Substitute
11	VT	Vertical Tabulation	27	ESC	Escape
12	FF	Form Feed	28	FS	File Separator
13	CR	Carriage Return	29	GS	Group Separator
14	SO	Shift Out	30	RS	Record Separator
15	SI	Shift In	31	US	Unit Separator
			127	DEL	Delete

Figure 5-7 ASCII code as it relates to data communications.

ASCII BITS PER CHARACTER VERSUS THE DECIMAL EQUIVALENT

Bit positions 1, 2, 3, 4:		Bit positions 5, 6, 7:							
		000	100	010	110	001	101	011	111
		0	1	2	3	4	5	6	7
0000	0	NUL	DLE	SP	0	@	P	`	p
1000	1	SOH	DC1	!	1	A	Q	a	q
0100	2	STX	DC2	"	2	B	R	b	r
1100	3	ETX	DC3	#	3	C	S	c	s
0010	4	EOT	DC4	$	4	D	T	d	t
1010	5	ENQ	NAK	%	5	E	U	e	u
0110	6	ACK	SYN	&	6	F	V	f	v
1110	7	BEL	ETB	'	7	G	W	g	w
0001	8	BS	CAN	(	8	H	X	h	x
1001	9	HT	EM	)	9	I	Y	i	y
0101	10	LF	SUB	*	:	J	Z	j	z
1101	11	VT	ESC	+	;	K	[	k	{
0011	12	FF	FS	,	<	L	\	l	¦
1011	13	CR	GS	–	=	M	]	m	}
0111	14	SO	RS	.	>	N	^	n	~
1111	15	SI	US	/	?	O	_	o	DEL

A	=	1	0	0	0	0	0	1	=	65 decimal
C	=	1	1	0	0	0	0	1	=	67 decimal
)	=	1	0	0	1	0	1	0	=	41 decimal

Binary counting numbers }	1	2	4	8	16	32	64

ASCII character	Bit position one					Bit position seven	

To cross-relate the above ASCII code chart that shows the bits per character to the decimal equivalent chart in Figure 5-7, place the ASCII character for which you want the decimal equivalent in the box marked "ASCII character." Using the above table, identify the bits (1 to 7) for the character. Place these bits in the seven boxes at the bottom. Add the "Binary counting numbers" (1, 2, 4, 8, 16, 32, and 64) to get the decimal equivalent. Add only the binary counting numbers that have a 1 in the corresponding box. For example, for the character C, we added 1 + 2 + 64 because there was a 1 below the 1, 2, and the 64.

the decimal equivalent for the character. For example, the ASCII 7-bit code for capital A is 1000001. Its decimal equivalent is 65. To prove this, boot your microcomputer and from the DOS prompt, hold down the Alt key while typing 65 on the numeric keypad (right side of keyboard). When the Alt key is released, the character A (upper case) will be displayed. You cannot display the ASCII characters 0 to 31 from the DOS prompt because they have special meanings to DOS. To check them, go into your word processor (for example, WordStar 2000) and use the Alt key and their decimal equivalents to display the ASCII 0 to 31 characters. Some network hardware removes (strips off) the parity bit of an ASCII character before transmitting it. This means it is only seven bits per character instead of eight when being transmitted over a communication circuit.

Extended Binary Coded Decimal Interchange Code (EBCDIC) is IBM's standard information code. This code has 256 valid character combinations ($2^8 = 256$) because there are 8 information bits and parity is carried as a ninth bit. You probably have heard people talk about a 9-channel tape drive. The 9-channel tape drive was developed originally to hold the IBM code with its 8 data bits and 1 parity bit. If used in asynchronous transmission, this code has 11 bits per character because there is 1 start, 8 data, 1 parity, and 1 stop bit. In synchronous transmission it has only 9 bits per character unless the parity bit is stripped off prior to transmission.

Binary Coded Decimal (BCD) code is a 6-bit code that has 64 valid character combinations ($2^6 = 64$). The BCD code was the logical extension from the earlier tab card-oriented Hollerith code. Depending on the specific hardware, this code can have 1 or 2 parity bits; therefore, it can be either 6 bits (if the parity bit is not transmitted), 7 bits (1 parity bit), or 8 bits (2 parity bits) during synchronous transmission. A start bit and a stop bit have to be added for asynchronous transmission.

Baudot code is one of the oldest codes of data communications. It is a 5-bit code that has only 32 possible character combinations; however, there are also two functions, called *letters* and *figures*. When one of these two functions is used, it sets the equipment so all characters typed after that point are in a different configuration than they were previously. In effect, this raises the number of valid character combinations to 58, just barely enough for simplified data communications. A version called *International Baudot* has a sixth bit added for parity purposes. Baudot code is used on the earlier teletype equipment and on very slow communication circuits (150 bits per second or less).

Efficiency of a Code Now that we have discussed codes, we must review network efficiency as it relates to a specific code set. One objective of a data communication network is to move the highest possible volume of accurate information through the network. The higher the volume, the greater the resulting network's efficiency and the lower the cost. Network efficiency is affected by such characteristics of the circuits as distortion and transmission speed, as well as by turnaround time, the coding scheme used, the speed of transmitting and receiving equipment, the error detection and control methodology, and the mode of transmission. In this section we will focus on the coding scheme and how the *efficiency of a code* affects transmission efficiency.

Transmission efficiency is defined as the total number of information bits divided by the total bits.

Each communication code structure has both information bits and redundant bits. *Information bits* are those used to convey the meaning of the specific character being transmitted, such as the character A. *Redundant bits* are used for other purposes such as error checking. Therefore, a parity bit used for error checking is a redundant bit because it is not used to identify the specific character, even though it may be necessary. As you can see, if you did not care about errors, the redundant error checking bit could be omitted. Also, message control characters, such as an END OF TEXT (ETX) character, are considered redundant bits. These bits are redundant by definition only because they are needed for accurate data communications, just as the periods and commas are required when you write a letter.

Figure 5-8 shows that the efficiency of the code (E_C) equals the bits of information (B_I) divided by the bits in total (B_T). This means that if you have an 8-bit code with 7 of the bits used to represent the character and 1 representing parity, then you have a code efficiency of 87.5 percent. This is calculated by taking the bits of information (B_I) and dividing by the bits in total (B_T): for example, $7/8 = 0.875$.

If you have a 6-bit code with 2 parity bits (8 bits total), then the efficiency of the code (E_C) is $6/8$ or 75 percent. As is evident by this comparison, some codes are more efficient than others.

The same formula (as shown in Figure 5-8) can be used to estimate the efficiency of an asynchronous transmission system. As an example, assume there is an 8-bit code structure where 7 bits represent the data and 1 bit is for parity. In asynchronous transmission there are usually 1 start bit and 1 stop bit. Therefore, the bits of

$$E_C = \frac{B_I}{B_T}$$

E_C: efficiency of the code

B_I: information bits

B_T: total bits

Figure 5-8   Efficiency of codes.

information (B_I) are 7, but the bits in total are 10 (B_T). The efficiency of the asynchronous transmission system is 7 bits of information divided by 10 total bits for an efficiency of 70 percent. It should be noted that if any other control characters are needed, such as message character counts or other control characters sent at the end of your transmission, the efficiency drops below 70 percent. On the other hand, if no start bit is used, the efficiency increases to $\frac{7}{9}$ or 77.8 percent.

The same basic formula can be used if an estimate is needed for the efficiency of a synchronous transmission system. In this case the bits of information (B_I) are calculated by determining how many "information" characters are in the message block. If the message portion of the frame or packet contains 100 information characters, using our 8-bit code, there are 7 bits times 100 characters, or 700 bits of information. Next, the bits in total (B_T) are the 700 bits of information, plus all the redundant bits that are inserted for control and security purposes. These other bits include the parity bit (eighth bit) that is appended to each character, the control bits in the flag at each end of the frame, the bits in the control field, the address field, the frame check sequence, and any internal control characters from the packet frame such as format identifiers, logical channel numbers, sequence numbers, and a couple of synchronization (SYN) characters.

For this example assume there are a total of 11 control characters for your message. Therefore, the number of redundant bits is 11 control characters times 8 bits per character, plus 100 bits (the parity bit for each of the 100 characters in your message) for a total of 188 redundant bits. The efficiency of this synchronous system is 700 bits of information (B_I) divided by 888 bits in total (B_T) for an efficiency of 79 percent.

This example shows that synchronous networks usually are more efficient than asynchronous networks and some codes are more efficient than others. The longer the message (1,000 characters as opposed to 100), the more efficient is synchronous over asynchronous. To extend our example further, assume we have a software or hardware scheme that strips off the individual parity bits for each character prior to transmission and puts them back on at the destination. The number of redundant bits (no parity bits) is reduced by 100; therefore, efficiency rises to 89 percent (700 bits of information divided by 788 bits in total). If the frame check sequences and other error checking techniques for synchronous transmission are good enough, you might consider stripping off the individual parity bits for each character prior to transmission in order to gain a 10 percent increase in throughput efficiency of data bits.

Throughput (TRIB) Many factors affect the *throughput* of a data communication network. Probably the most important are the transmission rate of information bits and the communication circuit bandwidth because bandwidth limits the absolute upper limit of speed. If terminals are multidropped, that is another factor because the circuit must be shared. If terminals are multiplexed, that becomes a factor because each terminal uses a reduced bandwidth (a subset of the total bandwidth on the circuit). Another factor is the capability of the front end processor to handle multiple incoming and outgoing communication circuits. If the front end cannot handle circuits or messages simultaneously, the capacity of the network is degraded. Software design is also a factor because it determines which protocol is used and whether transmission is in full duplex or half duplex. Propagation time, especially on satellite circuits, affects throughput. The time required for the host computer to process a request, perform a lookup, or update a database also is a factor in throughput. Error rates in hardware, in software, and on the communication circuit affect throughput because of possible retransmissions of the same message. The polling scheme (central control) or whether the system operates on an interrupt basis affects throughput. (For more on this topic, see the Response Time Evaluation section in Chapter 8.) Obviously, many items affect throughput. It is appropriate at this point to examine one of the major parameters of importance: how many usable characters of information can be transmitted per second.

The term *Transmission Rate of Information Bits* (TRIB) describes the effective rate of data transfer. It is a measure of the effective quantity of information that is transmitted over a communication circuit per unit of time.

The American National Standards Institute (ANSI) provides definitions for calculating the transfer rate of information bits. TRIB calculations may vary with the type of protocol used because of different numbers of control characters required and different time between blocks. The basic TRIB equation is shown in the Formula for Calculating TRIB box on page 162, along with an example. If you want to computerize the TRIB calculation, the book by Gilbert Held cited at the end of this chapter contains a 32-line Microsoft Quick Basic program to do so (Figure 2-5 on page 15 of Held's book).

CONNECTOR CABLES

Look back at Figure 5-1 to see the second component in our network. When the message leaves the microcomputer or other terminal and begins to move onto the network, the second component it encounters is the connector cable. When people discuss *connector cables,* the focus is on the standards (such as RS232 or RS449) and the data signaling or synchronization for the movement of synchronous data. Synchronization is achieved by having a start bit and a stop bit on each character (asynchronous) or sending SYN characters (decimal 22 in Figure 5-7) to the remote modem (synchronous).

RS232 (DB-25)/RS449 (DB-9)   When people talk about connector cables, they frequently refer to them as a RS232, DB-25, RS449, or DB-9. This is because each connector cable is based on a specified standard. By calling the connector by its standard designation, everyone knows precisely which connector is being discussed.

The RS232 standard is the most frequently mentioned. It was first issued in 1962, and its third revision, RS232C, was issued in 1969. The RS232D standard was issued in 1987 to expand on RS232C. The RS232D standard also is known as the EIA-232-D.

The *RS232* is the connector cable that is the standard interface for connecting data terminal equipment (DTE) to data circuit terminating equipment (DCE). The

FORMULA FOR CALCULATING TRIB

$$\text{TRIB} = \frac{\text{Number of information bits accepted}}{\text{Total time required to get the bits accepted}}$$

$$\text{TRIB} = \frac{K(M - C)(1 - P)}{M/R + T}$$

where K = information bits per character

M = block length in characters

R = modem transmission rate in characters per second

C = average number of noninformation characters per block (control characters)

P = probability that a block will require retransmission because of error

T = time between blocks in seconds, such as modem delay/turnaround time on half duplex, echo suppressor delay on dial-up, and propagation delay on satellite transmission. This is the time required to reverse the direction of transmission from send to receive or receive to send on a half duplex (HDX) circuit. It can be obtained from the modem specification book and may be referred to as *reclocking time*.

The following TRIB example shows the calculation of throughput assuming a 4800 bits per second half duplex circuit.

$$\text{TRIB} = \frac{7(400 - 10)(1 - 0.01)}{(400/600) + 0.025} = 3908 \text{ bits per second}$$

where K = 7 bits per character (information)

M = 400 characters per block

R = 600 characters per second (derived from 4800 bits per second divided by 8 bits/character)

C = 10 control characters per block

P = 0.01 (10^{-2}) or one retransmission out of 100 blocks transmitted—1%

T = 25 milliseconds (0.025) turnaround time.

If all factors in the calculation remain constant except for the circuit, which is changed to full duplex (no turnaround time delays, $T = 0$), then the TRIB increases to 4054 bits per second.

Look at the equation where the turnaround value (T) is 0.025. If there is a further propagation delay time of 475 milliseconds (0.475), this figure changes to 0.500. For demonstrating how a satellite channel affects TRIB, the total delay time is now 500 milliseconds. Still using the figures above (except for the new 0.500 delay time), we reduce the TRIB for our half duplex, satellite link to 2317 bits per second, which is almost one half of the full duplex (no turnaround time) 4054 bits per second.

newer RS232D is specified as having 25 wires and using the DB-25 connector plug like the one used on microcomputers. If this connector cable is attached to a microcomputer, people may refer to it simply as DB-25; if it is not attached to a microcomputer, they may refer to it as the RS232 interface.

Data terminal equipment (*DTE*) comprises the data source, the data sink, or both. In reality, it is any piece of equipment at which a data communication path begins or ends, such as a terminal. *Data circuit terminating equipment* (*DCE*) provides all the functions required to establish, maintain, and terminate a connection. This includes signal conversion and coding between the DTE and the common carrier's circuit, including the modem. A modem is DCE.

Figure 5-9 shows a picture of the RS232D interface plug and describes each of its 25 protruding pins. It is the standard connector cable (25 wires/pins) that passes control signals and data between the terminal (DTE) and the modem (DCE). This standard has been supplied by the Electronic Industries Association (EIA). Outside the United States, this RS232D connector cable is known as the V.24 and V.28. The V.24 and V.28 standards have been accepted by the international standards group known as the Consultative Committee on International Telegraph and Telephone (CCITT). These standards provide a common description of what the signal coming out of, and going into, the serial port of a computer or terminal looks like electrically. Specifically, RS232 provides for a signal changing from a nominal + 12 volts to a nominal − 12 volts. The standard also defines the cables and connectors used to link data communication devices. This is the cable that connects the modem to your microcomputer.

The RS232 has a maximum 50-foot cable length, but it can be increased to 100 feet or more by means of a special low capacitance, extended distance cable. This is not advised, however, because some vendors may not honor maintenance agreements if the cable is lengthened beyond the 50-foot standard.

As an illustration, let us present the cable distances for Texas Instruments' products. The cable length of the RS232 varies according to the speed at which you transmit. For Texas Instruments, the connector cable length can be up to 914 meters (1 meter = 1.1 yards) when transmitting at 1200 bits per second, 549 meters when transmitting at 2400 bits per second, 244 meters when transmitting at 4800 bits per second, and 122 meters when transmitting at 9600 bits per second. When end users operate at maximum distances, it is important to remember that they must meet the restrictions on all types of equipment used, including the electrical environment, cable construction, and cable wiring. This means that when you want to operate at a maximum cable distance, before proceeding it is necessary to contact the terminal and/or modem vendors to obtain their maximum cable distance.

The *RS449* standard has been adopted as U.S. Federal Standard 1031. The RS449 is shown in Figure 5-10. A 4,000-foot cable length can be used, there are 37 pins instead of 25 (useful for digital transmission), and various other circuit functions have been added, such as diagnostic circuits and digital circuits. In addition, secondary channel circuits (reverse channel) have been put into a separate 9-pin connector. This same 9-pin connector is used on the AT (Advanced Technology) microcomputers and is known as a *DB-9*. The serial port on your microcomputer may be either a DB-9 or a *DB-25*.

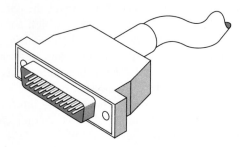

Pin   Circuit Name
1   Shield
2   Transmitted Data
3   Received Data
4   Request to Send
5   Clear to Send
6   DCE Ready
7   Signal Ground
8   Received Line Signal Detector
9   (Reserved for testing)
10   (Reserved for testing)
11   (Unassigned)
12   Secondary Received Line Signal Detector/Data Signal Rate Select (DCE source)
13   Secondary Clear to Send
14   Secondary Transmitted Data
15   Transmitter Signal Element Timing (DCE source)
16   Secondary Received Data
17   Receiver Signal Element Timing (DCE source)
18   Local Loopback
19   Secondary Request to Send
20   DTE Ready
21   Remote Loopback/Signal Quality Detector
22   Ring Indicator
23   Data Signal Rate Select (DTE/DCE source)
24   Transmitter Signal Element Timing (DTE source)
25   Test Mode

Figure 5-9   RS232D and V.24 interface (DB-25). The terminal connection to the modem is defined by the Electronic Industries Association (EIA) specification, which specifies the use of a 25-pin connector and the pin on which each signal is placed.

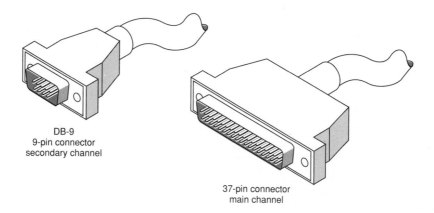

DB-9
9-pin connector
secondary channel

37-pin connector
main channel

37-Pin Connector		9-Pin Connector	
First Segment Assignment	**Second Segment Assignment**		
Pin Function	Pin Function	Pin Function	
1 Shield	20 Receive Common	1 Shield	
2 Signaling Rate Indicator	21 Unassigned	2 Sec. Receiver Ready	
3 Unassigned	22 Send Data	3 Sec. Send Data	
4 Send Data	23 Send Timing	4 Sec. Receive Data	
5 Send Timing	24 Receive Data	5 Signal Ground	
6 Receive Data	25 Request to Send	6 Receive Common	
7 Request to Send	26 Receive Timing	7 Sec. Request to Send	
8 Receive Timing	27 Clear to Send	8 Sec. Clear to Send	
9 Clear to Send	28 Terminal in Service	9 Send Common	
10 Local Loopback	29 Data Mode		
11 Data Mode	30 Terminal Ready		
12 Terminal Ready	31 Receiver Ready		
13 Receiver Ready	32 Select Standby		
14 Remote Loopback	33 Signal Quality		
15 Incoming Call	34 New Signal		
16 Select Frequency/ Signaling Rate Selector	35 Terminal Timing		
17 Terminal Timing	36 Standby Indicator		
18 Test Mode	37 Send Common		
19 Signal Ground			

Figure 5-10   RS449 interface and DB-9 connector. RS449 is a new EIA specification augmenting RS232C. This specification calls for use of a 37-pin connector. For those devices using a side, forward, reverse, or secondary channel, a second 9-pin connector is specified. RS449 provides for additional control and signaling.

For some of the new features, look at pin 32 (SELECT STANDBY). With this pin, the terminal can instruct the modem to use an alternate standby network such as changing from a private leased line to a public packet network, either for backup or simply to access another database not normally used. In other words, a terminal can be connected to two different networks, and the operator can enter a keyboard command to switch the connection from one network to another. With regard to LOOPBACK (pins 10 and 14), the terminal can allow basic tests without special test equipment or the manual swapping of equipment or cables.

With microcomputers, the RS232 and RS449 also are referred to as D-type connectors. The RS232 may be called a DB-25, and the 9-pin RS449 may be called a DB-9. Look at Figure 5-11 to see the microcomputer pin configurations for these two connectors.

There are also X.20 and X.21 interface cables. The *X.20* interface is for asynchronous communications, and the *X.21* is for synchronous communications. Each is based on only 15 pins (wires) connecting the DTE and the DCE. The lower number of pins requires an increased intelligence in both the DTE and the DCE. X.20 and X.21 are international standards intended to provide an interface with the X.25 packet switching networks discussed later in this book. A new RS530 standard also has been developed to replace the 37-pin RS449 connectors. The *RS530* is a 25-pin high speed interface for digital transmission at greater than 20,000 bits per second speeds. It uses the same 25-pin DB-25 connector plug.

Another option that may become available in the near future is a fiber optic cable in place of the standard RS232 electrical cables. Currently, by using fiber optic cable, we can locate a terminal 1,000 meters (3,280 feet) from a host mainframe computer. With a 1,000-meter fiber optic cable, these products can communicate at speeds ranging from 19,200 bits per second up to double that speed. Therefore, you get not only greater distance (1,000 meters) but also greater speed. This may be another example in which fiber optics will replace electronics in the future.

The *high speed serial interface* (HSSI) is beginning to appear in new products. HSSI defines the physical and electrical interface between the DTE and the DCE equipment. It was developed by Cisco Systems of Menlo Park, California, and T3plus of Santa Clara, California. They have submitted it to the American National Standards Institute, which also developed the EIA-232 and V.35 standards. HSSI allows data transfers over the connector cable at 52 million bits per second, whereas RS-449 cannot handle more than 10 million bits per second. HSSI is a 50-pin connector using shielded twisted pair cabling.

Data Signaling/Synchronization   As you learned earlier in this chapter, synchronous transmission is the movement of an entire message block at a time. Let us look at *data signaling* or *synchronization* as it occurs on a RS232 connector cable. Figure 5-12 shows the 13 most used pins of the 25-pin RS232 connector cable. On the left side is a microcomputer and on the right side is a modem.

Did you ever wonder what happens when you press the "send" key with regard to synchronous data transmission? When a synchronous block of data is sent, the microcomputer and the modem raise and lower electrical signals (plus and minus voltages of electricity) between themselves over the RS232 connector cable that connects a microcomputer to a modem. This usually is a nominal + 12 or − 12 volts.

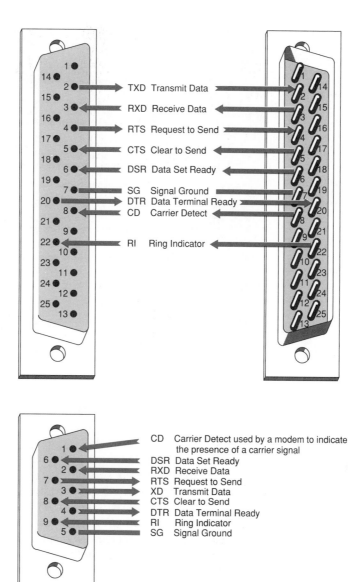

Figure 5-11 Typical 25-pin (RS232) and 9-pin IBM (PC/AT) modem connector for microcomputers.

For example, a modem with a RS232 interface might indicate that it is powered on and ready to operate by raising the signal on pin 6, DATA SET READY. (Data set is an older term for a modem.) When a call comes in, the modem shows the microcomputer that the telephone line is ringing by raising a signal on pin 22, the RING INDICATOR. Raising a signal means putting +12 volts on the wire or pin. The microcomputer may then tell the modem to answer the call by raising a signal on pin 20, DATA TERMINAL READY. After the modems connect, the modem

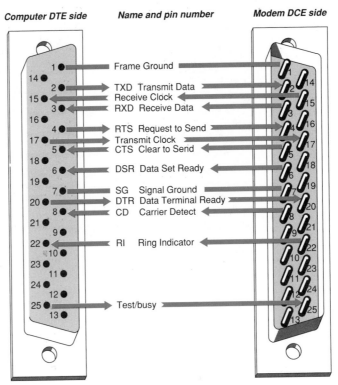

Computer DTE side   **Name and pin number**   **Modem DCE side**

Figure 5-12   RS232 modem control (13 most used pins).

may indicate the connection status to the microcomputer by raising a signal on pin 8, CARRIER DETECT. At the end of the session, the microcomputer may tell the modem to drop the telephone call (release the circuit) by lowering the signal on pin 20, DATA TERMINAL READY. The REQUEST TO SEND and CLEAR TO SEND signals go over pins 4 and 5, which are used in half duplex modems to manage control of the communication channel. Incidentally, some of these basic procedures may vary slightly from one manufacturer to another.

Follow the pins and signal direction arrows in Figure 5-12 as we discuss an example that handles the flow of a block of synchronous data. When the microcomputer operator presses the ''send'' key to transmit a block of data, pin 4, REQUEST TO SEND, transmits the signal from the microcomputer to the modem. This informs the modem that a block of data is ready to be sent. The modem then sends a CLEAR TO SEND signal back to the microcomputer by using pin 5, thus telling the microcomputer that it can send a synchronous block of data.

The microcomputer now out-pulses a serial stream of bits that contain two 8-bit SYN (synchronization) characters in front of the message block. A SYN character is 0110100 (decimal 22 in ASCII code). This bit stream passes over the connector cable to the modem using pin 2, TRANSMIT DATA. The modem then modulates this data block to convert it from the digital signal (plus and minus voltages of electricity) to an analog signal (discussed in the next section). From the modem this block of data goes out on to the local loop circuit that goes from your business premises to the telephone company central office. From there it goes on to the long distance interexchange channels (IXC) and the receiving end telephone company central office. Then it moves to the local loop, into the modem, across the connector cable, and into the host mainframe computer at the other end of the circuit as shown in Figure 5-1.

This process is repeated for each synchronous message block in half duplex transmission. The data signaling that takes place between the microcomputer and the modem involves the REQUEST TO SEND, CLEAR TO SEND, and TRANSMIT DATA pins. Accurate timing between blocks of data is critical in data signaling and synchronization. If this timing is lost, the entire block of data is destroyed and must be retransmitted.

MODULATION

In Figure 5-1, our message now leaves the connector cable and moves to the modem. Modems were discussed in Chapter 3 as one of the basic hardware components of a network. (To review the operation of a modem, see Figure 3-7.) The modem takes the binary electrical pulses received from the microcomputer and converts or modulates the signal so it can be transmitted. Modems perform either analog modulation or digital modulation, each of which can be accomplished in a variety of ways. These concepts will be discussed in the remainder of this section.

Analog Modulation   *Modulation* is the technique that modifies the form of an electrical signal so the signal can carry intelligent information on a communication medium. The modulated signal often is referred to as an *analog signal*. The signal that does the carrying is the carrier wave, and modulation changes the shape or form of the carrier wave to transmit 0s and 1s.

A continuous oscillating[4] voltage of arbitrary amplitude or frequency carries no intelligence. (The top of Figure 5-13 depicts amplitude.) However, if it can be interrupted or the amplitude altered so it becomes somewhat like a series of pulses that correspond to some known code (such as ASCII), then the oscillating signal can carry intelligence. In data communications this continuous oscillating voltage is called a *carrier wave* or simply a *carrier*. The carrier signal can be altered in many ways. The most common methods of *analog modulation* are amplitude modulation, frequency modulation, and phase modulation.

We call the equipment in which modulation takes place a *modulator*. If the modulator causes the amplitude of the carrier signal to vary, the result is called amplitude modulation, and so on for frequency and phase modulation. These modulators are, in fact, the modems located at each end of the transmission lines. The process of modifying a carrier wave so it carries a signal that can be interpreted is referred to as modulation, and the process of converting it back again so the original intelligence

---

[4]*Oscillate* means to swing to and fro or to vibrate.
Amplitude is the maximum swing to and fro above and below zero voltage.
Frequency is the number of swings to and fro in one second, as in cycles per second.

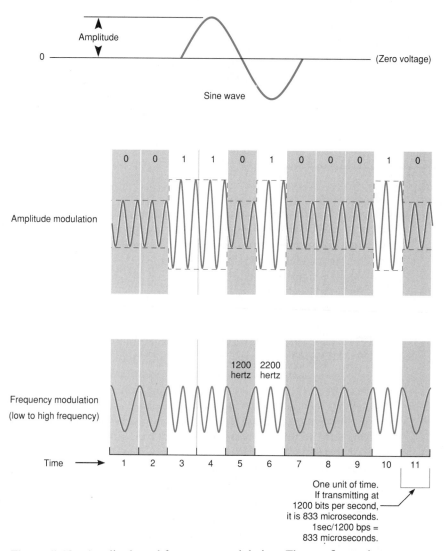

Figure 5-13 Amplitude and frequency modulation. The top figure shows amplitude as the height above or below the zero power level. The middle figure shows amplitude modulation, with the carrier wave carrying intelligence where the highest amplitudes represent binary 1s and the lowest amplitudes represent binary 0s. The bottom figure shows frequency modulation, with the carrier wave carrying intelligence where the high-pitched tones represent binary 1s (2200 hertz) and the low-pitched tones represent binary 0s (1200 hertz).

is recovered is called demodulation. In other words, the modem takes a digital signal from a computer or business machine and modulates it so it becomes a continuous or analog signal that can be transmitted over telephone lines, microwave towers, and so forth. In the demodulation process, the receiving modem interprets the modulated carrier signal (analog) and converts it back to a binary (digital) signal that is meaningful to the receiving computer or other business machine.

In *amplitude modulation* (AM), the peak-to-peak voltage of the carrier signal varies with the intelligence that is transmitted. The amplitude modulation shown in the middle drawing of Figure 5-13 depicts the peaks at the highest amplitude representing binary 1s and the peaks at the lowest (less power) amplitude representing binary 0s. Amplitude modulation is suitable for data transmission, and it allows efficient use of the available bandwidth of a voice grade line. However, it is more susceptible to noise during transmission (more errors) than is frequency modulation, which will be discussed next. In amplitude modulation, the height (amplitude) of the sine wave changes. These changes in the sine wave are represented by louder and quieter sounds.

Frequency modulation (FM), through the use of *frequency shift keying* (FSK), is a modulation technique whereby each 0 or 1 is represented by a different frequency. In this case, the amplitude does not vary. This type of modulation is represented by different tones. A high-pitched tone (higher frequency) equals a binary 1, and a low-pitched tone (lower frequency) equals a binary 0. The bottom of Figure 5-13 shows frequency modulation as a bit stream of 0s and 1s. Notice that the amplitudes are equal. Modems employing FSK may use three basic frequencies, such as 1700 hertz, 1200 hertz, and 2200 hertz. In this case, when no data is being transmitted, the carrier wave signal is 1700 hertz. When a stream of 0s and 1s is transmitted, the carrier wave switches between 1200 hertz and 2200 hertz, depending on whether it is a 0 or 1 that is transmitted. Figure 3-7 in Chapter 3 shows a modem using FSK.

Phase modulation is the most difficult to understand because there is two-phase (0° and 180°), four-phase (0°, 90°, 180°, and 270°), and eight-phase (0°, 45°, 90°, 135°, 180°, 225°, 270°, and 315°) modulation. Figure 5-14 shows *phase shift keying* (PSK) for a stream of 0 and 1 bits. Notice that every time there is a change in state (0 or 1), there is a 180° change in the phase. In a 180° phase change, the sine wave immediately goes in the other direction. A 180° phase change can be seen easily, but it is more difficult to see a 45° change in phase.

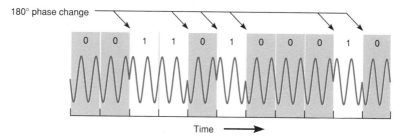

Figure 5-14 Phase shift keying (PSK). The sine wave changes 180° every time there is a change from 1 to 0 or from 0 to 1.

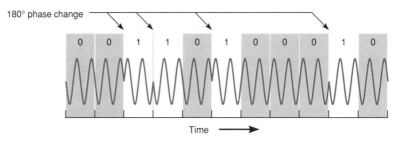

Figure 5-15   Differential phase shift keying (DPSK). The sine wave changes 180° every time a 1 is transmitted.

The other common type of phase modulation is *differential phase shift keying* (DPSK). In DPSK there is a 180° phase change every time a 1 bit is transmitted; otherwise the phase remains the same (see Figure 5-15). PSK and DPSK are two phase modulation techniques.

Different modulation techniques are used to obtain data rates of 2400 bits per second and above. At 2400 bits per second, a common technique is *quadrature phase shift keying* (QPSK). QPSK involves splitting the signal into four phases, so that a single frequency tone can take one of four values: 90°, 180°, 270°, or 360° of phase shift. Because a single tone can take any of four values, that tone can represent two bits of information. Note that this is more efficient than simple FSK, where two tones are required to represent one bit of information.

Other techniques are used for speeds above 2400 bits per second. For example, most 9600 bits per second modems use *quadrature amplitude modulation* (QAM). QAM involves splitting the signal into four different phases and two different amplitudes, for a total of eight different possible values. Thus, a signal tone in QAM can represent three bits (two to the third power). The problem with all high speed modulation techniques, however, is that they are more sensitive to imperfections in the communication circuit. The Bits/Baud section later in this chapter explains how a single tone or phase can represent two or even three bits of information.

The leased communication circuits provided by common carriers unfortunately tend to exhibit several types of imperfections, which limit the amount of information that can be transmitted across them. The two most common types of imperfections are envelope delay distortion and amplitude deviation distortion. *Envelope delay distortion* is caused by a phenomenon known as *dispersion,* in which different frequency components of a waveform propagate at different velocities. A complex waveform, such as that produced by a modem, typically is composed of many different frequency components. When the various components of such a waveform begin to propagate at different speeds, they cause the waveform to "spread out" in time. If the waveform spreads out too much, the receiving modem may not be able to interpret it correctly, thus causing errors. *Amplitude deviation distortion* is an undue amount of variation in the attenuation (loss of signal strength) versus frequency characteristics on the channel. Again, the result of excessive amplitude distortion is an increased error rate because of signal misinterpretation by the receiving modem.

To overcome distortion and transmit data reliably at data rates of 2400 bits per second and above, modem manufacturers developed a technique called *equalization.* Basically, equalization means the modem tries to compensate for imperfections in the communication channel. Equalization is the process of reducing frequency and phase distortion on a circuit by introducing time differences to compensate for the difference in attenuation or time delay at the various frequencies of the transmission band. Two types of equalization are commonly used today: compromise and adaptive equalization. *Compromise equalization,* which is used in medium speed modems, involves an equalizer that is set for average or compromise values based on observed communication circuit behavior over a large number of circuits. Compromise equalization is used at lower speeds (2400 bits per second) because at those speeds the equalization does not have to be as precise, and the circuitry for compromise equalizers is relatively simple and inexpensive. At higher data rates (4800 and 9600 bits per second), the results produced by compromise equalizers are inadequate, so a more sophisticated technique, *adaptive equalization,* is used. An adaptive equalizer is a device that continuously monitors the signal and adjusts the equalization to obtain the best transmission quality at any given time. In most modern high speed modems, this adaptive equalization is done by a microprocessor with a sophisticated equalization program.

Digital-to-Analog Conversion   Returning to our hypothetical signal in Figure 5-1, we observe that the digital side of the modem (the side connected to the terminal), has just received a synchronous block of data. It is represented as a sequence of direct electrical pulses (+ and − voltages) which, when counted into their individual 8-bit ASCII code structure, represent individual characters. The modem now takes each of these plus and minus voltages of electricity and converts them to an appropriate frequency. In other words, the modem carries out the *digital-to-analog conversion* process.

Let us develop another example using frequency shift keying (FSK), which involves modulating the carrier wave between two different frequency levels. Assume our modem is transmitting at a speed of 1200 bits per second, which means it can change between either of two different frequencies 1200 times each second of time. Therefore, every time the digital side of the modem receives + 12 volts of electricity, it transmits a frequency tone signal of 2200 hertz (2200 cycles per second). Conversely, every time the digital side of the modem receives − 12 volts of electricity, it transmits a signal of 1200 hertz. When no signals are received by the terminal, the modem falls into a middle frequency (1700 hertz), called its carrier wave (see Figure 5-16).

To transmit at 1200 bits per second, our modem has to attain a frequency of 2200 hertz and then hold that frequency pulse on the communication circuit for a time equal to 833 microseconds. The 833-microsecond timing factor is achieved by taking one second and dividing it by 1200 pulses per second; $1/1200 = 833$ microseconds. Also note that, as the modem is out-pulsing these different frequencies, it is doing it on the analog side of the modem (the side toward the local loop in Figure 5-1). At this point, the modem already has carried out its basic function of converting data from digital to analog form. At the other end of the transmission circuit, the

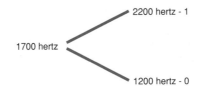

1. When there is no signal to transmit, the modem goes to its carrier wave (1700 hertz). Some modems use either the 2200 or the 1200 hertz as the carrier wave, instead of a third frequency.
2. When a +12 volt digital signal is received, the modem outpulses a 2200 hertz analog signal, which is a binary 1.
3. When a −12 volt digital signal is received, the modem outpulses a 1200 hertz analog signal, which is a binary 0.

Figure 5-16   The digital-to-analog conversion.

modem converts the data from analog to digital so the receiving computer can process it.

Basic Electricity   There are two general categories of electrical current: direct current and alternating current. *Current* is the movement or flow of electrons. The conventional flow of current is from + to −. Voltage is a measure of the potential difference between the + and − ends of an electrical circuit or battery. *Direct current* (dc) travels in only one direction in a circuit, whereas *alternating current* (ac) travels first in one direction (+) and then in the other direction (−).

The frequency of a continuous ac wave is the number of times per second that the wave makes a complete cycle from 0 to its maximum positive value, then through to its maximum negative value, and back to 0. Figure 5-17 shows three different *sine waves*. The top configuration shows one complete cycle, the second configuration two complete cycles, and the third configuration three complete cycles. Analog transmissions over telephone lines use the ac waveform known as a sine wave and are called analog or broadband signals.

Picture ac as the continuous flow of electrical current, first as a positive voltage (+) and then as a negative voltage (−). If it were a battery (it is not), the polarity of the battery terminals would reverse itself; the plus would become minus and then change back again. Because of these constant reversals in alternating current, first the electrical current flows in one direction and then it flows in the other direction. The plus (+) or minus (−) measurements are known as *polarity*. The number of times the polarity reverses itself every second is called the *frequency, hertz,* or *cycles per second*.

Picture dc as a circuit in which you have a battery (batteries are dc), so the electrical current always flows from the positive (+) terminal post to the negative (−) terminal post under the force of voltage. The electrical current flows in one

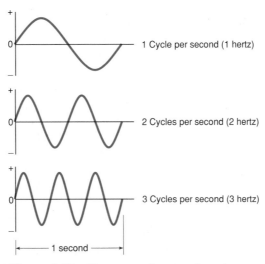

Figure 5-17   Sine waves (ac waveforms).

direction only; positive is always positive, and negative is always negative with direct current. Voltage is the pressure difference of the electricity between the two battery terminal posts; therefore, voltage is to electrical current as pressure in pounds per square inch is to a water pipe. Twelve volts is less pressure than 120 volts.

Leakage of the electrical current either at the terminal connector plug or as it passes over the connector cable causes distortion of your signal, and this in turn causes errors. Capacitance and inductance also cause distortion that can result in errors.

With *capacitance,* as we raise the voltage at one end of a communication circuit there is some delay before the voltage at the other end rises by an equal amount. The copper wire acts rather like a water hose in that it needs to be filled to capacity before the electricity applied at one end is received at the other end. The problem here is that if the pulses (+ and − voltages) are too short in duration, or if too many pulses are sent per second, then they become indistinguishable when they are received. The faster the pulse rate, the more difficult it becomes to interpret the received signal.

Inductance in a circuit is a force that resists the sudden buildup of electrical current. This resistance can be a cause of distortion and, therefore, of errors during transmission.

We use three common terms when discussing electricity. *Voltage* is defined as electrical pressure—the amount of electrical force pushing electrons through a circuit. In principle, it is the same as pounds per square inch in a water pipe. *Amperes* (amps) are units of electrical flow, or volume. This measure is analogous to gallons per minute for water. *Watt* is the fundamental unit of electrical power. It is a rate unit, not a quantity. You obtain the watt by multiplying the volts by the amperes.

Baseband/Broadband   Digital transmission generally uses direct current where the signals are represented as voltages of dc electricity being transmitted down the wire. These dc signals usually are sent over wire pairs of no more than a few thousand feet in length and are referred to as *baseband signals.*

Basically, baseband signaling is the digital transmission of electrical pulses. This digital information is binary in nature in that it only has two possible states, a 1 or a 0 (sometimes called *mark* and *space*). The most commonly encountered plus and minus voltage levels range from a low of $+3/-3$ to a high of $+24/-24$ volts. These baseband digital signals must be modulated onto the telephone company's interexchange channels by the modem for transmission to another city.

The binary 0s and 1s that are transmitted (groupings of these 0s and 1s make up a character) are represented by different levels of voltage such as $+12$ volts for binary 1 and -12 volts for a binary 0. The terminal outputs these plus and minus voltages (baseband signal), and they pass over the connector cable and into the modem. This is called a digital signal.

The modem then takes the digital signal and converts it to a *broadband signal* for transmission. Broadband signaling is the transmission of analog waveforms. The digital side of a modem (terminal side) accepts baseband signals, and the analog side (circuit side) accepts broadband signals.

Baseband systems pose a few other problems, some of which are caused by the laws of physics and others by vendors. In the laws of physics category, we find a lot of natural and humanly created noise in this band, as well as signal losses (attenuation) that limit the cable length more than with broadband. These restrictions affect layout and flexibility of use. Baseband cable lengths range from a few hundred feet to a mile or two, without using repeaters/amplifiers. A *repeater* or *amplifier* is a device that picks up the weak (attenuated) signal and increases its signal strength before passing it down the next cable segment or link. For example, repeater/amplifier devices are able to connect cable segments to create a 5- to 10-mile, or even longer, network link (see the accompanying box on Comparison of Digital and Analog Signals).

Digital Bipolar Signaling   *Digital signals* are discrete on and off signals as contrasted with the continuous form of analog signal. Notice in Figure 5-17 how the sine wave increases in a slow upward curve characteristic of a continuous analog signal. Also notice in Figure 5-18 how the digital square waveform increases from 0 to $+15$ volts instantly by going straight up, which is characteristic of a digital signal. Figure 5-18 shows various digital signals starting with the older *unipolar* and moving through two types of *bipolar* signals. In the figure, digital signals are drawn as square signals instead of the smooth curve sine wave analog signal. Notice that when there is no signal (a binary 0) in unipolar signaling, the voltage level is 0. In bipolar, the 1s and 0s vary from a plus voltage to a minus voltage. The voltage ranges from $+3/-3$ to $+24/-24$ volts, depending on the equipment used. The AT&T/Bell DDS (Digital Data System) system uses bipolar return to zero signals. Figure 5-19 shows the most common RS232 voltage levels. In Europe bipolar signaling sometimes is called *double current* signaling because you are going between a positive and negative voltage potential. Bipolar is used instead of unipolar because it permits faster pulse rates than is possible with unipolar signals.

COMPARISON OF DIGITAL AND ANALOG SIGNALS

An analog signal is simply a signal that varies continuously within a range of values. The signals from telephones, radios, and television generally are analog in nature. These transmission systems traditionally have been analog because digital circuit technology has only become practical within the last 20 or so years. It is interesting to note that Samuel Morse's digital telegraph (1837), which preceded Bell's analog telephone system (1876) by almost 40 years, was the inspiration for Bell's invention. Analog is the same as broadband.

In an analog system, data is represented by measurements on a continuous scale, so the accuracy of the machine is determined by the accuracy of the scale. An analog signal usually is represented as amplitude, phase, or frequency, the magnitude of which gives the value of some physical quantity like temperature or time. In our case, the quantities are the binary 0 or the binary 1. In other words, a high-pitched frequency might be a binary 0, and a low-pitched frequency might be a binary 1. Try this on a touchtone telephone by pressing the number 1 and then the number 2. You will hear two distinct tones. The frequency received by pressing 9 could be a binary 0, and the frequency received by pressing 2 could be a binary 1.

By contrast, digital communication is the transmission of discrete signals over a transmission channel. Normally it involves two discrete voltages for binary 0s and 1s. A digital receiver must be capable of correlating a received signal with a finite set of digital values or symbols. A digital signal is either on or off like a light switch, whereas an analog signal varies like a rheostat control, which allows you to vary the intensity of a light rather than just turn it on or off. Digital is the same as baseband.

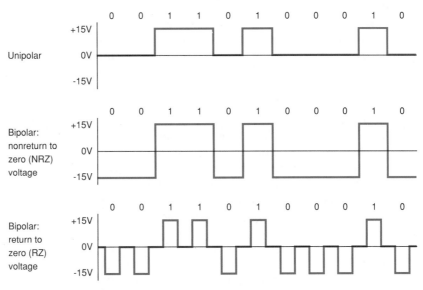

Figure 5-18   Unipolar and bipolar signals (digital).

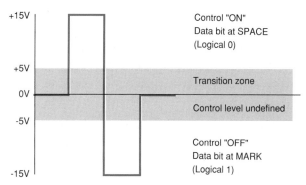

Figure 5-19   RS232C voltage levels. RS232C also
defines the level and polarity of the signals going to and
from the modem.

Digital Modulation   The subject of *digital modulation* can be confusing. Whereas it
once dealt only with modems that converted data transmissions to analog signals,
we now have voice transmissions that are converted to digital signals. The reason
for this change is that most circuits are of the older voice grade analog type. To use
them, we must convert data from digital to analog (continuous sine wave). Today's
newer circuits can handle digital signals, so both voice and data can be sent digitally.
In the future, all transmissions (voice, data, and image) will be sent digitally because
digital modulation is more efficient and produces fewer errors during transmission.

One digital modulation technique is called *pulse modulation*. It is used for transmitting digital information directly. In other words, an electrical digital signal is not
converted to an analog signal. Instead, the digital signal is converted to another
form, such as NRZ to RZ, as was shown in Figure 5-18, but it is still digital pulses
that are being sent down the circuit. Pulse modulation requires a different kind of
modem than is used for analog transmission.

Another type of digital modulation is *pulse amplitude modulation* (PAM), which
gives a different height digital pulse for each different plus or minus voltage (see
Figure 5-20). PAM is a digital form of the analog amplitude modulation shown in
Figure 5-13. A second type is *pulse duration modulation* (PDM), which gives a
longer timed pulse relative to the signal it is measuring. A third type, called *pulse
position modulation* (PPM), has more pulses per unit of time, depending on the
power of the signal it is measuring. These types of digital modulation normally are
used to convert analog signals to a digital form for transmission on local loops and
long distance interexchange channels/circuits (IXC).

Let us explore digital modulation further to see how a voice conversation (analog
signal) can be converted into a binary pulse stream (digital signal). Figure 5-21
illustrates how the original analog sine wave is converted into digital pulses of 0s
and 1s by using *pulse code modulation* (PCM). Each individual sine wave of the
conversation is sampled at a rate of 8,000 times per second. Therefore, 8,000 frames
per second travel down the line. If each frame contains eight bits (seven to encode
the frame and one for control), then the transmission speed on the circuit must be

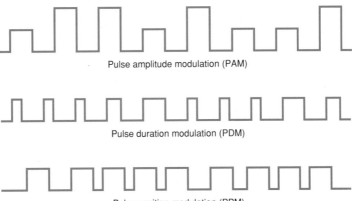

Pulse amplitude modulation (PAM)

Pulse duration modulation (PDM)

Pulse position modulation (PPM)

Figure 5-20   Pulse amplitude modulation (PAM), pulse duration modulation (PDM), and pulse position modulation (PPM). Notice how the three vary. With PAM, the height of the signals vary and the time between them is equal. With PDM, the width of the signals vary and the time between them is equal. With PPM, the width of the signals is equal and the time between them varies.

equal to 64,000 bits per second (8 bits × 8,000 frames per second). Basically, what you are doing is taking the original sine wave (top of Figure 5-21), encoding it with digital pulses of varying heights (amplitudes), and redrawing it (bottom of Figure 5-21) at the distant site to which you are transmitting the voice conversation. You can picture the reconstruction as having a group of vertical bars next to each other and, by connecting the tops of these bars, redrawing the sine wave. Look again at the top half of Figure 5-21 to see how the sine wave connects the midpoint of each of the eight possible amplitudes (heights).

Figure 5-21 assumes that only three bits (instead of eight) are used to encode each frame. This is done for simplification to make it easier to understand; actually, eight bits are used in pulse code modulation. As demonstrated in Figure 5-21, a set of three binary numbers (such as 011) codes each one of eight pulse amplitude heights. These bits are sent down the communication circuit to the distant station or terminal for reconstruction into the original sine wave. This serial transmission of binary pulses is the pulse code modulation mentioned above. Study this figure to see how each sample (the vertical bars are pulse amplitudes) is coded to PAM levels 1 through 8, but remember that in real life there are 128 levels rather than 8.

After these voice conversations are digitized, 24 of them are combined into one high speed circuit called a T-1. The T-1 circuit data rate is 1,544,000 bits per second.

With regard to 56,000 and 64,000 bits per second transmission speeds, most discussions on digital modulation describe a 64,000 bits per second circuit as the basic digital transmission channel. The 64,000 bits per second figure is arrived at by the pulse code modulation process. As described above, pulse code modulation converts a voice signal to a digital signal by sampling the voice 8,000 times per second. During the sampling, it detects changes in its waveform and then assigns each sample a

The signal (original sine wave) is quantized into 128 pulse amplitudes (PAM). In this example we have used only eight pulse amplitudes for simplicity. These eight amplitudes can be depicted by using only a 3-bit code instead of the 8-bit code normally used to encode each pulse amplitude.

After quantizing, samples are taken at specific points to produce amplitude modulated pulses. These pulses are then coded. Because we used eight pulse levels, we only need three binary positions to code each pulse.[1] If we had used 128 pulse amplitudes, then a 7-bit code plus one parity bit would be required.

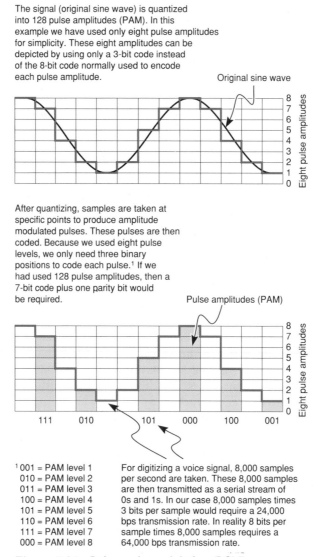

[1] 001 = PAM level 1
010 = PAM level 2
011 = PAM level 3
100 = PAM level 4
101 = PAM level 5
110 = PAM level 6
111 = PAM level 7
000 = PAM level 8

For digitizing a voice signal, 8,000 samples per second are taken. These 8,000 samples are then transmitted as a serial stream of 0s and 1s. In our case 8,000 samples times 3 bits per sample would require a 24,000 bps transmission rate. In reality 8 bits per sample times 8,000 samples requires a 64,000 bps transmission rate.

Figure 5-21 Pulse code modulation (PCM).

value ranging from 0 to 255. The value is then converted into an 8-bit binary number represented by 0s and 1s. Because there are 8,000 samples per second and 8 bits per sample, it takes 8,000 times 8 or 64,000 bits per second to turn a human voice into a digital signal when using pulse code modulation. The data is transmitted in 192-bit frames, followed by a framing bit. The *framing bit* synchronizes the clocks in both user and telephone company equipment. Each frame contains twenty-four 8-bit characters ($24 \times 8 = 192$ bits), as well as one framing bit to equal 193 bits. The frames are transmitted at a rate of 8,000 per second. Take 193 bits per frame, multiply it by 8,000 frames per second, and you get 1,544,000 bits per second.

Digital networks use amplifiers to amplify and retransmit the digital signal every few miles. In order to keep the amplifiers synchronized both with each other and the individual signal being amplified, the telephone company sets a standard called "maintaining a 1s density" in which the last bit in every 8-bit byte is forced to be a binary 1. This means that 8,000 bits of the 64,000 are dedicated to helping the amplifiers do their work, and only 56,000 bits actually carry the voice signal. Therefore, technically, a 64,000 bits per second channel uses 56,000 bits per second to carry the digitized voice signal and 8,000 bits to synchronize the signal as it moves between the various network amplifiers.

A newer standard, known as "binary 8 zero substitution" (B8ZS), allows the amplifiers to keep synchronization without "maintaining a 1s density." Obviously, this removes the need to dedicate 8,000 bits for synchronization; therefore, the full 64,000 bits per second channel carries the voice signal. When the entire channel of 64,000 bits per second is used to carry the signal, it is referred to as a "clear channel." The benefit of a clear channel is that it provides a slightly higher transmission speed because there are 8,000 more bits per second for the transmission, as contrasted with the older carrying capacity of 56,000 bits per second.

Pulse code modulation can be used to convert an analog voice signal to a digital stream of pulses for digital voice transmission. As might be expected, it is much easier to transmit data bits digitally because they do not have to be converted from an analog sine wave to a digital pulse. Some newer equipment allows you to digitize an analog voice signal and then send the digital transmission over a single voice grade communication circuit with a bandwidth of 4000 hertz.

Incidentally, as you may have guessed by now, other 0s and 1s can be interleaved between the 0 and 1 digital signals from the transmission we digitized in the Figure 5-21 example. This means a common carrier can convert from analog transmission to digital transmission and send two or more separate transmissions over a circuit that previously may have handled only a single voice call.

You have now encountered most of the concepts and terms that relate to analog and digital communications. These concepts have been discussed throughout the first five chapters of this book. You can review these terms by looking at the box Useful Terms Related to Analog and Digital Communications. If you are unable to see their relationship to either analog or digital communications, we suggest you review the areas you do not understand.

Bits/Baud   Bit and baud are terms used incorrectly much of the time. They often are used interchangeably, but they differ technically. In reality, the network designer or network user is interested in bits per second because it is the bits that are assembled into characters, characters into words, and thus business information.

A *bit* is a unit of information, whereas a *baud* is a unit of signaling speed. The plural of baud is baud. "Baud" and "bits per second" are not synonyms, but most data communication practitioners use them interchangeably. The *bit rate* and the *baud rate* coincide only when a code is used in which all bits are of equal length. Because this is true in most cases, we can use these two words interchangeably and they will be understood by data communication people. In transmission technology, one pulse generally is equal to a single-bit state—for example, 1200 baud generally implies a transfer rate of 1200 bits per second. Because use of the word "baud"

USEFUL TERMS RELATED TO ANALOG AND DIGITAL COMMUNICATIONS

ANALOG	DIGITAL
Broadband	Baseband
Alternating current	Direct current
Sine wave	Bipolar
	Unipolar
Amplitude modulation	Pulse amplitude modulation (PAM)
Frequency modulation	Pulse duration modulation (PDM)
Phase modulation	Pulse position modulation (PPM)
	Pulse code modulation (PCM)
Cycles per second	Pulses per second
Hertz	
Tone dialing	Pulse (rotary dialing)
Continuously variable	Binary in nature
	0 or 1
	On or Off
	Discrete signal
	Mark or space
Curved signal	Square signal
Frequency tone	
Audible sounds	
Carrier wave	

---

has proved confusing, we do not use it in this book. We use "bits per second" exclusively.

Baud is the signaling rate (pulse rate), which is the number of times per second the signal on the communication circuit changes. In other words, one simple method of increasing the rate of bits transmitted through a circuit is to combine pairs of adjacent bits into *dibits* ("di" = two). The object is to send each dibit as a separate signal element. Because the laws of information theory cannot be repealed, the process of transmitting two bits at the same time involves four (2^2) different signal states. One signal state represents 00, another 01, another 10, and the last one 11. Figure 5-22 shows how, by varying the voltage between 0 and 3 volts, the transmitting device can send two bits simultaneously. The upper half of this figure depicts the original bit stream of 0s and 1s which are represented by -12 volts for a 0 and $+12$ volts for a 1. Below that original bit stream is the bit stream of paired bits (dibits) and each of the four different voltage levels that represents each dibit. In other words, when the receiving device receives a $+3$ volts signal, it interprets that it has received the pair of bits "11." If the receiving device receives the $+1$ volt signal, it interprets that it has received a pair of bits "01."

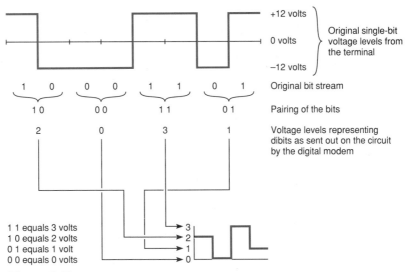

Figure 5-22 Dibits represented by different voltages (digital).

In another example, if a modem is able to change between any two frequencies 1,200 times per second, then the signaling rate is 1200 baud.

$$\frac{1 \text{ second}}{1200 \text{ baud}} = 833 \text{ microseconds (baud rate or pulse rate)}$$

The top half of Figure 5-23 shows a modem that has a carrier wave of 1700 hertz. It goes up to 2200 hertz when transmitting 1s and down to 1200 hertz when transmitting 0s. If this modem operates at 1200 baud, it means the modem is able to switch between 2200 hertz and 1200 hertz at a speed of 1,200 times each second. This in turn means the modem has a switching rate of 1200 baud and also a bits per second rate of 1200.

Now we can see how bits per second and baud differ. Looking at the bottom of Figure 5-23, notice how the modem now has four different frequencies to switch between 2200, 2000, 1400, and 1200 hertz. Also notice that each frequency now corresponds to a pair of bits rather than a single bit. This is still a 1200 baud modem, which means it can switch between any of the four frequencies at a speed of 1,200 times per second. The difference now is that transmission is two bits at a time. When the modem operates in the fashion of transmitting dibits, a 1200 baud modem is capable of transmitting at 2400 bits per second.

You might even imagine a modem that has 16 different levels of frequency. If it is able to switch among any of the 16 different levels at a 1200 baud rate, then it is transmitting at 4800 bits per second. This is because 16 different discrete identifiable signals are needed to transmit 4 bits at a time. It should be noted that modem makers never use 16 different frequencies for this type of transmission; they probably use a combination of two types of modulation, such as combining phase with amplitude modulation.

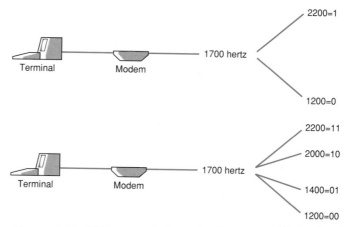

Figure 5-23   Dibit transmission using frequency shift keying (FSK).

Figure 5-24 shows that if transmission is 2 bits at a time (dibits), you have 4 different combinations. Transmission of 3 bits (tribits) at a time has 8 combinations, and 4 bits (quabits) at a time has 16 combinations.

In summary, baud is the signaling rate (also called pulse rate) that tells you how many times per second the signal changes. By transmitting two, three, or four bits with each change of signal, the modem can transmit more bits per second than there are baud on the circuit.

Dibits	Tribits	Quabits
00	000	0000
01	001	0001
10	010	0010
11	011	0011
4 combinations	100	0100
	101	0101
	110	0110
	111	0111
	8 combinations	1000
		1001
		1010
		1011
		1100
		1101
		1110
		1111
		16 combinations

Figure 5-24   Dibits/tribits/quabits.

The goal of a modem designer is to keep the baud rate as low as possible while making the bit rate as high as possible. The reasoning behind this is that if the baud rate is 1200, then the time available to identify the signal at the receiving modem is 833 microseconds (1/1200 = 833). If the baud rate is increased to 2400, then the time available to identify the incoming signal at the receiving modem is only 416.5 microseconds (1/2400 = 416.5). As a result, the receiving modem has only one half the time to identify the signal when the baud rate is 2400 compared to when it is 1200. Finally, most vendor literature misuses the word "baud," so it has become common practice to think of baud as equal to bits per second, even though this is not correct technically.

LOCAL LOOP

Our message that is flowing through the network components shown in Figure 5-1 now enters the *local loop,* sometimes called a *subscriber loop.* These are the circuits that go between your organization and the common carrier facility. These circuits normally are copper wires on telephone poles or underground. The newest local loops use rooftop antennas to transmit directly from a home or office via microwave, cable TV handling digital signals, or radio frequencies such as those used in cellular telephone local loops. In other words, the millions of miles of wire pair local loops that are strung along telephone poles or buried underground will be augmented over the next 20 years by alternative media for the local loop.

Before our signal leaves the local loop at the telephone company central office, we have to learn about station terminals, two/four-wire circuits, half duplex/full duplex, and amplifiers/repeaters as they relate to the movement of a signal between a terminal, the central office, and, ultimately, the other end of our network.

Station Terminals A *station terminal* is the *terminal block* for leased circuits or the *remote jack* (RJ) for dial-up circuits that terminates the local loop at your home or business. It is where you connect your modem or telephone. The upper half of Figure 5-25 shows the connection of a modem to a station terminal for a leased circuit; the lower half shows the remote jack connection for a dial-up circuit. The RS232 connector cable goes between the microcomputer and the modem, and a four-wire cable goes between the modem and the station terminal plug that terminates the local loop in your building.

Our signal has now passed over a major boundary point with regard to who is responsible for errors and the quality of circuits. It has left our modem and is now using the public local loop circuit of the telephone company or other common carrier.

Two/Four-Wire Circuits Data can travel either on a *two-wire circuit,* where there are only two wires from modem to modem, or on a *four-wire circuit,* where there are four wires from modem to modem (see the top half of Figure 5-26). The normal dial-up circuits are two-wire circuits, whereas private dedicated lease lines are four-wire circuits.

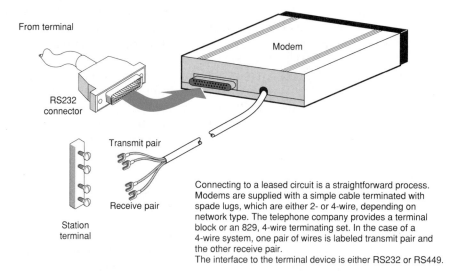

Connecting to a leased circuit is a straightforward process. Modems are supplied with a simple cable terminated with spade lugs, which are either 2- or 4-wire, depending on network type. The telephone company provides a terminal block or an 829, 4-wire terminating set. In the case of a 4-wire system, one pair of wires is labeled transmit pair and the other receive pair.
The interface to the terminal device is either RS232 or RS449.

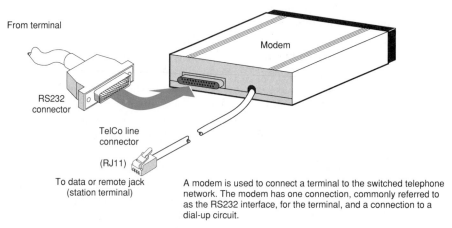

A modem is used to connect a terminal to the switched telephone network. The modem has one connection, commonly referred to as the RS232 interface, for the terminal, and a connection to a dial-up circuit.

Figure 5-25   Connecting the modem to the local loop.

Two-wire circuits have a problem with *echoes*. When people talk on a two-wire circuit, echoes may occur under some conditions. Echoes arise in telephone circuits for the same reason that acoustic echoes occur: there is a reflection of the electrical wave from the far end of the circuit. The telephone company provides echo suppression circuits to stop echoes during voice conversation. An echo suppressor permits transmission in only one, fixed, direction. These echo suppressors open and close on two-wire lines during data transmission. Echo suppressors were described in Chapter 2. Two- and four-wire circuits are discussed further in conjunction with half duplex in the next section.

Half Duplex/Full Duplex (HDX/FDX)   At this point our message can be traveling over the circuit in either half duplex or full duplex communications. Actually, there are three

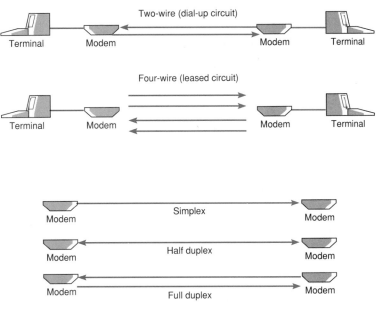

Figure 5-26   The top half shows transmission on a two-wire circuit and on a four-wire circuit. The bottom half shows simplex, half duplex, and full duplex transmission.

ways to transmit: simplex, half duplex, and full duplex (see the bottom half of Figure 5-26).

Simplex is one-way transmission such as you have in radio or TV transmission.

Half duplex is two-way transmission; however, you can transmit in only one direction at a time. A half duplex communication link is similar to a walkie-talkie link; only one "system" can talk at a time and the other must listen. Instead of using talk and listen buttons, computers use *control signals* to negotiate which system will send data and which will receive data. The most commonly used control signals for this type of communication are REQUEST TO SEND (RTS) and CLEAR TO SEND (CTS), which were explained earlier in this chapter in the Data Signaling/Synchronization section. The amount of time half duplex communication takes to switch between sending and receiving is called *turnaround time* (also called *retrain time* or *reclocking time*). The turnaround time for a specific modem can be obtained from its technical specifications (assume 20 to 50 milliseconds). For example, assume a message is sent from your modem to a distant modem. At completion of that message transmission, there is a certain amount of turnaround time while the modem at the receiving end changes from receive to transmit, as well as accounting for the REQUEST TO SEND and CLEAR TO SEND synchronization time delay (see Figure 5-27). Europeans use the term *simplex circuit* to mean a half duplex circuit.

With *full duplex* transmission, you can transmit in both directions simultaneously. Full duplex transmission does not require turnaround time because the transmit and receive are simultaneous. The messages can be transmitted in both directions at the

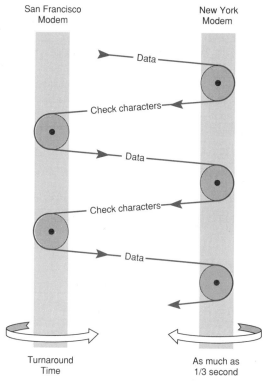

Figure 5-27   Turnaround time for half duplex. Data is sent from San Francisco to New York. At New York the modem must change its circuits from receive to transmit and carry out the synchronization (REQUEST TO SEND, CLEAR TO SEND) before sending the error CHECK CHARACTERS from New York to San Francisco. At San Francisco, there is another turnaround time before sending data again.

same time as shown in Figure 5-26. This is the opposite of half duplex, which transmits messages first in one direction and then in the other.

Half duplex and full duplex are different from two-wire and four-wire. Half duplex and full duplex are communication methods; two-wire and four-wire are circuits. Full duplex requires a front end processor or microcomputer that has the proper software for simultaneous two-way communication. Moreover, the local loop and circuits/channels must be four-wire circuits. Finally, with full duplex the terminal at your node must have the proper devices and functions so it can simultaneously receive and transmit data.

On the other hand, a two-wire or four-wire circuit is nothing more than a configuration that is supplied to you by the common carrier. All voice grade leased circuits are four-wire circuits. All dial-up circuits are two-wire circuits.

On a four-wire circuit it is easy to perform full duplex transmission (simultaneous transmission in both directions) because there are two wires in each direction to carry the message. If you want full duplex transmission on a two-wire circuit, you

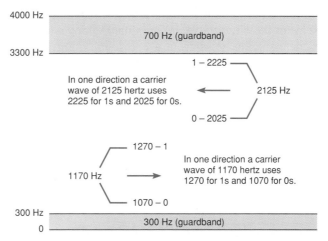

Figure 5-28   Full duplex on a two-wire dial-up circuit.

must use a special modem that creates two different frequency channels on the two wires, thus simulating a four-wire circuit (see Figure 5-28).

If you have a four-wire circuit using half duplex transmission, you also can keep both the send and receive signals from a modem operating simultaneously. This avoids the normal turnaround time for the modem's circuits because the REQUEST TO SEND signal leaves the modem on two of the four wires, whereas the receive side of the same modem is connected to the other two wires. This is *not* full duplex transmission; it is only a technique that is used to reduce the modem circuitry turnaround time to zero. Your messages still are sent in half duplex with this technique, but without the turnaround delay.

Amplifiers/Repeaters   Now that our message has left the modem and is in the local loop, the signal suffers attenuation. *Attenuation* is the weakening of the signal as it passes down a wire. It is caused by resistance. For example, copper wire pairs can experience attenuation or loss of signal strength because of weather. This occurs because the electrical resistance of wires rises with the temperature. Wet or humid conditions also increase attenuation because signal leakage occurs at insulators when they are wet. It should be noted, however, that there is an inherent resistance to the flow of a signal in any communication media, whether it is a copper wire pair, coaxial cable, microwave link, or optical fiber.

The telephone company places repeater/amplifiers at 1- to 10-mile intervals to increase signal strength lost to attenuation on local loops. The *amplifier* and its associated circuits are referred to as a *repeater* because it repeats the signal while increasing the signal's strength. Technically, repeaters do not filter out unwanted noise, but amplifiers do. The distance between the repeaters/amplifiers depends on the degree of attenuation because the signal strength cannot be allowed to fall too low. If too much attenuation occurs, it is increasingly difficult to distinguish the signal (message) from other noise or distortion always present on communication circuits.

On analog circuits it is important to recognize that noise and distortion always present on the circuit also are amplified, along with the increase in signal strength. This means some noise from a previous circuit link is regenerated and amplified each time the signal is amplified. This amplification has a definite effect on errors, creating the need to retransmit messages. Digital circuits are cleaner and more error free than analog circuits. A digital circuit with its associated digital amplifier re-creates a new signal at each amplifier station. For this reason, noise and distortion from the previous link of the network are not amplified each time the digital signal goes through an amplifier. This provides a much cleaner signal and results in a lower error rate for digital circuits. The benefit to users is that fewer messages have to be retransmitted because of errors.

TELEPHONE COMPANY CENTRAL OFFICE (END OFFICE)

After passing over the local loop, our message has reached the telephone company *central office* (see Figure 5-1), which is the switching center of the telephone company or other special common carrier. At the central office, the common carrier may perform circuit switching, or your circuits may be wired around the electronic switching system. Dial-up circuits are switched, and leased circuits are wired around the switching equipment. The central office also might be called an *end office* or *exchange office*.

Most common carriers today offer circuit switching like we have in the dial-up telephone system. By this method you cannot complete your call if the other telephone or circuit is busy. On the other hand, if you use a public packet switching common carrier, it can perform message switching because it can hold your message in a store and forward area and forward it when the other terminal or telephone is available. If you are using *leased circuits* (also called *private* or *dedicated*), your communication circuit is wired around this switching equipment in the telephone company central office. In other words, there is a direct circuit path from station terminal to station terminal. This method offers a much cleaner circuit with less noise and distortion, and with fewer retransmissions of messages because of errors. At the central office, your signal is amplified before being sent over the *interexchange channels* (IXCs), which are the long haul circuits that go between different end offices.

COMMUNICATION MEDIA (CIRCUITS/CHANNELS)

Our signal now has moved from the telephone company central office to the interexchange channels (IXCs) or long haul communication circuits. At this point, we might be using microwave circuits, satellite circuits, wire pairs, coaxial cables, or any other circuit medium that is available. The *medium* (or media if there is more than one) is the matter or substance that carries the voice or data transmission. It can be copper (wire), glass (fiber optic cable), or air (microwave or satellite). Our signal probably travels over wire pairs, coaxial cables, and microwave as it moves across the country or around the world.

A *circuit* is nothing more than the path over which data moves. Many people use the word "line" interchangeably with the word "circuit," although *line* is an older term that implies a physical wire or glass fiber connection. Circuit is more appropriate than line when you are speaking of satellite or microwave transmission. Sometimes the terms *circuit, channel,* and *line* are used interchangeably. Voice telephone lines sometimes are referred to as *trunks* or *trunk lines*.

Often an individual communication circuit is subdivided into separate transmission subchannels by the multiplexing technique. Some users refer to a channel when they mean a single transmission facility as well as when they mean a circuit that has been subdivided into numerous channels (more correctly, *subchannels*).

There is also the term *link*. There can be many links in a cross-country communication circuit because a link is any two-point segment of a communication circuit. A *two-point segment* is a circuit that goes between Point A and Point B (any two terminals or microcomputers); therefore, a multidrop circuit has many links as it traverses the country.

Many different types of transmission media are in use today. The following sections describe the basic characteristics of several types of media, such as open wire pairs, wire cables (also known as twisted wire pairs), coaxial cable, microwave transmission, satellite transmission, fiber optic cables, cellular radio, and several other miscellaneous circuit types. Each one is described thoroughly so you will understand how it operates.

These basic circuit types are packaged by the various common carriers to sell to the public. We call the circuits sold by the common carriers *communication facilities*. Chapter 7 describes specific communication facilities that are for sale or lease within the United States. Whereas the following sections describe the medium and the basic characteristics of each circuit type, the discussion in Chapter 7 describes how the circuit is packaged and marketed—in other words the basic communication facility that is available for purchase or lease from a common carrier. For example, Chapter 7 describes the available voice grade circuit services. If your organization has a private leased voice grade circuit between San Francisco and New York, the connection between the two cities might consist of wire cables, coaxial cable, and microwave transmission; therefore, a communication channel between San Francisco and New York can consist of several different types of communication media similar to the ones we will be describing here.

Open Wire Pairs   *Open wire pairs* are copper wires suspended by glass insulators on telephone poles (see Figure 5-29). They are spaced approximately 1 foot apart. While still familiar in many areas, they are being replaced by cables and other modern transmission media. Open wire pairs are rapidly becoming a part of the past.

Wire Cables (Twisted Wire Pairs)   *Wire cables* are insulated pairs of wires that can be packed quite close together (see Figure 5-30). Bundles of several thousand wire

Figure 5-29   Open wire pairs.

Figure 5-30   Twisted wire pair cables.

pairs are placed under city streets and in large buildings. In fact, your own house probably has a set of four wires connecting your telephone to the telephone company central switching office. Wire cables usually are twisted (*twisted wire pairs*) to minimize the electromagnetic interference between one pair and any other pair in the bundle. Wire cables also are being replaced by more efficient transmission media, such as coaxial cable, microwave, satellite, or optical fibers. The wire pair that connects your telephone to the wall plug is a wire cable. It is not twisted because it is so short and, if twisted, it would not have a nice appearance. Twisted pairs also are mentioned in Chapter 11 on Local Area Networks (see page 542).

Coaxial Cable   Figure 5-31 shows a single coaxial cable and a bundle of coaxial cables. Each individual *coaxial cable* consists of copper in the middle (the inner conductor) with an outer cylindrical shell for insulation. It is the outer shield, just under the shell, that is the second conductor. This type of circuit can transmit a substantially wider bandwidth than a twisted wire pair. Therefore, it is far more efficient to use a coaxial cable because it can contain many telephone conversations. A 2-inch diameter bundle of coaxial cables like those shown in Figure 5-31 can handle approximately 20,000 voice or data telephone calls simultaneously. Coaxial cables have very little distortion, cross-talk, or signal loss; therefore, they are a better transmission medium than either open wire pairs or bundles of twisted wire cables. Coaxial cables also are discussed in the context of local area networks in Chapter 11 (see page 544).

Microwave Transmission   A *microwave* is an extremely high frequency radio communication beam that is transmitted over a direct line-of-sight path between any two points. As its name implies, a microwave signal is an extremely short wavelength, thus the word *MICRO*wave. In general, wavelengths above 1000 megahertz (1GHz)[5] frequency are classified as microwaves. Microwave radio transmissions perform the same functions as cables. For example, Point A communicates with Point B via a through-the-air microwave transmission path, instead of a copper wire cable. Because microwave signals approach the frequency of visible light waves (see Figure 2-5 in Chapter 2), they exhibit the same characteristics as light waves, such as reflection, focusing, or refraction. As with visible light waves, microwave signals can be focused into narrow, powerful beams that can be projected over long distances. Just as a parabolic-shaped reflector focuses a searchlight into a beam, a parabolic reflector also focuses a high frequency microwave into a narrow beam. As the distance between communication points becomes larger, towers are used to elevate the radio antenna to account for the earth's curvature and maintain a clear line-of-sight path between the two parabolic reflectors (see Figure 5-32). A microwave acts as a carrier for hundreds of different simultaneous messages, whether standard voice telephone calls or data transmissions.

[5] 1 Hz (hertz) equals 1 cycle per second.
1 KHz (kilohertz) equals 1 thousand cycles per second.
1 MHz (megahertz) equals 1 million cycles per second.
1 GHz (gigahertz) equals 1 billion cycles per second.

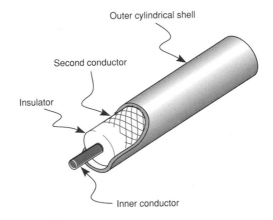

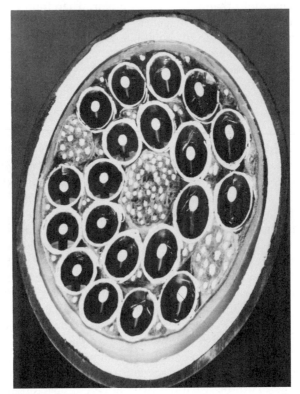

Figure 5-31 Coaxial cables. Exterior view (top) of a single coaxial cable and a cross-sectional view (bottom) of a bundle of 20 coaxial cables.

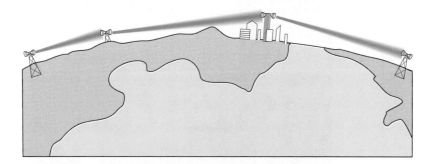

Figure 5-32   Microwave towers circling the earth (top). A microwave tower (bottom) with four long distance horns and two short haul dish antennas.

Figure 5-33 Short haul intracity microwave dish antenna.
Photograph courtesy of Motorola, Inc.

This transmission medium is the one most used for long distance data or voice transmission. It does not require the laying of any cable because long distance horn antennas with microwave repeater stations are placed approximately 25 to 30 miles apart. A typical long distance horn antenna might be 10 feet across, although over shorter distances in the inner cities the dish antennas might get down to 3 feet in diameter. In larger cities we now have microwave congestion; so many microwave dish antennas have been installed that they interfere with each other, and the air waves are saturated. This problem will force future users to seek alternative transmission media, such as satellite or optical fiber links. Figure 5-33 shows a short haul intracity microwave dish antenna. It can be used to connect two buildings or two local area networks several miles apart.

Satellite Transmission Transmission via *satellite* is similar to transmission via microwave except, instead of transmitting to another nearby microwave dish antenna, it transmits to a satellite 22,300 miles out in space. Figure 5-34 depicts a geosynchronous satellite in space. Figure 5-35 shows the satellite in operation.

One disadvantage of satellite transmission is that a delay occurs because the signal has to travel far out into space and back to earth (*propagation delay*). For half duplex transmission, the typical signal propagation time is approximately 0.5

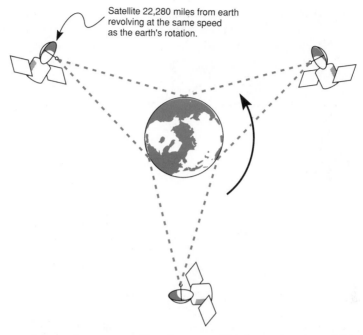

Satellite 22,280 miles from earth
revolving at the same speed
as the earth's rotation.

Figure 5-34 Geosynchronous satellites in space. This is a polar view of Earth with the satellites revolving around the equator.

second for the round-trip delay. This is because the message has to travel from Point A on the ground to the satellite, and then from the satellite to Point B on the ground (see Figure 5-35). In addition, the acknowledgment that the message was received without errors must do the reverse by going from Point B to the satellite and from the satellite to Point A. This is four links of 22,300 miles each, and 4 × 22,300 ÷ 186,000 equals 0.48 second. (Microwaves travel at 186,000 miles per second.) Moreover, there may be a further delay as the circuits from the ground station to your business office go through ground-based switching equipment. The delay is controlled by the common carriers to avoid disruptive voice telephone conversation. In data communications, however, this type of delay is disastrous if you are using half duplex transmission. This is so because when an individual message block is sent, you have to wait for a positive or negative acknowledgment before sending the next message. The use of full duplex is one way to solve this problem. Another solution is for the network to employ special devices for handling *satellite delay compensation* on half duplex circuits. See the accompanying Satellite Delay Compensation box for more details on this important problem.

Satellites use different frequencies for receiving and transmitting. These frequencies are in the ranges of 4 to 6 gigahertz (GHz), 12 to 14 GHz, and 20 to 30 GHz. (One gigahertz is equal to 1 billion cycles per second.) The older *C-band* transmits in the 4 to 6 GHz range and therefore requires a larger dish antenna.

Ku-band is the trasmission spectrum between 12 and 14 GHz. In addition to data

Figure 5-35 Satellite in operation transmitting to its ground station antennas.

transmission, the Ku-band is used to transmit television programs between various networks and individual television stations. One of the problems associated with Ku-band is *raindrop attenuation*. This problem occurs because waves that high in the spectrum are so short they can be absorbed by raindrops. It is not really a major problem but something engineers need to work around. One advantage of Ku-band is the waves are so short they can be caught and concentrated in much smaller dish antennas, such as those householders put on their roofs, thus permitting direct transmission between a satellite and the home. It is estimated that a dish antenna ranging from 30 to 48 inches in diameter is all that would be required for direct Ku-band transmission to your home.

Unlike the C-band, which has been the predominant commercial satellite bandwidth, the Ku-band is a high enough frequency that it does not interfere with ground-level transmissions, such as microwave and radar. In addition, very small aperture terminals (VSAT) can be used with the Ku-band. *VSATs* are small, inexpensive satellite dishes that significantly lower the cost for an organization wanting to enter a satellite network. A typical Ku-band satellite network provides either one-way or full duplex communications among VSATs installed at a large number of remote branch offices and a larger earth dish or "hub" installed at a central site. Major earth dish hubs can cost as much as several hundred thousand dollars. Companies such as Tymnet and AT&T Communications offer shared hub services to customers. This means users only have to buy inexpensive VSATs and not a significantly more expensive central hub dish. To put this cost in perspective, you

SATELLITE DELAY COMPENSATION

Satellite message delay, or path delay, must be taken into account when half duplex stop and wait transmission protocols are used. These protocols are described in the ARQ (Automatic Repeat reQuest) section of Chapter 9. For example, modems provide a variable timer to set the CLEAR TO SEND delay. The value of this timer usually is set to be greater than the round-trip delay (propagation time) of the overall path. In the case of a satellite, this path length is approximately 22,300 miles from earth to the satellite and 22,300 miles return, plus a possible several thousand miles more on terrestrial links between the satellite earth station and wherever your message is to be delivered. This propagation time easily can *exceed* 0.5 second. For this reason, a common practice is to set the CLEAR TO SEND delay on the modem to 700 milliseconds (0.7 second) for satellite transmission. On a terrestrial-based circuit, this CLEAR TO SEND delay might be set for only 50 milliseconds.

At this point you might wonder, "What is the CLEAR TO SEND delay?" The CLEAR TO SEND delay in a modem is the time from when it stops transmitting and waits for return of the acknowledgment that tells the modem whether the message was received correctly (ACK) or incorrectly (NAK) at the distant end of the telecommunication path. Remember, a message is sent; then transmission stops and waits until either an ACK or a NAK is received. Only then can the next message be sent. This wait time is set by the CLEAR TO SEND timer on the modem. Even on terrestrial-based circuits it might vary because there is a shorter propagation time for a message sent 10 miles than for one sent 3,000 miles.

With that in mind, it is reasonable to ask how you can reduce the delay time of 700 milliseconds without going to full duplex transmission or changing your software protocols. The answer is that some networks have *delay compensators* in which the acknowledgment is returned by the local delay compensator before the message is sent on the satellite link. Suppose the sender in our example sends Message 1. The delay compensator at the sender side of the satellite circuit (see figure below) sends an acknowledgment back to that sender. The sending terminal then is able to send Message 2 immediately, for which an acknowledgment is received immediately. After that, Message 3 can be sent immediately, and it also receives immediate acknowledgment from the delay compensator at its end of the circuit. By the time the third message has been sent, the receiver (the other end of the satellite circuit) may be ready to send back the actual acknowledgment to the first message stating whether it has been received correctly or incorrectly. Because the delay compensator provides the sending station with an acknowledgment before the data takes the satellite hop, the sender can immediately follow the first transmission with the second, and so forth. The delay compensator handles retransmission of blocks in error.

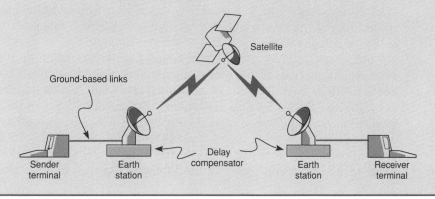

can lease one tenth of a satellite transponder for about $13,000 per month. This one tenth of a transponder can support a 120-node full duplex network. (*Transponders* in the satellite receive the incoming signals and retransmit them back down to earth.)

Current satellite networks primarily provide information services through data that is transmitted or received. Among the largest satellite users are news wire services, television networks, stock quotation services, and similar business data functions in which there is a download system. Through satellites, central television networks download news stories to subscribing television stations around the country or around the world. Similarly, stock quotations might be downloaded through a satellite network from the New York Stock Exchange to the ultimate user of that information.

Security poses a serious problem for satellite communications because it is easy to intercept the transmission as it travels through the air. Laser communication systems, which have begun to revolutionize long distance data transmission on earth, now are moving into the satellite arena. Whereas terrestrial-based fiber optic networks send pulses of laser light down hair-thin fibers of glass, future satellites will exchange information by transmitting laser beams across thousands of miles of empty space. Such laser intersatellite link (ISL) systems currently are under development in Germany, France, and the United States.

Laser ISL technology is a cousin of microwave communications. Information can be carried on a beam of laser light in much the same way that it is modulated onto a microwave signal. Whereas microwaves use a parabolic antenna, a laser satellite system uses an optical telescope to concentrate and aim the beam of light. At the target satellite, a receiving telescope captures and diffuses the laser signal, concentrates it, and focuses it onto a detector. One major laser ISL application is to cross-link military satellites in geostationary orbits at 22,300 miles altitude so they can communicate between themselves without having to rely on a vulnerable ground station back on earth.

Another issue is satellite crowding in space. There is now both orbit and frequency congestion among the various satellites. Figure 5-36 depicts a band of satellites around the earth, first as if you were looking from space, and then from earth. You can place only so many synchronous satellites around the band. Notice that this figure shows a 4° separation between each satellite. If you brought them too close together, they would touch. Because of frequency congestion—most of the available frequencies are in use today—we will have to launch larger satellites (fewer required) in the future, while also expanding available frequencies to meet future needs for satellite data, voice, and image transmission.

Look at the top half of Figure 5-36 and find your location on the globe. Then chart an imaginary line from where you are to one of the satellites. Notice how this line tends to go directly south, or possibly a little southeast or southwest, if you are in the United States. It is for this reason that satellite dishes in the United States usually face in a southerly direction and possibly southeast or southwest, depending on which satellite is being used for signal reception. Whereas Daniel Boone and Kit Carson looked for moss on the north side of a tree for compass direction, today's ''high-tech'' adventurer looks for the southerly direction of a satellite dish.

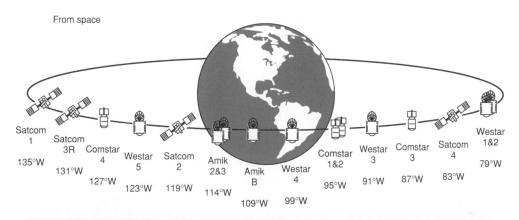

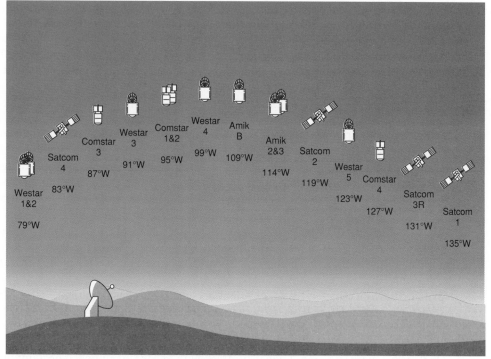

Figure 5-36 Geosynchronous satellite band around the equator.

Fiber Optic Cable *Fiber optics* is the newest technology for transmission of data, voice, and images over a continuous line. Instead of carrying telecommunication signals in the traditional electrical form, this technology uses high speed streams of light pulses that carry information inside hair-thin strands of glass called optical fibers. At the end of their journey, solid state electronics reconverts these pulses of light back into electrical signals so they can be processed by conventional microcomputers, terminals, and host mainframe computers. Fiber optic technology is a revolutionary departure from the traditional message-carrying systems of copper wires, microwave, or satellite radio signals. One of the main advantages of fiber optics is that it can carry huge amounts of information. This capacity (very wide bandwidth) makes it an ideal system for the simultaneous transmission of voice, data, and image signals.

As noted above, the optical fibers carrying the pulses of light are made of hair-thin strands of plastic or glass. Plastic is falling into disuse, however, because glass can be made into a purer product, enabling the signal to be transmitted over a longer distance before an amplifier/repeater is needed to increase the signal strength. A new, even purer *halide glass,* will bring improvements in the distance between amplifiers for fiber optic communications. Halide glasses are made from thorium, lanthium, and lutecium, whereas conventional glasses are made from silicon dioxide (sand). Because halide glass is purer, light can travel farther before it attenuates (degrades) enough to require amplification. The purer the glass, the less often the signal has to be amplified. For example, a windowpane made of halide glass could be 125 miles thick and still be translucent. Not having to amplify the signals as often would be an extremely important development because fewer amplifiers would be required.

When light signals are amplified today, they must first be converted back to electronic signals, amplified in power, and then reconverted to a light pulse for transmission down the next link of the fiber optic communication circuit. Not only does this process slow down the signal somewhat, but it also entails costly amplification equipment. *Light amplifiers* are being developed that can take a pulse of light, amplify its power without its having to be converted to an electrical signal, and pass it down the next link of the fiber optic circuit. Furthermore, having several thousand miles between amplifiers would significantly decrease the cost and complexity of undersea cables. Bell Laboratories reports it has been able to transmit readable optical signals for 3,700 miles without using a repeater. This development means significant progress is being made in this area, although it is still in the research laboratory.

British Telecom (England's major telephone company) has demonstrated the first all-optical light amplifier. This experimental amplifier amplifies and retimes light pulses directly, so they need not be converted back to electricity first as do conventional amplifiers. It operates at 140 million bits per second.

One of the current technological barriers with regard to optical fibers involves the inability of a pulse of light to switch between different communication circuits. There is no problem in transmitting light signals down an optical fiber, but if they could be switched as optical light pulses (rather than electrical pulses), we could gain a 30 to 50 percent increase in speed. Currently, an *optical switch* actually converts the signal back to an electrical pulse, switches it, and reconverts it back to an optical pulse for further transmission.

The process of switching without converting the light signal back to electricity is called *photonic switching*. Photonic switching diverts the light signal from one fiber optic line to another by changing a field of current between the incoming and outgoing circuit ports. These photonic switches are fashioned from materials such as gallium arsenide through which paths called *waveguides* are carved. Waveguides are described later in this section. The light beams travel down these waveguides, which are placed 5 to 10 microns apart, or about one tenth the width of a human hair. Problems arise when researchers try to build switches capable of handling more than 8 to 10 light beams. Today's photonic switches are still in the research laboratory, and they do not operate as fast as their electronic switch counterparts, although this limitation should be overcome soon.

AT&T and 21 other telecommunication companies have completed the first undersea cable to span the Pacific Ocean with a laser-powered, digital light wave communication system. The Hawaii 4/Transpacific 3 light wave system stretches nearly 7,200 nautical miles across the Pacific and requires nearly 250 undersea amplifiers located approximately 30 miles apart. This fiber optic cable system handles approximately 37,800 simultaneous telephone calls.

Figure 5-37 shows a fiber optic cable and depicts the idea of the optical core, the cladding, and how light rays travel in optical fibers. The optical core is very pure glass over which the pulses of laser light or light emanating from LEDs (light-emitting diodes) passes. The cladding is heat fused around the optical core and consists of glass that has a different refractive index, thereby making the light signals bounce down the optical core. Earlier cables, called *step index cables,* had mirror-like coatings around the optical core or a coating of plastic to cause this reflection.

An average cable bundle contains about 72 fibers, and a large cable contains about 144 fibers. A cable bundle for use within a building contains from 24 to 36 fibers. The earliest fiber optic cable systems were multimode, meaning they carried several light waves down the fiber simultaneously. But multimode cables were plagued by excessive signal attenuation (reduced optical intensity) and dispersion (spreading of the optical pulse). Single mode optical fiber cables transmit a single direct beam of light. It achieves higher performance, in part because the core diameter has been reduced from 50 microns to about 8 to 10 microns. This smaller diameter core allows the fiber to send a concentrated light beam farther than multimode because the light strikes the core/cladding boundary at a much smaller angle, causing less attenuation and dispersion.

The construction of an optical cable includes more than the optical core and cladding. Typically, the optical core is surrounded by its cladding, then protected by a layer of Kevlar (bulletproof vest material), and finally jacketed with some type of thermoplastic covering.

Optical modems convert electrical voltages from the computer or terminal into light pulses that are coupled into, and transmitted through, the optical fiber. The light sources commonly used are either light-emitting diodes (LEDs) or injection laser diodes (ILDs). Laser diodes are used for longer distances.

Fiber optic cable is an attractive security measure because it is almost immune to

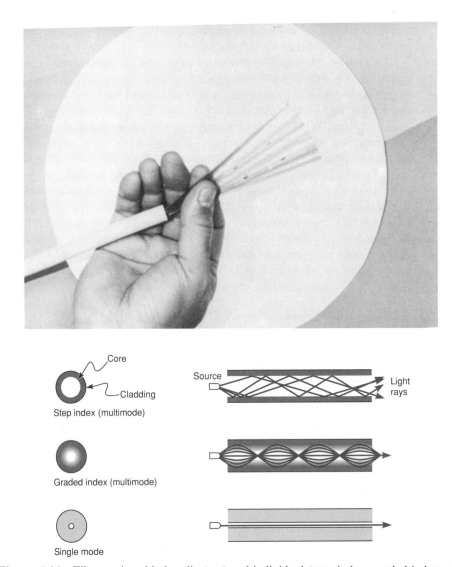

Figure 5-37 Fiber optic cable bundle (top) and individual (step index, graded index, and single mode) cables (bottom).

unauthorized access by tapping. Taps can be made by breaking the cable, polishing it off, and inserting a splice to detect the light. This method, which uses a T-splice adapter, gives a detectable light loss in fiber optic systems, so it can be detected. Another method, nicking, might be possible with a step index cable, which has a silica core and plastic cladding around it. The plastic cladding can be nicked so the light leaks out, although if too much light leaks out, the signal is lost. The nicking technique is almost impossible to accomplish in a graded index or single mode fiber because the optical core and the cladding are heat fused together. They are both glass, but of different refractive indexes.

The bad news for those who rely on the tap resistance of fiber optic cable is that it is becoming more tappable; the good news is that eavesdroppers can be detected. One way of tapping an optical fiber is through the use of *fiber identifier* hardware. By putting a *microbend* in the fiber cable and monitoring whatever light escapes, the fiber identifier can determine whether an optical cable is carrying traffic and the direction in which it is moving. Fiber identifiers are used to determine if an optical cable is carrying traffic before maintenance is performed or test signals sent down the optical fiber. Another method of tapping is at an existing T-splice because some T-splice connectors leak enough light to be detected. Most intrusion detection systems for single mode fiber links are designed to detect drops in signal strength and automatically set off alarms or shut off the signal. To detect anomalies in step index fibers, the system sends two signals that are balanced. Any variation in either of the signals creates an imbalance, and it is the imbalance that is detected. Imbalances occur when a light leak or tap is inserted onto the cable.

Splicing an optical fiber requires that a technician align the two fiber optic cores perfectly; otherwise some light leaks out. The optical cores must be joined precisely along six different dimensions: not only the x, y, and z dimensions, but also three angular dimensions. If the installer is not precise enough, light is lost and the signal degrades. In addition, the connections have to be strong enough to last thousands of hours while withstanding vibration and constant changes in temperature.

The basic technique for splicing, called *fusion splicing,* involves cutting the cable, polishing the ends of the splice, and then fusing them with a high voltage electricity torch. Given the thinness of the fiber, this process usually is done under a microscope by a well-trained technician. To lower the cost of this procedure, a number of companies have developed simpler methods. For example, General Telephone & Electronics has a kit that uses a diamond cleaver to cut the fiber, thus eliminating the need to polish the ends of the splice. The technician fits the cut fibers together, places a plastic collar over them, and pulls the fiber ends together in a device that aligns them automatically along all six axes. Other splicing kits also are on the market, and as these kits become simpler, the use of optical fiber cables will increase further.

Optical fibers are immune to electrically generated noise and, therefore, have a very low error rate. For example, a fiber optic cable might have a bit error rate of 10^{-9} (1 bit out of 1 billion) as compared with a 10^{-6} (1 bit out of 1 million) error rate found in metallic lines. Optical fibers also provide complete electrical isolation between transmitters and receivers, thus eliminating the need for a common ground. This provides electrical isolation from hardware and eliminates unwanted currents such as ground loop within an installation. For communications in a dangerous atmosphere, such as a petroleum refinery or a paint factory, it has another advantage because static spark is eliminated. For this reason, optical fiber cables may be the ideal solution in the robotic-controlled factory of the future. Communications within a factory, where many machines are operating, can be degraded severely by electrical noise, static electricity, and voltage fluctuations.

The small size and light weight of fiber optic cables offer users better opportunities to secure this medium physically. Because fiber optic cable is nonconductive, it is free from electromagnetic noise radiation and therefore is completely resistant to conventional passive tapping techniques. With passive techniques you do not actually cut into the communication medium but only get in close proximity to it. Finally, in most cases fiber optic cable is less restricted under harsh environmental conditions than its metallic counterparts. It is not as fragile or brittle as might be expected, and it is more resistant to corrosion than copper. The only chemical that affects optical fiber is hydrofluoric acid. Also, in case of fire, an optical fiber can withstand greater temperatures than copper wire. Even when the outside jacket surrounding the optical fiber has melted, a fiber optic system still can be operational in an emergency signaling system. One word of warning is in order, however. Care must be taken when these cables are pulled through a building so the cable is not separated; its tensile strength may not be as great as the tensile strength of some other cables, such as coaxial.

One of the biggest advantages of fiber optic cable is the bandwidth because this provides the potential of transmitting data at speeds up to 10^{14} bits per second. These bandwidth frequencies are 10,000 times greater than the upper ranges of radio frequency bands (microwave and satellite).

In the future, you will see the microprocessor chips (computers) operate completely on light pulses, not electricity. These optical chips soon will be optical computers.

One optical fiber-based network, the Fiber Distributed Data Interface (FDDI), provides a high bandwidth, general purpose interconnection between computers and peripherals, including the ability to connect local area networks to other networks. FDDI comprises a set of standards created by the American National Standards Institute (ANSI) X3T9.5 Task Group. Because FDDI is a token-passing ring local area network operating at 100 million bits per second over an optical fiber medium, it is described more fully in Chapter 11 (see page 529).

Cellular Radio Traditional mobile telephones win no awards for being there when you need them. The reason is that 20 channels typically are shared by 2,000 subscribers, and there are times when you cannot get a connection or even a dial tone. This situation is changing because of *cellular radio,* a form of high frequency radio in which antennas are spaced strategically throughout a metropolitan area (see Figure 5-38). A service area or city is divided into many cells, each with its own antenna. This arrangement generally provides subscribers with reliable mobile telephone service of a quality equal to a hardwired telephone system. Users (voice or data transmission) dial or log into the system, and their voices or data are transmitted directly from their automobile, home, or place of business to one of these antennas. In this way, the cellular radio system replaces the hardwired local loop.

This system has intelligence. For example, as you drive your automobile across the service area or city, you move away from one antenna and closer to another. As the signal weakens at the first antenna, the system automatically begins picking up your signal at the second antenna. With cellular radio, therefore, transmission is switched automatically to the closest antenna without communication being lost.

Today cellular radio is used widely by radio paging companies and users of mobile telephones. Figure 5-39 shows a cellular telephone, and Figure 5-40 shows two different uses of cellular telephones.

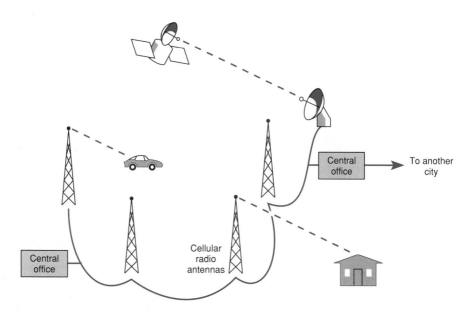

Figure 5-38 Cellular radio system.

Figure 5-39 Portable cellular telephone. Photograph courtesy of Motorola, Inc.

Figure 5-40   Uses of cellular telephones. Photographs courtesy of Motorola, Inc.

IBM and Motorola have joined to provide a new radio data network that will enable users with specially outfitted data terminal equipment (DTE) to access remote host mainframes via wireless radio links. The Motorola KDT 840 shown in Figure 5-41 is one of these DTEs. IBM's field service technicians have used this type of portable terminal for a number of years.

This network, called the *Advanced Radio Data Information Service* (ARDIS), is a 4800 bits per second service supported by 1,100 radio transceiver stations (like cellular radio antennas; see Figure 5-38) across the country. Each radio transceiver station is linked to one of 30 regional concentrator sites. The 30 regional concentrators in turn are linked to network control centers in either Chicago or Lexington, Kentucky. These centers track network usage, log-in authorization, and billing. Finally, users will connect their host processor to one of three customer communication controllers located in Chicago, New York, or Los Angeles. These three customer communication controllers connect to both the closest of the 30 regional concentrators and the other two customer communication controllers. The KDT 840s transmit their messages to the radio transceiver antennas.

Future cellular radio applications might include remote troubleshooting. Your automobile mechanic, for example, could use cellular diagnostic equipment to poll remotely your car's onboard computers and identify the cause of a problem. Most people think of a car telephone when anyone mentions cellular equipment, but in the very near future you will see many more applications. Cellular pay telephones will appear in taxicabs, buses, and trains. (They already are in airplanes.) Burglar alarm systems will use cellular radio because when burglars defeat alarm systems, 90 percent of the time they do it by cutting the telephone wires. Paramedic rescue units already use cellular radio.

The real future of cellular radio is based on the philosophy of dividing the entire United States, or even the world, into cells so a person can call from anywhere to anywhere. It would be easy to interconnect the cells of the entire United States with the cells of, let us say, France by using either satellite communications or fiber optic undersea cables. Most of us today think of a telephone as a fixed-location device (located in our home, school, place of business, or pay telephone booth), but the telephone is rapidly becoming a personal item. You will carry it with you, just as you might carry a calculator or a microcomputer today. Thirty years ago no one anticipated that we all would have electronic calculators small enough to carry with us. In the future, you will have small portable telephones, with the number assigned to you, and the telephone unit will be carried rather than connected to the wall of your home. AT&T already is offering personal telephone numbers that a person can use for life. These numbers use the 700 area code.

When you speak on a cellular telephone, anyone might be listening to your conversation. Cellular telephone calls are transmitted over the 870 to 890 megahertz frequency bands, which are easily accessible by today's scanners. Even though federal law says it is illegal to listen in on a cellular telephone call, it is virtually impossible to enforce this law because thousands of people own scanners. These devices have the ability to scan the frequencies and stop at the specific frequency your telephone call is using.

To complicate the issue, another federal law says that it is legal to use a scanner

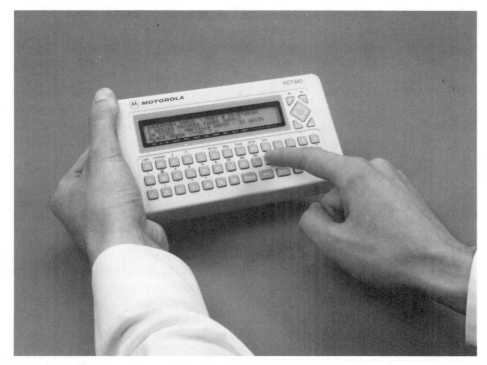

Figure 5-41   Cellular radio portable data terminal. Photograph courtesy of Motorola, Inc.

to listen in on telephone calls that are made by using a portable wireless telephone such as you may have at home. These wireless telephones transmit on a frequency of 46 to 47 megahertz bandwidth, and they also are easily accessible by anyone with a scanner. The wireless remote telephone in a home has a transmission range of only 500 feet or less between the handheld unit and the point at which it connects to the in-house telephone circuit, so a scanner listener has to be relatively close to the telephone user in order to scan the frequencies and pick up a specific telephone conversation.

Cellular telephone fraud is becoming a problem. Unscrupulous people purchase a cellular telephone and remove its security EPROM (erasable programmable read only memory). These people then replace the original EPROMs with "thumbwheel" EPROM substitutes. They do this by turning the wheels at random until they discover some other person's cellular telephone security code, at which point they can begin making calls on that code—at least until that person receives his or her next telephone bill. Some of the more sophisticated fraud perpetrators use scanners and laptop microcomputers to find large numbers of cellular telephone codes automatically. As yet this type of fraud is not very common, but owners of cellular telephones should check their bills immediately. Also, remember that you pay for both incoming and outgoing cellular airtime. Thus, you pay not only for calls you make, but also for those other people make to you.

A pager may be better for incoming calls than a cellular telephone if you want to save money and also have more security. For security reasons, you should not provide cellular telephone numbers to strangers. Instead, you should provide a beeper number for others to call you, and then you call them back on the cellular telephone. This procedure is more secure and also eliminates the cost of incoming cellular calls.

Miscellaneous Circuit Types   Other types of circuits are waveguides, tropospheric scatter circuits, short distance radio, infrared transmission, submarine cable, and FM band radio.

A *waveguide* is a conductive tube down which radio waves of very high frequency travel. These tubes may be as large as 2 to 15 inches across or as small as 8 to 10 microns etched into a circuit chip. Waveguides usually are placed in the back of microwave towers to transmit signals from the electronic equipment's repeater/amplifier to the dish antenna. They are used over very short distances, 10 feet or less. The American Telephone & Telegraph WT4 waveguide system can carry 230,000 two-way telephone calls simultaneously. Extremely small waveguides are now etched into chips for optical switches.

The *troposphere,* which extends upward from the earth about 6 miles, scatters radio waves and can be used for communication links of up to about 600 miles. *Tropospheric scatter* is especially useful in the South Pacific, where islands are separated by long distances. One problem with this method of transmission is that it requires very large antennas, on the order of 60×120 feet. Tropospheric scatter circuits can transmit television over shorter distances, and up to several hundred voice communications can be transmitted over a link of approximately 100 miles. Tropospheric scatter circuits are not advised for data transmission because of their high error rate. Obviously, microwave links, or even satellite circuits, are preferable.

Short distance radio is the type of transmission circuit used by walkie-talkies, police radio, taxis, and other community services. Depending on the distance involved, short distance radio might be used on the cellular radio circuits or it might be an independent high frequency radio. Citizen band (CB) radios are an example of short distance radios.

Infrared transmissions, like microwave, transmit their signals through the air. In this case, however, it is a light signal rather than a high frequency radio signal. Infrared and microwave actually are close together on the electromagnetic spectrum (review Figure 2-5 in Chapter 2). Infrared is slightly higher on the spectrum, however. It has made the transition from the radio portion of the spectrum to the light portion. A typical example of an infrared device is a television remote control.

Also like microwave, infrared requires a clear line-of-sight transmission, but both the signals and the distances can be improved by using repeaters. When compared to microwave, infrared's biggest disadvantage is that it is much more susceptible to attenuation from smoke, fog, and heat wave shimmering. It is not as susceptible to attenuation caused by rain, which is the primary weather condition affecting microwave. Both infrared and microwave are reliable for short distances (one half mile or less), but microwave works well for over ten miles when weather conditions are good. Infrared has several important advantages over microwave, and these may outweigh its disadvantages. It needs a far smaller beam-clearance area because infrared beams do not diverge or spread out as much. Infrared signals also can reach speeds of 45 million bits per second, making them useful in many video applications. Devices using infrared tend to be small and relatively easy to set up. The greatest advantage infrared has over microwave, however, is the lack of government regulations related to its use.

Submarine cables are transmission circuits that are placed in the oceans between the various continents. A popular form in use today is a bundle of coaxial cables. Bell Laboratories is developing a high speed underwater optical fiber cable to handle transmission speeds of 274 million bits per second, which would accommodate 4,000 voice channels and go across an ocean without any amplifiers.

The *FM band* is two 10-kilohertz-wide subchannels on the commercial FM broadcast band normally used by FM radio stations. These two bands can be used for broadcast transmission of business data at rates of 9600 to 19,200 bits per second. One advantage of this subcarrier technology is price. The receiving terminals cost about $100, and, unlike receive only stations used in satellite broadcasting systems, subcarrier terminals can be handheld devices that travel with the users. Of course, a satellite network has a far greater geographic range, but a single FM subcarrier can cover a 20- to 40-mile radius. One current use of FM band is the broadcasting of stock market price quotations to users who have the handheld FM receiving device.

CENTRAL SITE COMPUTER

Our message or signal has now passed from the microcomputer (see Figure 5-1), through the connector cable, modem, and local loop to the telephone company central office, over the circuits/channels to the distant city's telephone company end office, and through the modem. After being demodulated by the modem, our signal has reached the central site computer, which consists of a front end, a data channel, and the host mainframe computer that will process our message.

As we learned in Chapter 3, the front end controls the movement of our message from the remote terminal by means of a central control concept called polling. The data channel then moves the message from the front end into the memory of the host mainframe computer, which then processes the incoming message request. The *front end processor* is the basic network control point, controlling such functions as central control versus interrupt, polling/selecting, response time, error control, and logging.

Central Control Versus Interrupt   In our Figure 5-1 example, the front end processor probably is a *central control system*. This means that, when the "send" key on the terminal is pressed, the data signaling/synchronization cannot begin until the terminal is polled; that is, the front end sends a signal asking, "Do you have anything to send?" Because the "send" key has been pressed, the REQUEST TO SEND (pin 4 of the RS232 connector) can begin the data signaling/synchronization process as soon as the terminal receives the front end's poll. If this were an *interrupt system,* the terminal would interrupt the front end immediately when the "send" key was pressed. Local area network protocols are interrupt systems. To see how interrupt works, read the CSMA/CD section in Chapter 11.

Polling/Selecting   Polling and selecting take place in a centrally controlled system. *Polling* is the process of sending a signal to a terminal to give it permission to send messages it might have ready. *Selecting* is the process of sending a signal to a terminal to determine if it is in a current status that will allow it to accept a message from the central computer site. Most people tend to refer to both conditions as polling.

Polling is performed by the front end processor, although it can be performed easily by the host computer or a remote intelligent terminal controller. There are several types of polling such as roll call, fast select, and hub go-ahead.

With *roll call polling,* the front end processor consecutively works through a list of terminals, first polling terminal 1, then terminal 2, then terminal 3, and so on, until all are polled (see Figure 5-42). Roll call polling can be modified to prioritize terminals such as in the following sequence: 1, 2, 3, 1, 4, 5, 1, 6, 7, 1, 8, 9, and so on. Terminal 1 may have priority because of extremely heavy usage.

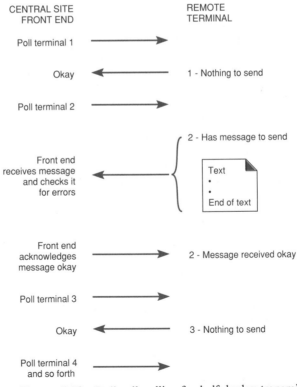

Figure 5-42   Roll call polling for half duplex transmission.

Typically, roll call polling involves excessive "wait time" because the front end has to poll a terminal and then wait for a response. The response the front end is waiting for might be an incoming message that was waiting to be sent, a negative response NAK indicating nothing is to be sent, or the full "timeout period" may expire because the terminal is temporarily out of service. Usually, a timer "times out" the terminal after waiting, say, one tenth of a second without getting a response. If some sort of failsafe timeout is not used, the system poll might lock up indefinitely on an out-of-service terminal. Incidentally, more sophisticated systems totally remove an individual terminal from the polling list after getting three consecutive timeouts.

Fast select polling schemes were developed to eliminate the time of waiting for a response when a terminal does not have a message to send, and to eliminate the timeout wait when a terminal is not operating correctly. In a fast select poll, the front end polls the terminals until the first incoming message is received. Assume we have 20 terminals and use fast select polling. The front end sends a poll character to terminals 1, 2, 3, 4, 5, and 6, and then, let us assume the first incoming message is received. If the first incoming message is from terminal 3, the front end stops polling and waits long enough to receive any incoming messages from terminal 6 (the last terminal polled). Next, the front end resumes polling at terminal 7 and polls terminals 7, 8, 9, and so on, until the next message is received. After waiting an appropriate time for receipt of any message from the last terminal polled, the front end once again resumes polling where it left off and continues to terminal 20. After polling all 20 terminals, it may automatically start the polling list again at terminal 1. With this type of polling scheme, the front end does not wait for a negative response from terminals with nothing to send, and, if a terminal is not operating correctly, it does not waste time waiting for a timeout before proceeding to the next terminal.

Hub go-ahead polling is used in multidrop configurations (see Figure 5-43). The front end passes the poll character to the farthest terminal on the multidrop circuit. That terminal then sends its message and passes the polling character to the next inbound terminal. That terminal also passes the poll to the next inbound terminal, and so on, until it reaches the terminal closest to the front end. The closest terminal passes the poll to the front end, and it restarts by again passing the poll to the

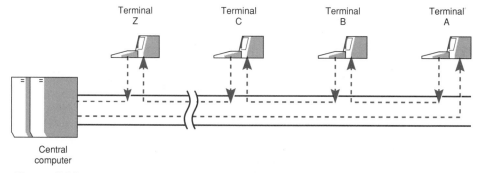

Figure 5-43 Hub go-ahead polling on a multidrop circuit.

farthest terminal. This technique relieves the front end of many polling tasks because the terminals themselves undertake the process of sending messages in a sequential fashion. It should be noted that hub go-ahead polling assumes more intelligence in each of the terminals so they can handle the poll properly. Intelligent terminals also are necessary because there must be a means of bypassing a terminal that is out of service and that would produce a polling break in the multidrop link.

KEY TERMS

Alternating current (ac)
Ampere (amp)
Amplifier
Amplitude
Amplitude modulation
Analog modulation
Analog signal
ASCII
Asynchronous transmission
Attenuation
Baseband signal
Baud
Baudot code
BCD
Bipolar
Bit
Broadband signal
Byte
Capacitance
Carrier wave
Cellular radio
Central control system
Central office
Channel
Character
Circuit
Coaxial cable
Coding scheme
Communication facilities
Connector cable
Current (electricity)
Cycles per second

DB-9
DB-25
DCE (data circuit terminating equipment)
Dedicated circuit
Dibit
Differential phase shift keying (DPSK)
Digital modulation
Digital signal
Digital-to-analog conversion
Direct current (dc)
DTE (data terminal equipment)
EBCDIC
Efficiency of a code
End office
Equalization
Exchange office
Fast select polling
Fiber optics
Four-wire circuit
Frame
Frequency
Frequency modulation
Frequency shift keying (FSK)
Full duplex
Half duplex
Hertz (Hz)
Hub go-ahead polling
Inductance

Information bit
Infrared transmission
Interexchange channel (IXC)
Interrupt system
Isochronous transmission
Leased circuit
Line
Link
Local loop
Mark
Medium/media
Microwave
Modulation
Open wire pair
Packet
Parallel mode
Parity bit
Phase modulation
Phase shift keying (PSK)
Polarity
Polling
Private circuit
Propagation delay
Pulse amplitude modulation (PAM)
Pulse code modulation (PCM)
Pulse duration modulation (PDM)
Pulse position modulation (PPM)
Reclocking time

Redundant bit	Space	Transponder
Repeater	Start bit	Trunk line
Retrain time	Station terminal	Turnaround time
Roll call polling	Stop bit	Twisted wire pair
RS232	Subchannel	Two-point segment
RS449	SYN	Two-wire circuit
Satellite	Synchronization	Unipolar
Satellite delay	Synchronous transmission	Voltage
compensation	Throughput	Watt
Selecting	Transmission efficiency	Waveguide
Serial mode	Transmission Rate of	Wire cable
Simplex	Information Bits (TRIB)	
Sine wave		

SELECTED REFERENCES

1. *Catalog of Technical Publications*. Florham Park, N.J.: AT&T Communications, January 1985 (AT&T Communications Publication 10000).

2. *Computerworld: Newsweekly for the Computer Community*. Published weekly by CW Communications, 375 Cochituate Road, Box 9171, Framingham, Mass. 01701-9171, 1967– .

3. *Computing Canada: The Newspaper for Information Processing Management*. Published biweekly by Plesman Publications, Ltd., 2 Lansing Square, Suite 2, Willowdale, Ontario M2J 5A1, Canada, 1975– .

4. Gofton, Peter W. *Mastering Serial Communications*. Berkeley, Calif.: Sybex, Inc., 1986.

5. Held, Gilbert. *Practical Network Design Techniques*. New York: John Wiley & Sons, Inc., 1991. [Page 15 contains a program to calculate information transfer ratios (ITRs).]

6. Lamberti, Allan. "New Directions for the Microwave Market," vol. 26, no. 4, April 1992, pp. 38–40.

7. *Network World*. Published weekly by CW Communications, Box 9171, 375 Cochituate Road, Framingham, Mass. 01701-9171, 1983– .

8. *Telecommunications: Covering the Total Spectrum of Communications Worldwide*. Published monthly by Horizon House-Microwave, 610 Washington Street, Dedham, Mass. 02026, 1967– .

9. Wiegner, Kathleen K. "Down to Earth," *Forbes*, vol. 148, no. 10, October 28, 1991, pp.190–191.

QUESTIONS/PROBLEMS

1. Must the input/output device at the remote end of a network always be a microcomputer? Explain why or why not.

2. How is data transmitted in parallel?

3. What feature distinguishes serial mode from parallel mode?

4. What are the three types of serial transmission and how do they differ?

5. Synchronization is another word for _____.

6. How do transmission errors affect messages in asynchronous and synchronous transmission?

7. What are SYN characters and what do they do?

8. Of what is a character comprised?

9. What purpose does the parity bit serve?

10. Many people use bit and byte interchangeably. Is this correct? Explain why or why not.

11. What is coding?

12. Briefly describe the four most important coding schemes.

13. What is transmission efficiency?

14. How do information bits differ from redundant bits?

15. Why are some codes more efficient than others?

16. How does data terminal equipment differ from data circuit terminating equipment?

17. What is a RS232?

18. What advantage does the RS449 have over the RS232?

19. What may replace the RS449?

20. What is the most commonly used connector cable?

21. What does data signaling accomplish and what happens if it does not work properly?

22. What does the modem do with a signal?

23. How is the carrier signal altered to carry intelligence?

24. Can amplitude modulation be used for data communications? Explain why or why not?

25. In what one way does frequency modulation differ from amplitude modulation?

26. Describe the two most common types of transmission imperfections.

27. What does equalization accomplish?

28. What are two types of equalization and when are they used?

29. To what does bipolar apply?

30. Why is bipolar signaling used?

31. What type of waveform is used when analog data is transmitted over telephone lines?

32. How does baseband differ from broadband?

33. What are three causes of signal distortion?

34. What is the function of a repeater?

35. What distinguishes the different types of pulse modulation from other types of modulation?

36. Are bits per second and baud the same thing? Explain.

37. Why are bits combined into pairs of dibits?

38. What is the local loop?

39. Where are two-wire and four-wire circuits used?

40. How do simplex, half duplex, and full duplex differ?

41. How does turnaround time slow communications?

42. Are two-wire and four-wire the same as half duplex and full duplex? Explain.

43. What causes attenuation?

44. How do analog amplifiers differ from digital amplifiers?

45. What is the function of the telephone company's central office?

46. What is the term that describes the path over which data moves?

47. Of the transmission media discussed in this chapter, which one is used most for long distance data or voice transmission and why?

48. What is the biggest problem in satellite transmissions?

49. In Ku-band satellite transmission, extremely short waves both create a problem and solve another one. Explain.

50. What is one of the major technological barriers preventing the widespread use of fiber optic communications?

51. Define microwave.

52. Optical transmission is achieved by sending _____ pulses down the optical core.

53. Name several advantages and disadvantages of fiber optic communications.

54. Cellular radio is said to be intelligent. Explain.

55. How does central control differ from interrupt at the front end processor?

56. How do polling and selecting differ?

57. How efficient would a 6-bit code be in asynchronous transmission if it had two parity bits, one start bit, and two stop bits? (Some very old equipment uses two stop bits.)

58. What is the transmission rate of information bits if you use EBCDIC (eight bits with one parity bit), a 400-character block, 9600 bits per second modem transmission speed, 20 control characters per block, an error rate of 1 percent, and a 30-millisecond turn-around time?

59. What is the TRIB in Question 58 if you add a half-second delay to the turnaround time because of satellite delay?

60. If a modem is able to switch between any two frequencies 2,400 times per second, what is the length of a pulse in microseconds?

61. Define current.

62. In what direction does direct current travel? Alternating current?

63. Define frequency, hertz, and cycles per second.

64. Define voltage, amperes, and watt.

65. If 24 digitized voice calls are on a T-1 circuit, why does it require a transmission speed of 1,544,000 bits per second?

66. How does "binary 8 zero substitution" (B8ZS) improve on the "maintaining a 1s density" standard?

67. Define clear channel.

68. What do the common carriers call the circuits they sell?

69. Describe one wireless radio network.

70. Discuss the legal issues of scanners, cellular telephones, and wireless telephones.

71. Discuss why pagers are more secure than cellular telephones.

72. How are infrared and microwave similar? How do they differ?

NEXT DAY AIR SERVICE CUMULATIVE CASE STUDY

Background on Next Day Air Service

The Next Day Air Service Board of Directors has accepted your recommendation to centralize communications along two major data links (Atlanta to Tampa and New Orleans to Tampa as shown in Figure 5-44). Both Atlanta and New Orleans have multiplexers. You really preferred the solution that you developed for Question 3 in Chapter 4, but Mr. Coone would not approve the purchase of five multiplexers (one each for Dallas, New Orleans, Atlanta, Orlando, and Tampa).

Now you have been asked to explore the feasibility of integrating both data and voice traffic onto a single transmission circuit. You must determine whether this is a viable option. In order to make this decision, you want to examine the current transmission circuits and assess their ability to handle the anticipated workload.

As you drive home after receiving this assignment, you realize that you are becoming much more involved with the firm's strategic planning initiatives. Suddenly your mind is ablaze with all sorts of thoughts regarding the expansion of Next Day Air Service's communication capabilities. For example, you think about recent major circuit and switch outages experienced by some of the leading common carriers. You realize that even though your operations were affected only slightly by these outages, it might be inevitable that NDAS someday will undergo a costly disruption of its communication network. You do not view such a situation as a major competitive threat because Next Day Air Service's principal competitors have similar networks, and all the parcel delivery services would be down in the event of a disastrous outage. You do,

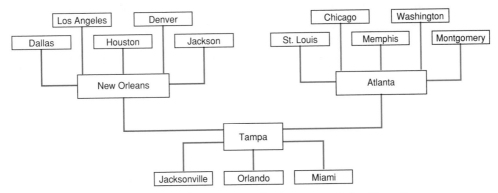

Figure 5-44 Next Day Air Service's communication network circuit configuration. Both of the circuits from New Orleans and Atlanta to Tampa are 19,200 bits per second leased circuits. All other circuits from the branch offices to the New Orleans, Atlanta, and Tampa hubs are 2400 bits per second circuits.

however, want to find a communication alternative that will provide NDAS with a competitive edge. For example, what if you could replace the existing network with some form of wireless communications? Microwave and satellite communications are viable alternatives. Perhaps some form of cellular radio could be considered as well. You decide to research these possibilities further and add this project to your ever-growing list of "things to do."

Questions/Problems for the Next Day Air Service Case

1. Calculate the TRIB for both the 2400 and 19,200 bits per second circuits in the Next Day Air Service network that is shown in Figure 5-44. Assume an average of 1,600 characters per message with a 1 percent probability for an erroneous transmission. The modems transmit with a 0.2 second turnaround delay. Both synchronous and asynchronous transmissions use an 8-bit ASCII code. The 2400 bits per second asynchronous circuits use 1 start bit, 1 stop bit, and each message block has 10 control characters for further error checking. The synchronous 19,200 bits per second circuits also use a 1600 character block, but each block has 55 control characters. Based on the transmission load data provided in Chapter 2 (Figure 2-18), are these TRIB ratings adequate?

2. If workload increases by 20 percent over the next year, will the existing transmission circuits meet the anticipated need? If not, would it be worthwhile to upgrade the dial-up circuits to higher speeds? What is your recommendation? As always, be prepared to defend your position.

3. What happens to TRIB if the reliability is increased on the 2400 bits per second circuits? What happens if reliability is decreased? Graph TRIB versus reliability to support your answer.

4. Based on the number of invoices/packages (bits per day) described in the previous chapters of the case, would NDAS require full duplex, four-wire circuits?

Chapter Six

NETWORK CONFIGURATIONS

This chapter describes network configurations. These configurations are the basic building blocks that are interconnected when we develop networks. Each configuration can stand alone as a single network, or several can be interconnected as in a wide area network (WAN).

INTRODUCTION

This chapter explains network configurations in enough detail, along with diagrams, that you can understand how they operate. By this time you already have mastered the fundamental communication concepts (Chapter 5) and data communication hardware (Chapters 3 and 4). This chapter draws the fundamental concepts and hardware together so you can see the many ways networks can be configured.

From the smallest network with just two or three microcomputers to a large network spanning long distances, data communication systems are organized into *networks*. It is the network that provides communications between all types of computers, printers, terminals, and many other pieces of hardware. Computers on a network typically are referred to as host mainframes, minicomputers, or microcomputers. Those network computers that provide usage of other peripherals, such as hard disks and printers, are called *servers*. They are so called because they provide service from the various peripheral devices to all network users. For example, *network servers* store and run the application programs for the other microcomputers on the network, and *database servers* store, update, and run the organization's database. A single computer can be both a network server and a database server.

Three Key Elements Any network has three key elements: media, nodes, and protocols. The *media* provide pathways over which data can travel; they also might be referred to as transmission facilities, channels, circuits, lines, or links. The transmission media are the various wires, cables, microwave links, satellite links, optical fiber cables, cellular radio, and so on. *Nodes,* which also are called *stations,* provide a means for inputting and outputting data over the transmission media. In data communications, a node or station is an input or output point on a network. These nodes might consist of switches, multiplexers, gateways, workstations, front ends, terminals, microcomputers, and the like. *Protocols* provide the common set of rules for managing the network pathways and the flow of the data. Protocols are software programs that tie the overall network together and make it a functioning entity. Of course, application programs are another type of software; they are separate from the protocol software that controls the flow of data between nodes.

As an example of the above three network elements (media, nodes, and protocols), have you ever thought of the group of friends with whom you closely associate as a network? These people are an informal information network because they exchange data (voice communications) among themselves. This information network transmits its voice communications over a type of medium: the air through which the sounds of your voices travel. Furthermore, this network employs a node for the voice communications. This node includes your voice box (larynx), mouth, and tongue to help form sounds, voice inflection, volume level, pitch, and so on. The group also observes various protocols or rules for exchanging information. These rules include asking for permission to speak or just starting to speak when you think the current speaker has finished. As you can see, a human network has the three components that are essential to the exchange of information in a network: your input/output node produces the output of speech, which travels over the medium of air, and becomes input to the other person's ears. To control the overall flow of speech you both observe learned protocols that govern your speaking behavior. Now we will examine the protocols that determine who speaks when; in a communication network these are central control or interrupt protocols.

Central Control Versus Interrupt   One of two basic protocols may be applied in a network of friends. The group may operate under a philosophy of central control or under one of interrupt communications. If the group uses *central control,* then one person might be the formal leader who gives other people permission to speak, much as a professor calls on students and each has a turn to speak. On the other hand, if the group operates under an *interrupt* philosophy, then each person interrupts with whatever it is he or she wants to say when the current speaker finishes a sentence or idea. Protocols also come into play with this informal information network in the form of which words might be inappropriate with different groups of people, the speed with which individuals speak, and so forth. In this situation your brain is the computer, and the basic rules of conversation you have learned over the years become the protocols by which you operate. As you will see, the communication network's protocols and the network's topology are interdependent.

TOPOLOGY

Networks can be classified by their *topology,* which is the basic geometric arrangement an individual network might take. The basic topologies used to lay out networks are called ring, bus, star, and mesh. They are used to configure an overall network, but you often only need to configure a single data circuit between two business offices. This is mentioned so you have the proper perspective on configuring an entire network as opposed to configuring a couple of data circuits between several business offices.

Ring Topology A *ring topology* connects all workstations in a closed loop, and messages pass to each node or station in turn. Figure 6-1 is a ring topology. The ring approach connects the cable in a ring or circular pattern. The upper half of Figure

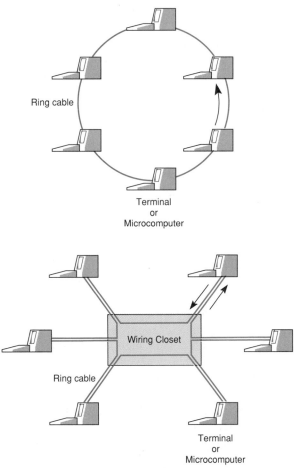

Figure 6-1 Ring topology. The upper half of this figure shows a basic microcomputer-to-microcomputer ring topology in which each microcomputer connects directly to the next one. Messages move in one direction. The lower half shows the same ring topology, but with the cable routed through a wiring closet for easy maintenance. The messages still move in one direction around the ring, but they go through the wiring closet in their circular pattern.

6-1 shows a basic ring topology in which each microcomputer is connected to the next one. The lower half of this figure shows the same ring topology, except all the cables are routed through a central *wiring closet*. Wiring closets are used because they make it easy to make repairs if the cable breaks. When this happens, it is easier to splice the cable, remove the microcomputer with the broken cable, and restore service to the other microcomputers on the ring. With the ring approach, data is transmitted around the ring in one direction only. The time required for the data to travel around the ring between the interconnected devices is called the *walk time*.

Each workstation on the ring has a unique address. Moreover, each microcomputer or server connects to the ring either with a T-shaped connector device or by direct connection to a network circuit card in the microcomputer. As the messages travel around the ring, a receiver unit at each node checks the address of the incoming signal and either keeps the message because it is the destination terminal or regenerates the signal and passes it on to the next device on the ring. Obviously, a terminal only keeps messages addressed to it. One advantage of ring networks is that when a node fails, usually only that node is lost; only a complete break in the cable is able to inactivate the entire ring. The usual protocol for a ring topology is called token passing. This subject is covered in Chapter 11 on Local Area Networks because ring topologies are found primarily in LANs.

Bus Topology   A *bus topology* connects all stations to a cable running the length of the network. The bus approach physically connects devices by means of cables that run between the devices, but cables do not pass through a centralized controller mechanism. In this situation, data *may* pass directly from one device to another, or it may be routed through a head end control point. The head end controller (see Figure 6-2) turns the message transmission around and sends it back down the cable in the opposite direction. With some bus networks, the message always must go to the head end and then back down the cable to whichever node or workstation it is addressed. Other bus networks allow the message to go directly to whichever node or workstation it is addressed without going to the head end first. Like ring topologies, bus topologies can be wired by using a microcomputer-to-microcomputer connection or by routing the cables through a wiring closet.

The term *bus* implies a very high speed circuit and a limited distance between the microcomputers, such as when all the nodes are in one building. These distances can be increased by using a repeater. The loss of a single node on a bus normally does not hinder the operation of the bus network unless the cable itself is cut. The microcomputers are attached to the bus by means of T-shaped connectors that break into the cable. Each tap causes a slight signal loss on the cable, although this is not a significant problem. Bus topologies are popular because hundreds of microcomputers can be connected to a single bus. Either token passing or carrier sense multiple access with collision detection (CSMA/CD) protocols are used with bus topologies. Both of these protocols are covered in Chapter 11, again because bus topologies tend to pertain primarily to LANs.

Star Topology   A *star topology* (sometimes called a *hub topology*) connects all workstations to one central station that routes traffic to the appropriate place. The star

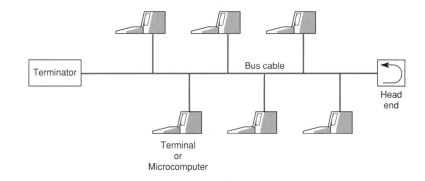

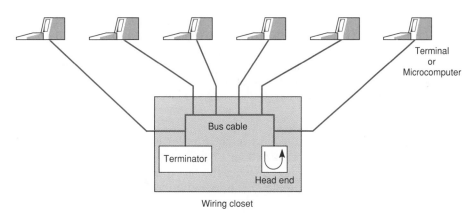

Figure 6-2   Bus topology. The upper half of this figure shows a basic microcomputer-to-microcomputer bus topology in which each microcomputer connects to the cable. Messages move from a microcomputer to the head end of the bus cable and then reverse direction. The lower half shows the same bus topology, but with the cable routed through a wiring closet for easy maintenance.

topology is a traditional approach to interconnecting devices in which each device is linked by a separate circuit through a central connection point or controller in a wiring closet. This topology is typified by many local area networks and PBX telephone switchboards in which all transmitted data must pass through a central control point to be transferred (switched) from the sender to the receiver. Figure 6-3 depicts a star topology.

When all the microcomputers (nodes) connect to a central point, should the central controller fail, the entire star network also fails. For this reason, it is critical for the central node to be able to handle traffic peaks; otherwise it may become overloaded at times of peak message transmission. Basically, the central controller in a star network is a message switch, the purpose of which is to switch the messages going between the different microcomputers.

We sometimes see combinations of the star and bus topologies in high-rise build-

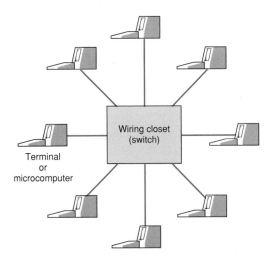

Figure 6-3 Star topology. The wiring closet in a star topology has a switch to make the connections from one microcomputer to another. This is different from ring and bus topologies employing wiring closets because messages in a star topology do not move in any specific pattern as they do with ring and bus.

ings. For example, the cables might run vertically in a bus topology between the floors of the building. At each floor, there might be a star topology for connecting the microcomputers. Put another way, the bus topology in these buildings is vertically oriented and the star topology is horizontally oriented.

Mesh Topology   In a *mesh topology,* any network node can communicate with any other network node. In a true mesh network, every node is connected to every other node by its own point-to-point communication circuit, but this is seldom implemented because of the extremely high cost. What we usually see is an arrangement in which one or more of the nodes become switching centers so they can interconnect any microcomputer with any other microcomputer. Regardless of how the microcomputer-to-microcomputer connection is achieved, any network that allows the interconnection of all its nodes to each other is a mesh network. Look at Figure 6-4 to see these two methods of interconnecting mesh networks. The public telephone system is an example of a mesh network using the switching center concept shown in the lower half of this figure. A mesh network using satellite transmission may be called a *hubless network* because there is no switching hub or node. The top half of Figure 6-4 is hubless, whereas the bottom half has a switching node. In some configurations, a mesh topology and a star topology are the same.

Physical Versus Electrical Topologies   It should be noted that *physical topology* is slightly different from *electrical topology.* The *electrical bus topology* is designed so every station receives every signal generated on the network media. In the *electrical ring topology,* the signal is regenerated and repeated as it passes from station to station. The ring and bus electrical topologies, however, can have one or both of two very

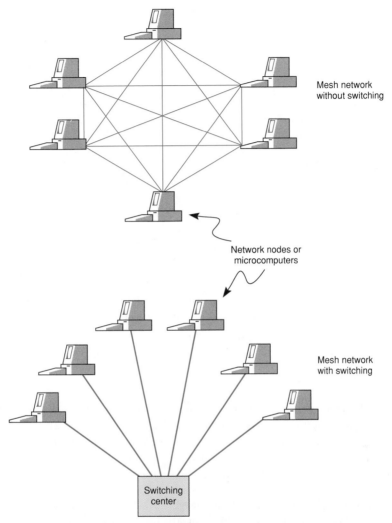

Figure 6-4 A network having a mesh topology allows any node to connect to any other node. This figure shows two methods of accomplishing such connections.

different physical topologies. In each electrical topology, you can choose between running cables from station to station in the ring or bus, or you can bring one cable from each station back to a central point called a *wiring closet* or *wiring hub*. The station-to-station and star physical topologies predominate in microcomputer-based LANs.

The station-to-station arrangement uses less wire and may be easier to install, but if the cable fails because of a bad connector or damage at any point along the way, the entire network goes down. The advantage of the star arrangement is that one bad cable or connector normally does not disrupt the network; if it does, the system can be restored quickly by unplugging the bad cable from the hub.

Figure 6-5   Wide area network (WAN) configuration. This figure shows the interconnection of ten U.S. cities through a switching center in Houston.

NETWORK CONFIGURATIONS

Whereas a topology defines the network's basic geometric arrangement, the *configuration* shows its actual or practical layout, including any constraints placed on it by software requirements (protocols) and physical hardware connections. Topologies are the building blocks of a network configuration. For example, a wide area network configuration might include all of the previously mentioned topologies.

Wide Area Network (WAN)   Some large networks are referred to as *wide area networks* (WANs). They link systems that are too separated, either physically or geographically, to be included in a small in-house network. In other words, wide area networks cover a large geographical area (see Figure 6-5). They usually transmit data over *public thoroughfares* (roads or streets) and, therefore, must use the communication circuits of a publicly registered common carrier (telephone company). A *common carrier* is a government-regulated private company that furnishes the general public with communication facilities, primarily circuits. Among the most noted examples of common carriers are AT&T, the Bell Operating Companies (local telephone companies), Bell Canada, US Sprint, and MCI.

Wide area networks use a broad range of communication media for interconnection and the nodes can be located as close together as a few city blocks or as far away as another country. They generally use microwave or satellite transmission, but they are not limited to these two media. As a result, wide area network is a general term referring to all networks that cover a broad area because the various nodes or stations are geographically separated by longer distances.

In other words, wide area networks are nothing more than the traditional long distance networks developed by business organizations and government agencies. These networks usually are made up of leased circuits configured to fit the business requirements of the organization developing such a network. An example of a wide area network is a packet switched network in which the user does not own the network but pays to use someone else's packet network. The point is that just by using the packet switched network, the organization has access to a wide area network covering a large geographical area.

Basically, a wide area network is any communication network that is configured in a manner that permits message, voice, or image signals to be transmitted over a widely dispersed geographic area. The voice telephone network can be regarded as a wide area network because it interconnects voice telephones throughout the world.

Metropolitan Area Network (MAN) A *metropolitan area network* generally spans a geographical area that encompasses a city or county. The various nodes may be anywhere from several hundred yards to 20 or 30 miles apart. The geographical boundaries of metropolitan area networks are not very tightly defined, but if someone talks about a statewide network, that normally is a wide area network instead of a metropolitan area network.

MANs interconnect various buildings or other facilities within a citywide area. In the example shown in Figure 6-6, this MAN is within the city of Sacramento. Now look back at Figure 6-5 to see how Sacramento fits into the wide area network. Notice that you can see more detail about the network as you look at each successive layer of the map (WAN in Figure 6-5 and MAN in Figure 6-6).

Backbone Network (BN) A *backbone network* is a large central network to which all the computers within an organization are connected. Backbone networks usually connect everything on a single company or government site. Looking at Figure 6-7, you can see that a backbone network at McClellan Air Force Base connects six different buildings or work areas on the base. Now look back at Figure 6-6 and you will see that McClellan Air Force Base is one of the nodes on the Sacramento metropolitan area network. Returning to Figure 6-7, it shows not only the backbone network interconnecting the facilities at McClellan Air Force Base but also a *gateway* at the fire station to access the broader Sacramento metropolitan area network. (Gateways interconnect networks.) As is evident, backbone networks are similar to metropolitan area networks, except they connect facilities covering a smaller geographical area and they normally are controlled by a single organization. Use of the word "backbone" can be confusing. Sometimes a corporation will refer to its wide area network as a backbone. The reason for using it this way is that all the corporate business functions are connected to the WAN; therefore, it is the corporate backbone.

Local Area Network (LAN) *Local area networks* are a group of microcomputers or other workstation terminal devices that are located in the same general area and connected by a common cable (communication circuit) so they can exchange information. For example, a LAN can be used within a building, on a business premises, or on a college campus. They cover a small area ranging from several hundred feet to several

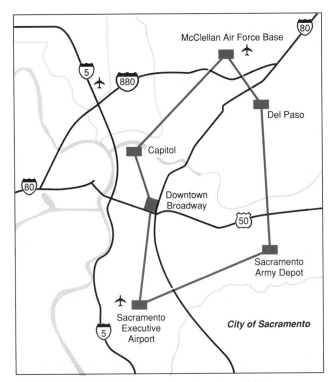

Figure 6-6 Metropolitan area network (MAN) configuration. This figure shows how McClellan Air Force Base interconnects with five other nodes in Sacramento.

miles. Local area networks are differentiated by the fact that their transmission media (circuits) generally do not cross any public thoroughfares (roads) and, therefore, do not have to be licensed by either the federal or state communication regulatory agencies.

In most LANs, devices with the processing power of a microcomputer are interconnected as shown in Figure 6-8. This local area network is located within the records building at McClellan Air Force Base in Sacramento. This eight-station LAN is used by personnel who maintain the military records within this building.

To see how network configurations build on each other, look again at Figure 6-8 to see how the local area network used in the records building connects to the backbone network in Figure 6-7. Moreover, the backbone network shown in Figure 6-7 is part of the metropolitan area network shown in Figure 6-6. Finally, the MAN in Figure 6-6 is part of the wide area network shown in Figure 6-5.

Local area networks can be configured easily to interconnect directly to a wide area network, to the backbone network of the larger organization, to a metropolitan area network, or to other local area networks, so that two or more LANs can transmit messages among their various terminals. In effect, a LAN covers the smallest geographical area, and a WAN covers the largest geographical area. Metropolitan

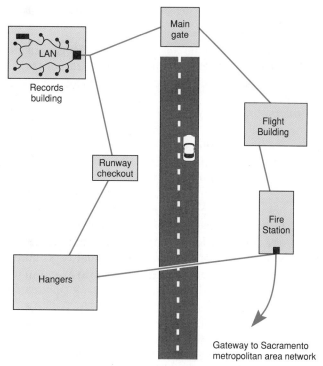

Figure 6-7   Backbone network (BN) configuration. This figure shows the interconnection of all the buildings on the premises of McClellan Air Force Base in Sacramento. Notice the gateway to the MAN that is shown in Figure 6-6.

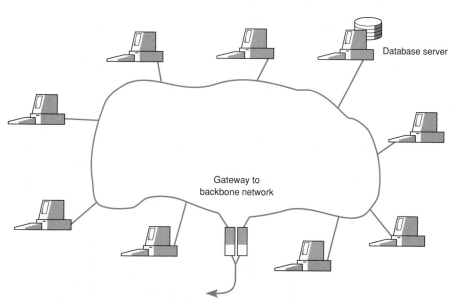

Figure 6-8   Local area network (LAN) configuration. This figure shows how the local area network within the Records Building at McClellan Air Force Base connects via a gateway to the base's backbone network shown in Figure 6-7.

area networks and backbone networks cover the geographical area between WANs and LANs. The details pertaining to local area networks are not covered in this chapter because an entire chapter is devoted to LANs (see Chapter 11).

Hybrid Networks Another popular term is hybrid networks. A *hybrid network* is a flexible or open-ended network that takes advantage of a mixture of different technologies or media to achieve a large wide area network or backbone network. A backbone network that interconnects all or many of the LANs within an organization can be called either a hybrid network or a wide area network interconnecting the LANs.

Hybrid networks have been in existence for years, but they were not given a label until recently. You can consider a hybrid network as any mixture of two or more network configurations combined in such a way as to optimize whatever it is the business entity wants to achieve. Hybrid networks may use a mixture of different types of transmission media (satellite, microwave, and so forth), dial-up communication circuits, private dedicated leased circuits, local area networks, and many other devices or protocols.

Point-to-Point Figure 6-9 demonstrates a leased circuit that is a *point-to-point configuration* because it goes from one point to another point. A point-to-point circuit means that an organization builds a private network and, in doing so, has a communication circuit going from its host computer to a remote terminal. Point-to-point circuits sometimes are called *two-point circuits*. This type of configuration is quite advantageous when the remote terminal has enough transmission data to fill the entire capacity of the communication circuit. When an organization builds a network using point-to-point circuits, many point-to-point circuits may emanate from the front end processor ports to the various remote terminals wherever they are located. When you use the dial-up telephone network to make a telephone call, that is a point-to-point connection.

Intelligent Terminal Controller Figure 6-10 shows a configuration that employs a *local intelligent terminal controller* (also called a *remote intelligent controller*) at the remote end of a point-to-point circuit. Such a configuration facilitates the point-to-point circuit connection to a local intelligent controller that has control of one or more terminals. Local intelligent terminal controllers frequently control 16 terminals simultaneously. The primary reasons for employing this device are to load the point-to-point circuit more efficiently and to serve as a security restrictor.

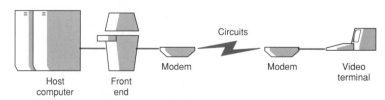

Figure 6-9 Point-to-point configuration.

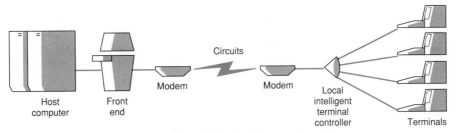

Figure 6-10   Local intelligent terminal controller configuration.

In addition, the local intelligent terminal controller is economical because more terminals or microcomputers can be attached to a single voice grade leased circuit. This is possible because the intelligent terminal controller uses the full bandwidth capacity of the leased line. Furthermore, it allows a large number of terminals in an office to share one leased line. Many metropolitan area networks and wide area networks use point-to-point circuits. As the next section shows, local intelligent terminal controller configurations also can be used in a multidrop network.

Multidrop   Figure 6-11 shows a *multidrop configuration* (also called *multipoint*). Notice that the first *dropoff* point (where a terminal is attached to the multidrop circuit) has only a single terminal, but the second dropoff has a local intelligent terminal controller managing a cluster of terminals. Either of these configurations is possible

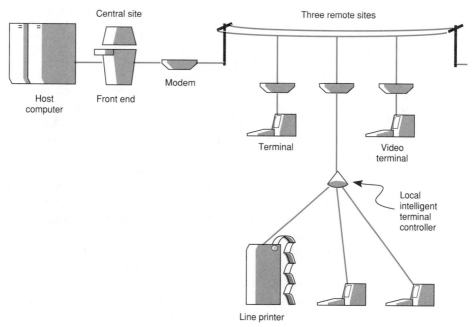

Figure 6-11   Multidrop configuration with three drops.

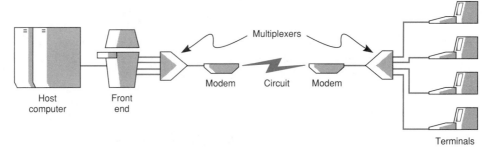

Figure 6-12   Multiplex configuration.

on a multidrop circuit. Organizations that design multidrop configurations do so to load the communication circuit more efficiently, reduce circuit mileage, and thus save money. When there are various branch offices or government agencies throughout a city or state, multidrop configurations can be a very efficient method of interconnecting these various locations. A WAN can consist of both multidrop and point-to-point circuits.

In a multidrop configuration, each dropoff point shares the line and is serviced or responded to in sequential fashion. In other words, only one dropoff point can use the circuit at a time. It is only because we can switch between the various dropoff points so fast that it appears each user has sole use of the entire circuit. It is not uncommon to have 50 or 60 terminals interconnected on a single multidrop circuit. There might be five to seven local intelligent terminal controllers (one per dropoff point) and perhaps six to ten terminals connected to each local intelligent terminal controller where that circuit has been dropped off at a branch office or agency.

Multiplex   Figure 6-12 shows a typical *multiplex configuration.* To *multiplex* is to place two or more signals on the communication circuit simultaneously. Multiplexing may be achieved by using either frequency division multiplexing or time division multiplexing. (These techniques were discussed in Chapter 4.)

The primary benefit of multiplexing is to save communication circuit costs between the host computer or business entity and many far-flung remote sites. Figure 6-13 shows how several levels of multiplexing can save on communication costs. Reading from right to left, the first level of multiplexing is where three locations of four terminals each are multiplexed onto a single IXC (interexchange channel) for transmission to a distant site. The second level multiplexes the resulting 12 signals over a single IXC circuit, for example, from Phoenix to Chicago. Finally, the third level multiplexes the combined 24 signals over a single IXC circuit from Chicago to New York. The modem pairs were left out to simplify this figure.

As you examine this illustration, think about how much more circuit mileage would be involved if you had a point-to-point circuit going from the front end to each of the 24 terminal device locations. Also, consider how an alternative configuration, such as multidropping (see Figure 6-14), might be used to connect the various terminal device locations, in contrast to one that uses multiplexing.

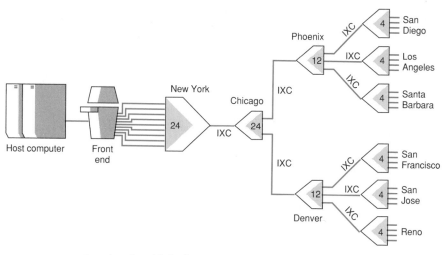

Figure 6-13   Levels of multiplexing.

PACKET SWITCHING NETWORKS

Packet switching is a store and forward data transmission technique in which messages are split into small segments called *packets*. A *packet switching network* is a special kind of wide area network. Packet networks often are referred to as *X.25 networks*, after the X.25 international standard on which they are based. They are value added networks (VANs) because the common carrier adds value by enhancing circuit features. When a message is sent from a terminal in a packet switching network, the message is divided into equal-sized packets and then transmitted

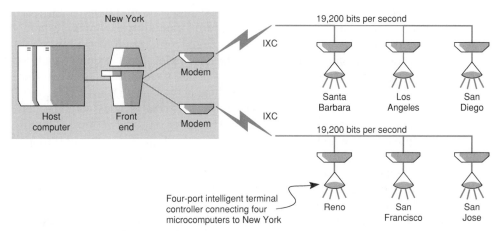

Figure 6-14   A multidrop configuration in which two multidrop circuits replace the multiplexed configuration shown in Figure 6-13.

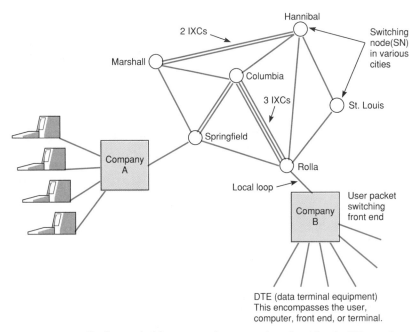

Figure 6-15   Packet switching network connecting six cities in Missouri.

through the network to the destination node. At the other end, the packets are reassembled into their original message and delivered to the appropriate destination terminal. Packets belonging to different messages or transactions can travel via the same communication circuits. Moreover, the action we call *switching* moves the packets from one circuit to another so they can reach their respective destinations. A virtual circuit is what connects the communicating terminals or microcomputers.

Virtual Circuits   A *virtual circuit* is a communication path used only for the duration of a specific message transmission. Virtual circuits use software that connects end points as though through a physical circuit. Address information is contained in the packets that carry source data to the destination. This circumvents typical hardware problems like data speed mismatch and helps retransmission when there are errors.

Figure 6-15 shows a packet switching network with a *switching node* (SN) at each end of the six cities connected to the network. These switching nodes route the messages through the network to whichever city and terminal they are addressed. Notice how packets originating in Columbia might be switched through both Hannibal and Rolla to reach St. Louis.

Switching nodes also may split messages into separate and individual packets. If the nodes do not split the message into separate packets, then the user's own computer or data terminal equipment (DTE) must complete this packetizing task. By the way, did you notice that some of the switching nodes are interconnected with several IXCs (communication circuits)? This is a distinct advantage to the packet switched service user because there is a built-in redundancy (in case of disaster) with regard to communication circuits between cities (switching nodes). How packetizing takes place is the topic of the next section.

Packetizing   Splitting messages into individual packets is called *packetizing*. Packets are assembled and disassembled either by the customer's data terminal equipment, or at the switching node by a *packet assembly/disassembly* (PAD) facility. In either case, packetizing is an almost instantaneous process, and data is transmitted in a virtually uninterrupted stream. The main functions of the PAD are to establish and clear the virtual telecommunication circuits, assemble the asynchronous characters received from the terminal into packets, transmit them on the virtual circuit, and, at the other end, disassemble packets received and reassemble them back into messages.

The Consultative Committee on International Telegraph and Telephone (CCITT) has defined a number of international standards that apply to packet switching networks. Among the more important ones are the following.

- **X.3** Defines the packet assembly/disassembly (PAD) and how it serves as the interface between asynchronous terminals, packet mode terminals, and other PADs in another distant packet switching network.
- **X.25** Defines the interface between data terminal equipment (DTE) and data circuit terminating equipment (DCE) that operates in a packet mode on public data networks. To simplify this, X.25 defines how terminals and packet switching nodes shall exchange packets between themselves.
- **X.28** Defines the interface between an asynchronous terminal and a PAD. Remember, the PAD is a hardware device that disassembles messages and puts them into packets for transmission and then reassembles the individual packets into their original messages when they reach their destination terminal.
- **X.29** Defines the procedures by which a terminal and a PAD facility exchange control information and user data.
- **X.75** Defines the procedures by which X.25 packet switched networks exchange data with other networks. The *X.75 gateway* is the gateway at each of the two networks.

A typical packet is a 128-character message block. In other words, no matter what the length of the original message, it will be split into one packet, but more likely into several 128-character-long packets. Notice that every packet is precisely the same size and contains the very same control characters within and/or surrounding the message. Once the message is packetized, either at your data terminal equipment (DTE) or at the network's switching node, it is ready for transmission. The top of Figure 6-16 pictures a typical packet. Notice the existence of a header address (the packet's destination), some control characters (if a message is broken into several packets, the software must number these packets so they can be reassembled at the other end of the communication circuit), up to 1024 bits of data (128 characters), and an error check (16 bits). The receiving switching node, therefore,

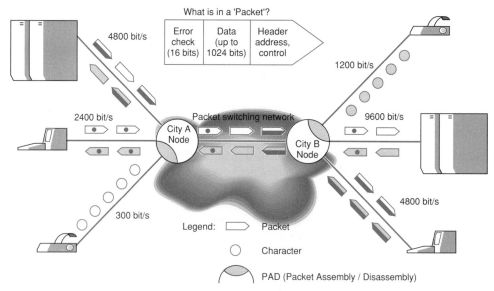

Figure 6-16   Packet switching concepts.

can ask to have the entire packet retransmitted if any bits in the packet are corrupted during its movement over the communication circuits.

The lower part of Figure 6-16 shows a packet switching connection between six different cities. The little boat-shaped figures (shown on the communication circuits) represent individual packets of separate messages. Notice how packets from separate messages are interleaved with other packets for transmission.

Although the packets in one data stream may mix with several other data streams during their journey, it is unlikely that packets from two different data streams will travel together during the entire length of their transmission. The two communicating terminals do not need to know through which intermediate nodes their data is routed. The packet network takes care of routing the packets by using either of two methods. The *first* method adds a destination and sequence number to each packet, in addition to information about the data stream to which the packet belongs. In this case, a route is chosen for each packet as it is accepted into the packet network. At the destination address, the packets are reassembled back into a continuous message by using the sequence number that tells the network where the packet belongs in the message stream. The sequence number is necessary because different routes may deliver packets at different speeds, making the data packets arrive out of sequence.

The *second* routing method sets up a virtual circuit. In this case, once a terminal informs a network of its desire to communicate with another terminal over the packet network, the network determines an end-to-end route and all packets for that transmission (message) take the same route. In other words, they use the virtual circuit that has been set up for that particular transmission. In this case the packet needs to contain only information about the stream to which it belongs; information about its destination or its position in the sequence of packets is not required.

For asynchronous transmission, the PAD at the sending end assembles the individual characters into 128-character packets, and then the PAD at the receiving end reassembles all the individual packets into their original character asynchronous message format. You might remember that the PAD assembles the characters of asynchronous transmission (character-by-character transmission) into a 128-character packet for transmission. As a result, low speed asynchronous terminals can use a packet switching network.

In the case of synchronous transmission, network users normally are responsible for packetizing their own synchronous messages. They use their own data terminal equipment or computers prior to transmitting the message to the switching node, although the switching node also can packetize the message.

Interleaving   Packet switching is popular because most data communications consist of short bursts of data with intervening spaces that usually are of longer duration than the actual burst of data. Packet switching takes advantage of this characteristic by *interleaving* bursts of data from many users to maximize use of the shared communication network.

Interleaving is achieved by assembling the bursts of data into packets that contain your message, addressing, control information, and error checking information. The packet switching network connects various cities, or other areas, with multiple circuit paths between them.

Switching   Packet switching networks generally are more reliable than other types of networks because they have *redundant circuits* between various cities (you saw this in Figure 6-15). This means that if a switching node or IXC circuit fails, an entirely different path might be utilized. Moreover, because *digital switches* are used, it is more reliable than older analog switching techniques.

At this point, we should compare circuit switching, store and forward switching, and packet switching. In *circuit switching,* communication circuits are switched between each other. If the entire circuit path is not available, you get a busy signal that prevents completion of your circuit connection (much like a dial-up telephone circuit). In *store and forward switching* (also called *message switching*), the entire transmitted message is accepted by the central switch and forwarded either immediately (the two circuits can be switched together at that moment) or at a later time when both circuits are free and can be switched together or when the receiving terminal requests its stored messages. In *packet switching* (which basically is a store and forward technique), your message is first split into the appropriate number of packets (normally 128 characters per packet) and then sent on to the receiving terminal. Usually, your message is forwarded immediately because packet switching networks are designed to have enough capacity (multiple circuits) to operate with immediate delivery. But some packet switched networks have the store and forward capability in case of communication circuit overloads, disastrous situations, an inoperable receiving terminal, or simply to offer electronic mail service.

The charges for using a public packet switching network are not related to the distance between the various switching nodes, as is true with other communication circuits. You generally are charged a basic price depending on the number of packets transmitted or the total usage time.

Many companies and government agencies set up their own in-house packet switching networks because it is a very efficient way to design private networks. A wide area network can transmit its messages as a packet network or through use of a centrally controlled roll call polling methodology. In addition, an organization can use many public packet switching networks on a number-of-packets-transmitted charge basis, as well as on a usage time basis.

One other point should be made. Any organization that does not want to develop its own in-house network and hire the required technical expertise is a prime candidate for public packet switched networks. Use of public data networks (virtually all of them use packet switching) eliminates many of the technical in-house expertise requirements and lowers overall network costs.

Frame Relay   *Frame relay* is an emerging packet switching technology that transmits data faster than the currently popular X.25 packet switching standard. Frame relay is simply a data link layer protocol that defines how frames of data are assembled and routed through a data network. (The data link layer is layer 2 of the Open Systems Interconnection seven-layer model of data communication protocols, the functions of which will be discussed in Chapter 9.) The frame relay technique provides higher performance than other wide area network packet switching technologies. It uses variable-length packets, and it has a total of only 48 overhead bits, which is approximately one quarter the number of bits required for implementation of the X.25 standard.

As an example of frame relay, look at Figure 6-17. The left side shows that when a X.25 packet leaves its Source A and moves through Node B, to Node C, to Node D, and finally to its Destination E, each intermediate node acknowledges the packet through which it passes. Under this protocol, Node B receives Packet 1 and acknowledges it as Acknowledgment 2 back to A, and so forth as it moves from node

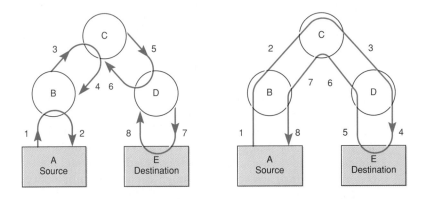

X.25 packet network   Frame relay packet network

Figure 6-17 Frame relay compared to X.25 packet switching. With X.25, each node sends an acknowledgment immediately on receiving a packet. With frame relay, the final destination terminal sends acknowledgment, making this technique faster than the X.25 technique.

to node. In a frame relay packet network such as we see on the right side of the figure, the Source A sends a frame as shown by Frame 1. As the frame moves between Node B, Node C, Node D, and on to Destination E, it keeps track of all the intermediate addresses. When Destination E receives the frame correctly, a single acknowledgment is sent back from E to Node D to Node C to Node B and ultimately to Source A as shown by the numbers 5, 6, 7, and 8.

To support frame relay, the intermediate addresses must be preserved. Moreover, the ability to return an acknowledgment to the correct sending device must be built into the intermediate nodes of the system. What we are seeing is replacement of the traditional X.25 packet switching standard with a frame relay methodology that basically works the same way, except it is many times faster during transmission because it has a more efficient message acknowledgment methodology.

Cell Relay Basically, *cell relay* is the same as frame relay, except it uses fixed-length packets of 53 bytes. This small, fixed packet makes cell relay more suitable for voice transmissions than is frame relay. This is so because voice transmission is not very tolerant of the receiving end's reassembly delay time that is caused by the variable lengths of frame relay packets. Moreover, the cell relay standard specifies higher speeds (45 million bits per second and above) because it is aimed at voice transmission.

In summary, you should consider using frame relay or cell relay when there is a need either to interconnect two local area networks or a local area network to a wide area network. This should be a consideration because both methodologies handle very high speed streams of packets. Another area for which cell relay is well adapted is the local area network-to-backbone network interconnection.

Fast Packet Multiplexing Another technology that is closely related to frame relay is fast packet multiplexing, an approach that is a significant improvement over the more traditional time division multiplexing. A *fast packet multiplexer* examines each channel for a packet and then transmits packets only from those channels that are active. The fast packet multiplexer must determine whether the channel has a packet ready to send or whether it is idle. As may be seen in Figure 6-18, the fast packet multiplexer skips over channels 2, 4, and 7 because they are idle during that cycle. This means the entire circuit bandwidth is given to channels 1, 3, 5, 6, and 8 because they are the only ones actively sending packets. A fast packet multiplexer handles packets from active channels in the same manner that a statistical time division multiplexer handles individual characters. When the first group of packets are sent, the fast packet multiplexer examines all the channels and sends packets only from the active channels, ignoring the ones that are idle.

One major difference between fast packet multiplexers and the more traditional time division multiplexers is that fast packet multiplexers can determine which packets are more important, such as packets belonging to a voice message (voice packets sometimes are called *talk spurts*). It has the ability to send the more important voice packets first and fast. This is an important feature because voice transmission is not very tolerant of delays, which are gaps in the spoken word. These gaps or delays are very distracting to the people carrying on the conversation. As you can see,

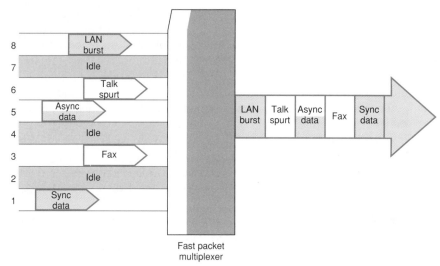

Figure 6-18   Fast packet multiplexing. This figure shows packets of voice (talk spurt) and data on eight channels that are multiplexed onto one outgoing high speed circuit.

fast packet multiplexers are able to multiplex both data and voice over the single transmission circuit.

Frame relay must be differentiated from fast packet multiplexing. The term *fast packet* refers to a method of transmitting packets in a packet switching network. Sometimes fast packet multiplexers are called *fast packet T-1 multiplexers* because the hardware is designed for use on T-1 circuits that transmit at 1,544,000 bits per second. To achieve greater packet transmission speed, fast packet multiplexers remove repetitive characters from data transmissions and gaps (when no one is speaking) from digitized voice transmissions. This multiplexing allows both the data and voice to be sent with less bandwidth. The remaining bandwidth can be used for more data or voice transmissions. Fast packet multiplexers also are more efficient because they use bandwidth as it is needed rather than dividing the T-1 circuit into 24 fixed channels.

Fast packet multiplexing is simply a faster packet switching technique that achieves greater speed because of its ability to use the bandwidth more effectively. Frame relay, on the other hand, can increase the speed of the fast packet process even further because it uses a more efficient acknowledgment technique and it has fewer overhead bits for control. Cell relay is even faster than frame relay.

PUBLIC DATA NETWORKS (PDNs)

Public data networks, which also are called *public timesharing networks,* and remote computing services are available for virtually any data processing application, business function, or information retrieval service that any organization might desire. Various governments and private companies offer network services to organizations that might wish to subscribe. Almost all these network services use the packet switching concept for transmitting data or messages.

Like most other networks based on the packet switching concept, public data networks also are value added networks (VANs). The concept of *value added networks* began when vendors leased circuits between cities, combined them into a packet switching network, started charging on the basis of message volume or amount of time used (rather than the traditional time and distance method), and sold the service to users. This was a first generation VAN. Second generation VANs came into being when the vendors selling these services identified additional user requirements and added them to the network. In this phase vendors added such services as electronic mail and security features. Today the third generation VAN is built around a microprocessor-based digital message switch similar to fully automated digital PBX switchboards. This provides more flexibility in configuring the packet switching value added network to fit more closely the system requirements of each individual user.

This digital message switching capability encourages large users (corporations and governments) to develop their own in-house third generation packet switched VANs. These VANs allow the user to interconnect an assortment of terminals, computers, and microcomputer workstations. Such packet switched networks can accept various line speeds and different protocols and can serve as a corporate backbone network to which all other networks within the corporation are connected. That is, they can accommodate private leased circuits, direct distance dialing, and connections to both public data networks and in-house local area networks. In Figure 6-15 you might visualize the switching nodes as being different corporate offices within the same organization.

Many information retrieval services, such as Dow-Jones News Retrieval Service, The Source, and Dialog, connect their computers to public data networks so their users can interconnect easily. Regardless of where the users might be located, they generally can connect through a local dial-up telephone call, or, as you might expect, they sometimes have a leased communication circuit to the information provider. Within the United States, numerous public data networks use packet switching capabilities, including the following.

- Infonet 1-800-342-5272
- Tymnet Global Network 1-800-872-7654
- ACCUNET/AT&T 1-800-222-0400
- IBM Information Network 1-800-727-2222
- CompuServe Network Services 1-800-848-8199
- SprintNet Data Network (formerly Telenet) 1-800-736-1130
- Mark*Net 1-800-433-3683
- DATAPAC (Canada) 1-613-781-6798

You should call these public data networks to obtain current prices for using their services. Their telephone numbers are included for this purpose.

Packet switched public data networks are available in most countries of the world. Some of these networks are PSS (England), Transpac (France), ARPAC (Argentina), Euronet (connecting major European cities), and Austpac (Australia). The European Economic Community (EEC) is promoting Euronet, a database information network for member countries.

As an example of public data networks using the new frame relay technology, Tymnet Global Network has a service it calls ExpressLane. The purpose of ExpressLane is to interconnect local area networks between the United States and Europe. The service uses frame relay technology transmitting at 1,544,000 bits per second over Tymnet's public X.25 packet switching network. This high speed frame relay transmission technique serves 160 cities in the United States. At present, ExpressLane's European connections are in London, Paris, Amsterdam, and Frankfurt, with many others planned for the future.

Organizations that use this frame relay service to interconnect their local area networks in the United States and Europe pay a flat monthly fee. For this fee, Tymnet provides the user with the components required for connection to the Tymnet network, including a bridge or router, all the necessary software, and a 56,000 or 64,000 bits per second access circuit. Organizations that use ExpressLane among the 160 cities in the United States pay a fee of $2,100 per month. Organizations that interconnect their local area networks in both the United States and Europe pay a fee ranging from $2,250 to $4,100 per month, depending on the charges for the international circuits.

DTS (DIGITAL TERMINATION SYSTEM)

A *digital termination system* is a communication service designed to provide flexible, low cost digital communications within a community. This configuration is nothing more than a local loop. It is the "last mile" to the final user premises, whether the premises is a private home, a large corporation, or a government agency. These local loop configurations have been dominated by the telephone companies and their copper wire pairs that are located either underground or on overhead telephone poles.

The pressing issue related to digital termination systems is bypassing. *Bypass* is any communication alternative that does not use the local telephone company's circuits. If private homes or companies want to bypass the local telephone company's local loop, they have a variety of options. Some of the competing common carriers might be those offering cable television (CATV), direct satellite transmission, intracity microwave transmissions, infrared transmissions, and cellular radio.

Two of the technologies that are available for voice or data over short distances (less than 15 miles), and that can provide 96 channels of voice or data transmission, are infrared and short haul microwave. Both of them, for example, can be used on college campuses to connect various buildings or two campus facilities that are not contiguous.

Infrared is a short distance transmission based on light. It is a low cost transmis-

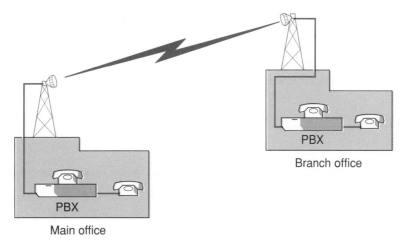

Figure 6-19 Digital termination system bypass using microwave.

sion medium and easy to install. Furthermore, there are no regulatory agency restrictions for infrared as long as transmission is within a single facility. Elaborate path alignment is not necessary, nor does it require frequency clearance or right-of-way clearance such as that required for microwave. The drawbacks of infrared are its restrictions to line of sight and its susceptibility to interference from smoke or fog.

Short haul microwave is based on transmission of a signal at specified frequencies within three frequency groupings (23 gigahertz, 18 gigahertz, and 2 to 10.5 gigahertz). Microwave requires frequency clearance from the regulatory agencies because it can interfere with nearby microwave antennas. An example of digital termination system bypass using microwave is shown in Figure 6-19.

Cellular radio units can be purchased or leased from telephone companies or independent vendors. Small *VSAT satellite antennas* also can be used, especially if a public packet switching vendor sets up a packet network on a satellite link.

As more corporations purchase digital switchboards (allowing them to own the central switch in their organization that controls both voice and data communications), they may be further tempted to use one of the digital termination systems to bypass the local telephone companies. Of course, the logic of bypassing is to save on costs by leasing fewer telephone company circuits. The bottom line on the DTS is that local telephone companies are losing revenues as more businesses link their offices directly with one another.

A recent example of bypassing occurred when Digital Equipment Corporation decided to link its corporate headquarters network to its employees' personal computers at their homes. To do this, DEC wanted to use Ethernet, a local area network that normally is used within buildings. When DEC approached its common carrier, NYNEX was not able to provide the wideband circuits required for Ethernet. DEC than turned to Cablevision Systems. This local cable television provider was able to supply both the circuits of the required bandwidth and a switching structure that was more compatible with Ethernet than the telephone company's switching system. DEC had Ethernet up and running on the Cablevision system within four days.

The Federal Communications Commission classifies the providers of digital termination systems as either limited or extended common carriers. *Limited common carriers* may operate digital termination systems in as many as 29 standard metropolitan areas. By contrast, *extended common carriers* may operate digital termination systems in no fewer than 30 standard metropolitan areas.

DRAWING A NETWORK

It is possible to draw networks either by using microcomputer-based software (see the next section on GrafNet Plus) or by using Figure 6-20. Use the following steps if you want to draw a network by hand.

1. Make several photocopies of Figure 6-20.
2. Cut out the required symbols (keep the symbol labels).
3. Tape the symbols in place by using double-sided tape.
4. Draw the lines with a ruler to connect the symbols.
5. Label the circuit lines you draw between the symbols with their appropriate speeds; that is, 9600, 19,200, 56,000, 1,544,000 bits per second, and so forth.
6. Look back at Figure 6-14 to see an example of a hand-drawn network configuration.
7. *NOTE:* Figure 8-29 on page 363 is a blank map of the United States. Remember, you can enlarge it on a photocopier.

GRAFNET PLUS SOFTWARE

The *GrafNet® Plus* software is an excellent package for drawing network maps. A restricted educational version, which is available at no cost to schools using this text, is intended for educational purposes only and is not for commercial distribution. Professors should contact their John Wiley & Sons sales representative or call John Wiley Sales Support at 1-800-225-5945 (ext. 6462) for a copy of the special educational version of GrafNet Plus. (Students should ask their professor to obtain this GrafNet educational program.) Companies or government agencies wishing to use the full commercial version of GrafNet Plus should write to Ms. Ranjana Sharma, Network Dimensions, 5339 Prospect Road, Suite 312, San Jose, California 95129, or call her at 1-408-446-9598, or send a facsimile request to 1-408-255-4576.

NOTE: Both versions of GrafNet Plus are graphics-based and require Microsoft Windows to run; therefore, you should have either Windows 2.1, 3.0, or 3.1, before attempting to use GrafNet Plus. If you do not have Windows, maps can be drawn by hand as explained in the previous section. GrafNet Plus runs on IBM or compatible microcomputers having 640,000 bytes of RAM, 4,000,000 bytes of available hard

Figure 6-20 Symbols for drawing network hardware configurations. Photocopy this page, cut out the symbols, tape them in place using double-sided tape, and draw the lines with a ruler to connect the symbols.

disk space, and running under Microsoft Windows 2.1 or greater. It can run with or without a mouse.

GrafNet Plus is an efficient software package for displaying and documenting a communication network spanning the world, a country, or a local area. In addition to drawing the network, network employees can use it to create and maintain a database of all the network nodes and links. GrafNet Plus plots the network on geographical maps. It is possible to zoom from a geographical view of the world to views of a country, a state, or selected regions as small as a square mile. GrafNet Plus also generates extensive reports of the network parameters. The network graphs and reports may be displayed on the screen or sent to a printer.

GrafNet Plus is easy to learn and use because of the simple pull-down menus and dialog boxes of the Windows user interface. GrafNet Plus has the following features.

- Presents network connections on U.S. and Canadian maps, state maps, maps of many other countries, and on world maps when using the global option
- Places nodes accurately on maps simply by entering an area code and a telephone number, or alternately by the latitude and longitude, which are obtainable from any world atlas
- Scales network views from a global view to a country, region, state, province, or other selected area
- Allows selective viewing and reporting of both links (circuits) and nodes (workstations, switches, multiplexers, and the like)
- Offers enhanced display features with full-color selection on a monitor
- Provides convenient network documentation with built-in report formats
- Provides customized page layouts with comprehensive print facilities
- Allows the easy exchange of network data and reports with other applications already in use—for example, the exchange of text file layouts from a word processor
- Prints maps of presentation quality

GrafNet Plus contains map information and coordinates for relating telephone numbers to the appropriate map locations. The database provides specific node locations in the following manner. The user simply enters the 3-digit area code and the 3-digit telephone number prefix (the first three digits of a 7-digit telephone number). GrafNet Plus then uses its database to locate the nodes on U.S., Canadian, or state maps. For international map locations, the user enters the country code in addition to the appropriate area code and telephone number prefix. On the other hand, the user can specify the geographical location of a node through its latitude and longitude (available from an atlas). Then GrafNet Plus consults the databases and displays each node in its proper location on the selected map. With convenient pull-down menus, the user can then link the nodes (draw the lines representing the circuits) and add other information, such as whether the node is a bridge, a multiplexer, a gateway, or some piece of other hardware.

Installing GrafNet Plus   GrafNet Plus must be installed on a hard disk having approximately 4 million bytes of available free space. Follow these steps to install GrafNet Plus.

1. Have in hand the three GrafNet Plus diskettes for the *"Special Version for Colleges and Universities."* They are the setup diskette and the North America utilities diskettes 1 and 2. You may want to print and read the README.DOC file on the setup diskette before continuing.

2. Place the setup diskette in Drive A. (Drive B also works.)

3. Switch to Drive A by typing A: and pressing the Enter key.

4. Type the word SETUP and press the Enter key.

5. Follow the instructions as they display on the screen. GrafNet Plus prompts when it is time to switch between diskettes. The educational version of GrafNet Plus includes only the maps for North America. In addition, some of the reporting functions have been removed from this version.

The setup program creates a main directory called C:\GRAF. At the end of installation, all the map, area code, and telephone prefix data is combined into a single file called MAP.DAT. This version includes four predrawn map files: TEST-NET.GNT, US-MAP.GNT, CANADA.GNT, and USNET.GNT.

How to Run GrafNet Plus   After GrafNet Plus has been installed, start Windows and then run GRAFPLUS.EXE from within Windows. The GrafNet main directory (C:\GRAF) contains the GrafNet Plus programs. The program that starts GrafNet Plus is GRAFPLUS.EXE: therefore, the full path to run GrafNet Plus is C:\GRAF\ GRAFPLUS.EXE. The GrafNet Plus icon under Windows is a small U.S. map.

GrafNet Plus Tutorial   This introductory tutorial will teach you the basic techniques for creating, displaying, and documenting networks by using GrafNet Plus. To begin, start Windows and then start GrafNet Plus. The initial screen of GrafNet Plus is the blank map of the United States as shown in Figure 6-21.

The top menu bar (see the top of Figure 6-21) contains the command menus related to GrafNet Plus. To pull down a menu, click on your choice with the mouse or hold down the Alt key and press the underlined character of the menu name (for example, Alt-F to pull down the File menu). To select a command from a pulled-down menu, either click the mouse on the command in the pulled-down menu or press the key for the underlined character in the command line of the pulled-down menu (see Figure 6-22). The initial screen shown in Figure 6-21 does not show the 48 individual states in the United States. To add the states, see the Adding State Boundaries to the U.S. Map box.

To begin the tutorial, let us load an existing sample network called TEST-NET.GNT. To do this, click on the File menu at the top of the screen to pull it down (see Figure 6-22). Select the Open command for the Open File dialog box to appear (see Figure 6-23).

The Open File dialog box presents a list of files currently in the C:\GRAF direc-

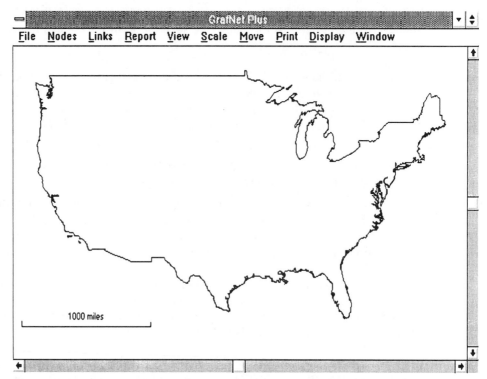

Figure 6-21   The blank map of the United States as shown in the opening screen of GrafNet Plus.

tory of GrafNet Plus. Use the mouse or the Tab key with the Up or Down arrow keys to scroll through the list of files. To select TEST-NET.GNT, scroll to that name and double click the mouse or press the Enter key when the light bar is on your choice. A sample network appears like the one shown in Figure 6-24.

Nodes are annotated symbols with the city name, and *links* are lines connecting the nodes. Notice how this network connects San Francisco to Detroit, Pittsburgh, Fairfax, and Sarasota. Now we will add a new network node at Boise, Idaho. To do this, click on the Nodes menu at the top of the screen to move to another screen like the one shown in Figure 6-25. Then select the Add Nodes command. The Add Nodes dialog box appears as shown in Figure 6-26.

Now we will add Boise to our map. Type Boise, ID in the Node Name box in the upper left corner of the screen (see Figure 6-26). Press the Tab key to move the cursor to the next box, which is Location. The area code for Boise is 208, so type 208 in the Location box and press the Enter key. (By the way, the area codes for U.S. cities are in the front section of most telephone directories.) After pressing the Enter key, the cursor moves to the Prefix box where you must enter a valid telephone number prefix for Boise. Recall that the prefix is the first three digits of a telephone number. Type 344 in the Prefix box and press the Enter key. These two

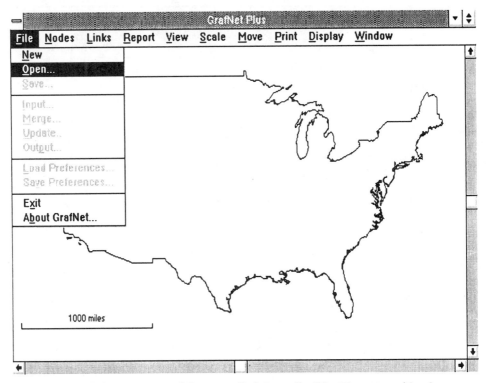

Figure 6-22 Select a command from a pulled-down GrafNet Plus menu either by clicking the mouse on the command in the pulled-down menu or by pressing the underlined character in the command line of the pulled-down menu.

ADDING STATE BOUNDARIES TO THE U.S. MAP

Wait until finishing the tutorial before trying the commands described in this paragraph. Did you notice in the Figure 6-21 GrafNet Plus start-up screen that the U.S. map shows no state boundaries? To add the internal state boundaries to this screen, click on the menu item Scale (see the top of the screen in Figure 6-22). When the pull-down menu appears, choose Countries, scroll to United States and click on it, click on the "Show Subregions" box, click on the "Scale" box, and the outline of the U.S. map in Figure 6-21 reappears with all the state boundaries showing. Use this same method for adding provinces to the map of Canada.

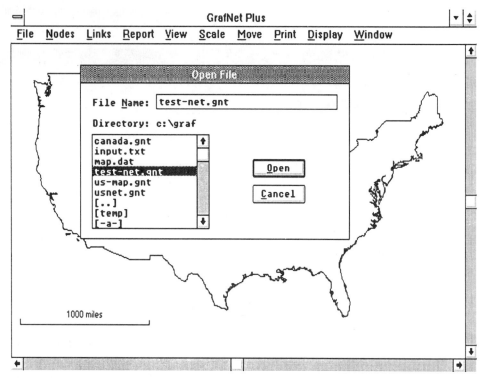

Figure 6-23 Select a GrafNet Plus file in the Open File dialog box. Scroll to its name in the directory c:\graf and double click to select it.

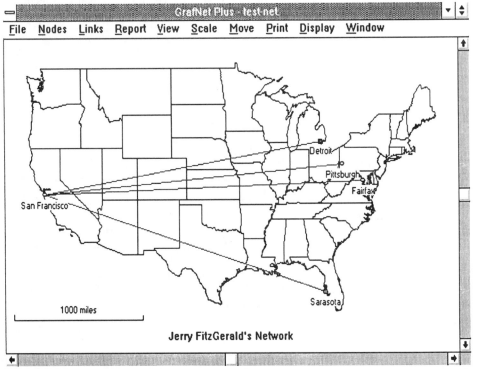

Figure 6-24 A sample network map in GrafNet Plus.

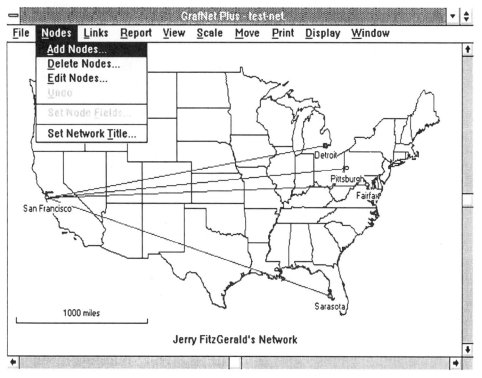

Figure 6-25 Add a node in GrafNet Plus by clicking on the Nodes menu at the top of the screen. Then select the Add Nodes command.

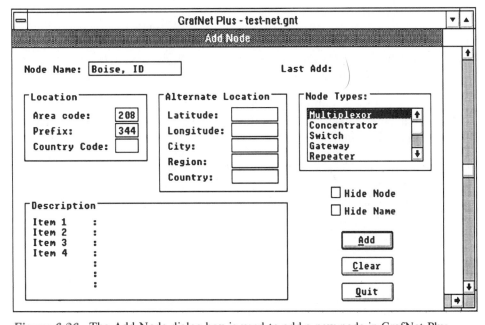

Figure 6-26 The Add Node dialog box is used to add a new node in GrafNet Plus.

253

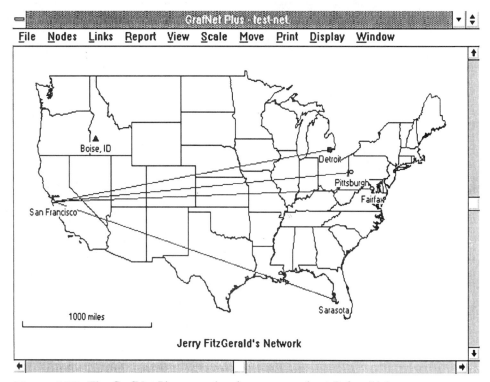

Figure 6-27   The GrafNet Plus map showing a new node at Boise, Idaho.

entries are all that is required for entering U.S. and Canadian nodes because you do not need the country code. GrafNet Plus is now able to locate Boise in its database of map coordinates.

Next, click on the word Multiplexer in the Node Types box. This places the map symbol for a multiplexer at Boise (a solid triangle in GrafNet Plus). Before leaving the Node Types box, scroll through the list to see the other types of nodes for which there is a unique symbol.

Finally, click on the Add box in the lower right corner to add the new node at Boise. The dialog box clears at this point so you can add another node. We are not going to add another node at this time, so close this dialog box and go back to your map by clicking on the Quit box. The map displaying the new node at Boise appears as shown in Figure 6-27.

NOTE: If you did not have the area code and prefix for Boise, you could have entered the latitude and longitude in the Alternate Location box on the Add Node screen (see Figure 6-26). The GrafNet Plus database would have located the node by using Boise's latitude and longitude instead of its area code and prefix.

Now examine Figure 6-27 and notice that no links (circuits) as yet connect Boise to any of the other cities on the map. To connect Boise to San Francisco, click on

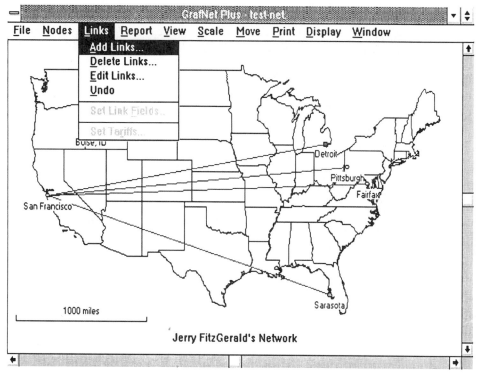

Figure 6-28   Connect Boise to San Francisco by clicking on the Links pull-down menu item at the top of the GrafNet Plus screen. Then select the Add Links command.

the Links menu item at the top of the screen (see Figure 6-27). When the Links pull-down menu appears, choose Add Links as shown in Figure 6-28. The Add Links dialog box then appears as shown in Figure 6-29.

The small box in the upper left corner of the Add Links dialog box is where you type the Link ID (see Figure 6-29). The Link ID is the name you assign to this link. Now type SF to Boise, ID in this box. Using the mouse, next move to the Nodes box, highlight San Francisco, and then click the Select button just below this box (Alt-S selects it if you do not have a mouse). Next, highlight Boise, ID in the same Nodes box and again click on the Select button just below this box. Notice that San Francisco and Boise, ID now appear in the Connections box to the right because you just connected them. Also notice that you can Unselect the connection by using this box if you made an error.

Now let us begin choosing some other characteristics for our new link. Move down to the Type box and click on Analog. Then move right to the Bandwidth box and click on 9.6–19.2 Kbps. To complete the link, move to the lower right corner, click on the Add box to draw the link, and then click on the Quit box so your map returns. Figure 6-30 shows the U.S. map with the new link from San Francisco to Boise.

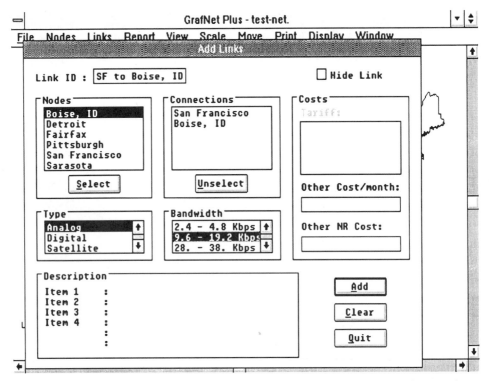

Figure 6-29   Use the Add Links dialog box to connect Boise to San Francisco on the GrafNet Plus map.

To print a title at the bottom of the new map, click on the Nodes menu at the top of the screen showing the map. Choose Set Network Title by clicking on it when the pull-down menu appears. A small window then appears in which "Jerry FitzGerald's Network" shows. Type a new title in this window. Then use the mouse to click on the Set box to add the new title. When the map reappears, it has the new title you have chosen at the bottom of the map.

To save a map, click on the File menu at the top of the screen showing the map. Choose Save from the pull-down menu by clicking on it. A small window then appears in which you type the filename you want to use for the map. TEST-NET.GNT initially appears in the window as the filename because this tutorial began with that file. You may want to change it to another name to save it. As with DOS, GrafNet Plus allows eight characters for the new filename and three for its extent.

To print the map, click on the Print menu at the top of the screen. Choose Print Network when the pull-down menu appears. The map then prints as shown in Figure 6-31. Note that your printer must be installed properly when setting up windows or it will not operate.

This ends the tutorial; but notice the many other menus to explore as you look across the top row of pull-down menu options in Figure 6-30. Some of these may not be available because some of the pull-down menus have been removed from the

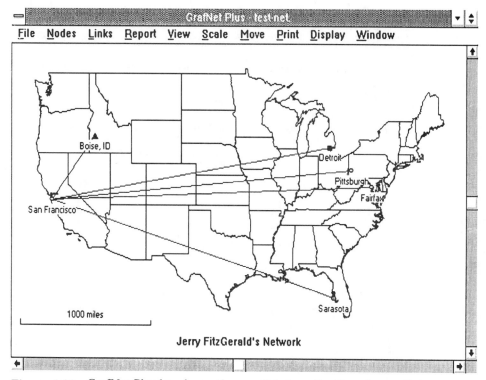

Figure 6-30   GrafNet Plus has drawn the new link from San Francisco to Boise.

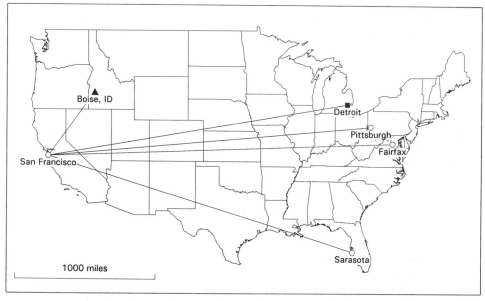

Figure 6-31   A printed copy of the completed network map from GrafNet Plus.

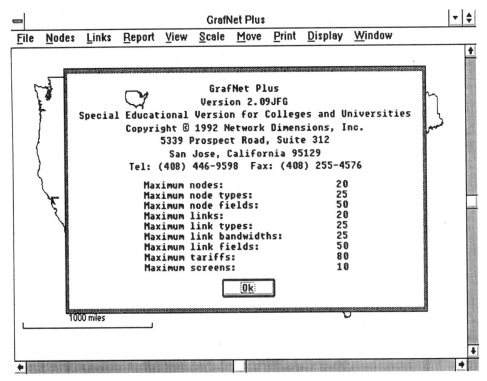

Figure 6-32   The About GrafNet Plus box.

educational version of GrafNet Plus. Figure 6-32 shows the limits for this educational version.

The full commercial version of GrafNet Plus does not have these limits. It offers detailed reports on nodes, circuits, and the like. It also has the ability to show tariffs (circuit costs), hardware costs, and numerous other geographical maps for plotting WANs. The full version has the global option for drawing maps that are worldwide in nature.

Our tutorial uses a U.S. map, but it is just as easy to draw a map of Canada, any province in Canada, or any state in the United States. To draw a map of Canada, click on the Scale menu at the top of the screen, and choose Countries when the pull-down menu appears. Then highlight Canada, click on the Show Subregions box, click on the Scale box, and GraftNet Plus presents a map of Canada on the screen like the one shown in Figure 6-33. The educational version of GrafNet Plus contains a file with a predrawn map of Canada; this file is named CANADA.GNT. To find it, click on the File menu at the top of the screen, choose Open when the pull-down menu appears, and then choose the file named CANADA.GNT. It also is possible to draw maps for each individual province in Canada.

To draw a U.S. state map, you also click on the Scale menu at the top of the screen. Choose Countries when the pull-down menu appears, scroll to the United

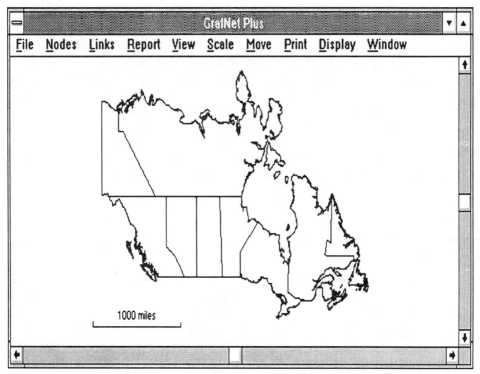

Figure 6-33   A GrafNet Plus map of Canada.

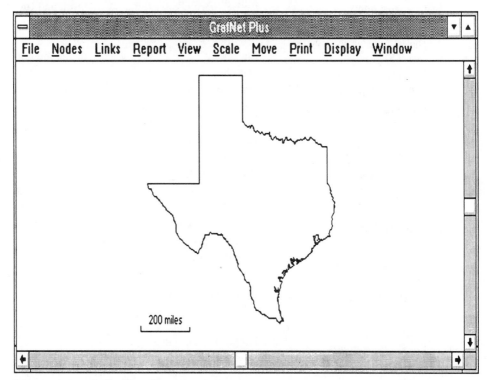

Figure 6-34   A GrafNet Plus map of Texas.

States, and choose it. After the U.S. map appears, click on the Scale menu again, choose Regions when the pull-down menu appears, and scroll to the state of your choice—Texas, for example. Choose Texas and GrafNet Plus presents a map on your screen like the one in Figure 6-34. Any state map can be drawn this way.

As you can see from this small tutorial, network map drawing software greatly simplifies the task of drawing network maps. This type of tool is indispensable to the network designer because it is easy to use and even easier to make changes when they are required because the network is changing. This software will be helpful when you reach the subject of network design in Chapter 8.

KEY TERMS

Backbone network (BN)
Bus topology
Bypass
Cell relay
Central control
Circuit switching
Common carrier
Configuration
Database server
Digital termination system (DTS)
Dropoff
Electrical bus topology
Electrical ring topology
Electrical topology
Fast packet multiplexer
Fast packet T-1 multiplexer
Frame relay
Gateway
GrafNet Plus
Hub topology
Hybrid network
Infrared
Interleaving
Interrupt
Link
Local area network (LAN)

Local intelligent terminal controller
Media
Mesh topology
Message switching
Metropolitan area network (MAN)
Multidrop configuration
Multiplex
Multiplex configuration
Multipoint
Network
Network server
Node
Packet
Packet assembly/ disassembly (PAD)
Packet switching
Packet switching network
Packetizing
Physical topology
Point-to-point configuration
Protocol
Public data network (PDN)
Public thoroughfare
Public timesharing network

Remote intelligent controller
Ring topology
Server
Short haul microwave
Star topology
Station
Store and forward switching
Switching
Switching node (SN)
Talk spurt
Topology
Two-point circuit
Value added network (VAN)
Virtual circuit
Walk time
Wide area network (WAN)
Wiring closet
Wiring hub
X.3
X.25
X.28
X.29
X.75

SELECTED REFERENCES

1. Briere, Daniel. "MANs Provide Digital Services at Low Cost," *Network World,* vol. 7, no. 46, November 12, 1990, pp. 1, 51, 54, 57, 60.

2. Derfler, Frank J., Jr., and Kimberly J. Maxwell. "Reliable Relays," *PC Magazine,* vol. 10, no. 15, September 10, 1991, pp. 377–379, 382–384, 386, 388–389, 392, 394, 398, 400, 402, 405.

3. Guy, Ken. "Fast Packet Multiplexing—A Technical Overview," *Telecommunications,* vol. 25, no. 6, June 1991, pp. 54–56, 58–59.

4. Heywood, Peter, and Elke Gronert. "Public Frame Relay Goes Global," *Data Communications,* vol. 21, no. 4, March 1992, pp. 77–80.

5. Johnson, William R., Jr. "Networking: A Strategic Advantage in Today's Global Marketplace," *Telecommunications,* vol. 26, no. 2, February 1992, pp. 27–28.

6. Kobielus, James. "Planned Super Networks Foreshadow 21st Century," *Network World,* vol. 8, no. 34, August 26, 1991, pp. 1, 43–45, 52.

7. Stallings, William. "Faster Packet Networks: A Trimmed-Down Specification Makes Frame Relay Faster Than a Speeding X.25 Packet," *Byte,* vol. 16, no. 12, November 1991, pp. 173–176, 178, 180, 181.

QUESTIONS/PROBLEMS

1. What is the primary function of a network?
2. What functions do servers perform?
3. Other than geographic differences, how do wide area networks differ from small local area networks?
4. What is a hybrid network?
5. How do local area networks differ from wide area networks or hybrid networks?
6. What are the three key elements of a network and how do they differ?
7. What are the basic topologies and how do they differ?
8. What is walk time and why is it important?
9. What are the most common ways to configure networks and how do they differ?
10. What primary benefit do local intelligent terminal controller, multidrop, and multiplex configurations have in common?
11. What is the technique in which messages are split into small segments and why is it used?
12. How is a virtual circuit distinguished from other circuits?
13. What is the function of a switching node?
14. What happens to messages when a PAD facility is used?
15. What features are common to every packet on a network?

16. Where does packetizing take place?

17. What does a packet contain?

18. Packets can be routed in either of two ways. What are they?

19. When packet networks are used, how does asynchronous transmission differ from synchronous transmission?

20. Why is packet switching popular?

21. How do packet switching networks differ from other networks in how they charge customers?

22. Packet switching networks generally are considered to be more reliable than other types of networks. Why is this so?

23. How do the three types of switching differ?

24. Why would an organization want to use a public packet switching network instead of developing a private packet switching network?

25. What is the difference between a public packet switching network and a public data network?

26. Why are public timesharing networks sometimes called value added networks?

27. When organizations develop their own packet switching value added networks, what are they called and what is their purpose?

28. Name four public data networks, including two outside the United States.

29. What is a digital termination system?

30. Explain the importance of bypassing.

31. Briefly discuss the advantages and disadvantages of the three types of digital termination systems.

32. How do limited common carriers differ from extended common carriers?

33. Select a set of characteristics that will serve to point out differences, advantages, and disadvantages of point-to-point and multidrop lines.

34. A _____ network is a mixture of two or more network configurations to achieve a large wide area network. Some organizations call this a backbone network.

35. Assume there are four terminals in each of the following cities: Detroit, New York, Chicago, and Washington, D.C. Each city has a four-level multiplexer and circuit leading to Atlanta. If Atlanta has a 16-level multiplexer, how many circuits are required to transmit all the data to Miami? *HINT:* Go to Chapter 8 and copy Figure 8-29 so you can draw this configuration or use GrafNet Plus.

36. Assume each city in Question 35 has its four terminals transmitting at the following rates:

    Detroit—9600 bps
    New York City—4800 bps
    Chicago—1200 bps
    Washington, D.C.—9600 bps

    How many voice grade circuits are required between Detroit and Miami if the Detroit/Miami modems can transmit at 14,400 bit per second?

37. What type of topology does the following illustrate?

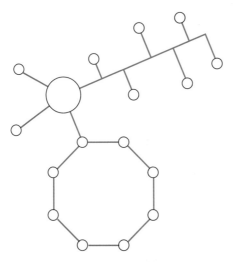

38. Can you configure a system that combines local intelligent terminal controllers, multi-drop, and multiplex configurations?

39. Identify several different packet networks.

40. Identify types of terminals and their locations for a network that is used by your organization, your department, or at your university or business.

41. Using Figure 6-11 as a guide, draw a multidrop configuration. *HINT:* Draw it on a copy of Figure 8-29 from Chapter 8.

42. Convert Figure 6-13 to both a multidrop configuration and a point-to-point configuration.

43. Name two types of servers on networks and state their purpose.

44. Why is a network's topology important?

45. What is a primary advantage of a ring network?

46. When discussing topologies, what does the term *bus* imply?

47. What is a primary disadvantage of a star topology?

48. What one feature distinguishes a mesh topology from other topologies?

49. State a logical progression of the primary network configurations.

50. How is a packet distribution network distinguished from a wide area network?

51. Discuss the international standards that apply to packet switching networks.

52. How do asynchronous and synchronous PADs differ?

53. Discuss why frame relay might replace X.25.

54. How does fast packet multiplexing differ from frame relay?

55. How does cell relay differ from frame relay?

56. Define fast packet multiplexing.

57. What is the primary advantage of fast packet multiplexing over statistical time division multiplexing?

58. How do you distinguish a topology from a configuration?

59. Use the GrafNet Plus software to draw a map connecting New York (multiplexer), Chicago (concentrator), and Los Angeles (gateway). Connect the three cities using digital 9600 to 19,200 bits per second circuits.

NEXT DAY AIR SERVICE CUMULATIVE CASE STUDY

Background on Next Day Air Service

You have done considerable work on the communication support for Next Day Air Service's outlying offices, but have for the most part neglected communications at corporate headquarters. Consequently, the next phase of your network activity will focus on the headquarters and its adjacent buildings.

The NDAS Board of Directors has expressed concern about the hodgepodge of computer equipment in its own offices. It recognizes that there is a more efficient way to process and communicate both raw data and meaningful information. At the same time, Mr. Coone is unsure about whether NDAS can afford a wholesale upgrade of equipment; likewise, he is doubtful about the "new" technologies that seem to be taking similar businesses in the Tampa area by storm. These "new" technologies include cellular telephones, LANs, and frame relay networks. Nevertheless, Mr. Coone acknowledges that a LAN does seem to be a logical step toward fulfilling the total integration of the NDAS information network. He likes the idea of installing a LAN at Tampa, which eventually can be connected to the WAN that interconnects all the other 15 offices.

As Mr. Coone's chief advisor, he has asked you to study the concept of establishing a single local area network for the entire headquarters. Because most of the offices are located in the main building, the idea of developing a suitable configuration (topology) for the LAN poses some interesting questions. The main building is a one-story structure with individual offices on each side of a corridor that runs longitudinally through the building as shown in Figure 6-35. Moreover, the fleet maintenance and dispatch offices are located in a small secondary building in the parking lot. This small building is only 50 feet in front of the main building. The maintenance and dispatch offices have not made any progress toward automating their operations; therefore, all the existing automation equipment is located in the main building. These include several microcomputers, a number of "dumb" terminals, a LAN, and the two minicomputers.

In addition, you have been authorized to purchase GrafNet Plus and Mr. Coone is eager to see the results. Because of his eagerness, you decide that when the GrafNet software arrives you will enter the existing circuits and diagram Next Day Air Service's current WAN. *NOTE:* Because the symbols in GrafNet Plus do not necessarily reflect the type of communication equipment Next Day Air Service has installed, you decide to use the following symbols: a triangle represents a city with a dial-up circuit, a square represents a city with a multiplexer, and a circle represents the company headquarters in Tampa. Be sure to indicate the speed of the circuit and the type of transmission. The city area codes and prefixes for NDAS's branch offices are shown in Figure 6-36.

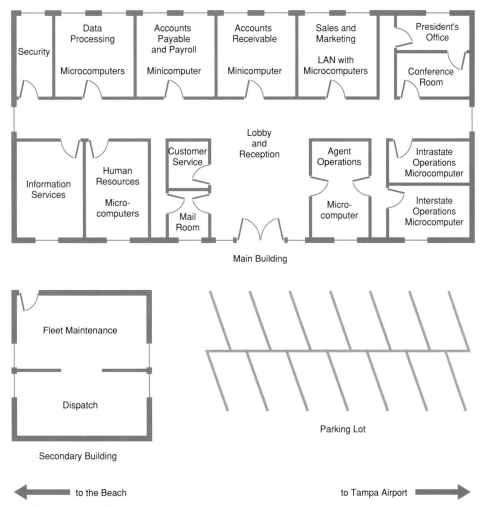

Figure 6-35 Facility map of the Next Day Air Service headquarters

Questions/Problems for the Next Day Air Service Case

1. Using GrafNet Plus, draw the configuration of Next Day Air Service's current WAN. Follow the instructions in the last paragraph of the case. Figure 5-44 also may be helpful. *NOTE:* If you are not using GrafNet Plus, use Figure 8-29 to draw the configuration map by hand. Alternatively, your professor may provide blank maps for hand drawing the network.

2. Assume that Next Day Air Service will take a conservative approach toward implementing a LAN. This means it will spend only the amount

City	Area Code	Prefix
Atlanta	404	355
Chicago	312	763
Dallas	214	939
Denver	303	458
Houston	713	224
Jackson	601	354
Jacksonville	904	356
Los Angeles	213	265
Memphis	901	274
Miami	305	325
Montgomery	205	244
New Orleans	504	733
Orlando	407	841
St. Louis	314	531
Tampa	813	253
Washington, D.C.	202	456

Figure 6-36 Next Day Air Service offices with area codes and prefixes for drawing the NDAS network map using GrafNet Plus.

needed to purchase the necessary hardware and software to create the LAN. In this approach, how could the existing equipment be configured to support a conservative LAN? What type of network topology might be appropriate?

3. The board of directors of Next Day Air Service has decided to authorize a one-time only, replace-selectively or replace-all-equipment approach. What would you replace and what type of equipment would you recommend? What type of topology would you install, taking into account both data messages and voice telephone calls from the WAN?

4. Make three photocopies of Figure 6-35 in the text. Use them to draw a star configuration having a digital PBX switch, a ring, and a bus topology connecting the various departments. Compare the three configurations.

5. Your answer to Question 1 was based on Figure 5-44 and it depicted a _____ configuration. Now look back at the original NDAS operations map in Figure 1-8. If you were to imagine that Figure 1-8 was a communication network configuration, what type of configuration would it be?

Chapter Seven

COMMUNICATION SERVICES (CIRCUITS)

This chapter defines common carriers, tariffs, and deregulation. It also describes the circuits that are available for voice and data networks, their transmission speeds (bandwidth), and how they are packaged for commercial use. Except for DIAL-IT 900, the costs (tariffs) of these communication circuits are presented in Chapter 8 where they are available for use in network design problems.

COMMUNICATION FACILITIES

The basic communication media, such as open wire pairs, wire cables, coaxial cables, microwave, satellite, fiber optic cables, cellular, infrared, and the like, were described in the Communication Media section in Chapter 5 (see page 190). In this chapter we present the circuits that are available commercially. They are derived or assembled from the basic types of media we described earlier. For example, in Chapter 5 you learned how wire pairs are used for circuits. In this chapter you will learn about T-1 circuits that use wire pairs to transmit. You also will learn about voice grade circuits that use wire pairs, coaxial cables, or microwave. In other words, common carriers put networks together by using both T-1 and voice grade circuits that are derived from the various types of media.

As a customer, you do not actually lease wire pairs or coaxial per se; you simply lease voice grade circuits. The common carrier decides whether it will use wire pairs, coaxial, or microwave for the voice grade circuits you are leasing. As you can see, the basic circuit types are used for creating the common carrier communication facilities that we will be describing here.

A *communication facility* is the medium that carries voice, data, or image transmissions from one point to another. These facilities (the media) may be physical, such as copper wires, coaxial cable, or optical fibers. On the other hand, the medium may be air, in which case the data communication facility transmits electromagnetic signals between microwave towers, satellites, cellular radio transmission antennas, and so on.

Even though there are separate data and voice communication facilities, technology is evolving toward a single communication facility that can handle voice, data, and image communications. The most prominent examples of such a facility are Integrated Services Digital Network (ISDN) and T-1 carriers, both of which will be described later in this chapter.

Once the various media are put together to form communication facilities, the common carriers offer them to the public as packages of *communication services*. An organization that wants to develop its own voice or data communication network can select from a variety of leased or switched (dial-up) communication services. If an organization chooses not to develop a private communication network, it may use the public packet switched network communication facilities. In this case the organization can use dial-up to gain access to the packet network, or it can lease a private circuit between the business premises and the entry switching node to the packet network. When leasing communication circuits, the organization pays a monthly lease and has these circuits available for its private use. If the organization uses the public packet switched network, it pays charges based only on its usage of the network. Usage charges may be based either on the *time* the network is utilized or on the *volume* of data packets transmitted. Using public packet switched networks relieves the user of network design problems, most network operations tasks, maintenance and troubleshooting, and other technical operations that are required when private leased circuits are used.

COMMON CARRIERS, TARIFFS, AND DEREGULATION

A *common carrier* is a government-regulated private company that sells or leases communication services and facilities to the public. Common carriers are profit-oriented businesses, and their primary products are communication circuits and related services for voice, data, and image transmissions. Because this marketplace has been deregulated in the United States, common carriers now supply a much broader range of computer-based services, such as the manufacturing and marketing of microcomputers, specialized communication hardware, software, and computer operations offered from the telephone company's central offices (switching centers).

Do not let the term *deregulation* confuse you. It simply means that these common carriers can enter into other types of business instead of offering only communication circuits. They still are regulated as to the prices they can charge for the communication circuit services offered. It is the other part of their business—computers, software, and other types of hardware—that is no longer price-regulated.

The biggest of the more than 1,200 common carriers in the United States and Canada are American Telephone and Telegraph (AT&T), the seven Bell Operating Companies (BOCs), Bell Canada, MCI Communications, US Sprint, and General Telephone and Electronics (GTE). Most carriers are small and offer communication facilities to a very small segment of the population, such as a 50- or 100-subscriber voice telephone network.

Tariffs   When offering communication services, common carriers are required to explain their offerings in writing. These are called tariffs.

A *tariff* is the schedule of rates (prices) and description of services that are to be received when a particular type of communication service is purchased or leased. The circuits are leased, but hardware may be either leased or purchased. The best example is the price structure for home telephones and the description of what is provided for the basic monthly fee. A monthly fee allows you to be connected to the dial-up telephone network; you must either buy the telephone or pay a small monthly fee for rental of the telephone instrument.

Tariffs are filed with the appropriate regulatory agency. There are two classes of regulatory agencies, federal and state. The best known regulatory agency is the *Federal Communications Commission* (FCC), a federal government agency that regulates interstate (between states) and international communications to and from the United States. The FCC has regulatory powers to compel common carriers to conform to the Federal Communications Act and its revisions. The federal government is continuing its deregulation of interstate communications to give common carriers more independence in the competitive business environment. Every common carrier engaging in interstate or international communications is under the jurisdiction of the FCC and is required to abide by its regulations.

The other regulatory bodies are the *Public Utilities Commissions* (PUCs) in each of the 50 states. These state Public Utilities Commissions are empowered to regulate intrastate (within a state) communications. Although the federal government is continuing its deregulation of common carriers, the individual state Public Utilities Commissions do not appear to be following the same course of action.

A common carrier wanting to sell communication services must have its services approved. To obtain this approval, it must file basic information with either the FCC or the state Public Utilities Commission. Such a filing provides details of its offered services, the charges for these services, justification for the charges, and so on. These documents, or tariffs, form the basis of the contract between the common carrier and the user of that common carrier's communication service (see the box on Sources of Tariff Information).

We also use the word "tariff" in another way. The Federal Communications Commission publishes numbered tariffs, or rulings, that the common carriers must follow. There are many tariffs, but two of the more controversial ones are Tariff 12 and Tariff 15. *Tariff 12* relates specifically to custom-designed networks. Common carriers for the first time are permitted to offer special pricing to an individual organization by filing a "custom" Tariff 12 dealing only with that one organization. This tariff allows large users of data communication services to bid for customized packages of voice and data services at large discounts off the standard pricing. The contracts generally cover periods of three to five years. In effect, this is similar to the discounting a merchandiser receives if it goes to a manufacturer and obtains a special discount if it buys 10,000 units of a product instead of 500 units. Tariff 12

SOURCES OF TARIFF INFORMATION

Teleresource Service
Bell Communications Research
Bellcore Customer Service
60 New England Ave.
Piscataway, N.J. 08854
201-699-2000
A service of the Bellcore Federal Regulatory Resource Center. Compiles and reviews FCC filings, rulings, and other sources of information. Provides daily updates to clients.

International Transcript Services, Inc.
2100 M St., N.W.
Washington, D.C. 20037
202-857-3800
Provides FCC document retrieval and copying services.

Fair Press Services
Division of Washington Information
    Group, Ltd.
P.O. Box 19352
20th Street Station
Washington, D.C. 20036
202-463-7323
Offers daily delivery of 43 categories and subcategories of FCC documents. Customers also receive the *FPS Daily Digest,* which is an index to FCC documents.

Lynx Technologies, Inc.
P.O. Box 268
Little Falls, N.J. 07424
201-256-7200
Provides a range of in-depth tariff information, including tariffs between the U.S. and other countries, within foreign countries, and from country to country overseas.

Downtown Copy Center
1114 21st St., N.W.
Washington, D.C. 20036
202-452-1422
Provides any FCC public document, including domestic and international tariffs for U.S.-based or other carriers filing with the FCC.

Center for Communications Management Information
11300 Rockville Pike
Rockville, Md. 20852
301-816-8950
Provides access to CCMI tariff analysts and other staff who interpret tariffs and explain their intricacies to users.

Telecommunications Information Services, Inc.
9 La Crue St.
Concordville, Pa. 19331
215-558-1770
Provides tariff information, as well as custom research and analysis of tariffs.

Tele-Tech Services
Division of Telecommunication Systems
Technology, Inc.
P.O. Box 757
McAfee, N.J. 07428
201-827-4421
Provides virtually all intrastate and interstate tariffs.

Valucom, Inc.
501 Church St., N.E., Suite 303
Vienna, Va. 22180
703-255-0700
Provides tariff information, custom research and analysis, and online database and tariff services.

also allows common carriers to enter into a facilities management operation so they can implement and manage an organization's entire communication requirements (voice and data).

Tariff 15 is the other controversial tariff. It permits American Telephone & Telegraph (AT&T) to single out certain customers to offer them discounted service prices in response to another competitor's offer, such as from MCI or US Sprint. Tariff 15 allows AT&T to match, but not beat, competitors' prices for communication services (circuits). The various common carriers and the Federal Communications Commission are constantly in disputes over both Tariff 12 and Tariff 15.

Deregulation   Although there are many similarities in the way data communication activities have evolved in the United States and in Europe, there also are many differences. One of the primary differences is that the data communication industry in the United States operates as a series of private companies that are regulated by the government, whereas in Europe and many other countries of the world the PTTs (Postal Telephone and Telegraph Services) are a government monopoly that owns, controls, and sells all voice and data communication services.

If the industry is regulated, as in the United States, it may be more innovative, cost effective, and able to develop new services faster. On the other hand, if the industry is a monopoly, as in many countries, it may be overburdened because it supports other government agencies (such as postal services) that drain its resources. Such a situation generally fosters an agency that is uneconomical and not very innovative or progressive regarding the development of new services. These statements are generalizations, however, and have notable exceptions.

Other differences might stem from the fact that government-owned monopolies may be run based on pressures created by unemployment, protection of industrial and technical markets, political considerations, national defense considerations, and cultural or social traits within a specific country.

The European environment is not a single sovereign market. It is plagued with many geographical, political, and economic differences. Their situation could be compared with trying to interconnect and achieve total compatibility in the data communication facilities between Mexico, Canada, and the United States. It is for this reason that the European PTTs are more sensitive than the United States to the need for international standards.

In all countries either the government has a regulatory agency to control privately run communication services and prices (a *regulation situation*), or it is the sole supplier of communication services (a *monopoly situation*). For example, in South America the federal governments are the sole suppliers of communication services, regardless of whether the service is voice or data. Germany's Deutschen Bundespost and France's Postes Telephonique et Telegraphique are the monopoly suppliers of communication services in those countries.

Like the United States, Canada has deregulated the communication environment and regulates only communication services and prices through its Canadian Radio-Television and Telecommunications Commission (CRTC). The Canadian CRTC is similar to the FCC in the United States. Mexico started deregulating Telefonos de

Mexico, known as TeleMex, in 1991. In England, the British Post Office Commission used to provide voice and data communication services. Until recently, the British Post Office was a government department (monopoly) that handled both mail and telecommunication services. Then it became a private company (the British government sold stock in this corporation), and now the British government regulates communications rather than being the monopoly supplier. Japan also has deregulated its communication industry and now regulates only communications. In Australia, there has been a massive deregulation of Telecom Australia's monopoly, and now it only regulates communications rather than being the sole supplier. In the Netherlands, the monopoly powers have been severely restricted, but they remain halfway between being a monopoly and a deregulated communication environment.

In a monopoly situation, private businesses cannot use communication circuits and telecommunication equipment unless they have been either manufactured, sold, or approved by the monopoly government agency. This restriction severely limits the growth of the country's businesses and reduces the country's economic growth. Growth is limited because we live in an information-based society, and any restrictions on the communication environment (whether voice or data) are bound to have a secondary effect on the entire economy.

In a country that has deregulated its communication environment, a regulation situation, businesses can use communication circuits from competing common carriers and communication hardware from many different vendors. Regulation occurs by controlling the prices common carriers charge for their services. In addition, the common carriers restrict the communication industry by requiring communication equipment manufacturers to meet various technical standards or specifications as to the type of signals that can be sent over the country's communication circuits. As an example, modem manufacturers must transmit signals that are within certain specified limits if they are to be approved for use in the United States. In reality, this not a burdensome restriction. It is a protective measure designed to ensure that one manufacturer's equipment does not harm another's or, especially, the communication circuits offered by various common carriers.

COMMUNICATIONS IN THE UNITED STATES

In the United States, 90 percent of the telephone system used to be run by American Telephone and Telegraph (AT&T). During the last few years of deregulation the 22 telephone companies owned by AT&T and AT&T itself were essentially divided in half (depending on your definition of half). The primary services retained and supplied by the first half are the local telephone services to your home or business premises, and the basic services retained and supplied by the other half (AT&T) are long distance telephone services.

Bell Operating Companies (BOCs)   Let us begin with the first half, which is local telephone service. The 22 individual telephone companies originally owned by AT&T were consolidated into seven *Bell Operating Companies* (BOCs). Some writers refer

Bell Atlantic
Bell of Pennsylvania
Diamond State Telephone
Four Chesapeake &
    Potomac Companies
New Jersey Bell

Ameritech
Illinois Bell
Indiana Bell
Michigan Bell
Ohio Bell
Wisconsin Bell

US West
Mountain Bell
Northwestern Bell
Pacific Northwest Bell

Bell South
Southern Bell
South Central Bell

Pacific Telesis (PACTEL)
Nevada Bell
Pacific Telephone

Southwestern Bell
Southwestern Bell

NYNEX
New York Telephone
New England Telephone

Figure 7-1   Seven Bell Operating Companies (BOCs), also called local exchange companies or Regional Bell Operating Companies (RBOCs).

to these as RBOCs, where the R stands for regional. Figure 7-1 shows how the United States was divided into these seven Bell Operating Companies. This figure gives the name of each of the seven companies and lists the original telephone companies that were grouped together to form each new Bell Operating Company. These are the telephone companies that supply telephones and local loop connections between your home or office and the telephone company end office (switching center) for voice and data transmissions.

Because of deregulation, the Bell Operating Companies now offer services other than communication circuits. Each of these seven companies has marketing agreements with manufacturers of office automation equipment, multiplexers, switchboards (PBXs), modems, cellular mobile telephone equipment, and so forth. The BOCs market equipment for these manufacturers. The next stage in the deregulation process is to allow these companies to manufacture their own equipment and computers. Of course, this will put them into direct competition with other computer manufacturers such as IBM and Digital Equipment Corporation. Now let us move on to the other half of the AT&T breakup.

American Telephone & Telegraph (AT&T)   The second half of this divestiture, American Telephone and Telegraph (AT&T), retained its old "long lines department," which handled long distance communication services. This part now is called *AT&T Communications*. AT&T also retained the Bell Laboratories (research division) and its manufacturing divisions, primarily Western Electric. As a result, AT&T's primary business is long distance communication services. Integrated with the long distance and networking operations is the manufacturing unit for information systems equipment. Other major divisions for AT&T are the Bell Laboratories research unit and AT&T International, which markets communication products abroad.

After the divestiture, AT&T was left as a single company (separate from the seven Bell Operating Companies) concerned primarily with long distance communication services. The other 22 telephone companies were spun off into seven regional Bell Operating Companies with the primary service responsibility of providing local telephone service. Of course, along with the AT&T divestiture came numerous other common carriers that are now in direct competition with AT&T for the long distance communication services market; the largest of these are General Telephone and Electronics, MCI Communications, and US Sprint. Moreover, the telephone instruments are no longer a monopoly item of these seven Bell Operating Companies or AT&T. Now it is up to you to decide whether you want to purchase your own telephone from another vendor or lease it from the telephone company.

Local Access Transport Areas (LATAs)   The service area of each of the seven Bell Operating Companies is broken into what are called *local access transport areas* (LATAs). These areas outline the geographic area *within* which the individual Bell Operating Company can offer service (*intraLATA*) and where it must turn service over to another supplier (*interLATA*), primarily AT&T, MCI, or US Sprint. These LATAs define the areas in which the *Local Exchange Companies* (also known as Bell Operating Companies) can provide local exchange and exchange access services.

Local exchange service is provided when the telephone company supplies a local loop. *Exchange access service* is provided when the local telephone company interconnects through the end office so your local loop can be connected to a long distance telephone company such as AT&T. Service *between* LATAs is provided by interexchange carriers like AT&T, MCI, or US Sprint.

Equal access is a vital issue brought about by deregulation. According to the terms of the deregulation agreements, local exchange companies (the BOCs) must provide all carriers of long distance services with access to local end office switches that are equal in type, quality, and price to that which they sell to AT&T affiliates. Exchange access may be equal, but this does not necessarily mean that all interexchange services are equal because the investment in maintenance, servicing, and equipment is the deciding factor in determining which carrier has the highest quality of service.

What equal access means in practice is that all the long distance carriers have equal use of the switches in an end office. If you want to place a pay telephone call with a specific carrier, for example, you first dial that specific carrier's access code before dialing the telephone number. The three major carrier access codes are 10288 for AT&T, 10222 for MCI, and 10333 for US Sprint.

LATAs have been modeled on the concept of Standard Metropolitan Statistical Areas (SMSAs). Where possible, LATAs are based on communities of interest and conform to state boundaries. Most states are comprised of several LATAs, but some of the sparsely populated states are a single LATA. A selected listing of Local Exchange Companies' LATAs is shown in Figure 7-2 where they are identified in general terms by state. There are approximately 200 LATAs in the continental United States. A number of them span state lines because they are based on SMSAs rather than political boundaries. (See LATA in the Glossary for additional information on LATA boundaries.)

The Bell Operating Company Pacific Telesis (PACTEL) has ten LATAs for California (Figure 7-3). As you can see from the figure, some of these LATAs are quite large. For example, a call from San Francisco north to the city of Eureka stays within one LATA service area, and so PACTEL collects the full long distance charge for it. By contrast, a call from San Francisco south to the nearby city of Monterey crosses the LATA boundary, and so the charges for the call are collected by a long distance interexchange carrier. This carrier can be AT&T, MCI, US Sprint, or any other supplier of long distance service that has been approved by the California Public Utilities Commission. As you can guess, each state has its own unique set of LATAs. Figure 7-3 shows only the LATAs for California.

Long Distance Common Carriers   In the United States, the three largest *long distance common carriers* are American Telephone and Telegraph, MCI Communications, and US Sprint. The following paragraphs discuss the long distance activities of these three carriers, especially those dealing with international telephone service.

American Telephone and Telegraph (AT&T) used to be the only long distance carrier in the United States. Since deregulation, it has expanded its services to include high speed data transmission, international toll-free dialing (like 800 numbers in the United States), and network management. AT&T is part of a consortium that is spending $3 billion to lay undersea high speed fiber optic cables that will improve transmission. In the area of telecommunication equipment, AT&T is well established in Europe and the Far East, including Italy, Spain, the Netherlands, and Indonesia. The overseas market is very big for AT&T, employing 22,000 people and generating about 15 percent of its $37 billion in annual revenues. Moreover, this market will grow further because AT&T is acquiring NCR Corporation. This acquisition is expected to add another 27,000 employees outside the United States and more than $3 billion to AT&T's international revenues.

MCI Communications Corporation (MCI) started in the United States as a small common carrier providing discount communication services. Today it is an international common carrier, providing direct dialing from the United States to 180 countries and international toll-free service to 25 countries. MCI began its international operations in 1983 when it bought Western Union International, Inc., from the Xerox Corporation. It continued expanding internationally when it bought RCA

Alabama	Evansville	Springfield	Philadelphia
Birmingham	Indianapolis	St. Louis	Pittsburgh
Huntsville	South Bend	Montana	Rhode Island
Mobile	Illinois	Billings	Single LATA
Montgomery	Cairo	Great Falls	South Carolina
Arkansas	Champaign	Nebraska	Charleston
Fort Smith	Chicago	Grand Island	Columbia
Little Rock	Forrest	Lincoln	Florence
Pine Bluff	Peoria	Omaha	Greenville
Arizona	Quincy	Nevada	South Dakota
Phoenix	Rockford	Single LATA	Single LATA
Tucson	Springfield	New Hampshire	Tennessee
California	Sterling	Single LATA	Chattanooga
Bakersfield	Iowa	New Jersey	Knoxville
Chico	Davenport	Atlantic Coastal	Memphis
Fresno	Cedar Rapids	Delaware Valley	Nashville
Los Angeles	Des Moines	North Jersey	Texas
Monterey	Sioux City	New Mexico	Abilene
Sacramento	Kansas	Single LATA	Amarillo
San Diego	Topeka	New York	Austin
San Francisco	Wichita	Albany	Beaumont
San Luis Obispo	Kentucky	Binghamton	Brownsville
Stockton	Louisville	Buffalo	Corpus Christi
Colorado	Owensboro	New York Metro	Dallas
Colorado Springs	Winchester	Poughkeepsie	El Paso
Denver	Louisiana	Rochester	Houston
Connecticut	Baton Rouge	Syracuse	Longview
Single LATA	Lafayette	North Carolina	Lubbock
Delaware	New Orleans	Asheville	Midland
Dover	Shreveport	Charlotte	San Antonio
Wilmington	Maine	Greensboro	Waco
D.C.	Single LATA	Raleigh	Wichita Falls
Washington	Maryland	Wilmington	Utah
Florida	Baltimore	North Dakota	Single LATA
Daytona Beach	Hagerstown	Bismarck	Vermont
Fort Myers	Salisbury	Brainerd-Fargo	Single LATA
Gainesville	Massachusetts	Ohio	Virginia
Jacksonville	Eastern	Akron	Culpeper
Orlando	Western	Cincinnati	Lynchburg
Panama City	Michigan	Cleveland	Norfolk
Pensacola	Detroit	Columbus	Richmond
Southeast	Grand Rapids	Dayton	Roanoke
Tallahassee	Lansing	Toledo	Washington
Tampa	Saginaw	Youngstown	Seattle
Georgia	Upper Peninsula	Oklahoma	Spokane
Albany	Minnesota	Oklahoma City	West Virginia
Atlanta	Duluth	Tulsa	Charleston
Augusta	Minneapolis	Oregon	Clarksburg
Macon	Rochester	Eugene	Wisconsin
Savannah	St. Cloud	Portland	Northeast
Idaho	Mississippi	Pennsylvania	Northwest
Single LATA	Biloxi	Altoona	Southeast
Indiana	Jackson	Capitol	Southwest
Auburn-Huntington	Missouri	Erie	Wyoming
Bloomington	Kansas City	Northeast	Single LATA

Figure 7-2   Selected list of local access transport areas (LATAs) by state (excluding Alaska and Hawaii).

Figure 7-3 Local access transport areas (LATAs) for California.

Global Communications in 1988 from General Electric Company. The latter acquisition secured its ties to many foreign telephone authorities. MCI has teamed with British Telecommunications PLC to provide a trans-Atlantic high-capacity fiber optic cable that will be able to handle its increased international traffic. In addition to offering long distance services within the United States, MCI offers what it calls Global Communication Service. This service negotiates transmission links with foreign telecommunication authorities, manages international voice and data networks, and provides billing in any currency.

US Sprint Communications Company (US Sprint) is the third largest long distance common carrier in the United States. It, too, has increased international traffic. Moreover, US Sprint is marketing multinational private networks and what are called carrier-select markets. Similar to equal access in the United States, carrier select simply means travelers can select the long distance carrier of their choice when dialing from another country. US Sprint has aligned itself with England's Cable & Wireless PLC to enhance its international markets. Their 50-50 partnership also is a fiber optic cable system. In addition, US Sprint owns an international public data network called SprintNet, which has links to 108 countries. It also is developing another private data network that will use switching hubs in 20 countries to link financial centers in Europe and the Pacific Rim.

As you can see, the international communication market has become a very competitive arena for American common carriers. It is a direct result of the deregulation of the telephone industry, not only in the United States but also in other countries. As a result, the general public and businesses worldwide are benefiting as the common carriers gain more freedom to compete in providing telecommunication equipment and services.

COMMUNICATION SERVICES OFFERED

The communication services described in this chapter may be supplied by AT&T, one or more of the seven regional Bell Operating Companies, MCI, US Sprint, General Telephone and Electronics (GTE), or one of the other common carriers. Companies like MCI and US Sprint are in competition with AT&T for interLATA (between LATAs) service, whereas the Bell Operating Companies and GTE handle the intraLATA (within a LATA) service.

Each of the following sections contains descriptions of selected services; usually, it is the most prominent service offered. These descriptions provide an insight into the types of communication services offered and a basis on which to carry out preliminary design analysis for various types of data communication network designs. The costs of these services (tariffs), except for DIAL-IT 900, are described in Chapter 8 under design step 12, Calculate Network (Circuit) Costs.

Private Circuit (Lease) Services   *Private circuit services* are those in which the user leases the service from the common carrier. In other words, private circuits are available for use by organizations twenty-four hours per day, seven days per week. In effect, they are for the exclusive use of the leasing organization. The communication facility that is provided when an organization leases a private circuit might be wire pairs, microwave, satellite, coaxial cable, or optical fibers. The common carrier provides only the communication facility or path over which messages travel. As mentioned earlier, users generally do not have a choice as to whether the specific type of circuit the common carrier provides is a wire pair, microwave, coaxial cable, or optical fiber. Private lease circuits are so much at the disposal of the lessee that one might think the circuits were owned by the organization, even though they are leased by payment of a monthly fee based on the mileage (distance between two nodes). These circuits are referred to as *dedicated circuits, leased circuits,* or *private circuits.*

Measured Use Services   *Measured use services* are communication services in which charges are based on how much the system is used. For example, a call from your home telephone is based on the length (time) of the conversation and how far (miles) the other person is from you. For a packet switched service, charges are based on a fixed per minute rate or how many individual packets of information are transmitted regardless of where the other party is located. With Wide Area Telephone Service (WATS), a fixed monthly fee is charged for a fixed number of hours of circuit usage. If the fixed time is exceeded, another per hour rate is charged. In other words, measured use services are those in which payment is based on utilization. Some of the primary services in this group are direct distance dialing (DDD), WATS, 800/900 service, and packet switching.

It is helpful to understand the distinction between a *leased circuit* and a *dial-up* (measured time) *circuit*. If you have a leased circuit from San Francisco to Los Angeles, it is one continuous and unbroken circuit path. In other words, this leased circuit is wired around any switching equipment at the telephone company central offices. By contrast, a measured time dial-up circuit goes through all the switching equipment in the telephone company central office; there is not one continuous and unbroken circuit path for your use. Every time a call is placed on a dial-up circuit, a new circuit path is established.

VOICE GRADE CHANNELS

Voice grade channels are analog circuits. They also are known as Series 2000/3000 Voice Grade Circuits. Technically, voice grade channels are for voice communication, remote operation of radio telephones, connection of private voice systems, interconnecting remote central offices, data transmission, remote metering, supervisory control of electronic devices, and facsimile machines. Everyone just refers to this as a voice grade equivalent channel. You might review Figure 2-6 in Chapter 2.

When this type of circuit is leased, it may include copper wire pairs, bundles of wire pairs, microwave transmission, coaxial cables, or even optical fibers. Normally, users are told if the voice grade equivalent channel is a satellite channel because network designers must take into account the propagation delay times associated with satellite transmissions. In addition, pricing structures for a satellite voice grade equivalent channel differ from those of wires, cables, or microwave.

Conditioning, or *equalization* as it sometimes is called, can be performed on communication circuits to improve their data transmission qualities. Because voice grade circuits transmit data in the voice bandwidth (300 to 3300 hertz), it is advisable to use conditioning or equalizing when transmitting at 4800 bits per second or greater, although it is not mandatory. This is because the signal suffers frequency/amplitude distortion or envelope delay distortion (changes in timing of the signal) during data transmission. An equalizer performs two functions.

First, it increases or decreases the amplitude of all the frequency components until they are the same amplitude as the reference component. This is accomplished by using the amplitude of the center frequency components of the voice grade channel as a reference (usually 1004 hertz). This action restores the frequency components of the signal to their former relative amplitude.

The second function of the equalizer is to delay each middle frequency component to the point where it is equal in delay to the edge components, so that after leaving the equalizer all the frequency components have the same relative delay. The higher frequencies attenuate faster than lower frequencies. The greater the bandwidth of the transmitted signal, the greater the degree of equalization/conditioning that is required. The different sets of requirements for attenuation and delay distortion are referred to as *levels of conditioning* for a circuit.

The user decides whether the circuit should be conditioned. AT&T offers two types of conditioning, which are used for point-to-point, multidrop, and switched configurations. *C type conditioning* has specific limits on attenuation distortion and envelope delay distortion. Such limits reduce line impairments so a data signal can get to its destination with less noise and distortion. Because there are fewer errors, fewer retransmissions are required. *D type conditioning* specifically limits noise and harmonic distortion. Again, this type of conditioning reduces line impairments, resulting in fewer errors and fewer retransmissions.

Modem manufacturers usually specify whether conditioning is required when using their modem on voice grade circuits. Most manufacturers of 9600 bits per second modems use adaptive equalization within the modem circuitry. By using the proper circuits, they control the amount of delay distortion introduced to offset that which is on the voice grade transmission channel. Conditioning/equalization therefore can be performed by the telephone company at its central office locations, or it can be performed continuously and automatically by the circuitry within modems.

In addition to conditioning, some local telephone companies such as New York Telephone (NYNEX) offer what is called a *straight copper circuit*. This is a pair of copper wires, and it is available only when the entire circuit is within the same telephone company central office. In essence, the straight copper circuit is comprised of two local loops connected at the central office. Because there are no repeater/amplifiers or loading coils in the circuit, the customer can use less expensive short haul modems (1 to 15 miles). Short haul modems also may be used on standard Series 3000 voice grade unconditioned channels, depending on the length of the circuit and the data rate.

Other similar private lease services include Series 1000 channels, which are low speed signaling and teletypewriter channels that vary from 30 to 150 bits per second. Because of their slow speed and their high cost (they may cost more than a voice grade data circuit), Series 1000 channels are falling into disuse and the telephone company is discouraging this offering.

WIDEBAND ANALOG SERVICES

Wideband analog services are used for either data transmission or alternate voice and data transmission. These services use analog circuits with a bandwidth that is wider than voice grade circuits. They are used for high speed data transmission, such as 19,200, 40,800, 50,000, and 230,400 bits per second. They also may be used in conjunction with a 50,000 bits per second switched service or high speed facsimile transmission. This type of communication channel may be delivered to the user as a Group 48,000 hertz bandwidth or as 12 individual voice grade channels (48,000 hertz ÷ 12 = 4000 hertz). It also is available as a Supergroup 240,000 hertz bandwidth. Organizations that need wider bandwidths use these channels to transmit greater quantities of data between facilities. Digital services are supplanting wideband analog services.

DIGITAL SERVICES

Digital services include point-to-point and multipoint configurations for the transmission of data in a digital manner. Analog modem conversion is not required, but you still need a DSU/CSU (digital modem). Digital service uses wire pairs, coaxial cable, microwave, or fiber optic cables. This type of service operates at 2400, 4800, 9600, 56,000, and 1,544,000 bits per second. It spans both the voice grade communication channels (4000 hertz bandwidth) and the analog wideband communication channels (greater than 4000 hertz). The advantage of using digital transmission is that digital modems are much less costly (although increased local loop costs may offset the lower modem cost) and the transmission error rate is far less than with analog circuits.

Digital services are replacing the traditional analog voice grade channels and wideband analog services, both of which supply analog circuits. Although digital circuits generally are leased, it is possible to get a switched digital circuit. Traditionally, an organization would lease a digital circuit between two of its facilities rather than leasing analog voice grade circuits or analog wideband circuits. This has changed because modern 56,000 bits per second switched services do not require a leased circuit—they are available on dial-up circuits.

The long distance carriers are able to establish these 56,000 bits per second circuit connections on demand (as needed by an organization) by using sophisticated digital cross-connect switching equipment. This does not mean that you can now use a 56,000 switched circuit from your home. What it does mean is that an organization can have 56,000 bits per second switched circuits installed from its headquarters to its branch offices. When a high speed data message is sent, such as from a Group 4 facsimile machine, the long distance carrier simply switches it to the proper circuit. This means the organization does not have to pay the full monthly lease rate on the circuit. Instead, it pays only for the amount of time it actually uses the 56,000 bits per second circuit. Switched digital services change the circuit's cost from a fixed price lease line to a measured time use charge. When the customer dials from the 56,000 bits per second DSU/CSU, a 56,000 bits per second circuit path is set up to the number at the remote branch location and data can be sent back and forth at 56,000 bits per second. This type of dial-up switched circuit is required for Group 4 facsimile machines. Moreover, international switched digital services offering either 56,000 or 64,000 bits per second speeds are available from the United States to numerous international locations.

The designer of a network first ascertains whether digital service is available in the area in which the organization wants to transmit and then compares the cost of digital service with the appropriate analog service such as the voice grade circuit or wideband analog services. ISDN and T-1 are specialized forms of digital services.

INTEGRATED SERVICES DIGITAL NETWORK (ISDN)

Integrated Services Digital Network is a leased service in which the common carrier offers a communication circuit with two 64,000 bits per second digital transmission channels and one 16,000 bits per second signaling channel (*2B + D*). This is a high speed digital transmission service over which you can combine simultaneous voice conversations, data transmissions, and image transmissions. ISDN uses coaxial cable or microwave.

The Consultative Committee on International Telegraph and Telephone (CCITT) has recommended standards on the physical and electrical specifications for the basic 2B + D user interface. There are two kinds of ISDN communication channels: basic and primary.

The *basic access service,* also called *basic rate,* is referred to as 2B + D because it consists of two 64,000 bits per second B channels and one 16,000 bits per second D channel. The B channels are used for all data other than control messages. The D channel is the conduit for "out-of-band" control messages and is used to specify, for example, what devices are connected at each end of the circuit link. The control messages give the network its intelligence. The two 64,000 bits per second B channels can handle digitized voice, data, and image transmissions, while any control messages/characters are sent simultaneously down the 16,000 bits per second D channel.

Primary access service, also called *primary rate,* is offered to commercial customers of an ISDN who want to hook up their PBXs or local area networks. It consists of a multiple group of 64,000 bits per second B channels. For example, primary rate consists of 23 B channels and one D channel (*23B + 1D*). It offers a 1,544,000 bits per second bandwidth divided into 23 B channels at a rate of 64,000 bits per second each and one D channel at 16,000 bits per second. Basically, 23B + 1D has the same capacity as a T-1 circuit (capacity of 1,544,000 bits per second) even though the mathematics is not accurate to the bit (23 times 64,000 bits per second plus 16,000 bits per second is equal to 1,488,000 bits per second). The slight difference between the two figures is unused capacity. Obviously, these are for high volume data transmission users. This 24-channel ISDN (23B + 1D) is the standard in North America, but Europe seems to prefer a larger ISDN (31B + 1D).

On the other hand, the basic access service is indeed a new communication facility because it is a circuit to either a business or a private residence that consists of two 64,000 bits per second paths plus one 16,000 bits per second circuit path. In either case, it probably will be a single communication circuit, wire, coaxial cable, optical fiber, microwave, or otherwise, into the user's facility.

The interconnection for the basic access service to your organization might be as shown in Figure 7-4. It involves a *network termination box* at the customer's site. Users get a single access communication circuit (local loop) that can carry 144,000

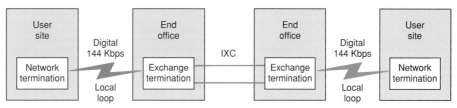

Figure 7-4   Integrated Services Digital Network (ISDN) showing use of network termination and exchange termination boxes.

bits per second (2B + D or 64K + 64K + 16K) between the user's premises and the local telephone company end office. The D channel uses a Q.931 message format that contains the calling party number, the type of service requested, any user-to-user information that must be transmitted, and so forth. The D channel is referred to as "out-of-band" signaling because it is outside of the B channel that carries voice, data, or image transmissions. Once the data transmission from the user site reaches the local telephone company end office, it enters an *exchange termination box.*

An exchange termination box in the first end office combines the signals (data, voice, and image) for further transmission over the IXC to the telephone company end office in the city to which the transmission is being sent. At the distant end office, the information enters another exchange termination box. From this point, the information is sent over another single access line (144,000 bits per second local loop) to the receiving user site. At the receiving premises, the information again enters a network termination box, and it is distributed to the appropriate station, node, terminal, or microcomputer.

AT&T now has a chip that can be incorporated into communication boards that are the interface for digital telephones, terminals, and microcomputers with the Integrated Services Digital Network. The chip implements the 2B + D ISDN standard. The chip also has the built-in capacity of formatting data (acting like a protocol converter) according to High-level Data Link Control (HDLC) protocols. If inserted into a microcomputer, the chip allows any microcomputer to integrate with this newer ISDN communication circuit.

In summary, ISDN is a digital communication circuit standard. The communication companies of the world believe ISDN will replace leased circuits and dial-up circuits as they presently are configured.

T CARRIER CIRCUITS

T carrier circuits are leased digital circuits with a transmission capacity of 1,544,000 bits per second moving over two pairs of wires. The *T carrier system* is the North American telephone industry standard for interconnecting digital communication systems. It is a hierarchy of digital transmission and multiplexing standards ranging from T-1 to T-4.

The North American Digital Hierarchy		
Digital Signal Format	Number of Voice Channels	Speed (bits/second)
DS-0*	1	64,000
DS-1	24	1,544,000
DS-1C	48	3,152,000
DS-2	96	6,312,000
DS-3	672	44,376,000
DS-4	4,032	274,176,000

*DS-0 is the signaling standard that divides frames into virtual channels.

T Carrier System			
T Carrier Circuit	Number of Voice Channels		Speed (bits/second)
	PCM	ADPCM	
T-1	24	48	1,544,000
T-1C	48	96	3,152,000
T-2	96	192	6,312,000
T-3	672	1,344	44,376,000
T-4	4,032	8,064	274,176,000

Figure 7-5 Digital signals in the North American Digital Hierarchy compared to T carrier circuits. PCM is pulse code modulation and ADPCM is adaptive differential pulse code modulation.

T-1 Circuits A *T-1 circuit* usually is defined as any digital communication system operating at a synchronous data rate of 1,544,000 bits per second. Data can be transmitted over a T-1 circuit at speeds ranging from 56,000 to 1,544,000 bits per second. Digitized voice uses 64,000 bits per second. By digitizing voice signals and multiplexing them with time division multiplexing, T-1 circuits allow for 24 simultaneous voice channels. T-1 circuits transport their data or voice messages according to a signaling format called DS-0. This is known as the *North American Digital Hierarchy;* therefore, *DS-0* defines the format of the signal that passes over a T-1 circuit. Compare the North American Digital Hierarchy (upper half of Figure 7-5) with the T carrier system (lower half of Figure 7-5).

DS-0 stipulates that data be transmitted in 192-bit frames, followed by a framing bit. The framing bit synchronizes the clocks in both user and telephone company equipment. Each frame contains twenty-four 8-bit characters (24 × 8 = 192 bits), plus 1 framing bit to equal 193 bits. The frames are transmitted at a rate of 8,000 per second. Take 193 bits per frame, multiply it by 8,000 frames per second, and you get 1,544,000 bits per second.

DS-0 divides frames into virtual channels. The DS-0 standard evolved from requirements for transmitting voice over T-1 links. Because T-1s are intrinsically digital, voice transmitted over a T-1 link must be digitized. The most common method of digitizing voice is pulse code modulation. With PCM, voice is digitized by sampling voice signals at the rate of twice the effective bandwidth (the bandwidth of a voice grade circuit is 4000 Hz), or 8,000 times per second. Each analog sample is digitized to a resolution of eight bits. Because there are 8,000 samples per second and each sample is eight bits, each voice signal requires a data rate of 64,000 bits per second (pictured in Figure 5-21), as opposed to the 56,000 bits per second for data. Note that the 8-bit character for data only uses seven bits for the data character, whereas the digitized voice uses all eight bits. Therefore, 8,000 parity bits for the 8,000 data characters are redundant (64,000 − 8,000 = 56,000).

Digitized voice usually is transmitted over T carriers, and new methods of digitizing voice are appearing each year. One of the newest methods is called *adaptive differential pulse code modulation* (ADPCM). This method digitizes voice at 32,000 bits per second instead of the traditional 64,000 bits per second used by standard pulse code modulation (PCM). As you can see in the lower half of Figure 7-5, the use of ADPCM makes the T-1 carrier twice as efficient because it can handle 48 voice channels (telephone circuits), rather than 24 as in pulse code modulation.

AT&T makes extensive use of pulse code modulation internally and transmits quite a bit of its information in pulse code modulated digital format over T carriers. The T-1 carrier uses two pairs of wires with digital amplifiers spaced approximately 6,000 feet apart to carry its 1,544,000 bits per second (24 voice/data circuits). The T-1 carrier is used for short haul transmission over distances up to approximately 50 miles. As a rule of thumb, a T-1 carrier with a capacity equivalent to 24 voice grade lease lines costs about the same per month as 12 to 14 individual voice grade lease lines might cost if leased separately.

Fractional T-1   *Fractional T-1,* which sometimes is called FT1, offers portions of a 1,544,000 bits per second T-1 circuit for a fraction of its full cost. Users who need more transmission speed than voice grade (19,200 bits per second) can have digital service at 56,000 bits per second, or a T-1 circuit at 1,544,000 bits per second. The jump from 56,000 to 1,544,000 bits per second is a costly one. For this reason, users now can lease individual 64,000 bits per second DS-0 channels on T-1 circuits. Each T-1 circuit has 24 DS-0 channels of 64,000 bits per second each (24 × 64,000 + 8,000 = 1,544,000 bits per second). The purpose of the 8,000 bits per second is for signaling, not data.

AT&T's fractional T-1 allows users to lease digital private lines in variations of 128, 256, 384, 512, and 768 thousand bits per second. US Sprint and MCI provide slightly different fractions. The European equivalent of the North American T-1 is called E-1, and its transmission speed is 2,048,000 bits per second.

T-2/T-3/T-4 Circuits   A *T-2 circuit* can transmit data at a rate of 6,312,000 bits per second. Basically, a T-2 circuit is a bundle of four T-1 circuits. Stated differently, a T-2 circuit has four times the bandwidth of a T-1 circuit.

A *T-3 circuit* allows transmission at a rate of 44,376,000 bits per second, although most articles refer to this rate as 45 megabits per second. This is equal to a bandwidth of 28 T-1 circuits.

T-3 circuits are becoming popular as the transmission medium for corporate backbone networks because of their 45 megabits per second capacity. At the low speed end, these T-3 circuits can be used as 672 different 56,000 or 64,000 bits per second channels. They also can be used simultaneously for both voice and data services.

As an example, a T-3 circuit can be cut into different fractions, just like a fractional T-1. An organization can use one or more of the 28 T-1 circuits (1,544,000 bits per second) between various sites, or it can use fractional parts of one of the T-1 equivalent circuits within a T-3 circuit. The common carrier divides one of the T-1s in the T-3 circuit into one one-half segment of a T-1 (768,000 bits per second) and two one-quarter segments of a T-1 (384,000 bits per second each). The organization then has flexibility in leasing various fractions of the T-1, such as three quarters, one half, or one quarter.

The traditional method of obtaining a T-3 circuit is via a piece of hardware called a *M-13 multiplexer*. This device gathers together 28 T-1 signals and uses two sets of time division multiplexing to produce a T-3 circuit. These multiplexers cost anywhere from $4,000 to $10,000 each. They are the T-3 equivalent of the digital channel bank for T-1s. A second method of obtaining a T-3 circuit is by having digital cross-connect switches, which sometimes are referred to as *digital access cross-connect systems* (DACSs). The third multiplexing alternative for T-3 circuits is to use a piece of hardware called an *add/drop multiplexer* (ADM). These devices allow the individual T-1 circuits to be added to, and dropped from, a T-3 circuit at a particular site. This is an especially useful hardware device if you want to multidrop T-1 circuits at an organization's various branch offices. T-1 multiplexers, digital channel banks, and digital cross-connect switches were described in the section on multiplexing in Chapter 4 (see page 128).

A *T-4 circuit* transmits at a rate of 274,176,000 bits per second. This is equal to a bandwidth of 178 T-1 circuits. Obviously, an organization using either T-3 or T-4 circuits must have a tremendous need to transmit very large quantities of data. Looking at the lower half of Figure 7-5, you can see that a T-4 circuit can carry 4,032 simultaneous voice telephone calls by using pulse code modulation (PCM). Alternatively, the 4,032 separate transmissions can be data transmissions between microcomputers.

SYNCHRONOUS OPTICAL NETWORK (SONET)

The *Synchronous Optical Network* (SONET) standard is being developed by the National Exchange Carriers Association, which is accredited by the American National Standards Institute (ANSI). This is a standard for optical transmission at gigabits per second speeds. For example, digital signals transmit on T-1 circuits at 1,544,000 bits per second and on T-3 circuits at 45,000,000 bits per second. SONET transmission speeds begin at the OC-1 (optical carrier level 1 will be discussed in a moment) level of 51,840,000 bits per second and ultimately will go as high as OC-256.

For example, other SONET transmission speeds are OC-9 at 466,560,000 bits per second, OC-18 at 933,120,000 bits per second, OC-24 at 1,244,160,000 bits per second, OC-36 at 1,866,240,000 bits per second, and OC-48 at 2,488,320,000 bits per second. One telephone company now has equipment carrying interoffice traffic on its fiber optic IXC circuits at 155,520,000 bits per second (OC-3) and 622,080,000 bits per second (OC-12). With speeds like these, it is easy to see why the telephone companies are installing optical fiber cable instead of copper cable when they install new circuits in cities for metropolitan area networks (MANs) or for cross-country links. As you have already learned, even the new undersea cables are optical fiber instead of copper.

The basic transmission frame for SONET is the *STS-1 frame,* which can be viewed as a matrix with 90 columns and 9 rows for a total of 810 characters (bytes). Each character of the frame is an 8-bit byte; therefore, each frame consists of 6,480 bits or 810 characters. STS-1 transmission is accomplished row by row and left to right until all the bytes are sent.

When STS-1 electrical signals are converted to optical signals, they are called *optical carrier level 1* (OC-1) signals. Each higher rate in the SONET fiber hierarchy is defined as a multiple of OC-1, with SONET data rates having been defined as high as OC-48 or 2.4 gigabits (2,488,320,000) per second. Each level above OC-1 is created by multiplexing. SONET is not yet fully implemented, but it is in the final stages of emerging into a standard for high speed fiber optic networks. Digital cross-connect switches or T-3 add/drop multiplexers (see previous section) still will be required to connect SONET networks with the existing North American network of T carrier circuits. Notice that the slowest SONET OC-1 optical transmission rate of 51,840,000 bits per second is slightly faster than the T-3 rate of 44,376,000 bits per second.

SATELLITE SERVICES

Several common carriers offer satellite channels for voice, data, facsimile, and various wideband applications. Basically, a *satellite channel* is defined as a four-wire equivalent voice grade circuit; therefore, users get a 4000 hertz bandwidth and a four-wire equivalent circuit. Available transmission rates can range from 300 to 19,200 bits per second for voice grade and 1,544,000 bits per second for T-1.

As was mentioned in the earlier discussion of voice grade circuits, users are notified when transmission is going over a satellite circuit because it may affect their protocols (rules by which two devices communicate). A half duplex protocol cannot be used successfully with satellite transmission unless satellite delay compensation is added. Instead, full duplex protocols must be used. Satellite channels usually are less costly than ground-based voice grade channels such as microwave transmission, wire pairs, and coaxial cables. If a greater capacity is needed, it is possible to lease a bundle or group of voice grade satellite channels to increase bandwidth beyond the standard 4000 hertz for a single voice grade channel.

The FCC has approved the use of a Direct Broadcast Satellite service to private homes. This means you can install a small (2.5-foot) dish antenna on your roof and receive television signals directly from medium-powered communication satellites orbiting some 22,000 miles above.

SOFTWARE DEFINED NETWORKS (VIRTUAL NETWORKS)

To make traditional leased voice grade circuits more competitive, it now is possible to lease a *software defined network* (SDN) communication circuit. SDNs are built on public switched networks to provide a private leased circuit for the leasing organization. The user leases a virtual circuit from Point A to Point B rather than a hardwired physical circuit as is normal with a voice grade leased circuit. Needless to say, a software defined network circuit costs less than a "physical" voice grade leased circuit.

Software defined networks are virtual lease line services. (Virtual circuits were discussed in the Chapter 6 section on packet switching.) These virtual network services enable customers to use dial-up facilities for extending private networklike functions to geographically dispersed sites that could not otherwise justify the cost of fixed-wire leased lines. A *virtual network* is a logical creation that provides a connection on a message-by-message basis, but it appears to be a dedicated circuit to the user. These networks are created within the memories of carrier network switches by programming the call-routing data. Firms use virtual networks to avoid the cost of leasing or purchasing network switching equipment and dedicated leased transmission facilities between their network nodes (stations).

All three of the major long distance carriers offer virtual networks. AT&T's service is called the Software Defined Network (SDN), US Sprint's is called the Virtual Private Network (VPN), and MCI's, Vnet. These services allow interconnection between most major U.S. cities and other major cities throughout the world. They also allow transmission speeds ranging from a very low 1200 or 2400 bits per second up to a high of 1,544,000 bits per second. Undoubtedly, the high end of this range should increase in the future. An example of how one virtual network operates is AT&T's Software Defined Network. It gives users control of their own special call-routing programs that are stored in AT&T's network. Customers can access the database containing the description of their network configuration and change the configuration as their network grows or as their business needs change.

The Global Software Defined Network (GSDN) is a private international virtual networking service. GSDN uses AT&T's Worldwide Intelligent Network to create a private virtual network between an organization's sites in the United States and its foreign sites. Software controls this network, making it appear to users that they have the features and performance of a dedicated physical network. When the network needs to be reconfigured, the network updates the software rather than physically moving circuits. GSDN is less expensive than international long distance service and requires much less commitment than configuring a network using standard leased circuits. This 9,600,000 bits per second service provides point-to-point virtual circuits that can handle voice, data, and facsimile. GSDN is available to Australia, Belgium, Canada, France, Italy, Japan, the Netherlands, Norway, Singapore, Spain, and the United Kingdom.

SWITCHED MULTIMEGABIT DATA SERVICE (SMDS)

The regional Bell Operating Companies offer *switched multimegabit data service* (SMDS) as an alternative to private network data transmission within the LATA areas (intraLATA) in which they operate. AT&T plans to offer an interLATA switched multimegabit data service. The new SMDS is aimed at local area network (LAN) interconnection. For example, it allows users to have Ethernet-to-Ethernet or token ring-to-token ring interconnection between two LANs at speeds equivalent to a T-1 circuit, or 1,544,000 bits per second.

Most of the regional Bell Operating Companies want to introduce SMDS at two transmission rates: *DS-1* at 1,544,000 bits per second or *DS-3* at 44,376,000 bits per second. Look back at the top half of Figure 7-5 and you will see how DS-1 and DS-3 compare. Data communication articles often refer to the ''DS-1 signaling rate'' instead of saying 1,544,000 bits per second. SMDS is a precursor to the full broadband Integrated Services Digital Network (ISDN) transmission and the full implementation of SONET at OC-3 rates (155,520,000 bits per second).

The advantage for users of SMDS is that today's most expensive element in a typical high speed wide area network is the circuit between different sites. Each circuit, whether it is a T-1 (DS-1 signal) or a T-3 (DS-3 signal) circuit, is a non-switched point-to-point connection that goes from Site A through the local Bell Operating Company end office to Site B. With SMDS, each corporate regional site requires only one circuit to connect to the BOC end office because messages on that circuit can be switched to the single circuit that goes from the BOC's end office to the organization's headquarters. Prior to SMDS, organizations had perhaps a half dozen incoming T-1 circuits to the central headquarters if they wanted to connect to six different regional offices. Now there might be only one or two (if required by capacity) T-1 circuits between the headquarters and the regional BOC end office containing the SMDS switch.

Switched broadband services like SMDS can be used to set up metropolitan area networks that operate at T-1 transmission speeds. Remember from Chapter 6 that metropolitan area networks (MANs) are networks within a metropolitan area. The IEEE 802.6 standard pertains to the development of metropolitan area networks; it defines their maximum diameter as 30 miles.

PERSONAL COMMUNICATION NETWORKS (PCNs)

American Telephone and Telegraph is exploring the possibility of offering a personal communication network (PCN) service. It recently asked the Federal Communications Commission for permission to start experimenting with the technology. AT&T is the first of the long distance carriers to consider offering a PCN service, although several of the regional Bell Operating Companies (BOCs), cable television operators, and specialty PCN firms have already applied for permission to start such services.

Personal communication networks use a wireless digital technology that can support both voice and data communications, as well as advanced network capabilities like Signaling System 7 switches that are located in the regional Bell Operating

Company end offices. Unlike traditional cellular telephone service, PCN is a complete network architecture. As such, it can be used instead of the local loop between homes or businesses and the regional BOC end office. In this case, it bypasses the local loop, thereby reducing basic revenues for the regional Bell Operating Companies that are bypassed. Instead of paying the regional BOC a monthly fee for the telephone service, you pay that same fee to the operator of the PCN. This means PCNs are in direct competition with the regional Bell Operating Companies controlling the local loops. If a long distance carrier like AT&T offers PCN service, it can be tied into that common carrier's long distance network. This tie-in can provide end-to-end digital connectivity for users in all the cities served by the PCN. In effect, it is like using cellular telephone technology to connect your home telephone to the worldwide telephone network.

The Federal Communications Commission has set aside the 1.8 to 2.2 gigahertz portion of the radio spectrum for personal communication networks. PCN technology has the potential to revolutionize data communications in the United States because users are able to communicate via small wireless handheld data terminals similar to the one shown in Figure 5-41 (page 210), laptop microcomputers, or desktop microcomputers. Picture a PCN user as having a laptop microcomputer with a small antenna for transmitting and receiving through-the-air messages.

DIRECT DISTANCE DIALING (DDD)

With *direct distance dialing* (also called *dial-up*), the normal voice telephone network is used for data transmission. The user dials the host computer telephone number, receives appropriate control signaling, enters passwords or authorizations, and connects to the host computer system.

Direct distance dialing uses an entirely different circuit path between the two telephone company central offices each time a number is dialed. Charges are based on the distance between the two telephones (in miles) and the time the connection is held open (the data transmission). The data communication user pays the same rate as the individual who uses the telephone for voice communication. Dial-up voice grade circuits have more noise and distortion than a private leased voice grade circuit because the signals go through the telephone company's central office switching equipment, although the newer digital switches bring DDD very close to the quality of a private leased circuit.

The telephone company does not make conditioning or equalization available for DDD circuits because each dialed call gets a different circuit path or routing. Equalization, however, can be obtained by using a more expensive high speed modem that performs automatic equalization after the call has been routed and connected. In addition, the DDD rate of transmission (bits per second) may be a little less than can be achieved on a private leased voice grade circuit because there is more noise and distortion on the circuit path. The point is that customers may have to transmit at a slightly lower bits per second rate to reduce the number of message blocks retransmitted because of errors. Direct distance dialing offers only two-wire connections; therefore, a special modem is needed to transmit simultaneously in both directions if full duplex transmission is required. This modem transmits in one direction by using one pair of frequencies and in the other direction by using a nonconflicting and different pair of frequencies. This was shown in Figure 5-28 in Chapter 5.

AT&T MEGACOM WIDE AREA TELEPHONE SERVICES (WATS)

The *AT&T Megacom WATS* is a special bulk rate service that allows direct dial station-to-station telephone calls, although it may be eliminated in the future. It can be used for both voice communications and data transmission. *Wide Area Telephone Services* (WATS) uses the 800 area code series in the United States. There also is an International Megacom WATS. It is available to 175 international locations, and it, too, uses the 800 area code numbers.

The 48 contiguous states are divided into 59 different WATS service areas. (Some states have more than one service area.) The geographical coverage of WATS from any one of these service areas is determined by the *band of service* to which the customer subscribes. For example, interstate service from California uses the following six bands:

- **Band 1:** Arizona, Idaho, Nevada, Oregon, Utah, and Washington
- **Band 2:** Colorado, Montana, Nebraska, New Mexico, and Wyoming
- **Band 3:** Iowa, Kansas, Minnesota, Missouri, North Dakota, Oklahoma, South Dakota, and Texas
- **Band 4:** Alabama, Arkansas, Illinois, Indiana, Kentucky, Louisiana, Michigan, Mississippi, Tennessee, and Wisconsin
- **Band 5:** Connecticut, Delaware, Florida, Georgia, Maine, Maryland, Massachusetts, New Hampshire, New Jersey, New York, North Carolina, Ohio, Pennsylvania, Rhode Island, South Carolina, Vermont, Virginia, Washington, D.C., West Virginia, Hawaii, Puerto Rico, and the U.S. Virgin Islands
- **Band 6:** Alaska

The state of California has two service areas, Northern California and Southern California, each of which is a different WATS band. The list of states served in bands 1 to 5 differs, depending on the state. For example, band 1 from Missouri includes Arkansas, Illinois, Iowa, Kansas, Kentucky, Nebraska, Oklahoma, and Tennessee. (Compare this with California's band 1 above.) As might be guessed, the first five bands out of New York are almost the direct opposite of bands 1 to 5 out of California. Band 5 out of California is similar to band 1 out of New York. When a customer subscribes to a band, such as band 4, service is automatic to all lower bands (in this case bands 1 to 3).

The WATS bands described above for *interstate WATS service* have no relationship to *intrastate WATS service*. California, for example, has a northern and a southern service area; therefore, WATS intrastate service can be for northern California only, southern California only, or statewide. Interstate WATS service does not include your home state; therefore, it is necessary to lease both interstate and intrastate WATS services if access is needed to your home state.

Interstate WATS service is available on the basis of the first 25 hours of usage, the next 75 hours, and over 100 hours of usage per month. Charges for either intrastate or interstate WATS are a flat fee for a specified number of usage hours.

If WATS service is used for data communications and the call holding time is less than 60 seconds, billing is for one minute of usage (one minute average call holding time). WATS service also is limited to one direction only; it is either *outward dialing* or *inward dialing*. Inward (In-WATS) and outward (Out-WATS) capability cannot be combined onto a single WATS circuit. The user has to subscribe to two circuits to have both inward and outward dialing.

AT&T combined all of its WATS and WATS-like services into a single family of WATS services. This new family of services includes Pro WATS I, Pro WATS II, Pro WATS III, Megacom WATS, All Pro WATS, the Pro WATS state plan, Multi-Location WATS, and the old WATS. AT&T's intent is to replace the usage-sensitive banded WATS scheme just described with a new one based on distance. This new distance-sensitive pricing structure is expected to benefit AT&T's WATS users by lowering their costs and simplifying network optimization.

AT&T MEGACOM®

As mentioned above, AT&T is replacing its banded pricing WATS service with a scheme based on distance. This new service is called AT&T Megacom, and it has two variations, the AT&T Megacom Service and the AT&T Megacom 800 Service.

The *AT&T Megacom Service,* which is outbound, is replacing outward dialing WATS. It gives users a new, simplified pricing structure that allows them to call anywhere in the United States, Puerto Rico, and the U.S. Virgin Islands with potential cost savings. This new pricing is based on the mileage and duration of each call, rather than on the geographic areas associated with the old WATS rates. Megacom eliminates the banded geographic pricing structure under WATS, and users are billed at the same rates for calls within the same area code, regardless of distance.

The *AT&T Megacom 800 Service,* which is inbound, is replacing inward dialing WATS. It introduces a slightly different toll-free calling that enables businesses to receive incoming calls in a cost-effective manner. With AT&T Megacom 800, users are able to receive calls from any location or selected groups of locations in the United States, Puerto Rico, Canada, Mexico, and the U.S. Virgin Islands. When you dial an 800 area code number, you are using either a Megacom 800 service or a WATS line. Again, billing is based on the duration of each call and the distance between the caller's area code and the area code of whomever is being called. International 800 service is now available to more than 50 countries.

If you have ever wondered how the 800 area code numbers work, see the accompanying How 800 Area Code Numbers Work box.

HOW 800 AREA CODE NUMBERS WORK

To see how a toll-free 800 call is handled, let us follow a call as it moves through the network. AT&T, MCI, and US Sprint all offer 800 services. We will assume that the number you want to dial is 1-800-999-5676 and that you have New York Telephone as your local telephone company.

When you begin dialing, New York Telephone sees this call as a 1+ number. This means it is a long distance call that should be assigned to AT&T, MCI, US Sprint, or the like. The local telephone switching equipment then checks the first six digits of the number, which in this case is 800-999. The local telephone company immediately knows it is an 800 call and one that should be switched to MCI because the 999 identifies it as an MCI call. If the first six digits were 800-542, the call would be switched to AT&T because 542 designates AT&T.

The local telephone company now routes the call to the MCI point of presence (POP) switching office. The *point of presence* is the switching office to which the local telephone terminates subscribers' circuits for long distance dial-up or leased line communications. At this point, whether the call is destined for MCI, US Sprint, or AT&T, it enters a large network database switch. The MCI switch receives all the information about the call, including the 800 number dialed and the telephone number from which the call originated. The MCI network database switch knows it has a call coming from, let us say, 212-591-6500 and going to 800-999-5676. The database switching computer might look at the time of day, the day of the week, or even a specific day of the year. After looking at these parameters, it then sends a message through the network. This message might say "I have a call coming from New York City" and the call starts moving across the country through the network to the destination number in less than a second.

In actuality, the destination number may not be the 800 number. Depending on the time of day, day of week, or specific day of the year, the switch knows from its database to translate the 800 number to another number. For example, if the call is made before noon on any day, it might convert the number dialed (800-999-5676) to 415-291-0616. After noon, the calls might be routed to another number in either the same city or some other city. Another option is for it to translate the 800 number to a number that connects to a dedicated access line (DAL) going directly to a corporate headquarters where a large group of people answer telephones. The concept of switching calls to different numbers based on the time of day means calls can be answered by people in Philadelphia in the morning and by people in San Francisco or even Honolulu later in the day.

In summary, the database switching computer receives the telephone number of the caller and the 800 number being dialed. It then establishes the time of day, the day of the week, or the day of the year so it can determine the telephone number or dedicated access line to which the call will be switched. As you can see, 800 numbers often switch their calls to some other area code and telephone number in a manner that is transparent to the caller.

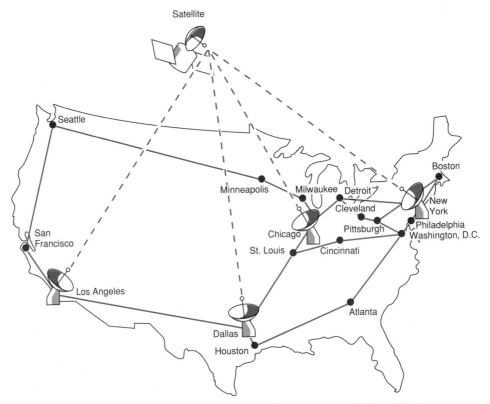

Figure 7-6   Packet switching network using satellite and terrestrial-based links.

PUBLIC PACKET SWITCHED SERVICES

Public packet switched services interconnect many cities and usually offer transmission speeds up to 1,544,000 bits per second. The network compensates for differences in transmission speed and different protocols between various switching nodes (SNs). The packet network also provides code conversion from one code to another. Data is segmented into 128-character (1024-bit) blocks or packets. Users access the service via private communication circuits, public dial-up circuits, or other packet switched networks. Figure 7-6 shows a packet switched network that has both ground-based circuits and satellite circuits. Each city represents a switching node.

In packet switching the user does not design or maintain the network. The customer may be, in fact, only a network user. This can be an advantage because it relieves customers of the many technical burdens related to designing and maintaining a private network.

As an example of a public packet switched service, American Telephone and Telegraph offers a service called *ACCUNET*®. This packet service is used throughout the United States and offers digital transmission speeds of 4800, 9600, and 56,000 bits per second. ACCUNET T1.5 (1,500,000 bits per second) and T45 (45,000,000 bits per second) support their high capacity networks by ACCUNET Customer Service Centers (ACSCs). Users access these ACSCs by a dedicated 800 number. ACSCs offer a combination of equipment and technical expertise to monitor network performance around-the-clock for seven days a week. The ACCUNET service conforms to the CCITT recommendations for the X.25 packet interface protocols.

The technical details on how packet networks operate were covered in the section on packet switching networks in Chapter 6.

DIAL-IT® 900

The *DIAL-IT 900 Service* allows many different users to call a 900 area code telephone number because it can handle 7,000 simultaneous incoming calls. These services have "sponsors" who arrange with AT&T to have their telephone number established. The sponsors have the responsibility of advertising this service to encourage people to call. Each caller is charged for the telephone call, although a sponsor may elect to pay the caller's charges, thereby making it a "free" call.

Two different arrangements are possible with DIAL-IT 900. The first is *information,* which may be either a prerecorded message or a live hookup. For example, the prerecorded call may be something as simple as a dial-a-joke service that allows callers to hear a recording of jokes. The recording originates at the sponsor's premises and so can be changed as often as the sponsor wishes. By contrast, live hookups allow callers to listen in on astronauts' conversations during space missions or to hear what is happening at a shareholders' meeting.

The second arrangement, a *call-counting* or *polling service,* allows callers to dial the 900 number to express preferences or vote on some question that is put to them by mail, over the radio, or through a television broadcast. This polling service requires two numbers, one for each opinion. It can require more numbers if callers are asked to express several opinions.

To explain how this service works, we must describe its cost. (All other costs are covered in Chapter 8.) When callers use the 900 service number, they are billed $0.45 per minute for 407 prefixes, $0.55 for the first minute and $0.35 for each additional minute for 350 prefixes, and premium rates for all other prefixes. (The prefix is the first three digits of the telephone number.) The sponsor can opt to pay for the call. Once the call volume exceeds 1,000 calls or call minutes per day, the sponsor earns

$0.02 for every call minute between 2,001 and 5,000

$0.03 for every call minute between 5,001 and 10,000

$0.04 for every call minute between 10,001 and 20,000

$0.05 for every call minute over 20,000

There are now discounts when the daily minimum average is 2,000 calls or 2,000 minutes of usage per day. The discounts range from 10 percent when the monthly charges are between $50,000 and $100,000 to a high of 23 percent when the monthly charges exceed $200,000.

AT&T also levies certain charges on the sponsors. With the prerecorded information arrangement there is a $250 flat fee, and the number must generate a weekly average of 2,000 calls per day per week. With the polling or voting arrangement, sponsors pay $25 per day for a minimum of 500 calls per day. If the call totals for either service fall below the minimum, sponsors are charged $0.25 for each call under the required total.

The DIAL-IT 900 Service has become controversial because numerous telephone subscribers have accidentally dialed, or their children have dialed, these numbers, and they have been billed with charges they consider unfair. The telephone companies now offer 900 number "blocking." With this feature, customers can ask to have outgoing 900 number calls blocked (stopped), so that anyone calling 900 numbers from a specific telephone is prevented from succeeding.

TELEX

Teletypewriter exchange service, or *telex*, is a data transmission exchange between two terminals. (It excludes voice communications.) Each subscriber has a keyboard-style terminal and can contact any other subscriber in the telex network. This is nothing more than an alternative to the voice telephone network, but it has the ability to transmit only hard copy between subscribers. Subscribers pay a monthly fee plus so many cents per minute of connect time. The connect time charge is only for the time it takes to transmit a message from one subscriber's terminal to another.

Western Union Corporation is the common carrier that offers telex service. In a major financial restructuring, Western Union has bought the ITT Worldcom telex network. These two telex services have been merged and combined onto the Easy-Link packet transport network to enhance Western Union's telex service. Even though there are an estimated 1.5 million telex subscribers worldwide, Western Union has experienced declining revenues in this area because customers are switching to facsimile devices, which are more affordable and can be used on the dial-up voice network. To meet this new market, Western Union has introduced EasyLink FAX^{SM} to accompany its reorganized EasyLink Telex^{SM} service.

FOREIGN EXCHANGE SERVICE (FX)

Foreign exchange service, or simply *FX service,* allows a user to call telephone numbers in another central office via the dial-up telephone network, but without incurring any charge other than that of a local call.

If an organization is located in the downtown center of a major city but most of its customers are in the suburbs, then it might lease a FX circuit. The telephones at the downtown company are connected directly to the telephone company's central office in the suburban area. In other words, a FX circuit is one that runs from your telephone instrument to the telephone company's end office in another area. When a FX circuit connects a downtown end office to a suburban end office, it allows distant suburban subscribers to have the same "free" dialing privileges as telephone subscribers in the nearby downtown area. When the telephone instrument is picked up by the suburban caller, the dial tone is directly from the downtown end office. If you list your company's telephone number in the suburban telephone book, people may call you at what appears to them to be a local number. In reality they reach you over the FX circuit.

The cost of FX service is the same as a voice grade private leased circuit plus the cost of a single telephone at the distant central office. Although this service may appear to be similar to intrastate WATS, it is not because the user does not have to dial the 800 area code and it accepts both incoming and outgoing calls.

COMMON CONTROL SWITCHING ARRANGEMENT (CCSA)

The *Common Control Switching Arrangement* is a private long distance dialed network. A switching arrangement allows interconnection of channels terminated in the switching equipment provided by the common carrier. The service is offered for large corporations and government agencies to interconnect several or hundreds of business operations, thus saving on telephone costs. A flat fee is paid for which the common carrier establishes a private telephone system interconnection for voice telephones, data hardware, and PBXs.

The largest CCSA is probably the U.S. government's Federal Telecommunications System (FTS). Many states also have set up private telephone systems that are designed, implemented, and maintained by the common carrier providing the CCSA service.

HOTLINE

The *hotline service* directly connects two telephones in distant cities. When either of the two receivers is lifted, the telephone rings at the other end of the connection. This is a point-to-point service and is available only in selected cities.

ELECTRONIC MAIL (E-MAIL)

Electronic mail is similar to voice mail except the user must key in (or type) the message so the recipient receives a textual-style printed message. Electronic mail is important in the office, but voice mail may be used as frequently.

One advantage electronic mail has over voice mail is that people tend to feel more comfortable delivering a lengthy or complex message in writing rather than leaving a verbal message.

Electronic mail, like voice mail, can be used to send messages to people when a two-way dialogue is not an immediate necessity. Thus, you can schedule future meetings, send messages to individuals or groups of people, overcome the problem of different time zones, and not worry if your recipient is unavailable when an electronic mail message is sent to an electronic mailbox.

Any user who has a portable terminal or microcomputer with a modem can connect to an electronic mail network. To review the features of an electronic mail system, reread some of the features that were listed in Chapter 2 for voice mail (see page 72); they are the same. Many firms have in-house E-mail systems on their wide area and local area networks.

Electronic mail systems must have standards governing their behavior if they are to operate properly. The two most important E-mail standards are the CCITT's X.400 and X.500. The *X.400* standard defines message handling for electronic mail. It operates at layers 6 and 7 of the OSI Reference Model (described in Chapter 9). X.400 defines user agents (UAs) and message transfer agents (MTAs), along with the names and addresses required for an electronic mail system. Each user has a mail agent, which is their user agent (UA). This UA allows the person using the system to type a message, include the recipient's address, and also receive incoming messages. The interface between two user agents is accomplished by a message transfer agent (MTA) that takes a message from a sender's user agent and delivers it to the UA to which it is addressed.

X.400 also defines a private and a public domain. A *private domain* is a private electronic mail system, whereas a *public domain* is a public electronic mail system that everyone can use, but with a charge. When an organization's private domain is connected to the common carrier's public domain, E-mail messages can be addressed on a worldwide basis. X.400 is very significant because it creates a standard for international user communications, just as there is a standard for interconnecting facsimile machines on an international basis.

X.500 is the directory service standard for Open Systems Interconnection (OSI) networks. It is the telephone directory of all possible users of an electronic mail system, and it governs the external behavior of the directory software. X.500 defines the standards for such things as the directory of user agents. This is the interface between the user and the directory, letting users access the directory. The primary purpose of the X.500 standard is to provide a worldwide directory for obtaining addresses to facilitate sending electronic mail messages throughout any public domain E-mail system and from or to any private domain E-mail system for which outside access may be allowed.

In summary, the X.400 standard defines how the E-mail system works, and the X.500 standard defines the directory of users so the proper address can be obtained in order to send E-mail messages. In a way, X.500 is similar to the current public telephone directories used to obtain another person's telephone number, and X.400 is similar to the public telephone company network that interconnects all the circuits so they work with each other even when a telephone call goes between different cities or countries.

As competition increases in the public telephone networks, you will be able to transmit both electronic mail and voice mail using your home telephone and microcomputer. All that is required for the electronic mail portion is a small interactive terminal and a modem.

Public electronic mail subscriber services are available from numerous sources that sell mailboxes connected to, and controlled by, that vendor's computer system. Some of the common ones are

Western Union Business Services	EasyLink
MCI International	MCIMail
General Electric Information Services	Quick-Comm
US Sprint Communications	Telemail
International Telephone & Telegraph	Dialcom
AT&T Information Systems	AT&T Mail
CompuServe	EasyPlex/InfoPlex
Tymnet Global Network	ONTyme
The Source Telecomputing	The Source

These mailboxes enable users to communicate with other subscribers at both local and remote sites. Although these public electronic mail services are less costly initially than an in-house corporate system, their capabilities are not always well suited to companies' needs. In addition, the levels of security required by a corporate user may not be met.

Most electronic mail is interoffice and intracompany; therefore, large corporations may do better by developing their own in-house electronic mail system. This system might be superimposed on the corporate local area networks or on any other existing networks. You even can put both electronic mail and voice mail on the same intracompany network. Several organizations also market PC-to-PC electronic mail packages. Market observers note that public E-mail firms will have to learn to connect with in-house E-mail or office automation packages such as IBM's PROFS, Wang's OAS, or DEC's All-In-One. The biggest challenge now is interconnecting public and private E-mail systems.

Implementation of an electronic mail system can be a shot of adrenaline to the corporate culture. Users find they can enter messages and get responses within hours, and they can check their mailboxes frequently, regardless of where they are within the corporate facilities, or even elsewhere in the world. E-mail usually changes both the communication patterns and the corporate culture of an organization. For example, upper-level executives tend to talk directly to employees several levels below them when using their electronic mail system. The corporate power structure, with its folkways and mores, usually precludes face-to-face or voice messages over several levels of management, but E-mail with appropriate carbon copies creates a more direct path down to the first level of employees.

Another impact of electronic mail on the corporate culture is that it allows employees to see the flow of information within the corporation, and they become aware that the company is using a system that is perceived as being attuned to the times.

Probably the most advanced and most useful communication systems have a combination of electronic mail and voice mail. Both are needed because many messages are better suited for voice, whereas others are more appropriate for the written documentation offered by an electronic mail system.

In the business office it might be too expensive and too time consuming to give every employee an electronic mail terminal, but most employees today have a telephone and can use voice mail. Electronic mail also requires more training. Furthermore, as observed earlier, human resistance to major change, such as going from voice conversations to typewritten conversations, makes implementation more difficult.

In summary, both electronic mail and voice mail are major factors in developing the automated office. Voice mail will become a major feature of the world's public telephone systems; electronic mail will become part of these telephone systems only when the user has an interactive terminal. In less developed countries it may be difficult enough to teach a person how to use a voice telephone, much less an interactive keyboard-driven terminal.

KEY TERMS

2B + D

23B + 1D

ACCUNET

American Telephone and Telegraph (AT&T)

AT&T Communications

AT&T Megacom

AT&T Megacom WATS

Basic access service

Bell Operating Company (BOC or RBOC)

Common carrier

Common Control Switching Arrangement (CCSA)

Communication facility

Communication services

Conditioning

Deregulation

DIAL-IT 900 Service

Dial-up

Digital service

Direct distance dialing (DDD)

DS-0

Electronic mail (E-mail)

Equal access

Equalization

Exchange access service

Federal Communications Commission (FCC)

Foreign exchange (FX) service

Fractional T-1

Hotline service

Integrated Services Digital Network (ISDN)

InterLATA

Interstate

IntraLATA

Intrastate

Leased circuit

Local access transport area (LATA)

Local Exchange Companies

Local exchange service

Long distance common carrier

MCI Communications Corporation

Measured use service

Monopoly situation

North American Digital Hierarchy

Optical carrier level 1 (OC-1)

Personal communication network (PCN)

Point of presence (POP)

Primary access service

Private circuit service

Private domain (E-mail)

Public domain (E-mail)

Public packet switched service

Public Utilities Commissions (PUCs)

Regulation situation

Satellite channel

Software defined network (SDN)

Straight copper circuit

STS-1 frame

Switched multimegabit
data service (SMDS)

Synchronous Optical
Network (SONET)

T carrier circuit

T carrier system

T-1/T-2/T-3/T-4 circuits

Tariff

Tariff 12

Tariff 15

Telex

US Sprint Communications
Company

Virtual network

Voice grade channel

Wide Area Telephone
Service (WATS)

Wideband analog service

X.400

X.500

SELECTED REFERENCES

1. AT&T Communications. *AT&T Catalog: Business Communications Systems* (catalog no. 3CS, published annually). Available from American Transtech, P.O. Box 45038, Jacksonville, Fla. 32232-9974.

2. AT&T Communications. *Catalog of Technical Publications* (PUB 10000 and 10000A). Available from Literary Data Center, Inc., G.P.O. Box C-9104, Brooklyn, N.Y. 11202.

3. AT&T Communications. *Local Access Transport Areas* (PUB SC 503-000). Available from AT&T Communications Consultant Liaison Program, 295 North Maple Ave., Basking Ridge, N.J. 07920.

4. AT&T Communications. *Network Communications: Applications & Services* (PUB 500-936). Available from AT&T Customer Information Center, 2855 North Franklin Road, Indianapolis, Ind. 46219.

5. AT&T Customer Information Center. *AT&T Documentation Guide* (PUB 000-11). Available from AT&T Customer Information Center, 2855 North Franklin Road, Indianapolis, Ind. 46219.

6. *Computerworld: Newsweekly for the Computer Community*. Published weekly by CW Communications, Box 9171, 375 Cochituate Road, Framingham, Mass. 01701-9171, 1967– .

7. Flanagan, William. *Guide to T-1 Networking: How to Buy, Install and Use T-1, from Desktop to DS-3*. New York: Telecom Library, Inc., 1990.

8. Giancarlo, Charles. "Making the Transition from T-3 to SONET," *Telecommunications,* vol. 26, no. 4, April 1992, pp. 17–20.

9. "How Do You Build an Information Highway?" *Business Week,* September 16, 1991, pp. 108–109, 112.

10. Johnson, Johna Till. "CSU/DSUs: In Search of Universal Access," *Data Communications,* vol. 20, no. 11, September 1991, pp. 79–110.

11. Kessler, Gary C. "Simplifying SONET," *LAN Magazine,* vol. 6, no. 7, July 1991, pp. 36–37, 39–40, 42, 44, 46.

12. *Network World*. Published weekly by CW Communications, Box 9171, 375 Cochituate Road, Framingham, Mass. 01701-9171, 1983– .

13. Slutsker, Gary. "Divestiture Revisited," *Forbes,* vol. 147, no. 6, March 18, 1991, pp. 118–119, 121, 124.

QUESTIONS/PROBLEMS

1. Define communication facility.

2. When an organization uses public packet switching networks, on what factors are the charges based?

3. Define common carrier.

4. Name three of the largest common carriers in North America.

5. Define deregulation.

6. A _____ is the schedule of rates and description of services offered by common carriers. What is it?

7. Who regulates common carriers and how is it done?

8. What is the primary difference between the evolution of data communication services in the United States and those in other countries?

9. Discuss the advantages and disadvantages of communication deregulation.

10. What aspect of communications is regulated?

11. Name four of the BOCs (also referred to as local exchange carriers or local telephone companies).

12. Define LATA.

13. How does local exchange service differ from exchange access service?

14. Why is equal access an issue?

15. What is the deciding factor in common carrier service quality?

16. Are customers able to specify the type of circuit when they contract for a private circuit?

17. Are leased circuits used exclusively by one user?

18. How do leased circuits differ from dial-up circuits?

19. Are voice grade circuits digital or analog?

20. Why is conditioning or equalization performed?

21. Why should a data communication manager know about something that seems as technical as conditioning?

22. How do wideband services differ from voice grade services?

23. When designing a network, what is the primary factor in deciding whether to use digital or analog service?

24. Why does the telephone company tell customers when they will be using satellite circuits?

25. Can the telephone company condition dial-up circuits? Why or why not?

26. What distinguishes ISDN from other services?

27. How do basic access service and primary access service differ?

28. How do network termination boxes differ from exchange termination boxes?

29. What are the two factors that distinguish T-1 circuits from others?

30. What is the T carrier system?

31. How does DS-1 differ from T-1?

32. How is digitized voice normally transmitted?

33. How many bits are in a DS-1 frame?

34. To what does the DS-0 standard apply?

35. What equipment multiplexes 24 voice channels onto one T-1 link?

36. What is the purpose of digital cross-connects?

37. How does a virtual circuit service differ from other types of circuits?

38. How do measured use services differ from private leased circuit services?

39. Can full duplex be used with direct distance dialing (dial-up)?

40. WATS is a special bulk rate service. How is WATS service charged?

41. How does AT&T Megacom service differ from WATS service?

42. What are the primary advantages of using public packet switched services?

43. Why might business firms wish to have 900 number arrangements?

44. What may replace telex services?

45. Give a simple example of FX service.

46. Describe the function of a Common Control Switching Arrangement.

47. Give a simple example of a hotline service.

48. What is the biggest challenge facing E-mail systems and why?

49. How does electronic mail change the corporate culture?

50. An organization can lease a private network but not have physical wires interconnecting the different nodes. What is this called?

51. What is a 2B+D? Define it.

52. What would be an ideal block length when using synchronous transmission over a packet switching network?

53. If Western Union tells you it offers a 100 words per minute telex service that uses characters consisting of seven bits plus parity, one start bit, and two stop bits (a word is six characters), what is the transmission rate in bits per second?

54. Identify and describe some of the private circuit (lease) services.

55. Identify various measured use services.

56. What is the difference between interstate/intrastate data communications and inter-LATA/intraLATA?

57. What is the difference between the FCC and a state PUC?

58. If you make a call from San Francisco to San Diego (California), is it intraLATA or interLATA?

59. Over which circuit is 64,000 bits per second common?

60. Which circuit uses a digital 1,544,000 bits per second transmission rate?

61. Suppose you contracted with AT&T for a DIAL-IT 900 number. On it you offered advice on a certain instructor's exam. Assume that you averaged 3,761 call minutes per day for the ten days prior to final exams and then canceled the DIAL-IT 900 number. Did you make any money?

62. Who decides whether voice grade circuits will be wire pairs, coaxial cables, or microwave?

63. Name and describe two controversial tariffs.

64. What is the most popular arrangement for common carriers to handle growing international telephone service?

65. Can you have switched services on both dial-up and leased digital circuits?

66. What device makes switched digital service possible?

67. What kind of circuit does a Group 4 facsimile machine require?

68. Distinguish between T-1, T-2, T-3, and T-4 circuits.

69. Describe how fractional T-1 operates.

70. Name the three ways to obtain a T-3 circuit.

71. Describe SONET.

72. What is the basic SONET transmission frame?

73. What is it called when STS-1 electrical signals are converted to optical signals?

74. Describe the regional Bell Operating Company switched service that interconnects two local area networks at T-1 circuit speeds. What purpose does it serve?

75. What is a personal communication network?

76. Why might PCNs revolutionize communications in the United States?

77. With what service is A&T replacing WATS?

78. Describe the telephone company service to customers called *blocking*.

79. Name the two major standards governing electronic mail.

NEXT DAY AIR SERVICE CUMULATIVE CASE STUDY

Background on Next Day Air Service

Assume that Next Day Air Service has an operational wide area network (WAN) in place, and a configuration for a local area network has been suggested. Now the board of directors is focusing on the kinds of communication facilities NDAS will need over the next several years. Recall that the current WAN uses dial-up to connect the remote offices to Atlanta and New Orleans and private leased circuits to connect these two hubs to Tampa.

Mr. Coone meets with you to discuss the future of communications for Next Day Air Service. He feels NDAS needs a network that can be expanded readily, but without having a major impact on the way Next Day Air Service conducts its routine business. He assumes Next Day Air Service will continue its current financial growth pattern, and he wants a recommendation on what may be necessary for Next Day Air Service to meet the competition. Next Day Air Service considers the Mississippi River as the East/West dividing line for the Continental United States. The projected growth trends for the United States are as follows.

Western U.S.: Traffic volumes to increase 120 percent over the next three years and one additional office will be opened every two months.

Eastern U.S.: Traffic volumes to increase by 60 percent over the next three years and one additional office will be opened every four months.

Questions/Problems for the Next Day Air Service Case

1. Based on your knowledge of NDAS's network, what would you suggest for the future to connect the remote offices to the hubs at Atlanta and New Orleans and the hubs to the corporate office in Tampa? Will the current facilities be adequate?

2. What specific voice service should NDAS acquire for customer inquiries concerning parcel deliveries?

3. The offices using modems to dial up the multiplexer in New Orleans have been reporting problems with garbled screens. You suspect a problem of circuit distortion. What would you suggest to remedy this situation?

4. Assume that Atlanta received permission to install a local area network. Atlanta wants to have access to the LAN located in Tampa. What type of service is aimed specifically at a switched LAN interconnection?

5. How could NDAS combine toll-free 800 number service (WATS) with interactive voice response (IVR) to better serve its customers?

Chapter Eight

NETWORK DESIGN FUNDAMENTALS

A perplexing problem when designing data communication networks is not whether the technology is available but how best to adapt its offerings to meet the changing and challenging networking needs of organizations. This chapter presents the fundamentals of designing data communication networks. It uses the systems approach to design, enumerating 13 detailed network design steps. We present several network design software packages at the end of this chapter (beginning on page 366). You can use this PC-based software to calculate network costs. The software is helpful when students have network design projects, especially when combined with the network drawing software described earlier in Chapter 6 (beginning on page 246).

INTRODUCTION

To help the network designer, this chapter makes numerous cross-references to other pages in this book. (See the box Page Number Cross-References for an explanation of these cross-references.)

This chapter uses a two-tiered approach in teaching how to design networks. The first part focuses on learning how to design by using manual or hand calculations, and the second part introduces computerized network design techniques. The reason for adopting this approach is that before you can proceed to computerized network design, you first need to understand the basics of how a communication network is conceived and designed. This approach is similar to the one used when you learned about basic mathematics: first you learned how to add numbers, and then you learned how to add them with a calculator.

It is not always possible to appreciate what a computer is doing when you are using computerized network design programs. For example, suppose you have a

---

PAGE NUMBER CROSS-REFERENCES

Many cross-references to other pages in this book appear throughout this network design chapter. *You should ignore them if you are familiar with the technical concept or term being discussed where the cross-reference appears.*

These cross-references are for the benefit of readers who may wish to start with the design chapter during the first week of class instead of reading Chapters 1 through 7 first.

The cross-references also may help more experienced readers who want to refresh their memories quickly about a technical detail.

Should you encounter an unfamiliar term or technical concept that is not cross-referenced to a specific page, you should refer to the Glossary (page 681), Index (page 723), or the detailed Table of Contents (page xii) to learn more about that term or concept.

---

computer program that calculates the airline mileage distance between two telephone company end offices. The technique used determines the vertical and horizontal coordinates of each end office and then employs those figures in a mathematical formula to calculate the mileage. This mileage then is multiplied by the circuit's cost per mile (tariffs were defined on page 269) to determine its monthly lease cost. When the computer program says that vertical and horizontal coordinates are used to determine the mileage, you may not understand what is meant unless you have read the first part of this chapter and calculated it yourself by using the vertical and horizontal coordinates. We describe how to use vertical and horizontal coordinates and give examples. In addition, important items such as needs assessment factors, feasibility factors, and evaluation criteria are discussed.

This chapter also includes basic line cost network design problems. We use the word "basic" because tariffs have become very complex since the United States deregulated the communication industry. The tariffs now apply to very small local access transport areas (see LATAs on page 274), and there are hundreds of different tariffs. As a result, it has become more difficult to use manual design methodologies when the number of nodes in a network exceeds 20 or 30. By reading this chapter and calculating the cost of a circuit link or designing a small three- to six-node network, you will gain an in-depth understanding of network design. The Computerized Network Design section later in this chapter introduces the art of network design using computer-based software tools.

THE SYSTEMS APPROACH TO NETWORK DESIGN

You should use the *systems approach* when planning a new data communication network, when enhancing a current network, or when planning for the use of public data networks (PDNs). In the systems approach, all influences and constraints are identified and evaluated in terms of their impact on the network design. Whether the network achieves success or just marginal utilization may be determined before a single piece of software or hardware is ordered. The key ingredient for success lies in planning based on the system's interface with the users. Far too often, data processing-oriented network designers take an equipment-oriented approach or a software-oriented approach. In today's world of data communications the designer must emphasize user *application systems*. For example, there are two major classes of data communication network users: the organization's management and its user personnel.

Managers must accept the network and believe in it, or they will not trust the data/information/reports they receive from it. If the information management receives is not Consistent, Accurate, Timely, Economically feasible, and Relevant (CATER), then management may not utilize the network to its fullest extent.

The *users* who work with the network on a day-to-day basis must be able to accept it, or their productivity may fall drastically. When productivity decreases, the cost of carrying out basic office functions may increase the cost of the final product or service by 10 to 50 percent. Office productivity recently has taken on added importance because we are moving from a predominantly manufacturing society to an information society that is service-oriented. In other words, proportionately more people are involved in information-related work than in manufacturing/ assembly work. We now need to move the industrial engineers from the factory environment into the automated business office and network environment.

Many businesses are drowning in data, while at the same time thirsting for meaningful information. To meet this challenge, we need databases from which we can identify, sort, and retrieve the necessary data so it can become meaningful information. Having this meaningful information is not enough, however. We still need to have a method for delivering it to managers and users. Delivery is accomplished by means of data communication networks, and these networks are what the following 13 steps will help you design.

THIRTEEN STEPS FOR NETWORK DESIGN

The following 13 steps should be used when designing a new data communication network. On the other hand, some steps can be omitted if a current network is being enhanced. For example, you might begin at Step 6 or Step 7 when enhancing a current network.

Your redesign may involve nothing more than setting up a gateway to connect to a public packet switching network. If so, you might go directly to Step 10 or Step 11. The exact sequence and number of steps are determined by the scope of the network design project. Even so, serious consideration should be given to all 13 steps. A detailed explanation of how to carry out the step is given for each.

1. Conduct a feasibility study
2. Prepare a network design plan

3. Understand the current network
4. Define the new network requirements
5. Identify the geographic scope
6. Analyze the messages
7. Calculate network traffic and circuit loading
8. Identify network security and control
9. Design network configurations
10. Evaluate software considerations
11. Evaluate hardware considerations
12. Calculate network (circuit) costs
13. Implement the network

As you progress through these 13 steps, keep in mind that the basic building blocks of a network are the following.

- Circuits, including voice grade lease or dial-up, wideband, digital, Integrated Services Digital Network (ISDN), T-1, SONET, SMDS, software defined networks (SDNs), satellite, and the like.
- Hardware, including microcomputers, terminals, modems, multiplexers, front end processors, host mainframe computers, intelligent controllers, routers, protocol converters, line adapters, and the like.
- Software, including protocols, OSI Reference Model, Systems Network Architecture (SNA), X.25, HDLC, SDLC, and the like.

From the viewpoint of a mechanical engineer, a network involves *pipes, pumps, and people* (PPP). In this context, pipes are the network circuits that carry the messages, pumps are the hardware and software that push and switch the messages through the network, and it is people who manage and use the network.

Your design will use circuits to connect the hardware, which will be controlled by the software (see Figure 8-1). Be sure to read Chapter 11 first if you are going to design a local area network.

1. CONDUCT A FEASIBILITY STUDY

The purpose of a *feasibility study* is to determine the possibility or probability of either improving the *current network* or developing a totally *new network*.

The first point that must be made about a feasibility study is that it may not be necessary to conduct one. Management may have performed it already in order to identify the problem or the purpose and objectives of the proposed network. Perhaps the scope of the proposed network already has been defined. Furthermore, it is entirely possible that either management or economic realities in the business environment have dictated that an online data communication network must be devel-

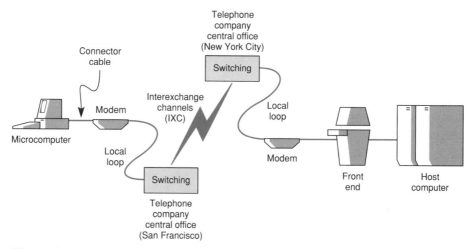

Figure 8-1 A simple network connecting a microcomputer in San Francisco to a host computer in New York. The circuits are the interexchange channels (IXCs), local loops, and the connector cables. The hardware is the microcomputer, modems, switching office, front end, and host computer. The software to run the network may be located within the microcomputer, switching office, front end, and host computer.

oped to meet the competition. If that is the case, it is no longer a question of whether to design a new network, but how it will be done.

For example, can you imagine any major airline deciding that a network costs too much or does not meet its objectives? If an airline decided against a network, it would cease to be competitive with the other airlines; therefore, the feasibility of a ''go/no go'' network decision is made even before the airline can start to think about a feasibility study.

Of course, we now are talking about a feasibility study that helps determine whether or not to proceed with a new network. The feasibility study also may be the basis for deciding whether to design a wide area network (WAN), metropolitan area network (MAN), backbone network (BN), or local area network (LAN). The Network Definitions box in Chapter 1 (page 5) defines these networks, and Figures 6-5 through 6-8 beginning on page 228 are diagrams of these four types of networks.

Needs Assessment Factors A primary responsibility in proceeding with a feasibility study is to define the problem clearly and put it in writing. *Problem definition* involves identifying all the problems that may indicate the need for a data communication network. These problems, called *needs assessment factors,* may be analyzed to determine whether they contribute to the need for this new network (see the accompanying Needs Assessment Factors box).

Once the problem has been defined in this way, the purpose and objectives of the new data communication network are identified, the scope or boundaries the network will encompass are established, and perhaps some preliminary ''magnitudes'' of cost can be identified.

NEEDS ASSESSMENT FACTORS

- Need to interconnect microcomputers
- Increased volume of inputs/outputs
- Need for distributed data processing
- Obsolete network hardware/software
- Inadequate file structures (database)
- Unsatisfactory movement of data/information throughout the organization
- Inadequate interfacing between application systems and staff
- Documentation not available in a timely manner
- Unreliability of current network
- Inability to maintain current network
- Inadequate security/privacy
- Decreasing productivity
- Inadequate training
- Future growth that requires new methods
- Competition that forces change
- Negative effect of old network on employee morale
- New network viewed as having a positive effect on investments, cash flow, and so forth
- Inadequate floor space for personnel or files
- Avoidance of future costs
- Need for more timely access to information for improved decision making
- Increasing flow of information or paperwork
- Need to expand capacity for business functions or manufacturing
- Need to increase level of service quality or performance
- Need for new methods and better exchange of information in conducting international operations
- Reduction of inventories
- Need for a paperless office
- Desire to take advantage of future technology
- Need to conform to international network standards

The feasibility study might include some preliminary work on the geographical scope of the network, or the physical areas of the organization that will be interconnected by it. It may be appropriate to develop a rough-draft geographical map of the intended network.

Deliverable for Step 1   At the completion of this data gathering, a short, written feasibility study report should be generated. This report is the instrument by which you tell management what the problem is, what you have found its causes to be, and what you have to offer in the way of a solution. This report also states the purpose or *objectives* of the network to be developed.

The feasibility study results might be presented verbally as well. A verbal presentation provides management with an opportunity to ask questions or discuss issues that may have a bearing on whether to proceed. Your feasibility study should help management decide whether to start a full program for the design and development of a new data communication network. It usually results in a *go/no go decision* for the WAN, MAN, BN, or LAN.

2. PREPARE A NETWORK DESIGN PLAN

At this point the feasibility study has been completed, and management has given its approval to proceed with the design and development of a data communication network. Be sure to note that in this chapter we are designing a totally new network. Some of the procedures discussed in the remainder of this chapter may be eliminated if you are merely enhancing a current network.

Feasibility Factors   In developing the plan, remember that a successful *network design plan* always takes into account the following three *feasibility factors*.

- *Technical feasibility* of the network
- *Operational feasibility* for the users who conduct their daily business by using the network, and for managers who rely on its reports
- *Economic feasibility* to keep the network within budgetary limitations

Network Goals   The first step is to take the statement on the purpose or objectives of the network from design Step 1 and divide it into three distinct goals. The *major goal* is the reason the data communication network is being built. The object is to ensure that the network meets these requirements. Next, *intermediate goals* are other gains the system can make while serving its major purpose, hopefully with little or no extra expense. Finally, *minor goals* are the functions that a communication network can perform for the organization, but for which it is not quite ready (future requirements). The major goals are mandatory; the intermediate goals are desirable; and the minor goals are "wish list" items.

There is no way to outline the exact steps the plan should follow because the network must be customized for the organization and application systems it serves.

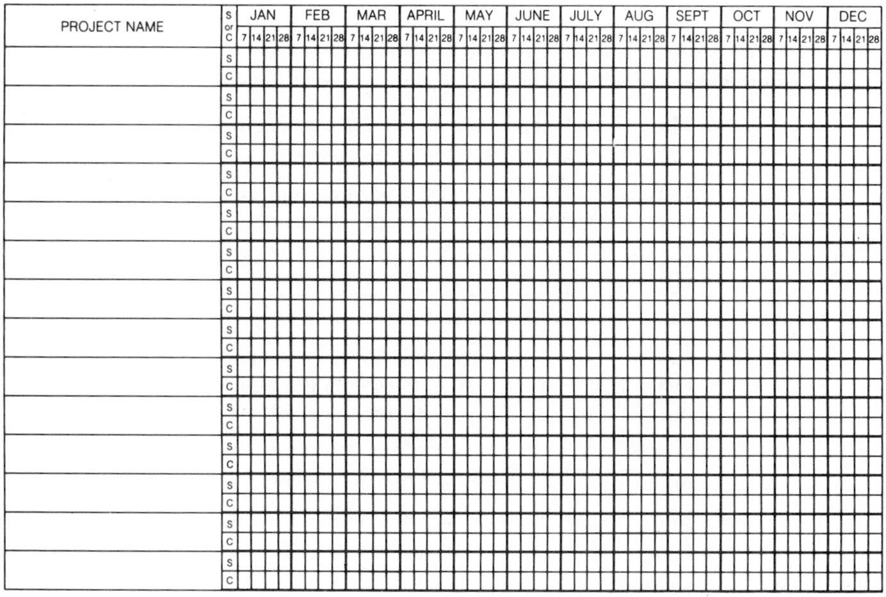

Figure 8-2 Gantt chart.

The goals the network is to achieve should provide the framework for the plan. For example, the major goal might be to speed up order entry and improve cash flow through better collections. The intermediate goal might be to integrate the accounting applications with the order entry operations. A minor goal might be to set up an electronic mail system sometime in the future. All too often network designers forget their priorities and concentrate on minor goals because of personal interest. When committed to writing, the goals serve as a constant reminder to avoid this trap.

The next step in developing a customized plan might be to identify the various departments that will use the network, sources of information, and a schedule for performing various activities. You can use a simple *Gantt chart* like the one shown in Figure 8-2 to plan the 13 design steps or you can use sophisticated planning software if it is available. In Figure 8-2, the horizontal axis represents units of time in weeks. List the different steps of your plan on the left vertical axis under Project Name. The S and C rows stand for "Scheduled" or "Completed," respectively. If you want to schedule a project step for June, you put Xs in the S row under June 7, 14, 21, and 28. As you complete the project, you put Xs in the C row to show the state of completion. We suggest using this Gantt chart to schedule the steps needed to complete your network design.

Network Evaluation Criteria   Finally, as the plan becomes finalized, develop some *evaluation criteria*. If evaluation criteria are developed at the beginning, then there is a yardstick at completion for measuring the success of the data communication network design, development, and implementation (see the Network Evaluation Criteria box). Insofar as possible, each criterion should be given a numerical value at the

NETWORK EVALUATION CRITERIA

- **Time** Are elapsed time, transaction time, overall processing time, response time, or other operational times reduced?

- **Cost** Are annual network cost, per unit cost, maintenance cost, or others, such as operational, investment, and implementation costs, reduced?

- **Quality** Is a better product or service being produced? Is there less rework because of the network? Has the quality of data/information improved? How can these quality factors be measured?

- **Capacity** Does the network have the capacity to handle workloads, peak loads, and average loads, as well as the long-term future capacity to meet the organization's needs in the next decade?

- **Scope** Was the network's scope properly defined? Does the network interconnect all the necessary business functions?

- **Efficiency** Is the network more efficient than the previous one?

- **Productivity** Has productivity of the user (information provider) and management (information user) improved? Is decision making faster and more accurate because of the information provided by this network?

- **Accuracy** Are there fewer errors? Can management rely more on this network than the old one?

- **Flexibility** Can the new network perform diverse operations that were not possible before?

- **Reliability** Are there fewer breakdowns of this network compared with the previous one? Is uptime very high with this network? The reliability/uptime of an online network is probably the best long-term criterion by which to judge its design and development.

- **Acceptance** Have the information providers, the information users, and the management accepted the network?

- **Controls** Are adequate security and control mechanisms in place to prevent threats to the network, such as errors and omissions, fraud and defalcation, lost data, breaches of privacy, disastrous events, and the like?

- **Documentation** Does the network have adequate written/pictorial descriptions documenting all its hardware, protocols, software, circuits, and user manuals?

- **Training** Are training courses adequate and are they offered on a continuous basis, especially for terminal operators? Are training manuals adequate and updated on a regular basis?

- **Network Life** Is the life of the network adequate? When a year is spent designing and implementing a network, its life should be of adequate duration to take advantage of the economies of scale.

beginning of the project. This value is used at project control points or on completion to provide the means of comparison that management needs to evaluate the success of the project. A method of risk ranking the evaluation criteria is described in Chapter 13 beginning on page 631. Ranking the evaluation criteria sometimes makes you reconsider the needs assessment factors or prompts you to rank them also.

These evaluation criteria can be used to evaluate the new data communication network after it has been developed. They also can be used to evaluate your own performance during the design and development of this new network. In this case, examine such items as whether development time schedules were on target. Were development costs within budget or was there a large cost overrun? Were any deviations from the original purpose or objectives and scope documented? Consider interactions with those affected by the network: Do they feel they were treated fairly, and are they satisfied with you and your design? Was there a lot of turnover on the project team during the design and development? As the plan is prepared (step-by-step approach), also develop evaluation criteria. If you ignore this step, someone else may do it and you may be judged by a set of criteria that do not relate well to your effort.

Deliverable for Step 2   The report at the end of Step 2 should discuss the technical, operational, and economic feasibility of the data communication network. The purpose of objectives from Step 1 should be divided into major, intermediate, and minor goals. In addition, the report should include a preliminary list of departments that are expected to use the network, as well as a tentative completion schedule. Finally, this report is incomplete if it does not contain a list of evaluation criteria.

3. UNDERSTAND THE CURRENT NETWORK

The object of this step is to gain a complete understanding of the current operations (application system/messages), including any network that is functioning. This step provides a *benchmark* against which future design requirements can be gauged. It should provide a clear picture of the present sequence of operations, processing times, work volumes, current communication network (if one exists), existing costs, and user/management needs.

Information Needs   To be successful at this stage, begin by gathering general information or characteristics of the environment in which the network must operate. Next, identify the specific applications that will use the new data communication network and any proposed applications that could use it in the future.

Learn something about the background of the industry in which the network will function (what competitors are doing in this regard), as well as about your individual company and the departments that are responsible for various applications.

Determine whether there are any legal requirements, such as local, state, federal, or international laws, that might affect the network.

Consider the people in different departments who will be affected by the network. Be sure to take into account the formal organization as shown on the organization chart, as well as the informal organizations within a specific department.

It is important to be aware that company politics might affect the design effort; people may tell you what they want to satisfy their personal interests rather than what is in the best interests of the organization.

You may have to develop a level 0 data flow diagram or an input, processing, output model[1] for *each* system that will use the data communication network. Your task is to identify each generic input to the network and each generic output. Describe and list each input, process, and output.

Identify the file formats so database planners can start to design the database and database access methodologies. You should be aware that transmission volumes increase dramatically when the network is used for database retrieval transactions and file transfers from microcomputers.

Techniques used to complete this step might include interviewing users, searching a variety of current records for message format and volumes, estimating and sampling for timings and volumes, and possibly comparing current application systems with similar ones that have been put on a data communication network.

Deliverable for Step 3   The documentation gathered during this step can serve as a future summary of the existing network. The report should include everything of importance learned during this step of the design. It is your written understanding of the network as it exists at the start of the design project. It should include any design ideas, notes on whether currently used forms or transmittal documents are adequate or inadequate, who was helpful or hindered progress, and any other impressions gained from interviews, meetings, data flow diagrams, flowcharts, sampling, inputs/outputs, and the like. In general, the report should contain information that can be referred to during the detailed development of the data communication network. It is the benchmark to be used for later comparisons. At the end of the network design, the question that may be asked is, "Are we better off with the new network than we were with the old one?" The benchmark information gathered at this stage will help answer this question.

4. DEFINE THE NEW NETWORK REQUIREMENTS

By the time the network design begins, certain items already should be established, such as definition of the problem, purpose or objectives, scope of the network, the major/intermediate/minor goals, evaluation criteria, general background information about the application systems that will use the network, and a thorough written understanding of the current network. With these items in hand, a list of *network requirements* can be developed. As you identify the new network requirements,

---

[1]*Fundamentals of Systems Analysis: Using Structured Analysis and Design Techniques,* 3rd ed., by Jerry FitzGerald and Ardra F. FitzGerald (New York: John Wiley & Sons, 1987). See pages 61–74 for data flow diagrams and page 290 for input, processing, output models.

keep in mind these two questions: "What is the purpose of the network?" and "What is the network to produce?"

The object of defining the network requirements is to assemble an overview of the functions to be performed by the *proposed network*. At this point, the data flow diagram (DFD) or the input, processing, and output model for each application system that will use the network might be of great value.

During the early stages of defining the network requirements, a review of the organization's long-range and short-range plans is advised. This review helps provide the proper perspective in which to design a network that will not be obsolete in a few years and that will meet the future requirements of the organization. These long- and short-range plans indicate such information as changes in company goals, strategic plans, development plans for new products or services, projections of sales, research and development projects, major capital expenditures, possible changes in product mix, new offices that must be served by the communication network, emphasis on security, and future commitments to technology.

It is during this step that the designer begins to formulate the details related to the required *circuit capacity* for handling average and peak message volumes, the various acceptable (and unacceptable!) *processing times* for applications and transactions, ways of increasing *productivity* for both managers and daily users, methods of improving *reliability* by increasing network uptime, and designing adequate *controls* to secure the network against unwanted events.

Prioritizing Requirements Once the network requirements have been identified, they should be prioritized (page 631 describes a risk ranking methodology for setting priorities). That is, they should be divided into *mandatory requirements*, *desirable requirements*, and *wish list requirements*. This information enables you to develop a minimum level of mandatory requirements and a negotiable list of desirable requirements that are dependent on cost and availability. Match these against your major, intermediate, and minor goals from Step 2. Mandatory requirements should match the major goals, desirable requirements should match the intermediate goals, and wish list requirements should match the minor goals.

Network requirements should be as precise as possible, regardless of the priority category into which they fall. For example, rather than stating "a large quantity of characters," state requirements in more precise figures such as "50,000 characters per minute plus or minus 10 percent."

At this point, try to avoid presenting solutions; only requirements are needed. For example, a requirement might state that circuit capacity should be great enough to handle 5,000 characters per second which will triple by 1995. It would be a mistake to state this as a solution by saying that a 9600 bits per second voice grade circuit is required. Solutions should be left for later, during Steps 9 through 12, when software and hardware considerations must be interrelated with the network configurations.

Moreover, it is necessary to identify each application that will use the network. If possible, also identify the message type each application uses. Knowledge of the applications helps not only now when identifying the network's requirements, but also later when identifying the geographical location for each node in the network.

Deliverable for Step 4   The report at the end of Step 4 includes information on the organization's long- and short-range plans, any future requirements that may have been uncovered, and some reasonable response times that are acceptable for the business operations being performed. These are not the potential response times the network must achieve. Instead, they are the response times workers require so they can complete their job tasks within a reasonable period of time. These response times make the network function for the benefit of the organization. Finally, the primary emphasis of this deliverable should be a detailed listing of the various requirements the new network must fulfill to achieve its goals. These requirements must be divided into three different priority categories: mandatory, desirable, and wish list requirements. One other item that should be included in this report has to do with message types. Take the general list of applications that are expected to use the network (this was developed during the Step 1 feasibility study) and list each application separately. As best as possible, list by application the specific message types that are to be transmitted over the network. Next, we are going to discuss response time, queuing, and simulation, which are useful when identifying the new network requirements.

Response Time   *Response time* in its simplest form is the time that elapses between the sending of an inquiry from a remote terminal and the receipt of the first character of the response at the same terminal. Therefore, response time includes transmission time to the computer, processing time at the computer, access time to obtain any needed database records, and transmission time back to the terminal.

The best indicator of response time for an undeveloped network is a set of statistics drawn from another operating network that supports the same application and uses the same protocol. In other words, examining a network with similar operating characteristics and applications is the best indicator of how well a planned network will perform. The problem is that finding such a duplicate system is almost impossible. If no similar network exists from which to draw performance data, then some predictive techniques must be used.

When using these predictive techniques, do not rely on average response times. Instead, always state the question as "*X* percent of all response times must be less than or equal to *Y* seconds." In other words, a typical statement might be that 95 percent of all response times must be less than or equal to three seconds. Mean and standard deviation of these figures might be used to identify the reliability of the final response time figure.

Cost and response time are inversely proportional. When the response time is shortened, the cost increases; when it is lengthened, the cost decreases. Factors that affect network cost include speed and capacity of the host computer, speed and size of the front end processor, capacity of the communication circuits, remote intelligent control devices, and software programs or protocols.

The specific components that contribute to response time are message input time, application processing time, and message output time, or

$$RT = MIT + APT + MOT$$

The *message input time* is the sum of the polling time, transmission time (including modem turnaround time and time for acknowledgment), and queuing time in a remote intelligent control device, front end processor, or host computer. The propagation time over the circuit usually is stable, but the other factors are determined statistically according to traffic volume. A typical input time might be 0.85 second.

The *application processing time* includes all program processing time and all input/output accesses to the database. As might be expected, these timings are variable, depending on message traffic and the number of transactions being handled by the host computer or by the server if it is a local area network (LAN). An example of a typical application processing time might be 0.75 second.

The *message output time* is the sum of the internal queuing in the host computer, front end processor, and any remote intelligent control devices, and the transmission time (including all modem turnaround, selection, and acknowledgment times). Again, the propagation time over the circuit usually is stable, whereas internal queuing is a variable figure depending on the current volume of transactions at the host/front end processor. An example of a typical message output time is 0.90 second.

If the sum of the typical average times is approximately 2.5 seconds, imagine what would happen if another half second were added for propagation delay time for satellite circuits or other delays, such as having to retransmit a large number of messages because of network-imposed errors. In a typical communication application, the component that becomes the most sensitive to increased volume is the application processing or database handling time in the host computer. Response time on a current network is easy to measure by use of a network analyzer (or even a stopwatch). Predicting it during the design stage, however, requires detailed network analysis involving queuing theory or simulation and a lot of common sense.

Queuing theory and simulation programs break the process into more segments than just message input time, application processing time, and message output time. Simulation takes into account such factors as terminal buffering, effect of an intelligent terminal control device, statistical time division multiplexers, mode of transmission used by the modem, communication circuit speed, communication circuit error rates, queuing at transmission nodes, front end, or host computer, line configurations such as point to point/multidrop/multiplex, message lengths, expected arrival times of messages, propagation delays, any priorities built into the system, average versus peak loads, central control versus interrupt, type of applications, speed of output devices, and intrinsic factors within the host computer, such as its hardware architecture, software, or protocols.

Queuing   Queuing theory allows for the definition of such elements as service time, facility utilization, and wait time at the host. A *queue* is a waiting line—of people to purchase theater tickets, of airplanes waiting to take off, or of automobiles stopped for a red light. When several network users send jobs to a shared printer, the jobs wait in the printer's queue until it is their turn. Single server and multiserver queuing relationships must work within the environment of network priorities. We cannot begin to explain, in this text, the techniques of statistical and queuing formulation. That should be reserved for a more advanced course, although modeling is introduced in a later section of this chapter. Estimations can be of the best or worst case. These techniques often yield average results that describe the average operational performance of a network. Statistical views of network performance based on queuing theory can vary from real performance by as much as 20 percent, but they can provide estimates of their own accuracy.

Simulation   *Simulation* is a technique to model the behavior of the communication network. Response time is viewed as an elapsed time incurred, which is part of the accumulation of the elapsed times of a series of individual events. Sophisticated programs can be written to simulate the action of a series of events, and these programs add up the elapsed times of each event. Simulation programs run on large machines and they can execute several thousand polls (polling was described on page 213) within a few seconds to generate a statistical view of the projected network. Simulators typically ignore error conditions because error conditions are the exception and not the rule. They can be built into sophisticated simulators, but this vastly increases the complexity of the programs. Queuing analysis can verify the predicted results of simulation. Vendors offer simulators to assist in examining the effects of many parameters on a communication network's projected performance such as

- Number of intelligent control units per circuit
- Number of terminals per intelligent control unit
- Printers/printer buffer size/printer speed
- Modem delay for turnaround
- Propagation delay
- Statistical time division multiplexer delay (if any)
- Line protocol overhead
- Message lengths/occurrences/rates
- Host computer processing delays
- Database access delays
- Multiple queues or single queues
- Polling/selecting

5. IDENTIFY THE GEOGRAPHIC SCOPE

By definition, to design means to map out, plan, or arrange the parts into a whole that satisfies the purpose or objectives. At the beginning of this step, you must review the list of applications that are expected to use the network and identify the location of each one. The purpose of this activity is to identify all the physical locations (geographic locations) that must be interconnected by the planned network. The rough-draft geographic map developed during the feasibility study should be examined at this point, and a more detailed and accurate version should be prepared.

Mapping the Network   A data communication network can have four basic levels of *geographic scope.*

- International (worldwide network)
- Country (within the boundaries and laws of a single country)
- City or state (within the boundaries of a specific city, state/province, or local governmental jurisdiction)
- Local facility (within a specific building or confined to a series of buildings located on the same contiguous property)

With regard to these four levels, a wide area network (WAN) includes international, country, or state geographic levels. A metropolitan area network (MAN) includes a city. A backbone network (BN) can include a city, but usually it includes an organization's facilities only within one small geographic area. A local area network (LAN) includes only local facilities and normally does not cross a public thoroughfare. At this point, you should be aware of a typical example of confusing communication terminology. Some companies call their "corporatewide network" a backbone network. This means they are referring to their wide area networks as backbone networks.

Usually it is easiest to start with the highest level, the international. Begin by drawing a network map with all the international locations that must be connected. At this level it is necessary only to interconnect the major countries and/or cities around the world. It is sufficient to have a map that shows lines going between the countries/cities. Details such as the type of circuit, multiplex, multidrop, concentrators, and the like have not been decided yet. See Figure 8-3 for an example of an international WAN. If the network does not cross international boundaries, then obviously this step can be omitted.

The next map you might prepare is the map for each country. Interconnections should be drawn between all cities within the country that uses the network. Again, a single line drawn between the cities is adequate because the type of configuration has not yet been decided. Figure 8-4 is a typical example of a country map intermixed with an international map because of the proximity of the two countries (the United States and Canada).

The next map to prepare is one of the city or state/province. This map can be divided into two levels. The first level uses a state map with lines drawn showing the interconnection among various cities within the state. Figure 8-5 is a state map. City maps are used at the second level. They show interconnection of various "local facility" locations within the city. Figure 8-6 is a city map. When two maps are used (both state and city), it does add another level. The advantage, however, is that it also decreases the complexity of simultaneously trying to design both intrastate circuits and intracity circuits. If either of these levels is omitted, the state-level maps may be the less vital. The city-level maps are needed to identify concentrator sites and multidrop locations, as well as individual terminal locations. At this point, lines are drawn only between the various interconnect points because configurations (multidrop, point-to-point, multiplex) have not been chosen.

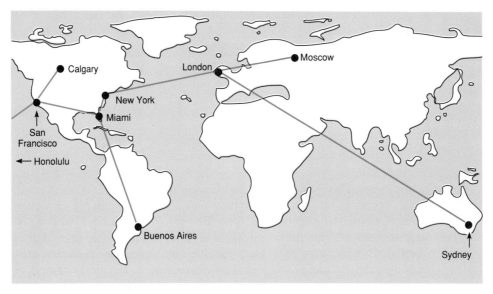

Figure 8-3   Example of a worldwide network map. A worldwide map is a wide area network (WAN).

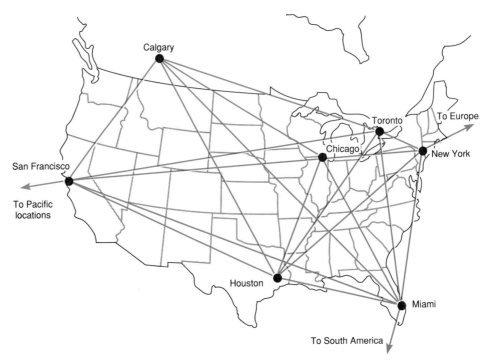

Figure 8-4   Example of a country map. A country map is a wide area network (WAN).

Figure 8-5 Example of a state map showing California.
A state map usually is a wide area network (WAN).

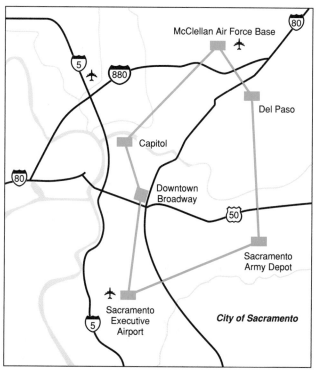

Figure 8-6 Example of a city map. A city map can be
either a metropolitan area network (MAN) or a backbone
network (BN).

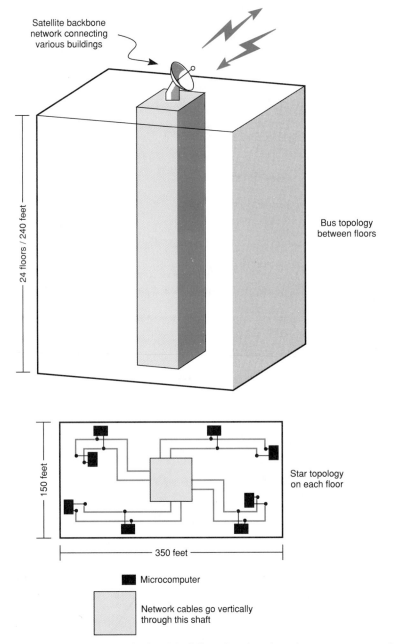

Satellite backbone network connecting various buildings

Bus topology between floors

24 floors / 240 feet

150 feet

350 feet

Star topology on each floor

■ Microcomputer

Network cables go vertically through this shaft

Figure 8-7   Example of a local building showing the microcomputers and cable layout on a floor.

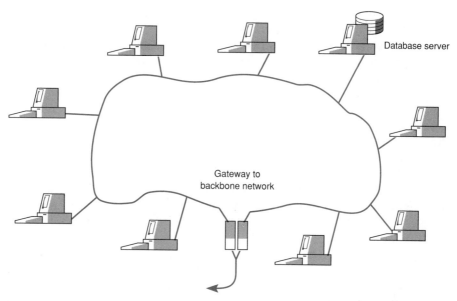

Figure 8-8 Example of a local area network (LAN) map. To add more detail, you can print on this drawing the name of the department in which each microcomputer is located.

The local facility "maps" are really pictorial diagrams because designers generally use blueprints or drawings of the building floor layouts (see Figure 8-7). Specific terminal locations can be identified on these pictorial diagrams. It is too early to identify concentrator/multiplexer sites, so this should be left until a later time. It is appropriate at this point to identify the location of current telephone equipment rooms that house communication circuits (voice and data). Another local facility map might be for a local area network (see Figure 8-8).

By the end of this task there are tentative locations for individual terminals and circuit paths for the local facility, intracity, intrastate, country, and international needs. To date, little is known about the volume of data that must be transmitted; nor is anything known about the type of hardware and software that might be required for this network.

Network Drawing Software Use the network drawing software that was described in Chapter 6 (page 246) to draw your maps for classroom projects. An alternative method is to use a photocopier to enlarge the map of the United States (see Figure 8-29 on page 363) and draw your network links on it. You also can use the photocopier's enlargement feature to obtain a single state map. For city maps, use the small inset maps of large cities found in a road atlas. Another option is to use Figure 6-20 (page 247) to draw a map, especially if it is for a local area network.

Deliverable for Step 5 The report at the end of Step 5 is the set of international, country, state, city, and local maps that were developed. Remember that the local maps might show a building, a floor layout, the interconnection of several buildings, or a local area network (LAN).

The next step is to analyze the specific messages, although this task can be performed simultaneously with development of the geographic maps and pictorial diagrams.

6. ANALYZE THE MESSAGES

The message analysis step may be combined with the previous step on identifying the geographic scope, but more often it is combined with the following step, which is calculate network traffic and circuit loading. It is identified as a separate step here so you clearly understand the level of detail that must be obtained during this very important step.

Characters per Message   In this step each *message type* that will be transmitted or received from each application system at each terminal location (node) is identified. In addition, each *message field* (data item/attribute) may need to be identified, along with the average number of characters for each field. Furthermore, it is necessary to identify *message lengths* and the *message volumes* that will be transmitted per day or per hour. It probably will be necessary to visit each location that will use the data communication network. These site visits are required to identify clearly each and every message type that will be transmitted or received. Because of these site visits, it may be desirable to combine Steps 5 and 6.

If the current system is a manual one, these messages might be on paper forms, but they also might be electronically generated messages or video screen formats on terminals. Each message should be described by a short title, and a sample of the message should be attached if there is a current equivalent. If there is no equivalent, all of the fields that are to make up the message must be identified in order to define the length of the message accurately. *Message analysis* sometimes reveals that the network will have to handle a greater volume of data than previously was thought.

After each message is described and samples of messages in the current system are collected, this data must be recorded. A simple form should be used to record this data, such as the one shown in Figure 8-9. The name of each individual message type is listed along with the number of characters in each message and a peak number if the length of the message can vary. It is always worth the effort to determine whether some of the messages have a peak number of characters per message. Peaks may occur during certain days of the year, hours of the day, or any other time unique to the business situation.

It should be noted here that most networks are built using the average number of characters for their basis because few organizations can afford the cost of a network built on the basis of the peak number of characters. The use of averages is even more prevalent when the choice is between average number of messages per day and peak number of messages per day.

Teller Inquiry System		
Message Name (Type)	Number of Characters per Message	Peak Number of Characters per Message
Passbook savings inquiry	22	28
Loan balance inquiry	82	82
Teller end-of-day closing	150	150

Figure 8-9   Messages and number of characters per message.

The network designer should note that a pure character count may be misleading with regard to the number of characters contained in the transmitted message. Header characters (identifying overhead-type characters within the message) and the data communication network control characters must be taken into account. The control characters can be such items as a consecutive message number, synchronization characters, carriage returns or tabulation characters when appropriate, and line control characters for the protocol (although the protocol may be unknown at this point). As a rule of thumb, 10 or 15 line control characters might be added to each message transmitted. Probably the best way to identify message lengths is to interview the people who run the current manual or computerized application system that will use the new network.

Number of Messages   Determining the volumes of messages is critical. Now that the average and peak number of characters for each message has been determined, the next step is to learn how many messages will be transmitted per day or per hour. To accumulate this information accurately, use Figure 8-10, which is a *network link traffic table*. As noted earlier, a *link* is an unbroken circuit path between two points.

The first item in the upper left corner is the identifier of a network link, which in this case is Calgary to San Francisco. Ultimately all of the links from Figure 8-4 would be listed in this column. The second column shows the name of the individual message type. The third and fourth columns show the average characters per message and the peak characters per message (if appropriate). The fifth and sixth columns show the average number of messages per day and the peak number of messages per day. The seventh and eighth columns show the average number of characters transmitted per day and the peak number of characters transmitted per day; these numbers are obtained by multiplying the characters per message by the number of messages per day.

Finally, when possible these traffic statistics (characters transmitted per day) should be divided into the hourly number of characters transmitted throughout the workday. This information can be used to spot problems with hourly peak volumes as the design progresses. For example, if a column total of the hourly number of characters transmitted between 9 and 10 A.M. has a volume that is 50 times the capacity of a single circuit network link, then a problem exists. The problem can

Network Link	Message Type	Characters/Message		Messages/Day		Characters/Day		Hourly Number of Characters Transmitted								
		Average	Peak	Average	Peak	Average	Peak	8-9	9-10	10-11	11-12	12-1	1-2	2-3	3-4	4-5
Calgary to San Francisco	Passbook savings Inquiry	22	28	1500	1650	33000	46200		12500	4000	4000	2000	1500	9000		
	Loan balance inquiry															
Down Totals						330,000	405,000									

Sum of This Column

Figure 8-10 Network link traffic table.

328

solve itself if you have some messages transmitted later, such as during the next several hours. Other solutions are to have some people work overtime or to design a network link that has the capacity to meet that peak one-hour volume, although cost may prohibit designing for peak volumes.

Even though the most important figure is the average number of characters transmitted per day, there may be important factors that cause peak volumes at various times during the day, week, or month. There also may be seasonal times of peak volumes because of holidays or legal requirements.

The designer should plan for varying volumes at different hours of the day. For example, in an online banking network, traffic volume peaks usually are in the midmorning (bank opening) and just prior to closing. Airline and rental car reservation network designers look for peak message volumes during holiday or other vacation periods. A military network designer finds extreme peaks in volume during crisis situations, and the telephone companies normally have their highest peak volume of calls on Mother's Day.

How to Estimate Message Volumes   You can calculate message volumes by counting messages in a current network or by estimating future messages. When possible, take a random sample for several weeks of traffic and actually count the number of messages handled each day at each location. If the application system is not on a network, you may have to physically count the paperwork forms.

If an online system is operational, network monitors/analyzers may be able to provide an actual circuit character count of the volume transmitted per hour or per day. Take care when selecting the sample of working days to ensure it is not an "out of normal" situation. When estimating message volumes for a network that does not yet exist, you can use conglomerate estimating, comparison estimating, or detailed estimating.

- With *conglomerate estimating,* representatives from each application system confer to develop estimates based on past experience.

- With *comparison estimating,* the network designer meets with people inside or outside the organization who have a similar system so they can supply estimates from their network.

- With *detailed estimating,* the network designer makes a detailed study of the overall application system and its future needs in order to develop subestimates, which then are added together to obtain the total volume of messages as we described above.

When making message volume estimates, be sure to take future growth into account so the network will meet the needs of the next decade. Do not worry about the accuracy of estimates at this point, although you should make them as accurate as possible. Accuracy may not be a major concern because of the stairstep nature of communication circuits. For example, assume a situation in which a voice grade circuit is used. It can be used to transmit at 19,200 bits per second, but to meet data volumes you need to transmit at 30,000 bits per second. This would require the lease of two voice grade circuits. The combined two voice grade circuits now have a maximum capacity of 38,400 bits per second, greatly exceeding the needed 30,000 bits per second. This overly simplified example demonstrates that if actual message volumes are higher than estimated, there may be plenty of spare capacity. On the other hand, the opposite problem may occur if estimates are too optimistic; the organization may be forced to lease two voice grade circuits when only one is needed. Hardware also can help because some modems can use compression to transmit at 38,400 bits per second using a single voice grade circuit.

Deliverable for Step 6   The report for Step 6 contains the list of messages with the number of characters per message (Figure 8-9) and the network link traffic table (Figure 8-10).

Now that individual message contents and the network link traffic table have been developed, there should be some feeling for the total volume of characters per day transmitted on each link of the proposed network. These are the volumes of characters transmitted from and to each local facility (node) where terminals will be located. The next step, which usually is carried out simultaneously with this step, is to determine network traffic and circuit loading.

7. CALCULATE NETWORK TRAFFIC AND CIRCUIT LOADING

Now that average/peak characters transmitted per day per link have been identified, work can begin on calculating the circuit capacities required to carry that traffic. They are based on the number of characters per message and the number of messages transmitted per hour or per day. They also can be augmented through the use of modeling.

At this point return to the geographic maps and pictorial diagrams (local facilities). Do these maps or pictorial diagrams still seem reasonable in light of the vast amount of further information that has been gathered during message analysis? At this time some of the maps or pictorial diagrams might be reconfigured slightly to further solidify the geographic configuration of the network. Remember to evaluate all the geographic maps: international, country, city/state, and local facilities.

Calculating Traffic on Each Link   The next step is to review all the network links over which data will travel. This may have been done when the network link traffic table was completed. If so, double-check at this time to verify that each message type was cross-referenced to the proper network link (columns 1 and 2 in Figure 8-10). If the hour-to-hour variation is significant, it may be necessary to take hourly peaks into account or adjust working schedules and work flow. For example, match the characters per day for each network link in Figure 8-10 with each network link that was shown on the country map (Figure 8-4). It is helpful when examining alternative configurations to list the characters per day for each link shown on Figure 8-10. It

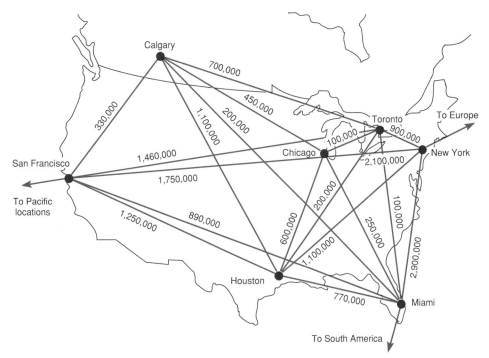

Figure 8-11   Link loading in characters per day for a point-to-point configuration.

is the column down totals (Figure 8-10) that really count. If the total number of characters transmitted in a single day on a single link is 330,000 or 405,000, then the network link has to operate at a speed that permits transmission of the 330,000 or 405,000 characters during the normal working hours. If it cannot meet this limit, certain adjustments have to be made. Now look at Figure 8-11. It shows San Francisco/Miami, 890,000; San Francisco/Houston, 1,250,000; and Houston/Miami, 770,000 characters per day. Later in the design, if the San Francisco/Miami traffic is multidropped through Houston, the total traffic on the Houston/Miami link will be 1,660,000 characters per day (890,000 + 770,000).

To establish *circuit loading* (the amount of data transmitted), the designer usually starts with the total characters transmitted per day on each link or, if possible, the number of characters transmitted per hour if peaks must be met.

Starting with the total characters transmitted per day, the network designer first determines whether there are any time zone differences between the various stations. This might be an international or national system with time zone differences that must be taken into account. For example, there is a three-hour time difference between Toronto and San Francisco. This means that if a host computer in Toronto operates from 7 A.M. until 4 P.M. (Toronto time), under normal circumstances there is only a five-hour working day in San Francisco, even assuming that someone is working through the lunch hour. By the time the people arrive at work in San Francisco at 8 A.M., it is already 11 A.M. in Toronto. Then Toronto shuts down its computer at 4 P.M., and it is still only 1 P.M. in San Francisco. This leaves the San Francisco facility with a workday that extends only from 8 A.M. until 1 P.M. The practical effect of this time difference is that the 1,460,000 characters (SF/TOR link in Figure 8-11) of data must be transmitted during a five-hour period rather than the eight-hour day you might expect. These effects have to be taken into account, or work schedules must be changed. Obviously, the Toronto host computer operating hours can be extended, or the San Francisco staff can start work earlier. There is no perfect solution to time zone differences, but the network designer must account for them.

Other major factors that affect circuit loading include the basic efficiency of the code used and TRIBs (see efficiency of a code on page 159 and TRIB on page 160). Synchronous transmission is more efficient than asynchronous transmission (page 153). The number of line control characters in the basic protocol affects line loading. For now, use 10 to 15 characters per message block. The application systems/ business future growth factors must be considered so the network will have a reasonably useful lifetime. Forecasts should be made of expected message volumes three to five years in the future. This growth factor may vary from 5 to 50 percent and, in some cases, exceed 100 percent for high growth organizations.

Some extra time should be allowed for transmission line errors (error detection and retransmission) that may result in the retransmission of 1 to 2 percent of the messages. Retransmission may be even higher when transmission is into or out of developing countries. The network designer also should consider a 10 to 20 percent contingency factor for the turnpike effect. The *turnpike effect* results when the network is used to a greater extent than was anticipated because it is available, is very efficient, and has electronic mail features. In other words, the network now handles message types for which it was not originally designed.

Other factors to consider when evaluating line loading might be whether to include a message priority system. Higher *priority messages* may require special identification and therefore may increase the number of characters per message. If the message mix changes and most messages become high priority over a period of time, then more characters will be transmitted during a working day. Moreover, a greater throughput may have to be planned to ensure that lower priority messages get through in a reasonable period of time. The learning curve of new terminal operators also may affect line loading. Operator errors and retransmissions are greater when a new system is being learned.

Another factor that might affect circuit loading is an inaccurate traffic analysis (confidence intervals). Try to account for any business operating procedures that might affect the network and volume of data transmitted.

Other factors that must be taken into account include the redundant characters and extra timing such as polling characters, turnaround time/synchronization characters, control characters in message frames and/or packets, modem turnaround time on half duplex circuits, message propagation time subtracts from the total useful throughput of data, printer time, lost time when statistical time division multiplexers are overloaded, and periods of high error rates. To calculate throughput, use the TRIB calculation from Chapter 5 (page 162).

Response Time Evaluation   At this point the network designer should review and establish some of the response time criteria that are required to meet the basic needs of the application system using the network. (Remember the response time equation presented earlier in this chapter.) Response time is a technical attribute of a network, but the application being run on the network is the primary factor that determines how short a response time is required. For example, a bank's automated teller machine (ATM) requires a very short response time, that is, 2.5 seconds or less. The bank requires a short response time in this situation because the customer is standing in front of the machine waiting to finish the transaction. On the other hand, the bank may be willing to accept slightly longer response times for terminals located inside the bank. For example, tellers may accept response times of 3.5 seconds, and loan officers entering new loan documents may accept response times of 5 to 7 seconds. The bank's network designer handles varying response times on the same circuit link by giving the highest priority to ATMs, second highest priority to the teller terminals, and third highest priority to loan officer terminals.

Finally, begin recording on the network maps and/or pictorial diagrams some of the bits per second transmission rates that will be required for each circuit link.

Link Capacity Requirements   Sometimes it is useful to show the transmission capacity required for each link. In Figure 8-11 we show the characters per day per link. Now add the bits per second transmission rate necessary for each circuit link. This helps when alternative network configurations, software, and hardware considerations are being developed and evaluated.

Look at the San Francisco to Houston link in Figure 8-11. It shows 1,250,000 characters per day. To convert characters per day to bits per second using asynchronous transmission, perform the following calculations.

$$
\begin{array}{rl}
1{,}250{,}000 & \text{characters per day} \\
\underline{\times\ 10} & \text{bits per character (asynchronous)} \\
12{,}500{,}000 & \text{bits per day} \\
\underline{\div\ 7} & \text{hours (assumes 7 working hours per day)} \\
1{,}785{,}714 & \text{bits per hour} \\
\underline{\div\ 60} & \text{minutes per hour} \\
29{,}762 & \text{bits per minute} \\
\underline{\div\ 60} & \text{seconds per minute} \\
496 & \text{bits per second transmission speed}
\end{array}
$$

Another example using synchronous block transmission might be the following. Assume each message is 200 characters long. This means 6,250 messages are transmitted per day (1,250,000 characters/day ÷ 200 characters/message). Also assume there are 10 control characters per message. This means there is a daily total of 62,500 control characters (6,250 messages × 10 control characters per message).

$$
\begin{array}{rl}
1,250,000 & \text{characters per day} \\
+\ 62,500 & \text{control characters} \\
\hline
1,312,500 & \text{total characters per day} \\
\times\ 7 & \text{bits per character without a parity bit} \\
\hline
9,187,500 & \text{bits per day} \\
\div\ 7 & \text{hours (assumes 7 working hours per day)} \\
\hline
1,312,500 & \text{bits per hour} \\
\div\ 60 & \text{minutes per hour} \\
\hline
21,875 & \text{bits per minute} \\
\div\ 60 & \text{seconds per minute} \\
\hline
365 & \text{bits per second}
\end{array}
$$

Neither of these two examples (asynchronous or synchronous) takes into account "other factors" such as the turnpike effect and retransmission because of errors. If you estimate that 1 percent of the blocks using synchronous transmission have to be retransmitted because of errors, that would add 63 more blocks of 210 characters each. If 1 percent of the asynchronous characters have to be retransmitted, that would add 12,500 more characters.

Deliverable for Step 7   The report for Step 7 adds the traffic analysis (messages and number of characters per day per link) to the documentation.

8. IDENTIFY NETWORK SECURITY AND CONTROL

Because the network probably will be the "lifeline" of information flow within the organization, *network security* and control are mandatory. All of the security and control mechanisms to be included in this data communication network must be taken into consideration during the detail design steps. As we stated earlier, we are well into an era in which information is the single most valuable resource within an organization. For this reason, it must be protected from all types of threats such as errors and omissions, message loss or change, disasters and disruptions, breach of privacy, theft, unreliability, incorrect recovery and restart, poor error handling, and viruses.

Control Spreadsheet Methodology   The methodology we use to identify areas in need of security and control requires development of a network *control spreadsheet*. The primary discussion describing development of this methodology is in Chapter 13, in the section How to Develop a Control Spreadsheet starting on page 624. For now, it is enough to know that this is the step in which you set up the control spreadsheet. Its development is continued through the remainder of the network design project.

The control spreadsheet shows the threats to the network and components or pieces of the network that must be protected. As the design effort continues, you identify controls that are needed to safeguard the components and stop the threats from occurring. As the controls are identified, they are related to the threats and components by placing them in the appropriate cells of the control spreadsheet.

The second edition of the book *Designing Controls into Computerized Systems* presents a risk ranked control spreadsheet methodology for designing controls into networks (see reference 6 at the end of this chapter). Moreover, Chapters 7 and 8 contain 94 control lists with hundreds of controls that can be used to protect data communication networks.

Deliverable for Step 8   The report for Step 8 contains three items: a control spreadsheet, a list of definitions for both the threats facing the network and the components of the network, and a controls list that describes the controls to be implemented into the new network.

9. DESIGN NETWORK CONFIGURATIONS

As you begin this step of designing *network configurations,* it is important for you to understand that Steps 9 through 12 are conducted together. That is, you proceed from one step, to the next step(s), back to an earlier step, and so forth—moving back and forth among the four steps. In other words, you design the network, evaluate software, evaluate hardware, calculate costs, and then return to redesign some aspect.

During this step of the systems approach to designing a data communication network, the designer uses all the information collected to date. Of special value are the network maps and the traffic/circuit loading data. These are used to configure the network in such a way as to achieve the required throughput at a minimum circuit cost. Begin this step by reviewing the maps and pictorial diagrams that show the links between the station/node locations.

Configurations Based on Network Goals   The object of this step is to configure the circuit paths between users and the host computer. The decision involves moving the stations/nodes about and making judgments with regard to software and hardware. In reality, this step is performed simultaneously with the next three steps. Some *goals* the network designer tries to achieve with regard to an efficient and cost-effective network are shown in the Goals of Network Design box. Be sure to read Chapter 11 first if you are designing a local area network.

Modeling Networks   The complexity of designing data communication networks presents the designer with many problems. The goal is to construct a system that provides adequate response time to the end user while ensuring the cost to deliver that response time is reasonable. To accomplish this goal, the designer must under-

GOALS OF NETWORK DESIGN

- Minimum circuit mileage between the various stations/nodes. Computer programs/modeling can help here.
- Adequate circuit capacity to meet today's data transfer needs, as well as those required three to five years in the future.
- Reasonable response times at individual terminals. Response time must meet the needs of each application.
- Reliable hardware that offers minimum cost, adequate speed and control features, a high Mean Time Between Failures (MTBF), and good diagnostic/serviceability features.
- Efficient software/protocols that can be used on a variety of circuit configurations including satellite circuits. One of the newer High-level Data Link Control (HDLC) protocols that can operate with various international standards (X.25) might be used. This permits the network to interconnect with national or international networks as well as with electronic mail systems, use multivendor hardware, and connect to public packet switched networks.
- A very high level of reliability (network uptime) must be met. This may be the most important factor. The network designer always should remember that when business operations move into an online, real-time data communication network, it is as if the company has closed its doors for business when the network is down.
- Reasonable costs (not necessarily the absolute lowest).
- Acceptance of the network by both day-to-day users and managers who must use its data or information.
- Just enough security and control for the highest risk application using the network.
- Compare the above goals with the mandatory, desirable, and wish list requirements developed during Step 4 to establish whether these design goals meet the stated network requirements.

stand the response time and cost tradeoff issues associated with data communication networks.

In this section we will discuss the design of multipoint polled networks. This type of network was chosen because it is a common class of data communication network and it presents difficult issues of how user transactions are handled in a system with multiple queues. Numerous queues tend to increase message delays.

As an example, when a user is ready to send a message to the host computer for processing, that message passes through many queues (wait times) or delay periods, as illustrated in Figure 8-12.

If there are other terminals sharing the circuit (multipoint), the queues and delays can compound or interfere with each other because usually only one terminal on a

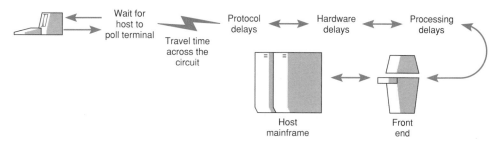

Figure 8-12   Message delay.

given communication circuit can communicate with the host computer at a given time. Therefore, if five terminals are on a circuit and each has a message ready to send, it is easy to see that the last terminal may have to wait until the others are finished. In addition, the computer may accept a message from Terminal 1 and then Terminal 2 and, before going to Terminal 3, send the response to Terminal 1's message, causing an additional delay for the others waiting for service. This example indicates some of the complexities, but the reader must understand that these are only a few of the delays encountered within data communication networks.

Fortunately, computer modeling techniques have been developed to help evaluate the problem and determine a solution. These modeling programs allow the designer to examine the issues without having to get involved with all the complexities of the problem. They are, if you will, "tools of the trade" and must be looked upon as *tools,* not push-button programs. A skilled user can derive good solutions by applying the tools successfully, whereas an unskilled user may apply the tools incorrectly and get totally different results.

A *model* is a body of information about a system gathered for the purpose of studying the system. A *mathematical model* describes the entities of a system with the attributes being represented by mathematical variables; the activities are described by mathematical functions that interrelate the variables. Given a mathematical model of a system, it sometimes is possible to derive information about the system by analytic means. Where this is not possible, it is necessary to use numerical computation for solving the equations of the mathematical model. *System simulation* describes the technique of solving problems by following the changes over time using a dynamic model of a system. A *dynamic mathematical model* allows the changes of system attributes to be derived as a function of time.

Analytical models generally make several assumptions to simplify the mathematics and provide results that can be evaluated easily and cheaply. Simulation models, on the other hand, can reflect the working of a network to any desired level of detail. The time and cost of development and program runs are directly proportional to the level of detail incorporated.

Let us illustrate some of the analytical and simulation modeling techniques used in a data communication network design. Consider a set of terminals connected to a host computer (CPU) via a multidrop line (Figure 8-13). The CPU and the terminals bear a central control relationship in the sense that the transmissions from the

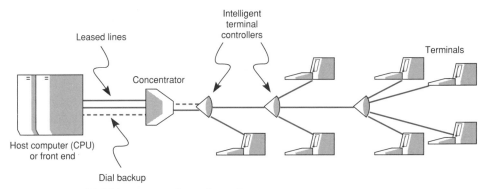

Figure 8-13   Multidrop network configuration.

terminals are controlled by the CPU or front end. Evaluating the performance of the network under the polling discipline is the task of the network designer. The designer uses modeling as a means to *predict* the performance of the network and answer such questions as: How does the response time of the network vary as a function of each terminal's load and the number of terminals? How is the response time affected by a specific polling discipline such as giving priority to outbound traffic (CPU to terminal) over inbound traffic?

With regard to analytical models, the designer resorts to queuing models to predict analytically the response time and throughput of a polled network. A general queuing model of a polled network is shown in Figure 8-14 and may be described as queues served in cyclic order with walk times. (*Walk time* is the time to switch service from one queue to another and includes the overhead time attributable to polling, propagation delay, modem synchronization time, and so forth.)

Messages arrive at a terminal according to a random process, which may be terminal dependent, and are queued for transmission. The server in this case is made available to each queue periodically, as defined by the polling protocol. The polling program also defines the amount of service received when the server polls a queue. Other characteristics of the network, such as poll message length and modem turnaround time, are modeled in the switchover time to go from Queue 1 to Queue 2, and so forth. The major difficulty in solving the above queuing model is the interrelationship between the queues at the various terminals. An exact model, therefore, has to solve an N-dimensional queuing process, which is a formidable task.

An analytical model requires a sophisticated user who is competent in mathematics for its development and use. When the user is discriminating, it can provide preliminary insights, but seldom can it yield numerical values of sufficient accuracy for the operational design of a network. To obtain a more realistic model capable of providing accurate numerical answers, we must resort to simulation. A point is reached at which a simulation model appears to be the easiest way of finding circuit utilization and response time. Because analytical models are so complex, it often is easier to use a simulation model to answer many of the questions posed by the network designer.

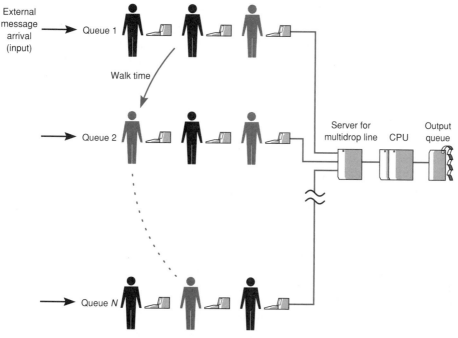

Figure 8-14   Queues model of polled terminals.

Simulation models allow users to enter a model of network traffic load and obtain an analysis of waiting times and response times in various parts of the network. The model may be tailored to the user's needs by entering parameter values specific to the network at hand. Alternatively, the user may prefer in some applications to rely primarily on the set of average values provided by the network. This set of values allows the simulation model to operate under a specific circuit discipline and is representative of many popular protocols currently in use.

Only the most complex networks need to be modeled. For classroom situations, we can design our network by using alternative configurations and compare the pricing of the network links. These configurations provide us with choices we call a choice set.

Choice Sets   When developing different network configurations, network designers have a variety of choices available to them. In other words, there is a *choice set,* which is a set of all available alternatives. Each alternative is a different network or a slightly modified version of another alternative. During the deliberations, the following decisions must be considered.

- Determine the choice set, that is, all possible network configurations.
- Divide the choice set into *attainable* and *unattainable choice sets*. The attainable set(s) contains only those alternatives that have a reasonable chance of

acceptance by management. Acceptance might be predicated on costs, software, hardware, circuit availability, or political factors within the organization.

- Review the attainable set of alternatives and place them in a ranked sequence from the most favored to the least favored, taking into account your evaluation criteria for choosing the most favored. The description of a risk ranking methodology is on page 631.

- Present the most highly favored alternatives to management for review and, it is hoped, approval.

The network designer also must know whether the proposed alternative is going to maximize something, optimize something, or satisfice something, or if it will be a combination of the three. To *maximize* is to get the highest possible degree of use out of the system without regard to other systems. To *optimize* is to get the most favored degree of use out of the system, taking into account all other systems; an optimal system does just the right amount of whatever it is supposed to do, which is not necessarily the maximum. To *satisfice* is to choose a particular level of performance for which to strive and for which management is willing to settle.

Task Dependence   During configuration development, the network designer must be aware that individual job tasks within the network may exhibit *task dependence;* that is, one task may be interrelated to another. The designer must consider three levels of job task dependence.

- *Random dependence:* a job task is required because of some other job task.
- *Sequential dependence:* one particular job task must precede or follow another job task.
- *Time dependence:* a job task is required at a set time with regard to another job task.

The network designer should assess various job tasks during the development and design of network configurations. Job task interrelationships must be studied with regard to future needs and growth because job tasks that are dependent today may not be after a new network is completed next year. Job tasks require an open-ended approach.

Evaluating Alternative Network Configurations   Now that the network maps/pictorial diagrams and traffic/circuit loading have been reviewed, line controls and modes of operation can be considered. This probably involves software and such factors as full duplex versus half duplex (page 186), whether a satellite link (page 196) is used, statistical multiplexers versus pure (transparent) multiplexers (page 125), modem speeds (page 92), intelligent terminal controllers (page 131), and how different configurations operate, such as central control versus interrupt (page 212), multidrop, or point-to-point (pages 232 to 233).

Various alternative configurations are shown. For example, Figure 8-11 shows a point-to-point configuration where each terminal node has its own communication

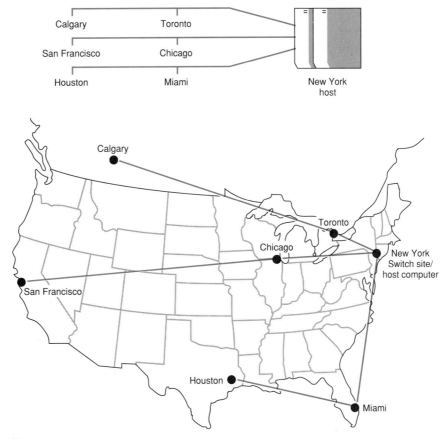

Figure 8-15 Multidrop configuration (also called multipoint).

circuit between all other nodes. Figure 8-15 shows the same cities connected using a multidrop circuit with New York as a center. Figure 8-16 shows the same cities connected using a multiplexed arrangement. The Houston site multiplexes San Francisco/Miami/Houston data to Chicago. Then Chicago multiplexes that data with the Chicago/Calgary/Toronto data and on to New York. Notice how the different configurations change overall circuit mileage. Circuits are paid for on the basis of dollars per mile per month; therefore, a minimum mileage configuration is also a minimum circuit cost configuration. Also notice that different numbers of modems are required in different configurations. For example, the point-to-point configuration requires many more modems than the multidrop configuration. Fewer modems obviously save on modem costs. Compare the number of modems required in Figures 8-11 and 8-15. Can you see that the multidrop configuration in Figure 8-15 requires 9 modems (3 in New York and 1 in each of the other 6 cities)? By contrast, the point-to-point configuration in Figure 8-11 requires a total of 41 modems (1 at each end of the 19 U.S. circuit links for 38 modems, and 3 more for the 3 international circuits).

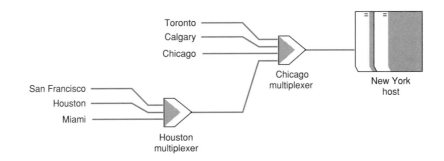

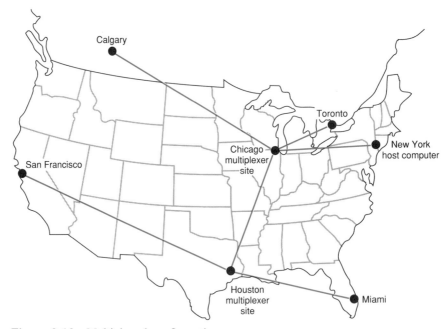

Figure 8-16   Multiplexed configuration.

Figure 8-17 shows a packet switching satellite network. This can be a private packet network or a public data network (PDN). Figure 8-18 shows a combination of a local area network, a packet satellite network, point-to-point, multiplex, and multidrop configurations. This configuration is a combination WAN and LAN.

This step requires choosing from among various network alternatives. The main constraints are the availability of software, hardware, and circuit links. These three factors are all interconnected and must be considered along with the performance and reliability that must be obtained. All these factors also are interrelated with regard to cost. Therefore, when alternative network configurations are developed, consider the software, hardware, circuits, performance, and reliability, and relate these five factors to your *cost/benefit analysis*. You can use the network drawing software described in Chapter 6 (page 246).

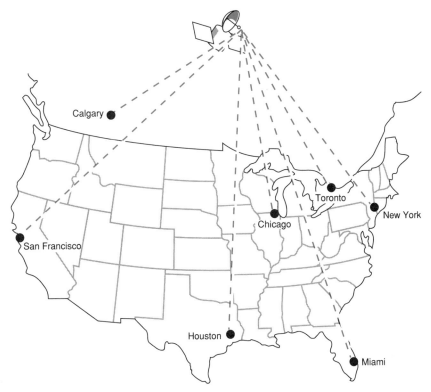

Figure 8-17 Public packet switching satellite configuration. This is a public data network (PDN).

Deliverable for Step 9   The report for Step 9 contains the network configuration layouts (maps) and a list of the goals to be achieved with this network. There also can be a model if modeling software has been used for the design project.

10. EVALUATE SOFTWARE CONSIDERATIONS

With regard to *software selection*,[2] the type of host computer may be a major constraint. The protocols (see Chapter 9) the host can handle may limit the types of terminals or other hardware that can be utilized. This limitation may be overcome by using protocol converters (page 133) or routers and gateways if the network includes a local area network (page 539).

Protocol Selection   This is the point at which *protocol selection* takes place. The software protocols determine the line control methodology/mode of operation. Deci-

[2] See FitzGerald and FitzGerald, *Fundamentals of Systems Analysis,* Chapter 10 (page 427). This chapter describes how to develop a Request for Proposals (RFP) for software.

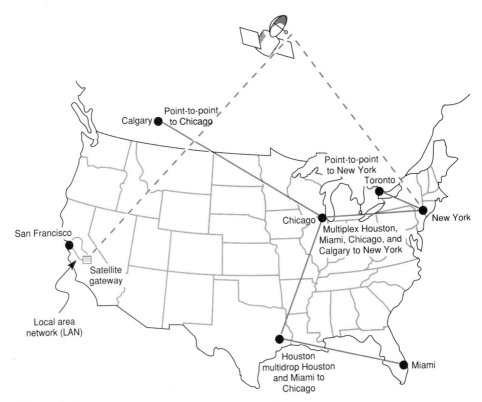

Figure 8-18   Multiple configurations.

sions must be made as to whether operations will be in full duplex or half duplex, asynchronous or synchronous, and at what speeds. For a new system one of the newer bit-oriented protocols should be selected, such as X.25, SDLC, or HDLC. The type of equipment already in place may be the determining factor in protocol selection. For example, Systems Network Architecture (SNA) may be the protocol of choice for an organization already using IBM equipment (page 427 in Chapter 9). The older byte-oriented protocols (such as Binary Synchronous Communications—BSC) probably are not a good choice because of their limitations on satellite links, slow half duplex operation, and inability to meet international standards. It is desirable to select a protocol that is compatible with the international standard seven-layer OSI model (page 417), although reality might dictate that another protocol be used for compatibility with existing hardware.

In addition to protocols/software, other network architectures/software that reside in the host computer and front end processors have to be considered. For example, telecommunication access programs (page 412) and teleprocessing monitors (page 415) may affect network operations. Security software packages in the host computer also can be a constraint. Finally, the host operating system itself may be a constraint to network control and operation, as might the database management system software.

Any software programs that are located out in the network should be reviewed. These may be at remote concentrators, remote intelligent controllers, statistical multiplexers, and terminals. Microcomputers also raise the issues of distributed data processing/remote application programs, micro-to-mainframe software (page 489), and local area network software. Be sure to read Chapter 11 first if you are designing a local area network.

The network designer can make a major contribution to the future by selecting a protocol that can grow, that is compatible with an internationally recognized standard, and that will not have to be changed for at least five to ten years. The protocol is crucial because the host computer network architecture must be able to interface with it. For example, the telecommunication access programs and teleprocessing monitor should be compatible with international standards. This means the OSI seven-layer model should be used as the basic skeleton when protocols are interfaced to host computer and front end software packages. Moreover, you might want to interface with a local area network at sometime in the future.

Another consideration is *internetworking,* which is connecting several networks together. Even though the OSI model is used widely, the Transmission Control Protocol/Internet Protocol (TCP/IP) is a reliable and universally supported alternative for internetworking. There also are other internetworking protocols.

Finally, software diagnostics and maintenance must not be overlooked. Determine how quickly either in-house people or the vendor can diagnose software problems and how quickly they can fix these problems. The concepts of Mean Time To Diagnose (MTTD), Mean Time To Respond (MTTR), and Mean Time to Fix (MTTF) will be discussed in Chapter 12; they apply to software packages as well as to hardware.

Deliverable for Step 10   The report for Step 10 contains tentative, but detailed, network configurations that show whether the network is to be point-to-point, multiplexed, multidropped, packet switched public data network (PDN), or a combination of these network types. These tentative configurations will be finalized in the next step. The report for this step also contains descriptions of the selected protocols, as well as documentation for both WAN and LAN software.

11. EVALUATE HARDWARE CONSIDERATIONS

Hardware selection[3] is easier to handle than software selection because hardware is a tangible item. Hardware was covered in Chapters 3 and 4, as well as Chapter 11 on LANs. Some pieces of hardware that need to be considered are

- Terminals/microcomputers
- File servers/database servers

[3] FitzGerald and FitzGerald, *Fundamentals of System Analysis,* Chapter 10 (page 425) and Request for Proposals (Appendix 3) for a methodology on how to develop a Request for Proposals (RFP) for hardware.

- Gateways/bridges/routers
- Intelligent terminal controllers
- Modems (analog/digital)
- Multiplexers (TDM/FDM/STDM/fast packet) and concentrators
- LAN medium access units (MAUs) for Ethernet
- LAN multistation access units (MAUs) for Token-Ring Networks
- Line-sharing devices
- Protocol converters
- Hardware encryption boxes
- Automated switching devices
- PBX/CBX switchboards
- Data protectors
- Various communication circuit types
- Port sharing devices
- Front end processors
- Host computers
- Testing equipment
- Channel extenders

Hardware Selection   With the above list in mind, the designer uses representations of the pieces of hardware and moves them about on the various network maps and pictorial diagrams. If you use the GrafNet software described in Chapter 6, it has specific symbols for multiplexers, concentrators, switches, gateways, repeaters, and different speed circuits, such as 2400 bits per second, or 64,000 bits per second. You can add the proper symbol at the city (node) where the item is located. For example, in Figure 8-16 you would show a multiplexer symbol at Chicago and Houston. By contrast, if you are drawing the network maps by hand, now is the time to make hardware configuration drawings like the ones shown in the top half of Figures 8-15 and 8-16. A full set of symbols for drawing configurations by hand is shown in Figure 6-20 on page 247. To save time, we suggest making photocopies of Figure 6-20, taping the symbols in place with double-sided tape, and then connecting the symbols by drawing the appropriate lines with a ruler. Whether you draw the configurations on a microcomputer or by hand, do not forget to make a list of the required hardware, such as nine modems, two multiplexers, six microcomputers, one server, one gateway, or whatever your network requires.

This experimentation with configurations should take into account the protocol/software considerations. The result should be a minimum-cost network that meets the organization's data communication (throughput) requirements. As a rule of thumb, remember that minimum circuit cost usually means minimum mileage. Meeting the organization's throughput requirements is no trivial task. Many organizations use computer simulation and modeling to carry out this task successfully.

Before ordering hardware, the design team should decide how to handle diagnostics, troubleshooting, and repair. It should be remembered that MTTD (*Mean Time To Diagnose*), MTTR (*Mean Time To Respond*), and MTTF (*Mean Time to Fix*) always apply to hardware. Vendor estimates of MTBF (*Mean Time Between Failures*) for hardware should be obtained by the design team. Issues that should be addressed include the types of test equipment (page 594) that are necessary and the structure of the network management group (page 586). Some hardware may have built-in diagnostic capabilities for its internal electronic circuits, as well as the ability to identify problems on the communication circuit.

Diagnostics go hand in hand with network service. The vendor's MTBF and ability to respond to service calls are essential factors that affect downtime of the network.

In summary, a network configuration that takes both hardware and software into account must be developed.

Deliverable for Step 11   The report for Step 11 contains the final maps (layouts) and configurations (multidrop, multiplex, and so forth) showing the appropriate nodes (cities or buildings). It also includes a list of the hardware that will be required to make the network operational, as well as the software/protocol requirements.

12. CALCULATE NETWORK (CIRCUIT) COSTS

Usually, it is a hindrance to propose cost limitations during the initial development of design alternatives. Of course, an effort always should be made to keep costs down; however, costs should not interfere with *preliminary* design configuration alternatives (choice sets). The point is that the various alternatives should be identified first; then costs should be related to the *attainable* design configurations. The first task is to identify the attainable and workable configurations, and the second is to identify the costs of those alternatives. Time should not be wasted on obtaining costs for configurations that are neither attainable nor workable.

Complexities of Network Costing   Estimating the cost of a network is much more complex than estimating the cost of a new piece of hardware. Many variables and intangibles are involved. Nevertheless, estimating the cost of a network is a necessary prerequisite to deciding whether implementation is justifiable. Some of the questions that must be considered are

- What are the major cost categories of the entire network? These may include
  Circuit costs
  Hardware costs
  Software costs
  Test and maintenance costs
  Network management costs
  Personnel costs

- What methods of estimating are available and what accuracy can be achieved?
- Can all costs be identified and accurately estimated?
- Can benefits be identified? Which benefits cannot be estimated in dollar terms and can they be measured in any other way?
- What criteria will management use when evaluating these cost estimates? (Refer to the evaluation criteria developed during Step 2.)

Because the specific method used to gather and compile network costs for presentation has to be tailored to meet the needs of the organization, several alternatives for cost analysis are presented here.[4]

Network Cost Analyzer   The *network cost analyzer* is a spreadsheet methodology. It is an excellent way to document specific network costs during a detailed cost analysis. The major costs are software, hardware, and circuit costs.

Figure 8-19 shows a network cost analyzer in which each cost category is listed horizontally across the top and each circuit link is listed vertically down the left side by network link. Each individual cost is placed within a cell, such as the circuit cost for the New York City to Los Angeles circuit. By adding the costs horizontally, you can obtain a *total link* cost for each network link. Some costs, like front ends, test equipment, host mainframe, and software, may have to be allocated among all the links on a fair basis. For example, a $300,000 front end serving 20 network links might be allocated at $15,000 per link.

Totaling down a column gives the total cost for a specific category of hardware or software. Finally, the grand total in the lower right corner shows the total cost of the entire network, including all circuit links and all cost categories.

Cost/Benefit Categories   Figure 8-20 shows various cost categories associated with data communication networks, as well as the various benefit categories. The most helpful items in this figure are the *direct costs,* the *indirect costs,* and the *intangible benefits.* Intangibles sometimes are very difficult to identify. Other benefits, such as direct and indirect cost reductions and revenue increases, must be identified in a manner that is unique to the organization for which the network is being designed. This figure can ensure that no critical cost or important benefit is overlooked. Figures 8-19 and 8-20 are used together. Also refer to the Local Area Network Cost Considerations box on page 549.

One of the most difficult aspects of calculating network circuit costs has to do with the circuits themselves because each type of circuit has different charges associated with it. When the network requires a mixture of circuits (for example, dial-up and satellite) or several communication vendors (for example, AT&T and MCI), these calculations become even more complex. The following sections will describe some of the differences in calculating the costs for traditional analog voice grade lease circuits, dial-up circuits, wideband analog circuits, all-digital circuits, T carrier

---

[4]FitzGerald and FitzGerald, *Fundamentals of System Analysis,* Review Chapter 10 (Economic Cost Comparisons) for an in-depth presentation of 12 different cost analysis methodologies.

Cost Category Network Link	Circuit Cost	Front End	Modems	Intelligent Controllers	Multiplexers or Concentrators	Microcomputers or Terminals	Software	Test Equipment	Personnel and Facilities	Total Cost for Each Network Link
New York City to Los Angeles	$1,420.71		$921.00				$200.00			$2,541.71
Total Cost for Each Category										Grand Total Network Cost

Figure 8-19 Network cost analyzer.

Costs	Benefits
Direct costs • Computer equipment • Communication equipment • Common carrier line charges • Software • Operations personnel costs • File conversion costs • Facilities costs (space, power, air conditioning, storage space, offices, etc.) • Spare parts costs • Hardware maintenance costs • Software maintenance costs • Interaction with vendor and/or development group • Development and performance of acceptance test procedures and parallel operation • Development of documentation • Costs for backup of network in case of failure • Costs of manually performing tests during a system outage • Security and control • Personnel **Indirect costs** • Personnel training • Transformation of operational procedures • Development of support software • Disruption of normal activities • Increased system outage rate during initial operation period • Increase in the number of vendors (impacts fault detection and correction because of "finger pointing")	**Direct and indirect cost reductions** • Elimination of clerical personnel and/or manual operations • Reduction of inventories, manufacturing, sales, operations, and management costs • Effective cost reduction, for example, less spoilage or waste, elimination of obsolete materials, and less pilferage • Distribution of resources across demand for service **Revenue increases** • Increased sales because of better responsiveness • Improved services • Faster processing of operations **Intangible benefits** • Smoothing of operational flows • Reduced volume of paper produced and handled • Rise in level of service quality and performance • Expansion capability • Improved decision process by provision of faster access to information • Ability to meet the competition • Future cost avoidance • Positive effect on other classes of investments or resources such as better utilization of money, more efficient use of floor space or personnel, and so forth • Improved employee morale • Keeping technical employees • Faster decision making

Figure 8-20　Cost/benefit categories.

Location	Vertical	Horizontal
Tulsa	7707	4173
San Francisco	8492	8719

$$\text{Distance} = \sqrt{\frac{(V_1 - V_2)^2 + (H_1 - H_2)^2}{10}}$$

$$D = \sqrt{\frac{(8492 - 7707)^2 + (8719 - 4173)^2}{10}}$$

$$D = \sqrt{2,128,234.1}$$

$$D = 1,459 \text{ miles}$$

Figure 8-21 Vertical and horizontal coordinates formula for determining air mileage between rate centers (end offices).

circuits, packet switched circuits, and satellite circuits. The first two sections (leased and dial-up) use a step-by-step approach because they are the most commonly used circuits today. Following along with these steps provides a good understanding of how intraLATA and interLATA charges work, as well as the use of vertical and horizontal coordinates for calculating circuit link mileages. This understanding is fundamental to your mastery of knowing how automated design tools arrive at their conclusions.

Voice Grade Leased Circuit Costs The major factors that have to be taken into account when figuring analog *voice grade leased circuit* (page 279) *costs* are the circuit link mileage, cost (*tariff*) for the circuit, and any circuit termination charges at each end of the circuit link.

The common carriers use a system of *vertical* and *horizontal coordinates* to determine the air mileage between central offices. Figure 8-21 shows the formula for calculating the vertical and horizontal coordinates to determine air mileage. You must know the vertical and horizontal coordinates to determine the distance between any two rate centers (telephone company end offices). The V and H coordinates for Tulsa and San Francisco are shown in Figure 8-21. Next, put the V and H coordinates for the rate center into the formula in Figure 8-21 and solve it to get the air mileage. (Note that the difference always is obtained by subtracting the smaller from the larger coordinate.) Round the mileage to the nearest whole number.

The term *rate center* is a telephone company term for the central or end office where the circuits terminate. For example, one end of a local loop goes to your business or home, and the other end goes to a rate center. It is called a rate center because it is used when calculating the rates charged for the provided service.

The Vertical and Horizontal Coordinates section at the end of this chapter (page 387) lists V and H coordinates by city only, even though they apply to individual end office locations throughout a city. For this reason, a given city may have many pairs of V and H coordinates. A list by city only is adequate for our design problems. You can obtain the complete set of V and H coordinates for all rate centers from FCC Tariff 10.

Each *FCC Tariff* is used for specific types of rate information. For example, Tariff 9 contains the rates and regulations for services provided among *AT&T* end offices and the type of "customer connection" to the end office. Tariff 10 contains the vertical and horizontal coordinates used to calculate the mileage between *central/end offices* (rate centers). Tariff 11 contains the rates and regulations for private line local channels provided by AT&T for local distribution of traffic. These local channels usually are provided by the local Bell Operating Company.

AT&T has at least one point of presence (POP) in each local access transport area. (LATAs were defined in Chapter 7 on page 274.) A *point of presence* (POP) is the end office to which your local loop is connected so that messages can go out on the long distance (IXC) circuits when your message transmission leaves the local LATA. These long distance IXCs are interLATA circuits; that is, they cross between LATAs.

The cost of a voice grade circuit is comprised of the following five cost elements (although number 4, conditioning, is optional).

1. Central or end office connection charge (station terminal) at each end of the IXC circuit. These station terminations are at the CO2 end offices in Figure 8-22.

   $16.40 per month per IXC circuit end

2. Mileage between the central or end offices (IXC circuits). Use V and H coordinates to calculate the mileage. It depends on the cities (rate centers) being connected.

3. Long distance (IXC) circuit charge. Use the mileage calculated in the previous step and the following table to determine the long distance (IXC) circuit charge. The following analog *interLATA* mileage charge is for the circuit between two end offices when this circuit crosses from one LATA to another.

Analog InterLATA Mileage Charges

	Monthly	
Mileage	Fixed	Per Mile
1–50	$ 72.98	$2.84
51–100	149.28	1.31
101–500	229.28	0.51
501 +	324.24	0.32

4. Cost of *channel options,* such as line conditioning (page 279), may be added. Conditioning is optional because some modems perform this function. *C type*

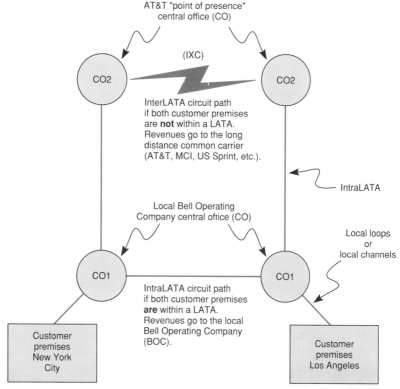

AT&T "point of presence"
central office (CO)

(IXC)

CO2

CO2

InterLATA circuit path
if both customer premises
are **not** within a LATA.
Revenues go to the long
distance common carrier
(AT&T, MCI, US Sprint, etc.).

IntraLATA

Local Bell Operating
Company central office (CO)

Local loops
or
local channels

CO1

CO1

IntraLATA circuit path
if both customer premises
are within a LATA.
Revenues go to the local
Bell Operating Company
(BOC).

Customer
premises
New York
City

Customer
premises
Los Angeles

Figure 8-22 Voice grade circuits. The central office (CO) also is referred to as a rate center or an end office. LATAs were described in Chapter 7. Figure 7-3 shows LATAs for California.

conditioning has specific limits on attenuation distortion and envelope delay distortion. Such limits reduce line impairments so a data signal can get to its destination with less noise and distortion (fewer retransmissions caused by errors). AT&T's Technical Reference Publication 41004 gives the exact specifications. *D type conditioning* specifically limits noise and harmonic distortion. Again, this type of conditioning reduces line impairments and, therefore, has fewer retransmissions caused by errors. There are seven levels of conditioning, but use these four levels for our design problems.

Type C
    Point to point $31/month
    Multidrop   52/month

Type D
    Point to point $22/month
    Multidrop   71/month

5. Cost of the analog *intraLATA* circuits (also called the local channel) must be calculated. This includes the circuit paths between CO1 and CO2 in Figure 8-22. If the user's site (your office) has the same end office (Bell telephone personnel sometimes call it a *wire center*) as the AT&T point of presence end office, use zero mileage in the next table to determine the cost. In the case of zero mileage, the cost is $66.87 for this local loop (local channel).

Analog IntraLATA Mileage Charges

Mileage	Monthly Fixed	Per Mile
zero	$ 66.87	zero
1–4	75.93	$6.34
5–8	78.24	5.77
9–25	101.31	2.88
over 25	111.62	2.48

All this complexity has been brought about by deregulation. Deregulation specifies that your local Bell Operating Company can charge for the local loops (local channels). These are the intraLATA circuits. AT&T, along with other long distance common carriers like US Sprint and MCI, can charge for the long distance interexchange channels (IXC). These are the interLATA IXCs.

AT&T, MCI, and US Sprint have at least one point of presence (POP) in each LATA (local access transport area). This point of presence is the end office to which your local loop must be connected when you want messages to go out on the long distance (IXC) circuits (interLATA).

Look at Figure 8-22 in which we have marked the central offices with numbers of CO1 and CO2. Central office 1 implies it is the local Bell Operating Company central office closest to your customer premises. It is the zero mileage charge local loop in the above table. For the $66.87 listed in this table, you get a circuit path from your customer premises (NYC) to CO1 and to CO2 when CO1 is both the local Bell Operating Company end office and the point of presence for the long distance carrier. This is true only when CO1 and CO2 are the same end office.

When the AT&T point of presence central office is not the same as the local Bell Operating Company central office, you must pay a mileage charge for the length of the circuit between the two central offices. In Figure 8-22 this is represented by the circuit that goes from central office 1 to central office 2. Sometimes these two central offices are the same, but usually they are not. Only a few companies that are lucky enough to be located next to the AT&T point of presence central office do not have to pay this extra (greater than zero mileage) intraLATA circuit mileage charge between CO1 and CO2. These lucky companies can use zero mileage calculation for the local loop link between central office 1 (Bell Operating Company) and central office 2 (AT&T) for their intraLATA circuits.

To calculate mileage charges when the AT&T point of presence is not at CO1, you determine the mileage between CO1 and CO2 and use the above intraLATA mileage charges. For example, if the mileage between CO1 and CO2 is 7 miles, the charge is \$118.63 instead of the \$66.87 zero mileage charge (7 miles $\times$ \$5.77 per mile + \$78.24 = \$118.63). For your design problems, make some estimates for this distance between the central offices (CO1 and CO2) because they are located throughout a city.

As you can see, we have given you only one analog intraLATA mileage charge table for this local loop mileage calculation. We have not provided all the local channel mileage tables because there are several hundred of them, they vary from state to state, and they vary between LATAs. Your local telephone company can supply them for your area. These rate tables are very long and are similar to the one above. This one is sufficient for your design problems, and it is enough to learn how to determine circuit costs. In any computerized network design software package, all the mileage charge tables are organized by area code and the first three digits of the telephone exchange number (the prefix).

You also should recognize that the rate tables (costs) are updated on a monthly basis. Although the costs you calculate here are representative, the rate tables for the entire United States would require approximately 4 million bytes of storage space.

Once you have calculated the cost for the local channel, there may be a few additional charges, depending on the current tariff structure. For example, there may be special access surcharges, and you may be charged for access coordination functions between AT&T and the Bell Operating Company. In your design problems you can ignore these because they are in a state of flux and change as deregulation continues. They usually are minor charges and will not affect your calculations significantly.

Now figure the cost of the circuit in Figure 8-22 if CO1 to CO2 at the New York end is 31 miles, and CO1 to CO2 at the Los Angeles end is 9 miles (assume no conditioning).

1. Central office connection charges for each end of the IXC between the CO2 in New York and the CO2 in Los Angeles: \$32.80 (2 $\times$ \$16.40)

2. V and H coordinates from the end of this chapter (page 387).

	V	H
New York City	4997	1406
Los Angeles	9213	7878

Based on the formula in Figure 8-21, the mileage is 2,443 miles.

3. InterLATA mileage charges (NYC to LA). In Figure 8-22 this is the circuit between CO2 and CO2.

$$
\begin{array}{rl}
2{,}443 & \text{miles} \\
\times\ 0.32 & \text{per mile} \\
\hline
\$781.76 & \\
+\ 324.24 & \text{fixed charge} \\
\hline
\$1{,}106.00 & \text{per month}
\end{array}
$$

4. Conditioning is not required. Assume the modems perform conditioning.

5. Local loop cost (intraLATA mileage charges) for customer premises (NYC) to CO2 and customer premises (LA) to CO2.

NYC to CO2 (New York end)

$$\begin{array}{rl} \$ & 2.48 \text{ per mile} \\ \times\ & 31 \text{ miles} \\ \hline \$ & 76.88 \text{ (this is the charge for CO1–CO2)} \\ + & 111.62 \text{ (the intraLATA fixed charge for NYC–CO1)} \\ \hline \$ & 188.50 \text{ per month} \end{array}$$

LA to CO2 (Los Angeles end)

$$\begin{array}{rl} \$ & 2.88 \text{ per mile} \\ \times\ & 9 \text{ miles} \\ \hline \$ & 25.92 \text{ (this is the charge for CO1–CO2)} \\ + & 101.31 \text{ (the intraLATA fixed charge for LA–CO1)} \\ \hline \$ & 127.23 \text{ per month} \end{array}$$

And so this private voice grade lease circuit would cost

$$\begin{array}{rl} \$ & 32.80 \text{ central office connection } (2 \times \$16.40) \\ & 1,106.00 \text{ interLATA (CO2 to CO2)} \\ & 0.00 \text{ conditioning} \\ & 315.73 \text{ intraLATA } (\$188.50 + \$127.23) \\ \hline & \$1,454.53 \text{ per month} \end{array}$$

On the other hand, if CO1 at the Los Angeles end is the AT&T point of presence central office, what is the new cost of the local loop (it was $127.23 above)? The new cost is $66.87, which is the zero mileage amount on the previous analog intraLATA mileage charges table.

Dial-Up Circuit Costs *Dial-up circuit* (page 290) *costs,* just as with leased circuits, have two different rate schedules. One is for interLATA/interstate and is billed by AT&T, US Sprint, MCI, or another long distance common carrier. The other is for intraLATA/intrastate and is billed by the Bell Operating Companies (BOCs) or other local telephone company.

Figure 8-23 gives the approximate rates for interLATA/interstate (long distance) calls as billed for AT&T, US Sprint, MCI, or another long distance common carrier. If you want to calculate the cost of an intraLATA dial-up call, we recommend calling your local telephone company business office to ask for its dial-up rate schedule. The dial-up rate schedule looks similar to the one in Figure 8-23 except the day rates for the initial minute and each additional minute are different. The rate mileage cutoff points also may vary because they may not go as high as 5,750 miles for intraLATA calls.

To calculate the cost of a long distance dial-up call, determine the air mileage between the calling party and the called party (use the V and H coordinates shown on page 388). Next, calculate the cost of the call by using the day rates in Figure

Discount Amount							
	Mon	Tues	Wed	Thurs	Fri	Sat	Sun
8:00 A.M. to 5:00 P.M.	Day Rate Period Full Rate						
5:00 P.M. to 11:00 P.M.	Evening Rate Period 35% Discount from Day Rate					Evening 35% Discount	
11:00 P.M. to 8:00 A.M.	Night and Weekend Rate Period 50% Discount from Day Rate						

	Day Rates	
Rate Mileage	Initial Minute	Each Additional Minute
1–10	$0.21	$0.14
11–22	$0.25	$0.17
23–55	$0.27	$0.19
56–124	$0.27	$0.21
125–292	$0.27	$0.23
293–430	$0.27	$0.24
431–925	$0.30	$0.26
926–1,910	$0.30	$0.26
1,911–3,000	$0.32	$0.27
3,001–4,250	$0.39	$0.31
4,251–5,750	$0.41	$0.33

Figure 8-23   InterLATA dial-up calls (also called direct distance dialing or DDD).

8-23. Do not forget to apply the appropriate discount when the call is an evening or night call.

Let us use the circuit given in Figure 8-22 (NYC to LA) and assume the organization uses a dial-up call instead of a private lease line. What would its monthly telephone bill be based on the interLATA rates given in Figure 8-23? Your first task is to determine how many minutes per day the telephone call lasts and whether there is one long call or many short calls each day. In this case, let us assume there is one six-hour call per day.

We already know from the previous V and H calculation that the mileage between New York City and Los Angeles is 2,443 miles. The six-hour call amounts to 360 minutes (6 hours × 60 minutes per hour). Based on the day rates in Figure 8-23, the daily cost is $97.25 for the long distance charges. To this must be added the basic monthly telephone bill from the local telephone company.

$$
\begin{array}{r}
359 \text{ minutes} \\
\times\ 0.27 \text{ per minute} \\
\hline
\$96.93 \\
+\ 0.32 \text{ for the first minute} \\
\hline
\$97.25 \text{ per day}
\end{array}
$$

Group 48 KHz Bandwidth (Wideband)

Mileage Band	Monthly Cost	
	Fixed	Per Mile
1–50	$ 165.28	$12.34
51–100	165.28	12.34
101–500	567.28	8.32
501–1,000	1,447.28	6.56
1,000+	3,617.28	4.39

Supergroup 240 KHz Bandwidth (Wideband)

Mileage Band	Monthly Cost	
	Fixed	Per Mile
1–50	$ 387.38	$29.18
51–100	387.38	29.18
101–500	1,342.38	19.63
501–1,000	3,407.38	15.50
1,000+	8,577.38	10.33

Figure 8-24 Wideband analog circuit costs.

The monthly cost is $2,139.50 plus the basic monthly telephone bill from the local telephone company. We assumed 22 working days per month (22 days × $97.25). If you look back to the previous private lease line cost calculation, you will see that it was only $1,454.53. As you can see, this organization would do better to lease a circuit rather than use dial-up circuits. The crossover from dial-up to lease depends on how many minutes per day are used when connected via the dial-up circuits. Dividing $1,455 by $97 shows that dial-up cost exceeded lease line cost on the fifteenth day.

Wideband Analog Circuit Costs Wideband service (page 280) from AT&T provides for 19,200, 40,800, 50,000, 56,000, and 230,400 bits per second transmission speeds. transmission speed depends on the modem being used. Remember, the modem determines the bits per second speed, but you still need a circuit having enough bandwidth to carry the speed at which the modem transmits. With wideband analog circuits, you lease either a *Group 48,000 hertz bandwidth* (equivalent to 12 voice grade circuits) or a *Supergroup 240,000 hertz bandwidth* (equivalent to 60 voice grade circuits). There is a monthly end office connection charge (station terminal) of $28 per circuit end ($28 × 2). The *wideband analog circuit costs* for both Group 48 KHz and Supergroup 240 KHz, which are shown in Figure 8-24, are based on the mileage between end offices (use V and H coordinates to calculate the mileage). In 1989 AT&T applied to the FCC to detariff wideband service because wideband is analog and the trend is toward digital services. AT&T is expected to continue providing the service to current users but will phase it out gradually by not accepting new wideband customers.

Digital Circuit Costs We calculate *digital circuit* (page 281) *costs* exactly the same way we did earlier for voice grade circuits, with one exception. The interLATA mileage

Digital InterLATA Mileage Charges			
		Monthly	
Speed	Mileage	Fixed	Per Mile
2400, 4800, or 9600	1–50	$ 72.98	$2.84
bits per second	51–100	149.48	1.31
	101–500	229.48	0.51
	501 +	324.48	0.32
19,200 bits per	1–50	$ 87.57	$3.40
second	51–100	179.07	1.57
	101–500	275.07	0.61
	501 +	389.69	0.38
56,000 bits per	1–50	$232.00	$7.74
second	51–100	435.00	3.68
	101–500	571.00	2.32
	501 +	1,081.40	1.30

Figure 8-25   Digital circuit costs.

charges in Figure 8-25 should be used for all-digital circuits instead of the voice grade circuit charges given earlier in the analog interLATA table. The tariff in Figure 8-25 is for transmission at 2400, 4800, 9600, 19,200, and 56,000 bits per second.

T Carrier Circuit Costs   The *T carrier circuit costs* (T-1, fractional T-1, or T-3) are shown in Figure 8-26. T carrier circuits were described in Chapter 7 starting on page 283.

Packet Switching Costs   Packet switching was described in Chapter 6 (page 235). Using AT&T's ACCUNET® packet network as an example, we find that three elements can be used for calculating *packet switching costs:* the private leased access line, the transmission speed per port, and the number of packets transmitted.

With ACCUNET, users must assemble/disassemble their own packets and send them via a *private lease line* to the AT&T point of presence end office that handles packet switching. Therefore, you must calculate the private voice grade circuit cost as we did earlier for a voice grade circuit. This cost depends on the mileage between the customer's premises and the AT&T point of presence end office. For example, when calculating this cost, use the previous analog voice grade mileage charge tables.

The cost element for *transmission speed per port* depends on how fast you want to transmit. This monthly charge is

- $495 for 4800 bits per second
- $645 for 9600 bits per second
- $1,225 for 56,000 bits per second

T Carrier InterLATA Mileage Charges			
		Monthly	
Speed	Mileage	Fixed	Per Mile
T-1	1–50	$1,800.00	$ 10.00
at 1,544,000	51–100	1,838.00	9.25
bits per second	101+	2,038.00	7.25
T-3	1–50	$6,000.00	$175.00
at 44,376,000	51–100	7,500.00	145.00
bits per second	101–200	10,500.00	115.00
	201+	13,500.00	100.00
Fractional T-1	1–50	$277.00	$ 10.79
at 256,000	51–100	567.00	4.98
bits per second	101+	943.00	1.22
Fractional T-1	1–50	$ 415.00	$ 16.19
at 384,000	51–100	851.00	7.47
bits per second	101+	1,416.00	1.82
Fractional T-1	1–50	$ 525.00	$ 20.45
at 512,000	51–100	1,076.00	9.43
bits per second	101+	1,789.00	2.30
Fractional T-1	1–50	$ 788.00	$ 30.67
at 768,000	51–100	1,614.00	14.15
bits per second	101+	2,683.00	$ 3.46

Figure 8-26   T carrier circuit costs.

To determine how many terminals can be connected to the port, you need to know that a 4800 bits per second port has the capacity of four virtual circuits, a 9600 bits per second port has eight, and a 56,000 bits per second port has forty.

Finally, the packet charge is based on *how many packets are transmitted* each day. To determine this monthly charge, you have to estimate or count the amount of packet traffic on the network. Remember that a packet is 128 characters long. The charges are $0.75 per kilopacket (1,000 packets) for Monday through Friday, 7:00 A.M. to 6:00 P.M. All other times are $0.38 per kilopacket. Design Steps 6 and 7, described earlier in this chapter, explain how to estimate message traffic.

To obtain the costs of using packet switching public data networks (PDNs), call any of the following services for their charges in your area.

- Infonet 1-800-342-5272
- Tymnet Global Network 1-800-872-7654
- ACCUNET/AT&T 1-800-222-0400

Satellite Circuit Usage Charges (Full-Time Usage)	
Speed of Transmission in Bits per Second	Monthly Charge
56,000	$ 955.00
64,000	1,061.00
128,000	1,909.00
192,000	2,653.00
256,000	3,395.00
384,000	5,092.00
768,000	6,365.00
1,544,000	9,548.00
Shared earth station terminal charges. There is a $3,714 monthly charge for each transmit/receive terminal.	

Figure 8-27   Satellite circuit costs.

- IBM Information Network 1-800-727-2222
- CompuServe Network Services 1-800-848-8199
- SprintNet Data Network (formerly Telenet) 1-800-736-1130
- Mark*Net 1-800-433-3683
- DATAPAC (Canada) 1-613-781-6798

Instead of being charged for the number of kilopackets transmitted, some PDNs charge for connect time when the access is via a dial-up call. To calculate the cost, you have to add the cost of the dial-up call to the cost-per-minute of connect time.

Satellite Circuit Costs   The leased digital *satellite circuit* (page 287) *cost* depends on the speed of transmission. To use satellite circuits, an organization must put a satellite dish on one of its buildings. The transmission then goes from the building to the satellite, to a shared earth station, and then to the destination of the message. In addition to the transmission speed charge, there is a shared earth terminal charge for each satellite circuit at the shared earth station. See Figure 8-27 for an example of satellite circuit costs.

Hardware Costs   The following costs are for selected pieces of communication hardware. These *hardware costs* are representative averages and therefore might not reflect the latest discounts. For this reason, you should contact hardware vendors directly or check prices in reference guides like Auerbach or Datapro. You also may request a BLACK BOX® hardware catalog by calling 1-412-746-5565. Vendors can provide specifications for any piece of hardware you might want to use. (You also can call or write to vendors for the cost of specific communication software pack-

Hardware	Approximate Purchase Cost
Modem (300–2400 bits per second)	$ 200
Modem (2400–9600 bits per second)	600
Modem (19,200 bits per second)	1,000
Modem (V.32 up to 38,400 bits per second)	1,400
Video terminal	800
Microcomputer	2,000
Multiplexer (8 ports)	1,400
Statistical multiplexer (16 channels)	4,000
Server	3,000
Gateway/bridge/router	4,000–7,000
Printer (laser)	2,000
Front end	10,000
Intelligent terminal controller (4 ports)	2,000
Network analyzer	4,000
Multiport modem with 4 ports (9600 bits per second)	1,000
Digital modem (DSU/CSU) at 56,000 bits per second	850
DSU/CSU with 6 ports at 56,000 bits per second	1,900
T-1 modem (DSU/CSU) at 1,544,000 bits per second	1,500
Protocol converter	1,000

Figure 8-28   Selected hardware costs.

ages.) Figure 8-28 offers selected examples of hardware costs that can be used in network design projects.

When organizations want to use only monthly costs, they match monthly circuit costs by adjusting the hardware costs to a comparable figure. That is, instead of using the purchase price of the hardware, they apply a 5 percent discounting rate. Using Figure 8-28, take the cost of the piece of hardware, multiply it by 0.05, and use the resulting amount as the monthly lease cost. For example, the V.32 modem costs $1,400; therefore, the V.32 modem's monthly lease cost is $70 (1,400 × 0.05 = 70).

Further Design Ideas   If you want to compare more alternative circuit types than were presented in this chapter, we suggest you call AT&T to obtain detailed tariffs for AT&T Megacom WATS (Wide Area Telephone Service), AT&T Megacom, and AT&T Megacom 800. These communication services were described in Chapter 7. Their costs are not presented here because some require maps of the bands emanating from specific telephone exchange local areas. You need the WATS maps and rates for the specific area of the United States in which you are located. Call AT&T at 1-800-222-0400 or your local AT&T business office for this information.

Figure 8-29   United States map.

You also can use the software that is described later in the Computerized Network Design section of this chapter.

The DIAL-IT 900 Service charges were included with the description of that service in Chapter 7. Perhaps you can think of an idea to make money with this service!

There are design problems for you to complete at the end of this chapter. Also consider developing your own network design problem from scratch. All you need to do is identify the cities you want to connect, draw them on a map, determine the bits per second traffic volume between these cities so you know what type or number of circuits are required, and calculate the costs (circuits, modems, terminals, multiplexers, and the like), using the previous material. Put each cost element onto a network cost analyzer (Figure 8-19) as you perform these calculations. Figure 8-29 can be used to draw your network. Use a photocopier to enlarge it.

Deliverable for Step 12   The report for Step 12 is the cost of the circuits. It also may include hardware and software costs. It should be presented as succinctly as possible by using the network cost analyzer shown in Figure 8-19. Use a photocopier to enlarge Figure 8-19 for this purpose, then use correction fluid to remove the dollars listed across the top row, and insert your own numbers in their place.

13. IMPLEMENT THE NETWORK

At this point there are two more subtasks.

- Sell the network both to management and to the users who will have to work with it. This is a verbal presentation.

- Implement the network. This probably is the most difficult task of all because the various pieces of hardware, protocol/software programs, network management/test facilities, and communication circuits must be assembled into a working network.

Selling the Proposed Network to Management   When presenting the network to gain management and daily user acceptance, the designer should be prepared for objections to the proposed network. Basic objections usually follow these lines.

- The cost is too high, or it appears too low for what the network is supposed to be able to do.
- The performance is not good enough, or it is more than required at this time.
- The new network does not meet the goals, objectives, and policies of the organization/departments that will be using it.
- The response or processing time is either too slow or too fast with respect to other operations within the organization.
- The network is not flexible enough. If changes are made in other areas, the network may collapse and the investment will be wasted.
- The quality, capacity, efficiency, accuracy, or reliability of the new network does not meet management's criteria.
- Certain management personnel may dislike or distrust the network design team's motives, personalities, or presentation methods.
- The list of evaluation criteria that was prepared earlier in Step 2 should be reviewed so you can be ready for questions on any criteria that were not met.

Implementing the Network   The implementation process begins *after* management has agreed to install and finance the new network. Implementation consists of the installation of the new network and the removal of the old network. It involves hardware, protocols/software, communication circuits, a network management/test facility, people, written procedures that specify how each task in the network is performed, training, and complete documentation of the operating network.

The steps involved in implementing a new data communication network can be very complex and demanding. A detailed *implementation plan* should be developed to enable implementation to proceed as smoothly as possible. The plan should specify who will do what and when they will do it. For this to be done properly, Gantt charts, the Program Evaluation Review Technique (PERT),[5] or a microcomputer-based planning tool should be used.

The design/implementation team must take into account the earliest lead times that are required to order hardware, software, and circuits. In many cases these items cannot be delivered immediately. In addition, some lead time is needed for testing the protocols and software to ensure they operate in conjunction with the

---

[5] FitzGerald and FitzGerald, *Fundamentals of System Analysis*, Gantt charts, pp. 170–173; flowcharts, pp. 551–561; PERT, pp. 536–548; DFD, pp. 61–74.

hardware and circuits. Both hardware and circuits may have to be implemented in various parts of a building, city, state, throughout the country, or even internationally. For this reason, it is imperative that a decision is made as to how the new network will be implemented. Four basic approaches can be used.

- All at once. All nodes and the host computer are started up at the same time (a one-for-one changeover).
- Chronologically, and in sequence, through the network. Start with the first application system, implementing the portions of the network that must be implemented with it, and then move on to the second application system.
- In predetermined phases. Similar areas within the network are started up at one time, and other areas are started up later.
- Pilot operation. Set up a pilot or test facility to ensure the operation is as expected before an all-at-once or chronological cutover is made.

Once the hardware is in place, the circuits have been installed, and the protocol/ software is operating, training of the users can begin, although when possible it should be started earlier. It is advantageous to obtain test terminals so terminal operators can use their particular application system in a training/test mode months before they do so in real life. Precise written procedures are required on how the terminal operators are to operate the application system for data input and manipulation. Written descriptions on how to retrieve and interpret the information and data output should be provided to management.

The training should include individual operator training, extensive written training manuals, and a methodology for continual updating of these manuals. At this point, the use of Computer Assisted Instruction (CAI) should be considered. With CAI there are no written manuals; all the training techniques and procedures are stored in the computer system, and the operators use their terminals for training as well as for standard business operations. Developers of most newer systems place much emphasis on the "user-friendliness" of their systems, providing extensive online help screens.

The network management and test center is a vital link in the network. This group must be in operation *before* the network is cut over to an operational status because reliability, or uptime, is the single most important criterion for user acceptance.

Evaluating the Operating Network Finally, after the network is operational, conduct follow-ups for the first six months or so to ensure that all parts of the new network actually are operating and that no minor activities or operations have been overlooked.

After the network is considered fully operational, a reevaluation should be performed 6 or 12 months later. This is a critical review of operator or user complaints, management complaints, efficiency reports, network management trouble reports, an evaluation of statistics gathered on items such as errors during transmission and characters transmitted per link, and a review of peak load factors. Of course, it also should include a complete review of the original evaluation criteria so the success of the design, development, and implementation of the new data communication network can be determined.

Deliverable for Step 13   In summary, 13 steps are performed to design a new data communication network. Although some steps may be omitted when a current network is enhanced, an orderly plan still must be followed. As the project closes, pull all the documentation together and arrange it in a binder that contains 13 separate sections, one for each step carried out. The final report also should contain the implementation plan, a description of problems encountered, and any required approvals.

COMPUTERIZED NETWORK DESIGN

Deregulation of the communication industry has brought unprecedented change to the way in which communication services are provided. Prior to deregulation, one common carrier offered end-to-end services and all requests for service were directed to this one common carrier. Today it takes several carriers and sometimes many different business transactions to accomplish the same thing. Nowhere is this new reality more pronounced or more complex than in the area of private line services. Where there once was one interstate private line tariff, there now are many interLATA tariffs—not to mention intraLATA tariffs and those of the various other competing private line suppliers.

Today's sophisticated network users are turning to automated network design tools as a means of calculating network costs and for the continual redesign of their voice and data networks. Such network design tools can be a major investment, ranging in price from several thousand dollars to over $50,000. On the other hand, rather than purchasing mainframe-based network design tools, some organizations opt to use them on a timesharing basis.

Network Design Tool Functions   Network design tools can perform a number of functions. The functions we will cover in this section are cost analysis, performance analysis, map and configuration drawing, and network configuration optimization.

Cost analysis requires that the vendor from whom the network design tool is purchased continually update the databases of LATAs (local access transport areas) and tariffs (prices). These databases contain tariff filings and LATAs for the various common carriers from whom the organization leases its data communication circuits. Depending on the sophistication of the network design tool, the databases might contain both interLATA and intraLATA tariffs.

The cost analysis portion of a network design tool should allow users to experiment with different tariffs and select from a variety of configurations. These different arrangements allow users to select multidrop circuits in a long haul or intraLATA common carrier's central office. The object is to allow users to explore the consequences of changing between different communication circuits or different common carriers, resulting in a minimal cost network.

Performance analysis allows users to estimate the response times and throughput of their network. It is important to note that these network design tools only provide estimates, which may vary from the actual results. Some network design tools estimate performance for a generalized class of network, such as any multidrop network, but other network design tools are built specifically for one type of network.

Map and configuration drawing packages provide documentation on how the network is to appear and the equipment it will contain. Network design software supplies predrawn maps on which the network designer lays out the various WAN, MAN, BN, and LAN configurations. Network drawing software was introduced in Chapter 6 (page 246).

Configuration optimization (sometimes called *topology optimization*) enables users to design the optimal layout of a network. Network design tools usually identify the optimal layout by interactively trying various combinations of configurations until the one that shows the lowest network cost is determined. Most modeling packages are able to optimize networks containing multidrop circuits, concentrators placed strategically throughout the network, and packet switches. The final result as to how "good" the optimization is depends on the algorithm used by the network design tool vendor.

Optimization is a CPU intensive process; therefore, large networks require a mainframe to optimize. Alternatively, microcomputers can be used for optimizing networks of less than 500 nodes. Optimization usually is based on establishing some given performance constraints and having the optimization algorithm optimize the network using these constraints. For example, the user might specify the maintenance of a three-second response time and require that the program lay out and optimize a least cost multidrop network based on 50 nodes. Beyond the three-second response time and the locations of the 50 nodes, the user also may specify other parameters such as the common carrier, transmission media, traffic volume statistics, basic characteristics of the terminals, microcomputers, host processors, front end processor, and the protocol that is to be used.

A sophisticated network design tool should be capable of analyzing hybrid networks that include multidrop, concentrators, and packet switching. Furthermore, the tool should allow users to modify items such as protocols, tariffs, circuit configurations, equipment characteristics, and such performance objectives as two- or three-second response time requirements.

Because the run time for one of these tools tends to increase as the square of the number of sites, users may need to reduce run times to those that can fit on a microcomputer. This is achieved by dividing the network into segments and optimizing different portions of it, such as different regions of the country or various multidrop segments.

To help you understand how some of these network design tools are used, the following sections describe several of them. The first one, Cost Analysis for Multiple Locations (CAML), is used to estimate the price of various dial-up services, such as long distance direct dialing, PRO-WATS, Megacom, and WATS. Next, the Private Line Pricer (PLP) is used to analyze the pricing of a wide range of private line circuit configurations. It provides comparative price information. MIND-Data/PC is used to price, manage, optimize, and design multipoint private line data networks.

It gives a graphic portrayal of what the network will look like when the various links are connected. The AUTONET tool generates minimal cost networks for mesh, multipoint, and point-to-point networks. Finally, we include the GrafNet Plus network display and documentation system that is used to draw network maps.

Cost Analysis for Multiple Locations (CAML)   The *Cost Analysis for Multiple Locations* (CAML) software is by SAV-NET USA, Inc., Route 202 and Hillside Ave., P.O. Box 236, Bedminster, N.J. 07921 (1-908-781-0950). It allows users to do a simple, quick pricing of several AT&T long distance services. To accurately predict savings, you must price each individual call under all possible long distance plans, but it often is not practical to do this. CAML can demonstrate the potential savings for AT&T WATS, AT&T Megacom WATS, AT&T Pro WATS, and direct dial long distance rates.

The output of the CAML program is based on the actual prices for the various services it itemizes. CAML uses numerous rules of thumb to make assumptions about uniformity of calling patterns and call durations. It is quite accurate in most cases. To gain an understanding of this accuracy, try entering data from actual AT&T bills and compare the estimates to the actual amounts. Occasionally, the program can be fooled when the data is not what it considers to be "normal." In most cases, however, the predicted result is quite close to the actual result.

The CAML software is available to professors adopting this text. (Students should ask their professor to obtain it.) Please contact your John Wiley sales representative or call John Wiley Sales Support at 1-800-225-5945 (ext. 6462). CAML is on a single 360,000 bytes 5.25-inch diskette for any IBM or compatible microcomputer. It runs from the floppy diskette in either Drive A or Drive B, or from a subdirectory on a hard disk. It requires DOS 2.1 or greater and 256,000 bytes of RAM (memory).

To install CAML on a hard disk, make a subdirectory and copy the contents of the diskette into the subdirectory by using the DOS COPY *.* command. To run the program, log onto the hard disk subdirectory containing the CAML files, or log onto Drive A or Drive B if you are using the floppy diskette. Type the word CAML and press the Enter key.

The main menu shown in Figure 8-30 follows the SAV-NET/CAML welcome and disclaimer displays. Selecting an option from this or any other CAML menu is simple. You can use the arrow keys to move the highlighted bar to the option of your choice and press the Enter (Return) key to select the desired option, or you can press the function key (F1, F2, and so forth) that corresponds to your selection option and selection takes place immediately.

You may want to start CAML by pressing the F3 function key at the main menu. This permits you to customize the program with your name and address, thereby personalizing your printed reports. Press F2 if you want to view the rates (tariffs).

Press F1 at the main menu to run CAML, and you will see the main data entry screen, which is shown in Figure 8-31. Move around the screen with the arrow, tab, and Enter keys. You can edit entries with the Insert and Delete keys. When all the entries have been completed, press the End key to proceed.

Read the Following Field Descriptions Carefully! Complete understanding of the various input fields and the assumptions made regarding these inputs must be under-

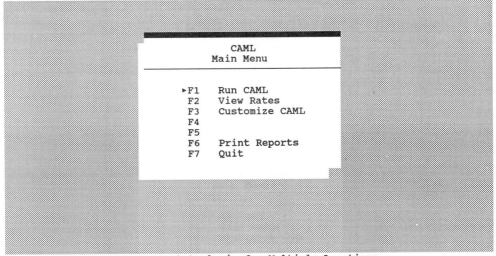

CAML - Cost Analysis for Multiple Locations

Figure 8-30 Cost Analysis for Multiple Locations (CAML) main menu.

stood if you want to obtain accurate estimates. Moreover, small mistakes made during entry can greatly decrease the accuracy of the output report. Relate the following field descriptions, such as Unrounded Minutes, to Figure 8-31.

Unrounded Minutes (less than one minute rounding)   Enter the number of minutes of real daytime usage per month. If you are entering this information from an actual bill, the entry should be calculated with sub-minute accuracy. That is, if a call lasts 1.2 minutes, it is billed as 1.2 minutes and not as 2 minutes. On

```
                        Direct    Credit
                        Dialed     Card
                        ------    ------
           Domestic
                                            Geographic Distribution
      Unrounded Minutes:  _____            ------(in Miles)-------
        Rounded Minutes:  _____   _____   1-300     300-900      900+
Total Interstate Calls:  _____   _____   33___      33___       33___

         International
                                            Approx. Distance to POP
      Qualified Minutes:  _____   _____   ----------------------
 Total Qualified Calls:  _____   _____            5__
   Avg. Monthly Expense: $_____  $_____
                                            Include Evening/Nite? (Y/N)  N

                                            Include Intrastate? (Y/N)    N
                         Actual Usage - Not Rounded
```

CAML - Cost Analysis for Multiple Locations

Figure 8-31 CAML data entry screen.

AT&T bills, WATS and Pro WATS are examples of sub-minute billed calls. Some other common carriers (OCCs), such as MCI or US Sprint, also bill in sub-minute increments. The rounding factor is critical to understanding and calculating potential savings. A past bill is not required to use this program. You can enter the estimated number of minutes for network design problems.

Rounded Minutes (one minute rounding)   Enter the number of daytime minutes of usage for one month. Unlike the Unrounded Minutes mentioned above, this data should come directly from an AT&T or OCC long distance bill in which calls are timed to the greatest minute. That is, a 2.1 minute call is billed as 3 minutes and not as 2.1 minutes. A past bill is not required to use this program. You can enter the estimated number of minutes for network design problems.

Total Interstate Calls   Enter the total number of calls made during the month. For example, if there are 6 calls per day and 22 days per month, then the total number of calls is 132 (6 × 22). This should correspond to the total number of calls entered in the minutes fields, including both Rounded Minutes and Unrounded Minutes if you have entries in both fields. If either the Rounded or Unrounded Minutes section is completed and no entry is made under Total Interstate Calls, CAML fills in this field automatically, CAML assumes the average call lasts 4 minutes. Obviously, allowing CAML to guess the average call length and number of calls makes the output less accurate than if you use the actual number of calls. Allow CAML to estimate the average call length only when you do not have the actual number.

Geographic Distribution (in Miles)   Calling patterns can be simulated by telling CAML the percentage of calls that are made to the three mileage bands (1–300, 300–900, 900+) shown on the data entry screen. If no entry is made in this section, CAML assumes the calling pattern is equal among all geographic tiers and assigns 33 percent to each band.

If you have a known pattern differing from the CAML assumption, you should enter this distribution as a percentage in the appropriate field(s). For example, if you are in New York and 50 percent of the outgoing calls are to locations in the northeastern United States that are 300 or less miles from New York, then you enter 50 in the 1–300 miles band. You then enter 25 in each of the other two bands if that is their distribution, or use the delete key for the two 33s shown in those two bands and allow CAML to calculate them for you. If you make entries in any or all categories, and they do not add up to 100, all calls are allocated in the proportions your entries indicate. When CAML's output differs from an actual bill, correcting the geographic distribution often makes the estimated output amount closer to the actual amount.

Approximate Distance to POP   The mileage for a T-1 circuit is used to estimate the cost of T-1 service and voice grade private line access to AT&T Megacom WATS service. This number should be the mileage between your end office and the nearest AT&T Megacom point of presence (POP). If you do not enter a number here, CAML assumes it is 5 miles.

Include Evening/Nite Usage?   Enter a Y in this field if your billing indicates calls made during evening and night/weekend rate periods. After completing the remainder of the input screen, an additional window opens for you to enter the evening and night/weekend data. Follow the same rules stated above for entering either Rounded Minutes or Unrounded Minutes.

Include Intrastate Usage?   Enter Y in this field if you want to include the costs of intrastate usage. CAML does not contain intrastate rates or pricing data, so you need to know the cost from an actual bill or be able to estimate this value. Contact your local telephone company for intrastate rate tables. If you enter a Y in this field, an additional window opens after you complete the remainder of the input screen so you can enter the intrastate data.

The intrastate cost window requests items that can be found on the bill of an existing AT&T customer. If your firm uses another carrier for intrastate calling, you must determine the cost as though AT&T were the carrier. If you know this charge and you are not a Pro State user, enter your intrastate long distance cost followed by the Pro State discount and monthly cost for your jurisdiction. If you are a Pro State customer, enter the billed cost and enter 0 (zero) for the discount followed by the monthly Pro State cost. CAML applies the discount entered to the cost and includes it in the output and analysis.

After entering the data, press End and Enter for CAML to calculate the costs (see Figure 8-32). CAML then displays the costs. A menu at the bottom of the screen allows you to choose F1 to edit inputs, F2 to review the current inputs, F3 to print, or F4 to return to the main menu. You also can print from the main menu.

```
                                              ═Rates current as of 03/15/90═
               LD           PRO/ML          Mega/ML        Wats/ML
            --------     ------------      ------------    ------------
DOMESTIC                                   (0 T1s          (2 lines)
                                            2 lines)
Direct      $230         $220/176          $619/606        $287/257
Card        $74          $67/63            $63/63          $74/74
Intrastate  $0           $0/0              $0/0            $0/0

INTERNATIONAL

Direct      $0           $0/0              $0/0            $0/0
Card        $0           $0/0              $0/0            $0/0
Supp Disc   $            $(0)/(0)          $               $
            --------     ------------      ------------    ------------
Total       $305         $287/239          $683/669        $361/331
ML Savings  $            $47               $13             $30
% Savings                16.5%             2.0%            8.3%

     ▶F1     Edit Inputs        F2    Review Current Inputs
      F3     Print              F4    Return to Main Menu

             CAML - Cost Analysis for Multiple Locations
```

Figure 8-32   Video display of CAML costs showing that direct dial-up long distance (LD) calls are a little more expensive than AT&T's Pro WATS (PRO/ML).

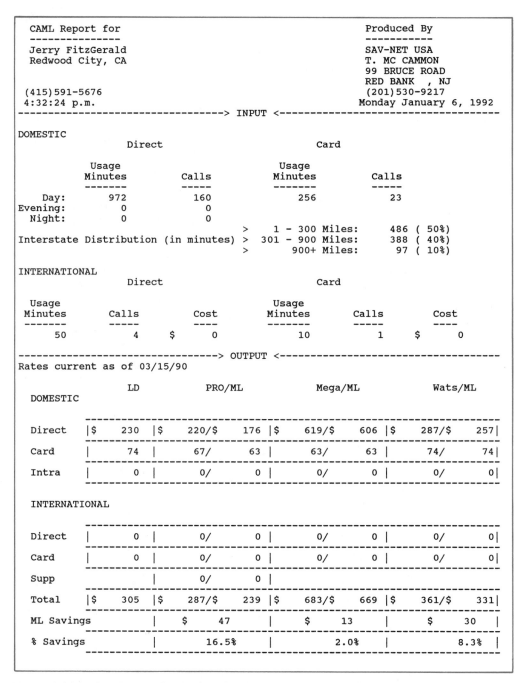

```
CAML Report for                              Produced By
---------------                              -----------
Jerry FitzGerald                             SAV-NET USA
Redwood City, CA                             T. MC CAMMON
                                             99 BRUCE ROAD
                                             RED BANK  , NJ
(415)591-5676                                (201)530-9217
4:32:24 p.m.                                 Monday January 6, 1992
-------------------------------> INPUT <-------------------------------

DOMESTIC
                  Direct                          Card

            Usage                          Usage
            Minutes         Calls          Minutes         Calls
            -------         -----          -------         -----
    Day:      972            160             256             23
Evening:        0              0
  Night:        0              0
                                >   1 - 300 Miles:      486 ( 50%)
Interstate Distribution (in minutes) > 301 - 900 Miles:  388 ( 40%)
                                >        900+ Miles:       97 ( 10%)


INTERNATIONAL
                  Direct                          Card

  Usage                                   Usage
  Minutes        Calls         Cost       Minutes        Calls         Cost
  -------        -----         ----       -------        -----         ----
     50            4        $    0            10            1        $    0

-------------------------------> OUTPUT <-------------------------------
Rates current as of 03/15/90

                  LD            PRO/ML          Mega/ML          Wats/ML
   DOMESTIC


  Direct    |$    230  |$    220/$   176  |$   619/$  606  |$   287/$   257|
            --------------------------------------------------------------
  Card      |     74   |     67/     63   |    63/    63   |    74/     74|
            --------------------------------------------------------------
  Intra     |      0   |      0/      0   |     0/     0   |     0/      0|
            --------------------------------------------------------------

  INTERNATIONAL

            --------------------------------------------------------------
  Direct    |      0   |      0/      0   |     0/     0   |     0/      0|
            --------------------------------------------------------------
  Card      |      0   |      0/      0   |     0/     0   |     0/      0|
            --------------------------------------------------------------
  Supp      |          |      0/      0   |
            --------------------------------------------------------------
  Total     |$    305  |$    287/$   239  |$   683/$  669  |$   361/$   331|
            --------------------------------------------------------------
  ML Savings|          |  $     47        |  $    13       |  $     30    |
            --------------------------------------------------------------
  % Savings |          |     16.5%        |      2.0%      |      8.3%    |
            --------------------------------------------------------------
```

Figure 8-33 Printed report for CAML showing both the input and the output.

Print reports   If you want to create a printout or create a file of the input and output data, you do so either by choosing that option from the output screen menu (F3) or by choosing Print Reports from the main menu (F6). Figure 8-33 shows a CAML printed report.

If you want to create a file, choose that option from the print menu for an entry screen to appear. First, enter the name of the file you want to create. The filename should conform to DOS with a maximum of eight characters for the filename and three characters for the extension. If you do not enter a filename, CAML uses the default CAML.FIL for the file's name. Next, enter your name, location, and telephone number (or that of someone for whom you are creating the report). When you have finished, press the End key. CAML saves the data in an ASCII file in the CAML directory unless you specify otherwise.

If you want to create a printed report, choose that option from the print menu for an entry screen to appear. First, enter your name, location, and telephone number (or that of someone for whom you are creating the report). When you have finished, press the End key. CAML checks to be sure the printer is operational. If it is, CAML prompts you to press the Enter key to begin printing. If you have a dot matrix printer, be sure the paper is aligned before printing; otherwise the output spreads over two pages.

Review Input   If you are at the output screen and want to review the values entered in the various fields, move the light bar to the Review Current Inputs (F2) option and press the Enter key. The input screen scrolls into view. When finished, press Enter to return to the output screen.

Edit/Change Input   If you are at the output screen and want to enter new data or edit existing data, move the light bar to the Edit Inputs (F1) option to return to the input screen. After editing, press End to return to the output screen.

The remaining four field descriptions explain the LD, PRO/ML, Mega/ML, and WATS/ML. These four headings appear in the columns in both Figure 8-32 and Figure 8-33.

LD (Long distance)   This column shows the calculated long distance cost based on n calls of t length, where n is the number entered or assumed from the number of calls input and t is the total minutes of usage divided by n. The numbers in this column are approximate—they approximate the rates of real long distance calls by upward rounding. That is, if the actual average call length is 4.2 minutes, calls are priced as though they average 4.7 minutes. Even though the variance is 0.5 minute, this method of approximation works. The total cost of AT&T Calling Card calls is similarly rounded and added to this column, as are international and intrastate costs if they have been entered.

International costs are equal to the value you entered in the input section. Daytime rates are used for the Calling Card service. Although they are not displayed, any evening and night usage you may have entered in the input section is included here.

Pro/ML (AT&T Pro WATS)   This column is calculated based on the tariffed rates for the AT&T Pro WATS service. Then all applicable volume and usage discounts are applied, as are international usage discounts. It includes fixed monthly costs for the Pro WATS service. These figures are totaled. The savings and percentage of savings from using this plan versus regular long distance are displayed.

Mega/ML (AT&T Megacom® WATS) This column is calculated based on the tariffed rates for the AT&T Megacom WATS service. It includes applicable fixed monthly rates. Any AT&T Calling Card and international discounts (AT&T World Connect® rates) are applied. Then these items are totaled. The savings and percentage of savings from this plan versus regular long distance are displayed.

The cost for access is included in the price of service; it is approximate, and it is based on a composite of various intrastate access tariffs. You should be aware that access costs vary widely from state to state and by type of access (T1.5 and voice grade). The number of lines or T1.5 access lines required is calculated using the Poisson distribution; it is accurate only to a total of 100 virtual lines. Also note that, if intrastate information was entered, the displayed cost under Megacom service is the same as for the Pro State costs under the Pro WATS section mentioned above. Intrastate Megacom service may be less or more costly, but intrastate pricing is beyond the scope of CAML.

WATS/ML (AT&T WATS) This column is calculated based on the tariffed rates for the "virtually banded" version of the AT&T WATS service. All volume and usage discounts are applied, including those for the AT&T Calling Card service and international calls. These items are totaled. The savings and percentage of savings from this plan versus regular long distance are displayed.

Note that the cost for the required dedicated access lines is included in the price of the service. Also note that, if intrastate information was entered, the displayed cost under WATS services is the same as for the Pro WATS section mentioned above. As with Megacom, intrastate WATS service may be less or more costly, but intrastate pricing is beyond the scope of CAML.

Private Line Pricer The *Private Line Pricer* (PLP) is a PC-based software tool that is used for estimating the cost of voice grade lease lines. The Private Line Pricer database of tariffs is updated monthly. It runs on an IBM PC, AT, XT, PS/2, or compatible with a hard disk. It requires DOS 2.0 or higher. It also requires a minimum of 512,000 bytes of random access memory and a minimum of 5 million bytes of available space on the hard disk.

A working educational version is available for the Private Line Pricer. This version contains a database of ten area codes that students can use to see how varying circuit connections are priced. This version also runs on IBM PCs or compatible and requires 512,000 bytes of memory; however, it does not require a hard disk like the full version. The educational version is delivered on one floppy diskette. To obtain the educational version, professors may contact Ms. Mary McCarthy at Economics and Technology, Inc., 1 Washington Mall, Boston, Mass. 02108, or by calling her at 1-800-225-2496 or 1-617-227-0900 if you are in Massachusetts. Professors also may obtain it by contacting their John Wiley sales representative or by calling John Wiley Sales Support at 1-800-225-5945 (ext. 6462). (Students should ask their professor to obtain it.)

Private Line Pricer deals with a wide range of private line circuit configurations, from simple two-point end-to-end services to complex multicarrier, multipoint configurations. The Private Line Pricer's database contains information about the location and availability of service for every telephone exchange in the 48 contiguous states. Moreover, optional tariff libraries include over 100 different interLATA and intraLATA tariffs and rate schedules for a full range of analog and digital, voice and data, and terrestrial-based services. This software allows you, quickly and automatically, to do the following.

- Calculate recurring and nonrecurring charges for simple and complex private lines
- Prepare accurate budgets and network cost estimates
- Verify common carrier billings
- Identify least cost routing for two-point circuits
- Compare the rates and service options of different carriers
- Retrieve data on any telephone exchange in the 48 contiguous states
- Build and maintain your own circuit database, which can be integrated with those of other microcomputer and mainframe applications
- Reprice existing circuits when rates change

To put what Private Line Pricer does into perspective, we should look at what must be done when the price of a simple two-point circuit is calculated manually. It may be useful to refer to Figure 8-22 while reading how this is accomplished. In addition, you should be aware that firms dealing in tariffs are more specific in how they reference tariffs. In the following steps the tariffs are referred to as NECA (National Exchange Carriers Association) tariffs and AT&T (American Telephone & Telegraph Company) tariffs to distinguish the part of the tariff that applies to the particular step. In this example AT&T tariffs deal with the interLATA connections, and NECA tariffs deal with the intraLATA connections.

Step 1   Obtain vertical and horizontal coordinates for the wire center (same as a rate center or end office) that serves each customer's premises (NECA Tariff 2). This is the switching facility in which the subscriber's local loop terminates.

Step 2   Determine the LATAs in which the origin and destination NPA-NXXs are located (NECA Tariff 2). The *NPA-NXX* is the first six digits of the telephone number, with the *NPA* portion being the area code and the *NXX* portion being the prefix or exchange code. For example, an NPA-NXX of 212-736 is for the 212 area code and 736 is for a midtown Manhattan prefix. Obviously, the last four digits of the telephone number are not included in 212-736.

Step 3   Obtain vertical and horizontal coordinates for all AT&T central offices (the same as the AT&T point of presence) in the two LATAs that provide the desired type of service (AT&T Tariff 10).

Step 4 Obtain vertical and horizontal coordinates for the wire center (end office or rate center) that serves each AT&T central office or point of presence (AT&T Tariff 10).

Step 5 Calculate the distance between the wire centers (end offices) serving the customers' premises and each of the central offices (points of presence). This must be done for each central office located in the same LATA as the customer premises. This calculation uses the same basic formula as the one shown in Figure 8-21, except that letters have been substituted to designate the customer's premises and the point of presence.

$$\text{Distance} = \sqrt{\frac{(V_C - V_P)^2 + (H_C - H_P)^2}{10}}$$

where (V_C, H_C) = coordinates of the wire center serving the customer's premises,
(V_P, H_P) = coordinates of the wire center serving the central office (point of presence).

Step 6 Calculate the interLATA distance between the central offices using the formula given in Step 5. This must be done for the central offices closest to each customer's premises. Sometimes you can select another central office to reduce the total price of the circuit.

Step 7 Apply Tariff 9 and 11 rates to the local circuits and interLATA circuit.

Step 8 Add the special access surcharge and message station recovery charge if applicable.

Step 9 Add the optional charges, such as those for conditioning, multiplexing, and signaling.

As you can see, this is a fairly complex exercise. The Private Line Pricer does the work for you in just a few seconds. It uses a three-step process during which the user answers questions that appear on the screen.

1. After entering the Private Line Pricer program, you select the type of service in which you are interested. The screen with these services is shown in Figure 8-34.

2. After answering the questions from the Service Description screen, you proceed to the Circuit Description screen (Figure 8-35) where you fill in the required circuit end points and tariffs.

3. The third screen (Figure 8-36) summarizes the circuit prices. The next three screens provide details of the prices for each circuit leg. These are for the local loop to the point of presence at one end (Figure 8-37), the local loop to the point of presence at the other end (Figure 8-38), and the interLATA circuit linking the AT&T point of presence in each LATA (Figure 8-39).

```
| ETI PRIVATE LINE PRICER                                            |
|             SERVICE DESCRIPTION                                    |
|_____|
|                                                                   |
|                                                                   |
|                                                                   |
| SELECT SERVICE:                                                   |
|   A.  Analog voice                                                |
|   B.  Analog data                                                 |
|   C.  Digital data (2.4 - 56.0 kbps)                              |
|   D.  High capacity digital (1.544 Mbps)                          |
|   Q.  Return to previous menu                                     |
|                                                                   |
| Calculate nonrecurring charges (Y for Yes, N for No):        Y    |
| Specify 2- or 4-Wire (Type 2 or 4):                          2    |
| Does signalling apply to this circuit ? (Y for Yes, N for No): N  |
|_____|
```

Figure 8-34 Private Line Pricer Service Description screen. This is the first step in which the desired service and options are selected. In this instance, the user has selected interstate jurisdiction, analog voice service (two-wire), no signaling, and nonrecurring charges.

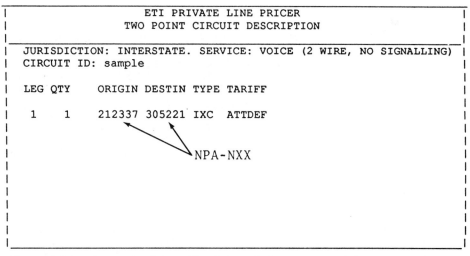

```
| ETI PRIVATE LINE PRICER                                            |
|          TWO POINT CIRCUIT DESCRIPTION                             |
|_____|
| JURISDICTION: INTERSTATE.  SERVICE: VOICE (2 WIRE, NO SIGNALLING) |
| CIRCUIT ID: sample                                                |
|                                                                   |
| LEG QTY     ORIGIN DESTIN TYPE TARIFF                             |
|                                                                   |
|  1    1     212337 305221 IXC  ATTDEF                             |
|                                                                   |
|                         NPA-NXX                                   |
|                                                                   |
|_____|
```

Figure 8-35 Private Line Pricer Circuit Description screen. This is the screen in which the user fills in the required circuit information. The user has selected "sample" as the circuit name. This circuit connects 212-337 (New York, New York) with 305-221 (Miami, Florida), and it uses AT&T's end-to-end tariff with "default" routing.

```
| ---------------------------------------------------------------------- |
|                    ETI PRIVATE LINE PRICER                             |
|                    CIRCUIT PRICE SUMMARY                               |
| _____|
| CIRCUIT ID:       SAMPLE                                               |
| SERVICE :         VOICE              JURISDICTION: INTER               |
| CIRCUIT FILE:     TESTFIL            PRICEOUT DATE :   JUN 27 1989      |
|                                                                        |
| LEG QTY    ORIGIN DEST     TARIFF    EFF DATE    MONTHLY        NRC     |
|                                                                        |
|  1    1    212337 101328   ATT11     050289 $    170.12 $   1079.49    |
|  2    1    104607 305221   ATT11     042189 $    150.22 $    986.82    |
|  3    1    101328 104607   ATT9      021189 $    708.40 $    392.00    |
|                                                                        |
|                                                                        |
|                                                                        |
|                                                                        |
|                                                                        |
| TOTAL CHARGES                                 $   1028.74 $   2458.31  |
|                                                                        |
| _____|
```

Figure 8-36 Private Line Pricer Circuit Price Summary screen. This screen displays the total monthly and nonrecurring charges for the circuit using AT&T's point of presence (POP) closest to each customer's premises. In this instance, the circuit connects the point of presence 101-328 in New York's zone 1 with the point of presence 104-607 in North Dade, Florida. The NPA 101 is the area code for the AT&T POP end office. You cannot dial the POP, which is why you may not recognize the area code number.

```
| ---------------------------------------------------------------------- |
|                    ETI PRIVATE LINE PRICER                             |
|                    CIRCUIT PRICE DETAIL                                |
| _____|
|CIRCUIT ID:    SAMPLE                                                   |
|FILE      :    TESTFIL   JURISDICTION: INTER    LEG    :   1 OF 3       |
|CARRIER   :    ATT       TARIFF:    ATT11       SERVICE:   VOICE        |
|                                                                        |
|               NPA-NXX EXCHANGE   LEC  STATE    --V--  --H--  LATA      |
|ORIGIN      :  212337  NYCMNY18   NYTC NY       4998   1407   132       |
|DESTINATION:   101328  NYCMNY50        NY       4993   1409   132       |
| _____|
|                                                MONTHLY       NRC      |
|MILEAGE CHARGE :              2 MILES      $      159.57 $   912.49     |
| SURCHARGE:                                $        0.00 $     0.00     |
|ACCESS COORDINATION CHARGE:                $       10.55 $   167.00     |
|                                                                        |
|                                                                        |
|                                                                        |
|                                                                        |
|UNIT PRICE:                                $      170.12 $  1079.49     |
|TOTAL CHARGES:         1  CIRCUIT(S)       $      170.12 $  1079.49     |
| _____|
```

Figure 8-37 Private Line Pricer Circuit Price Detail screen. This screen shows the price of the local loop that connects 212-337 (the customer's premises) in New York with its closest AT&T point of presence (101-328) using Tariff 11.

```
|                        ETI PRIVATE LINE PRICER                      |
|                        CIRCUIT PRICE DETAIL                         |
|_____|
|CIRCUIT ID:    SAMPLE                                                |
|FILE      :    TESTFIL    JURISDICTION: INTER    LEG   :  2 OF 3     |
|CARRIER   :    ATT        TARIFF:    ATT11       SERVICE:  VOICE     |
|                                                                     |
|             NPA-NXX EXCHANGE   LEC  STATE    --V-- --H-- LATA       |
|ORIGIN    :   104607  MIAMFLGR       FL        8351   528   460      |
|DESTINATION:  305221  MIAMFLCA  SBTC FL        8374   552   460      |
|_____ |
|                                              MONTHLY      NRC       |
|MILEAGE CHARGE :           11 MILES       $   139.67  $  819.82      |
|SURCHARGE:                                $     0.00  $    0.00      |
|ACCESS COORDINATION CHARGE:               $    10.55  $  167.00      |
|                                                                     |
|                                                                     |
|                                                                     |
|                                                                     |
|UNIT PRICE:                               $   150.22 $   986.82      |
|TOTAL CHARGES:          1   CIRCUIT(S)    $   150.22 $   986.82      |
|_____|
```

Figure 8-38 Private Line Pricer Circuit Price Detail screen. This screen shows the price of the local loop that connects 305-221 (the customer's premises) in Miami with its closest AT&T point of presence (104-607) using Tariff 11.

```
|                        ETI PRIVATE LINE PRICER                      |
|                        CIRCUIT PRICE DETAIL                         |
|_____|
|CIRCUIT ID:    SAMPLE                                                |
|FILE      :    TESTFIL    JURISDICTION: INTER    LEG   :  3 OF 3     |
|CARRIER   :    ATT        TARIFF:    ATT9        SERVICE:  VOICE     |
|                                                                     |
|             NPA-NXX EXCHANGE   LEC  STATE    --V-- --H-- LATA       |
|ORIGIN    :   101328  NYCZ 1         NY        4993  1409   132      |
|DESTINATION:  104607  MIAMI          FL        8350   529   460      |
|_____ |
|                                              MONTHLY      NRC       |
|MILEAGE CHARGE :          1098 MILES      $   675.60  $    0.00      |
|CO CONNECTION CHARGES: ( 2)               $    32.80  $  392.00      |
|                                                                     |
|                                                                     |
|                                                                     |
|                                                                     |
|                                                                     |
|UNIT PRICE:                               $   708.40 $   392.00      |
|TOTAL CHARGES:          1   CIRCUIT(S)    $   708.40 $   392.00      |
|_____|
```

Figure 8-39 Private Line Pricer Circuit Price Detail screen. This screen shows the pricing for the interLATA circuit (IXC) linking the two AT&T points of presence in each LATA (101-328 in New York's zone 1 and 104-607 in Miami) using Tariff 9.

This easy-to-use software tool provides the data and analytical capability that are needed to design and manage lease line networks. Furthermore, it eliminates the need for tariff tracking, manual lookups, and repetitive calculations. The Private Line Pricer has several components.

The *Standard Private Line Pricer* is the basic ETI package for pricing interstate circuits using AT&T Tariffs 9, 10, and 11 and the Local Exchange Companies' (Bell Operating Companies) special access tariffs. The AT&T Tariffs cover the IXC or long haul circuits, and the special access tariffs cover the customer-to-central office circuits. The standard PLP package of eight diskettes includes

- Complete 48-state vertical and horizontal coordinates database
- Two-point and multipoint pricing
- Carrier default routing for end-to-end circuits
- User-specified routing and carriers
- Services for analog voice, analog data, digital data, high capacity digital services, and T-1 circuits

The Standard Private Line Pricer can be made more powerful by adding any or all of the following options. (The entire package with all options is delivered on 13 diskettes.) *OCC PAK* is used to price interstate private lines provided by Other Common Carriers. The major ones include Contel ASC, Contel Federal Systems, MCI, National Telecommunications Network (NTN), US Sprint, and USTS (ITT). Where available, pricing includes analog voice, analog data, digital data, and high capacity digital services. The OCC PAK can be used to

- Evaluate rate and service offerings of competing carriers
- Compare routing options
- Verify carrier billings

State PAK is used to price intrastate private lines for the 48 contiguous states. It uses the tariffs for AT&T's interLATA circuits, the Bell Operating Company's special access services (customer-to-central-office circuits), and BOC intraLATA circuits. State PAK includes rates for analog voice, analog digital, analog data, digital data (2400, 4800, 9600, and 56,000 bits per second), and high capacity digital services (1,544,000 bits per second). The State PAK can be used to

- Analyze the impact of newly approved tariff filings
- Design a cost-effective network
- Estimate telecommunication costs for budgeting purposes
- Verify carrier billings

Optimizer PAK routes the end-to-end circuits of interstate carriers to minimize total monthly charges. It can be used to

- Minimize costs for two-point circuits
- Evaluate routing and carrier options
- Evaluate competitive carriers' bids

Network Optimizer (MIND-Data/PC®)   The totally new for 1992 *MIND-Data/PC* software is a comprehensive program for designing and managing private line networks. To obtain the university/college educational version of the MIND-Data/PC network design optimization package, write to Mr. David Rubin, Network Analysis Center, 6900 Jericho Turnpike, Suite 300W, Syosset, N.Y. 11791, or call him at 1-516-364-2255. The educational version is being supplied only to colleges and universities; it is not given to students. The educational version is a complete system—there are no limits on the number of nodes—and it is updated each September.

The MIND-Data/PC software consists of two major segments: the software that performs the calculations, and the complex database of tariffs and vertical/horizontal coordinates that are cross-referenced to area codes plus the first three digits of the telephone number.

MIND-Data is an interactive tool for pricing, managing, optimizing, and designing all types of private line data networks. It optimizes a centralized (polled) or mesh (packet or Transmission Control Protocol/Internet Protocol—TCP/IP) data network in terms of performance (response time and circuit utilization) and cost. The package runs on a microcomputer, and the results can interface with PC- or mainframe-based software. For example, MIND-Data/PC can perform several types of analysis, including the following.

- Design and analysis of packet switched networks.
- Reliability analysis of how the network performs in different failure modes.
- Analysis of the dynamics of a multinode circuit LAN/mesh network.
- Management tool to help telecommunication managers document, analyze, and manage their communication networks.
- Design of international networks.

This software package is a sophisticated microcomputer-based *network optimization* package for telecommunication professionals who

- Have responsibility for strategic or tactical network planning
- Need cost-effective analytical tools to carry out network analysis and design
- Perform network modeling to maintain desirable cost/performance ratios
- Perform continuous reviews of circuit pricing (tariffs) and reconciliation of billings back to planned network costs

MIND-Data is capable of response time analysis and topological design, and it allows the determination of network costs versus performance tradeoffs. The complete software package offers the capability of designing a network with anywhere from 2 to 16,000 nodes. Some tasks that MIND-Data can perform are

- Analyzing response time for both Binary Synchronous Communications (BSC) and Synchronous Data Link Control (SDLC) protocols. The protocols and other design parameters can be varied to customize your design analysis.
- Mixing of line speeds (bits per second) on different circuit links in a network.
- Drawing the layout of the network, presenting the layout on the video monitor, and printing it with a graphics subsystem.
- Pricing the network using built-in tariffs. The package uses AT&T Tariff 9 (interoffice between two different central offices) and other tariffs serving various wire centers for major metropolitan areas (NECA4 and Tariff 11). Tariffs include voice grade and digital data service (DDS) ranging from 2400 to 56,000 and 1,544,000 bits per second.
- Calculating the mileage between telephone company central offices by using a vertical and horizontal coordinates database interconnected with the LATA database.

MIND-Data covers a complete range of performance issues, along with the standard issue of designing and laying out a network. For example, it can answer a whole host of questions such as

- What is the response time for a given application profile and mix by location?
- What line speed is required?
- At what response time level is the network cost-sensitive?
- What is the impact on response time if lines are upgraded from 4800 to 9600 bits per second?
- What are the cost tradeoffs between several point-to-point circuits versus a multidrop circuit?

This package operates on an IBM AT or compatible computer. It also operates on an IBM/XT or IBM/PC; however, the AT's greater processing speed makes its use much more desirable. (A 386 or 486 is preferred.) MIND-Data also supports LAN installations. This computerized network optimizer functions *only* within the hard disk environment. In addition, it requires

- DOS version 3.0 or higher
- At least 640,000 bytes of memory (RAM)
- 22 million bytes of available hard disk storage space
- A color graphics adapter card (not a monochrome)
- A color monitor or monochrome
- Printer for reports

To load and execute, this package needs approximately 490,000 bytes of memory. Of the 640,000 bytes of RAM installed in the machine, approximately 40,000 bytes are used by DOS. Because memory-resident background programs and print spool-

Host: Tampa, Fla.
Circuit: 1 4800 bps voice grade

NODE	STREET ADDRESS	CITY	ST	ACEX	WIRE-CNTR V	H	VOICE GRADE CENTRAL OFFICE	
HOST	HEADQUARTERS	TAMPA	FL	813222	8172	1147	TAMPA	81611133
T1	OFFICE 121	TAMPA	FL	813229	8172	1147	TAMPA	81611133
T2	OFFICE 936	TAMPA	FL	813224	8172	1147	TAMPA	81611133
T5	OFFICE 994	TAMPA	FL	813221	8172	1147	TAMPA	81611133
T6	OFFICE 566	TAMPA	FL	813628	8160	1135	TAMPA	81611133

Figure 8-40   MIND-Data report. ACEX is a combination of the area code (813 for Tampa) and the first three digits of the telephone number. WIRE-CNTR shows the vertical and horizontal coordinates for a specific end office. The user chooses the identifier for each node, such as host, T1, and T2.

ers also occupy RAM, you must calculate the available memory space to allow enough capacity for MIND-Data to operate. It might be desirable to remove temporarily any other memory-resident RAM programs if you do not have enough RAM.

The program and data files consume over 22 million bytes of disk space. About 1 million bytes of disk space should be reserved for network files created during the design sessions; therefore, it is advisable to have 23 million bytes of available storage space on the hard disk.

MIND-Data uses a menu-driven approach with the F1 key for help. When using the package for the first time, read the user guide before starting so you understand the command structure. The menu-driven command line structure allows you to step through the system and move to whatever task you want to perform, such as

- Identify a type of transaction within an application
- Set up the nodes to design a new network
- Add nodes to a current network
- Save your network design
- Optimize the network to obtain costs or a response time analysis
- Print the reports showing costs, response time analysis, and so forth as shown in Figure 8-40
- Graphically display and print your network as shown in Figure 8-41
- Magnify a portion of your network by using the geographic zoom capability (see Figure 8-42 and Figure 8-43).

It is recommended that you design a two-node circuit on the first attempt, and then expand that into a four- or five-node network before proceeding with something more complex. Also note that MIND-Data/PC uses *ACEX* to represent the area code (AC) and the prefix of the telephone number (EXchange office). ACEX in MIND-Data/PC is the same as NPA/NXX in the Private Line Pricer software.

The educational version of MIND-Data is delivered on diskettes that contain the installation programs, various program files for calculations, database files for area codes, vertical and horizontal coordinates, LATA databases, and a demonstration

Figure 8-41   A wide area network (WAN) layout using MIND-Data/PC.

file called DEMO.BNF. The installation procedure is described in the documentation you will receive with your educational version.

AUTONET/MeshNet and AUTONET/Designer   This software has two parts: AUTONET/MeshNet, which generates minimal cost mesh networks, and AUTONET/Designer, which generates minimal cost multipoint and point-to-point networks. To obtain copies of AUTONET, write to Mr. Boris Dortok, Network Design and Analysis Corporation, 505 Park Ave., New York, N.Y. 10022, or call him at 1-212-688-5432. The university/college educational version of AUTONET costs $150. This software requires an IBM AT or compatible computer (preferably a 386 or 486), Windows 3.0, EGA, 4 million bytes of memory, 12 million bytes of hard disk space, a mouse, and a math coprocessor.

AUTONET/MeshNet generates minimal cost network design for mesh topologies in which any node can communicate with any other node in the network. It synthesizes network designs subject to user-specified traffic routing, capacities, and connectivity requirements.

This tool consists of a Graphical User Interface (GUI) and a Network Synthesizer. The user interacts with the GUI to specify network requirements as input data. The GUI then interacts with the AUTONET Tariff Databases to extract all relevant cost information and combines it with user-supplied data consisting of node, equipment, traffic, and physical link specifications to produce a network description. The Network Synthesizer then applies optimization algorithms to the network de-

Figure 8-42 Western United States state display with node identifiers, state names, and zoom using MIND-Data/PC.

scription to produce a network design. Users can display the results on the computer screen or send them to the printer for a paper copy. Users also can introduce network modifications to generate new designs until the results fit their needs.

AUTONET/Designer generates minimal cost network designs for multipoint and point-to-point topologies. It synthesizes network designs subject to user-specified traffic requirements. Moreover, AUTONET/Designer has the ability to specify optimal concentrator locations for a given geographical configuration.

Like its companion AUTONET/MeshNet, this tool consists of a Graphical User Interface (GUI) and a Network Synthesizer. In addition, it has a Concentrator Loca-

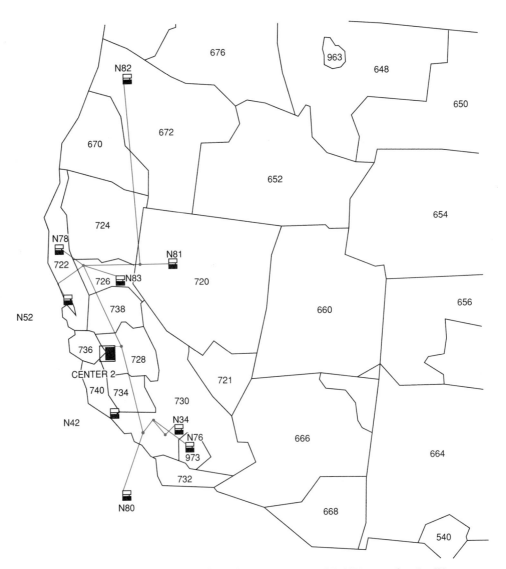

Figure 8-43 Selective MIND-Data/PC display, zoom, and LATA map for the Western United States. Notice the different boundaries between this LATA map and the state map shown in Figure 8-42.

tor. The user interacts with the GUI to specify network requirements as input data. The GUI then interacts with the AUTONET Tariff Databases to extract all relevant cost information and combines it with user-supplied data consisting of node, equipment, traffic, and link specifications to produce a network description. The Network Synthesizer applies optimization algorithms to the network description to produce a network design. Users are given the choice of specifying concentrator locations or having AUTONET/Designer find the optimal concentrator locations from a specified set of potential sites. The user can display results on the computer screen or send them to the printer for paper reports. Users also can introduce network modifications to generate new designs or modify the final design until the results fit their needs.

AUTONET/Designer has an unlimited network design capacity, bounded only by the available memory of the microcomputer. Up to 4,000 nodes can be supported on a microcomputer with 4 million bytes of memory. It allows a maximum of 50 drops on a multipoint circuit.

GrafNet Plus   The *GrafNet Plus* software was introduced in Chapter 6 where you will find its primary description and directions for obtaining a copy of the diskettes (page 246).

GrafNet Plus displays and documents communication networks on a worldwide basis. Network personnel use this software for creating and maintaining a database of network nodes and links. The software plots the network on geographical maps. You can use the zoom feature in the geographical views to narrow the view from a global display down to selectable areas as small as a square mile.

GrafNet Plus also generates extensive reports of network parameters. You can display the network graphs and reports on the screen or send them to a printer. GrafNet Plus is easy to learn and use, with the simple pull-down menus and dialog boxes of the Windows user interface. For example, GrafNet Plus

- Presents network connections on United States and Canadian maps, and on world maps with the global option.
- Places nodes on maps through simple entry of a telephone number, or alternatively by latitude and longitude information.
- Allows network views that can be scaled from a global view to a country, region, state, or other selectable area.

To compile network maps, the user enters an area code and a prefix for nodes in the United States and Canada and the country code for other nations. If desired, the user can specify the geographical location of a node by applying its latitude and longitude values. In this case, GrafNet Plus consults the two databases, relates the information, and displays each node on the selected map. With convenient pull-down menus, the user can then link the nodes and append extra descriptive information.

GrafNet Plus runs on an IBM PC/XT/AT or compatible computer with 640,000 bytes of RAM and 4 million bytes available on the hard disk. It uses Microsoft Windows 2.1x or higher, and a mouse; a color monitor is preferred.

VERTICAL AND HORIZONTAL COORDINATES

This section contains vertical and horizontal coordinates for several hundred cities in the continental United States. They can be used to calculate the mileages in design problems. We explained the calculation method in Figure 8-21. There are hundreds of these rate centers because each central or end office in a city is a rate center. This section contains only one set of V and H coordinates for each city because it is not necessary to have all the end offices for calculating the air mileage between end office locations when you are learning how to design network layouts.

	V	H		V	H
Abilene, Tex.	8698–4513		Blue Ridge Summit, Pa.	5518–1746	
Akron, Ohio	5637–2472		Boise, Idaho	7096–7869	
Albany, Ga.	7649–1817		Boone, Iowa	6394–4355	
Albany, N.Y.	4639–1629		Boston, Mass.	4422–1249	
Albuquerque, N. Mex.	8549–5887		Brewton, Ala.	8001–2244	
Alexandria, La.	8409–3168		Bridgeport, Conn.	4841–1360	
Allentown, Pa.	5166–1585		Bristow, Okla.	7799–4216	
Altoona, Pa.	5460–1972		Brockton, Mass.	4465–1205	
Amarillo, Tex.	8266–5076		Buffalo, N.Y.	5075–2326	
Anaheim, Calif.	9250–7810		Buffalo Peace Bridge, N.Y.	5074–2334	
Anniston, Ala.	7406–2304		Burlington, Iowa	6449–3829	
Antonia, Mo.	6880–3507		Burlington, Vt.	4270–1808	
Apollo, Tex.	8958–3482		Calais, Me.	3561–1208	
Appleton, Wis.	5589–3776		Cambridge, Mass.	4425–1258	
Asheville, N.C.	6749–2001		Camden, N.J.	5249–1453	
Atlanta, Ga.	7260–2083		Canton, Ohio	5676–2419	
Atlantic City, N.J.	5284–1284		Cape Girardeau, Mo.	7013–3251	
Augusta, Ga.	7089–1674		Carson City, Nev.	8139–8306	
Austin, Tex.	9005–3996		Casper, Wyo.	6918–6297	
Baker, Calif.	8888–7537		Casselton, N. Dak.	5633–5241	
Bakersfield, Calif.	8947–8060		Cedar Rapids, Iowa	6261–4021	
Baltimore, Md.	5510–1575		Centralia, Ill.	6744–3311	
Baton Rouge, La.	8476–2874		Champaign-Urbana, Ill.	6371–3336	
Beaumont, Tex.	8777–3344		Charleston, S.C.	7021–1281	
Beckley, W. Va.	6218–2043		Charleston, W. Va.	6152–2174	
Benton Ridge, Ohio	5847–2784		Charlotte, N.C.	6657–1698	
Berlin, N.J.	5257–1408		Chattanooga, Tenn.	7098–2366	
Bethia, Va.	5957–1491		Cheshire, Conn.	4755–1366	
Billings, Mont.	6391–6790		Chesterfield, Mass.	4595–1478	
Biloxi, Miss.	8296–2481		Cheyenne, Wyo.	7203–5958	
Binghampton, N.Y.	4943–1837		Chicago, Ill.	5986–3426	
Birmingham, Ala.	7518–2446		Chico, Calif.	8057–8668	
Bismarck, N. Dak.	5840–5736		Chipley, Fla.	7927–1958	
Blacksburg, Va.	6247–1867		Cincinnati, Ohio	6263–2679	
Bloomington, Ind.	6417–2984		Clarksburg, W. Va.	5865–2095	

	V H		V H
Clarksville, Tenn.	6988–2837	Fayetteville, Ark.	7600–3872
Clearwater, Fla.	8203–1206	Fayetteville, N.C.	6501–1385
Cleveland, Ohio	5574–2543	Findlay, Ohio	5828–2766
Cocoa, Fla.	7925–0903	Fitzgerald, Ga.	7539–1684
Collinsville, Ill.	6781–3455	Flagstaff, Ariz.	8746–6760
Colorado Springs, Colo.	7679–5813	Flint, Mich.	5461–2993
Columbia, S.C.	6901–1589	Florence, S.C.	6744–1417
Columbus, Ga.	7556–2045	Forrest City, Ark.	7555–3232
Columbus, Miss.	7657–2704	Fort Collins, Colo.	7331–5965
Columbus, Ohio	5972–2555	Fort Lauderdale, Fla.	8282–0557
Concord, N.H.	4326–1426	Fort Morgan, Colo.	7335–5739
Conyers, Ga.	7243–2016	Fort Myers, Fla.	8359–0904
Corpus Christi, Tex.	9475–3739	Fort Pierce, Fla.	8054–0737
Crestview, Fla.	8025–2128	Fort Walton Beach, Fla.	8097–2097
Crosby, N. Dak.	5495–6199	Fort Wayne, Ind.	5942–2982
Dallas, Tex.	8436–4034	Fort Worth, Tex.	8479–4122
Danville, Ky.	6558–2561	Framingham, Mass.	4472–1284
Davenport, Iowa	6273–3817	Frankfort, Ky.	6462–2634
Dayton, Ohio	6113–2705	Fresno, Calif.	8669–8239
Daytona Beach, Fla.	7791–1052	Gainesville, Fla.	7838–1310
Decatur, Ala.	7324–2585	Gastonia, N.C.	6683–1754
De Kalb, Ill.	6061–3591	Glenwood Springs, Colo.	7651–6263
Delta, Utah	7900–7114	Grand Forks, N. Dak.	5420–5300
Denver, Colo.	7501–5899	Grand Island, Nebr.	6901–4936
Des Moines, Iowa	6471–4275	Grand Junction, Colo.	7804–6438
Detroit, Mich.	5536–2828	Grand Rapids, Mich.	5628–3261
Dickinson, N. Dak.	5922–6024	Greeley, Colo.	7345–5895
Dodge City, Kans.	7640–4958	Green Bay, Wis.	5512–3747
Dodgeville, Wis.	5963–3890	Greensboro, N.C.	6400–1638
Dover, Del.	5429–1408	Greenville, Miss.	7888–3126
Duluth, Minn.	5352–4530	Greenville, N.C.	6250–1226
Eau Claire, Wis.	5698–4261	Greenville, S.C.	6873–1894
El Paso, Tex.	9231–5655	Greenwood, Miss.	7798–2993
Ennis, Tex.	8514–3970	Gulfport, Miss.	8317–2511
Eureka, Calif.	7856–9075	Hackensack, N.J.	4976–1432
Evansville, Ind.	6729–3019	Harlingen, Tex.	9820–3663
Fairmont, W. Va.	5808–2091	Harrisburg, Pa.	5363–1733
Fairview, Kans.	6956–4443	Hartford, Conn.	4687–1373
Fall River, Mass.	4543–1170	Hattiesburg, Miss.	8152–2636
Fargo, N. Dak.	5615–5182	Hayward, Calif.	8513–8660

	V H		V H
Helena, Mont.	6336–7348	Las Vegas, Nev.	8665–7411
Herndon, Va.	5644–1640	Laurel, Miss.	8066–2645
Hinsdale, Ill.	6023–3461	Laurinburg, N.C.	6610–1437
Hot Springs, Ark.	7827–3554	Lawrence, Mass.	4373–1311
Houghton, Mich.	5052–4088	Leesburg, Va.	5634–1685
Houston, Tex.	8938–3536	Little Rock, Ark.	7721–3451
Huntington, N.Y.	4918–1349	Littleton, Mass.	4432–1327
Huntington, W. Va.	6212–2299	Locust, N.C.	6613–1640
Huntsville, Ala.	7267–2535	Lodi, Calif.	8397–8532
Huron, S. Dak.	6201–5183	Logan, Utah	7367–7102
Indianapolis, Ind.	6272–2992	Longview, Tex.	8348–3660
Iowa City, Iowa	6313–3972	Los Angeles, Calif.	9213–7878
Iron Mountain, Mich.	5266–3890	Louisville, Ky.	6529–2772
Jackson, Mich.	5663–3009	Lubbock, Tex.	8598–4962
Jackson, Miss.	8035–2880	Lynchburg, Va.	6093–1703
Jackson, Tenn.	7282–2976	Lyons, Nebr.	6584–4732
Jacksonville, Fla.	7649–1276	Macon, Ga.	7364–1865
Jasper, Ala.	7497–2553	Madison, Wis.	5887–3796
Johnson City, Tenn.	6595–2050	Madisonville, Ky.	6845–2942
Joliet, Ill.	6088–3454	Manchester, N.H.	4354–1388
Joplin, Mo.	7421–4015	Manhattan, Kans.	7143–4520
Julian, Calif.	9374–7544	Marion, Ill.	6882–3202
Kalamazoo, Mich.	5749–3177	Mattoon, Ill.	6502–3291
Kansas City, Kans.	7028–4212	McComb, Miss.	8262–2823
Kansas City, Mo.	7027–4203	Medford, Oreg.	7503–8892
Kennewick, Wash.	6595–8391	Memphis, Tenn.	7471–3125
Key West, Fla.	8745–0668	Meridian, Miss.	7899–2639
Kingsport, Tenn.	6570–2107	Miami, Fla.	8351–0527
Klamath Falls, Oreg.	7510–8711	Midland, Tex.	8934–4888
Knoxville, Tenn.	6801–2251	Milwaukee, Wis.	5788–3589
La Crosse, Wis.	5874–4133	Minneapolis, Minn.	5781–4525
Lafayette, La.	8587–2996	Mobile, Ala.	8167–2367
Lake Charles, La.	8679–3202	Mojave, Calif.	8993–7899
Lake City, Fla.	7768–1419	Monroe, La.	8148–3218
Lamar, Colo.	7720–5403	Montgomery, Ala.	7692–2247
Lansing, Mich.	5584–3081	Mooers Forks, N.Y.	4215–1929
La Plata, Md.	5684–1528	Morgantown, W. Va.	5764–2083
Laredo, Tex.	9681–4099	Morristown, N.J.	5035–1478
Laredo, Tex.	9683–4098	Morristown, Tenn.	6699–2183
Las Cruces, N. Mex.	9132–5742	Muncie, Ind.	6130–2925

	V H		V H
Muskogee, Okla.	7746–4042	Plymouth, Mich.	5562–2891
Nashua, N.H.	4394–1356	Pocatello, Idaho	7146–7250
Nashville, Tenn.	7010–2710	Polk City, Fla.	8067–1067
Nassau, N.Y.	4961–1355	Pontiac, Mich.	5498–2895
Neche, N.D.	5230–5456	Port Angeles, Wash.	6206–9061
Newark, Ill.	6123–3527	Port Huron, Mich.	5367–2813
Newark, N.J.	5015–1430	Portland, Me.	4121–1334
New Bern, N.C.	6307–1119	Portland, Oreg.	6799–8914
New Brunswick, N.J.	5085–1434	Potsdam, N.Y.	4404–2054
New Haven, Conn.	4792–1342	Pottstown, Pa.	5246–1563
New London, Conn.	4700–1242	Poughkeepsie, N.Y.	4821–1526
New Market, Md.	5558–1676	Prescott, Ariz.	8917–6872
New Orleans, La.	8483–2638	Providence, R.I.	4550–1219
Newport News, Va.	5908–1260	Provo, Utah	7680–7006
New York City, N.Y.	4997–1406	Racine, Wis.	5837–3535
Norfolk, Va.	5918–1223	Raleigh, N.C.	6344–1436
North Bend, Nebr.	6698–4739	Reading, Pa.	5258–1612
North Bend, Wash.	6354–8815	Red Oak, Iowa	6691–4465
North Brook, Ill.	5954–3479	Redwood City, Calif.	8556–8682
Oakland, Calif.	8486–8695	Reno, Nev.	8064–8323
Ocala, Fla.	7909–1227	Richmond, Va.	5906–1472
Ogden, Utah	7480–7100	Roanoke, Va.	6196–1801
Oklahoma City, Okla.	7947–4373	Rochester, N.Y.	4913–2195
Omaha, Nebr.	6687–4595	Rockford, Ill.	6022–3675
Orangeburg, S.C.	6980–1502	Rock Island, Ill.	6276–3816
Orlando, Fla.	7954–1031	Rocky Mount, N.C.	6232–1329
Panama City, Fla.	8057–1914	Rosendale, N.Y.	4813–1564
Parkersburg, W. Va.	5976–2268	Roswell, N. Mex.	8787–5413
Pendelton, Oreg.	6707–8326	Sacramento, Calif.	8304–8580
Pensacola, Fla.	8147–2200	Saginaw, Mich.	5404–3074
Peoria, Ill.	6362–3592	Salina, Kans.	7275–4656
Petersburg, Va.	5961–1429	Salinas, Calif.	8722–8560
Petoskey, Mich.	5120–3425	Salt Lake City, Utah	7576–7065
Philadelphia, Pa.	5251–1458	San Angelo, Tex.	8944–4563
Philadelphia, Pa.	5257–1501	San Antonio, Tex.	9225–4062
Philadelphia, Pa.	5222–1493	San Bernardino, Calif.	9172–7710
Phoenix, Ariz.	9135–6748	San Diego, Calif.	9468–7629
Pine Bluff, Ark.	7803–3358	San Francisco, Calif.	8492–8719
Pittsburgh, Pa.	5621–2185	San Jose, Calif.	8583–8619
Plano, Ill.	6096–3534	San Luis Obispo, Calif.	9005–8349

	V H		V H
Santa Fe, N. Mex.	8389–5804	Troy, Ala.	7771–2136
Santa Rosa, Calif.	8354–8787	Troy, N.Y.	4616–1633
Sarasota, Fla.	8295–1094	Tucson, Ariz.	9345–6485
Scranton, Pa.	5042–1715	Tully, N.Y.	4838–1953
Searcy, Ark.	7581–3407	Tulsa, Okla.	7707–4173
Seattle, Wash.	6336–8896	Tupelo, Miss.	7535–2825
Seguin, Tex.	9161–3981	Twin Falls, Idaho	7275–7557
Shreveport, La.	8272–3495	Ukiah, Calif.	8206–8885
Sidney, Nebr.	7112–5671	Van Nuys, Calif.	9197–7919
Sikeston, Mo.	7099–3221	Waco, Tex.	8706–3993
Sioux City, Iowa	6468–4768	Wadena, Minn.	5606–4915
Sioux Falls, S. Dak.	6279–4900	Waldorf, Md.	5659–1531
Socorro, N. Mex.	8774–5867	Warrenton, Va.	5728–1667
South Bend, Ind.	5918–3206	Washington, D.C.	5622–1583
Spartanburg, S.C.	6811–1833	Washington, D.C.	5603–1598
Spokane, Wash.	6247–8180	Washington, D.C.	5632–1590
Springfield, Ill.	6539–3513	Waterloo, Iowa	6208–4167
Springfield, Mass.	4620–1408	Waycross, Ga.	7550–1485
Springfield, Mo.	7310–3836	Westchester, N.Y.	4921–1416
Stamford, Conn.	4897–1388	West Glendive, Mont.	5963–6322
Stevens Point, Wis.	5622–3964	West Palm Beach, Fla.	8166–0607
Stockton, Calif.	8435–8530	West Sweetgrass, Mont.	5829–7475
St. Joseph, Mo.	6913–4301	Wheeling, W. Va.	5755–2241
St. Louis, Mo.	6807–3482	White River Jct., Vt.	4327–1585
St. Paul, Minn.	5776–4498	Wichita, Kans.	7489–4520
St. Petersburg, Fla.	8224–1159	Williamsport, Pa.	5200–1873
Succasunna, N.J.	5038–1508	Williamstown, Ky.	6353–2636
Sunnyvale, Calif.	8576–8643	Wilmington, Del.	5326–1485
Superstition–Apache		Winchester, Ky.	6441–2509
Junction, Ariz.	9123–6669	Winston-Salem, N.C.	6440–1710
Sweetwater, Tex.	8737–4632	Winter Garden, Fla.	7970–1069
Syracuse, N.Y.	4798–1990	Winter Haven, Fla.	8084–1034
Tallahassee, Fla.	7877–1716	Woodstock, Ill.	5964–3587
Tampa, Fla.	8173–1147	Worcester, Mass.	4513–1330
Terre Haute, Ind.	6428–3145	Wyoming Switch, Minn.	5686–4521
Thomasville, Ga.	7773–1709	Youngstown, Ohio	5557–2353
Toledo, Ohio	5704–2820	Yuma, Ariz.	9385–7171
Topeka, Kans.	7110–4369		
Traverse City, Mich.	5284–3447		
Trenton, N.J.	5164–1440		

KEY TERMS

Application processing
time
AUTONET
Benchmark
Central office
Choice set
Circuit loading
Comparison estimating
Configuration drawing
software
Configuration optimization
Conglomerate estimating
Control spreadsheet
Cost analysis
Cost Analysis for Multiple
Locations (CAML)
Desirable requirements
Detailed estimating
Economic feasibility
End office
Evaluation criteria
FCC Tariff 9/10/11
Feasibility study
Gantt chart
Geographic scope
GrafNet Plus

Horizontal coordinates
Implementation plan
InterLATA
Intermediate goal
Internetworking
IntraLATA
Link
Major goal
Mandatory requirements
Map drawing software
Maximize
Message field
Message input time
Message length
Message output time
Message type
Message volume
MIND-Data/PC
Minor goal
Model
Needs assessment factors
Network configurations
Network cost analyzer
Network link traffic table
Network requirements
Network security

Operational feasibility
Optimize
Performance analysis
Pipes, pumps, and people
Point of presence (POP)
Private Line Pricer (PLP)
Problem definition
Queue
Random dependence
Rate center
Response time
Satisfice
Sequential dependence
Simulation
Systems approach
Tariff
Task dependence
Technical feasibility
Time dependence
Turnpike effect
Vertical coordinates
Walk time
Wire center
Wish list requirements

SELECTED REFERENCES

1. AT&T Communications. *Data Communications Using Voiceband Private Line Channels,* Technical Reference Publication 41004. Available from Literary Data Center, Inc., G.P.O. Box C-9104, Brooklyn, N.Y. 11202.

2. AT&T Communications. *Network Communications: Applications and Services,* Technical Reference Publication 500-936. Available from AT&T Customer Information Center, 2855 N. Franklin Road, Indianapolis, Ind. 46219. (Contains extensive circuit cost data. For more information, call 1-800-CLP-INFO or 1-800-432-6000.)

3. *AUTONET.* A software program available from Network Design & Analysis Corp., 505 Park Avenue, New York, N.Y. 10022, or by calling Mr. Boris Dortok at 1-212-688-5432.

4. *CAML—Cost Analysis for Multiple Locations.* A software program available from SAV-NET USA, Inc., P.O. Box 236, Bedminster, N.J. 07921-0236, or by calling Mr. John Leonard at 1-908-781-0950.

5. Cope, Patricia. "New Modeling Tools Help in Building LAN Internets," *Network World,* vol. 8, no. 51, December 23, 1991, pp. 1, 23–25.

6. FitzGerald, Jerry, and Ardra F. FitzGerald. *Designing Controls into Computerized Systems,* 2nd ed. Redwood City, Calif.: Jerry FitzGerald & Associates, 1990.

7. FitzGerald, Jerry, and Ardra F. FitzGerald. *Fundamentals of Systems Analysis: Using Structured Analysis and Design Techniques,* 3rd ed. New York: John Wiley & Sons, 1987.

8. *GrafNet Plus®.* A software program available from Network Dimensions, 5339 Prospect Road, Suite 312, San Jose, Calif. 95129, or by calling Ms. Ranjama Sharma at 1-408-446-9598, or send a FAX to 1-408-255-4576.

9. Held, Gilbert. *Practical Network Design Techniques.* Chichester, England: John Wiley & Sons, 1991.

10. *MIND-Data/PC®.* A software program available from NMI/Network Analysis Center, 6990 Jericho Turnpike, Ste. 300W, Syosset, N.Y. 11791, or by calling Mr. David Rubin at 1-800-765-4622, ext. 114.

11. *Private Line Pricer, AT&T Edition.* A software program available from Economics & Technology, Inc., 1 Washington Mall, Boston, Mass. 02108, or by calling Ms. Mary McCarthy at 1-800-225-2496.

12. Salamone, Salvatore. "Design Tools Optimize Networks, Reduce Costs, *Network World,* vol. 7, no. 11, March 12, 1990, pp. 1, 45, 48, 50, 52, 57.

13. Van Norman, Harrell J. "WAN Design Tools: The New Generation," *Data Communications,* vol. 19, no. 13, October 1990, pp. 129–130, 132, 134, 136, 138.

QUESTIONS/PROBLEMS

1. What is the key to designing a successful data communication network?

2. When should you use the systems approach to network design?

3. When planning communication networks there are two major classes of users to be considered. Who are they?

4. Why does this chapter have numerous page number cross-references?

5. Is a feasibility study always required before proceeding with network design? State your reason.

6. What is a primary responsibility of the feasibility study?

7. What does a feasibility study include?

8. What three factors should be taken into account when preparing a design plan?

9. On what should the design plan be based?

10. What are evaluation criteria and what is their purpose?

11. What is a major trap into which network designers or managers can fall?

12. What is a network benchmark and when is it established?

13. What is the value of examining long-range and short-range reports before beginning network design?

14. Define response time and what it includes.

15. What makes network costs increase with regard to response time?

16. What is a queue?

17. What purpose do simulators serve?

18. What is the response time formula and what does it include?

19. How are maps used in defining the geographic scope of a network?

20. What factors must be examined when analyzing messages?

21. How is message volume determined for a network that currently does not exist?

22. What is the relationship of traffic to circuit loading?

23. What is the turnpike effect and why is it important in network design?

24. What factors might affect circuit loading?

25. What methodology is used to identify network security and control?

26. What is the primary goal of a data communication network?

27. How does circuit loading differ from circuit capacity?

28. How do choice sets fit into the network design?

29. It can be said that some tasks in a network are based on dependence. What does this mean?

30. When choosing from among the various network design alternatives, what are the primary constraints that affect cost?

31. Discuss in general terms how software relates to network design.

32. Discuss in general terms how hardware relates to network design.

33. Should you always determine network costs first? Why or why not?

34. What are the ways to look at costing a network configuration?

35. What is the purpose of a network cost analyzer?

36. What cost/benefit categories are used to ensure no critical cost or important benefit is overlooked when estimating network costs?

37. What factors go into figuring the cost of voice grade circuits?

38. What method is used to calculate mileage between central offices?

39. What is the importance of rate centers in circuit cost calculations?

40. What do some of the FCC Tariffs contain?

41. Define a point of presence.

42. What five cost elements enter into calculating voice grade circuit costs?

43. What do voice grade leased circuits and dial-up circuits have in common with respect to circuit cost calculations?

44. What distinguishes the rate structure of wideband services from leased or dial-up circuits?

45. What three cost elements enter into calculating packet network costs?

46. What cost elements enter into calculating satellite circuit costs?

47. What four functions should computerized network design tools provide?

48. Describe the 13 steps a designer performs when designing a new data communication network.

49. Identify two or three critical points that should appear in a feasibility study final report.

50. Identify and define five or six key evaluation criteria.

51. There are four levels of mapping. Identify and describe them.

52. When analyzing messages, which of the following peak volumes is the most important, the character per message peak or the messages per day peak?

53. Why is minimum circuit mileage between various terminal locations important?

54. The following is an excerpt from last month's progress memo from the data communication analyst Jones to Mr. Smith, his manager.

> Mr. Allen, the Vice President of Marketing, called to ask whether anything could be done to improve the order entry network. I met with him and the Manager of Marketing Administration, Mrs. Johnson, and listened to their problems. We agreed on a short written definition of the problem, and determined that marketing field offices and salespeople, marketing headquarters, manufacturing, and distribution will be affected by any changes to the present network. Mr. Allen turned down my request to visit a typical field office because he feels Mrs. Johnson knows enough about their operation to fill me in. I met with the manufacturing planner, Mr. Williams, and the head of distribution, Miss Thomas. I obtained a general understanding of the current order entry network from Johnson, Williams, and Thomas. The design of the new network is under way now and will be completed soon. I then will prepare a cost estimate of the network design and will present both to you in my report next month.

Play the role of Mr. Smith and write a memo to Jones, commenting on his report. Be critical and try to determine any areas where Jones may not have done all he should have done.

55. Critique the following excerpts from a network requirements document:

- The network shall be easy to operate.
- The network shall have a Mean Time Between Failures of at least 1,000 hours.
- The network shall transmit in half duplex mode at 2400 bits per second.
- The network shall transmit at least 1,000 messages per hour.

56. The busiest link in a network carries 500,000 10-bit characters per 12-hour day. Allowing for a peak load equal to three times the average, for a 50 percent growth over the network life, and for a 10 percent error/retransmission factor, what is the minimum line speed in bits per second?

57. Calculate the air mileage (use V and H coordinates) from San Francisco to Denver and from Kansas City, Kansas, to Kansas City, Missouri.

58. In which step of the network design process would your plan start to identify the types of information to be collected, sources of information to be used, analyses to be performed, schedules of the various activities, and definition of the results to be produced?

59. Using Figure 8-11, convert the characters per day on the New York to Miami link to bits per second transmission speed, assuming asynchronous transmission (10 bits per character) and a six-hour workday.

60. What are some of the items that use transmission time but do not transmit business data and for which the designer must account?

61. Give examples of what factors might cause peak loads and discuss how the designer takes them into account when designing a data communication network.

62. Determine the cost of a voice grade (lease) circuit between Seattle, Washington (SEA) and Tampa, Florida (TPA). You need point-to-point C type conditioning. Use Figure 8-29 to draw the circuit.

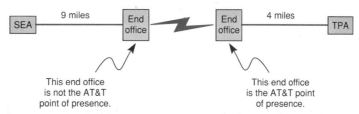

63. Assume in Question 62 that SEA uses a 16-channel statistical multiplexer transmitting at 9600 bits per second and TPA uses an 8-port multiplexer. Each end needs eight video terminals. What would it cost to purchase the necessary hardware? Also calculate the monthly lease cost of this hardware by using the rule of thumb given in this chapter for estimating monthly lease costs for hardware. Use the selected hardware costs in Figure 8-28 for these calculations. *HINT:* If you draw the circuit, you will not forget anything.

64. Assume the total number of transmitted characters per day from SEA to TPA in Question 62 is 400,000 and there is a six-hour workday. If a terminal operator can type 20 words per minute (six characters per word), how many terminal operators and terminals are required?

65. Assume 300,000 characters per day are transmitted from TPA to SEA in Question 64. How many terminal operators and terminals are required?

66. Can the circuit handle the combined traffic of Questions 64 and 65 at 9600 bits per second?

67. Using the circuit in Question 62, calculate the monthly dial-up cost of the circuit if nine 30-minute calls per day are made. Use the month of January 1993. Which costs more, this dial-up or the leased circuit in Question 62?

68. Convert the interLATA analog circuit cost in Question 62 to an interLATA digital circuit transmitting at 9600 bits per second. Does digital cost more or less?

69. Determine the cost of a multipoint circuit (private lease) from Seattle (SEA) to Salt Lake City (SLC) to Baltimore (BLT). Assume the following.

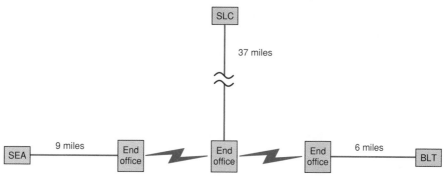

None of the three end offices is the AT&T point of presence, and assume there is no conditioning.

As a group project, use Figure 8-29 and choose four or five cities to interconnect. Draw your network and cost it out. Use whichever circuits you think are best and include the hardware costs. Record your costs on a copy of Figure 8-19.

70. Suppose you send a request for data to the central host database and your response gets back in three seconds. If the host database processing time is 1.5 seconds and your message takes 0.73 second to go from your terminal to the host, how long does it take for the message to return from the host to your terminal?

71. What is a model?

72. What is system simulation?

73. Define walk time as described in this chapter.

74. A mathematical model describes the entities of a network with the attributes being represented by mathematical variables. Use a dictionary and define both "entity" and "attribute."

75. Determine the cost of a voice grade lease circuit between Seattle, Washington (SEA) and Miami, Florida (MIA). You do not need any conditioning. Use the Private Line Pricer to calculate the circuit cost and the drawing in Question 62. Be sure to substitute Miami for Tampa in the drawing.

76. Run the network calculation in the READ.ME file on the Private Line Pricer diskette.

77. Each of the 13 steps of a data communication network design project requires some type of report. Name the deliverables required at the end of each design step.

NEXT DAY AIR SERVICE CUMULATIVE CASE STUDY

Background on Next Day Air Service

Thus far, the Next Day Air Service Board of Directors has been most pleased with your efforts. They are excited by your recommendations to bring Next Day Air Service into a networked information processing environment. But, with the pressing need to cope with a steady upsurge in business volume, the board cannot afford any additional delays in implementing a corporate headquarters local area network that is connected to the WAN. As a result, you have been given the added responsibility of implementing the LAN and interconnecting it to the WAN.

Talk about being overwhelmed! Not only has this project become much larger than originally intended, but now you are having difficulty keeping track of the progress of the many tasks that have been and remain to be carried out. Project management is becoming a key to the success of the entire network design effort.

You share these thoughts with an old college friend after a hard set of tennis. Your friend, who is a network manager for a large bank, suggests considering the use of one of the more popular network design software tools. They will provide some much-needed automation support, they are microcomputer-based, and they are relatively easy to use. Your friend also recommends that you identify and schedule the remainder of the tasks to complete the LAN/WAN design by using a Gantt chart. At first she recommended a PC-based scheduling package, but now has decided that a Gantt chart will be better because you will have more than enough to learn when you start using the new network design software tool.

Because of this conversation, you spend much of the weekend researching the relevant literature concerning these tools (that is, their cost, performance, features, ease of use, user satisfaction, and the like). You get lucky when you discover that the magazine *Data Communications* has just featured a comparison of several network design software tools. This research leads to the identification of several reasonably priced packages you could purchase right away. On Monday you discuss such an acquisition with Mr. Coone, and are pleased when he authorizes the immediate purchase of a network design package. It seems he is intrigued with the potential that such a package might possess.

You spend a few days learning how to use the software and then you begin designing and documenting the integrated WAN/LAN. Because you already have completed several of the network design steps, such as the network feasibility study, message analysis, and preliminary geographic maps, you are ready to move on to the final phases of the design effort. At this point, your attention is on the issues surrounding the actual network configurations. Specifically, you will be evaluating the hardware and software considerations, circuit costs, and the possible physical configurations of the WAN. When the WAN is completed, then you will be able to complete the LAN. Moreover, you realize that you need to learn a lot more about repeaters, bridges, routers, and gateways (discussed in Chapter 11) before you can design the internetwork connection between the WAN and the LAN. As always, be prepared to defend your position and recommendations.

Questions/Problems for the Next Day Air Service Case

1. President Coone has requested a short briefing on the status of the network design project for Next Day Air Service's wide and local area networks. The results of this briefing will be used for much of the president's presentation at the upcoming shareholders' meeting. Prepare a brief outline of your presentation, limiting your discussion to the 13 design steps to be performed in a network design effort.

2. Calculate the cost of a type C conditioned point-to-point leased voice grade analog circuit between Atlanta and Tampa. Use the formula in Figure 8-21 to calculate the mileage. Atlanta to the AT&T point-of-presence (CO2) is 12 miles and for Tampa it is 29 miles. (*HINT:* See Figure 8-22.)

3. Instead of leasing, calculate the cost of one dial-up connection between Atlanta and Tampa. Assume 8 hours per day and a month with 23 working days. Which costs more, dial-up or the leased circuit in Question 2?

4. How much more does the interLATA portion of the digital circuit (19,200 bits per second) cost than the interLATA portion of the analog circuit calculated in Question 2?

5. If you are using the Private Line Pricer (PLP), Network Optimizer (MIND-Data/PC), or AUTONET software, calculate the cost of a direct leased circuit between Houston and Miami or any other circuit link. Compare your answer with those of your classmates. If it is different, determine the reason for the difference. The purpose of this problem is to simulate a real-life situation, and not to obtain a specific answer.

6. Is it important to know who will be the users of the network? What are the two major classes of NDAS network users, and how is each involved with it?

Chapter Nine

PROTOCOLS AND SOFTWARE

This chapter defines the differences between protocols, software, and network architectures. Next, it follows the flow of a message through the network's various software packages. We explain in a simplified manner the seven layers of the Open Systems Interconnection (OSI) model. Other topics include telecommunication access methods, teleprocessing monitor software, frame (HDLC/X.25/SDLC), BSC, SNA, LU 6.2, SAA, TCP/IP, GOSIP, ONA, MAP, and telecommunication standards organizations.

PROTOCOL

A *protocol* is a strict set of rules or procedures that are required to initiate and maintain communications. Simply put, a protocol is a set of rules that allow two or more end points (microcomputers) to communicate. The What Is a Protocol? box describes the various types of protocols and their applications.

Protocols consist of syntax, semantics, and timing. The *syntax* of a protocol defines the bit stream (a series of 1s and 0s) by dividing it into fields. For example, the first 48 bits might be the source address, followed by 48 bits of destination address, and so on. *Semantics* defines the precise meaning of the bits within the field. For example, an address of all 1s (1111111) might be interpreted as a broadcast message that is sent to all network terminals. A control field of 1000001 might identify it as a *control message* rather than a *data message*. A control message might start or stop transmission, whereas a data message contains business information related to an application like payroll. *Timing* includes the data rate of the bit stream and pauses between acknowledgments in half duplex transmission.

When describing protocol syntax and semantics, we often refer to the Open Systems Interconnection (OSI) seven-layer model that is described later in this chapter. The data link control protocols in layer 2 of the OSI model are machine-to-machine protocols and are the ones discussed most commonly in the classroom.

WHAT IS A PROTOCOL?

Protocols are the rules two people use when they speak with one another or when two machines communicate during data communications. "Real-life" protocols govern our daily interactions. For example, they require that we not interrupt other people who are speaking until the time is appropriate. In the classroom, students raise their hands to be recognized, as opposed to shouting out what they wish to say. At a family holiday dinner table your speech might be a little more restrained than it is when you are with a group of football fans, your team is losing, and the person behind you just dropped an ice cream cone on your head.

The protocols for talking or typing data on a network are very rigid and must be followed. There are at least three distinct protocols: person-to-network, machine-to-machine, and person-to-person.

We follow *person-to-network* protocols to get on a network so we can transmit information. For example, when making voice telephone calls, the rules are simple: Pick up the telephone, listen for a dial tone before dialing, dial the telephone number, hang up if there is a busy signal, speak if the other party answers, and so forth. We learn these protocols as we grow up, and everyone can use them because they are very simple. We call these *microcomputer-to-network* protocols when we are using a microcomputer on a network—they are the process by which the microcomputer gets connected to the network.

Once connected to the network, there are *machine-to-machine* protocols. The software handles these protocols automatically so we do not have to interact with them. These protocols take care of such tasks as determining which terminal transmits at a given time, establishing how a message signals its beginning and its end, determining how the receiving terminal recognizes a transmission error, determining how a transmitter or receiver recovers from an unexpected break in the data flow, and establishing how the receiving terminal distinguishes between instruction bits like those for "End of message" and the bits that represent the characters of the message being transmitted. These protocols make possible the movement of messages across the network.

Next, *person-to-person* protocols govern how one user communicates with another user at the other end of the communication circuit, even though the other user may be a database or a microcomputer. These protocols (rules of behavior) allow us to speak with the person at the other end of the telephone line or to transmit information between two operators. Person-to-person protocols establish how we conduct ourselves when discussing business with the person at the other end of the circuit.

In summary, person-to-network protocols get us onto the network by establishing the circuit connection, machine-to-machine protocols move our data from Point A to Point B, and person-to-person protocols determine how we communicate with the other person or machine.

If there are all these different protocols, you may wonder how we learn to use them. Basically, it is easy. Again, let us use the telephone system as an example. The person-to-network protocol of the telephone system relates to our ability to dial the telephone and connect to the telephone network. The telephone company handles the machine-to-machine protocols because it makes sure the proper circuits are connected so the other telephone can ring. After the other person answers the telephone, we handle the person-to-person protocols when we ask, "Is Joy Poole in today?" and, on reaching Joy Poole, start our conversation.

Finally, moving from telephones to networks requires learning what needs to be entered so we can log-on to the network; that is, we must enter specific commands to invoke the person-to-network protocols. The microcomputer and network software together handle the machine-to-machine protocols that move our messages. After being connected to the network, we handle the person-to-person protocols by formatting our message, typing it, sending it, and interacting with the person or machine at the other end of the circuit.

These protocols make possible the exchange of information after a call (information channel) has been established. A *data link control protocol* specifies

- Which terminal transmits at a given time
- How a message signals its beginning and end
- How a receiver knows when a character or block of data begins and ends
- How a receiver recognizes a transmission error and asks for a message retransmission
- How a receiver sequences messages or characters within the message itself
- How a receiver distinguishes between instruction bits (such as those that indicate end of message) and bits that represent the actual message
- How a transmitter or receiver recovers when an unexpected catastrophe occurs, such as a break in the flow of data

The Microcomputer Protocols section in Chapter 10 decribes protocols that are specific to microcomputers.

SOFTWARE

Software programs are located at various points in the network. For example, the host computer might have such software packages as the operating system, the teleprocessing monitor, database management systems, security packages, and application programs. The front end processor probably has telecommunication access programs for network control. The remote intelligent terminal controller, switch, statistical time division multiplexer, or concentrator may have switching software, store and forward software, and control software packages that perform a subset of the telecommunication access program functions located at the front end processor. Farther out in the network there might be software packages located at or within a remote microcomputer so it can access the network.

Microprocessor chips have blurred the definition of software, which originally referred to computer programs. The term *firmware* is used increasingly to refer to that halfway point between hardware and software. Firmware is a microcircuit chip that contains the program functions to be performed. When the program functions are placed in an electronic chip, they operate much faster and are more secure from unauthorized change or modification.

You also can find protocols within various software, such as within the telecommunication access programs. This further blurs the distinction between protocols and software. Software can be any program, but protocols are specific software programs that control person-to-network, machine-to-machine, and person-to-person interfaces. Chapter 11 contains information on software that is specific to local area networks in the Ethernet, Token-Passing, ARCNET, and FDDI sections.

NETWORK ARCHITECTURE

Network architectures attempt to facilitate the operation, maintenance, and growth of the communication and processing environment by isolating the user and the application programs from the details of the network. Network architectures use both protocols and other software in their operation. The architectures combine the software and protocols to form a usable network.

Many people ask, "What is the reason behind network architecture when you have protocols and other software packages that actually perform the networking functions?" Quite simply, network architecture is the most cost-effective way to develop and implement a coordinated set of products that can be interconnected. The architecture is the "plan" that connects protocols and other software programs. This coordination is beneficial to both the network users and suppliers of hardware and software. The nine basic characteristics of a network architecture are

- *Separation of functions*. Because user networks and vendor products evolve over time, there must be a way to provide enhanced functions to accommodate the latest technology. With a network architecture, the network has a high degree of modularity so that changes can occur incrementally and with a minimum of disruption.
- *Wider connectivity*. The goal of most networks should be to provide optimum connection between any number of nodes, taking into account whatever levels of security might be required.
- *Resource sharing*. Network architectures allow shared resources, such as printers and databases. This, in turn, makes a network both more efficient and more economical to operate.
- *Network management*. The architecture must allow users to define, operate, change, secure, and maintain the network.
- *Ease of use*. With a network architecture, designers can focus their attention on the primary interfaces in the network and, therefore, make it user friendly.

- *Standardization.* A network architecture encourages software developers and vendors to use standard hardware and software. The greater the degree of standardization, the greater is the connectivity and the lower the cost.

- *Data management.* Network architectures take into account the management of data and the necessity to interconnect with various database management systems.

- *Interfaces.* The architectures also define interfaces, such as person-to-network, machine-to-machine (sometimes called program-to-program), and person-to-person interfaces. In other words, the architecture blends together the appropriate protocols (which are written as computer programs) and other software packages to produce a functioning network.

- *Applications.* Network architectures separate the functions required to operate a network from the organization's business applications. It is more efficient when business programmers do not need to be concerned with how the network operates.

SOFTWARE DESIGN

The data communication environment poses some unique problems for the program designer, the most basic of which is lack of control over the time dimension. In conventional batch processing, the designer plans the program so it can refuse to deal with inputs until conditions are just right. If things go wrong, the designer simply stops the "clock" and causes the program to abort. This luxury is not often available in the data communication world because inputs arrive at the computer at a time and sequence beyond the designer's control.

Four factors make data communication programs different from other software that control computers.

- Lack of control over input timing
- Communication errors
- Computer or circuit failures
- Real-time response requirements

What can the program designer do to deal with these factors? The first step is to ensure that the software provides proper *message accountability*. Basically, message accountability is a recordkeeping function that guarantees no inputs or intended outputs "fall through the cracks" and allows recovery from a communication or computer interruption to be accomplished with minimum damage to users.

For each incoming message this means

- Logging as soon as received
- Time tagging

- Address checking
- Format and, where possible, content error checking
- Receipt acknowledgment after logging and checking
- Diagnosing and acting constructively on errors
- Maintaining statistics on errors
- Stopping transmissions from terminals and lines that send an excessive number of errors

For outgoing messages it is important to

- Log at time of transmission
- Require acknowledgment and act constructively if acknowledgment is not received
- Provide a priority scheme to ensure that outgoing overloads are worked off in a rational manner
- Test the integrity of lines and terminals and maintain statistics on results
- Provide a rational means of disposing of messages that cannot be sent because of circuit or terminal errors

Another way to ensure message accountability is to combine inputs and outputs. The relationships that tie inputs and outputs together (that is, "input message type A yields exactly one output message type B") must be put to work by coupling them to the input and output logs. Such logs provide a continuous statistical accounting of work in process, detect any failures in obeying the relations, and provide the proper basis for recovery processes invoked after failures.

The second step is to conduct a *failure mode analysis*. In this process the software designer examines the consequences of each possible network failure for message integrity. These failures must be presumed to occur successively at each stage of program execution. Possible countermeasures are evaluated and selected for implementation by the software. This is an easy process to describe and a difficult and exhausting one to perform, but it is absolutely necessary if the resulting network is to have even minimal initial viability. It is likely that most of the network software will be devoted to dealing with the exceptions occasioned by communications, hardware, and people failure rather than to accomplishing the "mainline" network functions. The failure mode analysis, therefore, easily can turn out to be the major component in the design task.

Finally, all the principles of good noncommunication program design also apply. The chief of these are

- **Modularity:** Achieve *modularity* by breaking the functional job into small, "neat," functional modules and match the program structure to the functional structure.
- **Hierarchy:** Recognize the *hierarchy* of the functional modules and mirror it in the module calling relationships.

- **Generality:** Strive for *generality* by looking for the truly "primitive" functions, generalize their definitions, and clearly identify their basic parameters so that modules can be defined to perform groups of similar functions, rather than proliferating specialized modules.
- **Standardization:** Attain maximum *standardization* by designing the software using currently accepted industry standards, such as the OSI seven-layer model.

SOFTWARE TESTING

The same factors that make design of data communication software uniquely difficult also tend to make testing of that software more complex than in a batch environment. Because the timing and sequencing of "real-world" inputs are not always predictable, it is difficult to build confidence that any testing procedure has exercised the time relationships sufficiently to reveal all time-dependent pathological behavior in the program under test. Similarly, in testing the response of the program to environmental factors, such as communication errors and hardware failures, the network implementer has difficulty creating a sufficient variety of these events to ensure the program is tested thoroughly.

What can be done to ease these problems? There are three *software testing* areas on which the network implementer should focus.

- Test planning
- Test execution
- Test documentation

First, *test planning* is a function that often is forgotten until it is too late. The software test plan should be developed as part of the *software functional specification*. This approach helps ensure that

- The test focuses on proving the performance of the software, rather than proving that the programmer's concept of the software matches the design.
- Test support facilities, such as computer time, special test data, communications, and special test generation or data reduction programs, are identified early enough to plan their acquisition intelligently and efficiently.
- "Testability" of the software should be a design criterion. This also improves the "diagnosability" of errors and the overall maintainability of the software.
- All parties in the network development effort know the criteria by which the suitability of the software will be judged.

Second, *test execution* should be handled, if possible, by different personnel from those who developed the software. The objectivity introduced by an independent software test group pays off in improved performance and software integrity. Users must participate in the conduct of the testing if it is to be done effectively. Their involvement should increase progressively as the "bugs" are removed from the software and the detailed functional characteristics become more apparent. During this time, two things tend to happen. First, users can offer immediate, first-hand pragmatic judgments about discrepancies between specifications and actual performance. Often such discrepancies can be removed in simple ways, that is, by using the application knowledge of the users. Second, users are building knowledge of, and confidence in, the software.

Finally, *test documentation* often is an overlooked activity. "Coming events cast their shadows before them" is an adage that predates the software business by about 150 years,[1] but it has real importance in this current context. Almost all software failures, whether found during testing or weeks, months, or years after the software has been declared operational, "cast their shadows" during implementation and testing. Thorough, careful documentation of test planning, preparation, execution, and post-test analysis provides the best possible groundwork from which to analyze the failures and prevent their recurrence. It is important to recognize that more money frequently is spent on "maintaining" real-time programs (that is, fixing failures not found during testing and upgrading functional capabilities) than was spent on developing the programs in the first place. Good documentation is the foundation of any effort to keep software maintenance costs in line.

ARQ (AUTOMATIC REPEAT REQUEST)

One of the basic decisions the network designer must make is to determine how the network will recognize and correct transmission errors. A network that detects an error in data and has it retransmitted automatically is called an *ARQ (Automatic Repeat reQuest)* network. ARQ networks are of two types: stop and wait or continuous.

With *stop and wait ARQ*, after sending a block, the transmitting terminal waits for a positive acknowledgment *(ACK)* or a negative acknowledgment *(NAK)*. If it is an ACK, the terminal sends the next block; if it is a NAK, the terminal resends the previous block. Another possible response is a *WAK*, which means positive acknowledgment but do not transmit any more at this time.

ACK and NAK are 8-bit ASCII characters that tell the sending terminal whether the message was received with or without an error. If you examine Figure 5-7 in Chapter 5, you can see that a decimal 6 is an ACK and a decimal 21 is a NAK. An ACK signifies an error-free transmission, whereas a NAK signifies an error, which requires automatic retransmission of the message without interrupting the terminal operator. A WAK might be achieved by sending two ASCII characters, such as ACK and EOT (End Of Transmission). Stop and wait ARQ is half duplex transmission.

---

[1] Thomas Campbell (1777–1844), "Lochiel's Warning."

With *continuous ARQ,* the transmitting terminal does not wait for an acknowledgment after sending a block; it immediately sends the next block. While the blocks are being transmitted, the transmitting terminal examines the stream of returning acknowledgments. If it receives a NAK, the transmitting terminal usually (depending on the specific vendor's protocol programs) retransmits all the blocks from the one that was in error to the end of the stream of blocks sent. The terminal also may be able to retransmit only the block that was in error, although this method requires more logic and buffering at the terminals. Continuous ARQ is full duplex transmission.

Older protocols like BSC (Binary Synchronous Communications from IBM) usually employ the stop and wait ARQ. Newer protocols like X.25 and IBM's Synchronous Data Link Control (SDLC) use continuous ARQ for error recovery procedures. SDLC is the name of the protocol in IBM's Systems Network Architecture (SNA), which is covered later in this chapter.

When using various protocols with microcomputers, you may hear the term *sliding window protocols*. These are continuous ARQ protocols for full duplex transmission.

BASIC SOFTWARE CONCEPTS FOR WIDE AREA NETWORKS (WANS)

Before starting this discussion, you should know that software for a local area network is covered in Chapter 11.

To determine the network location of various software packages, look at Figure 9-1. For example, at the remote end of this data communication network, there may be six or more software packages located in various pieces of hardware, such as switches, statistical time division multiplexers, terminals, intelligent controllers, telephone company central office switches, remote concentrators, and, of course, microcomputers. With the exception of microcomputers, all these pieces of hardware use specialized software programs to perform specific functions required for network control or message movement. Microcomputers can accept more generalized software programs and, therefore, also can perform business application functions. The software programs located at the remote end of the network often are scaled-down subsets of the software located in the front end processor or the host mainframe computer located at the central site. From previous chapters, you already know the front end/host can perform switching, multiplexing, control functions, and any of the application programs that a microcomputer can perform.

Now look at the six software packages listed below the front end and host computer in Figure 9-1. When reading this chapter, you will learn that telecommunication access programs, along with the teleprocessing monitor, are software programs that bring messages into the host computer, get them ready for processing, and move them back out to the remote end of the network. The security software does just what the name implies—restricts access to the computer, programs, and stored database files. Application programs perform required day-to-day business functions. The database management system (DBMS) organizes, stores, and retrieves

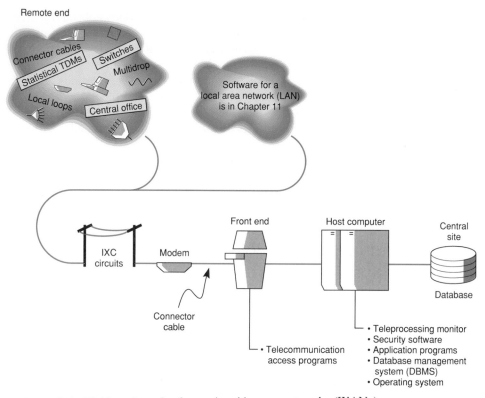

Figure 9-1   The location of software in wide area networks (WANs).

the organization's data/information. Finally, the operating system is the set of software programs that runs the host mainframe computer, controls, and coordinates among all the other software packages.

The intent of Figure 9-1 is not only to show where software packages are located at the front end or host computer but also to provide the basis for describing how your message flows as it moves through these software packages. Let us assume your message has left the remote microcomputer, passed over the connector cables, modem, telephone company end office, and IXC telecommunication circuits, and is now on its way through the modem and connector cables (at the central site) into the front end processor.

The message probably would not have been permitted to leave the microcomputer or remote terminal unless the *telecommunication access program* in the front end processor first polled the remote terminal and gave it permission to send the message. Note that the telecommunication access programs also can be located in the host computer, but only the older systems' architectures use the host. It is more efficient, and the processing loads are distributed better, if these programs are located in the front end processor.

IBM's communication software is a good example of dual location because it has telecommunication access programs both in the host computer (Telecommunications

Access Method—TCAM) and in the front end processor (Network Control Program—NCP).

After the telecommunication access programs bring the message in from the network, log it, check for errors, and perform any other functions this software is designed to do, the message passes from the front end to the host computer.

The *teleprocessing monitor software* package in the host now takes control of the message. The teleprocessing monitor software handles such functions as placing messages into input or output processing queues, file management, and sometimes database management, depending on the database management system. Its other functions are handling restart/recovery for problems, recording statistics for accounting purposes, keeping track of statistics for performance evaluation, handling communication tasks within the host computer such as processing requests and providing the interface with application programs or database management systems, checkpointing, error handling within the host, security checking, and performing various utility functions such as message switching or checking various control tables.

Once the teleprocessing monitor has placed a message into the host computer's input processing queue, the input message may go through a special *security software* package for review. A variety of security packages are available to check such functions as the validity of passwords, whether the password is a valid one for the originating terminal, whether the password allows access to the requested data, whether the originating terminal is allowed to make the request that was entered, whether both the password and terminal that sent the request are valid at the specific time of day the message entered the system, whether the terminal or password or both are restricted to specific application programs, files, records, data items, and the like.

Assuming a request passes all the security checks, the next step is for a specific *application program* to be called out to process the request that has been made. At this point the application program begins to process the request. Let us assume a *database management system* lookup is required to process this request.

Your database lookup proceeds something like this. The database management system software takes the database schema and matches it against the program subschema from the application program. *Schemas* delineate the specific logical data layout in the database, whereas *subschemas* delineate the specific logical data the program is allowed to retrieve.

Once the location of your data has been pinpointed on the disk, the database management system may ask the computer's *operating system* to physically read the disk because many database management systems do not physically read disks. When the data has been read from the disk and placed into a computer memory buffer, the database management system again takes control from the computer's operating system and sorts out the specific data the program subschema allows you to retrieve. The data is sent back to the application program, and processing of the message continues.

When the message processing has been completed, the results are passed back to the teleprocessing monitor and the response is put in the host computer's output queue.

Next, the telecommunication access programs in the front end take the message. They select the remote terminal that originated the request to determine whether it can receive the response. If the answer is yes, the response is transmitted to the terminal. At this time, the round-trip transaction has been completed.

Notice that this simple input transaction might have involved all six software packages in the front end and host computer shown in Figure 9-1. Furthermore, on the remote terminal end it may have involved any of several software packages in the microcomputer, intelligent terminal controller, and the like. This simple transaction may have gone through 50,000 lines of program code as it passed through the remote software packages, telecommunication access programs, teleprocessing monitor, security package, application program, database management system, and the host computer operating system. All this activity normally takes place in less than three seconds. Moreover, large networks can process 50 to 60 transactions per second and still offer a response time of less than three seconds.

TELECOMMUNICATION ACCESS PROGRAMS

The telecommunication access programs that used to reside in the host computer now reside in the front end processors, *switching nodes* (SNs) of a packet network, remote intelligent controllers, or microcomputers. Telecommunication access programs provide some of the following capabilities.

- Polling and selecting of terminals in a central control network
- Automatic dial-up answering of calls
- Code conversion
- Message switching and store and forward (although this might be in the host computer's teleprocessing monitor software)
- Circuit switching and port contention
- Logging of all inbound and outbound messages
- Error detection and retransmission when an error is detected

The front end processor functions enumerated in Chapter 3 can provide other ideas as to the type of software functions performed in many of today's front end processors.

In large networks, the most familiar communication software packages are the telecommunication access programs started by IBM. There are five such packages, and they are presented here as examples of the range of products for network control.

- Basic Telecommunications Access Method (BTAM)
- Queued Telecommunications Access Method (QTAM)
- Telecommunications Access Method (TCAM)

- Virtual Telecommunications Access Method (VTAM)
- Network Control Program (NCP)

Basic Telecommunications Access Method (BTAM)   The *Basic Telecommunications Access Method* provides the basic functions needed for controlling data communication circuits. It supports asynchronous terminals, synchronous communications, and audio response units. BTAM is a set of basic modules used to construct communication programs. Its use is recommended when there are ten or fewer circuits to support or when a specialized communication control program is required. BTAM requires knowledge of the terminal's operation, link discipline, and a basic knowledge of programming because BTAM users must write routines for scheduling and allocating facilities. The basic flow control and data administration routines also are the responsibility of the BTAM user. It is the least sophisticated of the five data communication software programs listed above, but it does contribute the lowest system overhead. BTAM provides facilities for polling terminals, transmitting and receiving messages, detecting errors, automatically retransmitting erroneous messages, translating code, dialing and answering calls, logging transmission errors, allocating blocks of buffer storage, and performing online diagnostics to facilitate the testing of terminal equipment.

BTAM resides in the central computer and is the interface between the front end processor and the user-written application programs. BTAM is an access method that provides support primarily for input operations. It will *not* perform, however, all the tasks that must be executed in most communication networks; therefore, it is not used widely in modern networks.

Queued Telecommunications Access Method (QTAM)   The *Queued Telecommunications Access Method* is an extension of BTAM and includes all the BTAM facilities except that it does not support synchronous communications; it supports only asynchronous terminals. QTAM provides a macrolanguage for the control and processing of communication information, including message editing, queuing, routing, and logging. It can schedule and allocate facilities, poll terminals, perform error checking routines, reroute messages, cancel messages, and the like. QTAM is not used much any more and has been replaced primarily by TCAM.

Telecommunications Access Method (TCAM)   The *Telecommunications Access Method* replaces and extends the older BTAM and QTAM. It resides in the host computer. The most significant features of TCAM are those for network control and system recovery. An operator control facility also provides network supervision and modification. It supports asynchronous terminals, synchronous communications, and audio response units. TCAM performs all the functions of BTAM and QTAM and handles the data communications in a network that uses a high degree of multiprogramming. Unlike the prior basic data communication software, TCAM has its own control program that takes charge and schedules the traffic-handling operations. In some cases it can handle an incoming message by itself without passing it to an application program—for example, routing a message to another terminal in a message switching system. TCAM also provides status reporting on terminals, lines, and queues. It has significant recovery and serviceability features to increase the security and availability of the data communication network. The checkpoint and restart facilities are much more capable than those of QTAM. TCAM has prewritten routines for checkpointing, logging, date and time stamping, sequence numbering and checking, message interception and rerouting, and error message transmission, and it supports a separate master terminal for the data communication network operator. TCAM can manage a network structured on Systems Network Architecture (SNA). *Advanced Communication Function*/TCAM (ACF/TCAM) also accommodates SNA/SDLC terminals. (SNA is described later in this chapter.) Most IBM networks today use TCAM or VTAM.

Virtual Telecommunications Access Method (VTAM)   The *Virtual Telecommunications Access Method* is the data communication software package that complements IBM's advanced hardware and software. It resides in the host computer. VTAM manages a network structured on SNA principles. It directs the transmission of data between the application programs in the host computer and the components of the data communication network. It operates with front end processors. The basic services performed by VTAM include establishing, controlling, and terminating access between the application programs and the terminals. It moves data between application programs and terminals and permits application programs to share communication circuits, communication controllers, and terminals. In addition to performing all the basic functions of the previous three data communication software packages, VTAM controls the configuration of the entire network, creates virtual connections, and permits the network to be monitored and altered.

When VTAM establishes sessions, one end of the session is understood to be the host and the other the terminal. VTAM makes the mainframe the primary end of the session and the remote terminal the secondary end. In technical terms, the host program is said to be the *primary logical unit* (PLU), and the terminal or microcomputer is considered to be the *secondary logical unit* (SLU). Only the primary logical unit can start a session, end the session, and perform key aspects of error recovery. When personal computers are linked to SNA hosts, they are considered to be secondary logical units just like terminals.

VTAM can be the sole telecommunication access method in the host, or it can operate in conjunction with the Network Control Program (NCP is described in the next section), which allows some of the network control functions to be offloaded to the front end processor.

Network Control Program (NCP)   The *Network Control Program* is a telecommunication access method located in the front end processors that control IBM's Synchronous Data Link Control (SDLC) communications between host computers and remote terminals. (SDLC is the protocol developed for SNA by IBM.) It also works with host resident VTAM software to route information through networks. NCP routes data and controls its flow between the front end processor and any other network resources. These other network resources can be the host mainframe computer or an intelligent control unit located either locally or at the remote end of the communication link. IBM's primary network control program is the Advanced Communication Function/Network Control Program (ACF/NCP). Network control programs reside in the front end processor, primarily in IBM's 3704, 3705, 3725, and 3745. NCP is *not* a replacement for TCAM or VTAM; it provides an interface with TCAM and VTAM by taking over some of their functions and moving them to the front end.

NCP can perform polling, error detection, error recovery, and intermediate routing. It provides some flow control (such as various types of message pacing), prevents network congestion, provides internetwork communication, and insulates VTAM from being overburdened by having to speak to an excessive number of other protocols. NCP version 5 supports dial-up lines and improves support for multidrop lines. It also supports SDLC's PU 2.1 functionality, enabling the front end processor to initiate sessions with remote terminals. With NCP version 5, one front end processor can communicate with other front end processors via an IBM Token-Ring Network. It includes load balancing across network bridges and backbone rings, port swapping, backup capabilities, and remote controller support. NCP is IBM's effort to move the telecommunication access method software out from the host mainframe to the front end processor. NCP is the only one of these five telecommunication access programs that actually resides in a front end processor; all the others reside in the host mainframe.

TELEPROCESSING MONITOR PROGRAM

As has been stated, some functions overlap between the telecommunication access programs and the teleprocessing monitor program located in the host computer. An example of this overlap is IBM's software package Telecommunications Access Method—TCAM (this is a telecommunication access program) and its Customer Information Control System—CICS (this is a teleprocessing monitor), both of which reside in the host computer. IBM's front end has its own program called the Network Control Program—NCP (this also is a telecommunication access program). TCAM and NCP overlap; therefore, functions such as polling/selecting can be performed from either the host computer or the front end processor.

Teleprocessing monitors are software programs that directly relieve the host computer's operating system of many tasks involved in handling message traffic between the host and the front end or the host and other internal central processing unit (CPU) software packages (such as the host database management system). Generally speaking, teleprocessing monitors perform such functions as message handling, access methods, task scheduling, and system recovery.

Whereas the telecommunication access programs access and move data into and out of the host computer, the teleprocessing monitor acts as the interface with the telecommunication access programs on one side and with all of the host computer's software on the other side. Teleprocessing monitors must be the interface with various operating systems, computer architectures, database management systems, security software packages, and application programs.

Typical teleprocessing monitors offer such features as the ability to deal with protocols, the ability to interact with various operating systems and hardware, and the ability to serve as the interface to database management systems and telecommunication access programs.

Teleprocessing monitors can offer some type of security. For example, a security package should accommodate a unique password and identification for each terminal operator and allow access only to the specific functions assigned to that operator password and/or terminal identifier. It can assign highly sensitive functions to a specific terminal or a group of terminals. Some security features might be security sign-on fields, darkened password fields, and a complete log of terminal sign-ons, including any security violations.

Other tasks conducted by teleprocessing monitors are logging of all messages (both input and output), accounting procedures for cost control, restart and recovery procedures in case of failure, utility features that carry out special maintenance tasks, and queue management of both inbound and outbound message queues, as well as the ability to place priorities on messages and/or queues. A teleprocessing monitor should have the ability to interact with multiple front end processors, terminals, microcomputers, and various data communication transmission speeds. The monitor provides input/output job task queue management, various methods of instituting priorities for certain transactions or jobs, file and database management, application program management, task and resource control, restart and recovery procedures in case of failure, and special utilities that carry out tasks often enough to warrant setting them up as a utility feature (OSI model layer 6). It keeps track of accounting features and operating statistics and isolates various programs or parts of the system from other programs or parts of the system. In other words, a teleprocessing monitor can be considered a "mini" operating system with data communication interfaces.

The world's most widely used teleprocessing monitor is the *Customer Information Control System* (CICS), which was developed by IBM to meet the demand for high volume transaction processing systems. In today's world it may not be perfect, but even IBM's direct competitors implicitly acknowledge that there are few alternatives to CICS. Whatever comes along to supplant it will be an evolving CICS rather than a totally new replacement. CICS is a table-driven teleprocessing program that offers 64 layers or systems it can service. Like any other teleprocessing monitor, CICS runs in conjunction with the host computer's operating system. CICS takes over the communication-related tasks that previously were handled by the operating system, thus allowing the operating system to concentrate on other control tasks or application programs.

The teleprocessing monitor will increase in importance and almost equal the operating system for performing job tasks as we move toward more online data communication-oriented networks, and especially as we move into the world of distributed systems and databases.

In summary, protocols are rules in the form of programmed instructions for handling messages in a network environment. Telecommunication access programs use the protocols to control and move messages from remote terminals to the host computer. Teleprocessing monitors control and move messages within the host computer.

OSI SEVEN-LAYER MODEL

The *OSI seven-layer model* is the plan by which communication software is designed. The widely implemented OSI model facilitates control, analysis, upgradability, replacement, and management of the resources that constitute the communication network. It also makes it much easier to develop software and hardware that link incompatible networks because protocols can be dealt with one layer at a time. Whichever standard is followed, the use of layers in designing network software and applications is strongly recommended.

One of the most important standards-making bodies is the *International Organization for Standardization* (ISO), which makes technical recommendations about data communication interfaces. (The abbreviation ISO comes from its French name, which sometimes causes confusion in English-speaking countries.) During the late 1970s, ISO created the Open System Interconnection (OSI) subcommittee whose task was to develop a framework of standards for computer-to-computer communications. The resulting effort produced the *Open Systems Interconnection Reference Model*, which is referred to as the OSI Reference Model. This seven-layer model serves as a framework around which a series of standard protocols are defined.

The seven-layer OSI model is put into practice as software that handles the transmission of a message from one terminal or application program to another distant terminal or application program. As its nickname implies, this software is divided into seven layers. One way to understand the OSI model is to view it as seven different software programs. This approach clarifies what each layer of software does in handling a message.

You can view the OSI model as though it were a seven-story office building with people working on each floor. Moreover, you can assume the people on each floor belong to separate departments; therefore, the people on each of the floors carry out different job tasks.

Like workers in a modern office building, data or messages can enter or exit the building only by the front door on the first floor. Because the company's business system applications, computers, and terminals are located on the seventh floor, the firm's employees carry out their job tasks (business applications) on the seventh floor. Thus, all messages start on the seventh floor, go down through floors six, five, four, three, two, and one, and then leave the building via the front door on their way to whomever they are addressed.

All messages have to go from the seventh floor and stop at each floor on the way down to the first floor because the employees on floors six through one have to process the message in some way before it goes out the front door. This is similar to what the OSI seven-layer model does. It processes messages, not in a single software program, but in seven different programs that are referred to as *layers*.

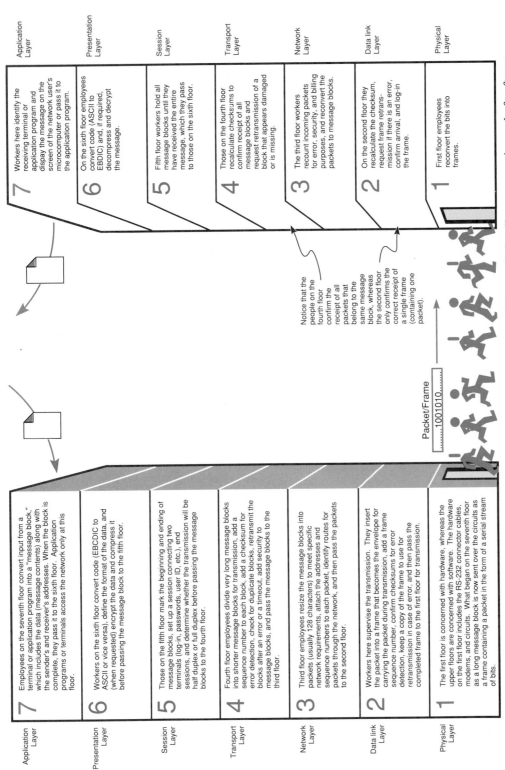

Figure 9-2 This figure depicts the OSI model as a seven-floor office building in which people handle messages instead of software programs doing the work. A message to be sent across the network enters the OSI software at the seventh floor, travels down to the first floor, goes out the front door, travels across the network, and reaches the other building, where it travels through the front door and up to the receiving terminal on the seventh floor of that building.

Right building (receiving):

7 — Application Layer
Workers here identify the receiving terminal or application program and display the message on the screen of the network user's microcomputer or pass it to the application program.

6 — Presentation Layer
On the sixth floor employees convert code (ASCII to EBDIC) and, if required, decompress and decrypt the message.

5 — Session Layer
Fifth floor workers hold all message blocks until they have received the entire message, which they pass to those on the sixth floor.

4 — Transport Layer
Those on the fourth floor recalculate checksums to confirm receipt of all message blocks and request retransmission of a block that appears damaged or is missing.

3 — Network Layer
The third floor workers recount incoming packets for error, security, and billing purposes, and recovert the packets to message blocks.

2 — Data link Layer
On the second floor they recalculate the checksum, request frame retransmission if there is an error, confirm arrival, and log-in the frame.

1 — Physical Layer
First floor employees recovert the bits into frames.

Notice that the people on the fourth floor confirm receipt of all packets that belong to the same message block, whereas the second floor only confirms the correct receipt of a single frame (containing one packet).

Packet/Frame
......1001010......

Left building (sending):

7 — Application Layer
Employees on the seventh floor convert input from a terminal or application program into a "message block," which includes the data (message contents) along with the sender's and receiver's addresses. When the block is complete, they pass it to the sixth floor. Application programs or terminals access the network only at this floor.

6 — Presentation Layer
Workers on the sixth floor convert code (EBCDIC to ASCII or vice versa), define the format of the data, and (when requested) encrypt the data and compress it before passing the message block to the fifth floor.

5 — Session Layer
Those on the fifth floor mark the beginning and ending of message blocks, set up a session connecting two terminals (log-in, passwords, user ID, etc.), end sessions, and determine whether the transmission will be half duplex or full duplex before passing the message blocks to the fourth floor.

4 — Transport Layer
Fourth floor employees divide very long message blocks into shorter message blocks for transmission, add a sequence number to each block, add a checksum for error detection, check for duplicate blocks, retransmit the blocks after an error or a timeout, add security to message blocks, and pass the message blocks to the third floor.

3 — Network Layer
Third floor employees resize the message blocks into packets (usually 128 characters) to meet specific network requirements, attach the addresses and sequence numbers to each packet, identify routes for packets through the network, and then pass the packets to the second floor.

2 — Data link Layer
Workers here supervise the transmission. They insert the packet into a frame that becomes the envelope for carrying the packet during transmission, add a frame sequence number, confirm checksums for error detection, keep a copy of the frame to use for retransmission in case of error, and then pass the completed frame to the first floor for transmission.

1 — Physical Layer
The first floor is concerned with hardware, whereas the upper floors are concerned with software. The hardware on the first floor includes the RS-232 connector cables, modems, and circuits. What began on the seventh floor as a long message block is now sent over the circuits as a frame containing a packet in the form of a serial stream of bits.

Each of these seven layers or programs has a name assigned to it, beginning at the top layer (seventh) and progressing to the bottom layer (first). The layers (starting with layer 7) are application, presentation, session, transport, network, data link, and physical. Now examine Figure 9-2. Notice that the floors in our building are named similarly, with the seventh floor being the application layer and the first floor being the physical layer. A brief summary of the work that is done by the people on each floor appears to the right of the floor's name. In other words, these summaries state what the people do at each floor as the messages move from the application layer (seventh floor) down to the physical layer (first floor) and out the door on their way to a distant terminal, computer, or person. After studying this figure, you should realize that in the OSI model, it is not people doing the work—it is software programs. Instead of seven floors, there are seven layers of these software programs.

One other point should be noted. If there were an intermediate node between the two buildings in Figure 9-2, this node would

- Calculate and verify the checksum for each frame (packet)
- Possibly reroute the message to avoid congestion on the network's links

To expand further on these concepts, examine Figure 9-3 which shows the seven layers of software located at the host end of a network and the same seven layers located at the remote terminal end of a network. Notice that there are physical communications between the two machines (host and terminal) *only* at layer 1, the physical layer. In other words, the actual message data bits must move down from layer 7 to layer 1, across the communication circuits that interconnect layer 1 at the host end to layer 1 at the terminal end, and then back up to layer 7 at the other end of the communication link.

All other connections between layers 2 through 7 are known as *virtual links* because they are only theoretical; physical data bits do *not* move between them. For example, even though a software program at layer 5 at one end may "think" it is sending data directly to layer 5 at the other end of the link, it is not. This is only a virtual link because the data path is 5–4–3–2–1–1–2–3–4–5. Another way of looking at virtual links is to view them as logical links or logical connection paths. Logically, data may flow between any of the layers at either end of a communication link, but physically it must flow down to layer 1, across the communication media, and back up to layer 7 (or the layer to which it is addressed) at the other end of the communication circuit.

The purpose of these seven layers is to segment the various functions that must be carried out when two machines want to communicate. For example, suppose you want to start a conversation with your friend. You probably would *not* carry out the dialogue by saying, "Hi. Do you want to talk with me?", then wait for your friend's answer, and if he or she said yes, start the conversation. Machines must do things like this first!

In a real-life, human-to-human situation, the protocols used to get someone's attention or obtain permission to speak might include looking at the person, using

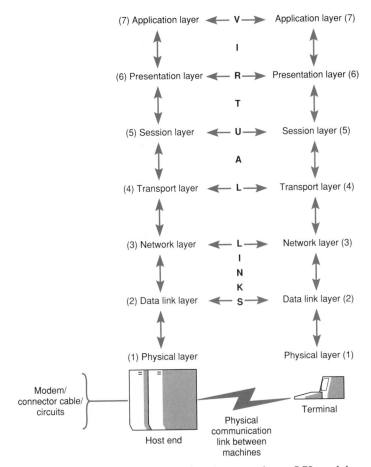

Figure 9-3 Communications using the seven-layer OSI model.
Information bits move only at layer 1.

body language, raising your hand in a classroom or a meeting, or just beginning to speak. These types of informal human ''protocols'' cannot be used in a data communication network situation because the terminals are not human, nor are they in face-to-face contact. As you learned when you read about establishing a dial-up telephone call, you must set up the communication link (communication circuit) first by dialing the telephone. Next, you establish your *session* by whatever it takes to identify the person or machine with which you want to communicate. Then you carry out the session by sending and receiving the business information (which is the purpose of your communication). Finally, you terminate the session (end your conversation with the other person or machine) and then terminate your link (disconnect the communication circuit) by hanging up the telephone.

The foregoing introduces the OSI seven-layer model, but remember that this is a *model* used by designers and programmers for developing communication software and protocols; it is not a single program. The following sections provide a more in-depth perspective of the tasks performed by each layer. The controls related to each layer are discussed in Chapter 13.

Layer 1: Physical Layer   The *physical layer* is concerned primarily with transmitting data bits (0s or 1s) over a communication circuit. The main purpose of this layer is to define the rules by which one side (host) sends a 1 bit so that the other side (terminal) defines it as a 1 bit when it is received. This is the physical communication circuit layer. At this layer we are concerned with very basic things like voltages of electricity, timing factors such as 1200 bits per second being equal to 833 microseconds per bit (1 sec/1200 bps $= 833$ μsec), full duplex or half duplex transmission, rules for establishing the initial connection, how to disconnect when the transmission is complete, and connector cable standards such as RS232 and RS449.

At this layer we are concerned with how the physical, electrical, and functional interchange takes place that establishes, maintains, and disconnects the physical link between DCEs (data circuit terminating equipment).

Remember that layer 1 is the basic link over which all data must pass. Layer 1 concerns hardware, whereas layers 2 through 7 concern software. Communication between layers 2 to 7 at a host and layers 2 to 7 at a terminal are only virtual (appearing to exist) communications. In reality, the messages must be passed down to layer 1 (physical layer) for the actual movement of the message between the host computer and a remote terminal.

Layer 2: Data Link Layer   The *data link layer* manages the basic transmission circuit established in layer 1 and transforms it into a circuit or link that is free of transmission errors. This error-free transmission link interacts closely with layer 3, the network layer. The data link layer accomplishes its tasks by transmitting frames and sending acknowledgment frames back to acknowledge the received data as in Automatic Repeat reQuest—ARQ. (We discuss some of the more common frames later in this chapter.)

Because layer 1 accepts and transmits only a serial stream of bits without any regard to meaning or structure, it is the task of the data link layer to create and recognize frame boundaries and check for errors during transmission. As you can see in Figure 9-2, the layer 1 protocol is handled in conjunction with the modem, connector cable standards, and communication circuits, whereas layer 2 requires intelligence (software) and therefore is located in some type of programmable device like a front end processor, network node, or microcomputer.

The data link layer establishes and controls the physical path of communications before sending your message down to the physical layer below it. The data link layer takes the data, which has been divided into packets by the layers above it, and physically assembles the packet for transmission by completing its frame. This assembly includes adding error detection, message type, and other control characters. If the protocol does not use packets, this layer assembles the message block into a frame, which is just another name for the block that is transmitted. Frames contain the message, along with other control and error detection characters.

A major task of layer 2 is to solve the problems caused by damaged, lost, or duplicate message frames so the layer above it (layer 3) can work with error-free messages. This includes error detection, correction, and retransmission, definition of the beginning and end of the message, resolution of competing requests for the same communication link, and flow control. The purpose of *flow control* is to keep a fast transmitting device from "drowning" a slow receiving device. Some mechanism or procedure must be employed to let the transmitting terminal know that the available buffer space at the receiver is filling to a critical level. This procedure and error handling are integrated, although the problem of one terminal overrunning another also is handled in some of the layers above this layer.

Typical data link level protocols are X.25, High-level Data Link Control (HDLC), Synchronous Data Link Control (SDLC), and some of the protocols used by your microcomputer.

Layer 3: Network Layer   The *network layer* provides for the functions of internal network operations such as addressing and routing. In other words, it provides services that move data through the network to its destination node/terminal. The network layer actually controls the operation of the combined layers, 1, 2, and 3. This sometimes is called the *subnetwork* or the *packet switching network function.*

Layer 3 provides control from one node (terminal) to another across the network. Basically, software at this layer accepts blocks from layer 4, converts them to shorter (resized) packets, and ensures that the packets get directed to their proper destination. A key issue is how to determine the route of the packet. It can be based, for example, on dynamic tables containing the various circuit routes that are updated frequently to show possible down circuits or circuits that currently are overloaded with data transmissions. After its routing has been established, the packet is passed down to the data link layer, which frames it and passes it down to the physical layer, which in turn pumps the data bits over the communication circuit to wherever the packets are addressed.

The network layer also is concerned with enabling simultaneous use of multiple links to increase information transmission performance. Among the issues addressed here are routing a message out of your network, flow control, end-to-end acknowledgments on the network for multilink paths, and host mainframe-to-network interfaces.

Routing of the packets is another task. At this layer there may be a database of routing tables to keep track of the various routes a packet can take and to determine how many different circuits are between any two individual packet switching nodes (review Figure 6-15 to see this concept). Packet routing also involves load-leveling the volume of transmissions on any given circuit, as well as knowing whether a circuit has failed.

There even can be an accounting function built into layer 3. An example is one that keeps track of how many packets or messages are transmitted for each organization so each group can be billed correctly; however, accounting functions usually are built into one of the higher layers of the seven-layer protocol scheme.

Layer 4: Transport Layer   The *transport layer* often is called the *host-to-host layer* or *end-to-end layer* because it establishes, maintains, and terminates "logical" connections for the transfer of data between end users. In practice, layers 4 through 7 are known as end-to-end layers, and layers 1 through 3 are known as protocol layers. The transport layer is responsible for generating the address of the end user, ensuring that all the packets of data have been received, eliminating duplicate packets, and ensuring that packets have not been lost during transmission. One major issue concerning front end processors, packet switching nodes, and host computers is which of these three hardware devices should ensure that all packets are received correctly at their destination and in their proper order. Even though the software takes care of this function, the problem lies in the fact that the software for this layer can be located physically in any one of these three devices.

The transport layer provides the facilities that allow end users to pass messages between themselves across several intervening circuit links, stations, or nodes. The layers below this layer (layers 1 to 3) are transparent (invisible) to end users. Layer 4 includes facilities to do all user addressing, data assurance (control), and flow control of messages from source to destination across either simple or complex networks. Even though the layer below this one (the network layer) actually is responsible for routing the packets, the transport layer initially establishes the packets (blocks) and the distant terminal address that is used for packet routing.

The transport layer deals with end-to-end issues, such as network addressing, establishment of virtual circuits, and procedures for entering and departing from the network. Only when we get above this layer do we start to discuss issues that are visible to end users.

At this layer we have moved out of the message protocols and into other software programs, peer-to-peer protocols between layers, and the vendor's network architectures. Probably the best known of these is IBM's Systems Network Architecture (SNA).

This layer might include the specifications for broadcast messages, datagram-type electronic mail services, accounting information collection, message priorities, security, response times, and a recovery strategy in case of failure.

The transport layer is known as a source-to-destination or end-to-end layer because a program at the source machine can carry on a virtual conversation with a similar program on a destination machine by using message headers and control messages. The physical path, however, still goes down to layer 1 and across to the destination machine.

At the lower layers (layers 1 to 3), the protocols are carried out by each machine and its immediate neighbors, not by the ultimate source and destination machines. These source/destination machines always are separated by many other pieces of hardware like front end processors, concentrators, multiplexers, message switches, and modems. Layers 1 to 3 are chained together in a sequential fashion, whereas layers 4 through 7 are end-to-end or computer-to-remote terminal software interfaces.

The transport layer also can multiplex several streams of messages onto one physical circuit by creating multiple connections that enter and leave each host computer. The *transport header* delineates which message belongs to which connection. There also is a mechanism at this layer that regulates the flow of information so a very fast host cannot overrun a slower terminal or especially an overburdened host. Flow control at the transport layer is a little different from flow control at the lower layers. The transport layer prevents one host from overrunning another host by controlling the movement of messages, whereas layers 2 and 1 control the physical flow (speed) of packets or frames. In fact, a lower layer can hold back data sent out by layer 4.

Layer 5: Session Layer   The *session layer* is responsible for initiating, maintaining, and terminating each logical session between end users. To understand the session layer, think of your telephone. When you lift the receiver, listen for a dial tone, and dial a number, you begin to create a physical connection that goes through layer 1 as a person-to-network protocol. When you start speaking with the person at the other end of the telephone circuit, you are engaged in a person-to-person session. In other words, the session is the dialogue the two of you carry out.

In addition, this layer is responsible for managing and structuring all sessions. Session initiation must arrange for all the desired and required services between session participants. Required services include logging on to circuit equipment, transferring files between equipment, using various terminal types or features, security authenticators, the software tasks for half duplex or full duplex, and the like.

Sometimes the session layer is referred to as the *data flow control layer* because it is responsible for establishing the connection between two applications or processes, reestablishing the connection if it fails, enforcing the rules for carrying on the session, and maintaining data flow control. The session layer also is concerned with establishing communications between given pairs of users and starting, stopping, and controlling those communications. For example, if the host mainframe is sending data to a printer that has a limited-size buffer, the established rules might be to send only one buffer-size block of data to the printer at any one time and then wait for the printer to signal that its buffer is empty before sending the next block of data. Layer 5 is responsible for controlling this data flow to avoid a buffer overflow (loss of data) at the printer.

This layer provides for session termination, which is an orderly way to terminate the session. It also provides the facilities to abort a session prematurely by such means as a break key. The session layer also might keep track of various accounting functions so the correct party receives the bill later. It may have some redundancy built in to recover from a broken transport (layer 4) connection in case of failure.

The session layer is very close to the transport layer, although it has more application-oriented functions than does the transport layer. Because the host computer's operating system supervisors generally handle the session layer, it would be easy to merge the session and transport layers into a single layer.

Layer 6: Presentation Layer   The *presentation layer* carries out a selectable set of message transformations and formatting to present data to the end users. This layer has such features as peripheral device coding, formatting, encryption, compaction, and code conversion.

This layer defines the end user's port into the network in terms of the code used, format, and any other attributes. Its job is to accommodate the totally different interfaces seen by a terminal in one node and what is expected by the application program at the host mainframe computer. For example, the layer 6 presentation services in IBM's Systems Network Architecture perform data compression, additions (such as column headings), translation (for example, program commands such as clear screen) from its machine language into local terminal commands, and so on. IBM's Customer Information Control System (CICS) teleprocessing monitor is a layer 6 service located in a host mainframe computer, although a product like CICS has many other functions beyond the presentation layer. At the presentation layer we are concerned with the displaying, formatting, and editing of user inputs and outputs.

Basically, any function (except those in layers 1 to 5) that is requested sufficiently often to warrant finding a general solution for it is placed in the presentation layer, although some of these functions can be performed by separate hardware and software (encryption). More generally, different computers have different file formats, so a file conversion option is useful as well as protocol conversion between incompatible hardware.

Layer 7: Application Layer   The *application layer* is the end user's access to the network. At this layer we are concerned with what the user is trying to do, namely, perform a business function. This task may be the generation of a form, creation of a policy, completion of a financial report, or any other number of products, such as spreadsheets. The purpose of the application layer is to provide a set of utilities for application programs. Each user program determines the set of messages and any action it might take upon receipt of a message. Other considerations at the application layer include network management statistics, remote system initiation and termination, network monitoring, application diagnostics, making the network transparent to users, simple processor sharing between host computers, use of distributed databases, and industry-specific protocols such as you might have in banking. This layer is where application programs, terminals, and computers access the network.

FRAME (HDLC/X.25/SDLC)

As mentioned earlier when discussing layer 2 of the OSI model, there are a number of data link level protocols. One of these is the *High-level Data Link Control* (HDLC), and another is IBM's *Synchronous Data Link Control* (SDLC). The HDLC SDLC, and X.25 protocols are very similar. They also are widely used data link control frame formats. HDLC is a standard from the International Organization for Standardization.

Many protocols are now standards and are referred to by the number of the standard, as in the case of *X.25*, which is the most popular international bit-oriented protocol. It defines the structure, contents, and sequencing procedures for transmitting data among DTEs, DCEs, and a public data network. It also defines the techniques used for error detection and recovery. It should be noted that X.25 only defines the requirements of a connection between data terminal equipment (DTE) and a public data network; it is not a standard connection between sets of data

8 bits	8 bits	8 bits	Variable	16 or 32 bits	8 bits
Beginning Flag 01111110	Address	Control	Message (Data Packet)	Frame Check Sequence	Ending Flag 01111110

Figure 9-4   A frame such as those for High-level Data Link Control (HDLC), X.25, or Synchronous Data Link Control (SDLC) protocols.

communication equipment from different vendors. Each equipment manufacturer must implement X.25 on its own hardware by using appropriate software.

The X.25 protocol pertains only to layers 1 to 3 of the OSI model. Layers 4 to 6 are more concerned with other software and network architecture, whereas layer 7 involves user application programs.

Figure 9-4 shows a typical *frame* from the HDLC, X.25, or SDLC protocols. Each frame begins and ends with a special bit pattern (01111110). This is known as the beginning and ending flag. The *beginning flag* references the position of the address and control frame elements and initiates error checking procedures. The *ending flag* terminates the error checking procedures. When you have contiguous frames, it also may be the beginning flag for the next frame.

The *address field* identifies one of the terminals. For point-to-point circuits it sometimes is used to distinguish commands from responses or to address a specific terminal device on multifunction terminals. This 8-bit field might contain a station address, a group address for several terminals, or a broadcast address to all terminals.

The *control field* identifies the kind of frame that is being transmitted, such as information, supervisory, or unnumbered. The *information frame* is used for the transfer and reception of messages, frame numbering of contiguous frames, and the like. The *supervisory frame* is used to transmit acknowledgments, such as to indicate the next expected frame, indicate that a transmission error has been detected, acknowledge that all received frames are correct, stop sending, and call for the retransmission of specified frames. The *unnumbered frame* is used for other purposes, such as to provide a command "disconnect" that allows a terminal to announce it is going down, or to indicate that a frame with a correct checksum has impossible semantics. Because control frames may be lost or damaged, just like information frames, they also must be acknowledged. A special control acknowledgment frame is provided for this purpose; it is called an *unnumbered acknowledgment*.

The *message field* is of variable length and is the user's message or request (data packet). This field may include a general format identifier, logical channel group numbers, logical channel numbers, packet-type identifiers, internal message DTE addresses (calling DTE and called DTE), packet sequence numbers, and, of course, the message that is being transmitted.

Notice that we have two types of sequence numbering here. In the previously mentioned control field we sequence number the individual contiguous frames. In the message field we sequence number the individual packets when the system breaks the message into multiple packets.

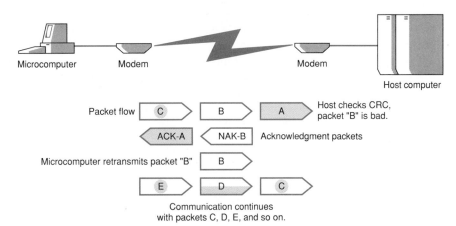

Figure 9-5   Data flow using the X.25 packet protocol in half duplex transmission.

The *frame check sequence field* provides a 16- or 32-bit cyclical redundancy checking (CRC) calculation that is placed in the field by the transmitting station. Upon receipt, the receiving station recalculates the CRC values and matches them to determine whether any errors occurred during data transmission. If the CRC values do not match, a request for retransmission is sent to the sending terminal station/node.

Figure 9-5 illustrates the flow of frames carrying packets on a communication circuit, although for this discussion, they will be called packets instead of frames. The figure shows the process of error detection and retransmission. This error detection and correction service is provided in layer 2 (the data link layer). In this case, a microcomputer is accessing a remote host computer via modems. As the microcomputer user types requests to the host computer, the protocol puts the data into packets and sends packets A, B, and C down the communication circuit. The protocol on the host side recalculates the cyclical redundancy check (CRC) on the packets and finds that packets A and C are complete, but that packet B was corrupted during transmission. Packet B is rejected and a negative acknowledgment (NAK) is sent back to the microcomputer. At this point the microcomputer retransmits packet B and then resumes communication with packets C, D, and E. Note that packet C has to be transmitted again, even though it was correct the first time. Sometimes this is called "go back *n*" error correction because transmission resumes from the corrected packet.

SYSTEMS NETWORK ARCHITECTURE (SNA)

To put the concepts of the OSI model, network architectures, HDLC, X.25, and SDLC protocols into perspective, we will examine how they operate when IBM's *Systems Network Architecture* (SNA) is used. IBM does not use the X.25 protocol. Instead, IBM uses its own Synchronous Data Link Control (SDLC) protocol, which

Before SNA	After SNA
The program code in the application programs handles both logical and physical control of the network resources (front ends, intermediate nodes, terminal controllers, circuits, and terminals).	VTAM manages network resources, physical network management is offloaded to the front end processor, and application programs issue SEND or RECEIVE macros to communicate with terminals.
Device-dependent code is in the application program.	No device-dependent code is in the application program.
Each host computer has its own dedicated circuits, networks, and terminals.	Several host computers share circuits, networks, and terminals.
Incompatible terminals require separate circuits.	All SNA terminals coexist on the same Synchronous Data Link Control (SDLC) circuit.
When the circuit is unavailable, the terminal is unavailable.	Many terminals still operate in the standalone mode if the circuit is unavailable.
The host computer processes all transactions.	The terminal controller processes many transactions.

Figure 9-6 Comparison of data communications before and after implementation of the Systems Network Architecture (SNA).

is almost identical to HDLC and X.25. The frames look the same (see Figure 9-4), but the internal bit structure or number of bits in any of the six fields may be interpreted a little differently. These protocols have been modified, however, so they now operate in the same manner. Figure 9-6 compares the differences both before and after implementing SNA.

SNA describes an integrated structure that provides for all modes of data communications and upon which new data communication networks can be planned and implemented. SNA is built around four basic principles. *First,* SNA encompasses distributed functions in which many network responsibilities can be moved from the central computer to other network components, such as remote concentrators. *Second,* SNA describes paths between the end users (programs, devices, or operators) of the data communication network separately from the users themselves, thus allowing network configuration modifications or extensions without affecting the end users. *Third,* SNA uses the principle of device independence, which permits an application program to communicate with an input/output device without regard to any unique device requirements. This also allows application programs and communication equipment to be added or changed without affecting other elements of the communication network. *Fourth,* SNA uses both logical and physical standardized functions and protocols for the communication of information between any two

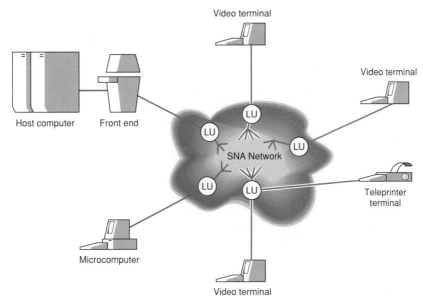

Figure 9-7   SNA session.

points. This means there can be *one* architecture for general purpose and industry terminals of many varieties, and *one* network protocol.

The appropriate place to begin understanding the concept of SNA is to look at it from the viewpoint of the end user (see Figure 9-7). The end user (terminal operator) talks to the network through what is called a *logical unit* (LU). These logical units are implemented as program code or microcode (firmware), and they provide the end user with a point of access to the network. The program code or microcode can be built into the terminal or implemented into an intelligent terminal controller, concentrator, or remote front end.

Before one end user of a SNA network can communicate with any other end user, each of their respective logical units must be connected in a mutual relationship called a *session*. Because a session joins two logical units, it is called a *LU-LU session*. Figure 9-7 depicts the interconnection of logical units when one end user wants to talk to another. The terminal user enters the request to talk to another terminal, and the network's software connects the two LUs.

The exchange of data by end users is subject to a number of procedural rules (protocols) that the logical units specify before beginning the exchange of information. These procedural rules specify how the session is to be conducted, the frame size, the amount of data to be sent by one end user before the other end user replies, actions to be taken if errors occur, the transmission speed, sequencing, what route the frame will take, what to do if the circuit fails, and the like. You can view it as though the SDLC software is performing the same tasks the people performed in Figure 9-2 on the first, second, and third floors. They are the machine-to-machine protocols.

If you compare the seven layers of the OSI model in Figure 9-2, the corresponding layers in IBM's SNA are (from the bottom up) physical control, data link control, path control, transmission control, data flow control, presentation control, and transaction services. As you can see, IBM has a similar seven-layer model.

Each logical unit (LU) in a network is assigned a network name. Before a session begins, the SNA network determines the network address that corresponds to each LU network name. This scheme allows one end user (for example, a terminal operator) to establish communication with another end user (for example, an application program) without having to specify where that end user is located in the network. These network names and addresses are used for addressing messages.

The flow of data between users moves between two logical units in a session. This flow of data moves as a bit sequence carried in a frame (see Figure 9-4) and generally is referred to as a *message unit*. The message unit also contains the network addresses of the logical unit that originated the message and the logical unit that is to receive the message. These are the basic protocols at work.

A session between a pair of logical units is initiated when one of them (the end user) issues a REQUEST TO SEND message. Once a session has been activated between a pair of logical units, they can begin to exchange data. This is where the Synchronous Data Link Control (SDLC) protocol handles the movement of data to have an orderly data flow.

A session between a pair of logical units is deactivated when one of them sends a deactivation request or when some other outside event interrupts the session. This outside event can be intervention by a network operator or failure at some other part of the network.

Network Addressable Units (NAUs) The logical organization of a SNA network, regardless of its physical configuration, is divided into two broad categories of components: network addressable units and path control network.

Network addressable units are sets of SNA components that provide services enabling end users to send data through the network and helping network operators perform network control and management functions. Physically, network addressable units are hardware and programming components within terminals, intelligent controllers, and front end processors. Network addressable units communicate with one another through the path control network (discussed in the next section).

There are three kinds of network addressable units in SNA (see Figure 9-8). The first one, the logical unit (LU), has already been introduced. The second kind is the *physical unit* (PU). This is not truly a physical device; it is a set of SNA components that provide services to control communication links, terminals, intelligent controllers, front end processors, and host computers. Each terminal, intelligent controller, front end processor, and the like contains a physical unit that represents the terminal, intelligent controller, or other device to the SNA network. The third kind of network addressable unit is the *system services control point* (SSCP). This also is a set of SNA components, but its duties are broader than those of the physical units and logical units. Physical units and logical units represent machine resources and end users, whereas the SSCP manages the entire SNA network or a significant part of it called a *domain*. A SSCP controls many other devices.

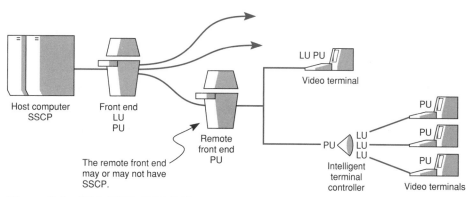

Figure 9-8   SNA SSCPs/LUs/PUs.

Just as sessions exist between logical units, sessions can exist between other kinds of network addressable units, such as a *SSCP-LU, SSCP-PU,* or *SSCP-SSCP session.* Figure 9-8 shows the location of LUs, PUs, and SSCPs in a network. In a family, the mother, father, and children are all PUs. You conduct a LU session when speaking with your father, mother, sister, or brother, but your mother or father is the SSCP controlling the children's LUs.

Systems Network Architecture defines a *node* as a point within the SNA network that contains SNA components. For example, each terminal, intelligent controller, and front end processor that is designed into the SNA specifications can be a node.

An expanded definition of a node is any microcomputer, minicomputer, mainframe computer, or database that constitutes a point on the network at which data might be stored, forwarded, input into the network, or removed from the network as output. Depending on which vendor's literature you are reading, they might refer to a node as a *station,* an *intelligent microprocessor-based device,* a *terminal,* or a *workstation.*

Each SNA node contains a physical unit that represents that node and its resources to the system services control point. When the SSCP activates a session with a physical unit (SSCP-PU session), it makes the node (terminal, intelligent controller, or front end processor) containing that physical unit an active part of the SNA network. It is convenient to think of a SNA node as being a terminal, intelligent controller, or front end processor within the network. Certain more powerful nodes also can be a SSCP.

Path Control Network   Remember that the logical organization of SNA is divided into two broad categories of components: network addressable units and the path control network. The *path control network* provides for routing and flow control. Logical units must establish a path before a LU-LU session can begin. Each SSCP, PU, and LU has a different network address, which identifies it to other network addressable units as well as to the path control network. Path control provides for the following.

- Virtual routing so all sessions can send their messages by different routes
- Transmission priorities
- Multiple links to maximize throughput
- Message pacing (flow control) to keep a fast transmitter from drowning a slow receiver
- Ability to detect and recover from errors as they occur
- Facilities to handle disruption because of a circuit failure
- Facilities to inform network operators when there is a disruption in the network

The path control network has two layers: the *path control layer* and the *data link control layer* (similar to layers 2 and 3 in the OSI model). Routing and flow control are the major services provided by the path control layer, whereas transmitting data over individual links is the major service provided by the data link control layer. It is in this area that Synchronous Data Link Control (SCLC) is used by links for serial bit-by-bit transmission of frames. The SDLC function includes the following activities (layer 2 of the OSI model).

- Synchronizing or getting the transmitter in step with the receiver
- Detecting and recovering from transmission errors
- Controlling the sending and receiving stations
- Reporting improper data link control procedures

The SDLC procedures sandwich each message into a frame for transmission. In the SDLC concept, the frame is the vehicle for every command and response and for all information that is transmitted using SNA. Figure 9-4 depicted the SDLC frame. All messages are put into this frame format for transmission from one node to another node *(a PU-PU session)*. The error checking for each message is incorporated in the frame check sequence portion of the SDLC frame.

A data communication network built on SNA concepts consists of the following (see Figure 9-9).

- A host computer
- A front end processor (intermediate node)
- Remote intelligent controller (intermediate node or boundary node)
- A variety of general purpose and industry-oriented terminals (terminal node or cluster node)
- Possibly local area networks or micro-to-mainframe links

APPC and LU 6.2   A newer part of IBM's Systems Network Architecture is *Advanced Program-to-Program Communications* (APPC). APPC often is referred to by its two components, *logical unit 6.2 (LU 6.2)* and *physical unit 2.1 (PU 2.1)*. It has been

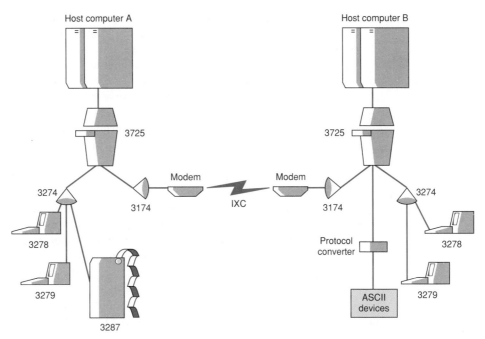

Figure 9-9   SNA network devices. The numbers refer to model numbers of IBM devices; 3725 front end processor; 3174/3274 controller; 3278/3279 terminals; 3287 printer.

defined by various users as an architecture, a high level program interface, a network operating system, and a protocol. IBM decribes APPC as a program interface and an operating system. As a high level program interface, LU 6.2 provides a set of conversion verbs that programmers can embed in programs when the program needs to communicate with another application, such as to access a database.

To accomplish this conversion, the programmer issues the LU 6.2 verb called "allocate" which in effect says, "I would like to converse with this other program." The programmer then issues a "send" command, which starts the program at the other end of the communication link. That program carries out its task (let us assume it is a database lookup) and returns the data to the original transmitting device. The advantage of this technique is that the user of a high level programming interface like LU 6.2 does not have to be sensitive to the location of the destination terminal or to networking, in terms of efficiency, encoding, or flow control. That is all taken care of by LU 6.2. Moreover, the host computer does not have to mediate the connection between the two end user terminals.

Until the advent of LU 6.2, or APPC, data communications meant two or more computers exchanging data in a predefined format. In the hands of skilled software developers and system designers, APPC/LU 6.2 allows programs on different computers to manipulate data interactively. This sometimes is referred to as providing users with protocols for peer-to-peer communications.

The term *peer to peer* can have two meanings when referring to communications. The first meaning is communication between two or more processes or programs by which both ends of the conversation exchange data with equal privilege and in which any physical differences between the computers are transparent to the application. The second meaning is communication between two or more network nodes in which either side can initiate sessions because no *primary-secondary* relationship exists, and in which either side is able to poll or answer to polls. Before the introduction of peer-to-peer communications, a primary-secondary relationship always existed where only one of the two nodes could initiate or start a communication session.

LU 6.2 can be viewed as a distributed operating system because it gives access to, and manages contention for, resources. An analogy might be one in which a computer's operating system allows the sharing of different resources, such as files and printers, without requiring the user to be aware of any other users. LU 6.2/APPC provides the same kind of capability in a network environment.

Although LU 6.2 allows communication between machines, it does not address file structures or any of the data stream questions. One of the strengths of LU 6.2 is that it can carry any data stream. Data structure incompatibilities are addressed at the presentation control layer (layer 6). You should be aware that LU 6.2 is contained in the data flow control layer (layer 5) of IBM's seven-layer SNA network architecture.

IBM's Systems Network Architecture supports nodes that are identified as physical units. It also defines logical entities in relation to these PUs and dictates how logical units interact. Advanced Program-to-Program Communications assumes the presence of both LU 6.2 and PU 2.1.

The physical unit protocols are those governing the manner in which a node on a SNA network can operate. (Remember that a node is any end point in the network.) The type of physical unit one can support dictates which node in the communication does polling, the status of the node (primary or secondary), whether multiple links can join adjacent nodes, and so forth.

Every node contains one physical unit that manages the telecommunication links connecting it to adjacent nodes. The component of PU 2.1 nodes that activates sessions with other PUs and LUs is called a *peripheral node control point* (PNCP). The PNCP becomes active when the node is operational.

The basic physical units include the following.

- PU 1.0 is an obsolete terminal controller protocol.
- PU 2.0 is an end node associated with minicomputers, 3274 display controllers, remote job entry (RJE) stations (such as 3770), and printers (such as the 3820) that attach only to host computers. PCs can emulate 3274s.
- PU 2.1 is a terminal controller, minicomputer, or microcomputer, and it allows connections to both hosts and any other PU 2.1 nodes.
- PU 4.0 is a communication controller or front end processor.
- PU 5.0 is a host processor.

PU 2.1 enables peer devices to communicate without host intervention. Each individual node with PU 2.1 capability can initiate a connection with other PU 2.1 intermediate nodes. LU 6.2 is a common set of programming verbs allowing communication among devices, but complete office networking cannot be achieved without the additional capabilities of PU 2.1. Before the advent of PU 2.1, the mainframe directed traffic through an intermediate node if a direct route from Point A to Point B was unavailable. Thus, a terminal wishing to converse with a non-IBM mainframe had to pass through an IBM host. PU 2.1 is the mechanism that allows you to use LU 6.2, which frees the host for other activities.

In summary, a SNA network is a collection of logical units, or LUs, linked by sessions. The LU is a "port" through which a user gains access to the services of a network. It can be a terminal, a microcomputer emulating a terminal, a printer, or an application program. It works at the application level and performs two tasks: it activates a session and it uses the session to communicate. A session is a logical connection between LUs that is independent of the physical nature of the connection. Think of it as a conversation between applications. The protocol used to perform the conversational duties is called a *LU session type*. There are a number of LU session types, as shown in the following list.

- LU 0 is a product-specific unit type for devices such as specialized store and forward controllers. Each product-specific LU 0 is unique.

- LU 1 is used for printers and remote job entry stations.

- LU 2 is used for the 3270 line of display stations.

- LU 3 is for older printer terminals that use pre-SNA programs.

- LU 4 was a precursor to LU 6.2, designed for low cost terminal-to-terminal and terminal-to-host communications.

- LU 6.0 and LU 6.1 are called intersystems communications and have been implemented in IBM's most popular teleprocessing monitor (CICS) and the IBM Information Management System (IMS) database.

- LU 6.2 represents a merger of the requirements of LU 0, LU 4, LU 6.0, and LU 6.1. APPC is LU session type 6, release 2, or simply LU 6.2. The purpose of LU 6.2 is to eliminate product-specific protocols and provide a common set of protocols that can be used for program-to-program (peer-to-peer) communications with or without a host computer.

- LU 7.0 is for 5250-type workstations.

APPC/LU 6.2 allows any two computers to communicate over any type of link, such as a local area network or telephone circuits. Moreover, LU 6.2 eliminates the primary-secondary relationships in micro-to-mainframe communications, thus allowing microcomputers to speak as equals to the host mainframe computer. LU 6.2 may be an opportunity to break the bonds of micro-to-mainframe emulation that are confining the microcomputer to virtually dumb terminal status in its communications with host mainframes.

Readers who would like to obtain a more detailed explanation of Systems Network Architecture should order IBM Manual GC30-3072, titled *Systems Network Architecture: Concepts and Products*.

SYSTEMS APPLICATION ARCHITECTURE (SAA)

IBM also has a newer broad architectural outline called *Systems Application Architecture* (SAA). It enables programmers to develop applications that can run on IBM personal computers, System/3*X*, System/370, 9370, 43*XX* mainframes, AS/400, and PS/2s. SAA is IBM's attempt to address the shortcoming of software incompatibility across its major hardware lines. As such, it represents the company's most important strategic direction since the debut of Systems Network Architecture (SNA).

SAA consists of four related components, one of which, Common Communications Support, should be a major improvement in the interaction between microcomputers, minicomputers, and host mainframes. The four components are the following. (Also see the Features of Systems Application Architecture box.)

- Common User Access. IBM has defined the basic elements of the user interface and how programs use them. The PC and PS/2 window-based interfaces use a mouse and are very icon-oriented.
- Common Programming Interface. IBM has selected several programming languages—initially Cobol, Fortran, and C—and services for use in writing consistent applications. Several programming services available on some IBM systems are available for use on other systems.
- Common Communications Support. IBM designated existing communication methods in the architecture, including the 3270 data stream, Document Content and Document Interchange Architectures, SNA Distribution Services, LU 6.2, SDLC, the Token-Ring, token bus, Ethernet LANs, ISDN, and X.25.
- Common Applications. IBM uses the first three elements to develop office applications that are common across hardware lines. IBM plans on a single product that works on diverse machines to perform document creation, document management, electronic mail, and decision support functions.

SAA is different from other network architectures. By allowing each application to be written once and then transported easily to another hardware platform, it facilitates the migration of mainframe applications to microcomputers.

The purpose of SAA is to gather all of IBM's incompatible operating systems, communication links, applications, and processors into one container. As an analogy, look at SAA as though it were an automobile dealership with vehicles of all makes, sizes, engines, colors, and so on. SAA provides a common methodology for garaging these vehicles (storing data), as well as instructions for driving each vehicle from Point A to Point B (data transmission).

SAA's primary goal is to make IBM's incompatible processors, operating systems, and applications compatible for use. Its purpose is to give users the option of

FEATURES OF SYSTEMS APPLICATION ARCHITECTURE

Common User Access Consistent application access across systems.

- Icons
- Color
- High resolution graphics
- Mouse support

Common Programming Interface Languages and services to be used for multisystem programs.

- Cobol, Fortran, and C programs
- Application generator like Cross System Product
- Procedure language like REXX
- Database interface like SQL
- Query interface like QMF
- Presentation interface like GDDM
- Dialogue interface like EZ-VU

Common Communications Support Methods of communicating between systems.

- 3270 Data Stream
- Document Content Architecture
- Document Interchange Architecture
- Intelligent Printer Data Stream
- SNA Distribution Services
- LU 6.2
- Synchronous Data Link Control
- IBM Token-Ring Network

Common Applications Single product for all systems incorporating

- Document creation
- Document library
- Personal services mail
- Decision support

sitting down at any PC, Personal System/2, or terminal and apply the same approach to access any data in the network.

If you plan to work with SAA, the manual called *IBM Systems Application Architecture: An Overview* should be on your bookshelf. It describes the details of SAA.

BINARY SYNCHRONOUS COMMUNICATIONS (BSC)

The *Binary Synchronous Communication* protocol is still in wide use because many organizations have not had the time or money to upgrade to the newer bit-oriented protocols like X.25, SDLC, HDLC, and others that are designed along the same lines as the OSI model. BSC is a byte-oriented protocol because it takes an entire 8-bit byte to send a command signal to the receiving station. With bit-oriented protocols such as X.25 or SDLC, the changing of a single bit within a frame's control byte sends a different command to the receiving station. BSC transmission takes place in a two-way, half duplex transmission mode with 8-bit byte commands.

Figure 9-10 shows a BSC message format. The SOH (start of heading—first character of message) is a fixed 8-bit character. The SOH is decimal 1 in ASCII coding as shown in Figure 5-7. It is followed by other header control characters that

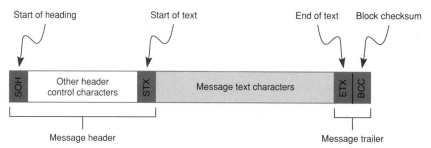

Figure 9-10   BSC message format (frame).

are used by the system for terminal addressing or other control purposes. The STX (start of text—decimal 2) is another special 8-bit character, as is the ETX (end of text—decimal 3). These two characters (STX and ETX) sandwich the message text characters so they can be identified easily. Finally, there is a block check character (BCC), which is a checksum at the end. The purpose of this block checksum is to detect any errors that occur during data transmission.

Notice that the BSC protocol does not place messages into tightly defined frames, nor does it handle any packet switching. It is an inefficient protocol because it is designed for half duplex circuits. BSC does not support loop circuits or mixing of terminal types. Different code structures cause serious problems. For example, the BSC protocol was designed to be used with Extended Binary Coded Decimal Interchange Code (EBCDIC), American Standard Code for Information Interchange (ASCII), or a 6-bit, 64-character code. BSC does not support hub go-ahead polling or some of the fast select polling scenarios.

Under BSC, the initiation of an error recovery procedure at one terminal station can cause line unavailability to other terminal stations until the recovery procedure is complete.

BSC half duplex operation works on the basis of sending one message block at a time to a distant terminal. The terminal must acknowledge the successful or unsuccessful receipt of each block before another one can be transmitted (stop and wait ARQ).

BSC does not provide complete error checking for all control and information transfer messages as does X.25 or SDLC. It does not provide any system-assigned block sequence numbering except for odd/even acknowledgments. Moreover, BSC cannnot be used on satellite circuits because the propagation delay time affects the stop and wait ARQ. Messages are delayed too long in satellite circuit transmission when you have to send a message block and receive an acknowledgment before you can send the second message block. This is because there is an approximate 0.5- to 0.6-second round-trip propagation time delay on a satellite circuit.

MANUFACTURING AUTOMATION PROTOCOL (MAP)

The *Manufacturing Automation Protocol* satisfies the special needs of factories, such as the networking of dissimilar devices, very fast access times, immunity from electrical or other interference on the communication circuits, reliability, ruggedness, and ease of maintenance and reconfiguration. This protocol is an overall organizational network that also can be used in an office setting for multiple tasks, such as word processing and other business functions. Its special use is in factory settings where, for example, it can enable scheduling from one of the terminal nodes, while simultaneously measuring paint thickness on a piece of metal with automatic sensing devices.

MAP is envisioned to provide high level communications among computers of various sizes and brands, along with a variety of programmable factory floor devices, such as robots, programmable controllers, vision systems, and microcomputers. MAP describes the network system that links everything together over a broadband backbone cable. Sometimes MAP is referred to as MAP/CIM. CIM, or *Computer Integrated Manufacturing,* means that computers are used to integrate the manufacturing, design, and business functions of an organization. Because it really describes concepts, it is a strategy or a road map rather than a network. Another name for the manufacturing automation protocol is MAP/TOP (for *Technical and Office Protocol*).

To date, the MAP model has six layers rather than the standard seven as in the OSI model. The missing layer is the presentation layer (layer 6). The basic backbone network endorsed by MAP is a token-passing broadband bus local area network that transmits at 1, 5, 10, or 20 million bits per second.

In summary, MAP is a type of OSI standard network that uses local area networking and optimizes factory applications. It endorses the IEEE 802.4 token-passing broadband bus network type using coaxial cable, broadband modulation, and token-passing access. MAP provides a multivendor device connection by using amplifiers, cable taps, splitters, terminators, and cable that are off the shelf rather than custom-made. IEEE 802.4 is described in Chapter 11 on local area networks.

DIGITAL NETWORK ARCHITECTURE (DNA)

The *Digital Network Architecture* is Digital Equipment Corporation's distributed network architecture. It is popularly referred to as *DECnet* and has five layers. The physical layer, data link control layer, transport layer, and network services layer correspond almost exactly to the lowest four layers of the OSI model. The fifth layer, the application layer, is a mixture of the OSI model's presentation and application layers. DECnet does not contain a separate session layer.

DECnet, like IBM's SNA, defines a general framework for both data communication networking and distributed data processing. The object of DECnet is to permit generalized interconnection of different host computers and point-to-point, multipoint, or switched networks in such a way that users can share programs, data files, and remote terminal devices.

DECnet supports both the Ethernet and X.25 protocols, and it has packet switching capabilities. An emulator permits Digital Equipment Corporation computers to be interconnected with IBM mainframes running in an SNA environment. The Digital Data Communication Message Protocol (DDCMP) is DECnet's byte-oriented protocol, which is similar in structure to IBM's Binary Synchronous Communications (BSC) protocol.

TRANSMISSION CONTROL PROTOCOL/INTERNET PROTOCOL (TCP/IP)

The *Transmission Control Protocol/Internet Protocol* probably is the oldest networking standard. It was developed for the U.S. Department of Defense's Advanced Research Project Agency NETwork (ARPANET). It allows reasonably efficient and error-free transmission between different systems, and it has been in place for about 15 years. Because it is a file transfer protocol, it can send large files of information across sometimes unreliable networks with great assurance that the data will arrive in an uncorrupted form.

When TCP/IP is used, data travels between sender and receiver applications inside segments created by TCP modules, which in turn travel inside packets of a special format called *IP-datagrams*. The IP-datagrams allow TCP segments that make up a long application data stream to take different routes through the network, much as packets in a packet switching network are able to travel by different data streams. TCP modules are active only at the communication path's end points where application data are inserted into or removed from TCP segments, which in turn are inserted into or removed from the IP-datagrams.

To understand TCP/IP, imagine the data being sent across the network as a document. This document has many typed pages. In fact, there are so many pages they must be separated into several stacks and placed in a series of separate interoffice envelopes. Each envelope is identified by a sequence number so the recipient knows the correct order in which to read the pages. Each of these interoffice envelopes then is inserted into a large mailing envelope with the destination office address added for mailing purposes. In our example, the typed pages represent application data, the interoffice envelopes represent TCP segments, and the large mailing envelope represents the IP-datagrams.

GOVERNMENT OPEN SYSTEMS INTERCONNECTION PROTOCOL (GOSIP)

When procuring new communication equipment, agencies in the U.S. government will be required to specify communication products that support the *Government Open Systems Interconnection Protocol* (GOSIP). You need to know why the OSI model originated if you are to understand what GOSIP is about. The OSI model was developed by a group of international users and vendors so they could move away from proprietary protocols that hindered the interconnection of networks. As you have seen, most vendors support the OSI protocols, either by using the seven-layer OSI model or by developing one that is quite similar.

GOSIP consists of a subset of the OSI protocols the government says it will use. In other words, GOSIP is a limited OSI model as defined by the U.S. government.

The main features it specifies are the ability to send and receive E-mail using the X.400 standard, and the ability to access and transfer files using File Transfer, Access, and Management. FTAM is the file transfer standard, and all FTAM systems must support at least T-1 circuits.

The GOSIP model supports IEEE 802.3 (Ethernet) over baseband or broadband, IEEE 802.4 (token bus) over 10 million bits per second broadband or 5 million bits per second baseband, IEEE 802.5 (Token-Ring), and X.25 packet switched networks. In addition, GOSIP specifies use of the *Connectionless Network Protocol* (CLNP) to provide a reliable end-to-end data path between networks. CLNP allows several local area networks to interconnect by masking the differences in their technologies. GOSIP also is moving toward ISDN as one of its requirements.

As you can see, GOSIP is not a true protocol or network architecture; it is a subset of protocols that vendors must fulfill if they want to sell their products to the U.S. government.

OPEN NETWORK ARCHITECTURE (ONA)

The *Open Network Architecture* is under development by an organization calling itself the Open Network Architecture Forum. This organization is run by Bellcore, a research group owned jointly by the seven Bell Operating Companies. ONA is not fully defined as yet, but it has two key parts. First, the *protocol model* describes a detailed methodology by which information and instructions are provided to, received from, or communicated within the network. Second, the *architecture model* is a conceptualization of the basic network functions required to make it more "open" or "closed." By openness ONA's developers mean the ability of any hardware or software to connect to and transmit over the network. The ONA model is described as a layered protocol for use between different information systems at their interfaces. The ONA model will be different conceptually from the internationally recognized seven-layer OSI model.

TELECOMMUNICATION STANDARDS ORGANIZATIONS

The world of standards rarely represents current realities. To set a standard, industry leaders must agree on the specific way something will be accomplished. A telecommunication standard may take one of many forms. It may exist as the definition of an architecture, the specification of a physical design, a set of protocols for interaction between two devices, or a set of conventions for behavior. Regardless of the form, the goal of the standard usually is to define interfaces between different stations or nodes. The driving force for defining standards is economics.

Standards are necessary in almost every business and public service entity. For example, before 1904 fire hose couplings in the United States were not standard, which meant a fire department in one community could not help in another community. The transmission of electric current was not standardized until the end of the nineteenth century. As a result, customers had to choose between Thomas Edison's direct current (dc) electricity and George Westinghouse's alternating current (ac) electricity. Before 1927, traffic signs and signals in the United States varied according to the plan adopted by each state, which meant drivers from one state often could not recognize signs when driving in other states. As an example, people who were color-blind might drive through red lights when visiting another state because red was the top of the three signal lights in their state, but it was at the bottom of the three signal lights in the state they were visiting.

The *standardization process* has three stages: specification, identification of choices, and acceptance. The *specification* stage consists of developing a nomenclature and identifying the problems to be addressed. In the *identification of choices* stage, those working on the standard identify the various solutions and choose the optimum solution from among the alternatives. *Acceptance,* which is the most difficult stage of the three, consists of defining the solution and getting the recognized leaders of the industry to agree on a single, uniform solution.

To understand why data communication functions are arranged in architectural layers (remember the seven-layer OSI reference model presented earlier in this chapter), let us review the functions that communication networks support to provide effective communications among end users (nodes). These functions generally include

- Establishing a transmission path
- Coding information into analog or digital form for transmission
- Ensuring that successive messages (groups of frames or packets) arrive successfully at the receiving node
- Establishing how to execute retransmission if a frame or packet is in error
- Establishing how to recover from a circuit failure
- Ensuring connectivity between different kinds of networks, including ones that are incompatible (*connectivity* ensures that two networks can talk with one another)
- Sending messages to the correct network node
- Incorporating optimization devices into the network, such as multiplexers, concentrators, port sharing devices, front ends, and switching devices
- Bypassing failed circuits or nodes
- Providing screen and printer formats, code conversion, programming languages, and protocol conversions for end users

Telecommunication standards, therefore, are protocols (rules) that have been agreed upon by pertinent industry and government standards-making bodies. As we discuss the most relevant standards, it is helpful to name and describe the most important organizations that define standards. The following organizations specify, identify, and agree on telecommunication standards.

International Organization for Standardization (ISO)   As noted earlier, the *International Organization for Standardization,* which is based in Geneva, Switzerland, developed the OSI seven-layer reference model, which was discussed at length earlier in this chapter. The membership of the ISO is comprised of the national standards organizations of each ISO member country. In turn, ISO is a member of the Consultative Committee on International Telegraph and Telephone (CCITT), whose task is to make technical recommendations about telephone, telegraph, and data communication interfaces on a worldwide basis. On issues of telecommunication standards, ISO and CCITT usually cooperate, but they are mutually independent standards-making bodies and they are not required to agree on the same standards. The American National Standards Institute (ANSI) is the United States' voting participant in ISO.

American National Standards Institute (ANSI)   The *American National Standards Institute* is the coordinating organization for the United States' national system of standards and is comprised of about 900 companies. ANSI is a standardization organization, not a standards-making body. Its role is to coordinate the development of voluntary national standards and to interact with ISO in order to develop national standards that comply with ISO's international recommendations. For example, the ANSI X.3 (PAD) Packet Assembler/Disassembler Committee recommends national standards for computers and office equipment suppliers.

ANSI also is developing a Fiber Distributed Data Interface (FDDI) for large backbone LANs. An FDDI network essentially is a counter-rotating token ring with a throughput of 100 million bits per second. This speed is much faster than the three IEEE 802 LAN standards; it is the fiber's ability to accommodate the speed that mandated the FDDI standard. Even though IEEE 802.3 (Ethernet), IEEE 802.4 (token bus and MAP), and IEEE 802.5 (token ring) all can be implemented with fiber, they do not take advantage of fiber's capacity. Ethernet and MAP specify a throughput of up to 20 million bits per second, and token ring specifies 16 million bits per second.

The FDDI standard contains two specifications: one for the physical layer and one for medium access control. The physical layer details the characteristics of the optical fiber transmission medium. These characteristics are determined primarily by the choice of signaling rate and fiber dimension. The specified data rate is 100 million bits per second using an encoding scheme called 4B/5B. The dimensions of optical fiber cable are specified in terms of the diameter of the core of the fiber and the outer diameter of the cladding layer. Chapter 11 on LANs has more information on both FDDI and IEEE local area network standards.

Consultative Committee on International Telegraph and Telephone (CCITT)   The *Consultative Committee on International Telegraph and Telephone* is the technical standards-setting organization of the United Nations International Telecommunications Union. It too is based in Geneva, Switzerland, and is comprised of representatives from over 150 national Postal Telephone and Telegraphs (PTTs), private telecommunication agencies, as well as industrial and scientific organizations. ISO is a member of

CCITT. The PTTs are telephone companies outside of the United States. For the United States, we can refer to them as the Bell Operating Companies (BOCs), American Telephone & Telegraph (AT&T), or common carriers. CCITT establishes recommendations for use by PTTs, other common carriers, and hardware and software vendors.

Institute of Electrical and Electronics Engineers (IEEE)   The *Institute of Electrical and Electronics Engineers* is a professional society in the United States whose standards committees focus on local area network standards. The IEEE 802.3 standard often is referred to as the Ethernet standard. It was the first and most entrenched standard of the three local area network standards. The 802.3 uses a bus topology, carrier sense multiple access/collision detection (CSMA/CD) access methodology, and it has been implemented using baseband media or fiber optics. The IEEE 802.4 is a token bus scheme used primarily on coaxial cable. This is the standard transmission methodology being pushed for the Manufacturing Automation Protocol (MAP) network mentioned earlier. The IEEE 802.5 token ring standard uses a token-passing access mechanism with baseband signaling over twisted pair wire media.

Another standard the IEEE is working on is the 1003.1 standard for portable operating systems in computer environments. It is based on the UNIX operating system and may be the first standardization of an operating system environment. Other countries have their own national standards-making bodies, too. For example, the British counterpart of IEEE is the Institution of Electrical Engineers (IEE).

Electronic Industries Association (EIA)   The *Electronic Industries Association* is an ANSI-accredited standards organization that develops a variety of standards, including equipment standards. Possibly its most prominent standard is the RS232 connector cable/plug. It also endorses other standards, such as the RS449 connector plug. Membership is drawn from manufacturers of telecommunication equipment and other electronics components.

National Institute of Standards and Technology (NIST)   Formerly known as the National Bureau of Standards in Washington, D.C., the *National Institute of Standards and Technology* is an agency of the U.S. Department of Commerce that develops federal information processing standards for the federal government. Among its many test facilities is the Network Protocol Testing and Evaluation Facility which has eight laboratories for research in the design, implementation, and testing of computer network protocols. This facility develops prototype implementations of protocols and then tests them in a variety of communication environments.

National Exchange Carriers Association (NECA)   The *National Exchange Carriers Association*'s T-1 Committee (accredited by ANSI) is comprised of representatives from domestic telecommunication manufacturers, carriers, users, and other interested parties. The T-1 Technical Subcommittee develops North American telecommunication standards. This committee, ANSI, and CCITT are developing standards for ISDN circuits. The I430 basic user network interface (also known as ISDN or 2B

+ D) details the physical and electrical specifications for an interface that supports two 64,000 bits per second digital channels and one 16,000 bits per second signaling channel. The I440/I441 details the message formats of the Q.921 and Q.920 message.

Corporation for Open Systems (COS)   The *Corporation for Open Systems* is a nonprofit corporation established in 1986. The organization has members from computer and communication equipment vendors and users. It was formed under the auspices of the Computer and Communication Industry Association. Although COS is not a standards-setting body, it was established to accelerate the introduction of products based on international standards, principally those based on the seven-layer OSI model.

The COS charter states that its purpose is to monitor OSI and Integrated Services Digital Network (ISDN) standards. It will develop standards for implementing layer 7 (the application layer) of the OSI model and the *X.400* electronic mail message-handling features (OSI layer 6).

The X.400 recommendation from the CCITT often is referred to as the *electronic envelope*. It specifies the format in which messages can be exchanged between various systems. The X.400 standard describes an electronic mail system using message transfer agents (MTAs) and user agents (UAs). The UAs are nothing more than mailboxes, including the software that helps with composing and addressing a message. The MTA gets the message from a mailbox to its various destinations.

The part of X.400 that has attracted the most attention is the P1 protocol, which specifies the rules for communication between one MTA and another MTA. The aim of the P1 protocol is to allow X.400 electronic mail systems to interconnect easily so users of each system have mail access to the users of all other systems. Among other things, it defines basic message delivery, date and time stamping, delivery notification, and type of information in the message. Most, if not all, of the hardware vendors are endorsing the X.400 standard. X.400 also is being endorsed in both the United States and Europe by various telephone companies in each country. In the world of digital transmission, ISDN can be regarded as a uniform voice and data transport scheme that incorporates a worldwide X.400 standard for transmission of electronic mail. (E-mail is discussed in Chapter 7.)

COS is a very powerful group because its members are important leaders in the world of communications. The COS goal is to stimulate the development of interoperable communication products from different vendors. In addition to promoting standards, COS operates a test center that focuses on such tasks as testing compatible ISO hardware/software and the ISDN network.

COS members contribute funds to the COS Strategy Forum, the primary decision-making body at the technical level. The Forum's numerous subcommittees deal with specific technical issues and are responsible for submitting recommendations to the Strategy Forum for its approval. Whereas the standards developed by the international standards-making bodies generally concentrate on a particular layer of the OSI model, COS users assemble a number of standards to produce a profile that supports a particular application or hardware. For example, COS is deeply involved in interconnecting and implementing various standards to achieve a successful MAP network.

Electronic Data Interchange (EDI)   EDI is the working name for Electronic Data Interchange for Administration, Commerce, and Transport *(EDIFACT)*. EDI allows the electronic interchange of business documents like purchase orders or invoices. These documents can have graphics as well as ASCII characters. It is the only standard ever specified for international EDI networks, and it has been embraced by the ISO as the premier standard for international EDI. The *Electronic Data Interchange* standard was formulated in 1985 by European and North American network users who were concerned that diverging sets of standards on the two continents would greatly inhibit international EDI.

EDI defines major components of the ANSI X.12 EDI standard. Although EDIFACT is supported by users in Europe and the Far East, Canadian and U.S. users have shown reluctance to embrace it because they already have invested in networks based on the EDI standard developed by the ANSI X.12 committee. Unfortunately, EDIFACT is not totally compatible with the X.12 standard.

Arcnet Trade Association (ATA)   In 1991 the *Arcnet Trade Association* was designated by the American National Standards Institute (ANSI) as a standards-setting body. The ATA has been responsible for defining the Attached Resource Computing Network (Arcnet) baseband token-passing protocol. The Arcnet protocol has been submitted to ANSI, which is expected to approve it as ANSI standard 878.1. After approval by ANSI, the ATA expects to submit the Arcnet protocol to the International Organization for Standardization for its sanction as a worldwide standard.

LEGALLY ENFORCEABLE STANDARDS

Legally enforceable standards are defined and enacted into law by the governments of various countries. In the United States, we have a law that provides criminal punishment for three types of computer criminals: those who gain access to federal computers, those who gain unauthorized access to computers at financial institutions that are covered by federal laws, and those who gain access to computers that hold national security data. The U.S. Department of Justice has a computer crime unit that is responsible for prosecuting crimes and encouraging stiffer penalties for convicted computer criminals. The FBI, U.S. Secret Service, and the military are all adding staff to address concerns about computer crimes. Moreover, many states now have their own laws on computer and communication security.

Federal Wiretap Statute   The *Federal Wiretap Statute,* which was enacted in 1968, protected only voice communications from interception. The primary thrust of this law was to prevent the illegal ''tapping'' of a telephone line or the illegal recording of voice telephone conversations. It was not until 1986 that an electronic privacy law was passed relating directly to data communications.

Electronic Communications Privacy Act of 1986   The *Electronic Communications Privacy Act* of 1986 makes it a federal crime to intercept electronic communications, such as data communications or electronic mail, or to tamper with the computers in a data network. The 1986 law prohibits the interception of data and image communications on private networks and the unauthorized access of network computers if stored messages are obtained or altered. Under this law, individuals are subject to penalties of up to $100,000 and ten years in prison if the crime is committed for commercial gain or malicious reasons. Fines for organizations can be up to $250,000. The privacy of network users also is protected under this law. Law enforcement officials need a court order to obtain electronic messages, and electronic mail services cannot disclose the content of messages transmitted over their service without the sender's authorization.

This act has been amended to define "access" to include the intentional transmission or distribution of unauthorized software that damages computer data, software, or hardware. This amendment relates directly to viruses. Felony penalties can run as high as five years in prison and a $250,000 fine. The act further specifies that anyone who unknowingly, but recklessly, transmits destructive software can face a misdemeanor penalty of up to one year in jail and a fine of $5,000. This amendment can make a person subject to a misdemeanor and a fine if that person accidentally, but recklessly, transmits a virus to someone else's computer. The amended law also extends the reach of the original law beyond just federal computers. It now includes any computer used in interstate commerce or communications. Finally, it allows civil actions that can result in the payment of damages to people who suffer losses because of computer abuse.

Computer Fraud and Abuse Act of 1986   Congress also passed the *Computer Fraud and Abuse Act* in 1986. This law expands federal jurisdiction of computer crimes. It refines and builds on the 1985 statute that covers only federal computers; the new law covers computer crimes involving private sector computers located in two or more states (interstate). It also hits the so-called pirate bulletin board systems that exchange computer passwords. Specifically, the law makes it a federal offense to access a computer in a fraudulent scheme to steal, and it makes it a felony to alter or destroy data, hardware, or software without authorization. The law also makes it a federal misdemeanor for an individual to traffic in computer passwords belonging to others, if there is a clear intent to defraud. The Computer Fraud and Abuse law imposes fines of up to $100,000 and ten years in prison for people who intentionally gain unauthorized access to computer systems to damage records or to steal records or cash.

Computer Security Act of 1987   The *Computer Security Act* was signed into law by President Reagan at the end of 1987. This act moves power away from the National Security Agency (NSA) and transfers it to the National Institute of Standards and Technology (NIST) by requiring NIST to establish security standards and training programs for federal agencies using unclassified information systems. NSA is an intelligence unit of the U.S. Department of Defense, and NIST is an agency of the U.S. Department of Commerce. The security of classified systems is still NSA's responsibility. The major impact of this law is to give total control of the data encryption standard (DES), which is used widely by both federal government agencies and private industry, to the National Institute of Standards and Technology.

Computer Virus Eradication Act of 1988   The *Computer Virus Eradication Act* was signed into law in 1988. Its purpose is to fight the spread of computer viruses. It provides for up to ten years in prison, a fine, or both, for anyone who "knowingly inserts into a program for a computer, or a computer itself, information or commands, knowing or having reason to believe that such information or commands may cause loss, expense, or risk to health or welfare." This law also prohibits giving such programs to others and allows for civil action against such perpetrators.

X.*NN* AND V.*NN* STANDARDS

The CCITT's X.*nn* and V.*nn* standards are recommendations for how particular electrical connections should be carried out. As you read the following recommendations, you should remember that terminals or microcomputers are referred to as data terminal equipment (DTE) and modems as data circuit terminating equipment (DCE).

The X.*nn* series concerns the connection of digital equipment to a public data network that employs <u>digital</u> signaling.

- X.1   User classes of service for public data networks.
- X.2   User facilities in a public data network.
- X.3   The packet assembly/disassembly (PAD) facility for asynchronous transmission in a public data network.
- X.4   General structure of the signals of the international alphabet number 5 code.
- X.12   ANSI standard for Electronic Data Interchange (EDI).
- X.20   Interface between DTE and DCE for asynchronous operation on public data networks. This interface cable connects modems to cables.
- X.20bis   Used on public data networks for DTE that is the interface to asynchronous V series modems. This interface cable connects modems to cables.
- X.21   Interface between DTE and DCE for synchronous operation on public data networks. This interface cable connects modems to terminals.
- X.21bis   Used on public data networks for DTE that is the interface to V series modems. This interface cable connects modems to terminals.
- X.24   List of definitions for circuits between DTE and DCE on public data networks.
- X.25   Interface between DTE and DCE for terminals operating in the "packet mode" on public data networks. It is known popularly as the X.25 gateway.
- X.26   Electrical characteristics for unbalanced polar or bipolar circuits for general use with data communications (identical to V.10—see V.*nn* series below). In Europe, polar or bipolar circuits may be called double current interchange circuits.

- X.27   Electrical characteristics for balanced polar or bipolar circuits for general use with data communications (identical to V.11). In Europe, polar or bipolar circuits may be called double current interchange circuits.

- X.28   DTE/DCE interface for start-stop data terminal equipment interconnections with the packet assembly/disassembly (PAD) facility in public data networks. It defines the interface between a nonintelligent terminal and PAD.

- X.29   Procedures for the exchange of control information and user data between a packet mode DTE and a PAD facility. It defines the procedure for governing the exchange of data between a PAD and a packet mode terminal.

- X.32   Defines a dial-up connection between the DTE and the DCE using a X.25 link (packets).

- X.75   Terminal and transient control procedures for data transfer systems on international circuits between packet switched networks using the X.25 protocol. It governs the interface between public packet switched networks (X.25), and it is the gateway at each of the two networks.

- X.121   International numbering plan for public data networks.

- X.400   Defines how a worldwide electronic mail system operates.

- X.435   Known as the EDI Messaging System and Services. It governs the transmission of Electronic Data Interchange (EDI) documents over the X.400 electronic mail system.

- X.500   Defines how to develop a worldwide directory of user names and their electronic mail addresses.

The V.*nn* series concerns the connection of digital equipment to a public telephone system that employs <u>analog</u> signaling.

- V.3   International alphabet number 5 (of which ASCII is one case).

- V.10   Same as X.26. In this case, when they talk about electrical characteristics, they are referring to communication between modems, which also may be called data circuit terminating equipment (DCE).

- V.11   Same as X.27. In this case, when they talk about electrical characteristics, they are referring to communication between modems, which also may be called DCE.

- V.21   Modem electrical characteristics for transmissions up to 300 bits per second. These modem electrical characteristic standards must be defined because the standard tones used in the United States seem to "discombobulate" the European telephone billing systems. As a result, many European countries have outlawed the use of standard American modems.

- V.22   Electrical characteristics for modems that operate up to 1200 bits per second in an asynchronous format on two-wire circuits.

- V.22bis   Electrical characteristics for modems that operate up to 2400 bits per second using asynchronous or synchronous transmission on two-wire circuits.

- V.24   List of definitions for interexchange circuits between DTE and DCE.

- **V.25, V.25bis, V.26, V.27, V.28, and V.29** As you move up the V-numbered series for electrical characteristics between modems, the speed moves up through 2400, 4800, and on to 9600 bits per second. In addition, various standards are set regarding half or full duplex, dial-up or lease lines, automatic dial capabilities, automatic call receipt capabilities, and so on. Of course, one of the primary purposes is to ensure the modem does not interfere with the public dial-up telephone system of the country in which it is operating or to which it is transmitting data.

- **V.32 (see V.32 in Chapter 3)** Electrical characteristics for a modem that operates at full or half duplex over two-wire direct dial networks and transmits at a speed of 9600 bits per second. It is capable of forward error correction. The modem signals at 2400 baud and encodes 5 bits per baud; 4 bits are for data, and 1 bit is for forward error correction. Therefore, even though the total transmission rate is 12,000 bits per second, only 9600 bits per second actually contain data. Full duplex transmission over two-wire circuits is not a new development because the V.22 and V.22bis modems had this capability. The secret behind the V.32 modem's ability to transmit at 9600 bits per second full duplex over two-wire circuits is a technique called echo cancellation. *Echo cancellation* isolates the received signal from the remote modem by eliminating interference caused by the transmitting signal, as well as reflections of the signal echoed back from the near-end and remote-end central offices. Echoes can be canceled because there is a small time difference between when they are received and when the main signal is received. This time difference is caused by propagation delays. Delay times are established when the modems independently clock between the near-end central office and the remote location.

- **V.33** Electrical characteristics using a leased line at 14,400 bits per second.

- **V.35** Electrical characteristics for a modem using a high speed transmission rate of 48,000 or 56,000 bits per second.

- **V.36** Electrical characteristics for modems using synchronous digital data transmission at 56,000 bits per second.

- **V.42** Data compression standard (see V.42 and V.42bis in Chapter 3).

- **V.54** Specifications for loop test devices for modems.

KEY TERMS

ACK

Advanced Program-to-Program Communications (APPC)

American National Standards Institute (ANSI)

Application layer

Application program

Arcnet Trade Association (ATA)

Automatic Repeat reQuest (ARQ)

Basic Telecommunications Access Method (BTAM)

Binary Synchronous Communications (BSC)

Computer Fraud and Abuse Act

Computer Security Act

Computer Virus Eradication Act

Connectivity

Consultative Committee on International Telegraph and Telephone (CCITT)

Continuous ARQ

Control message

Corporation for Open Systems (COS)

Customer Information Control System (CICS)

Data link control protocol

Data link layer

Data message

Database management system (DBMS)

DECnet

Digital Network Architecture (DNA)

Electronic Communications Privacy Act

Electronic Data Interchange (EDI)

Electronic Industries Association (EIA)

Federal Wiretap Statute

Firmware

Flow control

Frame

Government Open Systems Interconnection Protocol (GOSIP)

High-level Data Link Control (HDLC)

Institute of Electrical and Electronics Engineers (IEEE)

International Organization for Standardization (ISO)

Legally enforceable standards

Logical unit (LU)

LU 6.2

Machine-to-machine protocol

Manufacturing Automation Protocol (MAP)

Message accountability

Microcomputer-to-network protocol

NAK

National Exchange Carriers Association (NECA)

National Institute of Standards and Technology (NIST)

Network addressable unit (NAU)

Network architecture

Network Control Program (NCP)

Network layer

Open Network Architecture (ONA)

Open Systems Interconnection (OSI) Reference Model

Operating system

OSI seven-layer model

Path control network

Peer-to-peer

Peripheral node control point (PNCP)

Person-to-network protocol

Person-to-person protocol

Physical layer

Physical unit (PU)

Presentation layer

Protocol

PU 2.1

Queued Telecommunications Access Method (QTAM)

Security software

Semantics

Session

Session layer

Sliding window protocol

Software

Standardization process

Stop and wait ARQ

Synchronous Data Link Control (SDLC)

Syntax

System services control point (SSCP)

Systems Application Architecture (SAA)

Systems Network Architecture (SNA)

Telecommunication access program

Telecommunications Access Method (TCAM)

Teleprocessing monitor software

Timing (protocol)

Transmission Control Protocol/Internet Protocol (TCP/IP)

Transport layer

V.*nn* standard

Virtual link

Virtual Telecommunications Access Method (VTAM)

WAK

X.25

X.400

X.*nn* standard

SELECTED REFERENCES

1. Gillooly, Caryn. "Olympic LANs to Showcase Network Prowess of APPC," *Network World,* vol. 9, no. 19, May 11, 1992, pp. 1, 6.

2. Guruge, Anura. "IBM Radically Reformulates SNA," *Data Communications,* vol. 20, no. 5, April 1991, pp. 72, 74–77, 80, 82. [First article of two called "The New SNA."]

3. *IBM Systems Application Architecture: An Overview.* White Plains, N.Y.: IBM Corporation (IBM Publication GC26-4341).

4. *International Standards Index.* Denver: Information Handling Services. Annual index with bimonthly updates. Call 1-800-241-7824 for information about the index and its corollary publications.

5. Knight, Ivor. "Telecommunications Standards Development," *Telecommunications,* vol. 25, no. 1, January 1991, pp. 38–40, 42.

6. Layland, Robin. "The End for IBM's FEP?" *Data Communications,* vol. 20, no. 5, April 1991, pp. 73, 84–86, 88, 90, 92. [Second article of two called "The New SNA."]

7. Randesi, Steve, and Don Czubek. "SNA Goes for a Ride," *LAN Magazine,* vol. 7, no. 4, April 1992, pp. 109, 111, 113, 115, 117.

8. Rauch, Wendy. "SAA and NAS: The Promise of Distributed Computing," *Data Communications,* vol. 20, no. 3, March 1991, pp. 68–71, 73–75.

9. Rizzo, Tony. "SNA: A Fast Tour Through the Mainframe Networking World," *Network Computing,* vol. 2, no. 7, July 1991, pp. 88, 90, 92.

10. Stephenson, Peter. "The Peer Connection," *LAN Magazine,* vol. 6, no. 6, June 1991, pp. 121, 123, 125, 127–128.

11. *Systems Network Architecture: Concepts and Products.* White Plains, N.Y.: IBM Corporation, January 1981 (IBM Publication GC30-3072-0).

12. *Systems Network Architecture: Technical Overview.* White Plains, N.Y.: IBM Corporation, March 1982 (IBM Publication GC30-3073-0).

QUESTIONS/PROBLEMS

1. What are protocols? Describe their necessity.

2. What are the three components of a protocol and what is their purpose?

3. In social interactions we have person-to-person protocols. What are their counterparts in data communications?

4. How is software distinguished from firmware?

5. How is architecture distinguished from protocols and software?

6. What do network architectures make possible?

7. The most important network software resides at the host computer and front end. What are the types of software and what is the function of each one?

8. Where do telecommunication access programs reside?

9. Identify the five types of telecommunication access programs.

10. What is the purpose of the teleprocessing monitor program?

11. What is the most commonly used teleprocessing monitor program?

12. How is Automatic Repeat reQuest used?

13. What factors make data communication programming difficult? Indicate how these factors can be overcome.

14. What factors should network implementation take into account?

15. What is the plan or model by which software is designed?

16. What are the two most important standards-making bodies with regard to data communications and how do they differ?

17. What does the layered approach provide to data communication software development?

18. At what layer of the OSI model do communications over the circuit take place?

19. Layers 2 through 7 are said to be _____ because they are _____ .

20. If you were to portray the movement of data in the OSI model in its simplest terms, how would you describe it?

21. What are the most important points to remember about each of the OSI model's seven layers?

22. What is the most popular bit-oriented protocol and what does it do?

23. Describe the X.25 frame.

24. In cyclical redundancy checking for errors, what makes it work?

25. What are the four basic principles of Systems Network Architecture (SNA) and why are they important?

26. In SNA, how does the end user communicate with the network?

27. How does Synchronous Data Link Control (SDLC) relate to Systems Network Architecture (SNA)?

28. Describe the two logical components of a network designed by using SNA principles and explain how they differ.

29. What are the SNA sessions called?

30. What is a node?

31. What is the SNA program interface called?

32. Define peer-to-peer communications.

33. When you see the LU designation for protocols, what does it imply?

34. What is the purpose of Systems Application Architecture?

35. What distinguishes the BSC protocol from X.25?

36. To what type of environment is the MAP protocol particularly well suited?

37. The MAP protocol has only six layers. Which one is missing?

38. How does the DECnet architecture differ from the OSI model?

39. One protocol in particular is oriented toward file transfer. What is it?

40. What is different about the Bellcore Open Network Architecture?

41. Describe the three stages of standardization.

42. What is the purpose of a data communication standard?

43. Name three communication standards-setting organizations and one standard for each.

44. Outline four U.S. statutes related to communication security.

45. Use the following as a model to invent a line protocol for transmission between a central computer site and a remote terminal site.

Steps	Central Computer Site		Remote Terminal Site
1.	Poll Terminal A	⟶	
2.		⟵	Negative response code
3.	Poll Terminal B	⟶	
4.		⟵	Positive response code (changes terminal mode from idle to text mode)
		⟵	Text (first block of text)
		⟵	End of block code
		⟵	Parity check
5.	Parity received correctly	⟶	
6.		⟵	Text (second block of text)
		⟵	End of block code
		⟵	Parity check
7.	Parity received correctly	⟶	
8.		⟵	End of message
9.	Poll Terminal C	⟶	
10.		⟵	Negative response code

46. What does the following describe? The central computer sends a message saying, "Terminal A, do you have anything to transmit? If so, send it." If Terminal A has nothing to send, it replies negatively and the central computer goes on to Terminal B.

47. In the section titled Software Design, "acting constructively on errors" is cited as important for handling incoming messages. Assume a banking situation in which a withdrawal message is sent from a terminal to the central computer. Describe a "constructive action" for each of the following unusual conditions detected at the computer.

- Account number is garbled.
- Requested withdrawal exceeds account balance by a small amount, such as $100.
- Requested withdrawal exceeds account balance by a very large amount, such as $1,000.
- Incoming transaction is unreadable.

48. In the Software Design section, it is suggested that both incoming and outgoing messages be logged. Explain how these logs can be used to recover from a computer failure in a store and forward message switching system.

49. Propose a set of procedures for a store and forward message switching system that meets the requirements given in the Software Design section. Provide a rational means of disposing of messages. Assume there are three priorities of messages: delivery as soon as possible, delivery in 2 hours, and delivery in 12 hours. Assume terminals can be repaired in 6 hours and circuits in 1 hour if they fail. Assume that the messages are in English and that their average length is 20 words.

50. What are the three basic factors that make data communication programs different from batch programs?

51. What is the first step to ensure that the software provides proper integrity of the messages being transmitted?

52. Can you define the difference between protocols, software, and network architectures?

53. What is the biggest drawback of the Binary Synchronous Communications (BSC) protocol?

54. Which protocols use a continuous automatic repeat request (ARQ)?

55. When Systems Network Architecture (SNA) is used, can a remote front end processor have all three addressable units, such as LU, PU, and SSCP?

56. Summarize the basic functions of the X.25 protocol.

57. What is the difference between ISO and OSI?

58. Which standards-making body developed the RS232 standard?

59. What is X.400?

60. Name some "legally enforceable standards."

61. What are X.*nn* and V.*nn* standards?

62. Describe the networking protocol developed by the U.S. government as a standard for its agencies.

63. What is the purpose of the Connectionless Network Protocol (CLNP)?

NEXT DAY AIR SERVICE CUMULATIVE CASE STUDY

Background on Next Day Air Service

Having worked out the circuit costs for Next Day Air Service's WAN that joins all its branch offices, you are at a point in the overall design at which it is time to select the network protocols.

You begin by reviewing the physical layout of the network and the types and quantities of traffic. After reviewing NDAS's operational requirements at both its corporate headquarters and branch offices, you realize that the WAN will have voice call inquiries that do not require a direct connection to the LAN or a minicomputer. Moreover, invoices from the remote offices will be transmitted to a minicomputer or LAN in Tampa. You also have decided on an Ethernet LAN, but are unsure about the WAN protocol or how to make the WAN/LAN internet.

Along with the LAN issues that you have been addressing, you begin to consider suitable protocols for the WAN. You begin by investigating protocols and their various tie-ins to an overall architecture. After examining the alternatives, you narrow them to three choices: IBM's SNA, X.25, or running the entire WAN by internetworking several local area networks.

You have very little time to complete your analysis because you must make your recommendation fairly soon to the board of directors. This is imperative because you need to pursue a network architecture so that the much needed corporate LAN can be installed and used to support the organization.

Questions/Problems for the Next Day Air Service Case

1. Would IBM's System Network Architecture (SNA) be a feasible and desirable architecture for Next Day Air Service's integrated network? Explain why or why not.

2. If NDAS uses IVR for voice calls, the multiplexed WAN for invoices, and installs a LAN in both Tampa and Atlanta, it could have three networks. What are they? *HINT:* Review Questions 4 and 5 in Chapter 7. In this case, would a network architecture be necessary?

3. Discuss the differences between a person-to-network, a machine-to-machine, and a person-to-person protocol as they relate to the dial-up calls at NDAS.

Chapter Ten

MICROCOMPUTERS AND COMMUNICATIONS

This chapter introduces microcomputers and their use in networks. It covers microcomputer hardware, software, protocols, modems, electrical protection, the independent microcomputer in a network, micro-to-micro connections, and micro-to-mainframe links. We discuss local area networks in Chapter 11.

MICROCOMPUTERS

After the invention of the transistor by American Telephone & Telegraph's Bell Laboratories, the world of data communications and telecommunications began to move forward and dominate business operations at an unprecedented rate. Although the transistor is the heart of a data communication network, it was not until Intel's introduction of the microprocessor circuit chip that business data communication functions changed significantly.

A *microprocessor* contains transistors that switch electrical charges. Manufacturers form the transistors by impregnating a slice of silicone with chemicals that change the silicone to a transistor device. Microscopic metal tracks connect these devices so they crisscross the chip, making it look like a detailed city map. These tracks are the pathways over which the electrical signals travel between the transistors.

Unlike microcomputers, microprocessors have neither on-chip memories nor input/output connections to make them full-fledged microcomputers. Having these memory and input/output connections would consume valuable space on the chip and slow down the speed of the computer-on-a-chip. Instead, microprocessors use other devices to carry out these functions so they can concentrate on their primary function of high speed information processing.

A microprocessor chip becomes a *microcomputer* (also called a *personal computer* or *PC*) when it is connected to memory chips and input/output hardware or software devices. The central microprocessor chip in a microcomputer is approximately ½-inch square and has the ability to add millions of ten-digit numbers each second. By comparison, the early ENIAC computer was 8 feet high and 80 feet long, weighed 30 tons, and could add only 5,000 ten-digit numbers in a second.

Microprocessors actually are the heart of almost every piece of communication hardware. They not only form the basic computer within a microcomputer, but they also are the basic processing chip within intelligent data communication switches. Like their larger computer counterparts, microprocessors contain an arithmetic logic unit (ALU) for executing basic arithmetic and logic operations, registers that are short-term memories for storing data temporarily, and a control unit for regulating the flow of information between the memory chips and the logic unit in the microprocessor.

Data communications have changed the very way business enterprises operate. Today, a business uses many microcomputers in the automated office, micro-to-mainframe links, local area networks, standalone microcomputers, disk/file server database systems, local area network server systems, and microcomputer control systems that monitor and control almost anything, but especially data communications. In addition, hardware such as front end processors, modems, multiplexers, protocol converters, switches, and digital switchboards depend on microprocessor chips and the ability to interconnect with microcomputers. Today's powerful microcomputer has a 32-bit microprocessor chip in it. Popular microprocessor chips of this type are the Intel 80386/80486 and the Motorola 68030/68040. IBM uses the Intel chip, and Apple Computer uses the Motorola chip.

Because the focus of this book is on data communications, we will present only an overview on microcomputers and move directly to the interrelationships between microcomputers and communications. (Local area networks are covered in the next chapter.) For the business microcomputer, there are many different configurations. A configuration oriented toward business use (see Figure 10-1) might be a microcomputer that has approximately 640,000 bytes (characters) of internal memory, disk operating system software—*DOS* (the software that runs the microcomputer), a parallel input/output port for connection to a printer, a serial input/output port for connection to a modem for data communications, and disk storage. The disk storage may be an internal high speed hard disk with storage of 10 to 100 million bytes of information or one or two diskette drives with 360,000 to 1,400,000 bytes of information on each diskette. It is possible to connect either the parallel input/output port or the serial port to a data communication network, although generally the serial port connects to the modem which connects in turn to the network required for the business application.

The widespread use of microcomputers is accelerating the need for adequate communications throughout the entire business organization, as well as between the business organization and such outside entities as public data networks, bulletin boards, specialized databases, other companies, or government agencies. The individual standalone microcomputer can be made to be at least ten times more effective when it is networked with other microcomputers and, of course, other business entities.

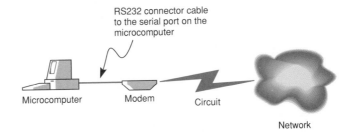

Figure 10-1 Typical microcomputer like the microcomputers used at the remote end of a network (lower half). The figure shows the location of the RS232 connector required for the microcomputer to communicate with other network devices (upper half).

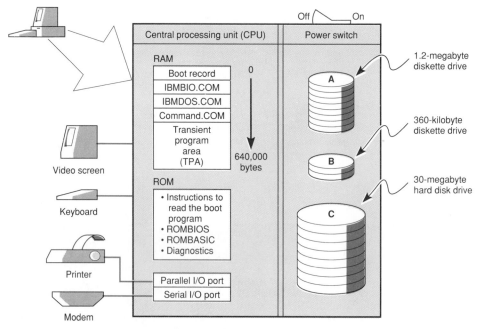

Figure 10-2   Microcomputer configuration.

The three most important items with regard to networking microcomputers are the operating system, modem, and communication software. For example, the first piece of software you encounter is the microcomputer operating system. For this discussion, we will use the IBM Personal Computer (PC) or PC-compatible microcomputer. Even though PC originally meant a specific microcomputer produced by IBM, today the terms *microcomputer* and *PC* are interchangeable.

Before moving on to the microcomputer communication software, protocols, modems, and micro-to-mainframe links, let us discuss the internal operation of a typical microcomputer. The microcomputer depicted in Figure 10-2 has a central processing unit (CPU) with both random access memory (RAM) and read only memory (ROM). *Random access memory* is the read and write memory in the microcomputer that stores programs and business applications. You can enter commands to write new programs or read data into this memory. This is your microcomputer's working memory. When you turn your microcomputer off, all the contents of the RAM are lost. *Read only memory* is a memory location in your microcomputer where data is stored permanently; it cannot be altered by the microcomputer operator. If you want to change the ROM memory, the circuit chip has to be removed from the microcomputer and erased electronically or with ultraviolet light. The ROM contains the basic start-up (boot) instructions. The information contents in a ROM can be copyrighted and even patented, making one microcomputer unique among others. When you turn your microcomputer off, all the contents of ROM are kept.

There are two diskette drives (A and B) and one 30-megabyte hard disk (C) in our example (Figure 10-2). There also are a video screen, both a serial and parallel input/output (I/O) port, and a connector plug for a keyboard. If you have ever wondered what happens when you turn on your microcomputer, let us go through the disk operating system (DOS) software boot scenario.

DOS Boot Procedure   Loading the DOS software and starting it is called *booting* the system. When you boot the microcomputer to use it, the following operations take place (follow along by looking at Figure 10-2).

- The power switch is turned on. This gives control to the ROMBIOS chip in the central processing unit.
- Fixed instructions in the ROMBIOS chip initiate diagnostic equipment checks to ensure that all components of the microcomputer are operating. These fixed instructions are the power-on self-test (POST) routines that check the memory, keyboard, initialization of various chips, disk drives, printer, and expansion boards.
- The ROMBIOS instructions load the boot record, and it checks the diskette in Drive A to determine whether the gate is open or closed. The *gate* is the lever you turn after inserting the diskette.
- If the gate is closed, the boot program is read from the Drive A diskette into the boot record in RAM. Control is given to the boot program.
- If the gate is open and you have a hard disk, the boot program is read from the hard disk (Drive C) into the RAM boot record and control is given to this program.
- If the gate is open and there is no hard disk, the microcomputer displays a message from the ROM telling you to insert the DOS boot disk into Drive A.
- The boot program reads the IBMBIO.COM (Basic Input/Output system) into the RAM. IBMBIO.COM handles the input and output commands for your microcomputer.
- The IBMBIO.COM program loads the IBMDOS.COM program.
- IBMDOS.COM executes the *CONFIG.SYS* file and loads *COMMAND.COM* (see the Three Essential DOS Files box).
- COMMAND.COM executes the *AUTOEXEC.BAT* file and turns control over to the microcomputer operator.

You now have control and can enter DOS commands to run your system. DOS controls every part of your microcomputer system and is the link between you and the microcomputer. As you already know, any application-level programs, such as spreadsheet programs, accounting packages, word processing packages, and communication software, must be able to operate with DOS because DOS controls everything—the hardware and the software.

THREE ESSENTIAL DOS FILES

COMMAND.COM   A file containing the program or instructions required to carry out a DOS command. It is the DOS command processor because this program interprets and carries out any command entered into the microcomputer. This object code file should never be changed by users.

CONFIG.SYS   A file used to set up your system. It controls various configuration features, particularly some aspects of the way memory is partitioned, loads special files called device drivers, sets up buffers, and performs various other functions. This file can be customized by users.

AUTOEXEC.BAT   A batch file automating routine tasks that need to be done before you begin working. It loads programs used for customizing hardware and software when starting (booting) your system. This file enables special programs to be available for use without entering them each time you start (boot) your microcomputer. This file can be customized by users.

Advanced microcomputer users should know that available memory space exists above 640,000 bytes. This extra memory is called either *extended memory* or *expanded memory*. Some of the operating system programs currently in RAM can be stored in this area by using various software programs. For example, the DOS files IBMBIO.COM, IBMDOS.COM, and COMMAND.COM can be stored in this extended memory between 640,000 and 1,000,000 bytes. Moreover, some application programs and communication software packages also can use the expanded memory above 1,000,000 bytes. This extended memory capacity is the reason why you see advertisements for microcomputers having 4 megabytes, 8 megabytes, or greater memory.

Use of extended memory requires a special software package called a high memory manager. This software is available either from various software companies, or it is in the DOS 5.0 operating system. We will not discuss extended memory in detail because it concerns microcomputer management and operation, and it does not have a significant impact on the operation of communication software.

Some DOS commands are known as internal commands and some as external commands. An *internal DOS command* resides in RAM (memory resident) and is available whenever DOS has been loaded. The COMMAND.COM file contains the internal DOS commands. *External DOS commands* are available, but they are contained on the disk (external to RAM) and must be called in from the disk every time you need to use them. When COMMAND.COM cannot find the command you entered via the keyboard in RAM, it calls it in from the external commands on the disk. Typical internal commands include DIR, COPY, RENAME, ERASE, TYPE, CLS, TIME, and DATE; typical external commands include DISKCOPY, FORMAT, and CHKDSK. These are described in your DOS documentation.

One other point should be made for clarification. There are two boot programs. The first and most basic one (ROMBIOS) has been programmed permanently into the ROM. This boot program can go out only to one of the disk drives (whichever one contains the DOS software) where it calls the much larger DOS boot program into the boot record in RAM. It is this second boot program that has a broader capability and can call in the rest of the DOS software programs.

Now that your computer is running, you have use of a video screen connected by a cable to the central processing unit, a keyboard for data entry, a serial port connected to a modem (although you will see in a later section that modems also can be installed inside the computer box itself), and a parallel input/output port that can be connected to a printer.

Microcomputers communicate with networks (the rest of the world) through the serial port, although it also is possible to communicate with a network through the parallel port. The programs you use with the microcomputer are located in the *transient program area* (TPA) shown in Figure 10-2. Notice that our microcomputer in this figure has a total memory space of 640,000 bytes. In RAM, the boot record, IBMBIO.COM, IBMDOS.COM, COMMAND.COM, and some DOS internal commands occupy some of the 640,000 bytes of memory space. The remaining unused memory space from the 640,000 bytes is the transient program area. Application programs or data reside in the TPA when you are using them. Examples of application programs are word processors, spreadsheets, and communication software.

OS/2 Boot Procedure   Instead of using the DOS operating system, you may want to use the *OS/2* operating system on your microcomputer. Figure 10-3 compares the DOS boot procedure with the OS/2 boot procedure. As you can see from this figure and the following description, the initial OS/2 boot procedure is similar to the DOS boot procedure, but it is more complex.

- When the power switch is turned on, the ROMBIOS chip loads the boot record.
- The boot record loads IBMBIO.COM.
- IBMBIO.COM loads IBMDOS.COM.
- IBMDOS.COM switches to protected mode, executes the CONFIG.SYS file, and loads the SHELL.EXE file.
- SHELL.EXE checks to see whether STARTUP.CMD exists.
- If STARTUP.CMD does exist, it loads CMD.EXE (similar to COMMAND.COM), which in turn executes STARTUP.CMD (similar to AUTOEXEC.BAT). Control is turned over to the microcomputer operator using OS/2 in protected mode.
- If STARTUP.CMD does *not* exist, the microcomputer operator is presented with two choices (DOS or OS/2 mode).

    If the DOS mode is chosen, COMMAND.COM is loaded, which in turn executes AUTOEXEC.BAT. Control is turned over to the microcomputer operator using DOS in real mode; that is, it is not in protected mode.

    If OS/2 mode is chosen, CMD.EXE (similar to COMMAND.COM) is loaded, which in turn executes OS2INIT.CMD (similar to AUTOEXEC.BAT). Con-

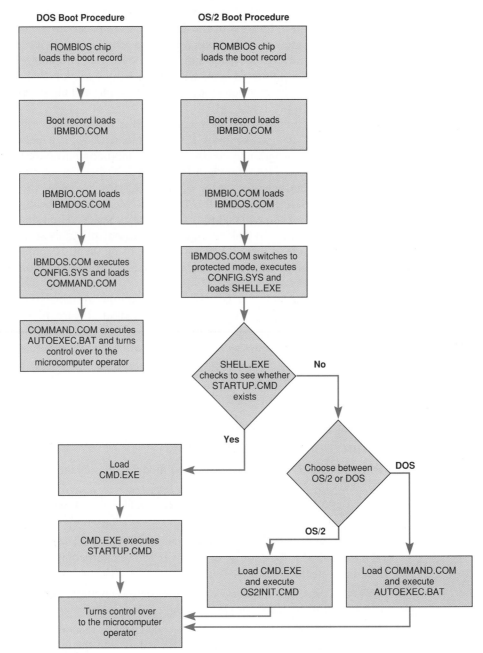

Figure 10-3 Comparison of DOS and OS/2 boot procedures.

trol is turned over to the microcomputer operator using OS/2 in real mode; that is, it is not in protected mode.

Diskless Microcomputer Boot Procedure   Regular microcomputers have disk drives, which is where they get the DOS operating system that allows the machine to boot and run. As the term implies, *diskless microcomputers* do not have disk drives. This lack of a disk drive means the microcomputers have no way of getting DOS to operate, so they cannot run.

A diskless microcomputer operates as follows. As you already know, a microcomputer with disk drives normally boots from either a hard disk or a floppy diskette when the power is first turned on. Because diskless microcomputers contain no disk storage devices, they are started with a special type of boot ROM (read only memory).

If you connect a diskless microcomputer to a local area network (LAN) and give it a remote boot ROM, it can run. The remote boot ROM is a small read only microchip (e.g., firmware) that plugs into the network interface card. When the local microcomputer is turned on, its ROM redirects the boot request to the microchip's encoded instructions that tell the diskless microcomputer where to find a server microcomputer on the network. The *network server* (a microcomputer that controls the network and contains the databases) then sends the proper boot information to the diskless microcomputer and starts it up. For example, when a local area network operates with Novell's NetWare, the network server's NET$DOS.SYS file contains a complete image of the diskette that would have been used if the diskless microcomputer had an A drive. This procedure enables the diskless microcomputer to run DOS as though it had a disk drive of its own. After booting, a diskless microcomputer operates like one with a disk when it is connected to a local area network.

Boot ROMs are not generic; they are hardware-specific and software-specific. It is therefore essential that you have a boot ROM tailored to both your specific network operating system and its network interface card.

You may wonder why anyone would want to have diskless microcomputers on a LAN inasmuch as it seems to entail extra effort and might be more costly. LAN security is enhanced significantly if the microcomputers used as workstations do not have any disk drives. When a LAN workstation operates without disk drives, it is impossible for the workstation user to make unauthorized copies of the entity's business data. This inability to make copies of files is what distinguishes diskless microcomputers from those with disks and what makes them desirable for networks in which security is a concern.

In addition, the diskless microcomputer forces users to store their data on the file server disk, which generally is more secure for two reasons. First, it is backed up on a regular basis, and second, it probably has backup electrical power to prevent electrical disasters.

Now let us examine the other aspects of microcomputers, including their serial ports, communication software, protocols, modems, micro-to-micro connections, micro-to-mainframe connections, and electrical protection for microcomputers and LANs.

SERIAL PORT (UART/USART)

When a microcomputer is to be used for the transfer of data, the RS232 connector cable must be plugged into the *serial port* (also called a *serial connector*) on the back of the microcomputer. This is the *COM1 port* used for data communications. If the microcomputer has two serial ports, the second one is known as the *COM2 port*. Two serial ports are now common on microcomputers because a modem uses the first one and a mouse or other modem uses the second one.

The *Universal Asynchronous Receiver and Transmitter* (UART) circuit chip is the device that serializes the stream of data bits for the COM1 and COM2 serial ports so they can transmit data. The UART chip handles asynchronous communications, whereas the *Universal Synchronous Asynchronous Receiver and Transmitter* (USART) chip handles both synchronous and asynchronous communications. The *UART/USART chip* executes the following four main tasks.

- It converts parallel signals coming from the microcomputer's central processing unit into a serial stream of bits for transmission out of the microcomputer, and it converts a serial stream of bits coming into the microcomputer into a parallel form for processing by the microcomputer.
- It adds the required start, stop, and parity bits to each synchronous character to be transmitted, and strips off those bits from received characters.
- It ensures that individual bits are sent out at the appropriate baud rate (bits per second), computes the parity bit on transmitted and received characters, and reports any detected errors.
- It handles the appropriate hardware handshaking signals required for two devices to communicate and reports on the status of incoming handshaking signals.

The UART/USART chip is not connected directly to the serial port RS232 connector plug on the microcomputer because the voltage levels inside the microcomputer are much lower than those used for serial transmission. The appropriate circuitry must be provided to modify the voltage levels. The voltages in a microcomputer are measured to the thousandth of a volt, whereas serial transmission might use ± 15 volts. The UART/USART and its associated circuitry often are incorporated on a *serial interface card,* which may be an optional accessory for a microcomputer. In other cases, the UART/USART is built into the microcomputer.

COMMUNICATION SOFTWARE FOR MICROCOMPUTERS

This section discusses why microcomputers are used for communications, what communication facilities are built into DOS, and other communication software packages. Microcomputers are used for many data communication tasks. Their primary uses are for accessing timesharing networks, transferring programs or data, communicating with other microcomputers such as in an automated office environment, using them on a local area network, and communicating with minicomputers and mainframe computers.

Microcomputer users may have databases of information available within their own organizations, but they also may want to use some of the many commercial databases that are available—for example, The Source, Dialog Information Services, Dow-Jones News Retrieval Service, and CompuServe Information Service. By using these commercial databases, you can obtain such services as airline schedules, electronic mail, medical advice, business financial information, educational information, news, weather, games/entertainment, home shopping/banking, and bibliographic information on specialized subjects. To connect your microcomputer to any of the commercial databases or other microcomputers, you need both a modem (modems for microcomputers are covered in a later section) and a communication software package.

The data you transmit or receive moves through the serial I/O port at the rear of the microcomputer, over the RS232 cable, into the modem, out of the modem, onto the circuits (telephone lines), and to the network you called (see the top half of Figure 10-1). You can use DOS to control this information flow, but it is more likely that, along with DOS, you will have a specialized communication software package because it is easier to use.

DOS Communications   First, let us discuss the capabilities of DOS for communications, and then we will move on to specialized communication software packages. With DOS Version 3.1 or higher, a communication command called MODE can control data transfer. Data is transferred in a serial fashion, and it is controlled by several characteristics or parameters that define how fast and in what form the data is transmitted. The *communication parameters* of your serial port must be the same as the serial port of the other microcomputers or commercial database services with which you want to communicate. Before you can use your communication port, you must set these parameters with the DOS MODE command or another communication package. The communication parameters that must be set for asynchronous transmission include

- **Baud:** How many bits per second are sent or received, for example, 1200 bits per second.
- **Parity:** The kind of error checking, such as odd, even, or no parity.
- **Data bits:** The number of bits per character. (DOS assumes seven bits per character.)
- **Stop bits:** The number of bits at the end of a character (usually one, but there can be two). Notice that you use asynchronous transmission.

When you use DOS Versions 3.1 to 5.0 to *initialize* (start) a serial communication port, the MODE command is entered in the following form:

MODE <port> <baud>,<parity>,<databits>,<stopbits>

The <> symbols indicate the parameters you must enter. Port is the name of the communication port; usually it is described as COM1: or COM2:. The remaining parameters are separated by commas, and they might look like this:

1200 for 1200 bits per second

E for even parity

7 for seven data bits

1 for one stop bit

The entry of the actual command when you are at the C:\> prompt appears as follows:

$$\text{C:\\>MODE COM1: 1200,E,7,1}$$

As you can see, DOS allows you to enter what is needed for data communications, although this is from the viewpoint of DOS Version 3.1 because earlier versions did not offer complete communication facilities. DOS Version 3.1 or later also includes three interfaces that are significant for networking applications: a file redirector, a file server, and NETBIOS.

The *file redirector* intercepts file requests and determines whether the file is local (resident on the microcomputer from which the request was issued) or remote (located on a microcomputer somewhere else in the network). If the file is remote, it routes the request to the *file server,* which can transmit, retrieve, and write to files anywhere in the network.

It is important to differentiate the DOS 3.1 standard from the NETBIOS standard. DOS 3.1 is the PC's operating system interface for applications. NETBIOS, on the other hand, is a pure communication interface that is independent of the PC's operating system. Many applications written for networks use the DOS 3.1 interface and do not use NETBIOS at all. In other words, a local area network vendor might use the DOS-provided NETBIOS, or the network vendor might supply its own *LANBIOS* to handle the network Basic Input/Output System.

NETBIOS The *NETBIOS* allows you to add such capabilities as networking to your microcomputer. NETBIOS implements several layers of the International Organization for Standardization's Open Systems Interconnection Reference Model for Data Communications (see Chapter 9). For example, in IBM's PC Network, NETBIOS resides in the ROM.

The acronym NETBIOS stands for *Net*work *B*asic *I*nput/*O*utput *S*ystem. It works at the session layer (layer 5) of the OSI model, which is the layer responsible for establishing, managing, and terminating connections for individual applications.

NETBIOS is a peer-to-peer communication protocol. In this case the term *peer to peer* refers to a network designed to support communications among intelligent machines. It allows microcomputers on a network to establish a connection between themselves and to communicate directly without having to go through a central host computer, file server, or other hardware device. It allows applications to talk directly to the network, instead of talking to DOS, which in turn talks to the network operating system. NETBIOS operates faster because it bypasses the DOS operating system.

NETBIOS provides an interface for applications and operating systems that need to address directly some other piece of system hardware. Application programmers call this interface *Interrupt 5Ch.* An application that issues an Interrupt 5Ch is telling the operating system that it needs to access the network interface card directly and use NETBIOS to communicate with another microcomputer via the network. Applications needing this type of interface are primarily communication programs, gateways-to-mainframes, and electronic mail systems (X.400). NETBIOS compatibility in an application is important only if that application has some need for direct and immediate network communications. All other application programs can use the DOS 3.1 interface to the network by using the MODE command. The NETBIOS communication has one major limitation: its inability to bridge incompatible networks. NETBIOS must be augmented with additional protocols to allow transmission across two incompatible networks. Remember that you might need a protocol converter for this purpose.

DOS 3.1 was the first version of DOS to include these multiuser function calls. A *function call* (also called a *primitive*) is a hook that DOS provides for application commands. For example, when a word processing application wants to open a file, it says "Open file" to DOS and DOS does it by using a function call. The function call is the part of DOS that understands the command from the application. DOS 3.1 has expanded the range of commands it understands to include multiuser commands. In other words, it has multiuser function calls for communications and networks. These function calls, particularly the extended open and the lock/unlock calls, are redefined specifically for networks.

To a programmer, the most important part of this interface is known as *Interrupt 21h.* An *interrupt* is a call that an application program issues to the operating system for a specific set of functions associated with that interrupt. When an application issues an Interrupt 21h call, it lets the operating system know it needs access to the functions that allow it to open and lock or unlock a file.

The two most important functions available via this Interrupt 21h are the extended open and the lock/unlock (also known as a physical lock). The *extended open function* allows an application program to open a file and specify how it will be used. For example, open the file and use it in a read only status. Or you can open the file and use it with a read/write status. The *lock/unlock function* goes to the disk and locks a physical range of bytes with the restriction specified via Interrupt 21h. It also is possible to lock portions of a file. This allows an application to open some part of a file, manipulate it freely, and leave the rest of the file open for others. This function is very important for database applications with multiple user micro-to-mainframe connections or local area networks.

Many people, preferring not to work at the DOS or NETBIOS level, purchase other communication software packages (see the next section) that take care of all these functions (sending commands to DOS and NETBIOS) and offer easy use through menu-driven user friendly screens.

Other Communication Software   The independent software packages used for communications do not require the use of the DOS MODE command. These packages offer provisions for logging on to a timesharing network, transmitting data files, calling other microcomputers or local area networks, and automatic dial and automatic answer facilities if someone else dials your microcomputer. More than 30 of these packages are available. Typical brand names of currently available communication software packages are ProComm Plus, CROSSTALK XVI, Smartcom III, Freeway Advanced, PC-Dial, MicroPhone II (for Windows), Relay Gold, WATSON, and so forth. The easiest way for you to understand what a communication software package does is to follow along as we describe ProComm Plus.

PROCOMM PLUS

ProComm Plus is a microcomputer communication package with an interface that makes connection between computers, bulletin boards, and electronic database services quick and easy. The 2.01 version provides fast access to commands and option screens through the use of Alt-key combinations. It also has pull-down menus and supports a mouse.

Help is always available in the Terminal window just by pressing Alt-Z. For readers who are familiar with pull-down menus, a single keystroke accesses the ProComm Plus pull-down menus. You already saw examples of pull-down menus in the discussion of GrafNet Plus (see Figure 6-22).

The ProComm Plus software supports 15 standard file transfer protocols, 3 user-defined external protocols, and 33 terminal emulations. Version 2.01 includes support for the ZMODEM and RAW ASCII protocols, and emulation for Data General 100/200/210 and DEC VT220/320 terminals. It also offers full 132-column support, and EGA/VGA systems can display extra lines of text in terminal mode.

ProComm Plus uses the ASPECT script language for its more than 400 commands. The ASPECT scripts are compiled for compactness, faster execution, and security. With ASPECT, users can create scripts that automate most of the ProComm Plus functions. As an example, you can build and store automatic log-on scripts. A *script* is the entire log-on sequence that contains all the necessary parameters for logging on to a specific database service or public data network (PDN). The purpose of scripts is to make the log-on as fast and painless as possible. The word ''script'' is derived from movies and television; a movie or television show has a written script for the actors to follow.

Additional options include a Host mode that functions like an electronic bulletin board system, allowing users to create custom screens, menus, and file listings. A unique ''File Name Clipboard'' can cut filenames directly from the screen and later paste them to the remote microcomputer for downloading. *Downloading* is the transfer of a program or data file from the host mainframe computer to a remote microcomputer. *Uploading* is the transfer of a program or data file from the remote microcomputer to the host mainframe computer.

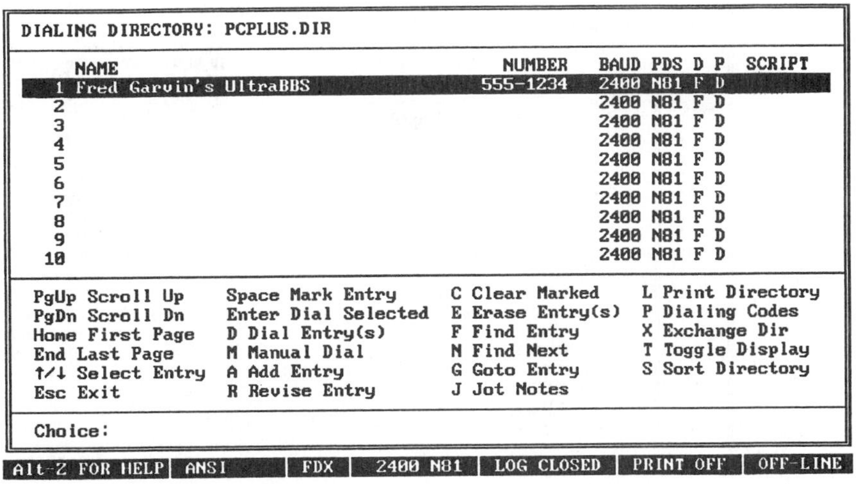

```
┌──────────────────────────────────────────────────────────────────────┐
│ DIALING DIRECTORY: PCPLUS.DIR                                          │
│                                                                        │
│       NAME                            NUMBER   BAUD PDS D P   SCRIPT   │
│    1 Fred Garvin's UltraBBS           555-1234 2400 N81 F D            │
│    2                                            2400 N81 F D           │
│    3                                            2400 N81 F D           │
│    4                                            2400 N81 F D           │
│    5                                            2400 N81 F D           │
│    6                                            2400 N81 F D           │
│    7                                            2400 N81 F D           │
│    8                                            2400 N81 F D           │
│    9                                            2400 N81 F D           │
│   10                                            2400 N81 F D           │
│                                                                        │
│   PgUp Scroll Up     Space Mark Entry      C Clear Marked   L Print Directory │
│   PgDn Scroll Dn     Enter Dial Selected   E Erase Entry(s) P Dialing Codes   │
│   Home First Page    D Dial Entry(s)       F Find Entry     X Exchange Dir     │
│   End Last Page      M Manual Dial         N Find Next      T Toggle Display   │
│   ↑/↓ Select Entry   A Add Entry           G Goto Entry     S Sort Directory   │
│   Esc Exit           R Revise Entry        J Jot Notes                         │
│                                                                        │
│   Choice:                                                              │
└──────────────────────────────────────────────────────────────────────┘
  Alt-Z FOR HELP   ANSI      FDX     2400 N81   LOG CLOSED   PRINT OFF   OFF-LINE
```

Figure 10-4   ProComm Plus Dialing Directory screen accessed by pressing Alt-D.

How to Use ProComm Plus   Running ProComm Plus is simple and straightforward. The program loads when you type PCPLUS at the DOS prompt. After a title screen, pressing one key takes users directly to the Terminal mode. From there, Alt-key combinations or pull-down menus lead users through setup options or directly to an online session. For example, Alt-S invokes extensive setup procedure options, and Alt-D moves users to the Dialing Directory (see Figure 10-4). Once in the Dialing Directory, users can immediately select an existing entry and place a call. Looking at Figure 10-4 you can see the highlight bar is at entry 1 for Fred Garvin's BBS. You would just press the Enter key to dial that number.

Look at the bottom of the Dialing Directory screen to see various other options for adding or revising directory entries. Adding new entries or revising old ones is easy; just press A to add or R to revise an entry. If you press R, ProComm Plus opens an options window (see Figure 10-5) for changing all relevant parameters. Once you make and save the changes, the added or revised entry becomes part of the Dialing Directory. Note that ProComm Plus not only dials the telephone for you, but it also automatically invokes the correct communication parameters (2400, NONE, 8, 1, FULL, DEFAULT, ZMODEM, ANSI, MODEM) for automatic connection to the network.

To make a call to any listed number, simply place the highlight bar at that entry and press Enter. Numbers not listed in the Dialing Directory can be dialed manually with the M (Manual Dial) option, which is one of the options at the bottom of the screen shown in Figure 10-4. Once connected, users normally follow the prompts provided by the service that was dialed (such as a bulletin board system or one of the commercial information services). ProComm Plus also allows users to dial a number of directory listings in sequence.

How to Upload and Download   Users can quickly upload files with the PgUp key or download files with the PgDn key. A protocol selection window provides a wide

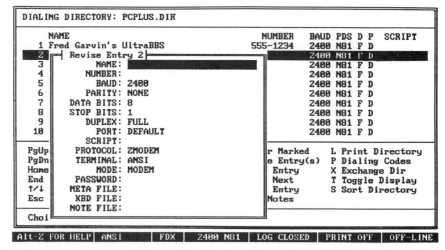

Figure 10-5 A ProComm Plus options window being used to revise entry 2 in the Dialing Directory. The highlight bar is positioned for the entry of a name.

range of popular protocols that are compatible with the requirements of the system being called. Figure 10-6 illustrates the protocols available with ProComm Plus. Many of these protocols are discussed later in this chapter in the Microcomputer Protocols section.

Once a compatible protocol is chosen, the user generally initiates an upload or download by entering the desired filename(s) and pressing the Enter key. ProComm Plus can automate much of this procedure with the ASPECT script language (if you

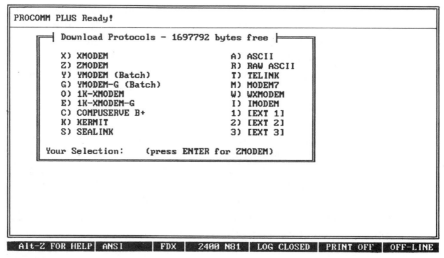

Figure 10-6 A screen showing all the protocols in ProComm Plus. You select the protocol that is used by the network to which you are connecting.

have written a script). The script even can be part of the Dialing Directory entry as shown in the right-most column in Figure 10-4.

When concluding a session, the user exits (disconnects) from the service by using the command provided by the service, presses Alt-X to exit ProComm Plus from the Terminal mode, and responds appropriately to the exit prompt.

WATSON (VOICE OR DATA)

Whereas a software package like ProComm Plus is used for the transmission of data, there also are combination packages that can handle both voice and data transmission. One such package is called WATSON, and another is PCDIAL LOG. As an example, WATSON's capabilities can be divided into the areas of telephone management, the modem and its software, and voice messaging.

WATSON is a microcomputer-compatible circuit board and software that combines voice mail and telephone management with the standard data communication facilities. Applications include a 500-entry electronic telephone book and database, a built-in 300/1200 bits per second modem, automatic telephone dialing, and redialing, dictation machine with true voice editing, and electronic calendar with alarms. WATSON VIS (for Voice Information System) upgrades the voice mail capabilities of the system to provide information to callers. The best way you can see how this package operates is to dial 1-800-6WATSON. (In Massachusetts, the number is 1-617-651-2198.) Do call by using a touchtone telephone so you can control this demonstration, record, and play back your own voice. WATSON digitizes your voice to record it onto the disk.

FILE TRANSFER VERSUS CAPTURE BUFFER

Asynchronous communication between microcomputers requires a pair of modems and a communication software package for the microcomputer. Most asynchronous software packages claim to support file transfer. Let us expand on this last point.

Most of the available microcomputer communication software handles the task of capturing data as it comes across the screen through the use of a memory buffer. When the memory buffer is full, the programs write the data to disk in a format specified by *your* microcomputer. This is not a true file transfer because the data is now in the operating format of *your* microcomputer rather than in the format of the sending microcomputer. This "capture buffer" system of downloading from a host computer allows you to store information from bulletin boards and other electronic databases, even though this information may not be in the exact file structure format that is needed for use in one of your programs, such as a spreadsheet or statistical package. These asynchronous communication software packages usually allow you to upload information to another microcomputer by sending a text file over the telephone lines. Again, this is not actually a file transfer because the receiving machine presumably is using the capture buffer method of saving the data.

True file transfer, either uploading or downloading, requires that *both* microcomputers use the same protocol and formatting. That is easy if the machines are identical. The problem arises when the machines at each end of the communication circuit are different or when different communication packages are used.

This consideration is mentioned here because one microcomputer user may develop something like a spreadsheet and want to transmit it for use by another person. Unless they have the same machines using the same protocol (asynchronous or synchronous communication software), the receiver may not be able to use the spreadsheet data without reformatting the information for his or her own spreadsheet. Use of the term *file transfer* implies the data is transferred and received in its original format. *Capture buffer* means the data is transmitted, but it is reformatted as it moves from the memory of the computer to a disk or video screen. Although this may not affect you now, it might in the future if you want to transmit various applications, such as a spreadsheet, among different microcomputer users.

MICROCOMPUTER PROTOCOLS

Any microcomputer communication package must include a transmission *protocol* if data is to be transmitted to some other location. When we discussed protocols in Chapter 9, we described the larger, more sophisticated protocols that are used in wide area networks. The most prevalent of these are the High-level Data Link Control (HDLC), the Synchronous Data Link Control (SDLC), and the X.25 packet switching protocol. These protocols handle flow control and the movement of data in large wide area networks (WANs) or for internetworking.

In this chapter, we will concentrate on protocols that can be used for interconnecting two microcomputers transmitting either asynchronously (character by character) or synchronously (block transmission). These microcomputer protocols are less sophisticated, take up less computer space, and are much easier to operate than the ones we described for host mainframe connections. Even though it is possible to use these simple protocols for transmitting from a microcomputer to a large centrally based host mainframe, the microcomputer in a microcomputer-to-mainframe connection (discussed later in this chapter) generally uses the more sophisticated protocol of the larger host mainframe.

Today, data transmission by microcomputers generally means the transfer of data files. All file transfer protocols have two characteristics in common. First, these protocols are designed to transmit error-free data from one computer to another. If this transmitted data is to be free of errors, some error checking routine must be included in the protocol. The second characteristic is that both the transmitting and receiving terminals must use the same protocol; that is, they must both agree on the communication procedures for such details as the block size, number of start and stop bits, error checking methodology, control characters, half or full duplex, and the like. Regardless of which microcomputer communication package is used, it probably will include one or more of the following *serial transmission protocols*.

X-ON/X-OFF   *X-ON/X-OFF* is one of the oldest protocols, dating back to the days of the teletype machine. Consequently, it was not really designed for use with computers. X-ON/X-OFF is good enough to use when only text is being transmitted, but it cannot handle machine language programs such as .COM or .EXE files. The basic concept of X-ON/X-OFF is quite simple. If Computer A sends something to Computer B and Computer B is free to receive, it acknowledges this by sending the X-ON signal. If Computer B is busy, it sends the X-OFF signal so Computer A can defer sending until Computer B is free.

As you can see, when two microcomputers communicate, some type of flow control is required. *Flow control* provides a mechanism for regulating data transfer between two communicating systems. For example, if one microcomputer is sending a long file to a printer, the printer probably cannot print as fast as the data can be sent. To avoid losing data, the printer sends an X-OFF character as its input buffer fills. This instructs the transmitting microcomputer to stop sending the file. After the printer has caught up and its input buffer is empty, the printer sends an X-ON character to resume the file transfer where it left off.

Under this protocol, when the receiving device is no longer willing to receive a string of characters, it sends an X-OFF character to the sending device. (The X-OFF character usually is the ASCII character DC3 or control S.) To restart transmission, the receiving device sends the X-ON character (usually the ASCII character DC1 or control Q) to the sending device. Because the X-ON and X-OFF characters can be destroyed or accidentally generated by communication line errors, this simple scheme can lead to confusion. As a result, more sophisticated protocols have been developed that use various cyclical redundancy error checks to turn on or off the flow of data between two modems.

XMODEM   The *XMODEM* protocol takes the data being transmitted and divides it into blocks. The block is similar to the frame we described in Chapter 9 (see Figure 9-4). Each block has a start of header character (SOH), a 1-byte block number, 128 bytes of data, and a 1-byte checksum for error checking. To start communications, the sending device (microcomputer) must receive a negative acknowledgment (an ASCII NAK character) telling it to start sending the data blocks. After receiving a block of data, the receiving device must wait for the circuit to clear before sending either a NAK character (this indicates an error was found through use of the checksum) or an ACK character if the block was received correctly. Blocks acknowledged with a NAK character are retransmitted. At completion of the session, the transmitter sends the ASCII character EOT (End of Transmission) and waits for an ACK character before terminating the session between the two microcomputers.

Even though this protocol was developed for micro-to-micro communications, it often is used for micro-to-mainframe communications where the host mainframe can support the XMODEM protocol. XMODEM is one of the protocols that uses a stop and wait ARQ (Automatic Repeat reQuest) half duplex mode of transmission. The 1-byte checksum for error checking is obtained by adding the decimal value of each ASCII character in the 128-character block, dividing the sum by 255, and retaining the remainder as the checksum that is transmitted to the other end of the communication circuit. The receiving microcomputer calculates its own checksum in the same way and compares it with the transmitted checksum. If the two values are equal, the receiving computer sends a positive acknowledgment (ACK) that informs the transmitter to send the next sequential message (block of data). If the two values are not equal, the receiver sends the transmitter a negative acknowledgment (NAK) to request a retransmission of the last message (block of data). Use of this checksum detects close to 95 percent of the errors.

Because the XMODEM protocol is in the public domain, it is readily available for software designers to incorporate into communication programs. For example, return to Figure 10-6 where you will see that XMODEM is the first protocol listed on the Procomm Plus Download Protocols screen. Some of the advantages of the XMODEM protocol are that it is easy to implement in a high-level language, it only requires a 256-byte buffer, it can transmit 8-bit characters, and it has an effective error detection scheme.

XMODEM-CRC *XMODEM-CRC* improves on the 95 percent accuracy of the XMODEM protocol. It replaces the checksum that adds the decimal value of each ASCII character with a more rigorous *cyclical redundancy check* (CRC) in which an integer is divided by a prime number. This improved version detects 99.969 percent of the errors.

XMODEM-1K *XMODEM-1K* increases throughput by as much as 87 percent by using data blocks of 1,024 bytes instead of the 128-character blocks of the original XMODEM. XMODEM-1K also uses a CRC error check and has a batch handling capability so you can execute multiple file transfers in a single operation.

WXMODEM *WXMODEM* (window XMODEM) speeds the transfer of data by allowing a transmitting modem to send data without waiting for the receiving device to acknowledge the successful receipt of each block of data (see the definition of continuous ARQ in Chapter 9). WXMODEM is a full duplex *sliding window protocol*. It divides a file into packets, each of which has a sequence number so the file can be put back into its proper order at the receiving end. It can send four packets (a "window") before receiving an acknowledgment.

YMODEM The primary benefit of the *YMODEM* protocol is CRC-16 error checking. CRC-16 is a 2-bytes-long cyclical redundancy check that detects errors at least 99.99 percent of the time. YMODEM also is able to transmit files. It does so by sending the ASCII STX (Start of Text) character at the beginning of a block, rather than the ASCII SOH (Start of Heading) character normally used. This identifies the block that follows as 1,024 bytes instead of the standard 128 bytes. In addition, two consecutive ASCII CAN (Cancel) characters abort a file transfer. When people speak of the YMODEM protocol, they mean the basic XMODEM-1K protocol with additional CRC-16 error checking and multiple file transfer capability.

YMODEM-G The *YMODEM-G* protocol is a streaming variation of the YMODEM protocol, and it is used with error controlling modems. An error controlling modem detects errors, but it does not correct them. This is a subtle point, but the two modems handle the error detection and erroneous block retransmission instead of the two microcomputers doing it. In a *streaming protocol,* the entire file is transmitted and then the acknowledgment is transmitted, followed by either a retransmission of the first block of data (there was an error) or the transmission of the next block of data (the prior block was received correctly). In effect, this is half duplex transmission between two modems even though it may appear to be full duplex.

ZMODEM *ZMODEM* is a newer protocol written to overcome some of the problems that occur when error-checked files are transmitted over packet switching networks like SprintNet or Tymnet. It is not a subset of XMODEM but instead incorporates features of several protocols. Its cyclical redundancy check is more powerful than that of XMODEM, and it uses a continuous ARQ. Like WXMODEM, it is a sliding window protocol. If the protocol detects an error when using a sliding window program, it retransmits only the packet that is in error. This means that only one erroneous packet must be retransmitted instead of the entire original block of data that was segmented into several 128-character packets. ZMODEM dynamically adjusts its packet size according to communication circuit conditions, and it uses a 32-bit CRC error check. Moreover, if ZMODEM aborts a file transfer, it can reinitiate the transfer from the point of the abort without resorting to retransmission of the entire file. ZMODEM usually is the preferred protocol of most bulletin board systems (BBSs).

KERMIT *KERMIT* is a popular protocol used with microcomputers. The KERMIT software is distributed free and unlicensed by Columbia University's Center for Computing Activities in New York City, although there may be a minimal charge ($5 or so) for the documentation and disk. Various versions of KERMIT can be located on public bulletin board systems and downloaded to your microcomputer. The KERMIT protocol was developed and is still copyrighted by Columbia University, which put it into the public domain as a free software communication package.

KERMIT is a RS232-based communication protocol designed to accommodate similar types of computers, operating systems, and file systems. It is suited especially to micro-to-mainframe connections for both IBM and non-IBM systems, but it works equally well with microcomputer-to-microcomputer or mainframe-to-mainframe connections. KERMIT communication-based programs provide error-checked transfer of text and, in most cases, binary files using both 7- and 8-bit codes. The only requirements are an asynchronous serial connection and KERMIT software running on each of the two communicating computers.

X.PC *X.PC,* developed by Tymnet, can construct packets on a microcomputer and send them to a network node for conversion to the synchronous X.25 standard format. Tymnet developed the X.PC protocol specifically for connecting asynchronous devices to packet switching networks. X.PC also can be used as a file transfer protocol for direct communication between microcomputers. X.PC provides error checking with automatic retransmission; it allows several different sessions to take place concurrently using only one modem and one telephone circuit; and it permits access to several different host mainframes from a single microcomputer.

Some people call X.PC an asynchronous version of X.25, even though the X.PC packet is not packaged the same way as the X.25 packet. Thus, special "translation software" is required for each dial-up transmission between a network using X.25 and the Tymnet network using X.PC protocol. The X.PC protocol uses a more comprehensive error detection scheme (cyclical redundancy check polynomial) than XMODEM. It also includes recovery procedures that are based on packet sequence numbers to ensure data integrity. Up to 15 logical channels can be accessed simultaneously allowing one microcomputer to be logged into 15 simultaneous applications, and it implements flow control through a rotating "window" algorithm that allows up to 15 packets per window and variable size packets up to 256 bytes long.

BLAST   *BLAST* is a *BL*ocked *A*Synchronous *T*ransmission program that incorporates the power and efficiency of High-level Data Link Control (HDLC) or Synchronous Data Link Control (SDLC) synchronous transmission protocols, but for use with asynchronous transmission. In this case, the blocks can be acknowledged negatively (NAK) in an out-of-sequence fashion. In other words, it uses continuous ARQ, thereby increasing data transmission efficiency. This protocol uses a cyclical redundancy error detection scheme (the ANSI CRC-16 polynomial), which is more effective than the one used by XMODEM. Both BLAST and X.PC result in a higher throughput than XMODEM. Because BLAST and X.PC both use sliding "windows," they allow propagation delays of up to approximately two seconds at 1200 bits per second transmission speed. For this reason, these protocols work on satellite links that have a longer propagation delay as messages move from earth to the satellite and back to earth. BLAST also works in full duplex mode. BLAST currently does not support any modem by name, but modem control parameters can be configured to match most available modems.

PC-BLAST II   The latest version of BLAST is called *PC-BLAST II,* and it works between microcomputers, minicomputers, and mainframes. It automatically converts data between different computers, as from MS-DOS to VAX/VMS to UNIX or even to IBM mainframes. BLAST can be operated in full duplex (simultaneous transmission in both directions), and it allows scripts that automate repetitive functions or routines and carries them out when you call on the script. PC-BLAST II is available to MS-DOS, UNIX/XENIX, MacIntosh, IBM mainframes, DEC VAX/VMS, and other popular computers.

MNP   *MNP* is Microcom Systems' networking protocol. Many of the newer asynchronous modems contain MNP modules in their circuits. There are six classes of MNP protocols. Class 1, the lowest level, is an asynchronous byte-oriented protocol that operates only in half duplex. Class 2 upgrades the Class 1 MNP protocol to operate at full duplex.

Class 3 takes asynchronous data from your microcomputer and changes it within the modem so that synchronous data is passed between the two modems. The data flow starts asynchronously at your microcomputer, becomes synchronous between the two modems, and is converted back to asynchronous data as it is handed to the microcomputer at the other end of the circuit. This type of protocol is becoming very popular because it increases the efficiency, speed, and reliability of data communications.

Class 4 adds data phase optimization and adaptive packet assembly. Data phase optimization reduces the overhead required for the protocol, thus making it more efficient. Adaptive packet assembly changes the packet size so larger packets are sent when the telephone circuit is a "good" one, but shorter messages or packets are transmitted when the circuit is "bad" or noisy.

Class 5 modems improve on adaptive packet assembly by automatically determining the optimum packet size for the line at any given moment. Class 5 also performs text compression of approximately 2:1. This compression effectively doubles transmission speed because only one bit is sent over the communication circuit for each two bits in the original message.

Class 6 can perform any of the functions of the first five classes and also includes what Microcom calls Statistical Duplexing™. Other vendors might call this *ping-ponging, pseudo-full-duplex transmission,* or *fast training.* With the *Statistical Duplexing* method of transmission, a modem transmits at very high speed in one direction at a time, but it can change direction very quickly (high speed turnaround time). This transmission method makes it appear that a microcomputer is transmitting in full duplex when it really is transmitting in half duplex. Class 6 includes universal link negotiation, which allows two modems to connect (*handshake*) and begin to communicate at 2400 bits per second and later increase the speed to 4800 or 9600 bits per second. One aspect of MNP Class 6 is that, as the speed increases from 2400 to 4800 to 9600 bits per second, the modems actually change "modulation schemes." MNP Class 6 allows different types of modems or those from different manufacturers to talk to each other, assuming they both use the MNP Class 6 protocol.

Microcom Systems uses the MNP protocol in its 19,200 and 38,400 bits per second dial-up modem that supports both asynchronous and synchronous data. It takes asynchronous data from your microcomputer and transmits synchronously between the modems by using statistical duplexing (ping-ponging).

MODEMS FOR MICROCOMPUTERS

From reading the earlier section on modems in Chapter 3, you should have a complete understanding of what a modem is and how it operates. We now want to present some specifics on microcomputer modems, although they perform the same basic tasks as the more powerful modems discussed in Chapter 3.

As your modem passes data between itself and the distant modem the protocol must carry out some type of flow control. To avoid loss of data, the average rate at which the receiving modem is able to accept data must be equal to or greater than the average rate at which the data is being sent. Therefore, if one modem is set to transmit at 1200 bits per second, then the receiving modem also must be able to transmit and receive at 1200 bits per second or greater. In addition, a mechanism must exist whereby the receiving modem can let the transmitting modem know it should stop transmitting, or at least slow down. This mechanism, known as flow control, is handled by the communication software package and is referred to as the protocol. The modem for your microcomputer can be either an internal modem or an external modem.

Internal Modems *Internal modems* are built into a circuit board that fits into one of the slots inside your microcomputer box. This circuit card contains the RJ-11 telephone jack plug, such as you have in your home telephone. By using the standard RJ-11 plug, you can connect the circuit card containing the modem directly to the telephone line's wall socket. Notice that you do not need the RS232 connector cable with an internal modem because the RS232 connects serial ports to external modems. Internal modems may not offer external indicator lights depicting the status of the modem or the circuit.

External Modems As the name implies, *external modems* are external to your microcomputer. They come in a small metal box and are connected to the serial I/O port (COM1) by using a RS232 connector plug and cable. Internal and external modems are the same, the only difference being their physical location (inside your microcomputer or as a separate external box). Once the external modem has been connected to the microcomputer, use the external modem's RJ-11 telephone jack to connect the external modem to the telephone company's wall plug (see Figure 2-9 on page 54).

Typical modem brand names are Hayes Smartmodem, Novation Auto-cat, Signalman, Racal Vadic, and Codex. Today's microcomputer modems usually operate at a speed of 300, 1200, and 2400 bits per second. Because 300 bits per second is very slow, it is recommended that you buy at least a 1200 bits per second modem, possibly with the option of being able to transmit at 2400 bits per second or even higher. As more public database systems offer 2400 bits per second transmission rates, microcomputer users are advised to transmit at higher speeds to save on telephone line usage costs and on the per hour charge rates of public databases.

Micro-to-Modem Connectors The serial port (COM1 or COM2) on your microcomputer may have a 25-pin RS232 connector plug or, if it is a PC/AT or PS/2 microcomputer, a 9-pin plug. All you must do is ensure that whatever plug you need comes on the modem you purchase. Several types of plugs are available for connecting cables to your microcomputer serial port. You already saw both the 25-pin and 9-pin plugs in Figure 5-11 in Chapter 5. In the world of microcomputers, these also are called D-type connectors (DB-25 and DB-9) because they are shaped somewhat like the letter D.

There also are *smart cables*. For example, all you do with the IQ Technologies[1] Universal Smart Cable is plug in the cable and set two switches. It automatically

---

[1]IQ Technologies is at 22032 23rd Drive S.E., Bothell, Wash. 98021-4497. You may call 1-206-483-3555 or FAX an inquiry to 1-206-485-8949.

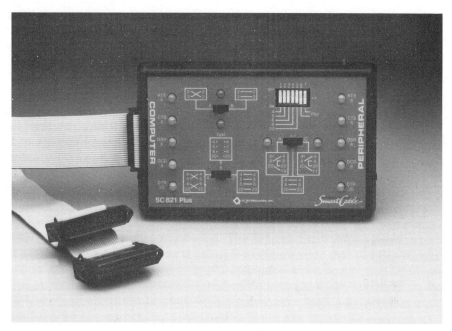

Figure 10-7   Smart Cable Maker (SC821 PLUS) used for a cable connection between two serial devices. Photograph courtesy of IQ Technologies.

matches all the data and handshake control lines when you flick a switch. This cable is an intelligent serial interface that looks at the RS232 signals from the microcomputer and the peripheral and uses its own built-in logic circuitry to make all the right connections. There also are smart cables for Macintosh, laptop, and PC/AT-style microcomputers.

Another option is a Smart Cable Maker (see Figure 10-7). It is both an intelligent cable and a diagnostic instrument because it interconnects two RS232 asynchronous serial devices while simultaneously providing a display of the interface configuration. When the Smart Cable Maker has the connection working properly, you can leave the cable in place, or you can use the cable connection information provided by it to build a permanent cable.

MICRO-TO-MICRO CONNECTIONS

Data can be transferred between two microcomputers by uploading it (using a micro-to-mainframe connection) to the host mainframe computer and subsequently downloading it to another microcomputer. Another method is to connect the microcomputers by using a local area network. Although both alternatives work well, they may be too costly for users who do not require online, real-time data transfer between the two microcomputers. Two inexpensive *micro-to-micro connection* alternatives are to copy the data onto a diskette and give the diskette to the other microcomputer user or bring the two microcomputers close together so a null modem cable can be used with your communication software.

Copy to Diskette   This process uses the DOS DISKCOPY, COPY, or XCOPY commands to copy the file you want to transfer onto a diskette that you then send to the other person. If the file is too large to fit onto one diskette, you can use the DOS BACKUP command or one of the backup software packages on the market.

If you do not have a backup program, the following batch file can be used to copy all the files in a subdirectory onto several diskettes. It is used when there are more files than can fit onto one diskette. This batch file, called BACUP. BAT, uses the DOS XCOPY command and requires DOS 3.2 or greater. EDLIN or COPY CON are used to create BACUP.BAT. This is the program.

```
echo off
cls
attrib +a *.*
:next
cls
echo ^G
echo ..Insert a formatted diskette into Drive A:
pause
xcopy *.* A: /m /v
if errorlevel 1 goto next
if errorlevel 0 goto end
:end
echo ^G
echo ^G
echo ..You have finished. All of the files have been copied.
cd \
```

This batch program must have a .BAT extension, and it should be placed either in the root directory or in a directory created specifically to hold batch files. The batch files directory must be listed in the PATH statement of the AUTOEXEC.BAT file. Assuming this batch file is named BACUP.BAT, you can use it by logging onto the subdirectory containing the files you want to copy. You then type BACUP and press the Enter key. The program copies all the files in the subdirectory onto the diskette in Drive A and prompts you when to change diskettes as each one is filled.

If you want to copy the files onto the diskette in Drive B, change line 9 above to: XCOPY *.* B: /M /V. If you add /S to line 9, it copies all the files on the subdirectory of the current directory, plus all the files below it.

Null Modem Cable Connections *Null modem cables* allow transmission between two microcomputers that are next to each other (six to eight feet apart) without using a modem. If you discover that the diskette from your microcomputer will not fit into another one, that transmitting over telephone lines is impossible, or that you cannot transmit data easily from one microcomputer to another for any reason, then it is time to get a null modem cable.

First, bring the two microcomputers close together. Next, obtain a null modem cable (more on the pin connections in a moment). The cable runs from the serial communication port on the first microcomputer to the serial communication port on the second one. The cable is called a "null" modem cable because it eliminates the need for a modem. You can either build a null modem cable or buy one from any microcomputer store. Null modem connector blocks are available to connect between two cables you already own.

To transfer data between two microcomputers, just hook the null modem cable between them and call up one of the computers by using the communication software you normally use. To do so, put one microcomputer in answer mode and get the other one to call it, but skip the step of dialing the telephone number. After the receiving computer has answered that it is ready, the data can be sent, just as you would on a normal long distance dial-up connection.

With null modem cables, a higher bits per second rate is accomplished easily; transmission can be 9600 bits per second, for example. This may be a great advantage for high volume data transfers from microcomputer to microcomputer because your modem might limit transmission to 1200 bits per second or less. Basically, a null modem cable switches pins 2 and 3 (TRANSMIT and RECEIVE) of the RS232 connector plug. A null modem wiring configuration is shown in Figure 10-8.

PC-to-PC Communications Several packages are available for the transfer of data between IBM PCs. These packages include the required cables and can be purchased for approximately $100. With this method, the two PCs are connected via their serial or parallel ports; special communication software makes them operate as though connected with a null modem cable. These *PC-to-PC communication* software packages are great improvements over the null modem cable. The two microcomputers are still only six to eight feet apart. In addition to data transfer, some PC-to-PC software allows printer sharing between two microcomputers.

To explain this method of transferring data between two microcomputers, we will discuss a product from Traveling Software called *LapLink*. This product performs file transfers similarly to a telecommunication program that downloads or uploads files to or from a mainframe. If you want to interconnect two microcomputers using this or a similar product, you will receive a diskette containing the necessary software and a special cable that has two plugs on each end of the cable. The cable has two plugs so that either a 25-pin or a 9-pin port can be used, depending on which one is on your microcomputer.

To use such a product, link the serial or parallel ports of each microcomputer by connecting the cable, and then load the software into both microcomputers. Either microcomputer can control the sending and receiving of files. LapLink transfers

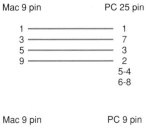

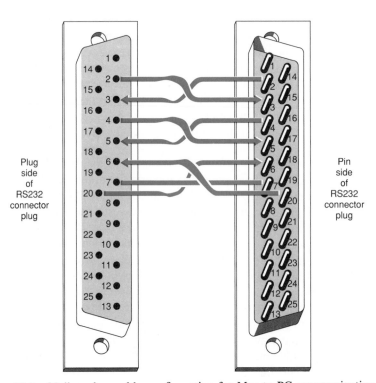

Figure 10-8 Null modem cable configuration for Mac-to-PC communications (upper half) and PC-to-PC synchronous communication (lower half).

files at 115,200 bits per second (serial) and 200,000 bits per second (parallel). As you can see, this is much faster than the 9600 bits per second used for a null modem cable. The software performs error checking during file transfer. It is possible to transfer more than one file at a time because entire DOS directories, including their subdirectories, can be transferred. LapLink understands DOS directory structures and permits movement between hard disk directories on either microcomputer.

Mac-to-PC Communications   As Apple Macintosh moves farther into the business environment, it is inevitable that files will have to be transferred between a Mac and a PC (personal computer by IBM or compatible). *Mac-to-PC communication* creates two problems. The first one is getting your files from one system to the other. The second is making sure the files are in a format that can be recognized by the application program of the microcomputer that is to use them. Any of several strategies may work, depending on the type of file and application software at the destination microcomputer.

The easiest solution is to use a combination of application software on the two microcomputers so the separate file translation step is eliminated. This works if the files can be used by the application without modification or if the files are straight text.

Another solution is to buy external drives for both the Macintosh and the PC. These external drives read and write disks from the other microcomputer. Most PC-compatible drives for the Macintosh plug into the Apple SCSI or serial port, although Apple requires an adapter card and works only with the SE or Mac II. The choice between a PC drive for the Mac or a Mac drive for the PC probably depends on which machine is used the most.

Other Mac-to-PC solutions are to send files via a modem and telephone lines or, if the microcomputers are in close proximity, to use a null modem cable. The communication software can transfer the files, but it does not convert the file formats from Mac to PC or PC to Mac.

Converting a Mac modem cable (called Mac-Hayes) to make it a null modem cable requires opening the 25-pin connector and reversing the wires leading to and from pins 2 and 3. See Figure 10-8 if you want to build a null modem cable.

The communication software on both microcomputers can be started after the cabling is connected. This may require telling it that a direct connection is being used rather than a modem, depending on the software. Remember that you do not dial a telephone number because the microcomputers are only six to eight feet apart. For example, with the CROSSTALK communication software the "Go local" command must be given so the programs know they are communicating without a modem. In addition, both programs must be set for the highest speed that is common to both microcomputers, the number of data bits (eight) must be established, and the programs must be set for the same number of stop and parity bits. Finally, the communication protocol, such as XMODEM or KERMIT, must be selected so that error-free data transfer can take place, after which the null modem file transfer can occur.

Commercial software that includes the cable is available. Two popular packages are MacLink Plus and LapLink Mac. Both include special communication programs for the Mac and the PC that permit selection from an onscreen directory of files you want to transfer.

When *MacLink Plus* is used, the two microcomputers can be connected with the supplied cable or via a modem and telephone line. After they are connected, you begin by running the PC program and then change to the Macintosh where control of the file transfers actually takes place. The lists of files from both systems are viewed with typical Mac scrolling; the contents of different PC disks and directories can be viewed just as is done with Mac disks and folders.

The program must be told the direction the files are to move, the original format of the files, and the new format to which the files are to be converted. By using the mouse, you then just click on the list of files to be transferred and the software does the work, including the format conversion and notifying you when it is finished. Transfers can be at speeds of up to 57,600 bits per second.

LapLink Mac works for a Macintosh the same way its namesake LapLink works for a PC or compatible. It differs from MacLink Plus, however, because file transfer is controlled from the PC instead of the Macintosh. LapLink Mac does not convert file formats. The screen is divided into two scrolling lists to display the current directory for the PC and the current folder for the Macintosh. The cursor and single keystroke commands are used to select and copy any file or group of files in either direction. Several sorting options are available for file display, and the user can switch among directories and folders. In addition to file transfer, LapLink Mac allows you to delete or rename files and to create new subdirectories and folders.

PC-to-Printer Communications

The easiest way for several microcomputers to share one printer (accomplish *PC-to-printer communication*) is to install a *printer sharing* option, although this is not necessary if you have a local area network because printers can be shared by connecting them to this LAN. Traditionally, a simple mechanical switch called an *A/B switchbox* has been used for such a connection. When using this option, you connect two microcomputers and one printer to the same switchbox. Its operation is very simple. When the switch is turned to A the printer is connected to Microcomputer A, and when the switch is turned to B the printer is connected to Microcomputer B. The disadvantage of such a mechanical switchbox is its inconvenience—it must be close to both microcomputer operators, or they will have to walk some distance to turn the switch so they can use the printer.

Today, we have automatic printer sharing devices containing a microprocessor and program chips. These chips allow the automatic printer sharing device to scan all the inputs coming from the various microcomputers. When it senses data coming in from one microcomputer, it stops scanning and passes that data to the printer. When the incoming data stream ends, the printer sharing device continues its scanning to look for input from one of the other microcomputers.

These automatic scanning printer devices usually are sold with two-, four-, or eight-plug capacities. Therefore, you can have up to eight microcomputers sharing a single printer, which normally is a laser printer. These devices cost from $200 to $600, and they are available with either parallel or serial ports. Parallel usually is recommended because of its greater speed, especially if you are transmitting graphics to the printer. Depending on the manufacturer, there usually is a maximum limit of 150 feet between the microcomputer and the printer sharing box.

At this point, you might note that organizations tend to want a local area network for two reasons: to share files of data or to share printers. If the organization's primary reason for setting up a local area network is to share a printer, it might cost less and require less software and hardware maintenance if a printer sharing box were used in place of a local area network.

BULLETIN BOARD SYSTEMS (BBSs)

A *bulletin board system,* or BBS, is a type of dial-up communication in which anyone with a modem can participate. In its most basic form a BBS runs on a host microcomputer that is equipped with a single telephone line modem. Users dial into the BBS via dial-up telephone lines and then log-on to the bulletin board system. If the BBS operator has a multiple line system, several users can log-on at the same time. (The number depends on the number of lines.) Once logged on to the BBS, users can leave public messages for other people who log-on later, they can upload files to or download files from the BBS, they can leave questionnaires or surveys for other users to complete, or they can run specially written programs that are external to the BBS through what is known as a "door." Bulletin board systems have been around for years; it is estimated that there are 32,000 bulletin boards in North America and 45,000 worldwide.

The business world is beginning to take notice of bulletin board systems, both for their positive and negative aspects. Among the positive aspects is the case of an organization that starts a BBS to increase its business; it sets up a multiple line BBS supporting several simultaneous users. For example, if the organization collects data, the BBS can provide online questionnaires for the public to call in and enter their data. Another example is an organization that uses electronic publishing to make newsletters and other information available online. Online databases can be made available on a BBS when an organization wishes to share data with the general public. Software vendors use bulletin board systems to offer the latest information on troubleshooting or alternate uses of features in their software. Finally, shareware software programs can be put on a BBS for distribution and trial usage prior to purchasing the complete package and its documentation.

To see how a corporate bulletin board works, call the Computer Insider at 1-313-375-1771. Once connected to the Computer Insider BBS, you will find message areas, file areas, bulletins, a newsletter, a mail door, and a database door. This is not only a chance to learn about corporate bulletin boards, but you also will receive a wealth of general computer information for the price of a telephone call.

Most of the negative aspects of bulletin board systems deal with viruses or legal issues. (As you will see later, these two issues are the same in some cases.) As everyone who reads a newspaper or watches television news is aware, *viruses* can cause major problems for both networks and organizations. They frequently are spread by employees who download infected programs to their employers' computers. These infected programs can arrive via downloading from a bulletin board system. As a result of viruses being spread by file transfers, many organizations have stringent rules regarding employees who bring their own copies of programs to run on the organization's computers. Some firms look upon illegal software very seriously and consider its use a cause for immediate dismissal. Employees often naively believe they are doing no harm if they bring in an illegal program. These employees not only violate the copyright laws and make their organization vulnerable to legal action for copyright infringement, but they also may cause considerable disruption and excessive expenditure of resources if their illegal program has a virus.

Those who operate a BBS should note that bulletin board operators may be targets of defamation and libel lawsuits. Electronic bulletin board operators are being compared with newspaper and book publishers, who can be held liable for defamatory and libelous statements printed in their publications. If a bulletin board user leaves a libelous message on the bulletin board, both the board operator and the writer may be held liable. This liability could apply to companies, universities, or even individuals who operate their own bulletin boards. Making a user's private messages available to others, using a bulletin board for illegal purposes, or placing a virus into a computer system by means of a bulletin board transmission are other actions for which the BBS operator can be held liable.

The magazine *Boardwatch* (available at computer stores) is a guide to thousands of regional and specialty bulletin boards. Three popular public bulletin boards are the following.

- Prodigy is the simplest to use but has fewer esoteric and high-tech boards. The cost is $50 for a start-up kit and $12.95 per month. In addition, you may be charged for long distance calling with any of these services. Call 1-800-776-3449 for information on Prodigy.
- CompuServe is far richer in boards, chat lines, and reference materials. The cost is $50 for a start-up kit, $24 a year, and $12.80 per hour of connect time. Call 1-800-848-8199 for information on CompuServe.
- GEnie is a bargain at $4.95 per month, which buys access to 100 boards and services on evenings and weekends. If you want a richer menu with live online forums, add $6 per hour of connect time. Call 1-800-638-9636 for information on GEnie.

Because most bulletin boards operate using the same parameters, here are some tips to make their use easier. Unless the BBS instructions indicate otherwise, before dialing make sure the modem and software are set for 300 bits per second, full duplex, originate mode, 8-bit word length, one stop bit, and no parity bit. When you or your communication software dials the BBS, you hear the dial tone first, then the dial pulses or tones, the ring, and finally the BBS microcomputer answers the telephone and issues a long, high-pitched tone that disables the echo suppressors. Your microcomputer then answers, and the connection to the BBS is complete. Once connected, the BBS presents a menu of choices showing what you can do in that particular bulletin board system.

If the parameters just described do not work, try 1200 bits per second in place of 300 bits per second because the higher speed is increasing in popularity. With 1200 bits per second, there still is a high-pitched tone, but a "connect prompt" may not appear on the screen. If a series of random characters appears, they usually are caused by line noise or a bad dial-up circuit. When this happens, hang up and start over by redialing.

Because many bulletin boards can handle only one caller at a time, good etiquette requires that calls be limited to fewer than 10 or 15 minutes and that only one call per day be made to a specific BBS. Use different passwords on each BBS to prevent hackers from impersonating you on another BBS. If you download software, copy it onto a floppy diskette rather than the hard disk to prevent hackers from embedding a program designed to erase your hard disk files.

Some common BBS commands are H or ? to get a help menu; G, Q, BYE, or OFF to sign off; Ctrl-C to interrupt a command; Ctrl-S to pause the system output; and Ctrl-Q to resume the output.

MICRO-TO-MAINFRAME CONNECTIONS

Organizations that rely heavily on microcomputers often find that rapid growth requires substantial new investments in hardware and software to allow these microcomputers to talk among themselves and especially to the mainframe host computer with its massive corporate databases. Obviously, the local area network is one solution, and this will be covered in the next chapter. At this point it is more appropriate to discuss the idea of a single PC micro-to-mainframe connection, or the clustering of microcomputers together in such a way that the clustered group of microcomputers possesses a *micro-to-mainframe link*.

Various options can be used to connect microcomputers and mainframes. The simplest and least expensive way is to use a *terminal emulation* capability without software. A more sophisticated way of making a micro-to-mainframe link is to employ a system that uses both a hardware board and some software. This type of terminal emulation is a link that permits file transfers, while also allowing users to capture and manipulate the mainframe-extracted data. Such links allow the microcomputer to emulate the video data terminal (VDT), the printer, and a control unit over the remote link.

Probably the most used data transmission method is found in the download environment for batch processing. Remember that downloading is the transfer of a program or data file from the host mainframe computer to a remote microcomputer and uploading is the transfer of a program or data file from the remote microcomputer to the host mainframe.

In today's data processing environment, we have moved from batch processing, through real-time individual transaction processing, on to distributed processing, and we are now in a file transfer environment. The massive volumes of data that are transmitted when files are transferred instead of individual transactions have exerted great pressure on our communication links. Software resides at both the host and the microcomputer to handle downloading and uploading. Finally, most host mainframes today must be able to accommodate both IBM-compatible PCs and Apple microcomputers.

Factors in Micro-to-Mainframe Selection   When choosing a micro-to-mainframe link, you should consider a number of factors.

- Which mainframes are supported by the software or hardware circuit board?
- Which mainframe operating systems are supported?
- Which microcomputers (IBM or Apple) are supported at the remote end?
- Which communication protocols are supported?
- Which microcomputer operating systems are supported?
- Which mainframe database file structures can be accessed?

In addition, determine

- The amount of memory required in the emulation board
- Whether the data is reformatted automatically before being transferred from the host mainframe to the microcomputer
- The total price for the software and any circuit boards required at the microcomputer end of the link

PC-to-Host Communications   Communication links between an IBM-compatible PC and an IBM host allow a microcomputer to emulate an IBM 3270 terminal and capture information for storage in another format. The software and hardware to do this usually are based on IBM 3270 protocols, Systems Network Architecture (SNA), or LU 6.2.

To make *PC-to-host communication* possible, the PC must be able to emulate an IBM 3270 terminal before connecting to an IBM 3270-based network. One popular method is to use an emulation board like an IRMA circuit board from Digital Communications Associates. (Other vendors also sell 3270 emulation boards.) Remember, however, that all hardware and software products *must* be tested prior to acquisition to determine whether the product actually can perform all the protocol requirements. This testing can be accomplished by contacting the network control center to request that the technicians monitor the connection via a data line monitor and watch for protocol violations or other problems. The best way, however, is for the mainframe owner to provide a list of tested and authorized products that can be used for PC-to-mainframe connections. Establishing this PC-to-mainframe connection is a three-step procedure.

First, the systems programming and communication groups at the host mainframe site must generate (sysgen) a new set of system software that describes the microcomputer as a participating 3270 terminal. The term *sysgen* is used when system software is generated for a mainframe computer.

Second, the hardware emulation board must be purchased and the circuit (usually coaxial cable) installed between the PC and the IBM 3174 or 3274 control unit. The emulation board is fitted into an expansion slot in the microcomputer, and the coaxial cable connects to the emulation board. The emulation board communicates with the 3174/3274 control unit, which in turn communicates with the front end and host mainframe. This communication is independent of whatever programs may be running in the microcomputer.

Third, you must run the emulation program to make the PC act like a 3270 terminal. This software can be customized to emulate any kind of 327X terminal or keyboard. Because the emulation board has its own microprocessor chip and memory, it functions separately from its own host microcomputer DOS environment. With this emulator, your PC now can operate in two modes: regular microcomputer mode (using DOS) or terminal emulation mode (using the emulation board) when you use the micro-to-mainframe communication link. You can switch between these two modes without losing your screen of data because the emulation board's memory is independent of the microcomputer's memory. It is analogous to having in one box two microcomputers that share the same keyboard and video screen.

To download data from the host mainframe computer, the PC-to-mainframe link must be able to support the mainframe access protocol, which is what the emulation board does. For example, if the PC-to-mainframe link can communicate with a certain DBMS that resides in the host mainframe, it may access files located in that database. Another task that must be performed is to reformat the files from their form as stored in the database at the host mainframe to a form that is manageable at the microcomputer. This process usually takes place at the mainframe. After the data is reformatted, it is transferred to the microcomputer. In other words, the mainframe converts the data files into data interchange format (DIF), document content architecture (DCA), ASCII, or worksheet (WKS) file formats and then downloads them to the emulator board residing in the microcomputer.

We now have *ISDN terminal adapter cards* for microcomputers. These cards permit the attachment of PCs to Integrated Services Digital Network (ISDN) circuits (2B + D) so they can transmit at 56,000 or 64,000 bits per second to a mainframe or public data network (PDN).

The Attachmate Corporation[2] has a free 5.25-inch demonstration diskette called NOW!. It portrays the operation of their 3270 PC-to-mainframe software. This demonstration shows how NOW! can automate repetitive, time-consuming procedures and replace them with quick, single keystroke operations, such as those for retrieving mainframe-based E-mail, unattended file transfers, data retrieval, and even downloading mainframe graphics.

Single Microcomputer   At the microcomputer end of the micro-to-mainframe link, there may be a single microcomputer or a clustered set of microcomputers. Figure 10-9 shows a single microcomputer on a micro-to-mainframe connection. This connection depicts an IBM PC connected to an IBM 3174/3274 cluster controller by means of a coaxial cable or a modem link. If the link is a coaxial cable, the microcomputer most likely is within 2,000 feet of the mainframe. If it is a modem link, then the microcomputer can be any distance from the mainframe. The cluster controller is

---

[2] Attachmate Corporation, 13231 S.E. 36th Street, Bellevue, Wash. 98006-9930, or call 1-206-644-4010.

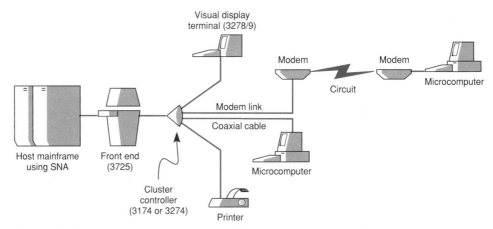

Figure 10-9   Single PC in a micro-to-mainframe connection. The bottom shows the microcomputer connected via a coaxial cable. The top shows the microcomputer connected via a modem link.

attached to the front end. Integrated hardware and software packages are available for the IBM PC; these packages allow it to emulate a 327*X* visual display terminal and plug directly into the cluster controller (either a 3174 or a 3274). Usually, the link between the microcomputer and the cluster controller is a coaxial cable, but it also can be a data communication modem attachment. This is a popular micro-to-mainframe connection because data is transferred to and from the mainframe system by capturing or generating screen images on the microcomputer when using an emulation board.

Clustered Microcomputers   To set up a clustered set of microcomputers, the user need only plug an emulation expansion board into a powerful host microcomputer (probably an 80386 or 80486) and attach to it some inexpensive PCs or dumb terminals. The host microcomputer in this situation is the server for the clustered microcomputers. Such a cluster promotes the complete functionality of several fully configured microcomputers. Today's advanced equipment allows clusters of up to 31 users to be built around one host microcomputer. The expansion board in the host microcomputer provides a microprocessor, random access memory, and two serial ports. Because each new expansion card has its own processor and memory, it puts little strain on the host microcomputer. Multiple-user software for clustering runs on the host microcomputer, along with the host copy of DOS, thereby allowing two disk volumes to be shared by all users for data storage. The software allows shared use of printers attached to the host microcomputer and permits ordinary DOS requests to be executed on the host.

A more sophisticated cluster set of microcomputers is one in which a specialized piece of hardware called a micro-to-mainframe server is the host at the microcomputer end of the micro-to-mainframe link. The *micro-to-mainframe server* is dedi-

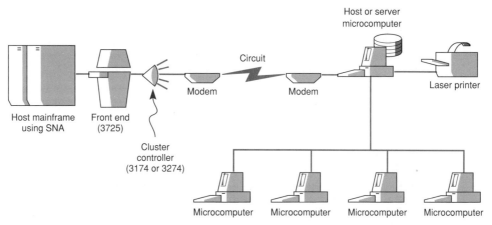

Figure 10-10 Clustered microcomputers in a micro-to-mainframe connection. The host or server microcomputer at the remote end provides required data, facilitates sharing of the printer or disk storage, and handles the communication tasks between the mainframe and the remote end of the link.

cated to providing any required data or file conversions, shared printer or shared disk storage facilities, and the tasks required for communication between the host mainframe and the clustered set of microcomputers on the micro-to-mainframe link. As circuit cards get more powerful, it is difficult to tell the difference between a dedicated micro-to-mainframe server for clustering microcomputers on a micro-to-mainframe link and a more powerful local area network (LAN). These clustered microcomputer groups are referred to as a *multiuser system micro-to-mainframe link.*

Figure 10-10 depicts five microcomputers connected to a single host mainframe. The host or server microcomputer acts as a cluster controller and controls the other four microcomputers. Each of the other microcomputers is attached to the host microcomputer by means of a high speed data communication link. With the proper software and hardware emulation boards in the host microcomputer, data can be transferred to and from the host mainframe computer, and the data can be modified while it is in the possession of any of the microcomputers on this link. A major advantage of this method is that it requires only one remote modem (instead of five) to connect all the locally multidropped microcomputers to the host mainframe computer.

When there is a clustered set of microcomputers, one of them (usually the host) can serve as either a disk server or a file server. Any of the other microcomputers attached to the host microcomputer therefore can store data on this disk and retrieve data from it, although there is a difference between disk servers and file servers.

Disk Servers A *disk server* is a hardware and software combination that treats the hard disk of the clustered group of microcomputers as though it were one large disk usable by all the microcomputers in the cluster. Each of the local microcomputers treats the disk as though it were a local peripheral device. Disk servers allow file sharing only by designating certain areas of the disk as public (each microcomputer can use a different public area), and these public areas are able to be read by any microcomputer in the cluster. For example, if the hard disk were to be partitioned into C:, D:, E:, F:, and G:, then each microcomputer in the cluster shown in Figure 10-10 would have its own disk space. Disk servers are somewhat dangerous because anyone can easily write on someone else's files, destroy their files accidentally, or read their files. Control is effected primarily by being a "good neighbor."

File Servers   A *file server,* on the other hand, has the further software intelligence to decide what to do with requests for writing to the disk storage and for reading from the disk storage. For example, the hard disk has only one partition (C:), but the software separates the files stored by each of the five microcomputers in the cluster shown in Figure 10-10. It can manage the storage more efficiently, and it can handle problems of security, such as putting various "locks" on records or files for security. File servers handle file serving on a file-by-file basis, meaning a user can set up his or her own files with read and/or write protection enabled or denied. File servers are far more elegant and convenient than disk servers. In a business environment, it is recommended that the organization always purchase software that enables it to use the philosophy of a file server. This should be done to protect valuable business data from theft, accidental erasure or modification, accidental breaches of privacy, and sabotage.

PC-to-Mainframe Using APPC   Advanced Program-to-Program Communications (APPC) can link PCs and mainframes without installing emulator circuit cards. One of these, *APPC/LU 6.2* (Advanced Program-to-Program Communications/Logic Unit 6.2), allows applications on microcomputers and mainframes to speak directly to each other. LU 6.2 should help in the area of application program development because it allows microcomputers to connect at the application software level.

Corporate users are implementing LU 6.2, an IBM communication protocol. LU 6.2, as further defined by IBM's APPC/PC (Advanced Program-to-Program Communications/PC), helps determine the requirements for establishing a *program-to-program link* between microcomputers and mainframes. Both APPC and LU 6.2 were described in Chapter 9. When you are at the program-to-program level, you are doing much more than transmitting screens (remember emulation) between the host mainframe and the microcomputer. LU 6.2 allows cooperative applications to exchange data more easily when they are running under different operating systems and when the systems are written in different languages. With APPC/PC, microcomputers should be able to communicate with mainframe systems while retaining full standalone processing capabilities. This protocol is IBM's input to the industrywide effort to establish a program-to-program communication link. As you might imagine, this would be a great improvement over terminal emulation, which just passes the screens back and forth.

IBM's Operating System/2, the first product to support the company's Systems Application Architecture, will let its PS/2s be integrated into IBM's SNA environment. OS/2 consolidates user access to a group of application program interfaces, including Advanced Program-to-Program Communications and NETBIOS. The

OS/2 operating system includes connections for the IBM Token-Ring Network and the PC Network.

Mac-to-Host Communications Most Mac-to-host file transfers are accomplished with IBM 3270 terminal emulation hardware and software. Vendors are starting to create applications that let the Macintosh serve as a front end processor to the IBM host, allowing cooperative processing by the Mac and the mainframe. This *Mac-to-host communication* is difficult to accomplish, however, because the two environments are so different.

Apple has a *MacWorkStation* developers' toolkit that allows programmers to write Mac-to-host applications that look and feel like the Macintosh user interface. Digital Communications Associates has a MacIRMA 3270 board that allows the Mac to be used as a front end to the IBM host computer when coupled with MacIRMA Graphics and their Application Programming Interface (API). Avatar Corporation also has a developer's tool called the MacMainFrame Programmers Toolkit. It helps programmers develop applications for the Macintosh in an IBM host environment.

Security A significant problem in the use of micro-to-mainframe links is in the area of control and *security*. When a portion of the organization's data is downloaded to a microcomputer, this data becomes subject to manipulation outside of the host mainframe programs that were intended to control and validate it. It frequently happens that the movement of data or programs to a remote microcomputer, the editing of that data, and the return of that data to the host mainframe database bypass many host edit controls or security features. This means the *host mainframe database* may gradually become polluted with corrupted data. This problem is magnified when many microcomputers are on a micro-to-mainframe link. See Chapter 13 for an in-depth discussion on security.

Speed Another ongoing development in the area of micro-to-mainframe links is the *transmission speed*. The 1200 or 2400 bits per second speed that we use in microcomputer communications usually is inadequate for transmitting data between a mainframe and remote microcomputer or a clustered set of microcomputers. In practice, 9600 bits per second is barely adequate for a clustered set of microcomputers; 19,200 or 38,400 is better. We are moving very rapidly toward the fully digital 56,000 bits per second and the 64,000 bits per second Integrated Services Digital Network (ISDN) speed of transmission for micro-to-mainframe connections. For those micro-to-mainframe links that go over a coaxial cable (with its approximate 2,000-foot limitation), it is quite easy to transmit at 19,200 bits per second. The point is that as we progress technologically with our micro-to-mainframe links, your microcomputer will have the ability to talk directly from a program within itself to a program in the host mainframe computer, and this will be accomplished at faster and faster data transfer rates. Terminal emulation is slowly but surely being phased out as the method for micro-to-mainframe connections. It is being replaced by LU 6.2 or local area networks.

Even though the micro-to-mainframe connection is a powerful communication link in the business environment, the next chapter covers an even more powerful one: local area networks.

ELECTRICAL PROTECTION FOR MICROS AND LANS

If you believe your microcomputer or local area network communications are immune to electrical power fluctuations, you may have serious problems, and possibly even physical damage to hardware or data files. We are concerned with two sources of power fluctuations: telephone companies and electric power utilities. *Telephone companies* provide electricity to communication equipment in buildings via telephone lines. The telephone companies only protect communication circuits from surges (power increases they call spikes) of over several hundred volts of direct current (dc). *Electric power utilities* provide electricity to buildings via the building wiring systems. The utilities only protect building electrical wiring systems from power surges of over several thousand volts. These surges can be catastrophic to your microcomputer, and even more so to files on a hard disk. *Surge protection devices* protect our equipment from power increases.

Communication Circuit Surge Device   Communication circuits may have an electrical spike that can destroy data on a disk. The normal voltage on a telephone line is 48 to 96 volts direct current, and it sometimes reaches a few hundred volts for ringing the telephone bell. The newer 32-bit microprocessor chips that operate at 32- and 40-megahertz speeds may be affected by the shorter and weaker spikes that did not affect earlier versions of these chips. *Spikes* are high magnitude, split-second voltage increases on communication circuits that can disrupt computer operations or communications and even damage equipment. They can be caused by many things, the most important of which is lightning that strikes on or near a communication circuit and causes a huge increase in voltage. Spikes are read as fault signals, thereby causing malfunctions, loss of a data communication circuit, or damage to data on a disk.

What you need is some method of protecting the communication system from surges that telephone circuits may let slip through to your building premises. A *surge* is an increase in voltage, and a *sag* is a decrease in voltage. Surges destroy modems, and sags cause loss of the communication circuit carrier wave. Protection is needed between the modem and the incoming telephone circuits. You should be aware that the telephone company's protection devices may not respond until the voltage on an incoming telephone line (*not* the electricity from the public utility) approaches several hundred volts. Keep this fact in mind when you think about protection devices for your telecommunication equipment, especially the PBX switchboards.

Several commercial devices are available that can perform the surge protection operation on telephone circuits/modems. One device has two modular telephone plugs (RJ-11 type) housed in a plastic body with a three-pronged 120-volt electrical plug sticking out from the back. The user plugs the electrical plug into the 120-volt ac power outlet, then plugs the modem into one side, and connects the other side to the wall socket for the incoming telephone line.

Because some of these devices cost only $20, it may be cost effective to purchase surge protection devices for the modem on your microcomputer, as well as for a larger network that uses communications, such as a local area network or a cluster of microcomputers with a micro-to-mainframe connection through modems. Small devices are available that plug into the telephone jack for protection of modems from spikes, surges, and sags. Although this type of equipment usually is purchased for the larger digital PBX switchboards, it can be used to protect individual modems, software, and microcomputers from incoming surges that can burn out microprocessor chips in the modem.

To give your microcomputer and disk units complete protection from fluctuations in electricity, you may need different types of protection, although they can be built into the same box.

Electrical Power Surge Device   Consider a device that protects against surges in power. The power we are talking about here is the electricity produced by electric utilities to provide light and power to our homes and businesses. Electric utilities tend to refer to voltage increases on electric power lines as surges, whereas communication workers tend to refer to voltage increases on communication circuits as spikes. You should be aware that some surge protectors can handle electrical and communication power increases because they have both three-prong connector plugs for 120-volt electricity and RJ-11 plugs for communication circuits. Surge protection devices may cost anywhere from $20 to $100. They protect equipment from *transients,* which are short-duration high amplitude surges, and spikes of voltage. These are caused when a utility switches lines, nearby power lines are hit by lightning, there is intermittent operation of nearby electrical motors, a large group of lights is turned on, or there is other electrical noise (which is electrical interference superimposed on the normal voltage sine wave).

Electrical noise occurs when power lines pick up high frequency waves and "hash" from automobile ignition systems, transformers, fluorescent lights, static electricity, and lightning storms. Voltage fluctuations (sags and surges) are variations on the magnitude of incoming voltage. Sags are fluctuations caused by voltage loss during power transmission, uneven regulation of the voltage, and intentional lowering of voltage by utilities during peak operating periods—commonly called a brownout.

Brownouts are long-term undervoltages that may last a few minutes or even hours. The electric utilities often initiate brownouts when peak demand exceeds generating capacity and they have to reduce the amount of power provided to their customers. Brownouts cause computer malfunctions and hardware damage the same way an instantaneous sag does by depriving the logic circuits, modems, and disk drives of the level of voltage they need to operate properly.

By contrast, *blackouts* are extended zero-volt conditions that may last for minutes, hours, or even days. The causes of blackouts include ground faults, accidents, lightning strikes, or other acts of nature. The most obvious effect of a blackout is a system crash. Damage to disk drives and other system components occurs when a blackout causes a sudden power loss.

A surge protection device provides instantaneous regulation of voltage input, but you should not expect too much from such inexpensive devices. They are designed primarily to protect against surges; little protection is provided against sags because it takes some type of battery or capacitor to do this effectively. All such devices have a minimum of filtering to clean up electrical noise.

For these devices to work effectively, the ground should not have a resistance greater than 5 ohms. (An *ohm* is a unit that determines the amount of difficulty an electric current encounters when trying to move. An insulator like glass has a high ohmic value, whereas a conductor like copper has a low ohmic value.) A surge device connects the active electrical wires to the ground. If the surge protector detects a surge, it very quickly becomes a short circuit (very low resistance path) between the conductor on which the surge appears and the ground conductor, thus draining away the surge before it can get to a sensitive piece of electronic equipment. The surge device should clamp the line (shunt the surge) at a value of voltage approximately 10 to 15 percent over the value expected on the line. Some surge protectors built to shunt a surge of electricity from the 120-volt ac power also have RJ-11 plugs so they can shunt a surge coming in on the telephone lines supplied by the telephone company.

Power Line Conditioner (PLC)   You also may need *power line conditioners* that protect against "dirty" power and very minor undervoltages or sags in power levels. They also protect against surges. You can see what dirty power does when a power drill or blender causes interference on your television set. A full-featured PLC not only isolates electrical noise, but it also regulates the voltage to the microcomputer. In other words, these devices control both the quality and quantity of power to microcomputers. Typically, PLCs use an isolation transformer to filter out any electrical noise. Voltage regulators also maintain power quantity by keeping power within an acceptable range.

Microcomputers are quite susceptible to sags, which are undervoltages lasting approximately eight milliseconds or longer. Undervoltages can cause electronic systems to lose memory if the voltage falls below approximately 87 percent of its rated voltage. They also might cause a microcomputer to reboot suddenly. A typical power line conditioner converts ac input of 95 to 130 volts into a constant 120-volt level.

Some power line conditioners can handle very short voltage variations as great as +15 or −15 percent, regulating them down to a +3 or −3 percent level of electrical variation. What you get is protection against very minor sags, surges, and dirty electrical power.

Uninterruptible Power Supply (UPS)   A third device you should consider for protecting microcomputers, communications, and especially local area networks is an *uninterruptible power supply* that allows your system to continue functioning, even if there is a total loss of power. These devices also protect against sags, surges, brownouts, and blackouts, and may include built-in power line conditioners. When the power goes to zero, the system automatically switches over from the public utility-furnished electrical power to the unit's built-in batteries. Because this function involves a switching time, the faster the UPS system can switch over to batteries, the less the likelihood that you will lose valuable data or cause hardware damage. Switchover might take from 2 to 8 milliseconds.

On the other hand, a continuous UPS system has no switchover time because it operates on batteries and generates true sine wave power at all times. You want true sine wave power output instead of a square wave because square wave power may damage electronic circuits if it is used for a lengthy period of time. Even though they cost a bit more, a continuous UPS is preferable to one that switches from public utility power to batteries.

UPS backup systems usually are rated in watts; you might see them advertised at 90 watts, 200 watts, 400 watts, 600 watts, and so forth. Some of the systems have a *volt-amps* (VA) *rating* that is approximately the same as watts. Moreover, some systems now show the ratings in both watts and volt-amps. If you want to convert volt-amps into watts, the phase angle (0) between the voltage and current waveform must be known. The cosine of this angle or "power factor" times volts times amps equals real power in watts:

$$\text{Watts} = \text{Volts} \times \text{Amps} \times \text{Power Factor}$$

For instance, computer installations usually have an average power factor of 0.89 lagging. The current waveform lags behind voltage. In other words, the typical computer loads are inductive rather than capacitive because most loads are inductive or resistive. Capacitive loads are rare and usually are canceled out by the larger inductive component. Therefore, if 400 watts of power are needed, the UPS should be rated at 450 volt-amps. A quick conversion equation is to divide the watts by 0.89 to get the volt-amps:

$$\frac{400 \text{ watts}}{0.89} = 449.44 \text{ volt-amps}$$

Another method of calculating the needed UPS size is to look at the name plate on the back of each microcomputer, printer, and monitor and record their voltage and amperage requirements. Multiply these figures together to get the volt-amps requirement for each device. For instance, a monitor drawing 0.6 amps at 120 volts requires 72 volt-amps (VA).

The needed UPS size is determined by adding the number of watts used by your microcomputer, modem, video monitor, and printer. (Many users do not include the printer because it requires so much electrical power.) If this total is 400 watts, then you should buy a 400-watt, 450 volt-amp UPS system to serve as backup.

If you intend to run the system on backup batteries for a long period after the loss of power, let us say more than 20 minutes, then you should buy a UPS backup that has a rating approximately 25 percent higher than the total wattage or volt-amps of the system. Using the previous example, you would want a 500-watt UPS even though your equipment uses only 400 watts. This extra wattage is needed to avoid overheating the UPS system electrical components and possible burnout of the unit. UPS systems are far more expensive than surge devices or power line conditioners. Backup power supply systems may cost anywhere from $250 for a 200-watt system to $700 for a 450-watt system. Prices vary depending on whether there is a built-in power line conditioner and whether the UPS switches over to batteries or uses its own batteries all the time (no switchover time) for continuous protection.

The importance of surge/sag devices was highlighted by a Bell Laboratories study that found the number one electrical problem faced by microcomputers is voltage sags. They account for 87 percent of all electrical problems monitored.

Static Electricity   One other form of electricity that may "zap" your system is *static electricity*. Now that we have discussed how to protect ourselves from incoming electrical problems, whether they originate from the telephone circuits or from electrical power, we need to consider our own self-generated static electricity. As we walk across a floor, we can generate a charge of static electricity that can be as high as 15,000 volts. Touching a circuit board or a disk unit while carrying that much static electricity can cause problems that result in permanent damage, erasure of data from a disk, or just an ordinary misread by a disk unit. To avoid such problems, always make sure that the equipment is grounded and that you have discharged any static electricity from your body (by touching a ground) before handling new circuit boards or removing them from your microcomputer. The best practice is to touch anything that is metal and grounded before you start working inside the computer.

If you have such problems as unexplained data losses, unexplained lockup of microcomputer keyboards, scrambled information, and intermittent unexplainable bugs, the microcomputer operators may have too much static electricity in their bodies. To solve this problem, make sure their chairs are placed on an antistatic grounding mat. This is a floor mat that is grounded in such a way that stepping on it or wheeling a chair across it causes the person or chair to be "drained" of any static electricity. Also check to make sure the microcomputer electric plugs are grounded properly.

KEY TERMS

A/B switchbox
AUTOEXEC.BAT
Blackout
Booting
Brownout
Bulletin board system (BBS)
Capture buffer
COM1/COM2 port
COMMAND.COM
Communication parameters
CONFIG.SYS
Cyclical redundancy check (CRC)

Disk server
Diskless microcomputer
DOS
Downloading
Electrical noise
External DOS command
External modem
File redirector
File server
File transfer
Flow control
Handshaking
Internal DOS command
Internal modem

ISDN terminal adapter card
KERMIT
LANBIOS
LapLink
LapLink Mac
Mac-to-host communication
Mac-to-PC communication
MacLink Plus
MacWorkStation
Micro-to-mainframe link
Micro-to-mainframe server
Micro-to-micro connection

Microcomputer

Microprocessor

MNP

Multiuser system micro-
to-mainframe link

NETBIOS

Network server

Null modem cable

Ohm

OS/2

PC-to-host communication

PC-to-PC communication

PC-to-printer
communication

Peer-to-peer

Personal computer (PC)

Ping-ponging

Power line conditioner

ProComm Plus

Program-to-program link

Protocol

Random access memory
(RAM)

Read only memory (ROM)

Sag

Script

Serial port

Sliding window protocol

Smart cable

Spike

Static electricity

Statistical duplexing

Streaming protocol

Surge

Surge protection device

Terminal emulation

Transient program area
(TPA)

Transients (electrical)

UART/USART chip

Uninterruptible power
supply

Universal Asynchronous
Receiver and
Transmitter (UART)

Universal Synchronous
Asynchronous Receiver
and Transmitter
(USART)

Uploading

Virus

Volt-amp rating

WXMODEM

X-ON/X-OFF

XMODEM

YMODEM

ZMODEM

SELECTED REFERENCES

1. Brinker, Scott J. "Corporate Bulletin Board Systems: Customer Support and More in the 1990s," *Telecommunications,* vol. 25, no. 11, November 1991, pp. 33, 35–36.

2. Byrd, Mike. "Improving Information Access," *PC Magazine,* vol. 10, no. 5, April 30, 1991, pp. 101–104ff. [Cover story on asynchronous communication software.]

3. *Byte: The Small Systems Journal.* Published monthly by McGraw-Hill, 1 Phoenix Hill Lane, Peterborough, N.H. 03458, 1975– .

4. Carrell, Jeffrey L., and David Greenfield. "Across the Great Divide: PC-to-Mac Connections," *PC Magazine,* vol. 11, no. 9, May 12, 1992, pp. 173–174, 176.

5. *Datapro PC Communications.* Published monthly by Datapro Research Corp., 1805 Underwood Boulevard, Delran, N.J. 08075, 1986– .

6. Dvorak, John C., and Nick Anis. *Dvorak's Guide to PC Telecommunications.* Berkeley, Calif.: Osborne/McGraw-Hill, 1990.

7. FitzGerald, Jerry. *Online Auditing for Microcomputers.* Redwood City, Calif.: Jerry FitzGerald & Associates, 1987.

8. Freed, Les. "High-End PC-to-Mac LAN Solutions," *PC Magazine,* vol. 11, no. 9, May 12, 1992, pp. 203, 206–207, 211, 216, 218, 220–221. (See also related boxes on pp. 182, 190, 198–199.)

9. Gofton, Peter W. *Mastering Serial Communications.* Berkeley, Calif.: SYBEX, 1986.

10. Gralla, Preston. "Printer Sharing Without a Network," *PC/Computing,* vol. 4, no. 11, November 1991, pp. 267–272.

11. *Info World: The PC News Weekly*. Published weekly by Popular Computing, 1060 Marsh Road, Suite C-200, Menlo Park, Calif. 94025, 1979– .

12. Magidson, Steve. "Portable Connectivity," *Network Computing,* vol. 3, no. 5, May 1992, pp. 80–81, 84–89.

13. *PC Tech Journal for the IBM Systems Professional*. Published monthly by Ziff-Davis Publishing Co., 1 Park Avenue, New York, N.Y. 10016, 1983– .

14. *PC Week*. Published weekly by Ziff-Davis Publishing Co., 1 Park Avenue, New York, N.Y. 10016, 1983– .

15. *Personal Computing*. Published monthly by Hayden Publishing Co., 10 Mulholland Drive, Hasbrouck Heights, N.J. 07604, 1976– .

16. Rizzo, John. "PC-to-Mac File Exchange: A Range of Approaches," *PC Magazine,* vol. 11, no. 9, May 12, 1992, pp. 181–182, 187. (See also related boxes on pp. 197–199.)

17. Rizzo, Tony. "Building Enterprise Applications: Bridging PCs and Mainframes," *Network Computing,* vol. 2, no. 6, June 1991, pp. 50–51, 54–56, 58.

18. Salem, Joe. "Tools for Wide-Area Communications: Bulletin Board Software," *PC Magazine,* vol. 10, no. 14, September 10, 1991, pp. 231–232, 239–243ff.

19. Wolverton, Van. *Running MS DOS,* 5th ed. Redmond, Wash.: Microsoft Corporation, 1991.

QUESTIONS/PROBLEMS

1. In what way was the advent of the microprocessor circuit chip significant?
2. What two items are required to network microcomputers?
3. Define the two types of memory found in microcomputers.
4. Describe the purpose of COMMAND.COM, CONFIG.SYS, and AUTOEXEC.BAT.
5. What is the purpose of DOS?
6. Describe the two types of DOS commands.
7. How does a diskless microcomputer boot up?
8. Explain the primary benefit of diskless microcomputers.
9. This chapter discusses both communication software and the software for microcomputer protocols. How do these two types of software differ?
10. What are the three interfaces required for networking applications?
11. What distinguishes a file redirector from a file server?
12. In the context of NETBIOS, what does peer-to-peer mean?
13. What is the primary function of NETBIOS?
14. Briefly describe the function of Interrupt 5Ch.
15. It is said that NETBIOS communication is limited because it cannot allow transmission across two incompatible networks. Name one way this limitation can be overcome.
16. What is a function call?
17. Briefly describe the function of Interrupt 21h.
18. List three commercial communication software packages.

19. What are the two ways in which files are uploaded and downloaded and how do they differ?

20. What two characteristics are common to all file transfer protocols?

21. Why is flow control necessary in microcomputer communications?

22. Four ways protocols handle the requirement for error-free communication between microcomputers are discussed in this chapter. What are they?

23. Name five sliding window protocols.

24. Why are sliding window protocols gaining in popularity?

25. Briefly describe how a sliding window protocol works.

26. With regard to micro-to-mainframe communication protocols, what are some of the problems that were mentioned in this chapter? Can they be overcome?

27. Name some file transfer protocols.

28. Why did Tymnet develop X.PC?

29. What does the script do in a protocol?

30. Some of the microcomputer protocols in the chapter deal with asynchronous microcomputers. Two of them send asynchronous data over synchronous networks in unique ways. Name the two protocols and describe how they use synchronous networks.

31. What is ping-ponging?

32. What is handshaking?

33. What are the two types of microcomputer modems and how do they differ?

34. Six ways to transmit data between microcomputers were mentioned in this chapter. What are they?

35. When connecting Apple and IBM microcomputers for communications, what two items must be purchased?

36. What two problems are associated with transferring files between Macintosh microcomputers and IBM compatibles and how can they be solved?

37. Two communication programs were described for handling Apple and IBM communications. What are they and how do they differ?

38. Several legal issues pertain to bulletin board systems. What are they and how do they affect both users and bulletin board operators?

39. What are downloading and uploading?

40. What options are available for connecting microcomputers to mainframes?

41. How would you go about establishing a micro-to-mainframe connection for IBM PCs or compatibles?

42. What is the purpose of emulation in micro-to-mainframe connections?

43. Why are connections between Macintosh microcomputers and host mainframes so difficult?

44. What are the functions of a network server on a micro-to-mainframe link?

45. What is the primary advantage of clustering a set of microcomputers for a micro-to-mainframe link?

46. How do disk servers differ from file servers?

47. What is one of the most troublesome problems related to micro-to-mainframe links?

48. It was stated in this chapter that some of IBM's newer features link microcomputers and mainframes in new ways. What are some of these ways?

49. What practical effect is the use of digital communications having on micro-to-mainframe links?

50. Why must you be concerned with electrical protection for your microcomputers or local area networks?

51. How do electrical spikes, surges, and sags differ?

52. What needs to be protected from fluctuations in electricity?

53. What are the four types of protection for microcomputer equipment?

54. Name the three sources of electricity that can erase microcomputer disks, damage chips, or cause disk misreads.

55. How many bits wide is the transfer path in the Intel 80386 and Motorola 68030 microprocessor chips?

56. If you have a microcomputer, compare the specifications of your system with those enumerated in the seventh paragraph of this chapter.

57. What is the difference between RAM and ROM?

58. Define booting.

59. Define DOS.

60. Are short haul modems and null modem cables the same thing? Explain your answer. The answer is in the chapter, but use the Glossary too.

61. What is DOS's command processor called?

62. What is a TPA?

63. What is NETBIOS?

64. What is the difference between a "file transfer" and a "capture buffer" transfer of data?

65. Which is the simplest (least sophisticated) protocol described in this chapter?

66. If a RJ-11 telephone jack plug is used for a two-wire circuit (this is the same line as the one on your telephone at home), what plug is used on a four-wire circuit? *HINT:* See Glossary.

67. Figure 10-10 uses one modem pair to connect five microcomputers to the host. How many modem pairs are required if the philosophy of Figure 10-9 is used?

68. Which is more powerful, a disk server or a file server?

69. When is it appropriate to use null modem cables?

70. What is the difference between a microprocessor and a microcomputer?

71. Describe the functions of UART and USART.

72. What is the purpose of a serial interface card?

73. Why is the UART/USART chip not connected directly to the serial port RS232 connector plug on the microcomputer?

74. Describe the YMODEM-G protocol.

75. How does an error controlling modem differ from other modems?

76. What is a smart cable?

77. What is the purpose of an A/B switchbox? Name one advantage and one disadvantage of this device.

78. What is the purpose of an automatic printer sharing device?

79. What are the two primary reasons for organizations wanting to have a local area network?

80. Why would an organization choose to use a printer sharing device instead of setting up a local area network?

81. Describe a micro-to-mainframe server.

82. How does a brownout differ from a blackout? Why should you be concerned about either one of them?

NEXT DAY AIR SERVICE CUMULATIVE CASE STUDY

Background on Next Day Air Service

After much heated discussion, the board of directors has decided to relax its demand for an internetworked LAN/WAN. To reduce costs, voice call requests for information will use the multiplexed network (WAN) and the Tampa employee who responds will use the LAN or a micro-to-minicomputer connection at headquarters. You realize that in the future some form of distributed processing using the Atlanta LAN may be a necessity.

Because Next Day Air Service already has purchased several of the latest model microcomputers as upgrades for the older personal computers that were used by the Sales and Marketing Division, you begin to examine the possibility of using one of these machines as a LAN server. The big question is the best way to accomplish the inquiry and processing functions. Should it be a micro-to-mainframe (actually a minicomputer) connection or a local area network or a combination of the two?

In an unrelated matter, Mr. Coone has read a report submitted by a division manager who is concerned about electrical problems the corporate headquarters is experiencing. Mr. Coone has asked you to examine where electrical problems could affect the network and to develop some possible solutions. You believe the problems might be created by a nearby manufacturing plant when it begins operations every morning. You suspect this because the electrical problems only seem to happen shortly after you arrive at work each morning and again in the evening.

You discuss these situations with your project group. The subject of microcomputer protocols resurfaces while you are exploring the different possibilities for linking the remote offices directly into the server at Tampa versus using voice calls to Tampa employees. Next Day Air Service requires rapid response to queries and expects all data concerning shipments and orders to be accessible to all remote requesters.

Questions/Problems for the Next Day Air Service Case

1. How can some of Next Day Air Service's microcomputers be connected to one of the minicomputers?

2. Why would Next Day Air Service want to install uninterruptible power supplies or surge protectors on its network equipment?

3. Assume that NDAS allowed its customers to dial into the Tampa LAN server. In this case, which protocol would be best: X-ON/X-OFF, XMODEM, or XMODEM-CRC?

Chapter Eleven

LOCAL AREA NETWORKS (LANS)

This chapter introduces the concept of local area networks and defines their use. It describes how to install a local area network, its topologies, and its protocols. Other subjects are Ethernet, token passing, Arcnet, FDDI, operating systems, servers, software, bridges, routers, and gateways, cabling, costs, implementation, management, LAN selection, and LAN security.

INTRODUCTION TO LANs

Today's "hot button" is linking microcomputers into a network that provides the standard business office functions of word processing, electronic mail, file sharing, file transfer, printer sharing, and processing capabilities. A large organization may have numerous local area networks connected together, and also have them connected to the organization's host mainframe computer. Today, another alternative is to connect the LANs together in such a way as to eliminate the host mainframe altogether. A local area network-to-host mainframe connection is just like the micro-to-mainframe connection, except it has the additional capability of being able to connect many microcomputers to form an interdepartmental or intradepartmental network that is independent of the host mainframe but connected to it.

A *local area network* is a group of microcomputers or other workstation devices that are located in the same general area and connected by a common cable (see Figure 11-1). The network is located within a small or confined area. Although it is not confined like a computer or a micro-to-mainframe link, it definitely is more restricted than the large corporate or government wide area or backbone networks that go between cities and even countries. A LAN interconnects microcomputers, word processors, minicomputers, facsimile machines, voice/data PBXs, executive workstations, and other hardware, for the purpose of communicating among themselves and ultimately with the host mainframe computer or public data networks (PDNs).

A LAN covers a clearly defined local area: a single building, a group of buildings within a business firm's property, a campus, or a confined area within a city if the

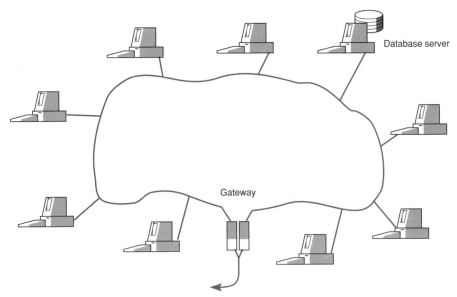

Figure 11-1   Local area network (LAN) configuration.

conditions are correct. It is not limited to communication within that defined local area because LANs provide easy access to the outside world through a gateway to other networks. Aside from their limited spread of a few miles, local area networks have a capacity for very high speed transmission. With lower speed transmission being available on standard telephone circuits, a LAN has added functionality because it can provide speeds from 50,000 to 100 million bits per second. Today's local area networks commonly operate at 2 to 10 million bits per second. Bandwidths are available to support very high speed transmission for fully animated motion of graphics, full-color video, digital voice telephone conversations, or any other high data rate analog or digital signals an organization may want to place onto a LAN.

Local area networks operate outside of the government's "regulated" environment, so an organization wanting to install a LAN does not have to be licensed or obtain approvals from any federal or state communication regulatory bodies.

ENTERPRISE-WIDE NETWORKS

The ability to interconnect local area networks that also interconnect with other networks has led to the term *enterprise-wide network*. For example, if we connect two local area networks it is an *internetwork;* if we connect several buildings it is a facility-wide network; but if we connect all the networks within an organization it is an enterprise-wide network. Some organizations may call their enterprise-wide network a backbone network (BN). In other cases, the enterprise-wide network includes all three network types (LAN, BN, and WAN).

The various network configurations were introduced in Chapter 6. Now we want to discuss how local area networks (LANs) relate to wide area networks (WANs), metropolitan area networks (MANs), and backbone or enterprise-wide networks. As we progress through this section, we will see how changes in networking technologies sometimes make it difficult to distinguish the various types of networks from one another.

Wide Area Networks (WANs) Versus LANs   *Wide area networks* (WANs) are nothing more than the traditional long distance networks developed by business organizations and government agencies. Wide area networks usually are made up of leased circuits configured to fit the unique business requirements of the organization developing such a network. The primary difference between a wide area network and a local area network (LAN) is that WANs cover a wider geographical area and the circuits usually are leased from common carrier telephone companies, whereas LANs are local communication networks usually contained within a single building, campus, or corporate facility in which there is no requirement for the communication circuit to cross a public road or someone else's property. Starting with the LAN in the upper left corner of Figure 11-2, you can see the relationship between a LAN, BN, MAN, and WAN.

Metropolitan Area Networks Versus LANs   A *metropolitan area network* (MAN) generally spans a geographical area that encompasses a city or county. The various nodes may be anywhere from several hundred yards to 20 or 30 miles apart. What constitutes the geographical boundaries of a metropolitan area network is loosely defined, but a statewide network normally is called a wide area network instead of a metropolitan area network. MANs interconnect various buildings or other facilities within a citywide area, which generally means they are much larger than LANs. Like WANs, they also use leased common carrier circuits and intersect both public roads and other people's property. In Figure 11-2, McClellan Air Force Base is one facility in the Sacramento area that is interconnected by means of a MAN.

The concept of metropolitan area networks is relatively new to networking. The two primary standards governing MANs are the IEEE 802.6 and the Fiber Distributed Data Interface (FDDI). Under IEEE 802.6, frames are segmented into fixed-size packets for transmission. This protocol supports four priority levels of messages, as well as circuit-switched voice traffic. Its performance is independent of distance and the number of nodes on the network, making IEEE 802.6 also suitable for high speed local area network data transmissions. Many of the regional Bell Operating Companies are considering using the IEEE 802.6 standard on public MANs. These public MANs, known as switched multimegabit digital service (SMDS), are discussed in Chapter 7.

The FDDI standard also is being considered for use in both MANs and LANs. The FDDI is a fiber optic token ring that runs at very high speeds—100 million bits per second. FDDI uses a multiple token-ring protocol that generates a new "free" token at the end of a frame. This technique allows the network to transmit multiple frames simultaneously. We cover FDDI in more detail later in this chapter.

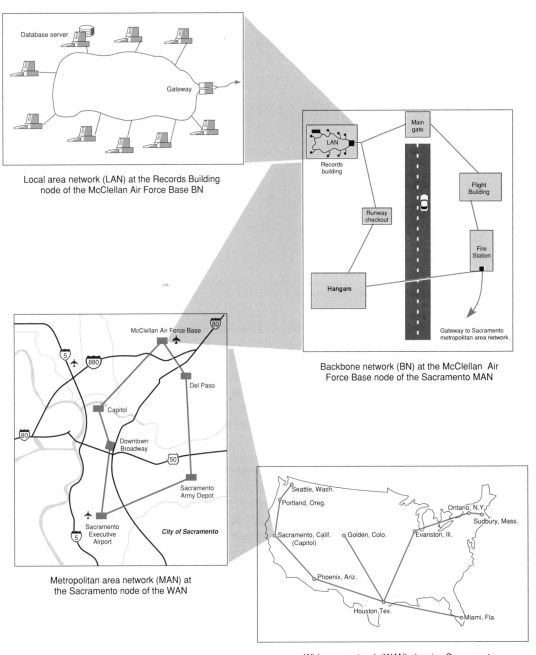

Local area network (LAN) at the Records Building
node of the McClellan Air Force Base BN

Backbone network (BN) at the McClellan Air
Force Base node of the Sacramento MAN

Metropolitan area network (MAN) at
the Sacramento node of the WAN

Wide area network (WAN) showing Sacramento
connected to nine other cities throughout the U.S.

Figure 11-2 Shows the hierarchical relationship of a local area network (LAN) to a backbone network (BN) to a metropolitan area network (MAN) to a wide area network (WAN). See the Network Configurations section in Chapter 6 (page 228) for more about how these four networks relate to one another.

Backbone Networks (BNs) Versus LANs   A *backbone network* is a large central network to which all the computers within an organization are connected. Backbone networks usually connect everything on a single company or government site. On the other hand, a backbone network may be an enterprise-wide network if it connects everything within a company, regardless of whether it is throughout the country or even across international boundaries around the world. This blurs the distinction of how we define enterprise-wide, backbone, and wide area networks. A backbone network can have one or numerous LANs attached to it. The Records Building LAN in Figure 11-2 connects to the McClellan backbone.

At the beginning of this section, we mentioned that changing technology makes it difficult to distinguish these various types of networks from one another. Moreover, local area networks were defined earlier as being confined to a small area, not crossing public thoroughfares, and as being exempt from government regulation. Now it is possible for a number of local area networks to be internetworked so they can operate as a wide area network without interconnecting through either a MAN or a BN. If several local area networks are located in different parts of the country, they can be interconnected to operate like a wide area network through the use of LAN gateways and high speed circuits. Figure 11-3 shows a satellite circuit interconnecting two LANs so they operate like a WAN. T-1 and microwave circuits also can be used to interconnect LANs. As you can see, rigid definitions no longer apply to this area of communications.

INSTALLING A LOCAL AREA NETWORK

There are two basic reasons for developing a local area network: physical sharing and logical sharing. *Physical sharing* refers to one microcomputer sharing a device attached to another microcomputer. For example, one microcomputer can share a printer or disk drive that is located in another microcomputer at another station or node. The main benefit of physical sharing is cost savings, especially in the area of sharing laser printers.

Logical sharing refers to business applications that may require several users to access the same data files. For example, a single logical database might be maintained so two or more microcomputers can share the contents of the database.

Most microcomputers are not delivered with an interface port that can be connected to a second microcomputer. (The exception is Macintosh microcomputers, which have a built-in capability called the AppleTalk port.) As a result, one of the first things that must be done when installing a local area network is to open each microcomputer and install a special network circuit card. Next, each microcomputer must be connected to the other microcomputers in the local area network via wire pairs, coaxial cable, or optical fiber. Finally, the local area network software must be loaded into each microcomputer installed on the local area network. The following five sections are a more detailed explanation of how to install a simple local area network.

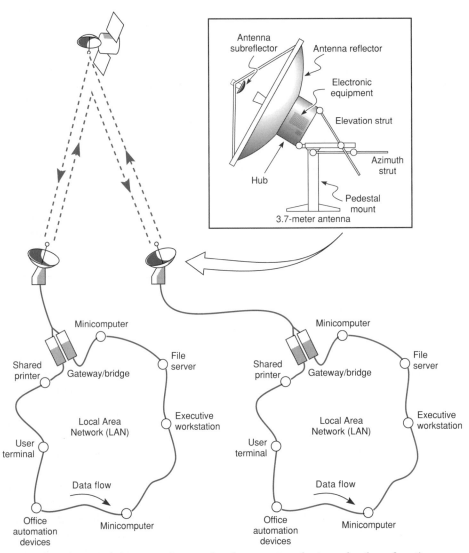

Figure 11-3 Satellite link connecting two local area networks to make them function as a wide area network.

- Circuit cards and cabling
- Server microcomputer or user microcomputer
- Installing the LAN software
- Developing a network profile
- The log-in process

Circuit Cards and Cabling   Assuming you already know which local area network you want to purchase and you have the circuit cards, cables, and software in hand, the process might proceed as follows. Each microcomputer that is to be connected to the LAN must be opened so you can install a *network circuit card* in one of its available slots.

Next, each microcomputer must be cabled to the other microcomputers in the network. The most common way of doing this is to connect the microcomputers together in a *daisy chain arrangement*. The first and last microcomputers in the chain are given a terminating plug to indicate to the network that no other microcomputers are attached to the chain. Most simple networks use a 9-pin plug similar to the one used on the serial communication port (COM1). This cable is plugged into the newly installed circuit card, and the other end is plugged into a circuit card in the next microcomputer to be connected to the LAN. Each network circuit card has two 9-pin plug positions.

In a simple inexpensive local area network, these cable lengths range from approximately 15 to 100 feet. Incidentally, a small local area network of this type might cost $300 to $400 for the first microcomputer on the network and $200 to $300 for each additional microcomputer. This cost includes the circuit cards, a cable for each microcomputer, and the appropriate network software.

The local area network software may require the setting of certain DIP switches or the moving of a jumper on the network circuit card. A *jumper* is a small connector that fits over a set of pins on a circuit card; it is used to connect the pins together. Now that the circuit cards have been installed and the cables have been connected from circuit card to circuit card in each microcomputer, we must decide which microcomputers are to be designated as servers and which are to be designated as users.

Server Microcomputer or User Microcomputer   In a typical local area network, distinctions are made among the various types of microcomputers as to their network function. For example, *server microcomputers* have resources such as printers or disk drives that are available for use by other microcomputers on the LAN. On the other hand, *user microcomputers* (sometimes called *client microcomputers*) need to use the resources made available by the server microcomputers. Typically, the most powerful microcomputer on the LAN (probably an 80386 or 80486) is assigned to be the server. This is called the *dedicated server* approach.

Some local area network software does not require this distinction between a dedicated server microcomputer and the user microcomputers. If the local area network does not require this definition, it can be classed as a *peer-to-peer network* in which any microcomputer can function as both a server and a user. A peer-to-peer network gives every microcomputer access to all of the network's resources.

In a network of peers, any microcomputer can share its hard disk and printer with any other microcomputer. The network's users create names for their local printers and disk volumes and designate them as sharable network resources. Other users map their printer ports and DOS drive letters for the hard disks to these resource names from the DOS prompt. Unlike server-based networks similar to those operating with Novell's NetWare, peer-to-peer networks allow you to share resources attached to any microcomputer without going through an intermediary like a central microcomputer server. On the other hand, if one of the network's microcomputers does not have a hard disk or a printer, you might as well configure it as a user microcomputer.

At this point of the installation you have installed the circuit cards, connected the microcomputers by daisy-chaining the cable between them, and made some decisions about which microcomputers are to be servers and which are to be users. The most difficult part comes next: installing the network software on each of the LAN's microcomputers.

Installing the LAN Software   This section deals with two LAN installation issues. The first is the amount of memory available to the network and how it relates to loading LAN applications. The second discusses the steps required to install the LAN's software.

As you learned in Chapter 10, BIOS (Basic Input/Output System) is a set of programs within the DOS operating system. The DOS BIOS is designed to operate within a single microcomputer environment; that is, it is not designed to work on a network. To enable DOS to communicate over a network, IBM defined an extension to the operating system called *NETBIOS* (NETwork Basic Input/Output System). Local area networks require NETBIOS to connect DOS (a single-user operating system) to the network hardware cards installed in each of the network's microcomputers. Local area network vendors have their own software (sometimes called LANBIOS) to serve as the interface with DOS through the NETBIOS.

It is important to recognize that local area network software resides in the memory of each microcomputer on the network. Because DOS is limited to 640,000 bytes of total random access memory (RAM) space, this can have a detrimental effect on the applications run at each of the network's microcomputers. As you already know, DOS uses some of this memory, any necessary TSR (terminate and stay resident) programs use some of this memory, and now the local area network software also must use some of this memory space. The point is that if too much of the 640,000 bytes of memory is used for these purposes, there may not be enough memory to run your word processor, spreadsheet, or other applications requiring a large amount of memory.

Some of the smaller local area networks only use from 2,000 to 15,000 bytes of memory, depending on the number of microcomputers on the LAN. The microcomputer designated as the network server always uses more memory (30,000 to 50,000 bytes). One of the solutions to this problem, which is used in larger local area networks, is to buy a *memory expansion card* or add memory to the motherboard so the LAN software can be loaded outside of the 640,000 bytes of RAM in DOS. This is a very practical solution when you have a large LAN with a single dedicated server because this extra memory card is required only in the server microcomputer, and not in the other user microcomputers on the LAN.

The actual process of installing the LAN's software consists of installing the network operating system, creating a station profile for each microcomputer, and logging onto the LAN. Installing the LAN's *network operating system* (LAN software) can be done in two ways, depending on whether you have a small, inexpensive LAN or a much larger one. At this point, you should be following the instruction procedure in the documentation manual to install the LAN operating system software onto the hard disk of the server.

The larger networks, like Novell, completely replace DOS with their own network operating system. One minor disadvantage of this procedure is that you must re-format the hard disk of the microcomputer that is to function as the server. On a smaller LAN, DOS is not replaced; it is installed on all the LAN's microcomputers.

Next you need to establish a network name for each microcomputer and load the *LANBIOS* (Local Area Network Basic Input/Output System), which is the LAN operating system software that makes the interface with DOS. At this point, the network operating system (LANBIOS) is loaded onto the microcomputer that just booted up. This microcomputer, along with every other LAN microcomputer, must have a unique network name because all messages must be addressed to a specific microcomputer, and this unique network name is its address on the network. At this point the LAN software has been installed, and now it is time to develop a network profile.

Developing a Network Profile   The next step is to establish a network profile for each microcomputer on the LAN. This *network profile,* also called a *station profile,* specifies what resources on this microcomputer are available for network use by other microcomputers and which devices or people are allowed what access to the network. The network profile normally is configured once when the network is set up, and it remains in place until someone makes a change. In a local area network, the server hard disk may have various attributes that can or cannot be accessed by a specific network user. Furthermore, a specific password may be required to gain access to the network (boot up).

If a device such as a hard disk on one of the network's microcomputers is not included on the network profile list, it cannot be used by another microcomputer on the network. For example, if you have a hard disk (C:) on your microcomputer and your microcomputer is connected to this LAN but the hard disk is not included on the network profile assignment list, then no other microcomputer on the network can access the hard disk on your microcomputer.

In addition to profiling such devices as disks and printers, you must configure a *user profile* for each person who is expected to use the LAN. The user profile adds an element of security to the LAN; therefore, each device and each user are assigned various access codes (names). When the LAN is operating, only those users with the correct code can use a specific device. Some local area networks even have special auditing files to keep track of who uses which resource.

By now the circuit cards have been installed and connected together with the cables, the server has been designated, the LAN's operating system software has been installed, a network profile has been recorded for each device, and a user profile has been recorded for each user. Now it is time to log-in to the network.

The Log-In Process   The last step is the log-in process. It is at this point that the intelligence of the software makes all the connections between the microcomputers, users, and devices like hard disks and printers. In larger local area networks like Novell, this is done automatically when you turn on the microcomputer because DOS has been replaced completely by the Novell version of DOS and its LANBIOS routines.

In smaller local area networks, the process of connecting to the LAN can be carried out by putting the proper commands into your AUTOEXEC.BAT file or by allowing the user to boot up with DOS and then enter the commands from the DOS prompt. Only two or three commands are required, depending on the local area network software.

The first command is a log-in command to identify the name of the user, the microcomputer (the unique network name for your microcomputer), and the name of the server containing the hard disk or printer you wish to use. A second command might assign, for example, the DOS designation D: to the hard disk on the server microcomputer. This command tells your microcomputer to look to the server microcomputer when you read or write to D: rather than to an internal disk on your own microcomputer. A third command might redirect any printing sent by an application on your microcomputer to the server microcomputer's printer rather than to the printer attached to your microcomputer.

At this point the local area network should be operational. The only tasks left are to make any necessary adjustments to the LAN and possibly debug it.

It should be noted that there are some very inexpensive printer sharing local area networks. These are not true local area networks because they do not allow sharing of files; they only share printers. In addition, they do not require circuit cards. They use their own software, and the two microcomputers are connected together by using the serial port (COM1). These inexpensive printer sharing LANs are discussed later in the Zero-Slot Sub-LAN section.

LEGAL ISSUES

There is a legal issue regarding the use of software on local area networks. This is a question of whether network users have the legal right to run a program purchased for a single user's computer on a local area network. The law says they do not! You must obtain a multiple user, per server, or a site license if you want to use single-computer software on a network. If we, as software users, blatantly violate the single-computer software license agreements, we may find that less software is available for sale in the future. Furthermore, many companies and government agencies now terminate employees who knowingly violate the licensing agreements for software they have purchased. Honesty and integrity are always the best paths to follow in this world of easily copied software.

One approach to controlling the number of copies of a particular application software package on a LAN is to use *LAN metering software*. This software controls the number of users who are allowed to access a particular software package at one time. A number of packages are available for this purpose, including ARGUS/n, Certus LAN, LANshell, LANtrail, LTAuditor, Netmenu, PreCursor, SiteLock, and Turnstyle.

The Software Publishers Association (SPA) in Washington, D.C., has an audit program for checking the number of illegal software copies on a network. Call 1-202-452-1600 for a copy of this audit program. The SPA consists of approximately 700 software publishers, and the audit program searches for copies of software produced by these companies. The SPA kit includes an application that scrutinizes directories in search of specific applications. You can eliminate illegal copies by searching for multiple copies of an application. If you have bought only one copy of a specific single-computer license application and find ten copies in use throughout the firm, your organization does not have control of its software resources. This situation may invite either legal action by a software producer or an unwanted virus spread through illegal software copying.

It is important to note that schools and training organizations must follow the same copyright laws as corporations and individuals. Special arrangements often can be made for site licenses or multiple license purchases. Moreover, many software producers offer special educational versions (like some of the software offered in conjunction with this book—see the Preface) or specially reduced prices for educational institutions.

WORD PROCESSING ON A LAN

Word processing on a local area network is similar to other word processing where only one microcomputer is used. For example, if you want to make changes to a report, the first thing you do on a single microcomputer is load the word processor by typing the appropriate command. With a LAN, you also type the command to load the word processor, but the microcomputer's network circuit card and LAN-BIOS send the command to the file server, which then decides whether the request can be handled. In this case, the file server learns the word processor is a read only program that is shared among users. Such a program can be used by many people at the same time, but none of them can modify it. The file server then loads the word processing program into your requesting microcomputer's memory, and the opening screen of the word processor appears on your screen.

To begin working, you request the file containing the report you want to modify. The microcomputer sends this command to the file server, which looks for the requested file and loads it into the memory of your microcomputer so you can begin working on it.

Suppose two other people are using the word processor while you are working on this file and they also decide they want to use the same file. When they request the file, the file server sends a message telling them the file is in use. In other words, the network locks out everyone else who may want to use that file at the same time you are using it. If you want to prevent everyone else from using this file at any time, it can be stored in a private directory to which only specified users are allowed access.

Now assume you finish modifying this file and type the command to save the modified version. Once again the file server takes your request, along with those of other network users, and acts on each request in turn. Then you type the print command, and the network begins the printing process.

The information to be printed is used to create a print image file that goes into the print queue or spooler. A record containing information about each file to be printed is stored in another file. Next, each print image file is transferred in its turn from the print queue to the appropriate printer. This process is executed in the background by a print program that is invisible to users. It takes place so efficiently that printing continues while the file server is carrying out other tasks in the foreground.

Let us illustrate this LAN process further with the following scenario. Laura, the manager of a communications department, plans to write a book on LANs with assistance from some of the other people in her department. Her first task is to create an outline that indicates how she plans to develop this book. Laura begins with an abstract describing what the book will contain, and then she adds chapter titles and subheads for each chapter. Next she chooses type fonts, page margins, page headers and footers, tab settings, and other style or format parameters that determine what her book will look like. Finally, Laura compiles a distribution list of those who are to work on the book, assigns a writer to each chapter, and determines which writers are to have access to chapters written by others. To achieve the last objective, she sets up security levels, with some chapter authors having greater access to chapter files than others.

When Laura saves her document, it is sent to the network server, which controls access to the file and keeps track of each chapter author. When Kevin, one of the chapter authors, accesses his microcomputer, he sees the book's abstract, Laura's instructions, and the chapters assigned to him. He can begin writing immediately and does not have to be concerned with the book's format. By preparing the outline and the book's format, Laura is assured the entire book will conform to a single format. If Kevin needs to refer to something written by one of the other authors, he will be able to read that chapter but not modify it.

Before the advent of local area networks, this process was more complicated. In the situation just described, Laura would have copied her file to a diskette and delivered it by hand. Kevin would have done his writing, copied it to a diskette, and returned it to Laura. This would have been accomplished without the benefit of referral to other chapters. Now Laura can send her file over the network by typing its path, filename, and Kevin's network address.

LAN TOPOLOGIES

Every network has a *topology,* which is the way the pieces of the network are connected together. In other words, it is the shape or geometric arrangement of network stations, which in turn determines the flow of information across the network. Local area networks are constructed using three basic topologies: the ring, the bus, and the star. Each of these three topologies can be used alone, or they can be combined together to form a *hybrid topology*. Chapter 6 has a much more detailed description of topologies (starting on page 222) that distinguishes between a configuration and a topology.

Ring Topology   A *ring topology* (shown in the top of Figure 11-4) connects all the terminals or microcomputers with one continuous loop. Within this loop the data travels in one direction only, making a complete circle around the loop.

Bus Topology   A *bus topology* (sometimes called a *tree topology*) is shown in the middle of Figure 11-4. With this topology each of the terminals or microcomputers is connected to a single cable that runs the entire length of the network.

Star Topology   A *star topology* (shown in the bottom of Figure 11-4) connects all the terminals or microcomputers to the central computer, each with its own incoming data circuit. Data flows back and forth between the central controller hardware and the terminal.

Knowledge of LAN topologies is important for comprehending the following sections on LAN architecture standards. As we saw in Chapter 6, there are both physical topologies and electrical topologies. These differences will become more evident as we discuss the IEEE 802, Ethernet, token-passing, Arcnet, FDDI, and AppleTalk LAN standards.

IEEE 802 STANDARDS

The *IEEE 802* series of standards is one of the most important for local area networks. The following 802 standards will be described in the next several sections.

- **802.1** is the basic IEEE specification for local area networks. It provides the basis for network architecture, network management, and internetworking.
- **802.2** is the data link layer (OSI model layer 2) specification for the following three physical access methods (that is, 802.3, 802.4, and 802.5).
- **802.3** is the standard for local area networks using the carrier sense multiple access/collision detection (CSMA/CD) access method. The standard has become popular because of its use in Ethernet local area networks (Ethernet).
- **802.4** is the standard for local area networks using the token-passing bus access method (token-bus).
- **802.5** is the standard for local area networks using the token-passing ring access method (token-ring).
- **802.6** is the standard for metropolitan area networks (MANs).

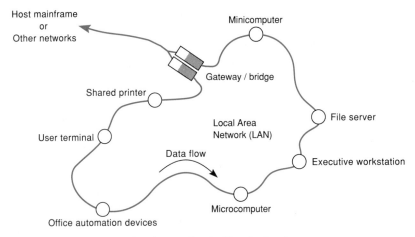

Local area network with a ring topology

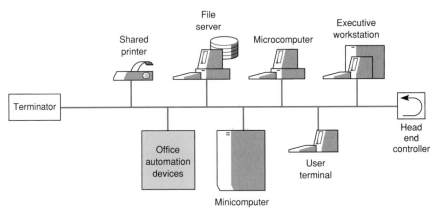

Local area network with a bus topology

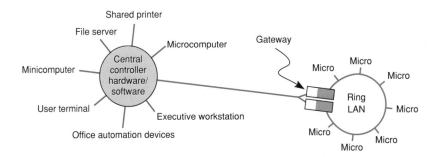

Local area network with a star topology with an attached ring

Figure 11-4　The three LAN topologies: ring, bus, and star.

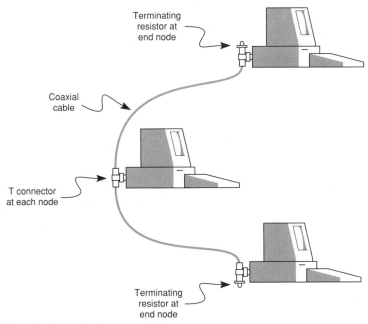

Terminating
resistor at
end node

Coaxial
cable

T connector
at each node

Terminating
resistor at
end node

Figure 11-5   A three-station Ethernet LAN using coaxial cable.

ETHERNET LANs

The first local area network architecture standard is also the one that has been available the longest. *Ethernet* is a 10 million bits per second carrier sense multiple access/collision detection (CSMA/CD) baseband technology. (At this point, do not be concerned about the detailed definitions of CSMA/CD and baseband because they are defined in the next two sections.) The IEEE 802.3 family of standards defines the Ethernet LAN standard. Ethernet is a bus-oriented wiring scheme that uses a shielded coaxial cable to make the connection between stations (nodes).

When we make LAN connections using regular coaxial cable, we call it *Thick Ethernet;* when we make them using the smaller 52-ohm coaxial cable, we call it *Thin Ethernet* or *Cheapernet*. With thick coaxial cable there can be 1,600 feet between the repeaters, but thin coax requires repeaters every 600 feet. Figure 11-5 shows a coaxial cable Ethernet connection. Today, both twisted wire pairs and fiber optic cable can be used in place of coaxial cable.

Baseband/Broadband   *Baseband* is a single channel, whereas *broadband* provides multiple channels. Baseband can carry only a single transmission at any one moment, whereas broadband splits the bandwidth into many channels. As a result, with broadband more than one transmission can occupy the LAN cable at the same time. Another view is that broadband is placed on a multiplexed signal. Baseband transmits by using basic digital electrical voltages and, therefore, occupies only one channel for which it uses the entire bandwidth.

Baseband is less complex than broadband, and usually it is less expensive because it does not need modulation devices (modems) for each microcomputer connected to the LAN. Baseband, however, is limited to a single channel (one message transmission at a time). This means that we cannot intermix all signals (voice, data, and image) on the same network if it is baseband. In local area networks, baseband may be best for organizations that constantly rearrange terminals, computers, and other devices. Reconfiguration is easier because there are no modems.

The broadband world presents somewhat more variation because of its ability to provide multiple channels. Vendors, therefore, can offer a combination of access methods, such as frequency division multiplexing (FDM), which is television-type channel selection, time division multiplexing (TDM), or any other approach on a given channel of the LAN. Whereas baseband electrically pulses the cable with a voltage or current switched between two different voltage levels, broadband divides the signaling into allocation slots, such as we see on television channels. Broadband also may use frequency modulation, amplitude modulation, phase modulation, or pulse modulation (electrical or optical) in its modulation devices.

Baseband uses only a small portion of the coaxial cable capacity and achieves a highly efficient data throughput with a straightforward circuitry. This technique, however, precludes the simultaneous use of the cable for other services such as video. By contrast, broadband uses modulation devices to subdivide the coaxial cable into many channels. As an analogy, think of these modulation devices as similar to multiplexers that allow a cable television system to carry 25 different channels of television over a single coaxial cable into your home. If they used baseband, the coaxial cable would be able to carry only one channel at a time; therefore, you would need 25 cables to receive 25 television channels.

A primary drawback of broadband is the expense of the modulation devices. Broadband allows unlimited distance because these modulation devices can be connected easily with amplifiers to amplify the signal, just as is done with the dial-up telephone networks used worldwide. This is no longer a very great advantage because repeaters/amplifiers now are available for baseband LANs, although they are somewhat more limited in distance. Because of these amplifiers, cable layout is very flexible, and cable distances are no longer important. For example, if another segment of cable is needed to install a new user workstation, we simply put an amplifier on the cable to bring the signal to that workstation up to a usable level.

CSMA/CD   The CSMA/CD Ethernet protocol must be termed "somewhat more ordered chaos." The carrier sense multiple access (CSMA) protocol is very simple in concept. Do not get on the network and transmit at random—listen first! If anyone is there, refrain from transmitting. When it gets quiet, take the network and send your message. This eliminates a certain number of collisions (messages interfering with each other), but a small problem remains. Because of network propagation delay, two users who are located some distance from one another can both listen to the channel, find it empty, and begin to transmit simultaneously. They follow the carrier sense rule, but their messages still collide. Therefore, let us add another piece to this concept.

Instead of just listening before we talk, we should listen while we talk as well. If we detect a collision during transmission, we wait and then retransmit. This is *collision detection* (CD). Two users still can attempt to retransmit at the same time, so to rectify this problem we add an algorithm into the network. Instead of each user retransmitting immediately after the end of the message, it is held back until some random time interval after the colliding message disappears. This does not eliminate collisions completely, but it reduces them to manageable proportions. This approach allows rather high utilization of the network by many users while still providing the flexibility necessary to accommodate intermittent traffic. This access method is called *CSMA/CD*.

As an analogy of the CSMA-CD protocol, let us suppose that you are involved in a conversation with a small group of friends (four or five people) sitting at a restaurant table. As the discussion progresses, each person tries to interrupt or "get the floor" when the previous speaker completes whatever it is he or she is saying. For example, you might be listening to one of your friends, while trying to judge when the person is going to stop talking so that you can immediately get into the conversation to say whatever it is you want to say. To determine when your friend is about ready to stop talking, you take into account the subject matter being discussed, whether the idea is reaching a logical conclusion, your friend's facial expressions, body language, voice intonations, and the overall attention level of the other members of this small group. Usually, the other members of the group "give the floor" to the first person who interrupts at the precise moment the previous speaker finishes talking, with an adequate amount of volume (not argumentative), and with a proper answer or a complementary comment related to the 'gist" of the conversation.

Notice how a small group of people tend to use a CSMA/CD protocol when talking. The point is that the carrier sense protocol of a LAN is patterned on a real-life situation. The way your conversation works is identical to the way a collision detect system works. A terminal listens, interrupts, and sends its message. As long as no other terminal interrupts during the short time period the message is traveling on the local area network, everything is all right.

For the sake of comparison, do you remember how a central control protocol works? It is used by large host mainframe computer networks with front end processors for polling the terminals on the network. With central polling, the front end or host mainframe computer polls each individual terminal or terminal controller and gives it permission to transmit. In other words, central control polling is analogous to a classroom situation in which the professor calls on the students who raise their hands. In a classroom situation, the professor acts like the front end central controller. To gain access to the class, the students raise their hands or make some other appropriate motion and the professor recognizes them so they can ask a question or make a comment. When they have finished, the professor again takes charge, or possibly recognizes someone else and allows that person to make a comment or ask

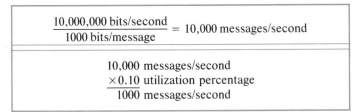

Figure 11-6   Local area network capacity.

a question. As you can see, even the central control protocol (polling) is patterned after a real-life type of protocol.

Now let us examine how the transmission speed helps get your messages through a local area network based on the Ethernet CSMA/CD protocol. The upper half of Figure 11-6 shows that if you take a 10 million bits per second transmission speed and divide it by 1,000 bits per message, you have a theoretical 10,000 messages per second capacity on the network. The lower half of the figure shows that if you take this theoretical 10,000 messages per second capacity and use only 10 percent of that capacity, you have the ability to send 1,000 messages per second. Therefore, if you have a message length that is 1,000 bits long and a collision detect protocol with a transmission rate of 10 million bits per second, you theoretically can transmit 1,000 messages per second and have very few collisions.

If you assume the network designer has specified only a 10 percent network utilization, then the network is empty 90 percent of the time (that is, no messages are being transmitted). In this situation you could transmit 1,000 messages every second, and the network still would be empty 90 percent of the time. In reality, it would not be totally empty because some of that time would be used to make up for collisions and retransmission of data that was received with an error.

The point is that if you have 100 terminals on a local area network, then each terminal can send ten 1000-bit messages each second. This amounts to using only 10 percent of the network's 10 million bits per second capacity. As a result, collisions are reduced significantly. Designers recommend not exceeding a network utilization rate of 25 percent.

CSMA/CD sometimes is referred to as *CSMA/CA* (for collision avoidance). Basically, CSMA/CD and CSMA/CA are equivalent, except that collision avoidance is alleged to be a more efficient method of transmission than collision detection. *Collision avoidance* requires that time slots be reserved for each station, which lowers performance when there are a large number of nodes. (The AppleTalk Protocol section later in this chapter presents additional detail on CSMA/CA.) By contrast, with collision detection, once a station detects an impending collision between two packets, a jamming signal is sent and both sending stations wait a random period before trying again.

Ethernet LANs transmit data in frames sometimes called *datagrams*. Certain bits are added to the user's data to enable correct transmission. Frame size depends on the protocol that encapsulates the user data to provide addresses, check fields,

Preamble	Start frame delimiter	Destination address	Source address	Length	Data + Pad	Frame check sequence
7 bytes	1	2–6	2–6	2	0–1500	4

Maximum size: 1500 bytes

Figure 11-7 Ethernet 802.3 frame. The most significant difference between "true" Ethernet and IEEE 802.3 Ethernet is the Pad field. True Ethernet defines the smallest data field as 46 bytes; the 802.3 Ethernet allows a zero-length data field and pads the frame to the proper length.

message type (whether it is a message for control purposes or a message containing business data), and other needed information.

Figure 11-7 shows the Ethernet 802.3 *frame* used for transmitting data. The Ethernet specification provides precise detailed definitions of the lowest two layers (physical and data link) of the OSI seven-layer model. It describes the carrier sense multiple access with collision detection (CSMA/CD) protocol, as well as the physical and electrical characteristics of a baseband coaxial cable medium. The original Ethernet specification was for thick coaxial cable, sometimes called *10Base5* or Thick Ethernet. Today, thin coaxial cable (*10Base2*) is rapidly replacing the original thick coax. When you hear someone mention Cheapernet or Thin Ethernet, the speaker is referring to thin coaxial cable.

Moreover, when you see a specification like 10Base2, it means the transmission speed is 10 million bits per second, it uses the baseband transmission methodology, and it has a maximum distance of 200 meters between repeaters or microcomputers. Broadband Ethernet also is available as a *10Broad36* network. Again, 10Broad36 means 10 million bits per second, broadband, with a maximum distance of 3,600 meters. Another addition to the standard is *1Base5* (1 million bits per second, baseband, at 500 meters). Notice that the terms *base* and *broad* are used in these specifications to define baseband or broadband transmission.

10Base-T   The *10Base-T* standard also is part of the IEEE 802.3 family of standards. It is the standard for running 10 million bits per second Ethernet local area networks over *unshielded twisted pair* (UTP) wiring. In this case, the name 10Base-T means 10 million bits per second, baseband, and the T means it uses *twisted pair wiring* (actually unshielded twisted pair). It is different from coaxial cable-based Ethernet LANs that have a bus topology in which the microcomputers interconnect via the same physical cable segment. Instead, 10Base-T stations connect in a star topology so that only one microcomputer goes down if a wire is cut. The 10Base-T specification allows for a bit error rate of no more than 1 in 100 million, which is the same as coaxial cable-based Ethernets.

In contrast to the established Ethernet versions that set distance limits of 500 meters for the original Ethernet and 200 meters for Cheapernet, the 10Base-T standard does not specify maximum distances from workstations to the central wiring hub. Rather, it establishes 100 meters as the target minimum distance. Three criteria must be met for the 10Base-T equipment to be interoperable.

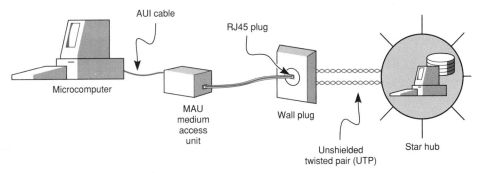

Figure 11-8 A 10Base-T LAN connection.

• The equipment must transmit and receive with an error rate within the limits specified by the 10Base-T standard.

• It must be able to detect and report data collisions to the attached workstation.

• It must be able to disable transmission if it does not receive the proper 10Base-T link integrity test pulses.

Another difference between 10Base-T and coaxial-based Ethernets is that with 10Base-T the medium access unit (MAU) has to accommodate two wire pairs because one pair transmits the Ethernet signal and the other receives the Ethernet signal. The MAU is the device into which the microcomputer connects. A 10Base-T local area network uses a *medium access unit* (MAU) and an *attachment unit interface* (AUI) as shown in Figure 11-8. The AUI is the cable. 10Base-T is popular because it does not require new telephone wires. It is possible to interconnect microcomputers having 10Base-T compatible network interface cards and use the on-premises telephone wires that already are in place. Some 10Base-T network cards are manufactured so they can be plugged directly into the already installed twisted wire pairs.

TOKEN-PASSING LANs

The passing of an electronic token is the basis for the second type of LAN architecture. Token-passing LANs can have either a ring or a bus topology. The IEEE 802.4 standard defines a token-bus network, and the IEEE 802.5 standard defines a token-ring network. *Token-passing networks* are popular where access to the network is critical because there are no collisions and the network guarantees immediate access.

The *token access method* can be likened to a relay race in which the track belongs to you as long as you have the baton. When your run is finished, you hand the baton to the next runner and the track then belongs to that runner. In a token-passing network, the baton is called a *token,* which is a unique short electronic message that is generated when the network is turned on.

Token-Bus Network   In an IEEE 802.4 *token-bus network,* the token is a frame or packet containing both the token and the message. A *node* sends the token frame to the designated address. The receiving node copies the message and then returns the token to the sending node.

The network maintains a table of addresses for each node. The address bears no resemblance to where a node is located physically on the bus network. Instead, the address is the order in which a node receives the token. A node requiring the token frequently is listed several times in the table so it can receive the token more often. A node that is listed in the table many times is said to have a higher priority than other nodes (*token priority*). When a transmission is complete, the token passes from the node that just finished its transmission to the node having the next lower address in the table. When the lowest address node in the token bus has completed its transmission, it sends the token back to begin the process all over again. In a token bus, each node receives the token, inserts the information it wishes to send, and sends the token to its destination. At its destination, that node copies the information, adds the acknowledgment, and sends it back to the sending node, which then passes the token on to the next node for transmission.

Token-Ring Network   In an IEEE 802.5 *token-ring network,* an electronic token moves between the network nodes in one direction. This technique is the *media-access control* (MAC) protocol. With MAC, a node with a message to transmit waits until it receives what we call a *free token;* that is, it is free for use. It then changes the free token into a *busy token;* that is, it is in use. The node transmits a block of data (a packet or frame) immediately following the busy token. If another node wants to transmit a message during this time, no free token is available on the network so it must wait. The receiving node copies the data in the frame, sets the copied bit, and the frame continues around the ring, making a complete round trip back to the transmitting node. The transmitting node then removes the frame and inserts a new free token on the ring (see Figure 11-9). The token-passing media-access control protocol prevents messages from interfering with one another by guaranteeing that only one node can transmit at a time.

The tokens and messages travel from node to node in a sequential fashion, but the cables actually use a star topology. Token-ring networks use a wire hub to turn the logical ring into a physical star. IBM's Token-Ring Network uses a 4- or 8-station hardware box called a *Multistation Access Unit* (MAU) to connect the unshielded twisted wire pairs at the star hub. For example, the multistation access unit would be located at the star hub in place of the server shown in Figure 11-8. This MAU only connects microcomputers; it is not a microcomputer itself. Do not confuse this MAU with the medium access unit (also a MAU) that connects to the AUI on a 10Base-T Ethernet LAN.

Token-ring networks operate at 4 million and 16 million bits per second over unshielded twisted wire pairs (UTPs). The token ring is better known than the token bus because IBM supports the token-ring standard with its Token-Ring Network.

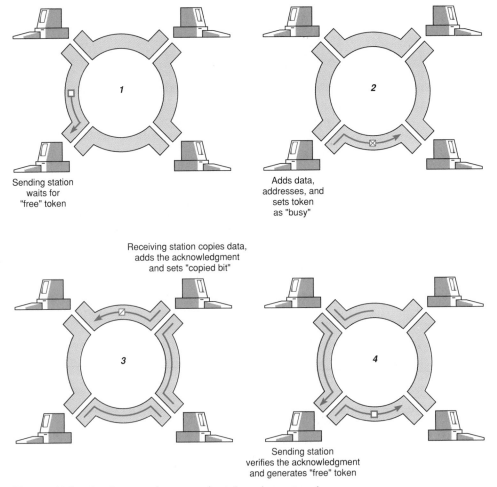

Figure 11-9   A token passing around a token-ring network.

ARCNET LANs

The next most common local area network operating system architecture is *Arcnet*™ (Attached Resource Computing Network), which the Datapoint Corporation developed in 1977 in response to the need for a low-cost PC LAN. Arcnet is a baseband token-passing bus or star architecture. It does not conform to the IEEE 802.4 or 802.5 token-passing standard; however, its low cost has made Arcnet very popular—so popular in fact that it is an established de facto standard. As a result of this popularity, the American National Standards Institute is expected to designate Arcnet as ANSI standard 878.1. The Arcnet Trade Association (ATA), which is accredited by ANSI to set standards, plans to seek approval of the International

Organization for Standardization to make Arcnet a worldwide standard after ANSI approves it.

Arcnet originally transmitted over a coaxial cable at 2.5 million bits per second. Transmission over twisted wire pairs or fiber optic cable was added later. The newer Arcnet Plus transmits at 20 million bits per second over coaxial cable. When Arcnet has a bus configuration, the maximum distance between microcomputers is 1,000 feet. When it has a star configuration with an active hub as the controller, the maximum distance for the coaxial cable is 2,000 feet from the microcomputer to the hub. Approximately 250 stations are possible on an Arcnet LAN.

FIBER DISTRIBUTED DATA INTERFACE (FDDI)

The use of high speed fiber optic local area networks is beginning to appear in user applications. The *Fiber Distributed Data Interface* (FDDI) is a set of standards created by the American National Standards Institute X3T9.5 Task Group. ANSI forwards the standards to the International Organization for Standardization (ISO) as they are adopted in the United States. The FDDI's primary competitor is the IEEE 802.6 Metropolitan Area Network (MAN) standard. Both FDDI and IEEE 802.6 can be used in citywide or companywide metropolitan area networks.

The FDDI standard is a token-passing ring LAN that operates at 100 million bits per second over an optical fiber medium. FDDI LANs control access by means of an electronic token that passes from one station to another. The FDDI token is a special media-access control (MAC) frame that allows only one station to transmit at a time. FDDI uses a "timed-token rotation" that limits the amount of time the station can hold the token before passing it to the next station. The FDDI standard assumes a maximum of 1,000 stations (nodes) and a 200-kilometer (120 miles) path that requires a repeater every 2 kilometers.

FDDI uses two counter-rotating rings called the *primary ring* and the *secondary ring*. Data traffic usually travels on the primary ring, although input data can travel on one ring and output data on the other. The secondary ring also can serve as a backup transmission path.

There are two types of FDDI stations: the *dual-attachment station* (DAS) and the *single-attachment station* (SAS). A DAS physically connects to both rings, whereas a SAS connects only to the primary ring (see Figure 11-10). Should a link fail, a DAS can recover by using the undamaged ring.

The FDDI media-access control (MAC) scheme uses a variation of the IEEE 802.5 token-passing ring standard discussed for token-ring networks. Like its 802.5 token-ring MAC, the FDDI MAC has a frame and a token. The frame carries the data while the token controls a station's access to the network.

To make a FDDI LAN work with an Ethernet 802.3 LAN requires that the entire Ethernet frame (shown in Figure 11-7) be encapsulated and incorporated into the FDDI frame format. The FDDI packet then passes over the FDDI network. Upon reaching its destination, the Ethernet packet is deencapsulated to get it off the FDDI LAN and back onto the Ethernet local area network.

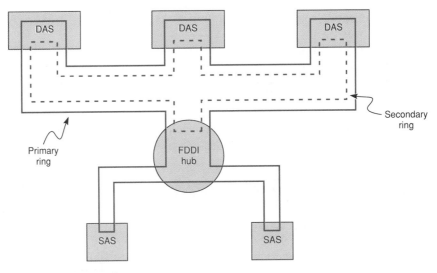

DAS: Dual-attachment station
SAS: Single-attachment station

Figure 11-10 Optical cable topology for a FDDI LAN. The FDDI has two rings. Data traffic normally travels on the primary ring.

APPLETALK PROTOCOL

Now that more businesses own Apple's Macintosh microcomputers, users want to interconnect not only with the IBM-based LANs, but also with Apple-based LANs. As you saw in Chapter 10, this is difficult because of their basic incompatibility.

All Macintosh microcomputers have a built-in network feature called *AppleTalk* that is used to interconnect Macintosh computers. This is a nonstandard set of protocols that spell out most of the functions in the seven-layer OSI model. It works with the Apple cabling system known as *LocalTalk*.

Like Ethernet, LocalTalk uses a carrier sense multiple access (CSMA) scheme to put packets on the network. It is different because it does not rely on collision detection (CD) as does Ethernet. LocalTalk uses a protocol called *LocalTalk link access protocol* (LLAP) for its carrier sense multiple access with collision avoidance (CSMA/CA). Rather than sensing collisions between data packets after they occur, terminals on an Apple CSMA/CA network send out a small 3-byte packet that signals their intent to put data on the network. This packet tells the other Macintoshes to wait until the data from the first Macintosh has been sent before attempting to send their data. If collisions do occur, they occur between these preliminary 3-byte packets instead of between the data packets. The LLAP does not guarantee that a packet will reach its destination, but it does ensure that all delivered packets will be error free.

LocalTalk transmits at 230,400 bits per second, it has a 1,000-foot cable length, and it supports 32 terminals. If the built-in LocalTalk capability does not meet an organization's needs, third-party vendors have developed data link protocols to support Ethernet, token-ring, and Arcnet networks that exchange data between Macintoshes and IBM-compatible PCs at 10 million bits per second.

LAN OPERATING SYSTEM SOFTWARE

Local area network operating systems are attracting attention because many organizations are moving major applications to network-based platforms. Problems arise in doing this because not all LAN operating systems are suited equally to every business situation. The *LAN operating system* is the software that runs and controls the network.

Software represents the major limiting factor in network availability or capability. The software provides the applications and, in addition, provides the conversion from protocol to protocol or equipment to equipment. As a result, it is the software vendors who ultimately drive the LAN market. Manufacturers provide hardware, but, just as happened in the mainframe computer industry, many software houses have emerged that specialize in application software, protocol conversion software, and operating system software. This specialized software in turn enhances network capabilities and makes integrated networks a reality.

Just hooking some microcomputers together with a cable does not make a network. It becomes a network when there are software programs to

- Move data back and forth between the server and the microcomputers
- Offer some type of data security at the server
- Direct traffic through the transmission medium (the cabling)
- Allow the microcomputers to connect and disconnect from the network
- Collect and compile network statistics for management and control of the local area network

If you have not yet read the earlier Installing a Local Area Network section, please do so because it describes the tasks performed by LAN software.

Local area networks have varying levels of capability, but they typically fall into three categories. At the highest level is the high-end full network LAN, next is the low-end DOS-based peer LAN, and the lowest level is the zero-slot or sub-LAN.

High-End Full Network LAN   A *high-end full network LAN* can interconnect with almost any other network, it can handle very large databases, it has a dedicated network server, and it uses sophisticated LAN software. These LANs really are network systems that can be configured either as a LAN or as a BN. Moreover, high-end LANs can be interconnected easily to form enterprise-wide networks or, in some cases, replace the host mainframe central computer. One example of a high-end network is Novell's NetWare 3.11.

Novell's network operating system, or the server operating system, is the heart of a NetWare network. It provides the functionality needed to run the network file system, manage memory, and schedule processing tasks. NetWare is a server-based system.

The user applications run on the server operating system. The network communication software is the link between the client/user microcomputer's DOS operating system and the network's operating system that is located in the server. In the server, the LAN vendor's network operating system replaces DOS. This communication software provides the protocols that allow data transmissions to take place. As you can see, three software components work together to enable communications: the network operating system in the dedicated server, the network communication software that interconnects the server to the user microcomputers, and the application systems that run on the server.

As to the hardware in a high-end network, it requires a powerful microcomputer for the server, a communication link (coaxial cable, fiber optic cable, or twisted pairs) between the server and the user microcomputers, user microcomputers or workstations, and special network interface circuit cards for the server and user microcomputers.

Low-End DOS-Based Peer LAN   A *low-end DOS-based peer LAN* has less capability and less sophisticated software than a high-end LAN. The low-end LANs have a limited number of nodes and they do not require a dedicated server, but the microcomputers do share their resources. One example of a low-end LAN is Artisoft's LAN-tastic 4.0.

Low-end LANs use the DOS operating system in conjunction with the LAN operating system and allow the sharing of any microcomputer hard disks without going through a central server, although one of the microcomputers in a low-end LAN can be designated as the server and the others as user microcomputers. These LANs also permit the sharing of printers. As you may recall, any microcomputer in a peer network can share its hard disk and printer with any other microcomputer. An inexpensive peer LAN interconnects from 10 to 300 user microcomputers by using a combination of DOS and its own software along with a special network interface circuit card in each microcomputer. Low-end networks do not require a dedicated server, but one can be designated as the server.

Zero-Slot Sub-LAN   The lowest level of capability for a local area network is the very inexpensive *zero-slot LAN* or *sub-LAN*. These are not full-fledged LANs—they do not require a network interface circuit card, and they connect via the RS232 port (COM1). Zero-slot LANs cost from one tenth to one half the amount of a more powerful LAN.

They are called zero-slot LANs because the zero-slot LAN adapter plug can be plugged into a serial or parallel port instead of taking up one of the microcomputer's expansion slots. (The slots are the location in the microcomputer box where you add circuit cards to gain extra memory or other enhancements.) Such a peer-to-peer device provides capabilities like file transfer, file sharing, printer sharing, E-mail, print spooling, and other benefits of networking. These LANs do not require a dedicated server. Instead, they provide direct access to the files on another user's hard disk.

Zero-slot LANs consist of intelligent hardware switches and adapters, software, or a combination of hardware and software. The zero-slot LAN operating system works in conjunction with DOS. Installing a zero-slot LAN usually takes only a short time because it does not require a circuit card. A full-fledged LAN takes much longer to install. These LANs can have a star, ring, point-to-point, or bus topology. They are able to handle up to 30 nodes, which can be increased by daisy-chaining several zero-slot LANs together.

LAN SERVERS

A *server* in a local area network really is a powerful microcomputer. A LAN server can be either a *dedicated server* in which serving the needs of the network is its sole function, or it can be a user microcomputer (sometimes called a client microcomputer) that also performs server functions. The purpose of a server is to make its attached peripherals (disk drives, printers, modems that connect to another network, facsimiles, and the like) available to the user microcomputers on the LAN. Figure 11-11 shows the various types of servers on a local area network.

The software running on a user microcomputer gives a network user access to the server. The LAN network operating system running on the server controls the files on the disk drive, printers, and so forth. Remember that high-end full network LANs use a dedicated server, low-end DOS-based LANs can have a dedicated server or just share resources among the user microcomputers, and zero-slot LANs can only share resources among the user microcomputers without the benefit of a server.

The most important characteristic of a server is the speed of its disk drive access and the speed of its microprocessor chip (for example, an 80486 running at 50 megahertz). There are many types of servers, including disk, file, network (sometimes called database), facsimile, and the like.

Disk Server   *Disk servers* divide the disk storage capability into fixed-size disk volumes called partitions (C:, D:, etc.). Each user is given one or more private volumes on which to store data. Because size is fixed and many volumes are required, it becomes a difficult administrative problem to add new users, manage existing users, and allocate disk space efficiently. In addition, there is a grave security risk because these files are only designated as public and private. Public means other users may be able to read or write on someone else's volume. As a result, users may lose data inadvertently, experience breaches of privacy, or have data modified improperly.

File Server   With *file servers,* a single file volume can be shared by many users and can be any size, limited only by the size of the disk storage itself. Each user can have one or more files. There is no administrative overhead for the movement of users and files. Moreover, security is addressed because the LAN software controls unique security locks such as volume locks, file locks, and record locks.

See the box on The Technical Differences Between a Disk Server and a File Server. Network servers function like file servers.

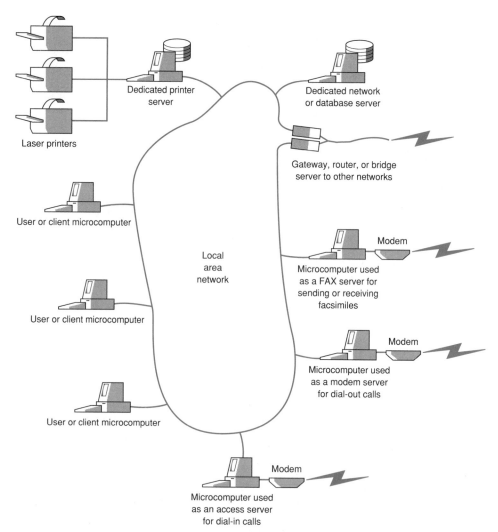

Figure 11-11   Different types of servers on a local area network.

Network Server   A *network server* is a dedicated microcomputer that provides special network application services for all the attached microcomputers. These services can include processing application programs, a shared file system, shared printers, and an electronic mail system. Network servers extend the facilities offered by file servers, local microcomputer applications, and operating systems. For example, a network server can provide a large-capacity file system extension to DOS that allows microcomputer users to share files more easily and have larger file storage areas available for their use. Network servers also can contain the necessary software to keep track of network resources, handle all the details of communications, provide network management services, and process applications.

THE TECHNICAL DIFFERENCES BETWEEN A DISK SERVER AND A FILE SERVER

DOS uses a file allocation table (FAT) to keep track of exactly where a particular file is stored on the hard disk. A disk server, however, has its own FAT. Without seeing a copy of this FAT, an individual user's microcomputer has no idea where its files are stored. To overcome this problem on a network, the disk server sends a copy of its FAT to the user's microcomputer, which then stores it in RAM. Using this FAT, the microcomputer can access its files on the disk server.

Imagine the situation if numerous microcomputers on the network received copies of the FAT and began saving files back to the disk server. Each copy of the FAT saved back to the disk server would overwrite (erase) the FAT file that existed prior to that update. If this happened, the integrity of the FAT would be lost very quickly.

With a disk server, the integrity of the FAT is maintained because the hard disk drive is divided (partitioned) into several user volumes (D:, E:, and so forth). Each volume is reserved for the exclusive use of a particular user microcomputer, which is what preserves the integrity of the FAT for that particular volume and user microcomputer.

By contrast, a file server contains special software that forms a shell around the computer's disk operating system. This shell software sends the disk access commands to the file server before DOS can receive them. The file server also maintains its own FAT. When a file is requested, the file server already knows where that file is located because of its FAT, so it sends the file directly to the user's microcomputer.

File servers are more efficient than disk servers because copies of the FAT do not have to be sent to each user microcomputer after it requests a file. Furthermore, the need to partition the server's hard disk drive into volumes is eliminated because the user microcomputer no longer needs to know where files reside.

Network servers usually have faster microprocessors. Today's high speed servers usually are built around an 80386/80486 chip or a 68030/68040 chip to gain a 32-bit-wide network interface and the 25 megahertz and up operating speed. Network servers also tend to have much larger disks. The 30- and 40-megabyte disks that accompanied the older 80286-based machines are now 100- and 300-megabyte disks. These sometimes are referred to as database servers (discussed next). The speed of these disks is faster because their average access time is in the area of 18 milliseconds and their platters spin at a higher rpm. The ruggedness or reliability of network servers is very important. Their disks must be far more rugged to handle the greater number of accesses, and they must have a much greater Mean Time Between Failures (MTBF) than the average hardware.

Some network servers are fault tolerant because the server box might contain two or three independent servers attached along a 32-bit-wide bus. The purpose of independent servers is to have the others handle the load if one of the microprocessors goes down; therefore, they are fault tolerant or, in theory, cannot fail. Some of them contain two or three disk controller circuit cards so they can handle the load if one of these cards fails. (See Control 26 in the LAN Controls section at the end of this chapter.) Servers are not just file servers anymore because they are more like network hubs, providing such services as terminal emulation or micro-to-mainframe connections.

Database Server A *database server* is more powerful and does more than a file server. For example, database servers provide the following functions.

- Centralize all the organization's operations on a database into one microcomputer
- Filter data to send only selected records to LAN workstations
- Track tables, indexes, and access paths by using a central system catalog
- Back up the database automatically
- Recover lost data and back out incomplete transactions
- Use a central data dictionary to relate data stored in different formats

The benefits provided by these features are that database servers reduce the amount of data moved between the server and the workstation, they reduce LAN workstation resource requirements, they offer the ability to grant and revoke access permission from a central location, they minimize lost data, and they prevent widespread data inconsistencies should the system fail. Sometimes the database server and the network server are the same microcomputer.

Facsimile (FAX) Server *Facsimile servers* on LANs are good for sending a FAX, but they are not so good for receiving them. Facsimile machines encode their images differently than microcomputer video monitors. Because they use two entirely different standards, it is difficult and slow to convert and read a FAX appearing on a video screen.

Printer Server *Printer servers* handle all the print requests on a local area network. These servers print everything sent to them from the various microcomputer workstations on the LAN.

Access/Modem Server *Access servers* or *modem servers* allow users to dial into or out of the local area network via the public dial-up telephone network. There is a subtle distinction between access servers and modem servers. Usually, dialing into the LAN is accomplished with an access server, whereas dialing out of the LAN is accomplished with a modem server. The access or modem server on the local area network accomplishes this gateway function with the aid of remote LAN software.

An access server connects to the LAN and retrieves applications from the network server's hard disk to run on its own CPU or to transfer files to the microcomputer that dialed into the LAN. Callers dialing into an access server can check their E-mail, transfer files, print files, run application programs, or send FAXs via the LAN's facsimile server. Access servers are ideal for database applications in which the amount of information moved is small and does not require installation of a router or high speed T-1 circuit.

The most common method of dialing into a LAN is by using *modem remote control*. In this case, the microcomputer that dials into the LAN remotely controls another microcomputer that also is connected to the LAN. The remote microcomputer uses a modem to dial into an access server microcomputer that is on a LAN. The remote microcomputer then runs *remote LAN software* on the microcomputer it dialed into so it can operate programs and access peripherals (such as printers and disks) on the LAN. Remote LAN software offers these features and adds the flexibility of node-to-node communications that allow users to share networked applications on a LAN with a remote dial-in microcomputer.

This remote LAN software can be used by developers and for technical support, group conferencing, and training. These packages offer such features as graphics support and a "chat box" in which users send prompts that automatically pop up on the screen of other remote users. Remote users can see the access server microcomputer screen as it accesses an application on a LAN, uses it for E-mail, or communicates via the chat box.

There is an inexpensive way to have an access server. Use one of the microcomputers that is connected via cable to the LAN and equip it with remote access LAN software, a serial port, and a modem. Then use this microcomputer as an access server on a one-at-a-time, first-come-first-served basis.

Remote access LAN software raises one serious question related to ethics and privacy because of a feature called "secret monitoring." It is possible for the software to be configured in such a manner that remote microcomputers can be monitored without detection. The question that must be asked is whether this type of monitoring violates the microcomputer operators' (workers') Fourth Amendment rights "to be secure in their persons, houses, papers and effects, against unreasonable searches and seizures."

Gateway, Router, or Bridge Server Although not generally viewed as being a server, gateways, routers, and bridges are three specialized pieces of hardware that connect LANs to other networks. They are being used more frequently to combine two networks within a single server box. Their functions are described in the next section. Combining two networks has brought the word "internetwork" into our vocabulary. *Internetworking* means interconnecting two or more networks.

INTERNETWORKING

The concept of an enterprise-wide network is replacing the reality of many independent networks located throughout an organization. The driving force behind enterprise networking is the shift toward an information-based business economy. Most business organizations operating in the new worldwide market realize that being a manufacturer or service provider requires an immense amount of information. This information must be stored, retrieved, analyzed, acted upon, and shared with others at a moment's notice. Interconnecting the organization's diverse networks is one way to meet this challenge.

An *internet* is a collection of local area networks interconnected by repeaters, bridges, routers, gateways, front ends or controllers, or direct nonswitchable links that join two specific networks (see Figure 11-3). When there is a large internet, the individual networks that are joined together are called *subnetworks*. Connection is made possible by using repeaters, bridges, routers, and gateways, or by going through the organization's central host mainframe computer.

Repeaters   *Repeaters* are very simple devices that pass all traffic in both directions between the LAN segments they link. Repeaters are not discriminating. That is, they are primarily hardware devices that relay everything they receive. The repeater's function is to extend the network cable beyond its normal limits. For example, a repeater allows you to create an Ethernet network several thousand feet in length, which is much more than the typical limit of less than 1,000 feet. This is possible because the repeater retimes the packets and reinserts them into each cable segment. In effect, the process begins again at each segment.

The repeater extends the size of a LAN by providing a connection point for additional cable segments that typically range in length up to 2,500 meters. The repeater regenerates signals from one segment to another, boosting the signal strength to carry data through the extended LAN. Repeaters operate at layer 1 (the physical layer) of the seven-layer OSI model.

Bridges   The purpose of a *bridge* is to increase the number of addressable nodes on a network or to link two geographically distant but similar networks that use the same protocol. For example, users on one LAN can address another LAN as though it were another node in their own network. Bridges operate at layer 2 (the data link layer) of the seven-layer OSI model.

Bridges are more sophisticated than repeaters because they operate by learning, filtering, and forwarding. When a bridge receives a packet, it determines the packet's source address and compares this address to its own internal *routing table*. If the *source address* is not in the routing table, then the bridge adds it. Thus, the bridge is said to *learn* the addresses of the devices on the network. If the *destination address* is not in the routing table, the bridge forwards the packet to all ports except the one on which it was received.

If the destination address is both in the routing table and on the same network segment as the source address, the bridge automatically discards the packet, which is a process known as *filtering*. The bridge can discard the packet because the station to which it is addressed will already have received and copied the message.

If the destination address is in the routing table but not on the same network segment, the bridge determines the port associated with the address and forwards the packet to that port, a process known as *forwarding*.

Bridges are a combination of both hardware and software. A typical bridge consists of a black box that sits between the two networks and has its own processor, memory, and software; its operations are transparent to the network user. A simple bridge can connect two Ethernet local area networks located in the same building.

This is useful if a LAN cable gets too long (that is, beyond its operational length limits) because you can divide one LAN into two LANs and connect them with a bridge. The top of Figure 11-4 shows a bridge going to another network or host mainframe computer.

Routers   *Routers* join two networks that may or may not be similar at layer 3 (the network layer) of the seven-layer OSI model. Not only are routers and bridges confused, but so are routers and gateways! A bridge is less complex and joins a network at the second layer, whereas routers operate at the third layer.

A router is another means of providing path control in a large internetwork environment because one major feature of a router is that it chooses the best route between two networks having multiple paths between them. Because a router knows its own location, as well as the packet's final destination, it looks in a routing table to identify the best path.

Routers must possess a higher level of software intelligence than either repeaters or bridges because they operate at the network layer of the OSI model. Routers allow the logical separation of an internetwork into many subnetworks by using an addressing scheme that distinguishes between *device addresses* and *subnetwork addresses*.

Routing systems use the *internetwork address* for routing decisions. They forward the packets with the router's own physical address instead of the sending node's physical address. For this reason you must display a packet's internet address if you want to know a packet's real source and destination node.

Routers use their routing tables to identify other subnetworks, the paths to them, and the relative efficiency of the paths. Whereas a bridge uses its forwarding table to make a simple forward or discard (filter) decision, a router uses its routing table to select the best route for each packet to follow to the next subnetwork.

A router only receives packets addressed to it by either a user station (source address) or another router. The router determines the next subnetwork to which the packet should go by the subnetwork address of the final destination contained in its routing table. The entire routing process occurs on a hop-by-hop basis.

A *brouter* is a special router that combines the functions of both a bridge and a router. For example, it may be able to route one or more protocols (such as TCP/IP and SDLC) to a specific network but bridge all other traffic. Bridges forward packets to their destination regardless of the protocol being used.

Routers are not the same as bridges because routers can perform other functions like identifying the best route between two networks. On the other hand, routers are not the same as gateways (discussed next) because gateways are able to translate data formats and open sessions between application programs. The point is that routers, bridges, and gateways perform the same basic task of interconnecting networks, but each is somewhat different from the others.

Gateways   *Gateways* are more complex than bridges because they are the interface between two dissimilar networks, including two different communication architectures. Gateways translate one network protocol into another, translate data formats, and open sessions between application programs, thus overcoming both hardware and software incompatibilities. Because gateways are more sophisticated than re-peaters, bridges, or routers, they operate at the higher layers of the seven-layer OSI model (layers 4 through 7). Gateways are used in micro-to-mainframe and micro-to-minicomputer communications. The classic IRMA card in a microcom-puter is an example of a gateway. Like bridges, gateways are combinations of hard-ware and software products. Gateways are designed for transparent operation, therefore, users do not need to know the protocol of the network from which they are requesting or sending data.

More complex gateways even take care of such tasks as code conversion (ASCII-EBCDIC). An example is a Systems Network Architecture (SNA) gateway that allows network users to access mainframe applications, data, and peripherals. With-out this SNA gateway on their local area network, each microcomputer would have to have its own 3270 hardware emulation card, coaxial cable, and mainframe con-troller port. The SNA gateway eliminates the need for additional hardware for the microcomputer, and it requires only one connection to the host computer because all data is sent through the local area network gateway.

A gateway, rather than simply forwarding or routing the packets, converts the packet to the protocol or network architecture of the destination to which the packet will be sent before sending it.

Gateways may be a standalone box, a front end connected to a mainframe com-puter, or even a special circuit card in the network server. Two systems might not be able to communicate because of restrictions on connectivity caused by addressing constraints, differences in input/output protocols, or different computer network architectures. In these cases, some type of gateway is necessary to allow the flow of data between them. There are three basic types of gateways: network-to-network, system-to-network, and system-to-system. Each one solves a specific interconnec-tion problem.

In the *network-to-network gateway,* two compatible X.25 networks need a gate-way because of internetwork domain problems. The X.25 network typically routes data and calls only within the boundaries of its own network definitions. As a result, each X.25 network is distinct and is controlled separately. If two such networks seek to communicate with one another, it is necessary for the calls to go through a special *X.75 gateway* node. The primary purpose of this X.75 gateway is to provide any necessary translation (particularly terminal address translation) for a call origi-nating in one network that is to go to a destination in another network. Such transla-tion is mandatory because the X.25 standard does not specify how an address is mapped into a user port. When a user in one X.25 network specifies an address in another X.25 network, a large portion of that address may not be comprehensible to the receiving network. For this reason the message is routed to a gateway for call processing. X.75 gateways are an integral part of the hardware furnished by packet switch manufacturers.

The primary function of the *system-to-network gateway* is to make the X.25 network available to a minicomputer system, as well as to some secondary functions related to the handling of asynchronous X.3 PAD functions. In either of these in-stances, the source of any data is assumed to be compatible with what the minicom-puter is expecting. When a client or user microcomputer wants to communicate with the network, however, it may encounter problems because of incompatibilities. For example, the gateway might connect directly into the minicomputer system bus on one side and into the synchronous line of the X.25 network on the other. The primary function of the system-to-network gateway is to take a protocol that is not understandable to the minicomputer and convert it to a form the minicomputer can understand.

By using a *system-to-system gateway,* you can connect one vendor's computer system to another vendor's computer system. When you are trying to interface two different computer systems, the gateway must provide both the basic system interconnection and the necessary emulation in both directions. The gateway probably would be made to look like the terminals or terminal controllers of one of the two computer systems, allowing the terminals of the second computer to attach to the first computer's controller.

The major difference between a system-to-system gateway and a system-to-network gateway is that the system-to-network gateway assumes the source of any data is compatible with whatever the computer system is expecting. By contrast, the system-to-system gateway assumes a basic difference in the systems themselves, such as character-oriented (asynchronous) versus block-oriented (synchronous), or other protocol and architecture differences between computers manufactured by different vendors.

Circuits Between LANs   Circuits connecting local area networks should be very high speed. When a LAN operates at 10 million bits per second, it slows the flow of packets between two LANs significantly if the connecting circuits are voice grade circuits with a transmission speed of only 19,200 bits per second.

The circuits interconnecting two local area networks should be T-1 (1,544,000 bits per second), T-3 (45 million bits per second), microwave at T-1 speeds, satellite at T-1 speeds, ISDN at a minimum of 144,000 bits per second, SMDS at T-1 speeds, or FDDI at 100 million bits per second. As you can see, the minimum speed should be at least 144,000 bits per second. This is a case in which faster is better.

LAN CABLING

The selection of a local area network topology can be influenced greatly by the type of cable that already exists in the building where the LAN is to be installed. Just as highways carry all kinds of traffic, from the tiniest economy cars to the largest trucks, the perfect *cabling* system also should be able to carry all kinds of electronic transmissions to all corners of the building.

Most LANs are formed with a blend of unshielded twisted pair (UTP) wires (ordinary telephone wire), fiber optic cable, and coaxial cable. You even can obtain a wireless local area network. An advantage of wireless might be that it runs on radio frequencies, thus eliminating the installation of wires, cables, or optical fibers. Obviously, a disadvantage is the lack of security. To protect the privacy of messages, users have to encrypt them before transmission on a wireless LAN.

Three transmission media dominate today's local area network installations: unshielded twisted pair (UTP) wires (which is current telephone technology), fiber optics, and coaxial cable. All types of media were discussed in the Communication Media section in Chapter 5 (page 190). The following paragraphs will discuss these three media and wireless as they relate to LANs.

Twisted Pairs   Today most office buildings already have *twisted pair* wires in place. Although initially it appeared that twisted pairs would not be able to meet long-term capacity and distance requirements, today this medium is one of the leading LAN cabling methodologies. Its extremely low cost (it often is in place already), the availability of both shielded and data grade twisted pair wiring that can handle higher transmission speeds, and the high data rates attainable on twisted wire pairs through the use of digital transmission methodologies make the cabling very useful. In addition, low cost repeaters/amplifiers allow the signal to be sent over greater distances, which overcomes the attenuation problem.

A BALUN makes it easy to connect twisted pairs to a coaxial cable. *BALUN* is an acronym for *BAL*anced *UN*balanced and refers to an impedance-matching device used to connect balanced twisted pair cabling with unbalanced coaxial cable. A BALUN is a small device about one-half inch in diameter and 3 inches long. One end has a standard RJ-11 telephone jack plug, and the other has a standard screw-in type of coaxial connector lead. One use for a BALUN is to direct signals to coaxial cables when two microcomputers are located some distance away from each other. At one microcomputer, you place a BALUN to direct the signal from the twisted pair wires onto a coaxial cable. At the other microcomputer, you use a second BALUN to take the signal off the coaxial cable and onto a twisted pair for entry into the microcomputer. The signal does not attenuate (lose power) as rapidly when it is going over a coaxial cable as it does when twisted pair wires are used; therefore, a slightly greater distance between the microcomputers can be attained by using coaxial cable.

Twisted pairs also are replacing coaxial cable in a number of applications in larger LANs like the 10Base-T Ethernet. Although twisted pairs never will supplant coaxial or fiber optic cables in a large broadband network, many cabling designers use them as feeder or drop cable to microcomputer workstations. Because of BALUNS, existing coaxial cable that is bulky, inflexible, and therefore troublesome to pull (install) can be replaced with more manageable twisted wire pairs. This is accomplished by cutting the coaxial cable and installing a tee connector with a BALUN that allows a twisted pair of wires to be routed to a microcomputer.

Twisted pairs can be unshielded as in regular telephone wiring, or they can be shielded with braiding or foil as shown in Figure 11-12. This figure also depicts a RJ-11 telephone jack plug that is connected to the telephone wire. The twists of the twisted pair eliminate *radio frequency interference* (RFI) and *electromagnetic interference* (EMI). They do this by aligning the two magnetic fields of the two wires in such a way as to diminish interference. The number of twists in a pair is important. In other words, the more twists, the less interference. *Data grade twisted pair* wiring has a higher number of twists per foot than the regular twisted pair wiring used in voice telephone applications.

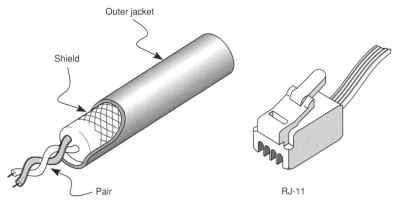

Figure 11-12 Twisted pair (shielded) and a RJ-11 telephone jack plug.

The other type of noise that twisting controls is cross-talk. *Cross-talk* is the interference a wire exerts over other nearby wires. RFI and EMI also can be controlled by shielding twisted pairs with some noise-reducing material such as foil or braiding. Cross-talk can be controlled in a multipair cable bundle by shielding each individual pair from the other pairs.

Fiber Optic Cable The second transmission medium is *fiber optic cable,* which uses a glass fiber that is drawn into a long cylinder to act as a "waveguide" for the light. Once the light is put into one end of the fiber, it becomes trapped in that fiber, bounces back and forth as though it were hitting a series of mirrors, and eventually comes out the other end. The light injectors generally are lasers or light-emitting diode (LED) transmitters. Lasers provide higher power than LEDs, but the LED is a less expensive method. The advantages of fiber optics are straightforward. It has tremendous bandwidth capability, it is impervious to electrical noise, and it is far more secure against tapping. It has more bandwidth available than we could fill with everything currently being transmitted, as well as anything we can think about in the future. The fibers are small, they do not pick up electrical noise, and they operate in extremely hostile environments such as open flames.

To make fiber optic cable readily usable for a multiple-user environment, it must be spliced. Cutting into fiber optic cable is relatively difficult. A few years ago, this task was performed by a technician with a microscope. Today, it is done by a piece of precision hardware that cuts the fiber, aligns it, and fuses it end to end.

Fiber optic cable is thinner than single twisted pairs (even unshielded ones) and therefore takes far less space when cabled throughout a building. It also is much lighter, weighing less than 10 pounds per 1,000 feet. Fiber optics can handle data rates of 100 million bits per second, and some vendors are boasting that 200 million bits per second speeds will be achieved soon. The ANSI Fiber Distributed Data Interface (FDDI) standard sets a speed of 100 million bits per second. A fiber optic cable can handle over 1,300 two-way conversations. By contrast, two twisted pairs are limited to about 24, although 96 are possible as you may remember from your reading about T-1 circuits in Chapter 7.

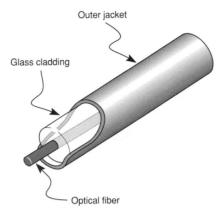

Figure 11-13   Fiber optic cable.

Because of the high bandwidth, fiber optic cabling is perfect for broadband LANs. With regard to distance between amplifiers, most of the time the distance is still only about 2,000 feet to 30 miles in the absence of an amplifier. From a data loss standpoint, fiber optics is not affected by dirty power, static electricity, or lightning strikes. Figure 11-13 shows the hair-thin glass fiber running down the middle of its glass cladding.

Coaxial Cable   The third type of transmission medium, *coaxial cable,* comes in all sizes, shapes, and characteristics. Each has some unique properties that can help or hinder design efforts. Cables are available in 52 ohms, 75 ohms, 93 ohms, and a number of impedances in between. An *ohm* measures the resistance. Coaxial cable usually supports frequencies up to 300 or 400 megahertz. If the correct cable is selected, it even can support frequencies into the gigahertz range. Coaxial cable sets the requirements for almost unlimited bandwidth support for LANs, and it is available at a reasonable price. As you might suspect, twisted pairs are the least expensive and fiber optic cables are the most expensive, leaving coax somewhere in between.

Coax is physically the largest of the three cable types. Depending on which coax you use, it may weigh anywhere from 20 pounds per 1,000 feet up to an astounding 90 pounds per 1,000 feet, which can have a detrimental effect on a dropped overhead ceiling, especially if it collapses because of the cable's weight!

Coax is not very flexible, so it cannot be bent around sharp corners easily. Unlike twisted wire, coaxial cable allows you to send information a greater distance before an amplifier is required. Coaxial cable is, by definition, shielded because its outer conductor also is a shield (see Figure 11-14). Some coaxial cables are doubly shielded. An example is Ethernet whose coaxial cables generally have both a foil shield and the second braided conductor shield. With Ethernet you can use the old thick coax (yellow in color) or the newer thin coax (52 ohms). Thin coax (Cheaper-net) is the more popular of the two coaxial cable types. With regard to the outer conductor, by now you should know that all electrical wiring requires two conduc-

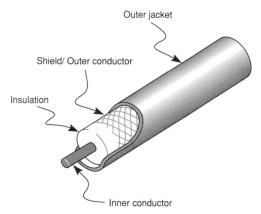

Figure 11-14 Coaxial cable.

tors to complete a circuit. For example, look at the wiring in your home or the twisted pair of a telephone wire. Coaxial cable uses its inner conductor as one of the two conductors and the braided shield (outer conductor) as the second conductor to complete the circuit.

Many people wonder why coaxial cable can handle higher speeds than twisted pairs. The reasons are complex, but the primary reason is that coax has a lower impedance than twisted pair. Most coaxial cable has an impedance of 60 to 75 ohms, whereas twisted pairs can have double that amount or an impedance as high as 130. A lower impedance means the wire impedes or resists the data signal less than a higher impedance. Because it encounters less resistance, coaxial cable can carry more data. It also can carry a higher bandwidth, which means it not only can move data at higher speeds, but it also can carry multiple signals simultaneously. Twisted pairs cannot handle broadband signals as well as coaxial cable.

Wireless LAN   *Wireless LANs* are an alternative method of "cabling" a local area network. They use the same protocols (Ethernet, for example) as other local area networks, but they transmit their data frames through the air rather than through coaxial cable, twisted wire pairs, or fiber optic cable. Several wireless LANs are available. Some require users to open their microcomputers for insertion of new circuit cards, but at least one does not require a new circuit card.

Wireless LANs have a transmission module that is connected to or placed very near the user's microcomputer. It is this transmission module that transmits the data frames to a control module. All wireless LANs do is operate without the need for cables—in effect, they are used in place of a building's cabling. Some wireless LAN vendors state distance limitations of their product in terms of feet (such as a maximum of 80 feet), and others state limitations in terms of the number of square feet covered. An example of the latter is where the transmission module might be able to interconnect all the microcomputers within a 50,000 square foot area.

One wireless LAN requires the user to install both a new card and a new driver in each microcomputer node. The user then regenerates the LAN operating system for the nodes supporting the wireless LAN. Another product does not require installation of either LAN cards or software drivers because the user connects "user PC modules" where they normally would connect the Ethernet cabling at the network circuit card. The user module then transmits the data frame through the air to a control module, which in turn connects to the server. The Altair Plus wireless LAN offers 500 feet between devices at 3,300,000 bits per second throughput, and it supports IEEE 802.3 Ethernet networks like 10Base-T, 10Base2, and 10Base5.

As mentioned earlier, the primary advantage of a wireless LAN is the avoidance of wiring, and the primary disadvantage is the need for data encryption to protect messages prior to their transmission through the air.

Installing Cables   You need to consider a number of items when installing cables or when performing cable maintenance.

- Before moving any cable, always inspect the ceiling above or the floor beneath, as well as the surrounding area, to see how the cables enter, exit, and are attached. In other words, check the "blind side."
- Before reconnecting any cables back into a network, test for continuity, polarity, or any shorts.
- Conceal all cable as much as possible to protect it from damage and for security reasons.
- When disconnecting a cable, always disconnect it at the central computer (CPU) end first, and always remove and tape one lead at a time. *Always* work with just one wire at a time.
- When connecting a cable, make all required connections on the floor end (remote) of the cable before effecting the final connection into the central computer (CPU) end.
- Properly number and mark both ends of all cable installations as you install them.
- Obtain a copy of the local city fire codes and follow them.
- Always update cable documentation records immediately upon installing a new cable.

To establish a management responsibility focused on cabling, you should adopt the following policies and procedures.

- Assess where the local area network fits into the total cabling distribution of the building or within the entire organization.
- Obtain documentation related to the existing wiring.
- Perform a physical inventory of any existing cabling systems and document those findings.
- Create diagrams of existing cable distributions.

- Establish an ongoing management program to keep track of all current and all newly installed cable.

- Establish a long-term plan for the evolution of the current cabling system to whatever cabling system will be in place in the future.

LAN COSTS

Over the last few years, low cost zero-slot sub-LANs based on communications using the microcomputer's serial I/O port have increased in both numbers and sophistication. Thus, they have become an extremely viable option for business. These low cost LANs offer some of the functionality of the higher priced networks, but typically they feature a cost per node (microcomputer workstation) of $100 to $250. This price does not include wiring a building. This is about one quarter to one fifth the cost of the more powerful LANs. These low cost LANs provide functions such as sharing printers, plotters, data, and disk storage devices, as well as micro-to-micro file transfer and print spooling.

The more expensive LANs, which have far greater capabilities, such as 10 million bits per second transmission rates and several miles of cable distance before requiring repeaters, cost from $250 to $1,000 per node. The more expensive LAN is the best option if you want to have file sharing and to install it throughout a building; but if you want to install a small two- to ten-node LAN within a single department (one or two rooms), you should seriously consider one of the inexpensive zero-slot LANs that use twisted pair wires and the COM1 port.

When users are asked how much it costs to install a LAN, they often answer $1,000 per connection. This figure may not be accurate for small LANs, but it probably is for larger LANs and the cost may be even higher. This is because there are some hidden costs. For example, the cabling in a large multifloor building can cost from $400 to $2,500 per microcomputer workstation. In addition, when you get a local area network, you begin needing the services of either a part-time or a full-time microcomputer local area network administrator or "guru." This is the person who makes sure the network keeps running, teaches people how to use the network, and does all the necessary chores such as updating software, performing various programming tasks, fixing broken cables, moving microcomputer workstations, and sometimes being responsible for LAN security.

If the LAN is very large, a management system is needed to keep track of the network, error rates on the network, the number of collisions among messages, and all the management tasks that must be performed on large-scale backbone networks. The costs jump even higher when you have a bridge, router, or gateway to another network, such as when internetworking or connecting to the organization's centrally controlled backbone network. The cost is higher because users transfer files (rather than single transactions) between databases, and people must learn new work habits. User training is another hidden cost because, for every hour of user training, there is one hour employees are unable to perform their normal daily routines. Finally, if the LAN has a database server, someone has to oversee security, optimize the disk storage (reorganize disk files), and ensure proper backup and recovery routines at the database server disk drive.

Use the box on Local Area Network Cost Considerations as a guide to identify all the costs related to your network.

IMPLEMENTING A LAN

Buying a local area network usually is easier than getting it to work. Before you buy, recognize that the LAN implementation process encompasses cabling the building, installing hardware and software, testing the LAN, training the users, establishing network security, managing the system, supervising the ongoing maintenance of the LAN, and planning future enhancements.

We already have discussed how to install a LAN, but during the LAN's implementation you must either install the cabling yourself or contract for someone to pull the wires through the building and extend them to each area where a workstation is to be located. Do not be surprised if the installation of the cabling costs far more than the purchase of the LAN itself.

Hardware installation means that you install each microcomputer or other workstation, along with any centralized items such as a shared printer or shared file or network server.

Software installation means that you install the LAN operating system onto the centralized disk/file/network server (if you have one) and onto the user microcomputers.

By the end of software installation, you should have the cabling in place, the user workstations connected, and the software up and running. At that point, testing can begin. Testing is the process that verifies all the LAN features and equipment are working as they should.

Training begins simultaneously with testing. Users must be trained in how to use the new local area network software commands so they can perform such functions as send their files to a shared printer and transfer or modify files in a shared file server environment. It is during this training that the various security restrictions on each user are established. Hopefully, the LAN software package has volume-locking, file-locking, record-locking, and password capabilities (discussed later in the LAN Security and Control section).

If it is a large local area network, then a software package or hardware monitor probably should be purchased for network management. This software is used for inventorying all the items in the network, as well as for monitoring the operating aspects of the network such as how many collisions occur between packets and the transmission error rates. (We discuss LAN management in the next section.)

The amount of energy and money devoted to maintenance depends on the complexity of the LAN. A part-time network supervisor probably can manage a small network used primarily for word processing and offering shared printers and disk files. On the other hand, a large network with, let us say, 100 users dispersed

LOCAL AREA NETWORK COST CONSIDERATIONS

- LAN software: Purchase or licensing cost of the local area network software.

- Application software: Purchase of multiple copies of application software or a network version, if available.

- Cabling: Cost of the cables and, more important, the cost of installing the cables in the building. Consider a wireless LAN.

- LAN hardware: Cost of concentrators, an uninterruptible power supply (UPS), MAUs, and other LAN hardware.

- LAN circuit cards: Cost of a network circuit card for each microcomputer on the LAN. Possibly the cost of extra memory for the server.

- Servers: Cost of the AT, 80386/80486 microcomputers to be used as network, database, printer, access/modem, or facsimile servers.

- Printers: Purchase of any printers required for the network.

- Fixed disks: Purchase of the larger capacity and faster access time fixed disk required on the network server.

- User microcomputers: Purchase of user workstations to be interconnected to the network server microcomputer. Also, the cost to upgrade currently owned microcomputers.

- Bridges/routers/gateways: Purchase of repeaters, bridges, routers, or gateways required for LAN-to-mainframe or LAN-to-LAN connections.

- Network administration: Cost of the network administrator or "guru." Even small local area networks with as few as five or ten workstations require, at the minimum, approximately 20 hours per week of network administration. The larger the network, the greater will be its personnel costs.

- Maintenance: Installation of future upgrades, fixing cables or other hardware "glitches," and correcting incompatibilities between network software and application programs.

- Training: Specialized training for the network administrator and all network users.

- Security: Costs related to network security such as specialized security software, changing passwords on a regular basis, or installing specialized hardware security devices.

- Backup: Backing up the network server database on a daily basis. Also may include purchase of specialized backup hardware and software.

- Future growth: Purchase the more expensive LAN if it appears the organization will grow enough to outgrow the capacity of a smaller LAN within three to five years.

- Network management: Hardware, software, and specialized training needed to develop a LAN network management system for ongoing redesign, monitoring, and diagnosing of problems.

- Facilities: Cost of rooms in a building, supplies, and the like.

- Consultant: Hiring of a local area network consultant specialist, either during the initial development or if severe problems occur.

throughout a multistory building requires the full-time effort of a LAN manager with top-notch technical and programming skills. As a rule of thumb, it should require one half of a full-time equivalent (FTE) person for administering a LAN with 15 stations, one and a half FTEs for 50 stations, and two FTEs for 100 stations. Large, sophisticated LANs require special monitoring hardware that may cost as much as a network workstation. Large organizations even have a small group of LAN management and maintenance personnel who install, manage, interconnect, and maintain all the individual LANs throughout the organization.

The 13 steps discussed in Chapter 8 can be used as the overall plan for designing and implementing a local area network. In addition, the initial network plan and its related documentation can be the benchmark on which future network enhancements are based.

MANAGING A LAN

Local area networks are used in many organizations as a "backbone" for communications among many communicating devices, such as terminals, microcomputers, shared printers, file servers, and office automation devices. As a result, LANs quickly are becoming critical networks within the organization. Network management encompasses a wide range of features necessary to plan, operate, control access to, and maintain a local area network. (Chapter 12 covers network management in greater detail.) Obviously, a small LAN with three or four microcomputers does not require extensive network management. Larger LANs with 50 to 200 workstation nodes, however, require a full-time network manager with the appropriate network management hardware, software, and testing equipment. Chapter 12 describes the Simple Network Management Protocol (SNMP), NetWare Management System (NMS), and SMT—Station Management for FDDI (pages 583 to 586).

A manager is required for such activities as adding new users to a network, removing user workstation devices from a network, reassigning security levels, fixing problems, moving devices, backing up servers, and installing new software. This manager should be responsible for incorporating new technology into the network and "fixing" the network should a catastrophic problem occur. Again, a small four- or five-node LAN does not require much management, but it seems that today's small LANs have a propensity for growing quickly into very large networks. These rapidly enlarged networks often become critical to the organization because of the organization's dependence on communication among the network's users and/or departments.

For network security, constant monitoring is necessary; it must be possible to keep track of which nodes currently are using the network and when they last logged on to the LAN. This can entail issuing individual passwords. Furthermore, the LAN software must operate properly with regard to volume locking, file locking, and record locking. LAN security is the last major section in this chapter.

Hardware and Software Tools   *Network management* relies on appropriate tools for monitoring network activity, network loading, network errors, network changes, and network security. The network manager probably has a dedicated microcomputer, appropriate software, and possibly specialized hardware used for the LAN management and analysis system. This system shows on the microcomputer screen the various facts and figures necessary to manage and control the overall LAN. The following are typical examples of this monitoring.

Network activity displays the number of packets on a network for the current second, minute, hour, or day. It also might show the elapsed time since a token loss was detected on a token ring or, if there is a collision detection system, the number of collisions within a certain period of time. Cumulative network downtime and network demand levels can be monitored.

Network loading displays the average load on a network and provides information on the busiest times of the day or hour. This information on loading can help in reconfiguring the network as it grows.

The *network error* display provides statistics necessary to identify a deteriorating network operation. It identifies and displays bad format packets, missing control characters, number of messages retransmitted because of errors, and so forth.

Server administrator software reports on usage, account maintenance, auditing, software licensing, and integrity monitoring.

Workstation cataloging gathers workstation hardware and software configuration information.

Menu generators assist in building application and function menus for workstation access to servers.

Network changes show network additions or deletions and keep track of the overall network configuration with regard to its users and the pieces of hardware attached to the network.

Network security includes restricting access to the LAN, virus protection, backup and recovery, physical and data security, and volume, file, and record locking. Chapter 13 is devoted to the security and control of networks, as is the last section of this chapter.

Organizations using local area networks find that managing them can be quite a challenge. Network managers need to know the answers to such questions as

- What are the network loads at any particular time?
- What channels are the most active?
- What types of errors are occurring?
- What will happen to the network when more terminals are added?

Several LAN management software packages are available to help network managers. The next section presents an example of local area network management and control software.

The LANVision Series   Triticom produces the LAN traffic monitoring software packages described in this section. A diskette containing demonstration versions of all seven programs is available for classroom use. The *LANVision* demonstrations are very effective because they simulate the operation of a LAN to show management statistics and other factors that are useful when managing a LAN. A LAN is not required to see these programs in operation. They run on IBM-compatible micro-computers having a hard disk. The seven demonstration programs are compressed onto one 3.5-inch diskette.

Professors wishing to obtain a copy of the LANVision Series demonstration diskette should contact their John Wiley & Sons sales representative or call John Wiley Sales Support at 1-800-225-5945 (ext. 6462). (Students should ask their professor to obtain this LANVision demonstration diskette.) Companies or government agencies interested in receiving additional information or a demonstration diskette should contact Mr. Barry Trent at Triticom, P.O. Box 444180, Eden Prairie, Minn. 55344, or telephone him at 1-612-937-0772, or send a facsimile request to him at 1-612-937-1998.

The LANVision software consists of seven separate LAN management software tools that perform the following tasks.

- **ARGUS/n: The LAN Station Monitor.** This software is used for monitoring Novell's NetWare LANs. It monitors up to 25,000 workstations, maintains a hardware inventory, allows operation of a remote workstation, determines what programs currently are being executed, shows a history of the programs that have been run, identifies hardware configurations, and performs many other tasks. The ARGUS/n InterNetwork package monitors up to five internet-worked NetWare LAN segments with up to 250 stations on each segment.

- **EtherVision: The Ethernet LAN Monitor.** This software monitors station frame counts, byte counts, and percentage of traffic generated by a station. It also sets alarms for intruder detection. EtherVision displays network utilization, station or network traffic, errors by station, frame size distribution, network load information, speeds, diagnostics, and many other statistics for managing an IEEE 802.3 Ethernet LAN.

- **TokenVision: Token-Ring LAN Monitor.** This software performs the same functions as EtherVision, except it is for use with either IEEE 802.5 or IBM Token-Ring LANs.

- **ArcVision: Arcnet LAN Monitor.** This software also performs the same functions as EtherVision, except it is for use with Arcnet LANs.

- **LANdecoder/e: Ethernet Protocol Analyzer.** This software captures and de-codes Ethernet protocols. You can see actual frame data (what is in the frame). You can select single frames from a particular station to analyze what is hap-pening to them, such as the reason for a specific frame being rejected. It also can be used to generate traffic for testing the capacities of a LAN.

- **LANdecoder/tr: Token-Ring Protocol Analyzer.** This software performs the same functions as LANdecoder/e, except it is for use with Token-Ring LANs.

- **BridgeIT!: Ethernet-Ethernet Bridge.** This software connects two Ethernet LANs, whether they are NetWare, TCP/IP, LAN Manager, VINES, 3+, DECNET, ISO, or any mixture of high-level protocols.

Although other vendors have LAN management software, Triticom offers a complete range that covers Novell's NetWare LANs as well as the three most popular LAN architectures: Ethernet, Token-Ring, and Arcnet. Triticom's demonstration diskette is an excellent tool for getting familiar with LAN management software. Each of the seven demonstrations contains more complete descriptions of what the tool does.

SELECTING A LAN

Selecting a LAN for your organization is no simple task. Today's LAN marketplace is crowded with numerous vendors, all claiming their product is the one you need. To complicate the situation, you may be sure that the simple small LAN you start with today may turn into a large multifloor, multibuilding, or enterprise-wide network at some time in the future! To choose the proper LAN, you should answer some basic questions, such as how many users there will be, how much data will need to be stored and transmitted, how easy it will be to add workstations, what cabling is needed, whose software should be selected, and how much security is needed. The 13 design steps in Chapter 8 will help in LAN selection, as will the 40 *key issues* for selecting local area networks that are examined in the following discussion. These issues are enumerated in the box on Local Area Network Selection Considerations.

One of the first issues that must be addressed is the *configuration* (see Glossary) and *topology* of the network. Is it best to have a star, bus, or ring network? The topology is influenced greatly by the decisions as to whose cable scheme is chosen and which topology is supported by which vendor. Although a star network may fit in quite well with sophisticated file servers and digital PBXs (switchboards), a bus topology may work equally well when wiring a large building. Ring topologies also work well, especially when it is a one-floor installation, although rings can be wired up and down throughout a large building. One option is to use a bus topology vertically (between floors) and a star topology on each floor.

The *protocol* is an important issue because it is here that you must decide whether you are going to use the token-passing approach or the carrier sense multiple access approach. Associated with the protocol decision is the decision on whether the system will be *baseband* (one message at a time) or *broadband* (multiple messages paths). These two considerations are critical when related to future growth because when you choose a protocol and baseband/broadband, you determine the LAN's future growth as to whether voice, data, and image transmissions can be added to the same cable.

In the *cabling* decision, you need to determine whether the existing telephone wiring (unshielded twisted wire pair), coaxial cable (93-ohm for IBM, 52-ohm for Thin Ethernet, and 75-ohm for CATV television cable), or fiber optics will be used. Remember that the cost of pulling the cables through the building may be greater than the cost of the cable itself. For this reason, a *wireless LAN* may be a more cost-effective alternative.

LOCAL AREA NETWORK SELECTION CONSIDERATIONS

- Configuration/topology
- Protocol
- Baseband/Broadband
- Cabling
- Wireless
- Number of nodes
- Number of users
- Servers
- Distance between nodes
- Workstation hardware
- Network circuit boards
- Connector cables
- LAN operating system
- Reliability
- Vendor service and support
- Ease of use
- Performance
- Vendor application support
- Application systems
- LAN management

- LAN support software
- Future growth
- LAN standards
- Bridges/routers/gateways
- Network hardware
- Security features
- Printer features
- Backup and recovery
- Electronic mail/voice mail
- Local disk files
- Documentation
- Electrical power protection
- Training
- Overall costs
- Outside consultant
- Legal issues
- Employee use policies
- Vendor contracts
- On-site spares
- Network manager

The maximum *number of nodes* (microcomputer workstations) probably will be an issue in the future, and it is one you must plan for now. Today you may be developing a local area network with only five or ten nodes, but will the LAN be able to grow to the size that may be required five years from now?

Along with the number of nodes, the *number of users* must be considered. In other words, how many people might use this local area network? Remember, you may have multiple users at a single node. Even though the number of nodes may not increase, as the number of users increases there may be an overload at the server. This overload might mean that the LAN operating system software is unable to handle user requirements and specific business needs such as database retrievals, processing application programs, electronic mail, and file transfer. Remember that multiple users at a single node can overload a LAN.

Another critical decision is the *server*. You must decide whether you are going to use a dedicated disk server for the central database. Moreover, you must decide whether there is to be a print server, an access/modem server, a facsimile server, a network server, or a separate database server.

The *distance between nodes* is another important consideration when selecting a LAN. On this topic you will have to check with each vendor, but you will find figures such as 100 to 1,000 feet per segment between each node, 3,000 feet from the network server to the microcomputer node, or possibly 7,000 feet end-to-end total network length. Remember, in today's world this is not an absolute limitation because you always can add repeaters/amplifiers to reamplify the signal and extend the medium for several thousand more feet.

The *workstation hardware* is a consideration. You already may have many of the microcomputer workstations that must be connected to the local area network. In this case, you must determine whether each piece of hardware the organization already owns or intends to connect to the local area network will function properly. Remember that one vendor's LAN software or hardware (network server) may not handle another vendor's hardware or software protocols.

Another consideration with the hardware is whether the required *network circuit boards* can plug into the equipment you already own. Are there enough slots? Do you need full- or half-length slots? The serial port probably will not cause any problem because you always can use a RS232 connector, but remember that PC/AT or PS/2 microcomputers may have a 9-pin plug instead of the 25-pin RS232. If you intend to use the parallel port for connecting to the LAN, however, make sure the proper connector plugs and cables are available. In other words, make sure you have the correct *connector cables*.

The *LAN operating system* is another critical consideration because the microcomputer operating system and the LAN's vendor-supplied software package must be compatible. They all must be able to work together and interface with the various nodes (microcomputer workstations or whatever hardware is connected to the LAN), as well as interface with the organization's application programs and host mainframe. At this point you also must take into account the *reliability* of both the vendor and the LAN operating system. You also must evaluate the level of *vendor service and support*. Other details pertaining to software evaluation include its *ease of use,* its *performance,* and the availability and kind of *vendor application support.* Speaking of applications, a review of the *application systems* is vital to be sure they can run on the proposed local area network.

Determine whether it is possible to actively *manage the LAN* and all of the related network elements. The previous section discussed managing a LAN as does Chapter 12.

Another consideration is *LAN support software.* For example, you must decide if third-party software, such as menu support, memory management, word processing, and spreadsheets, work with the LAN's operating system.

Future growth should be a major point to consider. In other words, you must determine whether the LAN can grow to meet the changing needs of the organization's application systems, geographic locations, interconnectivity, users, and hardware requirements. Is there enough built-in flexibility and modularity for the local area network to survive if or when *LAN standards* change?

Do not overlook the area of *bridges, routers,* and *gateways.* You must determine whether the LAN is going to interface with another corporate network, the organization's host mainframe, or some of the public dial-up networks outside of the organization. The question to ask is, What gateways are available to connect our network with the corporate host mainframe or other LANs within the organization? Consideration of other *network hardware* is necessary, including concentrators, multiplexers, fast packet, cell relay, direct microwave links, and the like.

A number of miscellaneous features also need to be addressed.

- *Security features* must be installed to protect each user's data. Remember, each user may have data of differing sensitivity or risk values. Another security consideration is whether users should have microcomputers without any disk storage devices attached to them. Consider virus protection, passwords, and file security controls. A later section in this chapter discusses LAN security as does Chapter 13.

- Various *print features* must be made available at the shared printer. Will some users need special purpose printers?

- Proper *backup and recovery* procedures must be provided. Certainly the server disk must be backed up, and recovery features for each user's disk files must be provided.

- Both *electronic mail* and *voice mail* are big features on local area networks, although you may opt not to put voice transmission on the LAN.

- Some users may be allowed to have their own *local disk files,* as well as have access to the disk files on the network server or host mainframe.

- Proper written *documentation* should be provided for all the hardware, software, nodes, users, and so forth.

- *Backup electrical power* or surge/sag protection may be required on both the electric utility power lines and any connecting telephone lines. What is being done to protect against static electricity?

- *Training* must be considered. You must examine both the cost of the training and the time required by each user to attend the various training sessions. Another consideration is who will perform the training.

- The overall *costs* of hardware, software, cabling (including installation) should be taken into account. A previous section covered LAN costs.

- An *outside consultant* may be required for some services.

- *Legal issues,* such as purchasing the proper software licenses and formulating policies on employee copying of software, must be addressed.

- *Employee use policies* should prohibit the use of personal diskettes and software on the organization's local area networks. Such policies help prevent the spread of computer viruses and the theft of privileged information. These policies also should address the connection of employee-owned hardware to the organization's LANs.

- *Vendor contracts* should require quick vendor response when service support is needed.

- *On-site spares* for critical hardware should be procured.

- A decision should be made as to whether there will be a *network manager* to run and administer the local area network.

LAN SECURITY AND CONTROL

One of the most important functions of LAN software is to provide a secure network. It does so by controlling the access of network users in various ways. Some network operating systems simply split the server's hard disk into sections called volumes or partitions. The disk server then assigns a volume or volumes to each network user. This is the *disk server* method of controlling security. Disk servers allow users to have greater access because they can use all the files in any volume to which they have access. Volumes usually are assigned public status (meaning everyone has read only access to its files), private access (a single user has both read and write access to its files), or shared access (all users have both read and write access to its files).

More sophisticated LAN network operating system software allows a greater number of access levels. This is the *file server* method of controlling security. File servers restrict users more than the disk server method because users have access only to specific files instead of to an entire volume of files. For example, a user might have the power to delete or create files, have no access to certain volumes or files, or just read access or write access. Access is a key network issue when many users want to share data.

Under an access level known as *volume locking,* a user who opens a volume can bar all other users from accessing any part of that volume by using a secret password. Some networks allow several users to view and modify different files within the same volume. This technique, which is called *file locking,* determines who can use each file within the volume. Certain file locking schemes permit several users to read but not write on the same file. Under the most precise level of network data access, known as *record locking,* only parts of files are locked. Users can read the same file in a volume simultaneously but are prevented from writing over the same records. True record locking is rare. Record locking schemes depend on both the network operating system and the application software that runs under it. Some operating system software supports record locking, but application programs must be written to take advantage of this feature. Some LAN software allows the LAN network manager to keep an audit trail of which network files a network user is working on and which network stations are exchanging information.

Finally, *password* access control is mandatory. For example, a multilevel secure LAN software package may have a security center that is a dedicated workstation offering centralized management of the network's security system. The types of security implemented might be

- Encryption of each packet before it is transmitted
- Physical or electronic keys that must be inserted into a network security device to gain access to the network

- Security windows, which define what type of data can be received and transmitted by a given user or a given microcomputer
- Volume, file, and record locking
- Password protection
- Virus protection, detection, and control. The following are some online sources of information on viruses: Computer Virus Industry Association's Virus Information Bulletin Board at 1-408-988-4004; National Computer Security Association's Bulletin Board at 1-202-364-1305; and National Institute of Standards and Technology's Computer Security Bulletin Board at 1-301-948-5717.

Build a Control Spreadsheet Chapter 13 contains a detailed step-by-step *Control Spreadsheet* methodology on how to identify, document, and evaluate the controls in a local area network. See the How to Develop a Control Spreadsheet section starting on page 624. You can conduct an in-depth security review of a specific local area network by completing a Control Spreadsheet for that LAN.

LAN Controls The following is a list[1] of specific *LAN controls* that can be used for controlling and protecting a local area network.

1. **Network Supervisor:** Designate a network supervisor or guru who has responsibility for the network and its security. This administrator assigns and manages user passwords or IDs, monitors audit trail reports, installs the LAN hardware and software, and ensures the honoring of software licensing agreements (that is, prevents the illegal copying of software).

2. **Physical Security:** Establish a strict physical security policy, especially for physical access to the network server and its hard disk. This means the network server, its hard disks, and its uninterruptible power supply should be located in a locked area that is covered by controlled access policies.

3. **Password:** Provide each user with a unique password for logging on to the local area network. These passwords should be changed at reasonable intervals, depending on the level of security required by the organization and the applications on the LAN. Immediately remove from the system any user passwords of terminated, transferred, or disgruntled employees.

4. **Log-off Policy:** Develop a policy requiring users to log-off when they leave their microcomputers unattended. Prevent microcomputers from being logged in when operators leave their desks for any extended period of time, such as during the lunch hour.

5. **Security Set-up:** Prevent the network installers from also setting up the network security. Have them teach the designated LAN administrator how to

---

[1]This list on LAN controls is one of 94 lists of controls enumerated in Chapters 7 and 8 of the book, *Designing Controls into Computerized Systems* (ISBN 0-932410-40-5). See reference 11 in Chapter 13.

set it up, and then have that person set up a security system that is unknown to the installers.

6. **Secure Cabling:** Secure the LAN cabling so it is concealed. For example, place it out of sight above drop ceilings or within walls. In addition, lock and restrict access to interconnection junction areas, such as wire closets where all LAN circuits begin, end, and interconnect.

7. **Cable Diagrams:** Develop and maintain cabling diagrams. This ensures ready knowledge of all local area network cable routing in the building. Up-to-date cabling diagrams are essential for timely troubleshooting.

8. **Diskless Microcomputers:** Consider using diskless microcomputers because they do not have internal disk storage that can be used improperly. Diskless microcomputers start with a special boot ROM that accesses DOS from the network server (see Chapter 10 for a discussion on the operation of diskless microcomputers). These microcomputers are more secure because operators cannot make unauthorized copies of the organization's data and they cannot use unauthorized software. The primary value of a diskless microcomputer is to protect against unauthorized file copying and viruses.

9. **Encryption:** Consider encryption, although it usually is unnecessary on a local area network. It may be needed if you are internetworking, connecting directly to wide area networks, or if you are installing a wireless LAN.

10. **Backup and Recovery:** Develop appropriate backup and recovery procedures for the LAN network server's hard disk. This also may require establishing backup procedures for the hard disks in any individual user microcomputers connected to the LAN.

11. **Documentation:** Maintain up-to-date documentation of the local area network hardware and software.

12. **Management Software:** Ensure that the LAN administrator has the proper management software. Such software is required to analyze the LAN, to look for network errors, and to assist in the continuing redesign and reconfiguration of the LAN to meet the organization's changing needs.

13. **Disk/File Server:** Use file server software, rather than disk server software, because it is more secure. File servers allow more control in restricting user access. For example, file servers can restrict access to individual files and, in some cases, even down to the record or data structure level. They use volume locks, file locks, and record locks to restrict access. By contrast, disk servers only allow volume locking, which means users are restricted only by the volume they can access, not the file. The most sophisticated servers are network servers and database servers.

14. **UPS Backup:** Have backup electrical power for the network server. In other words, install an uninterruptible power supply (UPS). Also install surge protection devices at both the network server and at all user microcomputers. Install surge protection devices on any incoming or outgoing circuits (access/modem server).

15. **Training:** Provide adequate training for LAN users to prevent the accidental breach of security or the accidental destruction of another user's data.

16. **Background Checks:** Perform background and reference checks prior to contracting with outside consultants for installing or troubleshooting a local area network.

17. **On-site Spares:** Keep on-site spares for critical hardware that must operate the entire time the local area network is running.

18. **Vendor Agreements:** Establish adequate vendor maintenance and service agreements to ensure quick vendor response when vendor support is required. Establish maintenance and service agreements with the common carrier that supplies the leased circuits used for internetworking.

19. **LAN Operating System Security:** Review the local area network operating system software for its security options, which determine the LAN's degree of security. For example, Novell's NetWare security includes the following.

   - Network access is based on user profiles assigned by the network supervisor. The five access levels are password, trustee, file, directory, and file rights.

   - The MONITOR server application locks the console keyboard until a password is typed.

   - Expiration dates and resource usage limits can be assigned to individual user accounts.

   - System supervisors can limit the amount of disk storage available to a user. Storage limitations can be placed on specific directories as well.

   - Allowable log-in days, time of day, physical locations, and number of incorrect log-in attempts can be limited for each user account.

   - Half-hour security checks determine whether a user can log-in (or is permitted to be logged in) during that time period, whether a user's account has expired or has been disabled, and whether a user's account has run out of funds.

   - Unauthorized or overdrawn user accounts are logged out automatically every half hour after the user has been given a five-minute warning.

   - A resource accounting feature allows network supervisors to charge users for connection time, the number of bytes read or written to disk, use of storage space on disks, or the number of requests made by a workstation. Rates can vary by the hour and by the day. Supervisors can assign credit limits and have the system monitor the users' account balances and log them off if they exceed their credit limits.

20. **Remote LAN Software:** Review the use of remote LAN software that operates programs and accesses peripherals on a remote microcomputer via a modem. This can cause a security breach if a remote user accesses LAN files. It also raises the issue of invasion of privacy because microcomputer users can be "observed" remotely without their knowledge.

21. **Download Policy:** Develop a policy for downloaded data. A significant problem with data downloaded via a LAN or micro-to-mainframe link arises when the downloaded data is subject to modification outside of the host mainframe control and security programs that are intended to control and validate this data. If this modified data then is uploaded to the mainframe, the central host mainframe database may become polluted with corrupted data. Downloaded data that is uploaded later also may be subject to the introduction of viruses, which could disable the host mainframe and invade the database.

22. **Dial-up Access:** Prevent dial-up access to the local area network when possible because LANs can be connected not only to the host mainframe, but also to one another. As these connections proliferate, it may become impossible to determine which outsiders have direct dial-up access to the sensitive databases located in the host mainframe computer.

23. **Software Security Package:** Consider purchasing a special software security package that resides in the network server and controls the local area network software. This is similar to the much more sophisticated security software packages that work in conjunction with the host mainframe operating system.

24. **Physical Locks:** Use locks, cables, anchor pads, alarms, and other security devices to prevent the theft of hardware connected to the local area network.

25. **CRC Error Checking:** Be sure the LAN software has some type of cyclical redundancy check (CRC) or polynomial block error check to detect transmission errors. When a message is sent from one station on the LAN to another, this checking allows the receiving station to verify that none of the data bits have been corrupted during transmission.

26. **Disk Mirroring/Duplexing:** Consider disk ''mirroring'' for database servers. (These are more sophisticated network servers.) Mirroring is useful when data must be available instantly all the time, and it ensures both the integrity and availability of the data. In mirroring, every time the hard disk is updated, the computer writes on two different hard disks on the same disk channel. This creates two mirror images of the database data. Disk mirroring can be accomplished only when the database server contains two physical disk drives because the records or data structures are written to both disks simultaneously. Should a problem develop with one disk, the second disk is available instantly with identical information on it. An alternative is disk ''duplexing'' in which the data is written to two hard disks on two different disk channels. Duplexing is even more redundant than mirroring because there are two disk channels.

27. **Legal Issues:** Ensure the awareness of users about the legal issue of using single-computer licensed software on local area networks. Software programs that have a single-computer license are not meant to be placed on local area networks; other types of licenses cover this application.

28. **Backup LAN Operators:** Ensure that several people in the user department know how to run the microcomputer system and the local area network.

29. **Server Uptime:** Check the "server uptime" intermittently to help detect if there has been an intruder. There may be cause for concern if the system has been operating all day, but the monitoring indicates that the server has been up for only one hour and there have not been any power failures.

30. **Virus Detection:** Install a dedicated virus monitoring, detection, and purging software package. It should check for all known viruses every time either the network server or a user/client microcomputer is booted. The software should be able to remove (purge) viruses.

KEY TERMS

1Base5
10Base-T
10Base2
10Base5
10Broad36
Access server
AppleTalk
Arcnet
Attachment unit interface (AUI)
Backbone network (BN)
BALUN
Baseband
Bridge
Broadband
Brouter
Bus topology
Busy token
Cabling
Cheapernet
Client microcomputer
Coaxial cable
Collision avoidance (CA)
Collision detection (CD)
Configuration
Control Spreadsheet
Cross-talk (noise)
CSMA/CA
CSMA/CD
Data grade twisted pair

Database server
Datagram
Dedicated server
Disk server
Dual-attachment station (DAS)
Enterprise-wide network
Ethernet
Facsimile server
Fiber Distributed Data Interface (FDDI)
Fiber optic cable
File locking
File server
Frame
Free token
Gateway
High-end full network LAN
Hybrid topology
IEEE 802 standards
Internet
Internetwork
LAN controls
LAN metering software
LAN operating system
LANBIOS
LANVision Series
Local area network (LAN)
LocalTalk

LocalTalk link access protocol (LLAP)
Low-end DOS-based peer LAN
Media-access control (MAC) protocol
Medium access unit (MAU)
Menu generator
Metropolitan area network (MAN)
Modem remote control
Modem server
Multistation Access Unit (MAU)
NETBIOS
Network activity
Network changes
Network circuit card
Network error display
Network loading
Network management
Network operating system
Network profile
Network security
Network server
Node
Password
Peer-to-peer network
Primary ring
Printer server

Protocol
Record locking
Remote LAN software
Repeater
Ring topology
Router
Secondary ring
Server
Server administrator
  software
Server microcomputer
Single-attachment station
  (SAS)

Star topology
Station profile
Sub-LAN
Subnetwork
Thick Ethernet
Thin Ethernet
Token
Token access method
Token-bus network
Token priority
Token-ring network
Topology
Twisted pair wiring

Unshielded twisted pair
  (UTP)
User microcomputer
User profile
Volume locking
Wide area network
  (WAN)
Wireless LAN
Workstation cataloging
X.75 gateway
Zero-slot LAN

SELECTED REFERENCES

1. Berline, Gary, and Ed Perratore. "Portable, Affordable, Secure: Wireless LANs," *PC Magazine,* vol. 11, no. 3, February 11, 1992, pp. 291–293, 297–298, 300, 303–305, 307–308, 310–314.

2. Brown, Ronald O. "Bridges and Routers: Network Traffic Cops," *InfoWorld,* vol. 14, no. 16, April 20, 1992, pp. 48–49.

3. Derfler, Frank J., Jr. "Connectivity Simplified: An Introduction to the Ways of Networking," *PC Magazine,* vol. 11, no. 6, March 31, 1992, pp. 251–252ff. (Two-part series in Connectivity section with overtitle "LAN Fundamentals 1." Includes Network Cabling Guide.)

4. Derfler, Frank J., Jr., and Steve Rigney. "Smart Links Between LAN Segments: Bridges and Routers," *PC Magazine,* vol. 10, no. 14, September 10, 1991, pp. 121–123ff.

5. Derfler, Frank J., Jr., et al. "LAN Fundamentals Part 2: Low-Cost LANs Grow in Features and Performance," *PC Magazine,* vol. 11, no. 7, April 14, 1992, pp. 299–300ff. (Second of two-part series in Connectivity section with overtitle "LAN Fundamentals 2. Includes boxes on Matching Network Protocols to the OSI Model and an Index to Connectivity Articles.)

6. Ellison, Carol. "Reaching Out with LAN Remote-Control Software," *PC Magazine,* vol. 10, no. 13, July 1991, pp. 301–304ff.

7. Fetterolf, Peter. "Connectivity: The Sum of Its Parts," *Byte,* vol. 16, no. 12, November 1991, pp. 197–198, 200, 202, 204–206, 208.

8. Herron, D. Keith, and Joanne T. Witt. "LAN Software Licensing Poses Problems," *LAN Times,* vol. 9, no. 6, April 6, 1992, pp. 45–46. (Part 1 of two-part article.)

9. Herron, D. Keith, and Joanne T. Witt. "LAN Software Licensing Poses Problems," *LAN Times,* vol. 9, no. 7, April 20, 1992, pp. 45–46. (Part 2 of two-part article.)

10. Kine, Bill. "Understanding the Requirements of 10Base-T," *LAN Times,* vol. 9, no. 8, May 11, 1992, pp. 27–28.

11. *LAN Magazine*. Published monthly by Miller Freeman, Inc., 600 Harrison Street, San Francisco, Calif. 94107, 1976– .

12. Mathias, Craig J. "Wireless LANs: The Next Wave," *Data Communications,* vol. 21, no. 5, March 21, 1992, pp. 83–87.

13. Sloan, John P., and Ann Drinan, eds. *Handbook of Local Area Networks.* Boston: Auerbach Publishers, 1991.

14. *Smart LAN Performance Test.* A software package available for $50 from Innovative Software, Attn: LAN Test, 9875 Widmer Road, Lenexa, Kans. 66215, 1-800-331-1763.

15. Udell, Jon, Tom Thompson, and Tom Yager. "Mix 'N' Match LAN: The Byte Lab Puts Together a LAN for Unix, Mac, and NetWare Clients," *Byte,* vol. 16, no. 12, November 1991, pp. 272–278, 280, 282, 284, 286.

QUESTIONS/PROBLEMS

1. It is said that a local area network-to-host mainframe connection is just like a micro-to-mainframe, except it has one additional capability. What is this capability?

2. Define local area network.

3. What are the distinguishing features of a LAN?

4. There are two reasons for developing LANs. What are they?

5. Briefly describe the steps that must be taken to install a LAN.

6. What is the most common way of cabling microcomputers together for a LAN?

7. Distinctions are made in local area networks between the different types of microcomputers. How is the distinction made?

8. In some local area networks, most of the microcomputers can talk only with the server microcomputer, but in others each microcomputer can talk with every other microcomputer. What are these two approaches called?

9. How is DOS affected by a LAN?

10. What is required to make DOS work on a network?

11. One of the problems associated with local area networks has to do with the memory in each of the microcomputers connected to the LAN. Describe this problem and one possible solution.

12. Briefly describe the steps that are required to install LAN software.

13. There are some inexpensive local area networks that are not "true" LANs. How do these differ from true LANs?

14. Discuss the legal issue of using single-computer license software on networks.

15. What is the difference between using a word processor on a single microcomputer and using one on a LAN?

16. What are the topologies of a local area network?

17. How do LAN topologies differ from LAN configurations?

18. What is a backbone network?

19. How does baseband differ from broadband?

20. Briefly describe CSMA, CD, and CA.
21. On what does packet size depend in a local area network?
22. Why should CSMA/CD networks be built with no more than 25 percent of their capacity dedicated to actual network traffic?
23. Define bit time.
24. What do the terms 1Base5, 10Base2, 10Base5, 10Broad36, and 10Base-T mean?
25. What two methods of LAN access are supported by the IEEE 802 committee?
26. How does a network using a token method operate?
27. Should you select a network because of its protocol or its performance characteristics?
28. How does a bridge differ from a gateway?
29. How are hybrid networks connected to user nodes?
30. How does a router differ from bridges and gateways?
31. What are the three types of gateways discussed in this chapter and how do they differ?
32. How do wide area networks differ from local area networks?
33. What one factor limits (or conversely, promotes) network availability and capability more than any other?
34. It is said that hooking some microcomputers together with a cable does not make a network. Why is this so?
35. Assume you want to install a local area network using IBM-compatible equipment. What must you know about the operating systems of the microcomputers?
36. Local area network software provides security. How is this done?
37. There are three ways to lock users out of local area network files (i.e., deny them access). What are they and how do they differ?
38. Remote LAN software provides several features. Name two.
39. Describe a legal issue involving remote LAN software.
40. What factor may have a great influence on selection of the local area network topology?
41. It is possible to have a local area network based on radio. Why would you want or not want to have a radio-based LAN?
42. What cable media normally are used in LANs?
43. What is the purpose of a BALUN? (Also see Balanced and Unbalanced in the Glossary.)
44. What feature makes data grade twisted pair wiring less susceptible to interference than regular twisted pair wiring?
45. What types of interference or noise can be found on twisted pair LANs?
46. Assume you want to install a LAN but are concerned about its cost. Realizing there are both inexpensive and expensive LANs, what features should you compare to help in the selection process?
47. What is required to implement a LAN?
48. Discuss why a network manager or "guru" is required for even small LANs.
49. What are the "tools of the trade" of a network manager and what is their purpose?
50. Discuss what makes LAN selection so difficult.

51. This chapter discusses a number of key issues that must be considered when selecting a LAN. Name six of these issues and elaborate on them.

52. What must a local area network do to justify its existence to management?

53. Look at Figure 11-6. Determine how many messages per second the local network can handle if it is designed for 100 percent utilization. (Technically, this is impossible because there would be too many collisions.)

54. What other two methodologies compete with LANs?

55. Define topology. Use the Glossary to contrast topology with configuration.

56. What might be an efficient combination of topologies for a LAN in a multistory building?

57. What is Ethernet?

58. _____ band uses direct electrical voltages, and _____ band uses a modulated signal.

59. How many transmission channels are on a broadband LAN?

60. Name two popular LAN protocols.

61. How many messages per second can your LAN handle if it has a speed of 2 million bits per second, 70-character messages using ASCII 8-bit code, no start-stops bits, and 25 percent utilization? See Figure 11-6.

62. What is the international standard gateway that links X.25 networks?

63. Why are wire pairs twisted as they run through the building's walls?

64. What is data grade twisted pair wiring?

65. Run the LANVision software demonstration package.

66. Discuss which of the 40 key issues for selecting a LAN would be the most important at your college, university, or company.

67. What are the four basic types of networks?

68. Some local area networks assign _____ levels to messages.

69. For what is the FDDI suitable?

70. Discuss why rigid definitions no longer always apply to network definitions.

71. When installing LAN software there are two important concerns. Name them.

72. What is the function of LAN metering software?

73. Why is it important to control illegal copies of software on a local area network?

74. What is the difference between Thick Ethernet and Cheapernet?

75. Two standards define token-passing networks. Name them.

76. There are two MAUs. Describe them.

77. Describe Arcnet.

78. How does FDDI work?

79. How does a FDDI LAN carry an Ethernet packet?

80. On what protocol is the AppleTalk LAN based?

81. This chapter states that LAN operating systems are attracting attention. Why is this?

82. What are the three levels of capability into which LANs typically fall?

83. What types of LANs use servers?

84. What is the most important characteristic of a server?

85. Name at least three types of servers.

86. What is an internet?

87. Name the devices that interconnect local area networks.

88. How are most local area networks formed?

89. Name the primary advantage and primary disadvantage of wireless LANs.

90. Discuss why it is important for organizations to enforce policies restricting use of employee-owned hardware and software and unauthorized copies of software.

NEXT DAY AIR SERVICE CUMULATIVE CASE STUDY

Background on Next Day Air Service

The local area network plan for Next Day Air Service has been developed into a workable configuration. Now you need to revisit the issue of LAN protocols and configurations so you can make a final recommendation for them. You also need to consider the operational and managerial procedures that will have to be adopted to ensure successful operation of the NDAS LAN.

The first issue to consider is the type of LAN you want to implement. Even though you decided on an Ethernet LAN (see the NDAS case in Chapter 9), you still can change your mind. The type of LAN should be analyzed carefully in view of its scope, configuration, protocols, and the methods by which users will be accessing corporate data. You realize that the larger a LAN becomes, the more likely it will be that one LAN will offer greater speed and reliability than some other. Internetworking also will become more important as the LAN and its utilization increases. You also realize that if Atlanta had its own LAN you could connect them through the WAN (but the transmission speed would be too slow), as you discussed in Chapter 7, Question 4, or as shown in Figure 11-3.

Mr. Coone is even more interested in the issue of how to manage the corporate local area network. Specifically, we need to investigate what should be managed, as well as how such management is to be enacted. For example, which departments or individuals should be responsible for creation and maintenance of the various corporate files that will be stored on the server? Will it be necessary for Next Day Air Service to hire a separate database administrator, or should this responsibility be integrated with the data processing operation? How will the procurement or development of new software applications be handled? Should there be one central office that controls and standardizes all acquisitions for LAN use, or should each user assume such responsibility? Then there is the area of network and equipment maintenance. In a multivendor environment, this can be a touchy point. Finally, you are aware that the topic of end user application development has been receiving quite a bit of attention. Because LAN management is so closely related to the kinds of applications users want to execute on a network, it seems worthwhile to consider incorporating end user application development efforts within the framework of LAN management.

The third issue should focus on local area network implementation. The cutover to a LAN will require some detailed coordination. For example, users must be trained, software must be installed and tested, management procedures must be evaluated, and the like. This will be a crucial time for NDAS. Indeed, the very success of its corporate LAN may well depend on the smoothness with which Next Day Air Service is able to make the transition into a networked environment.

Other issues that need to be considered at this time include such topics as repeaters, routers, bridges, gateways, and brouters and how they may fit into the situation at Next Day Air Service. The LAN's cabling, installation, security, and anticipated growth need to be addressed, as well as who or which remote offices can access the LAN. Finally, do not overlook the boxes on cost considerations (page 549) and LAN selection considerations (page 554).

Questions/Problems for the Next Day Air Service Case

1. Which is best for Next Day Air Service, a high-end full network, a low-end DOS-based peer LAN, or a zero-slot sub-LAN? Explain your choice.

2. In Chapter 6, you used Figure 6-35 to draw a configuration for a star, bus, and ring topology for the NDAS headquarters local area network. Now you must decide which LAN is going to be best for NDAS: Ethernet using coaxial cable, 10Base-T, token bus, or token ring. Which do you want to recommend? Justify your recommendation by listing three to five reasons why you chose one of the above LANs.

3. Make a copy of Figure 6-35 and draw the local area network you have selected for Next Day Air Service. This is your building map. Also draw a separate LAN map similar to the one shown in Figure 11-1. Use Figure 6-20 to draw the hardware symbols on the LAN map.

4. Using the LAN map you drew in Question 3, prepare a list for each microcomputer, identify which department owns it, and specify the use to which it will be put.

5. In which department would you locate the network (database), FAX, access (modem), repeater/bridge/router, and printer servers? State your logic for making these decisions.

6. Which do you think would be the three most costly items in the Tampa LAN?

7. Should NDAS mirror its database?

8. Run the LANVision software.

Chapter Twelve

NETWORK MANAGEMENT

This chapter discusses the basic management skills required to be a successful network manager. It also describes departmental functions, how to manage the department, required reports, network management software, error testing, and test equipment. Network control and troubleshooting, combining voice and data communications, and the Chief Information Officer also are discussed.

MANAGING THE DATA COMMUNICATION FUNCTION

One of the major growth sectors in both government and private business has been the internal "service function." The service functions have grown rapidly, and their management techniques need to be strengthened. These service functions include staff assistance, research departments, planning groups, coordinators, data processing departments, data communication networks, and the like. Such functions are organized to support manufacturing, sales, or the specific product or service for which the organization was conceived.

The primary responsibility of the data communication function is to move and convey data or information. This transfer of information may take place within a single department, between departments in an organization, or with entities outside the organization. Remember that *data* are nothing more than meaningless characters, whereas *information* takes these meaningless characters and assembles them into a fact or idea that can be used for decision making by managers. Information presupposes adequate communication because information is useless if it is not available when needed. Data communications add time value to information. Phrased another way, information that is only 75 percent accurate, but received in time to affect a decision, generally is more valuable than information that is 100 percent accurate, but received too late to be used in the decision making process.

The manager of a data communication function should always remember that data or information transmitted over any network must CATER to the needs of its users. *CATER* is an acronym that stands for *c*onsistent, *a*ccurate, *t*imely, *e*conomically feasible, and *r*elevant. Although the manager of the data communication function may not have direct responsibility for *consistency* or *relevancy* (those are the responsibility of the information owner/gatherer/developer), the data communication manager is responsible for ensuring *accuracy* (error-free transmission), *timeliness* (speed), and *economic feasibility* (cost-effective networks).

Information activities present a special organizational problem because they have to be both centralized and decentralized. The original developers or gatherers of data may be either centralized or decentralized, but the total organization is served best if the management of the data communication function is centralized with some of the network hardware and software decentralized. This may seem to be a dichotomy in today's world of distributed data processing and distributed databases. Nevertheless, the data communication management function should be centralized. It can be likened to the nervous system of the human body because it controls the paths over which all control messages and information flow. When viewed in this manner, it is obvious why centralized control is necessary to interconnect all the various terminals, CPUs, databases, and achieve internetworking.

The individual manager who is responsible for the data communication function must be adept at performing the five key management tasks of *planning, organizing, directing, controlling,* and *staffing*. Refer to the Five Key Management Tasks box to see what these five tasks include.

Because the information-based society is dominated by computers and communications, a manager's value to the organization is increased not only by knowledge but also by the *speed* at which that knowledge moves. Today's information-based economy is vitally concerned with the movement of voice conversations, data/information, and images (video/graphics). For this reason, today's manager is concerned with the entire telecommunication function, even though it may be referred

---

FIVE KEY MANAGEMENT TASKS

- *Planning* activities require . . .
  Forecasting
  Establishing objectives
  Scheduling
  Budgeting
  Allocating resources
  Developing policies
- *Organizing* activities require . . .
  Developing organizational structure
  Delegating
  Establishing relationships
  Establishing procedures
  Integrating the smaller organization
    with the larger organization

- *Directing* activities require . . .
  Initiating activities
  Decision making
  Communicating
  Motivating
- *Controlling* activities require . . .
  Establishing performance standards
  Measuring performance
  Evaluating performance
  Correcting performance
- *Staffing* activities require . . .
  Interviewing people
  Selecting people
  Developing people

to as data communications. The point is that effective communication managers must be aware of voice transmissions, data transmissions, and image transmissions; the information systems manager can no longer be concerned solely with data transmissions.

The manager might view a network as having *pipes, pumps, and people* (this concept was introduced in Chapter 8). Pipes are the circuits that carry messages (data/information), pumps are the hardware and software that push and switch the messages through the network, and people manage and use the network. The network manager's primary responsibility is to ensure that the pipes, pumps, and people all function as a cohesive unit for the benefit of the organization.

NETWORK ORGANIZATION

Network organization, as discussed in this section, focuses on the management and organization of the *people* running the network rather than on the physical organization of the network's communication circuits. Management must define a central control philosophy regarding the overall network functions. This means there is a single control source for all emergency problems, testing, and future planning. We discuss how to implement the management policies in two later sections of this chapter: Network Management and Managing the Day-to-Day Operations.

The data communication network organization should have a written charter that defines its mandate, operational philosophy, and long-range goals. These goals must conform both to the parent organization's information processing goals and to its own departmental goals. Along with its long-term policies, the organization must develop individual procedures with which to implement the policies. Remember that goals lead to policies, which lead in turn to procedures that detail how specific tasks are to be carried out so the organization can meet its goals. These policies and procedures, therefore, provide the structure that guides the day-to-day job tasks of people working in the data communication function.

The ultimate objective of the data communication function is to move data from one location to another in a timely fashion, and to provide and make available the resources that allow this transfer of data. All too often this major objective is sacrificed to the immediacy of problems generated by factors thought to be outside the control of management. Such factors might be problems caused by unexpected circuit failures, pressure from end users to meet critical schedules, unavailability of certain equipment or circuits, or insufficient information (on a day-to-day basis) to ensure that the network provides adequate service to all users. In reality, network managers must gather their own decision-making information to perform such essential tasks as measuring network performance, identifying problem areas, isolating the exact nature of problems, restoring the network (how to do this is discussed later), and predicting future problems.

Too many managers spend too much time on the management function of *controlling* because they must contend daily with a series of breakdowns and immediate problems. These managers do not spend enough time on the management functions of *planning* and *organizing* which are needed to develop a proper information base so they can foresee problems and reduce the need to drop everything to fix a breakdown (sometimes called *firefighting*).

Combining Voice and Data   A major organizational challenge is the prospect of combining the voice communication function with the data and image communication functions. Traditionally, voice communications were handled by a manager who oversaw the telephone switchboard systems and also coordinated the installation and maintenance of the organization's voice telephone networks. By contrast, data communications traditionally were handled by the data processing function (information systems department) because the staff installed their own communication circuits as the need arose, rather than contacting and coordinating with the voice communications management staff.

This separation of voice and data worked well over the years, but now changing communication technologies are causing enormous pressures to combine these two functions. These pressures are magnified by the high cost of maintaining separate facilities, the low efficiency and productivity of the organization's employees because there are two separate network functions, and the potential political problems within an organization when neither manager wants to relinquish his or her functional duties or job position. A key factor in *voice/data integration* might turn out to be the elimination of one key management position and the merging of two staffs into one.

We cannot present a perfect solution to this problem because it must be handled in a unique way within each organization. Depending on the business environment and specific communication needs, some organizations may want to combine these two functions and others may find it better to keep them separate. We can state unequivocally that an organization that avoids studying this situation might be promoting inefficient communication systems, lower employee productivity, and increased operating costs for its separate voice and data networks.

Typically, voice communications can require eight to ten times the budget needed for data communications. For example, an organization with a $1 million annual budget in data communication costs might find itself spending $8 to $10 million per year in voice communication equipment and transmission.

In communications we are moving from an era in which the computer is the dominant information systems function to one in which communication networks are the dominant information systems function. In some organizations the total cost of both voice and data communications will equal or exceed the total cost of the data processing function. Sometimes this cost factor is overlooked, ignored, or underestimated.

The integration of voice and data combines factors in voice technology, the office equipment market, the workstation market, and the network market. As a result, the manager who controls voice and data operations must be knowledgeable about workstations, office equipment, and network devices so they can be interconnected efficiently. In addition, this person needs to have an in-depth understanding of voice communications and especially digital PBX switchboards.

If you were to become the manager of a combined voice/data communication organization, some of your responsibilities and tasks would be to

- Plan, organize, direct, control, and staff the organization's entire voice/data network operation
- Acquire knowledge of public data networks and how to connect them to the organization's voice, data, and image networks
- Learn about the workstation and office equipment markets
- Develop and control the organization's backbone networks, including satellite, microwave, and other bypass (DTS) technologies
- Be responsible for micro-to-mainframe network connections
- Manage the organization's local area networks, as well as connect them to the organization's backbone network
- Be responsible for PBXs (switchboards)
- Plan, understand, and keep abreast of the latest technological developments in telephones
- Manage the day-to-day operations of all network functions
- Acquire communication-oriented hardware and software
- Manage the communication budget, with emphasis on controlling costs
- Develop a strategic (long-term) communication plan to meet the organization's policies and goals
- Combine voice, data, and image technologies

Merging voice and data promises many potential benefits, with some of the more important ones being lower costs, a competitive edge in meeting the organization's business needs, better strategic planning to anticipate the long- and short-term telecommunication needs of the organization's end users, improved use of new voice and data communication technology, and better cross-training between voice and data professionals.

The Chief Information Officer (CIO)   In our previous discussion on combining voice and data communications, we alluded to the problem of where the communication organization should be located within the business or government entity. This subject raises two other issues. Will the surviving organization be data communications or voice communications? To which higher organization will the communication manager report? This person could report to information systems (data processing), an administrative vice president to whom the previous voice manager reported, or to some other function.

Although any of these reporting relationships would work, we believe the information control function will be placed higher in the hierarchy of both private companies and government agencies as these organizations recognize that information is one of their *strategic resources*. In today's business environment we have accounting departments and senior vice presidents of finance to control the strategic re-

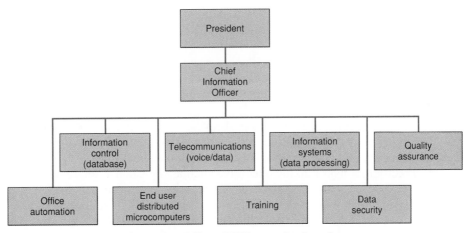

Figure 12-1   Chief Information Officer (CIO) organization chart.

source, "capital." It will be only a matter of time until we have a senior vice president and a single functioning department to control the organization's newest strategic resource, "information."

Because information is such an important strategic resource to organizations, a new executive function has emerged. This function is that of the *Chief Information Officer* who is a "czar" or "czarina" with the responsibility of overseeing all information within the organization. Figure 12-1 depicts a tentative organizational structure in which we have combined the voice and data functions. Notice that we have included the new vice-presidential-level position called Chief Information Officer (the president will have other vice presidents who are equal to the CIO). Also notice that, within this organizational structure, voice and data communications do *not* have to be combined. The Chief Information Officer could have both a Manager of Voice Communications and a separate Manager of Data Communications in place of the box marked Telecommunications. Also observe in the figure that the traditional data processing department has been divided into three major functions and five others.

- *Telecommunications* (voice and data) is responsible for ensuring that voice, data, and image transmission networks are available and optimized for all organizational users, including distributed local area networks that may not yet be internetworked.

- *Information Systems* (data processing) is responsible for running production jobs and operating the organization's centralized computers, as well as for system design and programming. Some organizations split this category into two separate functions: a production function responsible for running the organization's computers, and a design function responsible for designing and programming new application systems.

- *Information Control* (database) is responsible for identifying and controlling who can have use of which data, as well as being the custodian over all databases within the organization.

The other five functions (quality assurance, office automation, end user distributed microcomputers, training, and data security) are shown as examples of a large, well organized CIO department. Some organizations may add testing as an additional function.

Chief Information Officers perform three basic tasks. First, they oversee all the company's communication technology, including the traditional data processing functions, office automation systems, and telecommunications. Second, they report directly to a high ranking executive such as the Chief Executive Officer, Chairman, or President of the organization. Third, they concentrate on long-term strategy and strategic planning and leave day-to-day operations to subordinates.

The creation of the Chief Information Officer position is the direct result of new technology and the rise of information as a strategic resource. In the past, the traditional data processing department could handle the entire organization's needs for data processing, but this is no longer true. In many organizations the strategic resource *information* now is more important than the strategic resource *capital*. This shift dictates a realignment of responsibilities, the single most important one being in the area of voice and data communications. Having data or information that cannot be communicated or that is communicated too late is equal to not having the information at all. Most of the time managers are drowning in information; they have too much. The problem then becomes one of organizing the information (database) and communicating it (voice/data communications) more effectively. Today we are an information-based society, and this factor alone will cause us to restructure the communication management functions.

Another major topic that concerns the Chief Information Officer is security of the network and, even more so, security of data or information. Another organization (data security in Figure 12-1) should develop security standards and ensure that they are implemented and followed adequately. This organization should be separate from voice communications, data communications, and information systems. The internal audit function should review the security standards and enforcement performed by data security to ensure both adequacy and compliance. The data security manager should maintain independence by reporting directly to the Chief Information Officer. The next chapter covers the topic of security and control in greater detail.

How the telecommunication network manager functions and what is required of an effective manager is the subject of the remaining sections of this chapter. This discussion centers around how the needed management information is acquired through network management, managing the day-to-day operations, and test equipment.

NETWORK MANAGEMENT

In this section we address management of the organization's networks. Today's network managers are faced with a growing number of users, more microcomputer-based workstations, an increased use of applications, tremendously heavy traffic on all the communication circuits, local area networks, and internetworking.

Some network managers use the "old" rule of thumb that designates one person in the network department for every 50 to 100 terminals in the network. This yardstick probably is still adequate for today's networks because management would be assigning five to ten people to the day-to-day network management tasks needed for a 500-terminal network. The rule fails, however, with very large networks that have grown to, let us say, 5,000 terminals. In this case, the network manager cannot afford a corresponding increase in the number of staff to 50 or 100 people. This problem is not a serious one because both software and hardware network management systems are available.

One of the first network management tasks is to recognize the need for basic information on network status, network reporting, and network documentation.

Network Status As part of network organization and control, the present *network status* should be monitored and assessed continually by the design and analysis group (described later in this chapter) or the internal audit department. The data collected from a status review can be used both for future planning and for validating the performance of the network. Some questions that can be used in reviewing the network status are the following.

- Are the voice and data communication networks combined?
- Does the network manager report at a high enough level in the management hierarchy?
- Is the network manager within the Information Systems Department?
- How many independent data networks are in use throughout the organization?
- Are the networks application dependent or independent?
- What was the network availability (uptime) for yesterday, the last five days, the last month, and so on?
- Who manages the local area networks? Are they internetworked?
- What network reports and network documentation (described in the next two sections) are available?
- Is network management software being used?
- Are the security and control aspects described in Chapter 13 available?
- What is the data communication network's annual budget?
- What is the monthly communication cost or the total cost for last year? For voice? For data?
- Is the network critical to the organization's revenue-stream management, expense-stream management, cash-flow management, and so on?
- Is network operation erratic or difficult to monitor?
- Can trouble areas be pinpointed quickly (fault diagnosis)?
- Are 95 percent of all response times less than or equal to 3 seconds for online real-time traffic?

- Are management reports timely, and do they contain the most up-to-date statistics?
- How many hours per day or days per week are utilized for network operation versus network management functions?
- What is the inventory of hardware and where is each piece located in the network?
- What is the network configuration for all circuits?
- What is the inventory of software and where is each program located in the network?
- Does a formal network management organization exist with mandated goals, policies, procedures, and the like?

Network Reporting   Poor network reporting leads to an organization that is overburdened with today's problems (firefighting) and does not have time to address future needs. Management requires adequate reports if it is to address future needs. Information for these reports can be gathered from host computers, front end processors, network monitors, the network management group, local area networks, test equipment, and the like.

Technical reports that are helpful to management should contain some or all of the following *network reporting* details.

- Cumulative network downtime
- Detail of any subnetwork downtime
- Circuit utilization
- Response time analysis per circuit or per terminal
- Usage by various types of terminal stations such as interactive versus remote job entry
- Voice versus data usage per circuit
- Queue-length descriptions, whether in the host computer, front end processor, or at remote terminal sites
- Histograms of daily/weekly/monthly usage, number of errors, or whatever is appropriate to the network
- Failure rates for circuits, hardware, or software
- Utilization rate of critical hardware such as the host computer or front end processor
- File activity rates for database systems
- Local area network activity
- Network gateway failure statistics and daily activity
- Distribution of packet volume (for packet networks), or distribution of character volume per circuit link
- Statistical profile of network traffic

- Distribution of traffic by time of day and location
- Peak volume statistics as well as average volume statistics per circuit
- Correlation of activity between today and a similar previous period
- Correlation of queue-length statistics by time and volume to a similar previous period

Network Documentation *Network documentation* is mandatory for the control of any network. Some software packages document your network by managing the various lists of hardware and narrative descriptions. These same packages also can keep equipment lists and even draw network configurations. See the GrafNet Plus section in Chapter 6 (page 246) for an example.

In the area of microcomputers, a word processing software package might be all that is needed to maintain network documentation. On the other hand, perhaps one of the software packages for drawing or developing graphic presentations would be of assistance. Finally, a spreadsheet program might be useful to keep track of costs for the various circuits, pieces of hardware, and software.

Figure 12-2 depicts how network costs might be analyzed using a software program on a microcomputer. For example, the ShowText software that was used for drawing the network cost analyzer in Figure 12-2 is cited in reference 9 at the end of this chapter. Network documentation can consist of any of the following.

- Network maps or other descriptive documentation for each wide area network (WAN), metropolitan area network (MAN), backbone network (BN), or local area network (LAN)
  — Worldwide
  — Within a single country
  — Within a state or province
  — Within a city
  — Within a specific building or facility
- List of all dial-up network connections
- Manual of software and hardware standards
- Size and location of all local area networks
- List of all internetwork connections
- Circuit layout records
- Vendor maintenance records (MTBF, MTTD, MTTR, MTTF) with hardware, software, and circuit cross-references
- Software listings by hardware
- Software listings by network tasks performed
- All user site telephone numbers and individual contacts
- Hardware maintenance history logs located at each user site
- Circuit control telephone contact index and log (when possible establish a national account with the common carrier rather than dealing with individual common carriers in separate states and provinces)

HARDWARE OR SOFTWARE CATEGORY / NETWORK CIRCUIT LINKS	CIRCUIT COST	MODEM COST	FRONT END COST	NETWORK MANAGER SOFTWARE COST*	TOTAL COST FOR EACH NETWORK CIRCUIT LINK
NEW YORK TO CHICAGO					
CHICAGO TO DENVER					
DENVER TO SAN FRANCISCO					
SAN FRANCISCO TO LOS ANGELES					
LOS ANGELES TO SAN DIEGO					
TOTAL COST FOR EACH HARDWARE OR SOFTWARE CATEGORY					TOTAL COST

* Some costs may have to be prorated among several links.

Figure 12-2   Network cost analyzer.

- Serial number inventory (property control) of all network components
- Network switching criteria and redundancy locations
- Vendor contractual agreements and licenses for software
- Legal requirements to comply with local or federal laws, control, or regulatory bodies; also include legal requirements for other countries (international)
- Operation manuals for network operations personnel
- Vendor-supplied hardware operation manuals
- Software documentation manuals
- Escalation levels (where to go when the problem cannot be resolved)
- Preventive maintenance guidelines and schedules
- Record of user site tests required by network security monitor
- Disaster plan with recovery procedures
- Diagnostic techniques by hardware component or type of trouble

Monitoring Physical and Logical Parameters Network management is a key topic in networking. *Network management* is the process of controlling, monitoring, and running the network in such a way as to ensure its proper operation. There are two primary reasons for network management.

- To clear and recover from failures
- To improve the performance of a network with the admittedly impossible goal of "zero downtime"

A large organization's wide area network typically includes a host-based *network management system* that monitors the entire communication network. This includes the front end, modems, multiplexers, communication circuits, remote stations (nodes), and even local area networks that may be connected to the wide area network. The purpose of these software management systems is to collect operational statistics from the network devices.

The parameters monitored by a network management system fall into two distinct categories: physical network statistics and logical network information. Gathering statistics on the *physical network parameters* includes monitoring the operation of the network's modems, multiplexers, lines linking the various hardware pieces, and any other network devices. Monitoring the physical network consists of keeping track of circuits that may be down, tracing malfunctioning modems, and transmitting diagnostic signals from intelligent network devices (intelligent modems) to the central site. This type of monitoring may be done by using a "secondary" communication channel. In this case, statistical information is transmitted from the intelligent network device on a different frequency than the one carrying the actual network traffic.

Logical network parameters include performance measurement systems that keep track of user response times, the volume of traffic on a specific circuit, the destination of data routed across various networks, and any other indicators showing the level of service provided by the network. This type of management software operates in a passive manner, collecting the information and reporting it back to the central network operations control center. We cannot cover all the software available for network management in this section. Instead, we describe a few selections (NetView, Spectrum Services, ACCUMASTER Integrator, SNMP, NMS, SMT, and LANVision) to show the types of network management software packages that are available.

NetView IBM's *NetView* network management program is used for managing multi-vendor voice and data networks. This program combines and enhances the functions of five other IBM programs into a single software product that automates many network management tasks. It is designed for managing host network management services for Systems Network Architecture (SNA) networks. Prior network management programs that have been combined to form NetView include Network Communication Control Facility (NCCF), Network Logical Data Manager (NLDM), Network Problem Determination Application (NPDA), and some of the functions from

Virtual Telecommunications Access Method Node Control Application (VNCA) and Network Management Productivity Facility (NMPF).

We mention these five NetView programs to demonstrate that numerous network management programs are on the market. Among the functions NetView helps to automate are

- The ability of a centrally located person to test and monitor the status of analog communication circuits
- The ability to view a set of interactive displays and to execute commands against the displayed circuit or hardware in order to change something
- The ability to monitor and react to physical connectivity problems on multiple token-ring networks that are connected to the mainframe
- The online help facility that provides current dynamic network information status
- The help desk facility that isolates failed network components, provides suggestions on ways to fix the failure, and records incidents
- The ability to examine any network log and check the definitions to ensure that parameters are set properly
- The ability to monitor the network for out-of-service conditions and automatically reactivate all devices downstream from the failed resource

As NetView evolves, it is being integrated into a product called *SystemView,* which is to serve as a framework that will enable most of the diverse management activities of running a computer network to be integrated and, where possible, automated. SystemView management will go beyond the technical issues of managing a network and address other management tasks, such as financial administration, service level tracking, capacity planning, business planning, and management support for heterogeneous local area networks. In addition to managing the organization's networks, SystemView also can be used to manage the central host mainframe computers.

Spectrum Services   Another automated network management system is offered by one of the Bell Operating Companies and is called *Spectrum Services.* Pacific Bell provides this communication service to users on a contract basis. It uses proprietary hardware and software to diagnose network problems remotely, coordinate service restoration, detect degrading communication circuits, and maintain all the relevant information about a communication network, including network configurations. This service eliminates the user's need to track down the cause of a problem, deal with multiple communication service providers, determine responsibility for a problem, and correct the problem. Test engineers at the Pacific Bell response center test the user's system by means of remote hardware devices located at the user site. Spectrum Services gathers complete information about each user's communication network, stores this information in a database, monitors the user's network, and handles the basic failure control, testing, and problem management functions for the user's network.

There are even specialized software and hardware management programs that manage communication switches. Switches are pieces of hardware that switch circuits or messages among different terminals. They might be used by a corporate network, packet networks, cellular telephone services, and your normal dial-up telephone service. For example, the AT&T 5ESS switch can be used for circuit switching. To manage these switches, the user must check a separate operations system that collects diagnostic messages from the switch to determine its health. This other *switch management system* monitors telecommunication traffic moving through the switch to ascertain how well telephone calls are moving over the network.

ACCUMASTER Integrator®   To overcome the problems of coordinating some of the user tasks mentioned in the above paragraphs, AT&T has developed a network product adapted to its *Unified Network Management Architecture* (UNMA) standard.

The UNMA is AT&T's framework for end-to-end management and control of multivendor voice and data networks. Based on the OSI seven-layer model, this architecture focuses on integrating a variety of standalone network management systems. It has three domains: Customer Premises Equipment (CPE), local exchange carrier/PTT networks, and interexchange service. UNMA is supported by AT&T's family of products called ACCUMASTER.

The *ACCUMASTER Integrator* is a network control package that maintains a comprehensive inventory of all components in a user's network. It develops a map of network elements and connectivity to display this information. Icons, onscreen instructions in English, and a mouse make it easy for users to access the information they need.

One of the difficulties with complex networks is that any device with a problem triggers an alarm to alert network management that it needs attention. This alarm then triggers other alarms in related devices. Although these alarms provide an effective warning system, they tend to make it difficult for the network manager to isolate the problem so it can be solved. The Integrator correlates these alarms to isolate the fault. It also locates the source of the alarm to provide "ownership." This feature pinpoints who should be responsible for working on the problem, thereby eliminating the need for numerous people to work on solving the same problem.

The Integrator permits organizations to manage their own equipment (such as PBXs, LANs, mainframes, minicomputers, modems, and multiplexers), as well as certain operations related to central office switches, T-1 multiplexers, and other telephone company equipment in their network.

Simple Network Management Protocol (SNMP)   The *Simple Network Management Protocol* (SNMP) was derived from an earlier management protocol called *Simple Gateway Monitoring Program,* which in turn was derived from another protocol called the *High-level Entry Management System* (HEMS). The SNMP protocol originally was developed to control and monitor the status of network devices on Transaction Control Protocol/Internet Protocol (TCP/IP) networks, but now it is available for network management employing other network protocols.

SNMP is not an end user management system of its own; instead, it is the mechanism that enables network management. The SNMP protocol defines the communication between a manager and an object (the item being managed). SNMP is for use in an environment in which multiple management stations control the different manageable devices remotely over the network. It is used for managing network stations.

The *management station*, or *client*, sends SNMP messages to the remote stations that are to be controlled. The *remote station*, or *agent*, understands the request for information and returns the information requested. The *MIB* (Management Information Base) describes all the data that is available to the client. SNMP is expected to be even more powerful in the future as the MIB becomes more broadly defined so that more information can be accessed from the agent. The Internet Engineering Task Force, which oversees the SNMP standard, is developing a basic *Rmon MIB* that all LAN monitors can support.

The *Common Management Interface Protocol* (CMIP) is a competitor to SNMP. CMIP is a protocol for seven-layer OSI model networks. It monitors and keeps track of network usage and other parameters for user workstations and other nodes.

The question raised by the use of SNMP is whether network monitoring is really network management. SNMP monitors the network because it is a probe placed in remote stations. Some argue that true network management requires a monitor. A probe differs from a monitor because *probes* usually are placed in the network stations and report their results to a central point. By contrast, *monitors* are self-contained devices that monitor the network without receiving information from remote stations. Monitors are more powerful than probes because they can do such tasks as report excessive collisions on a local area network, report that the network is slowing down, report that a network link is down, and so forth. Analyzers are more sophisticated than monitors. Unlike monitors, *analyzers* look inside data packets to reveal the cause of the problem rather than simply report on its existence. In summary, a probe reports specific information from a remote station to a central site. A monitor continually checks the operation of a network and tells the network management personnel what is happening in the network, but it does not specify the cause of any problems. Finally, analyzers do all the work of a monitor, but they also help define the cause of a specific problem. All three are required for effective network management.

Many vendors, especially those marketing local area networks, are shipping their network products with SNMP already implemented. This gives network managers the ability to receive status information (MIBs) on the various network stations throughout their networks. SNMP is not meant to replace a comprehensive network managing and monitoring system because it only offers probes—it does not monitor or analyze.

NetWare Management System (NMS)   Novell's *NetWare Management System* allows local area network administrators to manage NetWare LANs and attached devices that are spread throughout an enterprise-wide network. The basic functions of NMS include network fault detection, performance, configuration, security, and accounting management. It has been designed as an open system, thereby allowing third-party vendors to integrate their services into the NetWare Management System.

Each server on the network must be equipped with a NetWare Management Agent (NMA), which is a set of three NetWare Loadable Modules (NLM) that relay statistics describing hardware, software, and data resources. NLMs are linkable modules written by either Novell or third-party suppliers to offer enhanced NetWare services. When linked, the modules work as though they are part of the NetWare operating system. Using the NLMs, the NetWare Management Agent collects such statistics from the server as memory usage and available disk space, as well as other data from the attached user or client workstations and hubs. The NetWare Management Agent also alerts the administrator in real time that potential resource allocation problems exist or that a preestablished alarm point has been reached, such as a network link overload. The NetWare Management Agent loaded into each server is similar to the Management Information Block (MIB) that accompanies the Simple Network Management Protocol (SNMP). Novell also supplies a NetWare Loadable Module that collects information about SNMP-based devices on a NetWare LAN using the MIB Agent.

The NetWare Services Manager polls the NetWare Management Agents to collect statistics from remote servers and the user workstations attached to each server. The NetWare Management Agent also can respond to polls from other network systems, such as IBM's NetView network management system.

A NetWare Management Map function automatically identifies NetWare-based servers, cable segments, routers, and client workstations within an enterprise-wide network and draws a graphical representation of the entire network. An optional NetWare Management Enhanced Map package allows a LAN manager to map network nodes into local building floor plans.

The significance of Novell's NetWare Management System is that it allows one console to manage the entire enterprise-wide network, and it also allows third-party vendors to incorporate their own products into the NetWare Management System architecture.

SMT—Station Management for FDDI As you learned in Chapter 11, the Fiber Distributed Data Interface (FDDI) is a token-passing local area network with a ring topology. It operates by transmitting over fiber optic cable. Token passing means that the right to transmit on the LAN is passed between stations by an electronic *token,* which is a special type of frame called a media-access control (MAC) frame. The token controls transmission by allowing only one station to transmit at a time. Moreover, FDDI is a *timed-token rotation LAN* because it limits the amount of time a station can take to transmit frames before passing the token to the next downstream station.

Station management, which is known as *SMT,* involves the control and management of the FDDI network. To manage a FDDI station, SMT must deal with both the control of local hardware (terminal) and other information about the station parameters and operating conditions. Once the FDDI ring is operational, it can do this because information about the MAC (token), the physical layer (OSI model layer 1), and the remote station operation can be passed between stations in the form of a SMT frame.

The *SMT frame* is a special MAC frame that carries a unique header. This header allows these frames to be separated so their information can be used to manage the network. The station management (SMT) information contained within this unique SMT frame identifies the station, version number, transaction, and the length of the information field in the SMT frame. The information field is a sequence of control information, such as

- Upstream and downstream neighbor addresses that can be used for developing a logical ring map
- Status information providing a station's configuration and operating information
- Information for loopback testing
- Request-denied information
- Status report frames used by stations to announce station status or duplicate addresses
- Parameter information that provides the means for remote management of the station attributes, such as specifying new parameters, deleting existing parameters, or requesting and providing information about a station.

SMT for FDDI networks will grow more important as users become familiar with its capabilities for managing the local area network. As more progress takes place in the area of managing fiber optic networks, either SMT's capabilities will be used to manage the FDDI network or a standard management protocol like SNMP could be modified to operate on the FDDI fiber optic LAN.

LANVision Series   The *LANVision Series* of seven LAN management software tools was introduced in Chapter 11 on page 551. A "working" demonstration diskette is available showing how each of these tools operates.

MANAGING THE DAY-TO-DAY OPERATIONS

To put the day-to-day network management functions in perspective, Figure 12-3 depicts a typical organization chart for a data communication function that is organized within the information systems or data processing departments. In this organization chart (contrary to the Chief Information Officer organization chart shown in Figure 12-1), the data communication network manager reports directly to the director of information systems (the highest person in the Information Systems Department). Remember that the network manager function may report outside of the Information Systems Department if there is a Chief Information Officer, or it can include the tasks of managing the voice communications if they are a combined voice/data function reporting to the director of information systems. We will assume

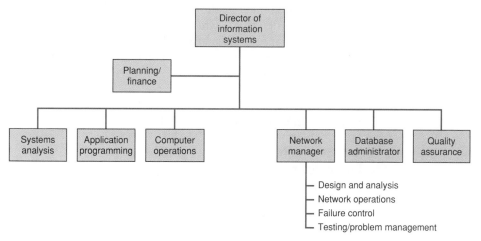

Figure 12-3 Organization chart for information systems.

here that the network manager is part of the Information Systems Department and that voice and data are not combined. We make this assumption so that we can identify and explain the four basic job functions of a data communication network manager: design and analysis, network operations, failure control, and testing and problem management.

Each of these functions involves specific tasks that require the utmost in management expertise and control of personnel, as well as in-depth technical knowledge. Let us examine these four functions.

Design and Analysis Function The *design and analysis function* is responsible for planning overall network design and for continuing analysis of the network. Management requires, for example, ongoing statistics on network performance and feedback on user satisfaction. Obviously, these statistics require close interaction with the other three job functions of the network manager.

This function is responsible for the development of operating procedures and standards for network personnel. The network designers use measurement tools, such as network models, optimizers, simulators, statistical measurements, and daily data collection routines, to plan and control the network. Network design should not be viewed as something that is done when the network is created and then forgotten. Network design and analysis is a continuing redesign of the network hardware, circuits, and software, and it continues for the life of the network.

As the people in this function analyze and redesign their network circuits, switches, other hardware, and software products, they may use either manual or automated design techniques. Chapter 8 presents a thorough 13-step systems approach to designing networks. We also discussed design and optimization software at the end of Chapter 8.

Establishing equipment selection criteria is one of the responsibilities of the design and analysis function. When determining the vendor of specific data communication products, a data communication manager must have a list of criteria to be met. The manager must determine which criteria are important for the specific network. For example, Chapter 11 discusses 40 criteria for selecting a LAN. Some criteria that should be considered when designing a network are

- Technical decisions
    Type of usage
        Wide area network (WAN)
        Metropolitan area network (MAN)
        Backbone network (BN)
        Local area network (LAN)
        Multipoint versus point to point
        Multiplex
    Protocol requirements
        Analog versus digital
        Synchronous versus asynchronous
        Electrical protocol (RS232, DB-9, DB-25, and the like)
        Compatibility with existing equipment
        Transmission speeds
- Vendor concerns
    Repair record: Mean Time To Repair (MTTR)
    Equipment reliability: Mean Time Between Failures (MTBF)
    Repair personnel
        Qualifications
        Location of nearest vendor technician (wait time)
    Documentation manuals
        Availability
        Usability
- In-house staff
    Qualifications
    Training requirements
    Problem diagnosis ability: Mean Time To Diagnose (MTTD)
- Cost decisions
    Lease versus purchase
    Industrial forecast (yesterday's technology at low cost versus tomorrow's technology for long term)
    Personnel costs to troubleshoot equipment
    Cost negotiation
        Volume purchases
        Maintenance
        Free training versus fee training
    Direct versus indirect costs
    Cost/benefit analysis
- Equipment diagnostics
    Diagnostic capabilities (front panel diagnostics or smart equipment)

Optioning of equipment (manual optioning via strapping or DIP switches versus automatic options via electronic circuitry with downline loading of options)

- Manageability of the hardware and software

Network Operations Function   The *network operations function* is responsible for the day-to-day operations of a network. The person or group performing this work maintains the ongoing communication services for the organization. They turn on the networks at the start of the business day and turn them off when the business day ends. One major function is the master network monitoring and daily gathering of statistics that are used by the network design and analysis people and, of course, by the network manager. This group may be the interface with irate users, as well as with the various hardware, software, and circuit vendors. This function or group of people often is combined with the next one, failure control.

Failure Control Function   The *failure control function* is handled by a central control group that receives telephone calls when problems occur and records the incidence of problems. This task may be performed by the network operations personnel. Basically, it is a help desk that is called when anything goes wrong in the network. This group has appropriate customer service representatives to record problems, report them to the testing and problem management group, follow up, and generally ensure that the network is back in operation as soon as possible. This group also might be responsible for change scheduling, coordination, and follow-up on any changes, whether they involve hardware, software, or circuits. In other words, this is the user's interface when there is a problem of any kind.

Failure control requires developing a central control philosophy for problem reporting and other user interfaces. This group should maintain a central telephone number for network users to call when any problem occurs in the network. As a central troubleshooting function, only this group or its designee should have the authority or responsibility to call hardware or software vendors or common carriers.

Numerous software packages are available for recording the information received from an incoming telephone call. The reports they produce are known as *trouble tickets*. The software packages assist the help desk personnel so they can type the trouble report immediately into a computerized failure analysis program. This type of package prints out a trouble report for follow-up and correction of the problem. It also automatically records and assembles various statistical reports to keep track of how many failures there have been for each piece of hardware, circuit, or software package. This software is different from the network management software that automatically collects data from stations (a probe) or analyzes circuit traffic. The software that produces trouble tickets is more similar to a very specialized word processor that has special features for statistical analysis.

Trouble tickets must be kept if a manager wants to do any type of problem tracking. Automated trouble tickets are better than paper because they allow management to gather problem and vendor statistics. There are four main reasons for trouble tickets.

- Problem tracking
- Problem statistics
- Problem-solving methodology
- Management reports

Problem tracking allows the network manager to determine problem ownership or, in other words, to ascertain who has responsibility for correcting any outstanding problems. Why is this important? Problems often are forgotten in the rush of a very hectic day of network problems. In addition, anyone might request the status of a problem. The network manager can determine whether the problem-solving machinery is meeting predetermined schedules. Finally, the manager can be assured that all problems are being addressed. Problem tracking also can assist in problem resolution. Are problems being resolved in a timely manner? Are overdue problems being flagged? Are all resources and information available for problem solving?

Problem statistics are important because they are a control device for the network operators as well as for vendors. With this information a manager can retrieve and compute availability of the network to its end users. The manager can determine whether problem solving by the network operators is excessive. These statistics also can be used to determine whether vendors are meeting their contractual maintenance commitments. Finally, they can be used to determine whether problem-solving objectives are being met.

Problem-solving methodology helps determine whether the problem priority system is working. You would not want a network operator to work on a terminal problem if an entire multidrop line consisting of dozens of terminals were waiting for a free technician. Moreover, a manager must know whether problem resolution objectives are being met. For example, how long is it taking to resolve problems?

Management reports are required to determine network availability, product and vendor reliability (Mean Time Between Failures), and vendor responsiveness (Mean Time To Repair). Without these reports a manager has nothing more than a "seat of the pants" estimate for the effectiveness of either the network's technicians or the vendor's technicians.

Regardless of whether this information is typed immediately into an automated trouble ticket package or recorded manually in a bound notebook-style trouble log, the objectives are the same. If the organization does not have a computerized package, then the notebook format is appropriate. The bound notebook, with two carbon copies for each original trouble report, should have prenumbered pages to avoid missing any of these reports. One page always should be kept at the "trouble log desk." Two carbon copies are useful because it may be desirable to give one copy to a vendor who is called in to correct the problem and one copy to the internal testing/problem management personnel.

When a problem incident is reported, the trouble log desk staff should record the following to the best of their ability.

- Who reported the incident
- The problem reporter's telephone number

- The time and date of the problem (not the time of the call) as closely as it can be identified
- Location of the problem
- The nature of the problem
- When the problem was identified
- Why the problem happened (probably unable to identify this in most cases)
- How the problem occurred (probably unable to identify this in most cases)

Once this information is recorded, the failure control personnel should use an electric time-and-date stamp machine to indicate when they received the incident report. The software adds the time and date in automated systems.

The purpose of this procedure is to mandate central control of all problems and totally eliminate unnecessary service requests to vendors. Remember that there may be many hardware or software vendors for a data communication network. In fact, a typical network might have different vendors for the following equipment: terminals, cable connectors, modems, multiplexers, circuits (sometimes even the local loops and the IXC circuits have different vendors), front end processors, host computer, local area networks, and probably two or three different vendors for the various software packages.

The purpose of the bound trouble log volume or the automated software is to record problems on paper so people will correct them and follow up, as well as to keep track of statistics with regard to problem incidents. For example, after a period of time using a centralized failure control group, the organization might learn that there were 37 calls for software problems (3 for one package, 4 for another package, and 30 for a third software package), 26 calls for modems evenly distributed among the two vendors, 49 calls for terminals, and 85 calls to the common carrier that provides the network circuits. Data of this type is valuable when the design and analysis group begins redesigning the network to meet future requirements. Also, hard statistics like this enable you to put more pressure on the vendor who supplied the software package with the high number of problems.

With regard to combining the network management and failure control functions, some organizations not only combine their job tasks, but also specify the amount of time they have to correct the problem. For example, they may be given 15 minutes to locate the problem and correct it. If they are not able to do this within the required time, they submit the trouble ticket to the testing and problem management function for more technical troubleshooting.

Testing and Problem Management Function   The purpose of the *testing and problem management function* is to establish test and validity criteria and coordinate the various testing functions. These test personnel maintain the complex testing equipment needed to diagnose problems quickly, and most of the time they fix the problem in-house. In other words, their mission is *troubleshooting*. Probably the group's single most important function is to interface with the failure control group. The failure control group, when it becomes aware of a problem, immediately passes this information to the testing group so they can diagnose the problem and identify what needs to be corrected. Depending on the severity of the problem, the network operations group may be notified as well. The complete problem-handling procedure may involve either fixing the problem in-house or notifying the appropriate vendor so that corrections can be made and the network can be operating again.

As soon as a problem is reported, the failure control group should immediately send a copy of the trouble log incident report to the testing and problem management group so they can diagnose the problem and possibly remedy it themselves. The testing and problem management group should report back to the failure control group as soon as they have diagnosed the problem so the time required to diagnose the problem can be recorded. In other words, the organization should keep track of *Mean Time To Diagnose* (MTTD), which is an indicator of the efficiency of testing and problem management personnel. This is the first of three different *times* that should be kept for future statistics.

For example, assume a vendor is contacted for correction of a problem. Either testing or failure control personnel should keep track of the time the vendor takes to respond. In other words, the *Mean Time To Respond* (MTTR) is identified. This is a valuable statistic because it indicates how well vendors respond to emergencies. A collection of these figures over a period of time can lead to a change of vendors or, at the minimum, can put severe pressure on vendors who do not respond to problems promptly.

Finally, after the vendor arrives on the premises, the last statistic to record is the *Mean Time To Fix* (MTTF). This figure tells how quickly the vendor is able to correct the problem. A very long time to fix in comparison with the time of other vendors may be indicative of faulty equipment design, inadequately trained customer service technicians, or even the fact that inexperienced personnel are repeatedly sent to fix problems.

One other statistic should be examined. It usually is developed by the equipment vendor, and it is called *Mean Time Between Failures* (MTBF). The Mean Time Between Failures of vendor-supplied network interface equipment should be very high, which is an indicator of *reliability*. When you ask for the Mean Time Between Failures, always find out whether it is a practical figure or a calculated figure. You want a calculated figure because it is far more accurate and realistic. Sometimes practical figures are developed on a theoretical basis and so are not dependable.

When we use the various mean times, we can work out a formula for calculating *network availability* (see Figure 12-4). The product (π) assumes a series of components that must all be operating for the network to be up and available (uptime). Here N is the number of network elements, such as modems, circuits, multiplexers, or network software.

Remember that the MTBF (failure) can be influenced by the original selection of vendor-supplied equipment. The MTTD (diagnose) relates directly to the ability of in-house personnel to isolate and diagnose failure of hardware, software, or circuits. This means that test personnel need adequate training. The MTTR (respond) can be influenced by showing the vendor how good or bad its response time has been in the past. The MTTF (fix) can be influenced by the use of redundant interface equipment, alternate circuit paths, adequate recovery or fallback procedures to earlier versions of software, and the technical expertise of internal or vendor staff. Because all four

$$\text{Network availability} = \frac{\text{Uptime}}{\text{Uptime} + \text{Downtime}} \times 100 = \text{percent of available time}$$

$$\text{Network availability} = \prod_{J=1}^{N} \frac{\text{MTBF}_J}{\text{MTBF}_J + (\text{MTTD}_J + \text{MTTR}_J + \text{MTTF}_J)}$$

$$N = \text{Total number of network elements.}$$

Figure 12-4 Network availability calculation.

of these mean time statistics are used to calculate network availability, their collection is vital if network performance is to be measured accurately and if performance is to be improved.

We can describe the total time to correct a failure as

$$\text{MTTRepair} = \text{MTTDiagnose} + \text{MTTRespond} + \text{MTTFix}$$

If the failure is fixed in-house, however, the MTTR (respond) is zero because in-house repair does not require a vendor to whom the mean times apply.

Another set of statistics that should be gathered are those collected on a daily basis by the network operations group who employ automated network management software (network monitors and analyzers). These statistics record the normal operation of the network, such as the number of errors (retransmissions) per communication circuit, per terminal, or whatever is appropriate. Statistics also should be collected on the daily volume of transmissions (characters per hour) for each communication link or circuit, each terminal, or whatever is appropriate for the network. This data can identify terminal stations/nodes or communication circuits that have higher-than-average error rates. It also can be used for predicting future growth patterns and failures.

Such predictions can be accomplished by setting up simple *quality control charts* similar to those used in manufacturing processes. Such programs use an upper control limit and a lower control limit with regard to the number of blocks in error per day or per week. Notice how Figure 12-5 identifies when the common carrier moved a circuit from one microwave channel to another (circuit B), how a deteriorating circuit can be located and fixed before it goes through the upper control limit (circuit A) and causes problems for the users, or how a temporary high rate of errors (circuit C) can be encountered when installing new hardware and software.

In summary, day-to-day management of the network requires four main functions, all of which have the primary goal of maintaining a high network *uptime* and a correspondingly low network *downtime*. The design and analysis function tries to design a reliable network and continuously redesigns it to accommodate new requirements and technologies. The network operations function oversees the network's daily operation. The failure control function coordinates activities to diag-

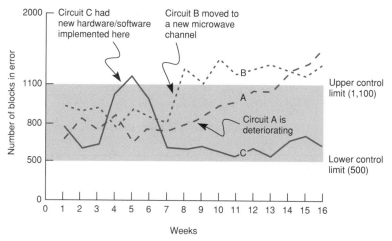

Figure 12-5   Quality control chart for circuits.

nose and repair problems when they occur or if the network goes down. It also keeps management apprised of how well the network is operating by providing required statistics that are indicators of the network's well-being. Finally, the testing and problem management function works with vendors and users to diagnose and fix problems in a timely manner.

TEST EQUIPMENT

Just a decade ago many data communication facility managers did not have test equipment. It was quite proper to depend on the telephone company when a circuit failed and on other communication vendors when hardware or software failed. Today everything is changed because of deregulation in the telecommunication market. For example, you might be using three or four "telephone companies," five or six hardware vendors, and two or three software vendors. This means that ownership of the proper test equipment is mandatory. Network management *must* be able to diagnose a problem (MTTD) and determine which telephone company, hardware vendor, or software vendor should be contacted for assistance when the problem cannot be fixed by on-site staff.

Basically, testing can be divided into the areas of analog testing, digital testing, and protocol testing. *Analog testing* involves troubleshooting on the analog side of the modem. Specifically, it means testing the analog communication circuits supplied by the common carriers.

Digital testing is similar to analog testing, except that it is aimed primarily at testing digital communication circuits. *Protocol testing* is aimed at testing the various sign-on/sign-off procedures (handshaking or line discipline), looking at the content of packets or frames, examining message propagation times, and other items related to software protocols.

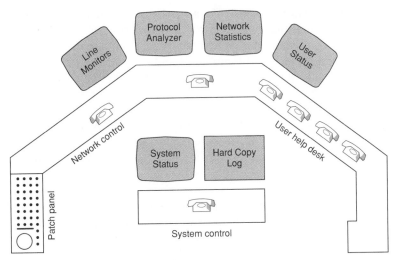

Figure 12-6   Network control center.

The typical network management toolkit of test equipment can cost $100,000 for a large network. Before defining specific test equipment, however, let us first present the concept of a network control center (see Figure 12-6) and the six basic categories of test equipment.

Monitors and analyzers generally are test sets that allow the operator to simulate specific message streams to test devices, communication circuits, or other workstations. A monitor looks similar to a portable microcomputer. Protocol analyzers offer both data and protocol analysis for SNA, X.25, HDLC, T1, DS0, frame relay, and the like.

Analog and digital test sets are found on any network that uses modems in conjunction with telephone company circuits. Most networks require both analog and digital test sets. These devices also look much like a portable microcomputer with a video screen and keyboard for data entry.

Patch panels provide electrical connection to all parts of the network. At the minimum, they provide centralized access to each network communication circuit. They often look like a large panel with a number of plugs or connectors that can be cross-connected between different communication circuits. Cross-patching permits the immediate replacement of a failed circuit with a spare circuit.

Data recorders do not always perform tests. They are used to tap into communication circuits and store on disk pertinent activities about various circuits. Basically, they are a monitor for collecting data, analyzing it, and printing out reports. Data recorders also look like portable microcomputers.

Handheld test sets are the least expensive and simplest type of network equipment. They can be inserted between two network devices to test voltages or to send and receive various test patterns of bits to isolate errors. They also are used to determine whether there is a problem with the RS232 connector cable.

Network management systems usually are microcomputers running software or the host mainframe that services the network. These network management systems are the latest in automated test equipment and may take over some of the functions performed previously by monitors and analyzers. They are used to identify errors, automatically run diagnostic tests, monitor the entire system, keep track of statistics, and prepare real-time management reports for the overall network management. Several of these systems were described earlier in this chapter, notably NetView, Spectrum Services, ACCUMASTER, SNMP, NMS, SMT for FDDI, and the LAN-Vision Series. Typical measurements that can be performed by the software in a network management system include, but are not limited to, the following four times.

- **Access time:** After the user requests service, *access time* is the average waiting time before the network can accept information for transmission. In a dial-up network, this service includes the total time between the user's dialing and receiving the answer, polling time, time until the CLEAR TO SEND signal is received from the modem, and so forth.

- **Block transfer time:** *Block transfer time* is how long the information is in transit between two end users. Modulation, propagation, and intermediate nodal/storage transfer times are included if the information goes across several network nodes.

- **Bit transfer time:** The *bit transfer time* (or bit transfer rate) is the total number of bits transmitted during a given time interval.

- **Disengagement time:** The *disengagement time* is the average waiting time between the user's request for disengagement and the actual disengagement from the network.

Some of today's line monitors and network analyzers use microprocessor chips to perform sophisticated network tests. In other cases, microcomputers are used, along with special software to perform network testing and monitoring. Techniques and devices for monitoring network performance can range from comparably simple analog and digital test equipment to highly sophisticated network monitors or analyzers and entire network management systems. Descriptions of the various types of test equipment follow.

Breakout Box   The most basic level of data communication monitoring and test equipment is analog test equipment. The *breakout box* is the next level up. It is a handheld device that can be plugged into a modem's digital side to determine the voltage values for the RS232 connector cable interface (25-pin cable), the V.24 interface, and others.

Bit-Error Rate Tester (BERT)   The *Bit-Error Rate Tester* (BERT) is a somewhat more sophisticated piece of digital test equipment than a breakout box because it sends a known pseudorandom pattern over the communication circuit. When this pattern is reflected back, the BERT compares the transmitted pattern with the received pattern and calculates the number of bit errors that occurred on the communication circuit. Various test patterns are used, and common pattern lengths are 63, 511, 2047, and 63511 bit patterns. The odd numbers allow simple circuitry in this test equipment.

Bit-Error Rate (BER) measurements can be made with this type of equipment. A BER is the number of bits received in error divided by the total number of bits received. Service personnel use BER measurements to tune the communication circuit and to make a subjective evaluation as to the quality of a specific circuit or channel. BER cannot be related directly to throughput because error distribution is not taken into account. Assume that 1,000 one-bit errors occur during a time interval of 1,000 seconds. If the errors are distributed evenly (one per second), the effect on throughput will be disastrous; however, if all the errors occur in a single second, the effect will be minimal.

Block-Error Rate Tester (BKERT)   The *BlocK-Error Rate Tester* (BKERT) calculates the number of received blocks that contain at least one bit error divided by the total number of blocks received; this is the *BlocK-Error Rate* (BKER). A BKER is more closely related to throughput than a BER. Assume a BKER measurement has been made and the BKER value is 10^2 (1/100). This means that out of every 100 blocks received, one contained an error; therefore, you would expect to see one retry for every 100 blocks transmitted (1 percent error rate).

Another error rate parameter (only for digital networks) is *Error Free Seconds* (EFS). EFS is similar to BKER except it indicates the probability of success rather than the probability of failure, and the block size is the number of bits transmitted in a one-second time period. For example, for a 4800 bits per second channel, the one-second block would contain 4800 bits.

On digital communication channels, AT&T Communications guarantees that 99.5 percent of all seconds of data transmission will be error-free seconds.

Fiber Identifier   The purpose of a *fiber identifier* is to locate a particular nonworking fiber without interrupting service on a fiber optic network. (Remember that a fiber cable may contain a bundle of 72 or 144 glass fibers.) The fiber identifier consists of a transmitter that injects a light signal, a detector that induces a low stress on the fibers allowing them to be searched without damage, and a receiver that emits an audible and visual signal when the fiber in question has been identified. The detector is a wandlike device that can detect the signal at splice locations simply by passing the wand near the splice. Because splices leak light, this is the place an illegal tap would be inserted on a fiber cable.

Cable Analyzer   The *cable analyzer* is a tester that checks LAN twisted pair wires for signal continuity, pulse distortion, parity, conductivity, connectivity, polarity reversals, and excessive noise in the data stream.

Self-Testing Modems   With *self-testing modems,* a test pattern is generated inside the modem (after appropriate buttons are pushed) that is as close as possible to the normal digital input (which is, of course, disconnected). The test pattern travels through the modem's circuitry, passes through an artificial telephone circuit, and is returned to its point of origin. The artificial telephone circuit acts as a local analog loop. The returning pattern is compared with the transmitted pattern, and the operator is advised of discrepancies via an indicator lamp.

Some modems also have digital or analog remote *loopback testing,* whereby the signal actually is sent over the communication circuit and is looped back to the originating modem by the remote modem. Then the signal is compared, and the operator is advised of any discrepancies. Figure 3-13 in Chapter 3 shows loopback testing.

Finally, some modems have internal circuit diagnostic checks whereby they can diagnose their own failures in case of circuit or chip failure. Self-diagnostics are made possible by the use of firmware and microprocessor chips. Newer modems contain some of the features of network analyzers. They actually keep track of poll times and other types of network analysis information.

Protocol Analyzer/Response Time Analyzer/Data Line Monitor   At this point our discussion of test equipment begins to be less clear-cut because there is so much overlap between the different types of equipment and the names used by the various vendors for their products. Today, protocol analyzers, response time analyzers, and data line monitors all tend to perform the same basic tasks.

Recognizing this overlap, however, we can distinguish between them by their original purpose. Basically, a *response time analyzer* checks the operation of the communication protocols in a polled network. It measures the amount of time that elapses from the initiation of polling until receipt of the response. A *data line monitor* not only performs response time analysis, but it also checks the actual data (both control and data characters) on the communication circuit. The functions of these two pieces of test equipment now overlap so much that we tend to roll them into one category called protocol analyzers because they check how the communication protocols are working.

Protocol analyzers measure the responses of all hardware in the network. This equipment can determine whether the network equipment is meeting specifications. These devices also allow you to see the content (bits) of a frame or packet during its transmission.

A typical piece of this equipment might measure poll-to-poll time, which is the time from the detection of the poll being sent to the terminal until the time that poll is again sent to the same terminal. This measurement is updated continuously as the polls are generated by the host computer.

Another typical measurement is poll or response time. This measurement starts at the second SYN character of the poll and is terminated by the second SYN character of the response. (You might review the Data Signaling/Synchronization section in Chapter 5.)

Other criteria with regard to protocol analyzers are the ability to offer hard copy (print information stored in its capture buffer) or to trap information when certain character sequences appear on the send or receive communication circuits. Some analyzers offer performance monitoring operations to help evaluate specific areas of network performance such as response time and link utilization. Protocol analyzers, response time analyzers, and data line monitors tend to look like a portable microcomputer, but with a few extra switches and buttons on the front panel. You can use these devices to check the interaction of software and hardware by looking at all the data passing in both directions on a communication circuit. This checking is mandatory with the new bit-oriented protocols because line control is no longer dependent on an entire byte to transmit the control message, but on a single bit within the 8-bit byte sequence.

Users can capture data in an external tape storage or internal memory, as well as freeze the most current data on the video screen. A protocol analyzer can show when a carriage return or a line feed occurs, as well as when a communication control code is transmitted. The technician can count the number of SYN characters, identify the eight bits of each field or character within a frame, and the like.

These devices have two basic categories, active and passive. *Active analyzers/ monitors* can generate data, are interactive on the circuit, and can emulate various terminals because they are programmable. *Passive analyzers/monitors* merely monitor and collect data to be examined later. It should be noted that this test equipment, especially active analyzers, can be a security risk because of its ability to generate data, interactively place it on a communication circuit, and do this while emulating another terminal located somewhere else.

A typical analyzer can monitor data, trap and count data for gathering communication circuit statistics, offer a video screen and printer, poll various stations, offer BERT capabilities, work with both asynchronous and synchronous systems, analyze various protocols, possess breakout box capabilities, and so forth.

Now it is possible to turn your microcomputer into a combined protocol analyzer, response time analyzer, data line monitor, and BERT tester. You accomplish this by using an internal PC adapter board, software, and an external RS232 interface unit that taps directly into your data line. The microcomputer can perform terminal and host emulation in asynchronous, synchronous, BSC, HDLC, and SDLC protocols. It displays a screen of EIA interface status indicators (RS232), the data rate, timing, code, SYN characters, and protocol setups. In other words, the integration of protocol analyzers, response time analyzers, and data line monitors has been achieved by incorporating them into a microcomputer.

Automated Test Equipment *Automated test equipment* consists of hardware (minicomputers or microcomputers) and specialized software packages. All of it has built-in microprocessor chips and programmable testing features. You should note that the programs able to perform this testing also can be housed within the host mainframe computer or a remote computer somewhere out in the network. Furthermore, the telephone companies offer centralized automated testing equipment that is located at the telephone company central office and used for monitoring your network.

This type of automated testing equipment performs such functions as diagnostic testing, polling, statistics gathering, protocol emulation, measurement of whether the bandwidth (circuit capacity) is being used efficiently, self-diagnosis of its own circuits, both analog and digital circuit testing, testing of centralized and remote switches, and automatic restart and recovery in case of a disastrous situation.

KEY TERMS

ACCUMASTER
  Integrator
Active analyzer/monitor
Agent
Analog testing
Analyzer
Automated test equipment
Bit-Error Rate (BER)
Bit-Error Rate Tester
  (BERT)
BlocK-Error Rate (BKER)
BlocK-Error Rate Tester
  (BKERT)
Breakout box
Cable analyzer
CATER
Chief Information Officer
  (CIO)
Client (microcomputer)
Common Management
  Interface Protocol
  (CMIP)
Controlling
Data
Data line monitor
Data recorder
Design and analysis
Digital testing
Directing
Downtime
Error Free Seconds (EFS)
Failure control
Fiber identifier

Firefighting
Handheld test set
Information
LANVision Series
Logical network
  parameters
Loopback testing
Management reports
Management station
Mean Time Between
  Failures (MTBF)
Mean Time To Diagnose
  (MTTD)
Mean Time To Fix
  (MTTF)
Mean Time To Repair
  (MTTR)
Mean Time To Respond
  (MTTR)
MIB (Management
  Information Base)
Monitor
NetView
NetWare Management
  System (NMS)
Network availability
Network documentation
Network management
Network management
  system
Network operations
Network reporting
Network status

Organizing
Passive analyzer/monitor
Patch panel
Physical network
  parameters
Pipes, pumps, and people
Planning
Probe
Problem-solving
  methodology
Problem statistics
Problem tracking
Protocol analyzer
Protocol testing
Quality control chart
Remote station
Response time analyzer
Rmon MIB
Self-testing modem
Simple Network Manage-
  ment Protocol (SNMP)
SMT frame
Spectrum Services
Staffing
Station management for
  FDDI (SMT)
Strategic resource
Testing and problem
  management
Trouble ticket
Uptime
Voice/data integration

SELECTED REFERENCES

1. *Auerbach Data Communications Management*. Published bimonthly by Auerbach Publishers (a division of Warren, Gorham & Lamont), 210 South Street, Boston, Mass. 02111-9990.

2. Carlyle, Ralph. "The Out of Touch CIO," *Datamation,* vol. 36, no. 16, August 15, 1990, pp. 30–32, 34.

3. Guruge, Anura. "IBM's System View: Adding Function to Form," *Data Communications,* vol. 20, no. 15, November 1991, pp. 99–100, 102, 104, 108, 110.

4. Henderson, Tom. "The Four, no Seven, Rules of Network Management," *LAN Times,* vol. 9, no. 8, May 11, 1992, p. 29.

5. Jander, Mary. "MIB Tools: Coping With the Not-So-Simple Side of SNMP," *Data Communications,* vol. 21, no. 3, February 1992, pp. 79–82.

6. Jander, Mary. "WAN Protocol Analyzers: Opening a Window on Fast Packet Services," *Data Communications,* vol. 21, no. 6, April 1992, pp. 69–70, 72–78, 80, 82.

7. *Journal of Network Management.* Published quarterly by Frost & Sullivan, Inc., 106 Fulton St., New York, N.Y. 10273-0028, 1989– .

8. *Network Management Systems & Strategies.* Published biweekly by DataTrends Publications, Inc., P.O. Box 657, Merrifield, Va. 22116-9822, 1989– .

9. *ShowText.* A software package available from TimeWare Corp., 2070 Touraine Lane, Half Moon Bay, Calif. 94019. [ShowText can draw tables like the one shown in Figure 12-2.]

QUESTIONS/PROBLEMS

1. What is the primary responsibility of the data communication function in an organization?

2. Why is it said that information activities present a special organizational problem?

3. From what part of the organization should the data communication function be controlled?

4. In the context of information CATERing to its users, for which of these concepts is the data communication manager responsible?

5. Name the five key management tasks the data communication manager must perform.

6. What two factors increase the value of the data communication manager to the organization?

7. To what do we refer when discussing network organization?

8. What should the written charter of the data communication network organization contain?

9. What are the objectives of the data communication function?

10. What are some of the factors that keep the data communication function from meeting its objectives?

11. Too many managers spend too much time on _____ and not enough time on _____ and _____.

12. Why is it said that combining voice and data is a major organizational challenge?

13. What has brought about the desire to combine the voice and data communication functions?

14. Which usually costs more, a voice telephone system or a data communication system?

15. In what areas would you need expertise if you were the manager of a combined voice and data communication system?

16. Name three benefits of combining the voice and data functions.

17. What type of resource is information?

18. How would you characterize the position of Chief Information Officer?

19. Describe the functions of a Chief Information Officer.

20. Briefly describe network status and how it is used.

21. What does management require to address future needs?

22. People tend to think of software when documentation is mentioned. What is documentation in a network situation?

23. Today's network managers face a number of demanding problems. Name three.

24. Network monitoring falls into two distinct categories. What are they and who does the appropriate monitoring?

25. Describe the four basic job functions of a data communication network manager.

26. How are trouble tickets used?

27. What do trouble tickets report?

28. Why is it important to have a centralized network failure control group?

29. Several important statistics related to network uptime and downtime are discussed in this chapter. What are they and why are they important?

30. How is network availability calculated?

31. In what way has deregulation influenced how testing is done on data communication networks?

32. Describe the three types of network testing.

33. Would you characterize the cost of a set of network management test equipment for a large network as being inexpensive, moderate, or expensive?

34. What are the six categories of network test equipment?

35. Network management systems deal with four times. What are they and why are they important?

36. Name three of the pieces of test equipment discussed in this chapter and indicate their use.

37. Calculate the percentage of network availability using Figure 12-4 and the following MTBFs for three network elements.

    MODEM   = 50,000 hours
    CIRCUIT   =   900 hours
    MULTIPLEXER = 40,000 hours

    In addition, the communications department collected the following annual number of hours for MTTD, MTTR, and MTTF.

    MTTD = 12,800 hours
    MTTR = 1,100 hours
    MTTF = 14,200 hours

38. If you have a very bad circuit and the MTBF is only 300 hours, how would that change the percentage of availability in Question 37?

39. Data or information transmitted over any network must CATER to the overall needs of the network users. Define the acronym CATER.

40. If the annual budget for voice telephones at the local university is $106,000, what is a good estimate of their data communication costs?

41. Will technology help or hinder the combining of voice and data communications? Explain.

42. If you were going to initiate a data communication network control department, what would be some of the major job tasks and what organizations would be set up in this department?

43. Assume you want to know the availability of a single modem. Use Figure 12-4 to calculate the availability if

    MTBF = 30,000 hours
    MTTD =   4 hours
    MTTR =   8 hours
    MTTF =   2 hours

44. If the modem is located in the village of Old Crow, 210 air miles north of Dawson City in Canada's Yukon Territory, the MTTR might be 96 hours (or possibly longer depending on snowstorms). Now what is the availability of the modem in Question 43?

45. If you were using a bit-error rate tester, would you use a BKER test for asynchronous transmission?

46. What are the two primary reasons for having the process of network management?

47. How does NetView differ from SystemView?

48. What is the Simple Network Management Protocol?

49. What is the name of SNMP's OSI competitor and how are they distinguished from one another?

50. How do probes, monitors, and analyzers differ?

51. What is the management of a FDDI network called?

52. Of the four mean times that were discussed in this chapter, which applies to vendors and which applies to in-house technicians?

53. What is the purpose of a fiber identifier?

54. How is a cable analyzer used?

55. What is a protocol analyzer?

56. What is NMS?

NEXT DAY AIR SERVICE CUMULATIVE CASE STUDY

Background on Next Day Air Service

Mr. Coones is very pleased because the network finally is in place and operating; but, as you expected, Next Day Air Service is experiencing growing pains as it adjusts to a new way of doing business and learns how to use the new network.

One recurring problem is that two departments disagree on which one should be responsible for dealing with the common carriers. The Human Resources Department originally set up the telephone system because no one else was able to do it. As a result, Human Resources controls the voice and facsimile communication system. The Information Services Department controls data communications, which is a natural outgrowth of its data processing and data communication responsibilities. Each of these departments believes it should be the contact for dealing with the common carriers, and each feels the other is getting in the way of its assuming its rightful place within the organization.

Because of your excellent past performance, Mr. Coone has asked you to study certain organizational issues pertaining to the control and operation of both voice and data communications. He wants you to analyze the operations of both departments and propose a method for streamlining the organization and fixing the problem. This analysis should address combining the voice and data communication responsibilities under a single manager. You may propose any reorganization that seems appropriate. Be sure to consider economies of scale when submitting any recommendations.

Consideration should be given to the type of individual who should manage this reorganization. Some of the factors that need to be evaluated are the traits and characteristics needed for successful leadership, the ability to understand systems that currently are in place, the ability to handle both data and voice networks, and the ability to analyze and manage future growth. The results of this evaluation will help determine whether such an individual exists within Next Day Air Service, or whether the firm needs to hire someone from outside the organization.

Another little problem occurred last week when NDAS experienced its first modem failure. Lee Coone had to ask Karen Lott to determine what failed on the 19,200 bits per second circuit. After fiddling with the problem for $1\frac{1}{2}$ hours, she finally called the modem vendor who then took 3 hours to get to the Tampa headquarters building. The good news is that the vendor's maintenance employee swapped a new circuit card into the failed modem and had it fixed in 15 minutes. Needless to say, Mr. Coone was not happy!

Questions/Problems for the Next Day Air Service Case

1. If the responsibilities for managing communications were to be consolidated into one department, which one would you choose and why? Base your answer on your knowledge of the communication management responsibilities exercised by both the Human Resources and Information Services Departments.

2. Would it be worthwhile to combine both voice and data circuits into a single network? Consider the future of NDAS and how it relates to continued communication growth.

3. Review Figure 1-9 and then develop an organization chart that reflects a realignment of the responsibilities for communications. Show separate organizational entities for both data processing and communications.

4. Consider the pros and cons of filling the new position of Voice/Data Communication Manager. Discuss the reasons why Next Day Air Service should promote someone from within the company to fill this new position. Now discuss the contrary reasons that explain why NDAS should hire someone from outside the organization for this position. Which position will you take? Why?

5. What was the MTTRepair on Next Day Air Service's first modem failure? Is this MTTRepair acceptable?

Chapter Thirteen

NETWORK SECURITY
AND CONTROL

This chapter describes why networks need security and control, what errors might occur, and how to control network errors. It also covers security in networks, the principles of a secure network, risk assessment, and how to identify, document, and evaluate the network controls by using a Control Spreadsheet. The remainder of the chapter describes several hundred controls listed in 15 different categories that relate to the control and security of a network. Chapter 11 discussed specific controls for the security and control of local area networks.

WHY NETWORKS NEED CONTROLS

Both business and government were concerned with security long before the need for computer-related security was recognized. They always have been interested in the physical protection of assets through such means as locks, barriers, and guards. Figure 13-1 shows the threats to a computer center, the data communication link, and the online nodes or stations (devices).

The introduction of computer processing, centralized database storage techniques, and communication networks has increased the need for security. Our concerns about security now are focused directly on the computer-related areas of the business function. This emphasis manifests itself in controls to *prevent, detect,* and *correct* whatever might happen to the organization through the threats faced by its computer-based systems. *Controls* are mechanisms that are implemented for the purpose of ensuring that the threats to a network are mitigated or stopped and that the components of the network are restricted, safeguarded, and protected from the threats. The Three Basic Categories of Controls box contains definitions for the three categories of controls.

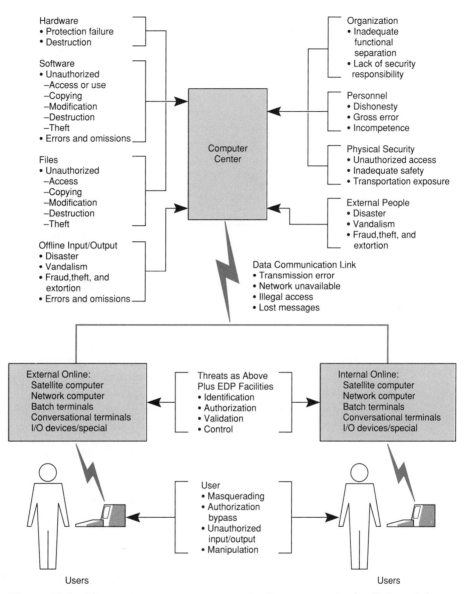

Figure 13-1   Threats to a computer center, the data communication link, and the online nodes.

Before moving on to network security, we want to present some short summaries of past computer crimes involving some aspect of communications. They will give you some idea of the types of crimes that have been committed. As you read the summaries, try to identify some controls that would have prevented, detected, or corrected the computer crime if they had been in force at the time the crime was perpetrated.

THREE BASIC CATEGORIES OF CONTROLS

Are the *preventive controls* adequate?

- Preventive controls mitigate or stop one from acting or an event from occurring. For example, a password can prevent illegal entry into the system, or backup circuits can prevent network downtime.
- Deterrent controls discourage or restrain one from acting or proceeding because of fear or doubt. They also restrain or hinder an event. For example, a guard or a security lock on a door may deter an attempt to gain illegal entry.

Are the *detective controls* adequate?

- Detective controls reveal or discover unwanted events, and they offer evidence of trespass. For example, software that looks for illegal network entry or a virus can detect these problems.
- Reporting controls document an event, a situation, or a trespass. For example, the same software that detects the illegal act or problem must report it immediately so a human being or some automated process can take remedial action.

Are the *corrective controls* adequate?

- Corrective controls remedy or set right an unwanted event or a trespass. For example, either computer programs or humans verify and check data to correct errors or fix a security breach so it will not happen again in the future.
- Recovery controls regain, make up for, or make good the effect of an unwanted event or a trespass. For example, software can recover and restart the communication circuits automatically when there is a data communication failure.

- The threat of computer viruses to a data communication network mandates that risk assessment and security controls be implemented. A *virus* is an executable computer program that propagates itself, uses another program as a carrier, sometimes modifies itself during or after replication, and typically is intended to create some unwanted event. This unwanted event may be simply a nuisance, or it may be more serious destruction of data files and programs.

  A massive viral infection of a network started one evening in 1988. Among the first targets were two science and research centers at Berkeley, California, and Cambridge, Massachusetts. The virus then targeted NASA's Ames Research Center in California, the University of Pittsburgh in Pennsylvania, and Los Alamos National Laboratory in New Mexico. By the next morning it also had *penetrated* computers at Johns Hopkins University (Baltimore) and the University of Michigan (Ann Arbor). This invading virus replicated itself so many times and so often that it overloaded the network, forcing the network operators to shut down for lack of computer cycles. It then moved on to Bellcore (Livingston, N.J.), SRI International (Menlo Park, Calif.), and New York University (New York City). It is noteworthy that the computers of AT&T's Bell Laboratories (Murray Hill, N.J.), of the University of Maryland, and of the Argonne National Laboratory (Chicago) were able to repel the virus. The point of this description is to demonstrate how quickly a computer virus can infect a nationwide network. In this example, it was less than one day.

- A second example of the need for network security is the case of a wholesale grocery firm in Los Angeles that fell victim to a band of hackers. The hackers commandeered the firm's messaging system and used it to run prostitution rings and pass drug information. The problem was identified when users complained about being unable to access their voice mailboxes because their passwords had been invalidated. Upon investigation it was discovered that hackers had overcome the security features of the system and reprogrammed the 200 voice mailboxes for their own use. The hackers accessed the system by using a toll-free 800 number maintained for the purpose of letting traveling employees call in for their messages. Once inside the system, the hackers used help programs to learn how to change security codes, thus denying access to authorized users. Among other things, the hackers sold stolen MasterCard, Visa, and American Express numbers via the voice messaging system. The system also was modified to provide information on the price of a kilogram of cocaine in New York.

- The massive fire that destroyed the central office switch of an Illinois Bell Telephone Company is a third incident demonstrating the need for security and backup. The fire cut voice and data communications to thousands of businesses in the western Chicago area. Many businesses, such as branch banks, cannot continue to operate as viable businesses if their voice and data communications are cut off for even a few days, let alone two weeks. The Walgreen Drugstore chain in Illinois reported that in the aftermath of the fire 180 of its 255 drugstores lost access to their central communication network.

- A gunman who was armed with a shotgun and a pistol entered a telephone company central office and took several hostages. He then began blasting away at the central office switch with the shotgun, causing an estimated $10 million in damages. Approximately 15,000 customers lost their telephone service but, to the credit of the telephone company, all service was restored within 22 hours.

- An illegal bookie in Australia tapped into the communication circuits of the legal bookmaking operations by using his telephone. The purpose was to know race results immediately, enabling him to pay off winners as fast as the legal betting establishments that are licensed by the government.

- An unknown person gained access to a computer terminal room by asking the janitor to open the door for him. He then picked the locks of the telephones and terminals, thereby gaining unauthorized access and use of timesharing facilities.

- An unknown person poured acid over telephone wires at the point where the wires entered a building that contained data processing and network equipment.

- At the time of the Persian Gulf War, Dutch hackers are reported to have ransacked U.S. Department of Defense computers at 34 sites, in some cases modifying or copying information linked to military operations in the Persian Gulf. Israeli officials said that an 18-year-old hacker had penetrated Pentagon computers and retrieved classified information related to the Patriot missile and other military secrets.

ERROR CONTROL IN NETWORKS

Before describing the control mechanisms that can be implemented to protect a network, you should realize that there are *human errors* and *network errors*. Human errors, such as a mistake in keying a number, usually are controlled through the application program. Network errors are controlled by the network software.

Errors are different from purposeful illegal acts like those described in the previous section. Errors occur as a result of doing your job, but illegal acts are planned events that can be carried out by employees or by outsiders. Illegal acts are more difficult to control than network errors.

There are two categories of network errors: *corrupted* (changed) *data* and *lost data*. The factors to consider when selecting an error control system are the maximum error rate that can be tolerated, the cost of increased accuracy compared with the cost of correcting errors, and the future cost of errors remaining in the received data or information.

What Are Network Errors?   Network errors are a fact of life in today's data communication networks. Depending on the type of circuit/line, they may occur every few minutes, every few seconds, or even more frequently. They occur because of noise on the lines. (Types of line noise are discussed in the next section.) No data communication network can prevent all these errors from occurring, but most of them can be prevented, detected, and corrected by proper design. Common carriers that lease data transmission circuits to users provide statistical measures specifying typical error rates and the pattern of errors that can be expected on the different types of circuits they lease.

Normally, errors appear in bursts. In a *burst error* more than one data bit is changed by the error-causing condition. This is another way of saying that 1-bit errors are not uniformly distributed in time. However, common carriers usually list their *error rates* as the number of bits in error divided by the number of bits transmitted, without reference to their nonuniform distribution. For example, the error rate might be given as 1 in 500,000 when transmitting on a public voice grade telephone circuit at 1200 bits per second. This means there is 1 bit in error for every 500,000 bits transmitted.

The fact that errors tend to be clustered in bursts rather than evenly dispersed has both positive and negative aspects. If the errors were not clustered (but instead were evenly distributed throughout the day), with an error rate of 1 bit in 500,000, it would be rare for two erroneous bits to occur in the same character, and consequently some simple character checking scheme would be effective. But this is not the case because bursts of errors are the rule rather than the exception. They sometimes go on for time periods that may obliterate 50 to 100 or more bits. The positive aspect is that, between bursts, there may be rather long periods of error-free transmission. Therefore, no errors at all may occur during data transmission in a large proportion of messages. For exa#ple, when errors are #ore or less evenly distrib#ted, it is not di#ficult to gras# the me#ning even when the error #ate is high, as it is in this #entence (1 charac#er in 20). On the other hand, if errors are concentrated in bursts, it becomes more difficult to recover the meaning and much more reliance must be placed on knowledge of the message #######[1] or on special logical or numerical error detection and correction methods.

Error prevention is achieved by using circuit conditioning and forward error correction devices, as well as by managing the network properly.

It is possible to develop data transmission methodologies that give very high *error detection and correction* performance. The only way to do the detection and correction is to send along extra data. The larger the amount of extra data sent, the greater the error protection achieved. However, as this protection is increased, the throughput of useful data is reduced. Therefore, the efficiency of data throughput varies inversely as the desired amount of error detection and correction is increased. Errors even have an effect on the length of the block of data to be transmitted when synchronous transmission is used. The shorter the message blocks used, the less likelihood there is of needing retransmission for any one block. But the shorter the message block, the less efficient is the transmission methodology as far as throughput is concerned. If the message blocks are long, a higher proportion may have an error and have to be resent.

The error rate in transmissions sent over the dial-up switched network varies from one time of day to another. The error rate usually is higher during periods of heavy traffic (the normal business day). In some cases the only alternative open to the user of these facilities is to transmit the data at a slower speed because higher transmission speeds are more error prone. Dial-up lines are more prone to errors than private leased lines because they have less stable transmission parameters, and because different calls use different circuits, they usually experience different transmission conditions. Thus, a bad line is not necessarily a serious problem in dial-up transmission; a new call may result in getting a better line. *Conditioning,* a service that is available on private leased lines, consists of special electrical balancing of the circuit to ensure the most error-free transmission.

What Causes Network Errors?   *Line noise* and *distortion* can cause data communication errors. In this context we define noise as undesirable electrical signals. It is introduced by equipment or natural disturbances, and it degrades the performance of a communication line. Noise manifests itself as extra bits, missing bits, or bits whose states have been "flipped," and the result is a degraded message content. Line noise and distortion can be classified into roughly 12 categories: white noise, impulse

---

[1]In case you could not guess, the word is "context."

noise, cross-talk, echoes, intermodulation noise, amplitude noise, line outages, attenuation, attenuation distortion, delay distortion, jitter, and harmonic distortion.

White or Gaussian Noise is the familiar background hiss or static on radios and telephones. It is caused by the thermal agitation of electrons and therefore is inescapable. Even if the equipment were perfect and the wires were perfectly insulated from any and all external interference, there still would be some white noise. White noise usually is not a problem unless its level becomes so high that it obliterates the data transmission. Sometimes noise from other sources such as power line induction, cross modulation from adjacent lines, and a conglomeration of random signals resembles white noise and is labeled as such even though it is not caused by thermal electrons.

Impulse Noise (sometimes called *spikes*) is the primary source of errors in data communications. An impulse of noise can last as long as 1/100th of a second. An impulse of this duration is heard as a click or a crackling noise during voice communications. This click does not affect voice communications, but it might obliterate a group of data bits, causing a burst error on a data communication line. At 150 bits per second, 1 or 2 bits would be changed by a spike of 1/100th of a second, whereas at 4800 bits per second, 48 bits would be changed. Some of the sources of impulse noise are voltage changes in adjacent lines or circuitry surrounding the data communication line, telephone switching equipment at the telephone exchange branch offices, arcing of the relays at older telephone exchange offices, tones used by network signaling, maintenance equipment during line testing, lightning flashes during thunderstorms, and intermittent electrical connections in the data communication equipment.

Cross-talk occurs when one line picks up some of the signal traveling down another line. It occurs between line pairs that are carrying separate signals, in multiplexed links carrying many discrete signals, in microwave links in which one antenna picks up a minute reflected portion of the signal from another antenna on the same tower, and in any hardwired telephone circuits that run parallel to each other, are too close to each other, or are not electrically balanced. You are experiencing cross-talk during voice communication on the public switched network when you hear other conversations in the background. Cross-talk between lines increases with increased communication distance, increased proximity of the two wires, increased signal strength, and higher frequency signals. Like white noise, cross-talk has such a low signal strength that it normally is not bothersome on data communication networks.

Echoes and echo suppression can be a cause of errors. (Echo suppressors were discussed in Chapter 2.) An echo suppressor causes a change in the electrical balance of a line. This change causes a signal to be reflected so that it travels back down the line at reduced signal strength. When the echo suppressors are disabled, as in data transmission, this echo returns to the transmitting equipment. If the signal strength of the echo is high enough to be detected by the communication equipment, it causes errors. Echoes, like cross-talk and white noise, have such a low signal strength that they normally are not bothersome.

Intermodulation Noise is a special type of cross-talk. The signals from two independent lines intermodulate and form a new signal that falls into a frequency band differing from both inputs. This resultant frequency may fall into the frequency that is reserved for another signal. This type of noise is similar to harmonics in music. On a multiplexed line, many different signals are amplified together, and slight variations in the adjustment of the equipment can cause intermodulation noise. A maladjusted modem may transmit a strong frequency tone when not transmitting data, thus yielding this type of noise.

Amplitude Noise involves a sudden change in the level of power. The effect of this noise depends on the type of modulation being used by the modem. For example, amplitude noise does not affect frequency modulation techniques because the transmitting and receiving equipment interprets frequency information and disregards the amplitude information. Some of the causes of amplitude noise may be faulty amplifiers, dirty contacts with variable resistances, sudden added loads by new circuits being switched on during the day, maintenance work in progress, and switching to different transmission lines.

Line Outages are a catastrophic cause of errors and incomplete transmission. Occasionally, a communication circuit fails for a brief period of time. This type of failure may be caused by faulty telephone end office equipment, storms, loss of the carrier signal, and any other failure that causes an open line or short circuit.

Attenuation is the loss of power the signal suffers as it travels from the transmitting device to the receiving device. Some power is absorbed by the transmission medium or is lost before it reaches the receiver. As the transmission medium absorbs power, the signal becomes weaker, and the receiving equipment has less and less chance of correctly interpreting the data. To avoid this problem, telephone lines have repeater/amplifiers spaced through their length. The distance between them depends on the amount of power lost per unit length of the transmission line. This power loss is a function of the transmission method and circuit medium. Attenuation increases as frequency increases or as the diameter of the wire decreases.

Attenuation Distortion refers to high frequencies losing power more rapidly than low frequencies during transmission. The received signal can thus be distorted by unequal loss of its component frequencies.

Delay Distortion occurs when a signal is delayed more at some frequencies than at others. If the method of data transmission involves data transmitted at two different frequencies, then the bits being transmitted at one frequency may travel slightly faster than the bits transmitted at the second frequency. An *equalizer* is a piece of equipment that compensates for both attenuation distortion and delay distortion. Equalizers are built into some modems, or the telephone company can perform equalization (conditioning) on private lease circuits and dial-up calls.

Jitter may affect the accuracy of the data being transmitted. The generation of a pure carrier signal is impossible. Minute variations in amplitude, phase, and frequency always occur. The signal may be impaired by continuous and rapid gain and/

or phase changes. This jitter may be random or periodic. Phase jitter during a telephone call causes the voice to go up and down in volume.

Harmonic Distortion usually is caused by an amplifier on a circuit that does not correctly represent its output with what was delivered to it on the input side. *Phase hits* are short-term shifts "out of phase," with the possibility of a shift back into phase.

HOW TO CONTROL NETWORK ERRORS

Error control implies (1) techniques of design and manufacture of data communication transmission links and equipment to reduce the occurrence of errors (an area that is outside the scope of this book), and (2) methodologies to detect and correct the errors that are introduced during transmission of the data. There are four approaches to error control: loop or echo checking, error detection with retransmission, forward error correction, and proper network management. The first three approaches are discussed below, but network management is so important that Chapter 12 is devoted to the subject.

Loop or Echo Checking   *Loop checking* or *echo checking* does not use a special code. Instead, each character or other small unit of the message, as it is received, is transmitted back to the transmitter, which checks to determine whether the character is the same as the one just sent. If it is not correct, then the character or block of data is transmitted a second time. This method of error detection is wasteful of transmission capacity because each message (in pieces) is transmitted at least twice and there is no guarantee that some messages might not be transmitted three or four times. Some of this retransmission for a second or third time might not be necessary because the error could have occurred on the return trip of the character, thus requiring the transmitter to retransmit the character even though it was received correctly the first time. This type of error checking does provide a high degree of protection, but it is not as efficient as other methods. It sometimes is confused with full duplex transmission.

Error Detection with Retransmission   Schemes for *error detection with retransmission* are built into data transmitting and receiving devices, front end processors, modems, and software. These schemes include detection of an error and immediate retransmission or detection of an error and retransmission for up to ten tries and then notification that there is a circuit problem. Error detection and retransmission is the simplest, most effective, and least expensive method of reducing errors in data transmission. It requires the simplest logic, needs relatively little storage, is best understood by terminal operators, and is most frequently used. Retransmission of the message in error is straightforward. It usually is called for because the transmitter received a negative acknowledgment. Various methods are used to determine that the message that has just been received has, in fact, an error imbedded in it.

Three common *error detection methods* are parity checking, *M*-of-*N* codes, and polynomial checking.

Parity Checking If you examine a character from the ASCII coding structure, it soon becomes apparent that one of the eight bits encoding each character is redundant. That is, its value is determined solely by the values of the other seven and therefore is unnecessary. Because this eighth bit cannot transmit any new information, its purpose is to confirm old information. The most common rule for fixing the value of the redundant bit uses the parity (evenness or oddness) of the number of 1s in the code. Thus, for an even parity code system using ASCII,

- Letter V is encoded 0110101. Because the number of 1s is 4, already an even number, a 0 is added in the parity (eighth) position, yielding V = 01101010.
- Letter W is encoded 0001101, which has an odd number of 1s. Therefore, a 1 is added in the parity position to make the number of 1s even, yielding W = 00011011.

A little thought will convince you that any single error (a switch of a 1 to a 0 or vice versa) will be detected by a parity check, but nothing can be deduced about which bit was in error. Moreover, if the states of *two* bits are switched, the parity check may not sense any error. Of course, it may be possible to sense such an error because the resulting code, although correct as far as parity is concerned, is a code that is "forbidden," for example, undefined or inappropriate in its context. Such detection requires more circuitry or software. Many networks today do not use parity because it cannot correct errors and is only about 50 percent accurate in detecting errors. Moreover, some networks remove the parity bit before transmission and replace it at the receiving terminal. Thus, transmission requires only 7 bits per character instead of the less efficient 8 bits per character. When parity is used, networks are described as having *odd parity, even parity,* or *no parity.*

Another parity checking technique is the *cyclical parity check* (sometimes called *interlaced parity*). This method requires two parity bits per character. Assuming a 6-data-bit code structure, the first parity bit provides parity for the first, third, and fifth bits, and the second parity bit provides parity for the second, fourth, and sixth bits. Figure 13-2 shows even parity when using the cyclical parity check on a 6-bit code.

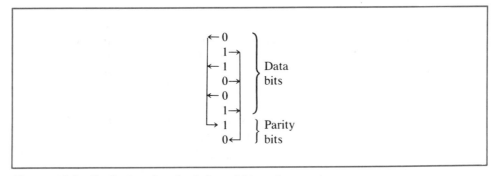

Figure 13-2 Cyclical parity check for a 6-bit code.

M-of-N Codes The *M-of-N codes* (also called *constant ratio codes*) can indicate whether one of the bits was changed during transmission. For example, with a 2-of-5 code, there are always two 1s and three 0s representing a character. If this precise ratio (two 1s and three 0s) is not present in each received character, then an error has occurred during transmission of the data. One disadvantage of this system is that it makes many of the possible combinations unusable. For example,

$$C = \frac{N!}{M!\,(N - M)!}$$

shows how to calculate the number of usable code configurations when using one of these self-checking codes. C (the number of combinations) is determined by taking the various factorials of N and M, where N equals the total number of bits in the code and M equals the number of 1 bits in the code. With the example of a 2-of-5 code we have $C = 5!/2!\,(5 - 2)!$ or only 10 legal combinations. Obviously, this is far too few combinations; therefore, a 2-of-5 code is totally unusable except for transmitting numbers.

Some years ago IBM developed a 4-of-8 code, where 4 of the 8 bits were 1s and 4 were 0s. Any other combination was an error. This code was of limited value because there are only 70 valid combinations instead of 256. In addition, it does not have the option of stripping off the parity bit before a synchronous transmission and putting it back on upon receipt. On the positive side, this 4-of-8 code detects errors better than a single parity bit. It has the same error checking capabilities as the double parity bit in a BCD code structure shown in Figure 13-2.

Polynomial Checking *Polynomial checking* often is performed on blocks of data for synchronous data transmission. In this type of message checking, all the bits of the message are checked by application of a mathematical *algorithm*. For example, all the 1 bits in a message are counted and then divided by a prime number (such as 17), and the remainder of that division is transmitted to the receiving equipment. The receiving equipment performs the same mathematical computations and matches the remainder that it calculated against the remainder that was transmitted with the message. If the two are equal, the entire message block is assumed to have been received correctly. In actual practice, much more complex algorithms are used.

One of the most popular of the polynomial error checking schemes is *cyclical redundancy check* (CRC). It consists of adding bits (about 8 to 32) to the entire block. A communication protocol, using a 16-bit CRC, calculates a 16-bit number that is a function of all the data in the block being sent. This 16-bit number is added to the end of the message block. The receiver recalculates its own 16-bit CRC as the block is received. If the numbers are the same, everything is acceptable. If they are different, an error has occurred. Once an error is detected, the correction mechanism tells the sender to retransmit the message. The sender goes back to the last successful (prior) message and begins transmitting again. A 16-bit CRC detects every error that is 16 bits or smaller with 100 percent probability. In CRC checking the data block can be thought of as one long binary polynomial, P. Before transmission, equipment in the terminal divides P by a fixed binary polynomial, G, resulting in a whole polynomial, Q, and a remainder, R/G.

$$\frac{P}{G} = Q + \frac{R}{G}$$

The remainder, R, is appended to the block before transmission, as a check sequence k bits long. The receiving hardware divides the received data block by the same G, which generates an R. The receiving hardware checks to ascertain whether the received R agrees with the locally generated R. If it does not, the data block is assumed to be in error and retransmission is requested. A 25-bit CRC code added to a 1000-bit block allows only three bits in 100 million to go undetected. That is, for a 2.5 percent redundancy, the error rate is 3×10^{-8}. Today, 32-bit CRC codes are popular because they detect even more errors.

Forward Error Correction   *Forward error correction* uses codes that contain sufficient redundancy to permit errors to be prevented by detecting and correcting them at the receiving equipment *without* retransmission of the original message. The redundancy, or extra bits required, varies with different schemes. It ranges from a small percentage of extra bits to 100 percent redundancy, with the number of error detecting bits roughly equaling the number of data bits. One of the characteristics of many error correcting codes is that there must be a minimum number of error-free bits between bursts of errors. For example, one such code, called a *Hagelbarger code,* corrects up to six consecutive bit errors provided that the 6-bit error group is followed by at least 19 valid bits before more error bits are encountered. Bell Telephone engineers have developed an error correcting code that uses 12 check bits for each 48 data bits, or 25 percent redundancy. Still another code is the *Bose-Chaudhuri code,* which, in one of its forms, is capable of correcting double errors and can detect up to four errors.

To show how such a code works, consider this example of a forward error checking code, called a *Hamming code,* after its inventor, R. W. Hamming. This code associates even parity bits with unique combinations of data bits. Using a 4-data-bit code as an example, a character might be represented by the data bit configuration 1010. Three parity bits P_1, P_2, and P_4 are added, resulting in a 7-bit code, shown in the upper half of Figure 13-3. Notice that the data bits (D_3, D_5, D_6, D_7) are 1010, and the parity bits (P_1, P_2, P_4) are 101.

As depicted in the upper half of Figure 13-3, parity bit P_1 applies to data bits D_3, D_5, and D_7. Parity bit P_2 applies to data bits D_3, D_6, and D_7. Parity bit P_4 applies to data bits D_5, D_6, and D_7. For the example, in which D_3, D_5, D_6, $D_7 = 1010$, P_1 must equal 1 because there is but one 1 among D_3, D_5, and D_7 and parity must be even. Similarly, P_2 must be 0 because D_3 and D_6 are 1s. P_4 is 1 because D_6 is the only 1 among D_5, D_6, and D_7.

Now, assume that during the transmission, data bit D_7 is changed from a 0 to a 1 by line noise. Because this data bit is being checked by P_1, P_2, and P_4, all three parity bits now show odd parity instead of the correct even parity. (D_7 is the only

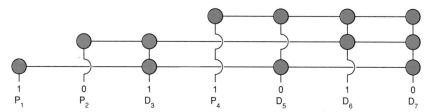

Checking Relations Between Parity Bits (P) and Data Bits (D)

0 = Corresponding parity check is correct 1 = Corresponding parity check fails			Determines in which bit the error occurred
P_4	P_2	P_1	
0	0	0	→ no error
0	0	1	→ P_1
0	1	0	→ P_2
0	1	1	→ D_3
1	0	0	→ P_4
1	0	1	→ D_5
1	1	0	→ D_6
1	1	1	→ D_7

Interpreting Parity Bit Patterns

Figure 13-3   Hamming code for forward error correction.

data bit that is monitored by all three parity bits; therefore, when D_7 is in error, all three parity bits show an incorrect parity.) In this way, the receiving equipment can determine which bit was in error and reverse its state, thus correcting the error without retransmission.

The lower half of Figure 13-3 is a table that determines the location of the bit in error. A 1 in the table means that the corresponding parity bit indicates a parity error. Conversely, a 0 means the parity check is correct. These 0s and 1s form a binary number that indicates the numerical location of the erroneous bit. In the example above, P_1, P_2, and P_4 checks all failed, yielding 111, or a decimal 7, the subscript of the erroneous bit.

The Consultative Committee on International Telegraph and Telephone (CCITT) has incorporated a forward error correction technique called *Trellis coding* into its V.32 specification of 9600 bits per second dial-up modems. Forward error correction is essential in certain circumstances. In some media like simplex communication links, there is no return communication channel to provide a negative acknowledgment (NAK), retransmission cannot be requested, or a message may be sent to thousands of receivers with no return message capability.

Satellite transmission is one area in which the argument for forward error correction makes sense. A round trip from the earth station to the satellite and back includes a significant delay. Error rates can fluctuate depending on everything from the transmission frequencies to the condition of equipment, sun spots, or the weather. Compared to satellite equipment costs, the additional cost of forward error correction is insignificant.

The use of forward error correction in broader markets such as modem-based communications is limited today because coding forward error correction algorithms is costly. With time, however, forward error correction circuit board modules will be replaced by chip-level devices. Chip implementations of forward error correction are coming on the market.

WHY NETWORKS NEED SECURITY

A few computer crimes and how to control errors were described in the previous sections of this chapter. LAN security and control also were discussed in Chapter 11. Now we will describe a sophisticated network penetration (illegal act) by someone using public data networks (PDNs). In this instance, the computer hacker entered the communication networks by using stolen MCI, US Sprint, and other voice communication network identification and passwords in the following manner.

The hacker first placed a call to a Philadelphia gateway node (switching node) of a PDN. Once that circuit was established, he placed a second call to a US Sprint gateway node in Chicago and used a second stolen access code to enter Sprint. Then he used the US Sprint linkage from Chicago to establish a third circuit with a Telenet gateway node in San Francisco, for which he used still another stolen access code. He then used one of the unprotected host computers maintained by Telenet as a switch before establishing a host-to-host circuit via Tymnet. This hacker then jumped through several other host computers, entered DATAPAC (a Canadian public packet switching network), and again used several host computers before reentering Telenet to attack the ultimate target computer.

With such a complex communication environment, the chance is remote that intermediate host computers would ever discover they were being used by a *perpetrator* as switches to go to another network. In fact, the host computer probably paid unknowingly for this perpetrator's communication charges. The people who are most likely to discover such a computer crime are the individual subscribers, for it is they who receive the dial-up telephone bills from the various network vendors.

In recent years organizations have become increasingly dependent on data communication networks for their daily business communications, database information retrieval, distributed data processing, and the internetworking of LANs. This commitment to data communications/teleprocessing has changed the potential *vulnerability* of the organization's assets. This change has come about because the traditional security, control, and audit mechanisms take on a new and different form in data communication-based systems. Increased reliance on data communications, consolidation of many previously manual operations into computerized systems, use of database management systems, and the fact that online real-time systems cut across many lines of responsibility have increased management concern about the adequacy of current control and security mechanisms used in a data communication environment.

Emphasis on network security also has increased as officers and directors of organizations have been sued and as government regulatory agencies have issued security-related pronouncements. Moreover, we have learned that losses associated with computerized frauds are quite simply many magnitudes larger per incident than those from noncomputerized frauds. These factors have led to increased vigilance in protecting the organization's information assets from many potential hazards such as fraud, errors, lost data, breaches of privacy, and the disastrous events that can occur in a data communication network.

To protect its data communication networks, the organization must be able to implement adequate control and security mechanisms within its facilities, including buildings, terminals, local area networks, local loops, interexchange channel circuits, switching centers, gateways, packet networks, hardware (modems, multiplexers, encryption devices, and the like), network protocols, network architecture software, test equipment, and network management control.

For example, Figure 13-4 depicts a typical network like the one an organization might develop. In such a network all the areas just mentioned require well-thought-out decisions (policies and procedures) to provide security and control. With the kind of network in Figure 13-4, the organization is vulnerable to many points of entry from an unwanted intruder (*hacker*). In fact, every terminal in the network is a potential entry point for an unauthorized intruder; this also is true of public dial-up access points.

The remainder of this chapter will discuss the various controls that might be used to prevent, detect, or correct threats. We also will present a Control Spreadsheet and risk analysis methodology for identifying the threats and their associated controls. The Control Spreadsheet provides a data communication network manager with a good view of the current threats and any controls that are in place to mitigate the occurrence of these threats. The risk analysis methodology can be used to rank threats or any other set of alternatives pertaining to the network.

LOCATION OF NETWORK CONTROLS

To implement a good security program in a communication network environment, you need to identify all the points at which control must be established. These are called *control points*. Once it is determined where these controls should be located, then it is possible to identify what individual controls actually are required in the network at each control point.

As an example, we have identified 18 *network control points* (that is, areas where control and security mechanisms must be implemented) for a wide area network (WAN), and they are shown in Figure 13-5. The network manager, quality assurance administrator, security officer, or the organization's EDP auditor should examine these areas to be sure the proper controls are implemented and functioning properly. The numbers in the figure correspond to the numbered list below. This list defines the control point and describes the general type of security required at each of these 18 control points.

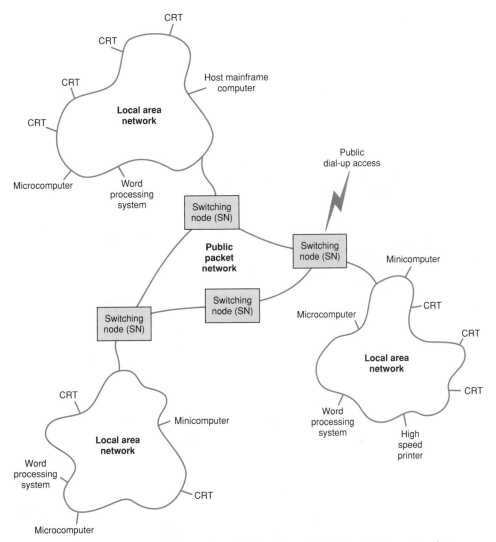

Figure 13-4 Internetworking several LANs by using a packet switching network to form a wide area network (WAN).

1. Physical security of the building or buildings that house any of the hardware, software, or communication circuits must be evaluated. Both local and remote physical facilities should be secured adequately and have the proper controls.

2. Operator and other personnel security requires implementing the proper access controls so that only authorized personnel can enter closed areas where network equipment is located or access the network. Proper security education, background checks, and the implementation of error and fraud controls fall under this control point.

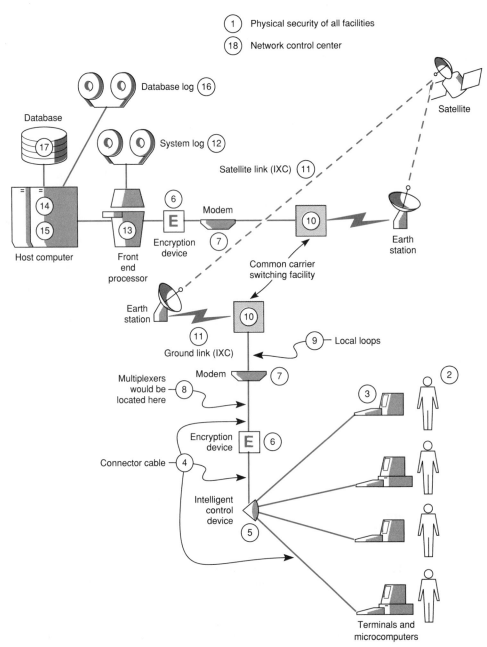

Figure 13-5 Network security control points.

3. Terminals and microcomputer workstations are a primary area in which both physical and logical types of security controls must be enforced.

4. Local connector cables and wire pairs that are installed throughout the organization's facilities must be reviewed for physical security.

5. Local intelligent control devices that control groups of terminals should be reviewed for both physical and logical programmed controls.

6. Hardware encryption is a primary control point, especially as it relates to the security of messages.

7. The modems should be reviewed as they relate to control and security at this point in the network. Modem theft may be a problem.

8. Multiplexers and concentrators, if they are used in the network, must be secured to prevent unauthorized entry, and they should contain backup circuits. Physical security and backup electrical power may be required at a remote site.

9. Local loops that go from the organization to the common carrier's switching facility should be reviewed. Encryption may be the answer here.

10. The physical security and backup of the common carrier switching facility (telephone company central office) should be evaluated. If this facility is destroyed, all the circuits will be lost. This review may include both central offices in a city and earth stations for satellite transmission.

11. The security/control mechanisms should be reviewed with regard to the interexchange channel (IXC) circuits. Encryption may be the answer here.

12. A major control point is the system log that logs all incoming and outgoing messages. There may be two logs: one used for network recovery and one saved for historical purposes.

13. The front end processor is another major control point to review. Teleprocessing access method software has controls. If there is a packet switching node (SN), it must be reviewed for security and control.

14. Within the host computer, any controls that are built into the software should be reviewed. Teleprocessing monitor software has controls and there also may be specialized security software.

15. Also within the host computer, any controls that are designed into the hardware mechanisms/architecture should be reviewed.

16. Another major control point, but only in database systems, is the database before-image/after-image logging tape. This should be reviewed for any controls that may be in existence. Many other security/control items of data are logged at this point.

17. In database-oriented systems, another control point is the database management system (DBMS) itself. The database management system software may have some controls that augment the security for the data communication network and control data flows.

18. The last control point is the network control center. This area has controls that relate to network management and operation, the test equipment, reports, documentation, and the like (see Chapter 12).

These 18 control points are the specific areas in which control features can be implemented and maintained within a wide area network. If you were to compare the 18 control points listed above with the control points in a local area network, you would see how the following items apply.

- Items 1, 2, 3, 4, and 18 apply to all types of local area networks (LANs)
- Perhaps items 7 and 8 as a medium/multistation access unit (MAU) or switch
- Item 11 but as the LAN cable instead of the IXC circuits
- Items 14, 15, 16, and 17 but with the server
- Item 6 if encryption were necessary

These network control points become the components in the Control Spreadsheet that we will be discussing in the next section.

HOW TO DEVELOP A CONTROL SPREADSHEET

To be sure that the data communication network and microcomputer workstations have the necessary controls and that these controls offer adequate protection, it is advisable to build a two-dimensional matrix we call a *Control Spreadsheet*. It incorporates all the controls that *currently* are in the network. We use this Control Spreadsheet tool as a means of identifying, documenting, and evaluating the existing controls in a network. Moreover, it becomes the benchmark on which to base future security reviews.

Identify the Threats and Components   The Control Spreadsheet is constructed by identifying, first, all threats facing the network and, second, all the network's component parts.

- A *threat* to the data communication network is any potential adverse occurrence that can harm the network, interrupt the systems using the network, or cause a monetary loss to the organization. For example, lost messages are a potential threat. Threats are events we do not want to occur.
- A *component* is one of the individual pieces that, when assembled together, make up the data communication network. A component can be viewed as the item over which we are attempting to maintain control. Thus, the components are the hardware, software, circuits, and other pieces of the network, including the people who run it.

Figure 13-6 contains a list of threats typically faced by a wide area network. Your first step is to identify the specific threats facing the network being reviewed. Notice

- **Errors and Omissions:** The accidental or intentional transmission of data that is in error, including the accidental or intentional omission of data that should have been entered or transmitted over the network. This type of exposure includes, but is not limited to, inaccurate data, incomplete data, malfunctioning hardware, and the methodologies and controls for handling errors at a remote distributed site or at the central computer site. It also includes the validation of data either at the time of transmission or during transmission.

- **Message Loss or Change:** The loss of messages as they are transmitted throughout the data communication network, or the accidental or intentional changing of messages during their transmission.

- **Disasters and Disruptions (Natural and Manmade):** The temporary or long-term disruption of normal data communication capabilities.

- **Breach of Privacy:** The accidental or intentional release of data about the organization or an individual, assuming that the release of this information is improper to the normal conduct of business in the organization.

- **Fraud or Theft:** The theft of information that should have been kept confidential because of its proprietary nature. This exposure also includes the theft of assets such as might be experienced in embezzlement, fraud, or defalcation.

- **Network Unavailable:** The reliability of the data communication network and its "uptime." Reliability of hardware, software, and circuits, and the maintenance of these items are chief concerns here.

- **Inability to Recover and Restart:** The recovery and restart capabilities of the data communication network, should it fail. In other words, how does the software operate in a failure mode? How long does it take to recover from a failure? Recovery and restart include backup for key portions of the data communication network and contingency plans for backup should any part of the network fail.

Figure 13-6   Threats faced by a wide area network (WAN).

that each threat has a short name consisting of two or three words and a sentence or two defining the threat.

Figure 13-7 contains a list of components that you will find in a wide area network. Just as with the threats, you first have to identify the components in the network being reviewed. Again, each component has a short name consisting of two or three words and a sentence or two defining the component.

The two- or three-word name for each threat and each component is what we place in the border cells of the Control Spreadsheet when we begin working on it.

As mentioned, identifying and documenting the controls in a network first requires identifying the *specific* threats and components that relate to whatever network the organization uses. In other words, the network being reviewed might be a wide area network (WAN), metropolitan area network (MAN), backbone network (BN), or local area network (LAN); therefore, the threats and components may vary somewhat depending on the type of network. The threats generally are the same

- **Host Mainframe Computer:** Most prevalent in the form of a central computer to which the data communication network transmits and from which it receives information. In a distributed network, with equal processing at each distributed node, there might not be an identifiable central computer, just some other equal-sized distributed computer. It might be a network server in a LAN.

- **Network Software:** The software programs that operate the data communication network. These programs may reside in the central computer, a distributed network computer, the front end processor, a remote concentrator or statistical multiplexer, or a LAN server. This software may include the telecommunication access programs, a comprehensive teleprocessing monitor program, or the LAN operating system software.

- **Front End Processor:** A hardware device that interconnects all the data communication circuits (lines) to the central computer or distributed computers.

- **Multiplexer, Concentrator, or Switch:** Hardware devices that enable the data communication network to operate in the most efficient manner or to interconnect networks. This might include bridges, routers, or gateways in a LAN.

- **Communication Circuits and Local Loops:** The common carrier facilities used as links (a link is the interconnection of any two stations/terminals) to interconnect the organization's stations/terminals. This includes the local loop that is the communication facility between the customer's premises and the telephone company's end office, as well as the LAN cabling.

- **Modems:** Hardware devices that are used for the conversion of digital data signals from terminals to an analog electrical form that is acceptable for transmission over the communication circuits. This might include a medium or multistation access unit (MAU) in a LAN.

- **People:** The individuals responsible for inputting data, operating and maintaining the data communication network equipment, writing software programs for data communications, managing the data communication network, and those working at the remote stations or terminals.

- **Microcomputers and Terminals:** Any or all of the input or output devices used to interconnect with the online data communication network.

Figure 13-7 Components that make up a wide area network (WAN).

regardless of whether it is a WAN, MAN, BN, or LAN, whereas the components tend to vary more. When reviewing the controls in an enterprise-wide network, you develop a separate Control Spreadsheet for each network that is interconnected.

After identifying the threats and components, the next step is to place the short name of each threat in the border cells across the top of the Control Spreadsheet as shown in Figure 13-8. You also place the short name of each component in the border cells down the left side of the Control Spreadsheet. The threats and components in Figure 13-8 were taken from Figures 13-6 and 13-7.

THREATS COMPONENTS	Errors and Omissions	Message Loss or Change	Disasters and Disruptions	Breach of Privacy	Fraud or Theft	Network Unavailable	Inability to Recover and Restart
Host Mainframe Computer							
Network Software							
Front End Processor							
Multiplexer, Concentrator, or Switch							
Communication Circuits and Local Loops							
Modems							
People							
Microcomputers and Terminals							

Figure 13-8 Empty Control Spreadsheet with threats and components.

Identify and Document the Controls   Once the specific network threats and components have been identified and their names have been placed in the border cells of the Control Spreadsheet, you can begin working on the network *controls*. During this step, you identify the current in-place controls and place the individual controls into each cell for each threat and component. To do this, you begin by describing each control and placing its description in a numerical list. For example, assume 24 controls have been identified as being in use in the network. Each one is described, named, and they are numbered consecutively 1 through 24. The numbered list of controls has no ranking attached to it: the first control is number 1 just because it is the first control identified. Figure 13-9 shows what a list of in-place controls looks like.

Next, each of the controls that has been identified is placed in the proper cell of the Control Spreadsheet. This is accomplished by reading the description of each control in the control list and then asking the following two questions.

1.   Which threats does this control *mitigate* or stop?
2.   Which components does this control *safeguard*, protect, or restrict?

For example, if the description of Control 1 is "ensure that the system can switch messages for a down station/terminal to an alternate station/terminal," then the number 1 should be placed in the very first cell in the upper left corner (see Figure 13-10). It is given this position because a control that ensures that the system can switch messages when a station is down helps stop errors, and it also is a control that safeguards or resides in the host computer and/or front end. Figure 13-10 also shows Control 1 in the cell that intersects between Message Loss or Change and Host Mainframe Computer, as well as in several other cells. The point is that by answering these two questions, you can place each control in the proper cells of the Control Spreadsheet.

One quick way to identify the cells into which a control fits is to use some coins. Look at Figure 13-10 to see how this works. First, read the description of the specific control to be placed into the cells. Then, place a coin over the name of each threat in the top border that the control might mitigate or stop. Next, place another coin over the name of each component in the left border that the control might safeguard or protect. The cell intersections show where that control's number should be placed.

Figure 13-10 shows the finished Control Spreadsheet with all its controls in the appropriate cells. As you can see, it depicts the interrelationship of each "in-place" control to the threat that it is supposed to mitigate or stop and the component that it safeguards, protects, or restricts.

Evaluate the Network's Control and Security   The last step in designing a Control Spreadsheet for a specific network is to evaluate the adequacy of the existing controls. This is accomplished by reviewing each subset of controls as it relates to each threat and component cell of the Control Spreadsheet. For example, the subset of controls

1. **Terminal Down:** Ensure that the system can switch messages destined for a down station/terminal to an alternate station/terminal.

2. **Message Switching:** Determine whether the system can perform message switching to transmit messages between stations/terminals.

3. **Store and Forward:** In order to avoid lost messages in a message switching system, provide a store and forward capability. This allows a message destined for a busy station to be stored at the central switch and then forwarded at a later time when the station is no longer busy.

4. **Logging:** Review the message or transaction logging capabilities to reduce lost messages, provide for an audit trail, restrict messages, prohibit illegal messages, and the like. These messages might be logged at the remote station (intelligent terminal), they might be logged at a remote concentrator/remote front end processor, or they might be logged at the central front end processor/central computer.

5. **Queue Control:** Transmit messages promptly to reduce risk of loss.

6. **Passwords:** Identify each message by the individual user's password, the terminal, and the individual message sequence number.

7. **ACK/NAK:** Acknowledge the successful or unsuccessful receipt of all messages.

24. **Dial-Up Modems:** Consider the following special controls on dial-up modems when the data communication network allows incoming dial-up connections: change the telephone numbers at regular intervals; keep the telephone numbers confidential; remove the telephone numbers from the modems in the computer operations area; require that each "dial-up terminal" have an electronic identification circuit chip to transmit its unique identification to the front end processor; do not allow automatic call receipt and connection (always have a person intercept the call and make a verbal identification); have the central site call the various terminals that will be allowed connection to the system; utilize dial-out only when an incoming dialed call triggers an automatic dial-back to the caller (in this way the central system controls the telephone numbers to which it will allow connection).

Figure 13-9   Controls list.

THREATS / COMPONENTS	Errors and Omissions	Message Loss or Change	Disasters and Disruptions	Breach of Privacy	Fraud or Theft	Network Unavailable	Inability to Recover and Restart
Host Mainframe Computer	1,2,3,4,6,7,24	1,2,3,4,5,7	1,8,11,13,16	6,8,24	6,8,24	1,13,16	
Network Software	1,2,3,4,6,7,24	1,2,3,4,5,7	1,8,16	6,8,24	6,8,24	1	
Front End Processor	1,2,3,4,6,7,24	1,2,3,4,5,7	1,8,13,16	6,8,24	6,8,24	1,13,16	
Multiplexer, Concentrator, or Switch	1,2,3,4,6,7,24	1,2,3,4,5,7	1,8,13,16	6,8,24	6,8,24	1,13,16	
Communication Circuits and Local Loops	12		10,15,16,18			15,16	
Modems	12,18,19,20,22,23	18,24	8,9,10,11,13,14,15,16,18	24	24	9,10,11,13,14,15,16,17,18	9,10,11,14,15
People	5,6	5,7		6,8,24	6,8,24		
Microcomputers and Terminals	6,24	2		6,8,24	6,8,24	1	

Figure 13-10   Control Spreadsheet with control numbers in the cells.

that are listed down a column below a threat are evaluated. The object of this step is to answer the specific question, "Do we have the proper controls and are they adequate with regard to each specific threat?" Using Figure 13-11, the Control Spreadsheet clearly defines the specific subset of controls that relate to the threat Errors and Omissions. Looking down the column below Errors and Omissions, we see they are 1, 2, 3, 4, 5, 6, 7, 12, 18, 19, 20, 22, 23, and 24. On the other hand, the subset of controls relating to the component Front End Processor are 1, 2, 3, 4, 5, 6, 7, 8, 13, 16, and 24. A control number in a cell signifies that the control represented by that number will mitigate or stop the threat at the top of the column while simultaneously safeguarding, restricting, or protecting the component in the left border cell of the row.

This type of review also can be performed on four specific subsets of controls. For example, individual subsets of controls can be evaluated as they relate to threats (columns), components (rows), individual cells, and empty cells that indicate a lack of control. Looking at Figure 13-11, we see a pictorial diagram describing the above four areas that should be reviewed. The Control Spreadsheet approach offers a perfect tool for a detailed microanalysis of the controls in a data communication network. It clearly shows the relationship between various subsets of controls and specific threat areas, component parts, individual cells, and empty cells. Use the Three Basic Categories of Controls box presented earlier in this chapter to help during your evaluation.

The step-by-step methodology that has been described here for designing and developing a Control Spreadsheet is described in much greater detail (it includes risk ranking) in Chapter 2 of the *Designing Controls* book (see reference 11 at the end of this chapter).

HOW TO CONDUCT A RISK ASSESSMENT

Very often it is desirable to conduct a risk analysis to establish certain parameters related to network security or some other aspect of the network. A *risk analysis* (same as a *risk assessment*) is used to assign levels of risk, ranging from high risk to low risk. It should be noted, however, that risk analysis does not necessarily have to rank only the risks the network faces. It can be used to rank many other criteria. For example, some of the uses of risk analysis are to rank

- Threats to a network
- Sensitivity of the network components
- Importance of network controls
- Criteria for selecting a local area network
- Network goals, evaluation criteria, needs assessment factors, or to prioritize network requirements
- Alternatives in the disaster plan or for backup
- Other business decision criteria such as network design alternatives

Threats \ Components	Errors and Omissions	Message Loss or Change	Disasters and Disruptions	Breach of Privacy	Fraud or Theft	Network Unavailable	Inability to Recover and Restart
Host Mainframe Computer	1, 2, 3, 4, 6, 7, 24	1, 2, 3, 4, 5, 7	13, 16	6, 8, 24	6, 8, 24	1, 13, 16	
Network Software	1, 2, 3, 4, 6, 7, 24	1, 2, 3, 4, 5, 7	1, 8, 16	6, 8, 24	6, 8, 24	1	
Front End Processor	1, 2, 3, 4, 6, 7, 24	1, 2, 3, 4, 5, 7	1, 8, 13, 16	6, 8, 24	6, 8, 24		
Multiplexer, Concentrator, or Switch	1, 2, 3, 4, 6, 7, 24	1, 2, 3, 4, 5, 7	1, 8, 13, 16	6, 8, 24	6, 8, 24	1, 13, 16	
Communication Circuits and Local Loops	12		10, 15, 16, 18			15, 16	
Modems	12, 18, 19, 20, 22, 23	18, 24	8, 9, 10, 11, 13, 14, 15, 16, 18	24	24	9, 10, 11, 13, 14, 15, 16, 17, 18	9, 10, 11, 14, 15
People	5, 6	5, 7		6, 8, 24	6, 8, 24		
Microcomputers and Terminals	6, 24	2			24		

Callouts:
- This column shows the subset of controls that mitigate or stop the threat Errors and Omissions.
- This row shows the subset of controls that safeguard the component Front End Processor.
- Some individual cells may be more sensitive to the network or the organization; therefore, the controls in these cells should be reviewed very closely.
- Empty cells show a lack of control, which may indicate a serious problem.

Figure 13-11   Evaluation of the network's control and security.

The methodology discussed here uses ordinal ranking. *Ordinal ranking* sequences threats or other decision criteria into a series ordered from high to low. For example, in an ordinally ranked list, the top item is perceived to be the most risky (sensitive, costly, and the like), the next item down is perceived to be the second most risky, the next item down is third most risky, and so forth. This risk ranking methodology combines the Delphi and Comparison Risk Ranking techniques.

Delphi Technique   The Delphi technique is carried out by a few experts who are chosen for their in-depth knowledge about the network, system, or environment being reviewed. This small group of experts is known as the *Delphi team*. The Delphi team members combine their knowledge into a consensus opinion by using a Comparison Risk Ranking Sheet. Delphi is the basis of today's "expert systems." The Delphi team is composed of three to nine key people who have the most up-to-date information about the network being reviewed. Key managers should be members of the Delphi team because it is they who deal with both the long-term and day-to-day operational aspects of the network. More important, their participation in the Delphi team means the final results can be implemented quickly, without further justification, because it is they who make the final decisions affecting the network.

Comparison Risk Ranking   The best way to describe how Delphi and Comparison Risk Ranking work together is to use an example. Suppose you want to conduct a risk assessment of one of your organization's networks. First, select the Delphi team, which then meets to review the threats that could affect the network being assessed. After reviewing the threats, the team members express and adjust their opinions until they arrive at a consensus about which threat might cause the most damage or delay. The process used to arrive at this consensus is called Comparison Risk Ranking.

The ranked list developed by the Delphi team progresses from the most damaging threat to the least damaging. Damage is only one criterion for ranking threats. Many other *judgment criteria* can be used, such as threats that are the most risky, the most sensitive, cause the greatest delay, create the highest dollar loss, are the most costly to recover, are the most time consuming to recover, the most dangerous, most difficult, most critical to the organization, most prone to liability judgments, most politically oriented, have the highest probability of occurrence, or any other concern relevant to the network being reviewed.

Once the Delphi team is chosen and the threats or other items to be ranked are identified, Comparison Risk Ranking is used to complete the process. *Comparison Risk Ranking* is a technique in which any list of items is entered onto a Comparison Risk Ranking Sheet to obtain an ordinal ranking of these items. This ranking sheet becomes the *decision model*.

An Example   Using our example of threats to a network, how do we determine which threats are most critical? Let us assume our Delphi team is composed of five members who have been chosen for their familiarity with the specific network, including its communication software, its hardware and circuits, its manual operational as-

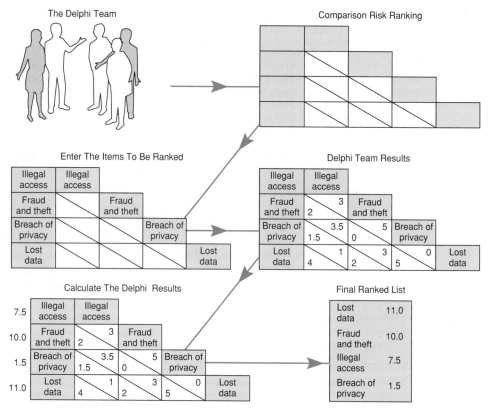

Figure 13-12   The Comparison Risk Ranking risk assessment methodology.

pects, its business functions, the types of data transmitted, and the total environment within which the network operates.

Figure 13-12 shows the basic steps of the Delphi and Comparison Risk Ranking process. To keep our example simple, we will use only four threats. The upper left corner in Figure 13-12 depicts the Delphi team. The second picture (upper right corner) shows a Comparison Risk Ranking Sheet. Following the arrows, the third picture shows the same ranking sheet with four threats entered into its border cells. In this short example, the threats to be ranked are ILLEGAL ACCESS, FRAUD AND THEFT, BREACH OF PRIVACY, and LOST DATA. The Delphi team leader proceeds by asking a series of questions (related to these threats) of the other Delphi team members. Each member of the Delphi team registers an opinion by casting a vote to indicate the *relative* damage inflicted by each threat when weighed against each of the other threats. Note that in this example the judgment criterion is, "Which threat will cause the most damage?"

Look again at the third picture in Figure 13-12 and assume the Delphi team leader's first question is, "Which is the greater threat with regard to our network: ILLEGAL ACCESS or FRAUD AND THEFT?" Notice the salient question here is the one bounded by ILLEGAL ACCESS in the top border cell and FRAUD AND THEFT in the left border cell.

Now look at the fourth picture in Figure 13-12 and you will see that the numbers 3 (ILLEGAL ACCESS) and 2 (FRAUD AND THEFT) already have been entered into this cell. Because there are a total of five votes in this cell (3 + 2), these entries confirm that there are five members on the Delphi team. Of these five members, three voted that ILLEGAL ACCESS is a greater threat to this network than FRAUD AND THEFT. The other two Delphi team members voted that FRAUD AND THEFT is a greater threat than ILLEGAL ACCESS.

After discussing this vote and counting the votes (3 and 2), the Delphi group leader moves down the column to the next item and asks, "Which is the greater threat: ILLEGAL ACCESS or BREACH OF PRIVACY?" The cell for this question shows that 3.5 Delphi team members voted for ILLEGAL ACCESS and 1.5 members voted for BREACH OF PRIVACY. The fractional votes of 0.5 on each side of the diagonal line in this cell reflect the fact that one Delphi team member thought ILLEGAL ACCESS and BREACH OF PRIVACY posed the same degree of threat. In other words, when someone votes that two threats are of equal concern, that person's vote is split with one half (0.5) recorded in each side of the two spaces provided for the item being ranked.

From this point, the Delphi team leader continues down the column and tallies the votes for the next question, "Which is the greater threat: ILLEGAL ACCESS or LOST DATA?" On reaching the bottom of the column, the team leader moves to the top of the next column to the right and asks the question, "Which is the greater threat: FRAUD AND THEFT or BREACH OF PRIVACY?" Moving down this column, the next question is, "Which is the greater threat: FRAUD AND THEFT or LOST DATA?"

On reaching the bottom of the column, the leader moves to the top of the next column to the right and asks the question, "Which is the greater threat: BREACH OF PRIVACY or LOST DATA?" In our very small example of only four threats, all the ranking sheet questions have been asked and answered.

These votes then are added together. Sum the votes down each column and across each row. The vote totals are shown to the left of the fifth picture in Figure 13-12. Now look at the last picture in the lower right corner of Figure 13-12 to see the completed Final Ranked List. This ranked list of threats was calculated from the Delphi team's Comparison Risk Ranking Sheet.

This process results in an ordinally ranked list of threats with the highest risk item at the top (11 votes in this example). After such a ranking, the numerical values in this list can be used as weighting factors, they can be applied to ranges of dollar loss figures, percentages can be developed, or previously derived dollar loss amounts can be modified and/or verified using these numbers. They also can be used to combine a single list of items (threats) that has been ranked twice, each time using a different judgment criterion. For example, the judgment criterion for one ranking might be, "Which threat will cause the greatest dollar loss?" and the other might be, "Which threat has the highest rate of occurrence?" (i.e., which would occur most often). Combining the two rankings provides one ranked list based on both dollar loss and probability of occurrence.

The use of the Delphi technique and Comparison Risk Ranking has

- Allowed the Delphi team members to divide their vote when the two threats were perceived to be equal (0.5 and 0.5)
- Prevented Delphi team members from being coerced into voting against their conscience because votes could be split easily, with some members voting for one threat and some voting for the other
- Guaranteed that each threat was compared with every other threat once and only once
- Made the Delphi team's work easier because it permitted only two threats to be compared at one time
- Kept the group's focus on the subject because only two items were compared at one time; discussion of nonrelated topics was minimized
- Provided a logical and nonpolitical tool with which to discuss differences
- Developed the group's consensus opinion quickly and logically
- Provided the means with which to use the "expert system capability" of the Delphi team members
- Included key management decision makers in the risk assessment
- Provided a high productivity tool that enabled the work to progress quickly
- Taken less than two hours of time to produce a usable risk ranking

A much more detailed step-by-step description of this risk assessment methodology is in Chapter 5 of reference 11 cited at the end of this chapter. Moreover, reference 12 describes a PC-based software package that automates this Comparison Risk Ranking/Delphi methodology.

BASIC CONTROL PRINCIPLES OF A SECURE NETWORK

Many organizations are not only developing complex networks, but they also are interconnecting them both together and to international networks outside the organization. The purpose of the following 30 *control principles* is to ensure adequate control and security in networks. Each control in a network should be evaluated and documented using these principles.

- Identify and define the specific threats related to each network.
- Risk rank the list of threats to determine which are the most important ones and which are the least important.
- As best as possible, try to have a preventive, detective, and corrective control for each threat. (The box on Three Basic Categories of Controls presented earlier in this chapter defines these types of controls.)
- A control's cost should be equivalent to the identified risk. It often is not

possible to ascertain the expected loss; therefore, this is a subjective judgment in many cases.

- An adequate system of internal controls is one that provides "just enough" control to protect the network. Just enough means the controls are those a *prudent person* would implement, taking into account both the risks and the cost of the controls. Just enough addresses both adequate control and cost-effective control while also taking into account the level of risk.

- The less complex a control, the better it is for the organization. As long as the control with the least complexity will perform adequately, it should be the control of choice.

- When a control has an override mechanism, make sure that it is documented and that the override procedure has its own controls to avoid misuse.

- Controls should apply to everyone, not just a few select individuals.

- Controls must be accepted by management (those who depend on the outputs and the reports of the network) and the users (those who use the network for their daily job tasks). Some network personnel may be both managers and users.

- When a control fails, the network should default to a condition in which everyone is denied access. A time of failure is the time of greatest vulnerability for a network.

- Institute the various security levels in an organization on the basis of "need to know." If you do not need to know, you do not need to access the network.

- It is desirable to implement entrapment controls in networks for the purpose of identifying the hacker who gains illegal access.

- Controls must be sufficient to ensure that the network can be audited. This means there should be transaction trails and historical records.

- Someone or some department must be accountable for the control and security of the network. This includes being responsible for the controls and their operation.

- The controls should be verified and tested. *Verifying* ensures that the control is present, and *testing* determines whether the control is working as it originally was specified.

- When designing network controls, assume that you are operating in a hostile environment.

- Always convey an image of security by providing continuous education and training.

- Continuously monitor the entire set of controls in the network.

- Identify backup controls in case there is a partial or full failure of the network. The principle here is that you achieve greater control during times of crisis if you have a depth of controls and possibly even redundant controls.

- Ensure that the organization has a comprehensive written control philosophy that encompasses all its networks.

- Make sure the controls provide the proper separation of duties. This applies especially to those who design and install the controls and those who are responsible for the everyday use and monitoring of the controls.

- Consider insurance as the last resort should all controls fail.

- Secrecy, by itself, is not a good control mechanism. You cannot be sure the control always will be secret.

- Controls should be reviewed periodically to be sure that they still are working and that they will work under a wide range of adverse conditions.

- Controls should still work, even when only one part of a network fails. For example, if a backbone network fails, all local area networks connected to the backbone should still be operational with their own independent control mechanisms providing protection.

- Automated controls (computer-driven) always are more reliable than manual controls that depend on human interaction.

- Controlling access (preventing) to networks is preferable to detecting and correcting an intrusion after it occurs.

- The control documentation should be considered a highly confidential or secret document. Furthermore, names, uses, and locations of network components should not be made readily available to the public.

- Recognize that there may be occasions in which a human must override a control. This may be a situation in which the network or one of its software or hardware subsystems is not operating properly and controls must be suspended temporarily. There should be a formal procedure to document this occurrence should it ever happen.

- Always assume your opponent (a hacker) is smarter than you!

ENCRYPTION

Encryption, a concept introduced in Chapter 4, is the process of disguising information by the use of many possible mathematical rules known as *algorithms*. Actually, *cryption* is the more general and proper term. *En*cryption is the process of disguising information, whereas *de*cryption is the process of restoring it to readable form. Of course, it makes no sense to have one process without the other. When information is in readable form, it is called *cleartext* or *plaintext;* when in encrypted form, it is called *ciphertext.*

The art of cryptography reaches far into the past and until recently has almost always been used for military and political applications. By today's exacting standards, such ciphers are insecure and therefore obsolete. They usually were alphabetic ciphers (rules for scrambling the *letters* in a message) designed for manual processing. Today's world of binary numbers and the speed of computers have given birth to a new class of cryption algorithms.

An encryption system has two parts: the algorithm itself, which is the set of rules for transforming information; and the *key,* which personalizes the algorithm by making the transformation of your data unique. Two pieces of identical information encrypted with the same algorithm but with *different keys* produce completely different ciphertexts. When using most encryption systems, communicating parties must share this key. If the algorithm is adequate and the key is kept secret, acquisition of the ciphertext by unauthorized personnel is of no consequence to the communicating parties.

The key is a relatively small numeric value (in number of bits) that should be easily transportable from one communicating node to another. The key is as it sounds: it is something that is small, portable, and with the aid of a good algorithm, it keeps valuables where they belong.

Good encryption systems do not depend on keeping the algorithm secret. Only the keys need to be kept secret. The algorithm should be able to accept a very large number of keys, each producing different ciphertexts from the same cleartext. This large "key space" protects the ciphertext against those who try to break it by trying every possible key. There should be a large enough number of possible keys that an exhaustive computer search would take an inordinate amount of time or would cost more than the value of the encrypted information.

Almost every modern encryption algorithm transforms digital information. *Scrambling* systems have been devised for analog voice signals, but it generally is agreed that their algorithms are not as strong as those used for digital signals made up of binary bits. The most recent advances in analog signal protection have not been in newer and better algorithms. Instead, they have been in the technology of high speed conversion of analog signals to digital information bits in preparation for encrypting them with digital algorithms. Another method of protecting analog voice data is to use spread spectrum (see Glossary) technology, but this is not an encryption technique. In any case, the vast majority of today's proprietary information is digital. For this reason we will discuss only digital techniques.

Encryption algorithms may be implemented in software or hardware. The software has some advantages in protecting stored data files and data in the host computer's memory. However, hardware implementations have the advantages of much greater processing speed, independence from communication protocols, ability to be implemented on dumb devices (terminals, facsimile machines, and so on), and greater protection of the key because it is physically locked in the encryption box. Unauthorized tampering with the box causes erasure of the keys. Hardware implementations have been reduced to the chip level because they are simply specialized microprocessors housed in small hardware boxes.

Many software packages are available for encrypting data before it is stored on the hard disk of your microcomputer. Among these are DataSafe, CryptMaster, WATCHDOG, Cipher, Desmodul, Secure, Private Line, and others.

Data Encryption Standard (DES)   By far the most widely used encryption algorithm is the *Data Encryption Standard* (DES). It was developed in the mid-1970s by the U.S. government in conjunction with IBM. DES is maintained by the National Institute of Standards and Technology—NIST (formerly the National Bureau of Standards—NBS) and often is referred to as NBSDES or DEA (Data Encryption Algorithm). The U.S. government recommends that DES be used for the encryption of commercial and *un*classified military data. The American Banking Association has endorsed its use for the commercial banking industry.

This combination of credentials makes DES the technique of choice by private institutions. This concept of "choice" is somewhat misleading. DES is the *only* algorithm endorsed by the government. The academic literature is full of alternatives, but practical reasons such as the necessity of obtaining insurance against third-party fraud and the lack of mathematical sophistication on the part of encryption system users presently leave little choice.

DES is classified as a *block cipher*. In its simplest form the algorithm encrypts data in independent 64-bit blocks. Encryption is under the control of a 64-bit key. DES expects a full 64-bit key, but it uses only 56 of the bits. (Every eighth bit may be set for parity.) Therefore, the total number of possible keys is 2^{56} or over 72 quadrillion combinations.

To put quadrillions into perspective, let us introduce the metric unit of femtoseconds. A *femtosecond* is one quadrillionth of a second, a unit so small that it is very difficult to associate with it in any meaningful way. Femtoseconds are incredibly brief. To look at it another way, there are as many femtoseconds in one second as there are seconds in 30 million years. If you are looking at 72 quadrillion (72,000,000,000,000,000) combinations, you can see that this is an unbelievably large number of combinations. Did you know that there is a measurement below femtosecond, called an attosecond? An *attosecond* is one thousand times shorter than a femtosecond. See the box on Speeds at Which Computers and Networks Operate for a better understanding of these times.

If you could test just one of these combinations each second, then one quadrillion combinations might take 30 million years to test! Seventy-two quadrillion combinations equals a time period of 30 million years times 72. Cryptographers who specialize in breaking these block ciphers have to test only half the combinations to obtain a 50/50 probability of arriving at the secret key. This testing is enhanced further by the use of very specialized mathematical algorithms that are designed to quickly invalidate large groups of these combinations. In addition, specially designed computers may be able to test 10,000 combinations each second. As a result, they never do have to test even one half of the 72 million combinations to "break" the secret key. On the other hand, the key might be changed daily or even hourly to defend against codebreakers.

DES ciphertext is composed of blocks containing highly randomized bit sequences. The algorithm is so thorough in its randomizing of any 64-bit block (almost without regard to the cleartext of the key) that the ciphertext almost always passes standard tests for randomness. In fact, the random quality of ciphertext is a crucial factor in the design of communication networks that convey ciphertext. Communication control characters (for message routing or error detection) cannot be mixed with ciphertext because there is always some probability that DES will generate one of these control characters and thwart the communications.

As a result, DES hardware usually is employed as shown in Figure 13-13. Communication protocols, parity, and checksums are in place with the message *before* it enters the originating DES hardware device. As is shown, this information may originate from a terminal, a front end, or a variety of communicating devices. The

SPEEDS AT WHICH COMPUTERS AND NETWORKS OPERATE

The speed at which computers work is measured in terms of seconds. For example, it may take one microsecond to add two numbers. A faster computer may add the same two numbers in only one nanosecond. The meanings of these very small numbers are shown below. Notice that the power to which the number is raised is equal to the number of zeroes in the denominator, except it is a negative power.

Millisecond is one thousandth (1/1,000) of a second or 10^{-3}
Microsecond is one millionth (1/1,000,000) of a second or 10^{-6}
Nanosecond is one billionth (1/1,000,000,000) of a second or 10^{-9}
Picosecond is one trillionth (1/1,000,000,000,000) of a second or 10^{-12}
Femtosecond is one quadrillionth (1/1,000,000,000,000,000) of a second or 10^{-15}
Attosecond is one quintillionth (1/1,000,000,000,000,000,000) of a second or 10^{-18}

milli   micro nano   pico   femto atto

$$1/1,000,000,000,000,000,000$$

10^{-3} 10^{-6} 10^{-9} 10^{-12} 10^{-15} 10^{-18}

The above numbers represent very small amounts of time. By contrast, the speed at which networks operate is measured in terms of bits per second. Transmission speeds are measured in the thousands, millions, and, increasingly, billions of bits per second. The meanings of these very large numbers are shown below. Like the small numbers above, notice that the power to which the number is raised is equal to the number of zeroes in the denominator, except it is a positive power.

Kilobits is one thousand (1,000) bits per second or 10^3
Megabits is one million (1,000,000) bits per second or 10^6
Gigabits is one billion (1,000,000,000) bits per second or 10^9
Terabits is one trillion (1,000,000,000,000) bits per second or 10^{12}
Petabits is one quadrillion (1,000,000,000,000,000) bits per second or 10^{15}
Exabits is one quintillion (1,000,000,000,000,000,000) bits per second or 10^{18}

kilo   mega   giga   tera   peta   exa

$$1,000,000,000,000,000,000$$

10^3 10^6 10^9 10^{12} 10^{15} 10^{18}

hardware encryption boxes normally are used on a link-to-link basis as depicted in Figure 13-13.

Placing the DES device between the modems can present a number of problems. First, most DES boxes are digital devices, and they usually do not accept the analog signals output by modems. Second, in asynchronous communications at least the start bit must be sent in the clear. Encryption can, and usually does, begin with the

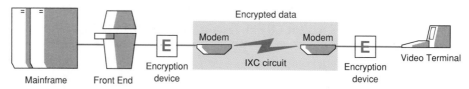

Figure 13-13   Encryption devices.

first data bit and end with the last. Similar problems can occur if synchronous timing signals are encrypted.

After encryption, the randomized information is transmitted to a network switch, computer, terminal, or other receiving device. The receiving DES hardware encryption device, which must be loaded with the *same* key as the originating DES hardware, then decrypts the information before it enters the receiving terminal device. Any communication protocols are verified *after* the decryption.

In some ways DES provides better error detection than standard parity or checksum techniques. If a single bit of any 64-bit ciphertext block is flipped during transmission, on decryption of that block the result will be 64 bits of random nonsense. This "error propagation" virtually ensures that parity and checksum will fail after decryption.

A more serious problem occurs if a bit is picked up or dropped during communication. The message loses 64-bit block "synchronization" at the point of the dropped or added bit, and the message decrypts into nonsense. The result can be the loss of an entire message.

This magnification of communication errors is not without its price. Since the *minimum* loss of information is usually 64 bits, a retransmission almost always is required if there is a single bit communication error.

DES is a member of a class of algorithms known as *symmetric*. This means that the key used to decrypt a particular bit stream must be the *same* as the one used to encrypt it. Using any other key produces cleartext that appears as random as the ciphertext. Symmetric algorithms can cause some problems in the complex area of *key management;* keys must be dispersed and stored with great care. Because the DES algorithm is known publicly, the disclosure of a *secret key* can mean total compromise of encrypted messages. Therefore, in order for two nodes in a network to establish communication of ciphertext, it is first necessary to generate and communicate a common key over a secure channel or send it by personal courier without using the network.

In addition to DES, users seeking data transmission protection have at least two other alternatives: proprietary algorithms and public key cryptosystems. A *proprietary algorithm* can be developed solely for the use of a single organization. Assuming that such algorithms are strong enough to withstand cryptanalysis, a few potential problems still remain. First, the cost to develop and implement a proprietary system is considerable and may even be prohibitive. Second, any algorithm developed by an outside party always is open to the question of how good it is at resisting attack. Finally, if the algorithm is to be used outside the United States, the National Security

Agency must approve it before it can be exported. We discuss public key cryptosystems next.

Public Key Encryption   *Public key cryptosystems* are inherently different from secret key systems like DES. Public key systems are based on one-way functions. Even though you originally know both the contents of your message and the public encryption key, once they are put together (encrypted) by the one-way function algorithm *public key*, they cannot be taken apart again unless you have the secret one-way function algorithm *private key*. One-way functions, which are relatively easy to calculate in one direction, are computationally impossible to "uncalculate" in the reverse direction. The message sender must look up the recipient's one-way encryption function in a public key directory and use it to encrypt the message. Receivers maintain their own secret private key or mating decryption algorithm for this one-way function.

The primary difference between a public key system (asymmetric) and a single key DES system (symmetric) is that in a public key system there are two different keys (public and private) and no secret keys are exchanged between communicating parties. Public key systems, however, do not eliminate the key distribution problem, but key distribution costs less than one tenth of what it costs for the symmetric class of algorithms like DES that require the same key at both ends of the link. The keys still must be distributed during system startup. A public directory that contains each participant's one-way encryption function public key is shared by the community. The strength of these systems lies in maintaining the secrecy of the decrypting function (private key) and the ability of the algorithm to withstand cryptanalysis. If someone solves the public key one-way function, the system is compromised. The one-way function is based on the difficulty in factoring very large integer numbers. The solution to this problem has eluded mathematicians for hundreds of years.

In public key encryption systems, the key needed to decrypt a message is different from the one used to encrypt it. The two keys are related distantly in a mathematical sense. The security of asymmetric systems depends on the extreme difficulty (analytic impossibility or computational infeasibility) of deriving one key from the other.

Asymmetric algorithms using two different keys can reduce the key management problem greatly. Each receiving node has its publicly available key (hence the name "public key") that is used to encrypt messages sent by any network member at that node to the other node. These public keys may be listed in a telephone book-style directory. In addition, each user has a private key that decrypts only the messages that were encrypted by its public key. The net result is that if two parties wish to communicate with one another, there is no need to exchange keys beforehand. Each knows the other's public key from the public directory and can communicate encrypted information immediately. The key management problem may be reduced to each user being concerned only with the on-site protection of its private key.

To visualize how a public key algorithm works, look at Figure 13-14. At the top of this figure is a public directory containing all the public keys for each organization using public key encryption. Our public directory contains five different banks.

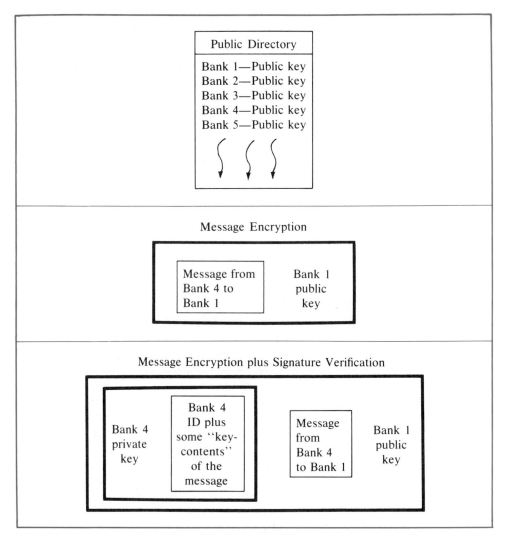

Figure 13-14   Public key encryption. The "key-contents" in this figure refers to unique information from the message, such as date, time, and the dollar amount.

To use the public key encryption methodology, a bank also has a secret key known as a private key; therefore, there are two separate keys, the private (secret) key and the public key. In this case, the bank places its public key into the public directory and carefully secures its own copy of the private key.

The middle of Figure 13-14 shows what an encrypted message looks like. When Bank 4 wants to send a message to Bank 1, it encrypts the message with the Bank 1 public key, which is obtained by Bank 4 from the public directory. This represents a straightforward encryption of a message between Bank 4 and Bank 1. Obviously, when the message is received at Bank 1, it decrypts the message using its secret private key.

For more complex encryption, Bank 4 can include its signature so Bank 1 also can verify the signature or, in other words, be sure that the message originated from Bank 4. This is known as *authentication*.

To perform a signature verification (see the bottom message of Figure 13-14), Bank 4 first encrypts its ID (signature) plus some of the "key-contents"[2] of the message, using the Bank 4 private key. This is its own private key and is known only to Bank 4.

Next, Bank 4 encrypts both the entire message contents and the already encrypted Bank 4 ID using the Bank 1 public key from the public directory. This means that the Bank 4 ID has been double-encrypted, first using the Bank 4 private key and then a second time using the Bank 1 public key. The message is then transmitted to Bank 1.

Upon receipt of the message, Bank 1 uses its private key to decrypt the entire message. At this point, Bank 1 is able to read the contents of the message, except for a block of data that still is encrypted (unidentifiable). Because the message was received from Bank 4, Bank 1 assumes that Bank 4 secretly encrypted its ID plus some key-contents of the message for signature verification purposes by using its private key. At this point, Bank 1 takes the Bank 4 public key (from the public directory) and decrypts the trailing block of data that contains the Bank 4 ID plus some key-contents of the message. Once decrypted, Bank 1 knows Bank 4 actually sent the message because the key contents in this block of data had a date, time, and dollar amount that matched those in the already decrypted message.

In this way, the public key system encrypts messages and also offers electronic signature verification without an exchange of keys among all the thousands of banks around the world. The public directory need only be updated as often as necessary. You can encrypt with a public key and decrypt with a private key, or you can encrypt with a private key and decrypt with a public key.

The asymmetric algorithms for public key systems are very different from symmetric algorithms like DES, but in practice their ciphertexts are similar when viewed from the data communication standpoint. Each produces ciphertext consisting of randomized bit patterns. There is almost always some degree of inherent error propagation; therefore, the practicalities of handling communication of both types of ciphertexts are for the most part identical where the message is encrypted before reaching the modem.

The world of cryptology is full of controversy and debate because national security always is the issue. Another underlying cause of this controversy is the fact that cryptology is an art rather than a science. Except for a few noteworthy exceptions, it is impossible to *prove* mathematically whether an encryption/decryption algorithm can be broken. Thus, the only route to breaking a cipher is an artful (and perhaps time-consuming and expensive) trial and error approach sometimes called "brute force." Debates about the security of ciphers often end with mathematical generalizations and seat-of-the-pants type expressions.

The next section describes a specific public key cryptosystem.

---

[2] The term *key-contents* means unique information from the message such as date, time, or dollar amount. It does not refer to the public and private keys.

RSA Digital Signature   The RSA cryptosystem was invented at MIT in 1977. The inventors of the initial algorithm founded RSA Data Security in 1982. RSA stands for Rivest, Shamir, and Adleman, the surnames of the three individuals who invented this public key cryptosystem.

Not only does the *RSA Digital Signature* authenticate the identity of the author of a message, but it also verifies the contents of a message. A basic property of the RSA cryptosystem provides the identification of the author in the following way. If you can decrypt a message from someone using that person's public key, the message must have come from that person because only the correct private key can produce an encrypted message that decrypts with the matching public key.

The RSA Digital Signature employs a cryptographic "hashing" algorithm to create a *message digest* that is unique to each message—very much like a fingerprint. If even one bit of the message is changed, roughly 50 percent of the bits in the corresponding message digest also change. Furthermore, the hashing algorithm is a one-way function; the message content cannot be reconstructed from the bits of the message digest. Encrypting the message digest with the author's private key produces the RSA Digital Signature, which then is attached to the message.

With its 128-bit message digest, the probability that different messages will have the same digest by coincidence is less than 1 in one trillion trillion. (That is, one trillion a trillion times.) This technique effectively ensures that two message digests will match only if the messages from which they are derived are identical on a bit-by-bit basis.

Let us examine how this works. Assume someone receives a file with an attached RSA Digital Signature. First, the signature is separated from the message. Then the recipient uses the message digest algorithm to compute an *independent message digest* based on the received message.

The recipient's program then decrypts the signature block with the author's (sender's) public key to obtain the original message digest and compares it with the independent message digest. If the two message digests match, the signature undoubtedly is authentic and unaltered (either by tampering, viral infection, or transmission errors) since its electronic signing. Figure 13-15 depicts this process.

Although the RSA Digital Signature is easy to produce and check, it is impossible to forge; therefore, it positively identifies the author (sender) of a message. Unlike a handwritten signature, it also verifies the contents of a message.

In 1989 the Department of Defense's Advanced Research Projects Agency (DARPA) established the *Privacy-Enhanced Mail* (PEM) program on its Internet network. This program is based on RSA's encryption and authentication algorithm, making it the Internet encryption standard. Internet links government, corporate, and educational institutions worldwide. With several million users and thousands of nodes, it is the world's largest network.

RSA Data Security and DARPA provide a free source code toolkit for implementing PEM. This toolkit, known as *RSA REF*erence Implementation (RSAREF), supports the following PEM-specified algorithms.

RSA encryption and key generation

MD2 and MD5 message digest functions

DES in cipher-block chaining mode

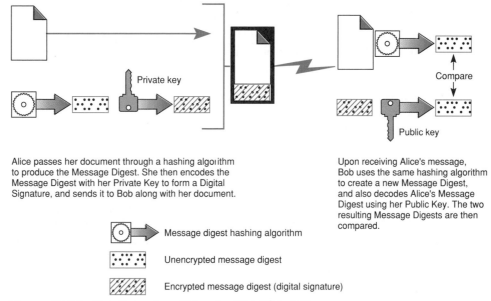

Alice passes her document through a hashing algorithm to produce the Message Digest. She then encodes the Message Digest with her Private Key to form a Digital Signature, and sends it to Bob along with her document.

Upon receiving Alice's message, Bob uses the same hashing algorithm to create a new Message Digest, and also decodes Alice's Message Digest using her Public Key. The two resulting Message Digests are then compared.

Message digest hashing algorithm

Unencrypted message digest

Encrypted message digest (digital signature)

Figure 13-15   Creating and verifying the RSA Digital Signature.

RSAREF is written in the C programming language as a library that can be called from an application program. It is free to all noncommercial (educational, research, testing, or individuals) users. To obtain a copy of the RSAREF toolkit, professors should write to the RSAREF Administrator, RSA Laboratories, RSA Data Security, Inc., 10 Twin Dolphin Drive, Redwood City, Calif. 94065, or send an E-mail request over Internet to: `rsaref-administrator@rsa.com`. Students should ask their professor to obtain a copy of RSAREF.

NETWORK CONTROLS

The remainder of this chapter contains more than 20 lists of specific controls that relate to network hardware, circuits, microcomputers, databases, the OSI seven-layer model, software, management, recovery, backup, and disasters. These control lists help you decide which controls may be best for a specific network. Note that we have *physical security* like that provided by locked doors, and we also have *logical security* that is provided by software, procedures, and the like.

Local Area Networks (LANs)   The security and control of local area networks was described in Chapter 11. For a list of the specific controls that relate to LANs, see the LAN Security and Control section starting on page 557.

Other Sources for Control Lists   In addition to the control lists provided in this chapter, the following two items may be of benefit. Their bibliographic information is in the Selected References section at the end of this chapter.

- The EDPAA's *Control Objectives* (reference 5) contains control lists in such areas as network security, network operations, access to network data, network performance monitoring, and hardware physical security.
- The *Designing Controls* book (reference 11) contains 94 control lists in such areas as viruses, illegal access, networks, facsimile machines, microcomputers, circuits, local loops, modems, and multiplexers. As an example, the list of controls for LANs that starts on page 558 of this text is from Chapter 8 of the *Designing Controls* book.

HARDWARE CONTROLS

Network hardware is discussed here in terms of the controls that relate to it. We will review *hardware controls* that relate to front end processors, packet switching controllers, modems, multiplexers, remote intelligent controllers, terminals, and voice telephone security.

Front End Processors   The *front end processor* that controls a centrally controlled data communication network can be one of the single most important areas for security and control. It is only a piece of hardware, but within it are software programs and protocols that control the access methods for data flow.

Some specific controls that might be housed within the front end processor are

- Polling of terminals to ensure that only authorized terminals are on the network
- Logging of all inbound and outbound messages (systems log) for historical purposes and for immediate recovery should the network fail
- Error detection and retransmission for messages that arrive in error
- Message switching that reduces the possibility of lost messages (there also can be circuit switching or packet switching)
- Store and forward techniques that help avoid lost messages (although store and forward opens up the possibility of a network programmer copying messages from the storage disk)
- Serial numbers for all messages between all nodes
- Automatic call-back on dial-up facilities to prevent the host computer from being connected to an unauthorized dial-up terminal
- Systems editing such as rerouting of messages and triggering of remote alarms if certain parameters are exceeded or if there is an abnormal occurrence
- Collection of network traffic statistics for long-term control of the total network

Packet Switching Controllers   A *packet switching controller* or switching node (SN) is similar to a front end processor, but it has some specialized features that pertain to the operation of a packet network. A packet switching controller can perform any of the control functions previously mentioned for front ends. In addition, it performs other specific control functions such as the following.

- Keeps track of messages between different nodes of the network.
- Controls the numbering of each packet to avoid lost packets, messages, or illegal insertions.
- Routes all messages. It may send different packets, containing parts of the same message, on different circuits (unknown circuit path). This may prevent an unauthorized user or perpetrator from receiving all parts of a sensitive message.
- Contains global and local databases that contain addresses and other sensitive data pertaining to each node. These databases can be cross-referenced with other written documentation when network nodes are reviewed for security.
- Keeps track of the sender of each message that is delivered on dial-up packet networks for control and billing purposes.
- Restricts the users to dial-up or allows use of leased circuits into the packet network.

Modems   The *modem* may be an interface unit either for broadband (analog) communication circuits or for baseband (digital) communication circuits. It does not matter which because these hardware units can perform any of the controls listed below, depending on the features installed by each manufacturer.

Modems can offer loopback features that allow the network manager to isolate problems and identify where they are occurring in the network. Some modems contain automatic equalization microprocessor circuits to compensate for electronic instabilities on transmission lines, thereby reducing transmission errors. Some modems have built-in diagnostic routines for checking their own circuits. Mean Time Between Failure (MTBF) statistics should be collected for modems because low MTBF indicates that downtime is excessive.

Some dial-up modem controls include changing the modem telephone numbers periodically, keeping telephone numbers confidential at both user sites and the central data center, possibly disallowing automatic call receipt at the data center (using people to intercept), removing telephone numbers from both local and remote dial-up modems, and requiring the use of terminals that have an electronic identification circuit for all dial-up ports. Finally, it may be desirable to utilize a *dial-out-only facility,* whereby the act of dialing into the network and entering a password automatically triggers a disconnect; the front end or host computer then dials the "approved" telephone number that matches the password used during the original dial-in. In other words, dial-in triggers a dial-out.

Multiplexers   Because many multiplexers are at remote locations, a primary control is to prevent physical access to the *multiplexer*. Another consideration is whether the multiplexer should have dual circuitry or backup electrical power because loss of a large multiplexer site can knock out several hundred terminals. Because time division statistical multiplexers have internal memory space, and some have disk storage, special precautions must be taken. Memories and disk storage make illegal copying of messages easier. Other controls include logging all messages at the remote multiplexer site before transmission to the host computer and manually logging all vendor service call visits.

Remote Intelligent Controllers   A *remote intelligent controller* can be a special form of multiplexer or a remote front end processor that is located several hundred miles from the host computer. These devices usually control large groups of terminals. All the controls that were mentioned for multiplexers also apply to remote intelligent controllers.

A review of software controls that can be programmed into this device is suggested. For example, daily downline loading of programs can help ensure that only authorized programs are in this device. Another control is the periodic counting of bits in the memory space. This identifies a minor program change so that a new one can be downline-loaded immediately. Each controller should have its unique address on a memory chip (instead of software) to thwart anyone who wants to change controller addresses. Remote logging of each inbound/outbound message should be considered seriously. If hardware encryption boxes are located in the same facility as the remote intelligent controllers, then access to these devices should be controlled by implementation of strict physical control procedures and locked doors.

Terminals—Human Error Prevention   The control of terminals or microcomputers in a data communication network has two basic aspects. The first concerns mitigating *human errors* made while running business application systems, and the second is providing *terminal security*. Controls to prevent, detect, and correct human errors are necessary because, of these two aspects, human errors cause the greater dollar loss. First, we will present a list of human error prevention controls, and then we will move into the second aspect, which is providing restrictive controls at remote terminals and microcomputers.

- Adequate operator training should be provided through self-teaching operator manuals and the periodic updating of these manuals.
- Dialogue between the operator and the application system should be kept simple. (Menu selection might be utilized.)
- Terminals should be easy to use and have functional keyboards.
- Preprinted forms for printing terminals and a fill-in-the-blank format (preprinted forms on a video screen) for video terminals should be considered.
- Instructions should be preprogrammed and available for recall when an operator needs help. Secured systems, where assistance should be more difficult to obtain, may be an exception.
- Operators should have restart procedures that can be used for error recovery during a transaction.
- Work area extremes in light, noise, temperature, and so on must be minimized if operators are to reduce errors to a minimum.

- Reasonably fast response times reduce errors because longer response times produce error-causing frustration in operators. Long response times also reduce productivity.
- Intelligent terminals can edit for logical business errors and verify data before transmission.

Terminals—Security Controls The remote terminal or remote microcomputer may be the single most important point for controlling security; specific controls *must* be enforced here. There are three general ways of restricting access to computer systems or databases, based on something you know, something you have, or something you are.

First, restricting access by *something you know* requires the use of some sort of secret identification code or password. These codes and passwords are issued to authorized users of the system, who should keep them confidential. To enter the system, users need enter only their password.

Second, access can be restricted by *something you have,* such as a key. The key might be a physical key like the one used to unlock the front door of your home or to start your automobile, or it can be an electronic key (secret encrypted numbers contained in a small circuit chip).

Third, to restrict access by *something you are,* one or more of your own physical characteristics is used as the unique identifier that permits your entry to the system. This might be a fingerprint, a handprint, an eye retina print, a voice print, signature verification, and so forth.

The following specific security controls might be implemented at the remote terminal/microcomputer location.

- Make sure terminals have a unique electronic chip built in that provides positive identification. With chips, the front end or host can identify each terminal electronically.
- Physically lock terminal on/off switches or have locks that disable the screen and keyboard.
- Keep terminals in a physically secure location.
- Lock off all the communication circuits after hours by positively disabling the communication circuits.
- Assign an individual password to each system user.
- Make available to each user a plastic identification card that runs through an identification card reader. Such cards replace the need for individual passwords.
- Use special log-in numbers that can be entered only by a key person in the department.
- Consider using a type of personal identification such as signature, fingerprint, voice, or hand image identification.
- Transaction-code each terminal. This prevents any transaction that is not re-

lated to the work area in which the terminal is located. In other words, the terminal is made transaction specific.

- Develop a security profile of the types of data being entered and the user log-in procedures. If a violation occurs, the terminal that was used can be shut down automatically. In addition, a terminal security report should be delivered to the manager of the user work area within 24 hours.

- Restrict terminals to read only functions.

- Sequence-number, time-stamp, and date all messages.

- Ensure that passwords do not print when they are typed.

- Ensure the proper disposal of hard copy terminal output.

- Allow intelligent terminals to perform editing on transactions before they are transmitted.

- When looking at the control and security of dial-up terminals, review the controls for dial-up modems that were listed previously in the section on modems.

Voice Telephone Security *Voice telephone security* is a means of restricting users when they use dial-up access to computer systems. We presented call-back restrictors for modems in the section on Port/Line Security Device in Chapter 4. At this point we want to describe a small, inexpensive device that can be used to restrict the potential telephone user from even dialing certain numbers.

This device, called a *telephone call restrictor,* is placed between the telephone and the wall jack into which the telephone plugs. It is about as large as a half carton of cigarettes, and it is placed directly over the current telephone wall plug. The call restrictor is plugged into the wall plug by using the RJ-11 telephone jack, and the telephone is plugged into the call restrictor. This little box is programmed by using DIP switches. It is able to keep telephone users from dialing various numbers such as 0, 411, 555, and 976. As you may know, not being able to dial 0 keeps the user from calling a Bell operator; 411 from calling local directory assistance, for which organizations are charged; 555 from calling long distance directory assistance; and 976 from calling certain services for which there is a charge, such as a sports message or the joke of the day. In case you did not recognize these numbers, most are the first three digits of a telephone exchange number such as 555-1212, which is long distance directory assistance when preceded by an area code.

This system also gives the caller a tone after a call has lasted three minutes; this feature is used to keep telephone calls as short as possible in order to save costs. As you might have surmised by now, someone who is intent on violating the system can remove the call restrictor from the wall with the appropriate tool—a simple screwdriver. In an unattended area, the call restrictor therefore has to have some type of heavy-duty wire case around it which is bolted to the wall. The call restrictor is intended for areas in which company employees are present and where numerous telephone users might use the telephone for voice calls. Another way to regulate telephone calls is through the switchboard (PBX) where it may be almost impossible to circumvent the controls.

Because voice telephone calls using cellular radio (discussed in Chapter 5) are transmitted over radio waves, they can be intercepted easily with readily available equipment. To avoid interception, you can buy cellular telephones that have built-in voice scrambling. California has a law that makes it illegal to eavesdrop on cellular telephone calls. Unfortunately, this is an impossible law to enforce. Who knows when someone is eavesdropping? What about the computer hacker who hears your credit card number or some other vital information?

When you place a cellular telephone call, the telephone sends out a burst of data that gives your telephone number, the number called, and your telephone serial number. Anyone who has a radio scanner can intercept this information because it is broadcast over the radio. A person who wants to spy on telephone calls does not have to sit next to a radio scanner to find out who is calling whom. With a little know-how, a microcomputer can do the job. One simply links up the microcomputer and has it record all the calls that are made. This is called *vacuum cleaning* because it sucks up the data transmitted during a telephone call. Vacuum cleaning can provide hackers with cellular telephone numbers that can be used easily for another breach of security called spoofing.

Spoofing is the relaying of telephone numbers gained through vacuum cleaning or other means, and reprogramming the telephones to make calls at another person's expense. With spoofing, people can get erroneous charges for calls placed fraudulently on their numbers. Spoofing with cellular telephones has a potential for causing far greater financial loss than the fraudulent use of stolen codes from traditional telephones. Losses can be great because you may know that a call came from a certain telephone number, but the number does not indicate the caller's location, which may change from moment to moment.

In addition to fraud, plain old-fashioned *eavesdropping* can become a serious breach of privacy. People should be careful of what they say when using cellular telephones because anyone with a scanner may hear the conversation.

Another potential problem is the ease with which the electronic serial numbers of cellular telephones can be changed. Serial numbers are nothing more than an integrated circuit chip glued into a socket. They can be pried loose easily and replaced with other chips that contain concocted or stolen serial numbers. As you can see, cellular telephone serial numbers do little more than give a false sense of security.

CIRCUIT CONTROLS

Some of the communication *circuits* that must be reviewed for controls are the wire pairs and cables that are placed throughout the user facility, the local loops that go between the user facility and the common carrier (telephone company), and the interexchange channel (IXC) circuits between cities.

The wire pairs and cables within the user facility should be made as physically secure as possible because this is where anyone wanting to tap the system would enter. It is 100 times easier to tap a local loop than it is to tap an interexchange channel. Ensure that the lines are secured behind walls and above ceilings, and that the telephone equipment and switching rooms (wire closets) are locked and the doors equipped with alarms.

Little can be done about local loops except to visit the common carrier switching facility. The visit can provide some idea about the physical security, fire protection, and disaster prevention controls implemented by the common carrier. If these controls are inadequate, about the only thing you can do is split local loops from your facility to two or three different common carrier switching facilities (telephone company end offices).

Encryption of messages is the only dependable method of providing security on interexchange channels. If the information is so sensitive that a breach of privacy or the insertion or modification of a message cannot be allowed, then encryption must be considered.

Fiber optic cables might be used for the internal cables within your facility. These cables offer security through their immunity to electrically generated noise, resistance to taps, isolation, and small size. They also have some very special benefits when used in a harsh environment. All of these were discussed in the Chapter 5 section on Fiber Optics.

MICROCOMPUTER CONTROLS

The driving force behind the use of microcomputers, especially in micro-to-mainframe connections and local area networks, is the desire of end users to use mainframe data with their own microcomputers located in their own departments. Users want to manipulate this data and have the ability to update mainframe databases in real time, as well as to interact with centralized host mainframe applications. Neither economics nor competition between different organizations is going to stop this development. As a result, *microcomputer security* is an extremely important issue in today's business, government, and scientific environments.

The security of a microcomputer workstation can be divided into three major areas. First, all the *physical security* features that might be in place at a central host mainframe site also must be considered at the remote microcomputer location. Many of the security features have to be scaled down because of cost or the "smallness" of the microcomputer. For example, a large halon fire suppression system might be located at a host mainframe site, but a small handheld fire extinguisher might be adequate for a remote microcomputer site.

Second, *data security* is the protection of data and programs at the central site, during transmission, and at the microcomputer site. The level of data security required determines whether you allow dial-up connections to the central site, which pathways through the network are allowed, whether the data is encrypted, and what security is imposed on the database at both the central and remote sites. Database controls are discussed in the next section of this chapter.

Network access security is the third issue related to the microcomputer connection. It does not matter whether the microcomputer is being used in a micro-to-mainframe link, a local area network, or a dial-up link through a public packet switched network. Network access security is critical in any of these uses. Network access security is restricting access to the data and programs. To achieve network security in relation to the microcomputer, the general protection objectives should be

- Verification of message origin and destination.
- Verification of the timeliness of a message.
- Detection, by the receiver, of any modification to the message or the sequence of messages.
- Detection, by the sender, of a fraudulent acknowledgment of the receipt or nonreceipt of a message.
- Prevention of unauthorized disclosure of messages to any person not having unique identification, such as passwords or cryptographic keys.
- Positive acceptance of all messages. Once the system gives evidence of acceptance, it should never be lost, distorted, without proper authorization, or duplicated.
- Special network security requirements to prevent an illegal entry at network restart time after the system has gone down or if it has been partially out of service.
- Notification to operational personnel, and specialized control reports as follow-up, when errors in message transmission, routing, formatting, or other anomalies occur.
- Control of access to the network and its facilities so that only authorized personnel have access. Complete audit trails should show who accessed what and when the access occurred.
- Rapid and automatic detection and notification of the type and location of any security breach.
- Safe storage of all messages in a front end, host mainframe, or LAN server system's log.

One very effective way of restricting access to a network is to use an add-in card or an EPROM (erasable programmable read only memory) chip to control the booting process. If the microcomputer cannot boot until a password is entered, users are restricted from entering the communication network even if they have their own copy of DOS or OS/2.

When a LAN workstation operates without disk drives, it is impossible for the workstation user to make illegal copies of the entity's business data. This is the way a diskless workstation operates. A microcomputer with disk drives normally boots from either a hard or a floppy diskette when the power is turned on. Because diskless workstations contain no disk storage devices, they are started with a type of boot ROM (read only memory) that actually is a microchip. When the local workstation is turned on, its ROM redirects the boot request to the network server. The network server then sends the proper boot information to the local workstation and starts it up. After booting, a diskless microcomputer workstation connected to a local area network operates just like one with a disk, except users are prevented from making unauthorized copies of files. This procedure was described in more detail in the Diskless Microcomputer Boot Procedure section of Chapter 10.

One note of caution should be mentioned. Many diskless microcomputers have expansion slots within the chassis that can be a security risk. With these slots it is possible for a perpetrator to insert a HardCard or other hard-disk-on-a-card into the expansion slot and copy data from the server disk. For security reasons, it is better to purchase a diskless microcomputer without these extra expansion slots. The tradeoff here is flexibility and cost against security.

Several security access software packages are available for microcomputers. For example, one package called WATCHDOG offers the following security features:

- IDs and passwords to prevent unauthorized access
- Restrictions on whether a user can read files, write to files, create files, delete files, or use the DOS commands based on user IDs
- Data encryption
- Audit trail monitors system directory accessed, program executed, date, and time
- Virus protection
- Ability to work with an optional circuit card to enhance security by combining the software security with hardware security

DATABASE CONTROLS

In the previous section, we discussed three major kinds of security related to microcomputers. One of these was data security, a subject so important that we want to discuss it in more detail. Security experts maintain that there is no foolproof way to protect the data in a microcomputer. Even so, *databases* must be protected, and so the following are some guidelines for making databases secure.

- Use software security features at the host, user microcomputer, and LAN server. Along with them, use the volume, file, and record locking features that might be available in the file server or network server installed at the microcomputer. Finally, use *all* the security features in the "security software package" that is installed on the host mainframe, microcomputer, or LAN server.
- Restrict entry to the system based on something the user knows (password), something the user has (key), or something the user is (fingerprints).
- Once a user is in the database, define the user's limits such as the ability to read, write, create, delete, search, modify, and the like.

- Appoint a database administrator who can grant or revoke various security privileges and also interact with different users on issues related to the databases. This person is the custodian of the databases and also ensures proper backup and recovery procedures.
- Use dial-back security devices to restrict entry.
- Consider data encryption. In addition to encrypting data for transmission over a network, if the need is for highly secure data, you can encrypt it prior to storage on the disk and then decrypt it when it is read from the disk. This ensures that the data is useless if someone steals the disk.
- Use disk mirroring or duplexing (see Control 26 in the Chapter 11 section on LAN Security and Control).
- Automate the disk backup procedures.
- Monitor and limit data downloading to microcomputers and the uploading of that data back to the host mainframe. When the data is in the host mainframe database, it may be protected adequately, but once it gets to the remote microcomputer, many of the controls that might prevent errors or other data corruption are lost.
- Do not keep extremely sensitive data online.
- Screen and classify both users and data. Not everyone must see everything. Some organizations, especially in government, assign different security clearance levels to users as well as to data, thus permitting users to see only what they "need to know."
- Use removable hard disks so they can be transferred to a locked storage area.
- Create a secure physical environment in the area around the database and the microcomputer workstation.

OSI MODEL CONTROLS

Protocols are simply the rules by which two machines talk to each other. The word "protocol" comes from the Greek *prōtokollon*, which was the first sheet glued to a papyrus roll; it was the table of contents.

As discussed in Chapter 9, the International Organization for Standardization (ISO) has developed a seven-layer model (OSI model) for protocols. A brief summary of the tasks performed by each layer, along with the controls that should be in each layer, follows. The *OSI model* is the most popular protocol model that has been approved by international standards-setting organizations.

Layer 1—Physical Link Control   Layer 1 consists of the cable, modem, and physical circuitry. It is concerned with transmitting a serial stream of data bits over the communication circuit. It cannot interpret and does not know that the data may be in packets or frames, nor does it know about error checking, and so forth. This is the physical link over which all data bits move.

Controls are needed to physically protect the connector cable, modem, and communication circuits. The primary goal at this layer is to control physical access by employees or vendors to the connector cables and modems. This includes restricting their access to the wiring closets in which all the communication wires and cables are connected. All local loops leaving the building should be physically secured and out of harm's way to prevent physical damage or an easy telephone tap. Formal procedures should be in effect to help identify breaches of security or illegal entries to the network when made at the physical layer. Finally, physical protection of the telephone circuits (IXC channels) is the responsibility of the common carrier (telephone company). You cannot do much about it, except to audit the telephone company's physical security procedures and possibly encrypt the data before it leaves your building to go out onto the public network.

Layer 2—Data Link Control   The second layer is responsible for packaging the packets or data into frames and getting them to layer 1. It also is responsible for calculating the error checking polynomial (CRC) and inserting addresses and so forth into the frame or packet.

Controls at this layer should have features such as sequence counting of frames, error detection and retransmission capabilities, identification of lost frames, and reduction of possible duplicate transmissions to zero. It should solve problems caused by damaged, lost, or duplicate frames, prevent a fast transmitter from drowning a slow receiver in data, provide limited restart capabilities in case of abnormal termination situations, ensure that some of the transmitted data characters are not misinterpreted as line control characters, increase flow control efficiency to ensure that the maximum number of frames can be sent without requiring an acknowledgment, properly terminate a session, and the like.

Layer 3—Network Control   Layer 3 is responsible for translating logical addresses (names) into physical addresses (nodes or devices). It also chooses the best circuit route if more than one is available and packetizes the original message into the designated packet lengths (usually 128 characters).

Controls in this layer ensure that all packets are received correctly and in their proper order at their destinations. This layer of protocol should accept messages from the host, convert them to packets, and ensure that the packets get directed toward their destination. Packet routing should be controlled here. In addition, there might be some global or local databases at this layer that should be kept secure. Control of congestion, such as too many packets on one channel, should be controlled by this layer. This layer also can contain billing routines for charging users and should be reviewed for possible problems such as errors, theft of time, or improper message charges.

Layer 4—Transport Control   Layer 4 is responsible for establishing and maintaining the connection and initiates the retransmission request when a packet arrives in a corrupted state. It sometimes is called the host-to-host layer.

Controls that should be checked at layer 4 relate to network connections because the transport layer might have to create multiple network connections to get the required number of circuit paths. Multiplexing might be invoked at this layer, so multiplexing controls should be reviewed. Also at this layer a program on a source machine carries on a conversation with a similar program on the destination machine using headers and control messages; therefore, some of the controls might be in the application programs. At the lower layers (layers 1 to 3) the protocols are carried out by each machine and its immediate neighbors rather than by the ultimate source and destination machines, which may be separated by many hardware devices and circuit links. Another needed control is one that determines whether the software at this layer can tell which machine belongs to which connection. Other controls that are performed at this layer, even though they may be performed elsewhere as well, are source/destination machine addressing and flow control (here it is flow of messages rather than flow of packets) so one machine cannot overrun another.

Layer 5—Session Control   The fifth layer supports the user's session and turns communication on and off between two workstations. If a temporary electrical disruption on the network breaks the circuit, it often can get the lower layers (1 or 4) to reestablish the connection before the application program or the operator is aware of a problem.

Controls that should be examined at this layer are the typical controls that relate to a terminal (dedicated or dial-up) such as passwords, log-in procedures, terminal addressing procedures, authentication of terminals and users, and correct delivery of the bill. Another control occurs when the transport control (layer 4) connections are unreliable; the session layer may be required to attempt to recover from broken transport connections. As another example, in database management systems it is crucial that a complicated transaction against the database never be aborted halfway through the routine because this leaves the database in an inconsistent state. The session layer often provides a facility by which a group of messages can be set aside so none of them is delivered to the remote user until all of them have been completed. This mechanism ensures that a hardware or software failure within the subnetwork never can cause a transaction to be aborted halfway through its processing. The session layer also can provide for sequencing of messages when the transport layer does not.

Layer 6—Presentation Control   Layer 6 translates formats from the application layer above it to provide a syntax (language) that is commonly understood by all devices throughout the network, converts code, and encrypts or compresses when necessary.

Controls at this layer might be software encryption, text compression, text compaction, and conversion of incompatible file formats so two systems can talk to one another. This layer also can take incompatible terminals and modify line and screen length, end-of-line conventions, scroll versus page mode, character sets, and cursor addressing to make them compatible. Simple errors at the remote terminal might be caused by the software at this layer.

Layer 7—Application Control   The seventh layer is the interface of the network with the application. It provides such functions as file transfer and electronic mail. It serves as the interface to the network by accepting message blocks to be sent.

Controls at layer 7 are related to the business system application programs used in the organization. These application layer controls consist of the tasks that ensure a valid connection between whatever application program is being used and the addressing or transmission of messages required by this business application. Because the purpose of layer 7 is to insulate application programs from the detailed technical task of transmitting messages, controls should ensure that no messages get lost, misdirected, or improperly modified by this layer of software. Many of the controls required here are the typical day-to-day logical controls that are built into the business application system itself, although layer 7 also should contain internal controls within the communication software to validate sender and receiver addresses.

NETWORK SOFTWARE CONTROLS

Controls that relate to network architecture software typically are associated with layers 4 through 7 of the OSI model. Additional architecture *software controls* relate to the mainframe computer operating system, teleprocessing monitor software, telecommunication access programs, databases, security software packages, and LAN operating systems.

Teleprocessing monitor software relieves the operating system of the many tasks involved in handling message traffic between the host and remote terminals such as line handling, access methods, task scheduling, and system recovery. Throughput is increased by offloading these data communication functions from the operating system to the teleprocessing monitor.

Some of the controls that should be reviewed for teleprocessing monitors are access controls, for example, who can sign on to a terminal, and who can access program routines (sometimes called *exits*). With regard to these exits, the code of each exit routine should be checked for correctness and security. These exit program modules should be placed in software-controlled libraries.

As an example, let us discuss IBM's teleprocessing monitor CICS (Customer Information Control System). There are too many security features in this package to provide exhaustive coverage here, but two selected examples are the LTERM and the sign-on table.

The *LTERM* is the logical terminal address. You can restrict a specific terminal (LTERM) so it can execute only certain types of functions. Obviously, this is a further restriction over and above the password the user may have had to use to enter the system. In addition, the LTERM restriction is transparent because the user's terminal is restricted without regard to the user entering any password or identification code. This restriction is based on the terminal itself and how the terminal is defined by the LTERM.

The *sign-on table* in CICS is one of 64 levels or systems. It is cross-referenced to the user's identification (password) and, therefore, can restrict various user identifications or passwords from using CICS. It is essential that you do not assign the security keys in the sign-on table to operators who may have a conflict of interest and that you restrict their transaction capability based on their identification or password. Notice that LTERM and the sign-on table have the ability to restrict what a terminal might access and they also restrict the terminal operator's access.

The vendor's "system generation" manuals or the teleprocessing monitor should be reviewed to determine whether the vendor built any security controls into the teleprocessing monitor.

Telecommunication access programs are vendor-supplied programs that control the transmission of data to and from the host computer and various data communication devices. The telecommunication access programs most likely reside in a front end processor, but they also can reside in the host computer.

Some controls for the telecommunication access program may be documented in the vendor's system generation manuals. The controls that were built in by the software vendor should be evaluated to be sure they protect application programs and databases in the host mainframe. As with teleprocessing monitors, user program routines (exits) and access methods need to be examined.

Another interface with the teleprocessing monitor is the very sensitive network control database. For example, there might be a *system database* containing global information about addresses and logical names of all peripheral devices, locations of system files, system timing parameters, task locations and priorities, peripheral device control tables, and system supply command lists. Because of its importance to the security of the entire system, data in the system database must be protected from copying or destruction.

Another critical database is the *network database* containing local information, such as the number of stations, polling and selecting lists, current station identifier, communication control port addresses, logical terminal identifiers, terminal device list, terminal poll and call sequences, dial-up numbers, and message and process information. The network database also must be protected from unauthorized copying.

The network database can be used to cross-check against manual documentation. Because it contains information such as the number of stations and logical terminal identifiers, a copy of the database can be matched against the written network documentation as a means of verifying the currency of the documentation.

The impact of any security software packages that restrict or control access to files, records, or data items should be reviewed. These packages are independent of the data communication software. Such a package may offer a unique password and identification of each terminal operator and allow access only to the specific functions assigned to that operator. For instance, it can assign highly sensitive functions to a specific terminal or a group of terminals. Some packages also offer encrypted security data, security sign-on fields, darkened password fields, and a complete log of terminal sign-ons that includes any security violations. They offer additional features, such as file security to the record or field level, terminal security, transaction security, batch reports on all activity, automatic sign-off of unattended terminals, and immediate online notification of security violations. With regard to LAN operating system software, it is important to review the vendor's security specifications.

Finally, network software should be protected in any disastrous situation such as a power failure. Restart and recovery routines should be available, and the system should have only one master input terminal for entering sensitive or critical commands. All default options should be identified, and the impact of default options that do not operate properly should be assessed to determine whether adequate software maintenance is available. In addition, all sensitive tables (passwords) should be protected in the memory.

MANAGEMENT CONTROLS

Network management requires setting up a central control philosophy for handling the overall network functions. The network manager should be independent of other managers in the data processing environment or even of the information systems department. Some of the general responsibilities of this job function are design and analysis, network operations, failure control, and testing/problem management. They were covered in Chapter 12.

Some network management controls include the following. The network management team should have a national account with the common carrier when possible. There should be a central call number to log all problems related to who, what, where, when, why, the telephone number, data, and time of a problem. The failure control group should compile statistics for their hardware such as Mean Time Between Failures (MTBF). The network hardware vendor often can supply these data. The network management people also should maintain statistics on the time from failure to recovery. In its most detailed form, this is the Mean Time to Repair which equals the Mean Time To Diagnose (MTTD) plus the Mean Time To Respond (MTTR) plus the Mean Time To Fix (MTTF). (Chapter 12 discusses how these Mean Times are used.)

In addition to central control for problem reporting, the network management group should maintain other statistics such as the cumulative network downtime, subnetwork downtime, circuit utilization reports, response time analysis, queue-length descriptions, histograms of daily usage (such as number of characters transmitted per day per circuit), failure rates of the circuits (such as number of retransmitted messages), local host and file activity statistics, local device error activities, network gateway failures, distribution of character and packet volume, distribution of traffic by time of day and location, peak volumes, and a statistical profile of all time-related network traffic. These reports, or similar ones, should be available for managing the network.

To control network documentation (some of this can be cross-checked for currency in the global or local network databases), a good network management team should have the following: circuit layout record, network maps, hardware and software cross-references, all network vendor maintenance records, software listings by network task and component, all user site telephone numbers and names of individuals to contact, a component maintenance history log, circuit-controlled telephone contact index, inventory of network components by serial number, network redundancy locations and switching criteria, vendor contracts, vendor contacts, and an up-to-date list of personnel working in the network center.

A control review of network management should ascertain the existence of appropriate operation manuals and a comprehensive description of how the network operates. There should be adequate recovery procedures, backup procedures, and disaster plans.

Not much can be done to control communication test equipment because it is in continuous use. Network management must recognize, however, that misuse can allow breaches of privacy or the insertion of illegal messages.

A network monitor (protocol analyzer) is mandatory when bit-oriented protocols like X.25 or LANs are used. The only control that can be put on such a device is a keylock for its switch. The keylock should be turned off and the key removed when the equipment is not being used. This prevents people from browsing over data as they pass through the data communication network. Loopback test equipment should be used to diagnose the location and cause of problems.

Microprocessor-based network analyzers permit checks for poll-to-poll or poll-to-response times. Such checks aid network management in assessing polling efficiency. Other, smaller handheld test devices, such as breakout boxes, allow test personnel to send test patterns of data bits to a modem through the RS232 or RS449 cable. The primary control for test equipment is to ensure that only qualified people use this equipment and that they use it only when necessary.

RECOVERY/BACKUP/DISASTER CONTROLS

Establishing a disaster recovery capability requires devising recovery procedures and backup for the entire environment (building) and for hardware, software, data, and communication networks. An extremely detailed and broad-scoped *disaster recovery plan* can bring the organization back to a functioning business in the event of almost any type of disaster. This plan should address various levels of response to a number of possible disasters and should provide for partial or complete recovery in the areas of

- The building (environment)
- System software and utilities
- Application programs
- Data center hardware
- Remote microcomputers and terminals
- Manual forms
- Data entry support
- Switching centers
- On-site and off-site database file storage and retention
- System operating procedures at the data center and at remote user areas

- Staff assignments and responsibilities during the disaster
- Adequate updating and maintenance of the disaster plan
- All communication networks (private leased backbone, local area networks, micro-to-mainframe, public dial-up, and so forth)
- All related communication hardware

A complete disaster recovery plan covering all these areas is beyond the scope of this text, but we intend to address the formulation of a data communication recovery disaster plan.

Recovery controls and *backup controls* within the data communication network encompass many areas. The person who reviews these controls may start at either end of the network (remote terminals or central host computer). The object is to check for *recovery procedures* and *backup hardware* throughout the network. Perhaps the most important question to ask is whether it is cost effective to back up each piece of hardware encountered between a remote terminal site and the central host computer. A related question is: Are there software procedures for recovery of data files, network databases, network software, and the like? Use of Figure 13-5 during the review of recovery, backup, and disaster controls helps ensure that all network control points are considered.

An important consideration is backup of the communication circuits. One option is to lease two separate circuits (that have been alternatively routed) to have one for backup. Another option is to utilize dial-up communication circuits as backup to leased circuits. Of course, another alternative is to have manual procedures that can be used if the circuit is down for a very short period of time, perhaps several hours at the maximum. Temporary satellite transmission is now an option.

There should be recovery and restart capabilities in the event of either a hardware or a software crash. Backup facilities should include backup power, possibly at both the local and remote sites.

A data communication network disaster plan should include a separate plan for each of six different areas: (1) the data communication network control center, (2) communication circuits, (3) switches, concentrators, microcomputer workstations, multiplexers, and intelligent terminal controllers, (4) common carrier (telephone company) facilities, (5) electrical power for the data communication facilities, user terminals, and lights, and (6) distributed local area networks.

A good data communication network disaster plan should take the following into account.

- The name of the decision-making manager who is in charge of the disaster recovery operation. A second manager should be indicated in case the first manager is unavailable.
- Availability and training of backup personnel with sufficient knowledge and experience in data communications.
- Recovery procedures for the data communication facilities (WAN, MAN, BN, or LAN). This is information on the location of circuits, who to contact for

backup data circuits and documentation, and preestablished priorities as to which data circuits should be reconstructed first.

- How to replace damaged data communication hardware and software that are supplied by vendors. Outline the support that can be expected from vendors, along with the name and telephone number of the person to contact.

- Location of alternative data communication facilities and equipment such as connector cables, local loops, IXCs, common carrier switching facilities, satellite, and public data networks (PDNs).

- Action to be taken in case of partial damage, threats such as a bomb threat, fire, water or electrical damage, sabotage, civil disorders, or vendor failures.

- Procedure for imposing extraordinary controls over the network until the system returns to normal.

- Storage of the disaster recovery procedures in a safe area where they cannot be destroyed by the catastrophe. This area must be accessible, however, to those who need to use the plans.

- A preestablished list of priorities that states what is to be fixed first. The section on How to Conduct a Risk Assessment (page 631) presented earlier in this chapter will be very helpful for this task.

KEY TERMS

Amplitude noise	Cross-talk	Encryption
Asymmetric algorithm	Cryption	Equalizer
Attenuation	Cyclical parity check	Error detection and
Attenuation distortion	Cyclical redundancy	correction
Authentication	check (CRC)	Error detection with
Backup controls	Data Encryption Standard	retransmission
Block cipher	(DES)	Error prevention
Burst error	Data security	Error rate
Ciphertext	Database controls	Even parity
Circuit controls	Decision model	Forward error correction
Comparison Risk Ranking	Decryption	Gaussian noise
Component	Delay distortion	Hacker
Conditioning	Delphi team	Hamming code
Constant ratio code	Detective control	Hardware controls
Control points	Dial-out-only facility	Harmonic distortion
Control principles	Disaster recovery plan	Human error
Control Spreadsheet	Distortion	Impulse noise
Controls	Eavesdropping	Interlaced parity
Corrective control	Echo	Intermodulation noise
Corrupted data	Echo checking	

Jitter	Phase hit	Scrambling
Judgment criteria	Physical security	Software controls
Key	Plaintext	Something you are
Key management	Polynomial checking	Something you have
Line noise	Preventive control	Something you know
Line outage	Privacy-Enhanced Mail (PEM)	Spike
Logical security		Spoofing
Loop checking	Private key	Symmetric algorithm
Lost data	Proprietary algorithm	Telephone call restrictor
M-of-N code	Public key	Terminal controls
Network control point	Public key cryptosystem	Threat
Network error	Recovery controls	Trellis coding
Odd parity	Risk analysis	Vacuum cleaning
Ordinal ranking	Risk assessment	Virus
Parity checking	RSA Digital Signature	White noise

SELECTED REFERENCES

1. Anderson, John C. "I Spy! Observations on Modern-Day Cryptography: A Brief History of Cryptography, With Comments on the State of the Art, and Answers to Users' Questions," *ISPNews,* vol. 3, no. 2, March/April 1992, pp. 1, 24–27.

2. *Auerbach Data Security Management.* Published bimonthly by Auerbach Publishers (a division of Warren, Gorham & Lamont), 210 South Street, Boston, Mass. 02111-9990, 1981– .

3. *Computer Fraud and Security Bulletin.* Published monthly by Elsevier International Bulletins, Mayfield House, 256 Banbury Road, Oxford OX2 7DH, England, 1978– .

4. *Computer Security Digest.* Published monthly by Computer Protection Systems, Inc., 150 North Main Street, Plymouth, Mich. 48170, 1988– .

5. *Control Objectives: Controls in a Computer Environment, Objectives, Guidelines, and Audit Procedures.* Carol Stream, Ill.: EDP Auditors Foundation, 1990.

6. *Data Processing & Communications Security.* Published quarterly by Assets Protection Publishing, P.O. Box 5323, Madison, Wis. 53705, 1976– .

7. Dayanim, Joshua F. "Disaster Recovery: Options for Public and Private Networks," *Telecommunications,* vol. 25, no. 12, December 1991, pp. 48–51.

8. *Disaster Recovery Journal: The Magazine for Contingency Planning and Security.* Published quarterly by Systems Support, Inc., 2712 Meramar Drive, St. Louis, Mo. 63129, 1987– .

9. *EDPACS: The EDP Audit, Control and Security Newsletter.* Published monthly by Auerbach Publishers (a division of Warren, Gorham & Lamont), One Penn Plaza, New York, N.Y. 10119, 1973– .

10. FitzGerald, Jerry. *Control-It® A Control Spreadsheet Methodology for Microcomputers.* Redwood City, Calif.: Jerry FitzGerald & Associates. (Four PC-based software packages. Free demonstration diskette available.)

11. FitzGerald, Jerry, and Ardra F. FitzGerald. *Designing Controls into Computerized Systems,* 2nd ed. Redwood City, Calif.: Jerry FitzGerald & Associates, 1990, ISBN 0-932410-40-5.

12. FitzGerald, Jerry, *Rank-It® A Risk Assessment Tool.* Redwood City, Calif.: Jerry FitzGerald & Associates. (An expert system software tool for IBM PCs or compatible that combines the Delphi technique with Comparison Risk Ranking. Free demonstration diskette available.)

13. Marcella, Albert J., Jr. *EDI Audit and Control.* Norwood, Mass.: Artech House, 1992.

14. *Risk Management Manual.* Published bimonthly by Assets Protection Publishing, P.O. Box 5323, Madison, Wis. 53705.

QUESTIONS/PROBLEMS

1. After reading the How to Conduct a Risk Assessment section, use Figure 13-16 to rank the seven reasons for attending college.

2. Today's security manifests itself in controls that _____, _____, and _____.

3. Define computer virus.

4. Define the two types of errors.

5. Errors normally appear in _____, which is when more than one data bit is changed by the error-causing condition.

6. If a network has a very high error detection and correction performance, what is sacrificed to have this error-free environment?

7. What time of day normally has more errors on dial-up lines?

8. Is there any difference in the error rates of lower speed lines and of higher speed lines?

9. Is there any difference in the error rates of dial-up lines and of private leased lines?

10. Briefly define noise.

11. How is line noise manifested?

12. Compare three of the 12 categories of noise and distortion.

13. Two of the 12 categories of noise and distortion discussed in this chapter are related to attenuation. How do they differ?

14. What are the three approaches to error control?

15. How does loop checking work?

16. Describe the three ways in which error detection with retransmission can be handled.

17. What is the simplest and least expensive method of reducing data transmission errors?

18. Name three common methods of detecting errors.

19. Briefly describe how even parity, odd parity, and no parity work.

20. Briefly describe how *M*-of-*N* codes work.

21. Briefly describe how polynomial checking works.

22. How does cyclical redundancy checking work?

To get good grades	To get good grades						
To please my parents		To please my parents					
To learn something useful			To learn something useful				
To get a BA or BS degree				To get a BA or BS degree			
To get a good job					To get a good job		
To party and have fun						To party and have fun	
To prepare for graduate school							To prepare for graduate school

Figure 13-16 Use this Comparison Risk Ranking Sheet to conduct a risk ranking on your most important reasons for attending college.

23. How does forward error correction work? What distinguishes it from other error checking methods?

24. A number of error detecting and correcting methods are discussed in this chapter. What distinguishes each one from the others?

25. Under what circumstances is forward error correction desirable?

26. It is said that the commitment to data communications has changed the vulnerability of the organization's assets. Why is this so?

27. What factors have brought increased emphasis on network security?

28. What is the first thing you must do when conducting a network security review?

29. A Control Spreadsheet shows all the _____ network controls.

30. Define threat.

31. Define component.

32. Briefly outline the steps required to complete a Control Spreadsheet.

33. What two questions must be asked when deciding which controls should be placed in which cell of the Control Spreadsheet?

34. Name at least six areas that should have controls in a data communication network.

35. Define encryption and decryption.

36. Older cryptographic systems were based on scrambling the _____ of a message.

37. Modern cryptographic systems are based on the _____ and the _____.

38. What must be kept secret in a good encryption system?

39. Does modern cryptography focus on analog or digital methods? Explain.

40. Is it possible to implement encryption algorithms in both hardware and software, or are they limited to one or the other?

41. What encryption standard is used for commercial purposes and unclassified military data?

42. Define block cipher.

43. When discussing the concept of "breaking" encryption algorithms, it is in terms of nanoseconds, femtoseconds, and attoseconds. To what do these terms refer?

44. What is a crucial factor in the design of communication networks that convey ciphertext?

45. What does it mean when an algorithm is classed as a symmetric algorithm?

46. To what does the term *key management* refer?

47. What are the three alternatives for organizations wanting to use encryption?

48. What is the inherent *difference* between proprietary (private) and public key systems?

49. What is the inherent *similarity* between proprietary and public key systems?

50. A number of hardware controls are discussed in this chapter. Discuss one of the most important and explain why it is important.

51. Describe the purpose of a dial-out-only facility.

52. Controls are important for time division statistical multiplexers because they have _____ and _____ that make illegal copying of messages easier.

53. Controls for remote intelligent controllers usually involve _____.

54. Controls for terminals have two entirely separate aspects. What are they?

55. Describe the three general ways of restricting access at the remote ends of a network.

56. What device can keep telephone users from dialing certain prefixes?

57. Describe three security problems when communicating by cellular telephone.

58. Controlling the security of local loops and interexchange circuits is difficult because they are owned by the common carriers. How can this problem be overcome?

59. Describe the three areas that need to be considered in controlling microcomputers.

60. Why is it necessary to maintain control over databases?

61. Describe the purpose of the controls at each layer of the OSI model.

62. Although network software controls are associated with the OSI model layers, teleprocessing monitor program and telecommunication access programs are also important control points. Describe the purpose of controls for each of these areas.

63. How does the system database differ from the network database?

64. What is the philosophy under which network management operates?

65. What is the purpose of a disaster recovery plan?

66. Why would you want to perform a risk analysis?

67. Define ordinal ranking.

68. What is a Delphi team?

69. Define Comparison Risk Ranking.

70. What are some of the judgment criteria that can be used to risk rank a data communication network?

71. Briefly outline the steps required to risk rank threats to a network.

72. Break the class into several teams, each of which conducts a small risk assessment of threats to a network. Identify four or five threats. Make some assumptions regarding the type of network. Finally, identify the judgment criteria that will be used to rank the various threats, rank the threats, and then identify network-oriented controls that would mitigate or stop each threat. Use Figure 13-17 for this exercise.

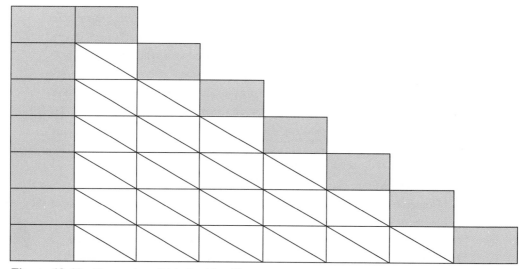

Figure 13-17 Comparison Risk Ranking Sheet.

73. If there was a 3-of-7 code, it could represent $C_3^7 = 7!/(3!4!) = 35$ distinct symbols, out of the $2^7 = 128$ bit combinations. We then could say that the 3-of-7 code is $35/128 = 0.273$ or 27.3 percent "efficient." How efficient would a 5-of-10 code be?

74. If the transmission speed is 9600 bits per second and a spike (impulse noise) hits the line for one tenth of a second, how many bits are destroyed?

75. Why does the 4-of-8 code not use a parity bit?

76. A frequently used form of checking of decimal numbers is the modulo nine check. A check digit is appended to each numerical quantity. The digit is the remainder, upon division by 9, of the sum of the digits in the original number. For example, if the original number is 73842, then the sum of the digits is 24 $(7 + 3 + 8 + 4 + 2)$. The check digit calculation is: $24/9 = 2 +$ Remainder of 6; therefore, the check digit is 6. The number with the check digit appended would then be 738426. Assume that during transmission there is an error that changes the number 738426 to the number 739426. Let us check the received number (739426). The sum of the digits is 25 $(7 + 3 + 9 + 4 + 2)$; therefore, $25/9 + 2 +$ Remainder of 7. Because 7 does not equal 6, the number has been detected as an error. Experiment with this method to find out under what circumstances it works and when it fails. If you are particularly industrious, look up "casting out 9s" in a mathematical dictionary or investigate this property in a book on number theory.

77. How efficient is the method given in Question 76 if we are transmitting 8-digit numbers? 12-digit numbers?

78. Using the format of Figure 13-3, encode the data character using 1011. Identify P_1, P_2, and P_4.

79. Do errors in data communications normally appear in bursts or are they distributed evenly over time?

80. What is the most frequently used approach to error control?

81. Look at Figure 13-5. To protect your message as it moves from the earth station to the satellite, which of the 18 control points is the primary one you should consider?

82. Is it possible first to encrypt with a public key and then to decrypt with a private (secret) key, as well as first to encrypt with the private key and then to decrypt that message with the public key?

83. Do packet switching controllers have job tasks beyond that of a typical front end processor?

84. What do you think are the three most important security controls that can be placed on a terminal?

85. Which layer of the OSI model performs controls such as error detection and retransmission or sequence counting of contiguous frames for transmission?

86. As the manager of a major data communication network, how many types of disaster plans might you consider?

87. What if you encrypted a file on your microcomputer and lost the "key." How long would it take you to break the key if

- Your microcomputer could test one key each second.
- There were only 25 million possible keys.
- The correct key showed up after testing 50 percent of the possible keys.

88. Name the three basic types of network controls.

89. This chapter discussed 30 principles for evaluating and documenting network controls. Discuss one of them and give an example of what could happen if you did not follow this principle.

90. The RSA Digital Signature was discussed in this chapter. What is its purpose?

91. Review the How to Develop a Control Spreadsheet section and then read the following case study. You should perform the following tasks in connection with the case study.

- Identify five or six general threats in the case. List these threats in the Threats column of Figure 13-18.

- Identify five or six general components in the case. List these components in the Components column of Figure 13-18.

- Place the names of the threats in the border cells across the top of the empty Control Spreadsheet provided in Figure 13-19.

- Place the names of the components in the border cells down the left side of the empty Control Spreadsheet provided in Figure 13-19.

- Read the case again and, using some interpretation, underline or identify all the controls that appear to be in the case.

- Number all identified controls.

- Place the controls (by number) in the appropriate cells of the Control Spreadsheet (Figure 13-19). This procedure (using coins) was explained in the How to Develop a Control Spreadsheet section.

- Analyze the control structure. Determine which controls are adequate and which new controls should be added. Use your own knowledge and the control lists in this chapter when identifying new controls that might be recommended.

Note: The following is a situation case, one that depicts a specific situation within an organization, rather than a full-length case study of an organization. The tasks are best performed by small teams of two or three students working together. There is no single answer in filling out Figure 13-19. You must seek a reasonable level of control for each cell. Some cells may have too many controls, and others may have none at all. Use your discretion to determine the "reasonable level."

MULTISYSTEM COMMUNICATION NETWORK

The Belmont State Bank uses an online data communication network for several of its business functions. This network is used for online inquiries of the passbook savings system and of the demand deposit accounting system (that is, the checking accounts).

This is a large bank with hundreds of branches that are connected to a central computer system. Each branch has a variety of terminals and terminal controllers connected to the central system by use of the public telephone network. Some of these terminals are on dedicated leased lines, and others use the dial-up telephone network.

The security team visited six branch offices to conduct threat scenario sessions with the local branch operations staffs. These threat scenario sessions provided a good perspective of branch management, operations personnel, security, and prevailing attitudes toward embezzlement and other threats.

This network uses video terminals, teleprinter terminals, transaction terminals, local intelligent controllers, a decentralized database, and a variety of other hardware devices and software programs. When possible, the bank purchases outside packages rather than developing application systems "from scratch."

Terminals at the branches and central headquarters sites are in physically secure locations. Vendors who perform maintenance are responsible for ensuring that the remote intelligent controllers, modems, and other devices operate effectively. Terminal operators use a four-digit numeric password, and each terminal is transaction-coded to accept only its authorized transactions. The nine largest branches are allowed direct entry of their wire transfer business, which constitutes 92 percent of the wire transfers sent or received by the bank. There are written procedures at the local branches. Employees at several branches have started using their own or locally purchased microcomputers to increase the efficiency and throughput of the system.

Instructions for training operators are given in an extensive training manual that is updated monthly. This manual is kept in a looseleaf format. It is maintained centrally, and the updates are distributed to the various branches.

The operator terminals are transaction-coded and have all the appropriate function keys; the software has various restart procedures and checkpoints that can be used to correct errors during a transaction. In some cases preprinted forms appear on the video screen so the operator can fill in the appropriate data.

During transmission, the front end processor performs error detection and correction and orders the retransmission of any message that is in error. A bit-oriented protocol is used. One of the good features of this system is its message switching with a store and forward capability. This gives everyone in the bank access to electronic mail. Wire transfer messages are switched from this computer to the more secure and separate wire transfer control system computer. When a user calls in, the central system calls that user back in order to control which telephone numbers are connected to its dial-up modems. Encryption currently is under consideration.

The application programs are maintained by local bank employees, although a few of the packages still use some outside consultants for maintenance. An effective program change control procedure is operational.

The communication network control group has line monitors and other devices that are required to maintain an effective uptime ratio for this network. The network has been operating at a 98.95 percent uptime. Some of the terminal operators, however, have begun to complain about slow response time, which has been measured at an average of three seconds.

THREATS	COMPONENTS

Figure 13-18 Identify threats and components.

Figure 13-19 An empty Control Spreadsheet.

NEXT DAY AIR SERVICE CUMULATIVE CASE STUDY

Background on Next Day Air Service

With the recent outbreak of computer and network viruses, the board of directors has become slightly paranoid and, finally, security conscious. Accordingly, Mr. Coone has met with you again. He is concerned that Next Day Air Service's networks, which are beginning to increase its market share, may become infected by one of these viruses. His first concern is how to prevent such an infection because it would shut down the network for several hours. Mr. Coone was angry enough when the first modem failure shut down one of the 19,200 bits per second circuits for 4¾ hours. You certainly do not want to have that happen again!

You recognize that a complete security and control review is needed. Because of this you review the Control Spreadsheet methodology and set about the task at hand.

Once the Control Spreadsheet is completed, you still have to address the cost, technical, and operational feasibility of any controls. The board of directors wants to prevent any threat that appears to be "excessive" by implementing either hardware or software controls. Of course, the board has to approve any controls before implementing them. Accordingly, you must be able to defend your security review and any resulting recommendations.

The board of directors has expressed concern that the common carriers do not provide adequate error and security controls. Mr. Coone has asked you to consult several common carriers to determine what level of error, physical, and data security they provide for the local loops and central office. As a result of investigating several common carriers, you compile the following table, which profiles the transmission error rates, security measures, and costs of five common carriers.

Common Carrier	Transmission Error Rates	Physical Security of Central Office	Security on Local Loop	Costs
Company A	1 in 500,000	Minimal	Adequate	Moderate
Company B	1 in 550,000	Adequate	Minimal	High
Company C	1 in 400,000	Very adequate	Adequate	Low
Company D	1 in 600,000	Minimal	Very adequate	High
Company E	1 in 450,000	Adequate	Adequate	Moderate

Now you must make a recommendation. You realize that it is possible to use more than one common carrier to provide a backup local loop if the security measures provided by a primary carrier are inadequate. These are very important factors when determining what security measures Next Day Air Service should incorporate in its security review.

Additional items that need to be investigated are circuit route diversification, service restoration guarantees, and alternative local loop carriers for backup and route diversity. It will require some research to determine what is available in your area.

Mr. Coone's next concern is that the database management system on the network server has not been given the proper attention with regard to security. Therefore, he has asked you to examine what security measures are appropriate for the database server. You develop the following list, which shows the six security items that should be considered.

1. Restrict entry to the LAN based on a password and a user ID.

2. Restrict the user's limits once in the database; for example, the ability to read, write, create, or delete files should be restricted to specified users.

3. Appoint a database administrator (DBA) who can grant or revoke security privileges in order to control the security function.

4. Consider using dial-back security devices to restrict unauthorized entry to the network.

5. Consider using data encryption. The data can be encrypted prior to storage on the disk and decrypted when it is read from the disk. This ensures that the data is useless to anyone who gains unauthorized access to the network.

6. Install disk mirroring on the server.

Identify the levels of access controls that are available and evaluate their effectiveness. The database management system on the server must be protected adequately because it is a valuable asset to Next Day Air Service.

Questions/Problems for the Next Day Air Service Case

1. Which common carrier shown in the preceding table provides the best error and security control? Explain your logic.

2. Use Figure 13-20 to build a Control Spreadsheet. Place in it the 30 controls from the LAN Controls section (page 558) in Chapter 11 of this text. Discuss any empty cells.

3. Use Figure 13-21 to risk rank the six security items for the NDAS network. Assuming that only four can be installed because of time constraints, which four would you choose to install?

THREATS COMPONENTS	Illegal Access	Errors and Omissions	Message Loss or Change	Disasters and Disruptions	Breach of Privacy	Fraud or Theft
Application or System Software Programs						
Host Computer or LAN Server						
Database Files						
Communication Circuits (IXC)						
Local Loops						
Modems						
Terminal Users (People)						
Microcomputers and Terminals						

Figure 13-20 Control Spreadsheet for the security review of Next Day Air Service's local area network.

Password User ID	Password User ID					
Restrict Read/Write/ Create/Delete		Restrict Read/Write/ Create/Delete				
Database Security Administrator			Database Security Administrator			
Dial-back Security				Dial-back Security		
Encryption					Encryption	
Server Disk Mirroring						Server Disk Mirroring

Figure 13-21 Comparison Risk Ranking Sheet for use in ranking the six security items for Next Day Air Service's local area network.

GLOSSARY AND ACRONYMS

ACCUMASTER Integrator® AT&T's network management program to manage multivendor voice and data networks from the host computer.

ACCUNET® AT&T's public digital packet switching network services for data communications.

ACF Advanced Communication Function. ACF is part of IBM's telecommunication access program called Network Control Program (NCP) that provides an interface with TCAM and VTAM. ACF also is part of the Systems Network Architecture concept.

ACK An ASCII or EBCDIC code character indicating a positive acknowledgment, that is, a message has been received correctly.

ACM Association for Computing Machinery. The ACM is an association of computer professionals.

Acoustic Coupler An older type of modem that permits use of a telephone handset as a connection to the public telephone network for data transmission.

Acronym A word formed from the initial letters or groups of letters of words in a phrase. An example is the word *laser,* which means *l*ight *a*mplification by *s*timulated *e*mission of *r*adiation.

ACU See **Automatic Calling Unit.**

ADCCP Advanced Data Communication Control Procedure. Pronounced "add-cap." This is a bit-oriented data link control standard approved by ANSI.

ADCU Association of Data Communications Users.

Address

1. A coded representation of the destination of data, or of its originating terminal. For example, multiple terminals on one communication circuit must each have a unique address.

2. Sometimes referred to as *called number.* The group of digits that make up a telephone number. For example, an address may consist of an area code, a central office, and a line number, such as 415-555-1212.

3. Source address or destination address.

ADMD ADministrative Management Domain. The X.400 electronic mail standard defines public and private domains. Public domains are administered by public common carriers, and private domains correspond to corporate electronic mail systems. The part of the mail exchange administered by the public domain is called the administrative management domain.

ADU See **Automatic Dialing Unit.**

AFIPS American Federation of Information Processing Societies.

ALOHA A system using a "transmit at will" access method. The name comes from a method of telecommunications whereby signals are beamed at satellites when transmission is ready to go. If it gets through, fine; if it does not, then the sender tries again. The ALOHA method of transmission was used first by Hawaiians who had satellite dishes beaming at communication satellites over the equator. It also was used for communicating with dishes in other Pacific Basin countries.

Alternating Current (ac) The electrical current used to power computers.

American National Standards Institute (ANSI) The principal standards-setting body in the United States. ANSI is a nonprofit, nongovernmental organization supported by more than 1,000 trade organizations, professional societies, and companies. It belongs to the Consultative Committee on International Telegraph and Telephone (CCITT) and the International Organization for Standardization (ISO).

American Standard Code for Information Interchange See **ASCII.**

Amplifier A device used to boost the strength of a signal. Amplifiers are spaced at intervals throughout the length of a communication circuit. Also called a *repeater*.

Amplitude Modulation See **Modulation, Amplitude.**

Analog Pertaining to representation by means of continuously variable physical quantities, such as varying frequencies.

Analog Signal A signal in the form of a continuously varying physical quantity such as amplitude, which reflects variations in the loudness of the human voice.

Analog Transmission Transmission of a continuously variable signal as opposed to a discrete on/off signal. Physical quantities such as temperature are continuously variable and so are described as "analog." The traditional way of transmitting a telephone or voice signal is analog.

ANI See **Automatic Number Identification.**

ANSI See **American National Standards Institute.**

API Application Program Interface. API is the way IBM links incompatible equipment for micro-to-mainframe links. Part of the NetView network management system, API allows applications on microcomputers and mainframes to speak directly to each other at the application software level, even though the equipment is from different vendors.

APPC Advanced Program-to-Program Communications. APPC is a part of IBM's Systems Network Architecture that provides peer-to-peer communications. It is a high level program interface that allows two application programs to communicate. Also called *LU 6.2* after its most important component.

AppleTalk A set of communication protocols that defines networking for an AppleShare network.

Application Level Control Pertains to the control of a specific application to safeguard, restrict, or protect it. For example, controls are implemented into a payroll application to prevent theft of the organization's assets.

Arcnet Attached Resource Computing NETwork. A proprietary token-bus local area network developed by the Datapoint Corporation.

Area Code A number assigned to the geographical subdivision or operating area to facilitate message and circuit switching. Called city code outside of the United States. See also **Numbering Plan Area.**

ARPANET One of the early packet switching networks. ARPANET was developed by the U.S. Department of Defense Advanced Research Projects Agency.

ARQ Automatic Repeat reQuest. A system employing an error detecting code so conceived that any error initiates a repetition of the transmission of the incorrectly received message.

ASCII   American Standard Code for Information Interchange. Pronounced "ask'-ee." An eight-level code for data transfer adopted by the American National Standards Institute to achieve compatibility among data devices.

Asynchronous Transfer Mode (ATM)   A communication switch that handles interface speeds ranging from 45 million bits per second on a T-3 circuit to 600 million bits per second. It multiplexes data streams onto the same backbone network by using cell relay techniques. ATM switches can handle multimedia traffic, such as data, graphics, voice, and video. The ATM technology was developed by the CCITT broadband ISDN working group, and it uses the IEEE 802.6 cell technology. ATM and the switched multimegabit data service (SMDS) are competing technologies for switching high speed data streams. See also **SMDS.**

Asynchronous Transmission   Transmission in which each information character is individually synchronized, usually by the use of start and stop bits. The gap between each character is not a fixed length. Compare with **Synchronous Transmission.**

AT&T Communications   The name of American Telephone and Telegraph (AT&T), reflecting its present emphasis on providing long distance communication services. AT&T is one of the oldest providers of communication equipment and circuits. It is commonly known as "Ma Bell" and was the parent organization of the various Bell Telephone companies before deregulation.

ATM

1.   See **Asynchronous Transfer Mode.**

2.   In banking, an automated teller machine.

Attenuation   The difference between the transmitted and received power caused by loss of signal strength through the equipment, communication circuits, or other devices. Expressed in decibels.

Attosecond   One quintrillionth of a second or $(1/1,000,000,000,000,000,000)$ 10^{-18}.

Authentication   In the context of transmission security, a method of guaranteeing that a message is genuine, that it has arrived unaltered, and that it comes from the source indicated.

Automatic Calling Unit (ACU)   A device that permits a business machine to dial calls automatically.

Automatic Dialing Unit (ADU)   A device capable of automatically dialing digits.

Automatic Equalization   Adjusting a transmission channel while sending data signals to reduce errors during transmission. Equalization is the process of reducing frequency and phase distortion of a circuit by introducing time differences to compensate for the difference in attenuation or time delay at the various frequencies of the transmission band.

Automatic Number Identification (ANI)   The process whereby a long distance common carrier provides its customers with a visual display of an incoming caller's telephone number.

Automatic Outward Identified Dialing   The ability of a switching system to identify the originator of an outgoing call without operator intervention.

Automatic Repeat reQuest   See **ARQ.**

Backbone Network (BN)   A large central network to which all the networks within an organization are connected; thus, it is the organization's backbone for communications. It usually is a network that interconnects everything on a single site, but it can be larger if it connects all the organization's terminals, microcomputers, mainframes, local area networks, and other communication equipment.

Balanced   The state of impedance on a two-wire circuit when the impedance to ground as measured from one wire is equal to the impedance to ground as measured from the other wire. A balancing network is a combination of electronic components that stimulate the impedance of a uniform cable or open wire circuit over a band of frequencies.

BALUN BALanced/UNbalanced. An imped-ance-matching device to connect balanced twisted pair cabling with unbalanced coaxial cable.

Band Elimination Filter An electrical device that blinds a receiving unit by blocking specific fre-quency ranges.

Bandpass Filter An electrical device that allows a specific frequency band to exit a device and attenuates or restricts all others.

Bandwidth The difference between the highest and lowest frequencies in a band. For exam-ple, a voice grade circuit has a 4000 hertz band-width. In more recent usage, bandwidth also means faster transmission in terms of bits per second. When people say they need more band-width, they need more transmission capacity or a greater number of bits per second trans-mission speed.

Bandwidth-on-Demand The ability to add more circuit capacity automatically and as needed. Instead of having several fractional T-1 cir-cuits, an organization can have one T-1 circuit and use inverse multiplexers to dedicate some of the channels to switched 56,000 bits per second usage. As one 56,000 bits per second channel fills to capacity, a second one is brought into service automatically for the next message transmission. See also **Digital Cross-Connect Switch.**

Baseband Signaling Transmission of a signal in its original state, that is, a signal in its origi-nal form, not changed by modulation. It is a digital signal and is usually direct electrical voltages.

Basic Access Service In ISDN, two 64,000 bits per second B channels for data transmission and one 16,000 bits per second D channel for signaling (2 B + D). See also **Primary Access Service.**

Basic Rate See **Basic Access Service.**

Baud Unit of signaling speed. The speed in baud is the number of discrete conditions or signal elements per second. (This is applied only to the actual signals on a communication circuit.) If each signal event represents only one bit condition, *baud* is the same as *bits per second*. When each signal event represents other than one bit, *baud* does not equal *bits per second*.

Baudot Five-bit, 58-character alphanumeric code used in transmission of information.

BCC See **Block Check Character.**

BCD Binary Coded Decimal. Six-bit alphanu-meric code used in transmission.

Bell System The seven telephone operating companies known as the Bell Operating Com-panies (BOCs).

Bellcore The short name for Bell Communi-cations Research, which is a research organi-zation formed by the seven Bell Operating Companies after the divestiture of American Telephone & Telegraph. AT&T's research or-ganization is the Bell Laboratories.

BER Bit-Error Rate. The number of bits re-ceived in error divided by the total number of bits received. An indicator of circuit quality.

BERT Bit-Error Rate Testing. Testing a data line with a pattern of bits that are compared before and after the transmission to detect errors.

Binary A number system using only the two symbols 0 and 1, which is especially well adapted to computer usage because 0 and 1 can be represented as ''on'' and ''off,'' or as negative charges and positive charges. The bi-nary digits appear in strings of 0s and 1s.

Binary Coded Decimal See **BCD.**

Binary Synchronous Communications (BSC or bisync) A half duplex, character-oriented synchronous data communication protocol devised by IBM in 1964.

Bipolar Coding A method of transmitting a bi-nary stream in which binary zero is sent as a negative pulse and binary one is sent as a posi-tive pulse.

BISYNC **BInary SYNChronous communications transmission.**

Bit

1. An abbreviation of the term *binary digit*.

2. A single pulse in a group of pulses.

3. A unit of information capacity.

4. Zeros and ones.

Bit-Error Rate (BER)   See **BER.**

Bit-Error Rate Testing   See **BERT.**

Bit Rate   The rate at which bits (binary digits) are transmitted over a communication path. Normally expressed in bits per second (bps). The bit rate should not be confused with the data signaling rate (*baud*), which measures the rate of signal changes being transmitted. See also **bps.**

Bit Stream   A continuous series of bits being transmitted on a transmission line.

BIU   Bus Interface Unit. In a local area network the BIU is the device located between the terminal and the cable. It provides the physical connection to the input/output bus. See also **Medium Access Unit (MAU)** and **Multistation Access Unit (MAU).**

BKER   Block-Error Rate. The number of blocks received in error divided by the total number of blocks received.

BKERT   Block-Error Rate Testing. Testing a data link with groups of information arranged into transmission blocks for error checking.

Block   Sets of contiguous bits or bytes that make up a message, frame, or packet.

Block Check Character (BCC)   The checksum at the end of a Binary Synchronous Communications (BSC) message. The block check character is used to check for errors in a detection with retransmission protocol.

Block-Error Rate   See **BKER.**

Block-Error Rate Testing   See **BKERT.**

Blocking   The inability of a PBX to grant service to a requesting user because the transmission channel is not available. The term refers primarily to PBX switchboards and central office switches that lack the ability to provide circuits to all users at all times. Contrast with **Nonblocking.**

BN   See **Backbone Network.**

BOC   Bell Operating Company. One of the 22 local telephone companies spun off from AT&T as a result of divestiture, and now reorganized into seven regional Bell holding companies (RBOC).

Booting   The process of turning on and loading a computer's memory with the operating system that allows it to function. The word comes from "pulling oneself up by one's bootstraps." Booting is of two types: cold boot and warm boot. A cold boot is the state when you initially turn your computer's power on. In a warm boot, the operating system is reloaded into the computer's memory. When you press the Control, Alt, and Delete keys simultaneously you throw the DOS operating system out of memory and reload a "new" copy. This is a warm boot.

bps   Bits per second. The basic unit of data communication rate measurement. Usually refers to rate of information bits transmitted. Contrast with **Baud** and **Bit Rate.**

Bridge   A device that connects two similar networks using the same protocols. Compare with **Gateway, Router,** and **Brouter.**

Broadband Circuit   An analog communication circuit that has a bandwidth of greater than 4000 hertz.

Broadband Ethernet   The 10Broad36 version of Ethernet, meaning that it transmits at 10 million bits per second in broadband with a maximum distance of 3,600 meters. Also called *IEEE 802.3*.

Brouter   A piece of hardware that combines the functions of a bridge and a router. See also **Bridge** and **Router.**

BSC See **Binary Synchronous Communications.**

BTAM Basic Telecommunications Access Method. BTAM provides the basic functions needed for controlling data communication circuits in IBM 360/370 systems.

Buffer A device used for the temporary storage of data, primarily to compensate for differences in data flow rates (for example, between a terminal and its transmission circuit), but also as a security measure to allow retransmission of data if an error is detected during transmission.

Bulletin Board System (BBS) A dial-up electronic bulletin board in which anyone with a modem can participate.

Burst Error A series of consecutive errors in data transmission. Refers to the phenomenon on communication circuits in which errors are highly prone to occurring in groups or clusters.

Bus A transmission path or channel. Typically an electrical connection with one or more conductors in which all attached devices receive all transmissions at the same time.

Byte A small group of data bits that are handled as a unit. In most cases it is an 8-bit byte and it is known as a *character*.

C Band The frequency range from 4 to 6 GHz that is used for commercial satellite communications.

C Type Conditioning A North American term for a type of conditioning that controls attenuation, distortion, and delay distortion so they lie within specified limits.

C1, C2, C3, C4, C5 Levels of conditioning offered on AT&T's voice grade lease circuits to improve the quality of transmission. Reduces attenuation and delay distortion.

Cable Assembly of one or more conductors (usually wire) within an enveloping protective sheath.

Cable Television See **CATV.**

Call-back Modem A modem that can be activated only with a password. When a user calls, the modem disconnects the call after receiving the password and calls back to the caller's predefined telephone number to establish a connection. Used in **Dial-back Only Facilities.**

Call Detail Recording (CDR) A private branch exchange (PBX) feature to keep track of telephone call costs so they can be charged to the proper department. Also called *Station Message Detail Recording (SMDR)*.

Call Management System A system that monitors voice calls in organizations to keep track of call traffic and other factors relevant to voice communications.

Camp-on A method of holding a call for a station when a busy condition is experienced, frequently signaling the station that a call is waiting, and automatically forwarding the call to the desired station when the busy condition is terminated.

Capacitance The ability to store energy such as small amounts of electricity. Capacitors can store and release energy. An inductor is another device with this ability.

Carrier An analog signal at some fixed amplitude and frequency which then is combined with an information-bearing signal to produce an intelligent output signal suitable for transmission of meaningful information. Also called *carrier wave* or *carrier frequency*.

Carrier Frequency The basic frequency or pulse repetition rate of a signal bearing no intelligence until it is modulated by another signal that does impart intelligence.

Carrier Sense Multiple Access See **CSMA/CA** and **CSMA/CD.**

Carrier Wave The basic frequency or pulse repetition rate of a signal bearing no intelligence until it is modulated by another signal that does impart intelligence.

CATV Originally Community Antenna TeleVision. Now also CAble TeleVision. It refers to the use of coaxial cable loops to deliver television or other signals to subscribers.

CBX Computerized Branch eXchange. See **PBX.**

CCITT See **Consultative Committee on International Telegraph and Telephone.**

CCSA See **Common Control Switching Arrangement.**

CD

1. Collision detection in the CSMA (carrier sense multiple access) protocol for local area networks.

2. Carrier detect occurs when a modem detects a carrier signal to be received.

CDMA Code Division Multiple Access. See **Spread Spectrum.**

CDR See **Call Detail Recording.**

Central Computer See **Host Computer.**

Central Office The switching and control facility set up by the local telephone company (common carrier) where the subscriber's local loop terminates. Central offices handle calls within a specified geographic area, which is identified by the first three digits (prefix) of the telephone number. Also called an *end office* or *exchange office*. Compare with **Tandem Office** and **Toll Office.**

CENTREX A widespread telephone company switching service that uses dedicated central office switching equipment. CENTREX CPE is where the user site also has Customer Premises Equipment (CPE).

Channel

1. A path for transmission of electromagnetic signals. Synonym for *line* or *link*. Compare with **Circuit.**

2. A data communication path. Channels may be divided into subchannels.

Channel Bank Equipment that performs multiplexing of lower speed, generally digital, channels into a higher speed channel. The equipment typically is in a telephone central office where it is connected to T-1 circuits.

Channel Extender A scaled-down front end that links remote host computers with the central host computer. It is used in place of a front end processor at the host end.

Channel Service Unit (CSU) A unit that can be called a *digital modem*. It performs transmit and receive filtering, signal shaping, longitudinal balancing, voltage isolation, equalization, and remote loopback testing for digital transmission. See also **Data Service Unit.**

Character A member of a set of elements on which agreement has been reached and which is used for the organization, control, or representation of data. Characters may be letters, digits, punctuation marks, or other symbols. Also called a *byte*.

Character Parity A technique of adding a redundant bit to a character code to provide error checking capability.

Cheapernet See **Thin Ethernet.**

Checking, Echo A method of checking the accuracy of transmitted data in which the received data are returned to the sending end for comparison with the original data.

Checking, Parity A check that tests whether the number of ones in an array of binary digits is odd (or even).

Checking, Polynomial A checking method using polynomial functions of the data transmitted to test for changes in data in transmission. Also called *cyclical redundancy check* (CRC). See also **CRC.**

CICS Customer Information Control System. CICS is the most widely used teleprocessing monitor program, and it resides in IBM host computers.

CIM Computer Integrated Manufacturing. A specification that integrates computers into the manufacturing, design, and business functions of an organization. See also **MAP.**

Circuit The path over which the voice, data,

or image transmission travels. Circuits can be twisted wire pairs, coaxial cables, fiber optic cables, microwave transmissions, and so forth. Compare with **Channel, Line,** and **Link.**

Circuit Loading   See **Line Loading.**

Circuit Switched Digital Capability (CSDC)   AT&T's dial-up service using full duplex, 56,000 bits per second digital circuits on an end-to-end basis. Also known as *ACCUNET Switched 56.*

Circuit Switching   A method of communications whereby an electrical connection between calling and called stations is established on demand for exclusive use of the circuit until the connection is terminated.

CIU   See **Communication Interface Unit.**

Cladding   A layer of material (usually glass) that surrounds the glass core of an optical fiber. Prevents loss of signal by reflecting light back into the core.

Class X Office   Hierarchical designation of telephone company switching facilities according to functions. Class 5 is an end office, Class 4 is a toll center, Class 3 is a primary center, Class 2 is a sectional center, and Class 1 is a regional center.

CLEAR TO SEND   See **CTS.**

Client   A microcomputer that connects to a local area network. Other names for it are user microcomputer, station, node, or workstation.

Cluster Controller   A device that controls the input/output operations of the cluster of devices (microcomputers, terminals, printers, and so forth) attached to it. Also called a *terminal controller.* For example, the 3274 Control Unit is a cluster controller that directs all communications between the host computer and remote devices attached to it.

Coaxial Cable   An insulated wire that runs through the middle of a cable. A second braided wire surrounds the insulation of the inner wire like a sheath. Used on local area networks for transmitting messages between devices.

Code   A transformation or representation of information in a different form according to some set of preestablished conventions. See also **ASCII, EBCDIC, BCD,** and **Baudot.**

Code Conversion   A hardware box or software that converts from one code to another, such as from ASCII to EBCDIC.

Common Carrier   An organization in the business of providing regulated telephone, telegraph, telex, and data communication services. This term is applied most often to U.S. and Canadian commercial organizations, but sometimes it is used to refer to telecommunication entities (such as government-operated suppliers of communication services) in other countries. In the United States, the prices these organizations charge are regulated by the U.S. Federal Communications Commission or state public utility commissions. See also **PTT.**

Common Control Switching Arrangement (CCSA)   A dedicated switched network leased by a user organization to handle communication requirements among its various locations.

Communication Interface Unit (CIU)   A device that provides the physical connection to the local area network. May also be called a *medium access unit* (MAU), a *Multistation Access Unit* (MAU), or a *transceiver.*

Communication Satellite   An earth satellite that acts as a telecommunication radio relay. Most communication satellites are in geosynchronous orbit approximately 22,300 miles above the equator, so they appear from earth to be stationary in space.

Communication Services   The population or entire group of all transmission facilities that are available for lease or purchase.

Compaction   In Systems Network Architecture, the transformation of data by packing two characters into one byte. The most frequently sent characters are compacted.

Comparison Risk Ranking   The process by which the members of a Delphi team reach a consensus on which threats to a network have the highest risk value. It produces an ordinally ranked list arranged from high risk to low risk.

Component One of the specific pieces of a network, system, or application. When these components are assembled together, they become the network, system, or application. Components are the individual parts of the network that we want to safeguard or restrict by using controls.

Compression In Systems Network Architecture, the replacement of a string of up to 64 repeated characters by an encoded control byte to reduce the length of the data stream sent to the LU-LU session partner. The encoded control byte is followed by the character that was repeated (unless that character is the prime compression character, typically the space character). Many other compression hardware and software schemes are available. See also **Data Compression.**

Computerized Branch Exchange (CBX) See **PBX.**

COMSAT Communications Satellite Corporation, a private U.S. company established by statute as the exclusive international satellite carrier and representing the United States in INTELSAT.

Concentrator A device that multiplexes several low speed communication circuits onto a single high speed trunk. A Remote Data Concentrator (RDC) is similar in function to a multiplexer but differs because the host computer software usually must be rewritten to accommodate the RDC. RDCs differ from statistical multiplexers because the total capacity of the high speed outgoing circuit, in characters per second, is equal to the total capacity of the incoming low speed circuits. On the other hand, output capacity of a statistical multiplexer (stat mux) is less than the total capacity of the incoming circuits.

Conditioning A technique of applying electronic filtering elements to a communication line to improve the capability of that line so it can support higher data transmission rates. See also **Equalization.**

Configuration The actual or practical layout of a network that takes into account its software, hardware, and cabling. Configurations may be multidrop, point-to-point, local area networks, and the like. By contrast, a topology is the geometric layout (ring, bus, star) of the configuration. Topologies are the building blocks of configurations. Compare with **Topology.**

Connector Cable The cable that goes between the terminal and the modem. It is usually either the RS232 or RS449 standard.

Constant Ratio or **M-of-N** A code in which the ratio of 1s and 0s in each character is maintained constant such as four 0s and four 1s.

Consultative Committee on International Telegraph and Telephone (CCITT) An international organization that sets worldwide communication standards.

Contention A "dispute" between two or more devices over the use of a common channel at the same time.

Control A mechanism, the purpose of which is to ensure that the threats to a network are mitigated or stopped and the components of a network are safeguarded, restricted, or protected. Controls ensure that the organization's assets are not exposed to undue risk. Controlling both threats and components reduces the organization's exposure to risk to an acceptable level. There are two levels of controls: system level controls and application level controls. See also **Application Level Control** and **System Level Control.**

Control Character A character whose occurrence in a particular context initiates, modifies, or stops a control operation.

Control Spreadsheet A two-dimensional matrix showing a three-way relationship between the controls in a network, the threats that are being mitigated, and the components that are being protected. The cells in a Control

Spreadsheet represent the exposures faced by the organization, and the controls listed in each cell represent the specific control enacted to reduce or eliminate the exposure. A Control Spreadsheet is a pictorial representation of the network and its controls.

COS   Corporation for Open Systems. An organization of computer and communication equipment vendors and users formed to accelerate the introduction of products based on the seven-layer OSI model. Its primary interest is the application layer (layer 7) of the OSI model and the X.400 electronic mail standard.

CPE   Customer Premises Equipment. Extra equipment the user purchases to enhance its CENTREX system. See also **CENTREX.**

cps   Characters per second. A data rate unit used where circuits carry bits forming a data character.

CPU   Central Processing Unit.

CRC   Cyclical Redundancy Check. An error checking control technique using a specific binary prime divisor that results in a unique remainder. It usually is a 16- to 32-bit error checking character.

CRT   Cathode Ray Tube. Commonly refers to a video monitor that uses a cathode ray tube for its screen display. Compare with **VDU.**

CSMA/CA   Carrier Sense Multiple Access (CSMA) with Collision Avoidance (CA). This protocol is similar to the Carrier Sense Multiple Access (CSMA) with Collision Detection (CD) protocol. Whereas CSMA/CD sends a data packet and then reports back if it collides with another packet, CSMA/CA sends a small preliminary packet to determine whether the network is busy. If there is a collision, it is with the small packet rather than with the entire message. CA is thought to be more efficient because it reduces the time required to recover from collisions.

CSMA/CD   Carrier Sense Multiple Access (CSMA) with Collision Detection (CD). A system used in contention networks. The net-

work interface unit listens for the presence of a carrier before attempting to send and detects the presence of a collision by monitoring for a distorted pulse.

CSU   See **Channel Service Unit.**

CTS   CLEAR TO SEND. A control signal between a modem and a controller used to operate over a connector cable.

Customer Information Control System   See **CICS.**

Customer Premises Equipment (CPE)   Equipment that provides the interface between the customer's CENTREX system and the telephone network. It physically resides at the customer's site rather than the telephone company's end office. CPE generally refers to voice telephone equipment instead of data transmission equipment.

Cyclical Redundancy Check   See **CRC.**

D Type Conditioning   A North American term for a type of conditioning that controls harmonic distortion and signal-to-noise ratio so they lie within specified limits.

DAA   Data Access Arrangement. A telephone switching system protective device used to attach uncertified telephone company equipment to the carrier network. Its purpose is to protect telephone company equipment at the end office.

DACS   See **Digital Access and Cross-Connect System.**

Data

1.   Specific individual facts or a list of such items.

2.   Facts from which conclusions can be drawn.

Data Circuit Terminating Equipment   See **DCE.**

Data Communications

1.   The movement of encoded information by means of electrical or optical transmission systems.

2.   The transmission of data from one point to another.

Data Compression The technique that provides for the transmission of fewer data bits without the loss of information. The receiving location expands the received data bits into the original bit sequence. See also **Compression.**

Data-over-Voice (DOV) When data and voice share the same transmission medium. Data transmissions are superimposed over the voice bandwidth.

Data Protectors Devices that protect the telephone company circuits from extraneous electrical signals. They limit the amount of power that can be transmitted to the telephone company central office.

Data Service Unit (DSU) A Channel Service Unit that, in addition, provides bipolar conversion functions to ensure proper signal shaping and adequate signal strength. It, too, is a form of digital modem. See also **Channel Service Unit.**

Data Set

1. In data communications a term generally synonymous with modem, which is a device that allows a digital terminal to transmit and receive data over an analog communication channel.

2. In data processing, a file of data.

DATA SET READY See **DSR.**

Data Sink See **DTE.**

Data Terminal Equipment See **DTE.**

Database A set of logically connected files that have a common access. They are the sum total of all the data items that exist for several related systems. In other words, a database might have several data items that can be assembled into many different record types.

Datagram An Ethernet packet.

db See **Decibel.**

DB-9, DB-15, DB-25, DB-37, DB-50 Refers to plugs with 9, 15, 25, 37, and 50 pins, respectively. The DB refers to the physical shape of the connector plug. DB-9 plugs into the COM1 serial port and CGA/EGA video cards/monitors. DB-15 plugs into the IBM PS/2 series and VGA video cards/monitors. DB-25 is a common RS232 connector that plugs into modems. DB-37 is the RS449 connector that plugs into modems. DB-50 is a connector plug used with host mainframes.

dBm Power-level measurement unit in the telephone industry based on 600 ohms impedance and 1000 hertz frequency. Zero dBm is 1 milliwatt at 1000 hertz terminated by 600 ohms impedance. See also **Decibel.**

DBX Digital PBX. An all-digital switchboard.

DCE Data Circuit Terminating Equipment. The equipment installed at the user's site that provides all the functions required to establish, maintain, and terminate a connection, including the signal conversion and coding between the data terminal equipment (DTE) and the common carrier's line. It usually is the modem.

DDD See **Direct Distance Dialing.**

DDS AT&T's Digital Data Service for transmitting data digitally.

Decibel (dB) A tenth of a bel. A unit for measuring relative strength of a signal parameter such as power and voltage. The number of decibels is ten times the logarithm (base 10) of the ratio of the power of two signals, or ratio of the power of one signal to a reference level. The reference level always must be indicated, such as 1 milliwatt for power ratio.

Dedicated Circuit A leased communication circuit that goes from your site to some other location. It is a clear unbroken communication path that is yours to use 24 hours per day, seven days per week. Also called a *private circuit* or *leased circuit.*

Delay Distortion A distortion on communication lines that is caused by the different propagation speeds of signals at different frequencies. Some frequencies travel more slowly than others in a given transmission medium and, therefore, arrive at the destination at slightly different times. Delay distortion is measured in microseconds of delay relative to the delay at 1700 Hz. This type of distortion does not affect voice, but it can have a serious effect on data transmissions.

Delay Equalizer   A corrective device for making the phase delay or envelope delay of a circuit substantially constant over a desired frequency range. See also **Equalizer.**

Delphi Group   A small group of experts (three to nine people) who meet to develop a consensus when it may be impossible or too expensive to collect more accurate data. For example, a Delphi group of communication experts might assemble to reach a consensus on the various threats to a communication network, the potential dollar losses for each occurrence of each threat, and the estimated frequency of occurrence for each threat.

DES   Data Encryption Standard. DES, the most widely used encryption algorithm, uses a 64-bit key. It was developed by IBM and the U.S. National Institute of Standards and Technology (formerly the National Bureau of Standards) and endorsed by the American Banking Association.

Dial-back Only Facilities   Used to prevent security breaches. When a user calls and provides a password, the modem breaks the connection and dials back to a predefined telephone number that matches the password. This technique prevents unauthorized terminals from gaining access to a network.

Dial Tone   A 90 Hz signal (the difference between 350 Hz and 440 Hz) sent to an operator or subscriber indicating that the receiving end is ready to receive dial pulses.

Dial-Up Telephone Network   See **Direct Distance Dialing.**

Dibit   A group of two bits in which each possible dibit is encoded as one of four unique signals. The four possible states for dibits are 00, 01, 10, and 11.

Digital Access and Cross-Connect System (DACS)   Another name for a digital cross-connect switch.

Digital Cross-Connect Switch   Used by long distance common carriers to establish 56,000 bits per second circuit connections for organizations on an as-needed basis. May be called a *Digital Access and Cross-Connect System* (DACS). See also **Bandwidth-on-Demand.**

Digital Modem   See **Channel Service Unit.**

Digital Network Architecture (DNA)   The byte-oriented framework within which Digital Equipment Corporation designs and develops its communication products for networking and distributed data processing. DNA is based on layers, many of which are similar to the OSI model.

Digital PBX   A PBX (switchboard) designed to switch digital signals. Telephones used in a digital PBX must digitize the voice signals. Computers and terminals can communicate directly through the digital PBX which functions as a point-to-point local area network.

Digital Signal   A discrete or discontinuous signal whose various states are discrete intervals apart, such as $+15$ volts and -15 volts.

Digital Termination System   See **DTS.**

DIP Switch   Switches for opening and closing leads between two devices, such as microcomputers or printers. Usually located on circuit boards.

Direct Current (dc)   The electrical current used for digital signaling.

Direct Distance Dialing (DDD)   A telephone exchange service that enables the telephone user to call other subscribers outside the local area without operator assistance. In the United Kingdom and some other countries, this is called *subscriber trunk dialing* (STD).

Discrete Files   A set of data items and record types for one specific application. A discrete file is a separate, individual file for one application.

Diskette   A disk for storing microcomputer files made of thin, flexible plastic and enclosed in a protective jacket. The most popular sizes are 5¼ inches and 3½ inches. Also called *floppy disk.*

Distortion The unwanted modification or change of signals from their true form by some characteristic of the communication line or equipment being used for transmission, for example, delay distortion and amplitude distortion.

Distortion Types

1. *Bias:* a type of distortion resulting when the intervals of modulation do not all have exactly their normal durations.

2. *Characteristic:* distortion caused by transients (disturbances) which, as a result of modulation, are present in the transmission circuit.

3. *Delay:* distortion occurring when the envelope delay of a circuit is not consistent over the frequency range required for transmission.

4. *End:* distortion of start-stop signals. The shifting of the end of all marking pulses from their proper positions in relation to the beginning of the start pulse.

5. *Jitter:* a type of distortion that results in the intermittent shortening or lengthening of the signals. This distortion is entirely random in nature and can be caused by hits on the line.

6. *Harmonic:* the resultant process of harmonic frequencies (due to nonlinear characteristics of a transmission circuit) in the response when a sinusoidal stimulus is applied.

Distributed Data Processing (DDP) Remote communications are required to accomplish a computer-based task. A network of geographically dispersed, but logically connected, data processing nodes with sharing of network server, printers, host applications, databases, and so forth. Contrast with **Telecommunications.**

DOS Disk Operating System. A program or set of programs that instructs an IBM or IBM compatible disk-based computing system to schedule and supervise work, manage computer resources, and operate and control peripheral devices, including disk drives, keyboards, video monitors and screens, and printers. The most popular operating systems for PCs are MS-DOS from Microsoft (Bellevue, Washington) and PC-DOS from IBM.

Download The process of loading software and data into the nodes of a network from the central node. Downloading usually refers to the movement of data from a host mainframe computer to a remote terminal or microcomputer.

Drop In data communications, the connection made for a terminal on a transmission line. Also called a *node* or *station*. See also **Multidrop.**

DSR Data Set Ready. A modem indicates it is ready to function by raising a DSR signal. Pin 6 of the 25-pin RS232 connector indicates that the modem is on and ready to operate by sending the signal from the modem to the microcomputer's DTE side.

DSU See **Data Service Unit.**

DTE Data Terminal Equipment. Equipment comprising the data source, the data sink, or both that provides for the communication control function (protocol). Data termination equipment is actually any piece of equipment at which a communication path begins or ends, such as a terminal. The data sink is the receiving device.

DTS Digital Termination System. A form of local loop. It connects private homes or business locations to the common carrier switching facility.

Dual Cable A two-cable system in local area networks in which the cable provides two physical paths for transmission, one for transmitting and one for receiving, instead of dividing the capacity of a single cable.

Duplexing An alternative to the process of mirroring, which occurs when a database server mirrors or backs up the database with each transaction. In mirroring, the server writes on two different hard disks on the same disk channel. Duplexing is more redundant, and therefore even safer than mirroring, because the database is written to two different hard disks on two different disk channels. Compare with **Mirroring.**

E-Mail   See **Electronic Mail.**

EBCDIC   Extended Binary Coded Decimal Interchange Code. A standard code consisting of a set of 8-bit characters used for information representation and interchange among data processing and communication systems. Very common in IBM equipment.

Echo Cancellation   Used in higher speed modems to isolate and filter out (cancel) echoes when half duplex transmissions use stop and wait ARQ (Automatic Repeat reQuest) protocols. Needed especially for satellite links.

Echo Checking   See **Checking, Echo.**

Echo Suppressor   A device for use in a two-way telephone channel (especially circuits over 900 miles long) to attenuate echo currents in one direction caused by telephone currents in the other direction. This is done by sending an appropriate disabling tone to the circuit.

Echoplex   A method of checking data transmission accuracy by returning characters to the sending station for verification of data integrity. Also called *echo checking*.

ECMA   See **European Computer Manufacturers Association.**

EDI   See **Electronic Data Interchange.**

EIA   See **Electronic Industries Association.**

802 Standards   See **IEEE 802.1, IEEE 802.2,** and so on.

Electron   An elementary particle made of a tiny charge of negative electricity.

Electronic Data Interchange (EDI)   Electronic Data Interchange for Administration, Commerce, and Transport. Standardizes the electronic interchange of business documents for both ASCII and graphics. Endorsed by ISO. Defines major components of the ANSI X.12 EDI standard.

Electronic Industries Association (EIA)   Composed of electronic manufacturers in the United States. Recommends standards for electrical and functional characteristics of interface equipment. Belongs to the American National Standards Institute (ANSI). Known for the RS232 interface connector cable standard.

Electronic Mail (E-Mail)   A networking application that allows users to send and receive mail electronically.

Electronic Switching System (ESS)   A type of telephone switching system that uses a special purpose stored program digital computer to direct and control the switching operation. ESS makes possible custom calling services such as speed dialing, call transfer, and three-way calling.

Emulate   When changing from one computer to a ''new generation'' computer, existing programs frequently cannot run on the new equipment. To save the cost of reprogramming, computer vendors provide software and hardware (emulators) that accept old programs and translate them to the new computer's machine language. In other words, the new computer equals the old computer's ability to run the programs.

Encapsulation   A technique in which a frame from one network is placed within the data field portion of the frame in another network for transmission on the second network. For example, it enables a message initiated on a coaxial cable-based Ethernet local area network to be transmitted over a FDDI fiber optic-based network and then placed onto another Ethernet LAN at the other end.

Encryption   The technique of modifying a known bit stream on a transmission circuit so that it appears to an unauthorized observer to be a random sequence of bits.

End Office   The telephone company switching office for the interconnection of calls. See also **Central Office.**

ENQ   A control character used in ASCII and EBCDIC data communication to indicate an inquiry.

Enterprise-Wide Network   The network that results when all the networks in a single organization are connected together.

Envelope Delay Distortion   A derivative of the circuit phase shift with respect to the frequency. This distortion affects the time it takes for different frequencies to propagate the length of a communication circuit so that two signals arrive at different times.

EOB   A control character used in ASCII and EBCDIC data communications to indicate end of block.

EOT   A control character used in ASCII and EBCDIC data communications to indicate end of transmission. It terminates the transmission.

Equalization   The process of reducing frequency and phase distortion of a circuit by introducing time differences to compensate for the difference in attenuation or time delay at the various frequencies in the transmission band.

Equalizer   Any combination (usually adjustable) of coils, capacitors, or resistors inserted in the transmission circuit or amplifier to improve its frequency response.

Error Control   An arrangement that detects the presence of errors. In some networks, refinements are added that correct the detected errors, either by operations on the received data or by retransmission from the source.

ESS   See **Electronic Switching System.**

Ethernet™   A 10 million bits per second local area network developed by the Xerox Corporation. It uses coaxial cable or twisted pair wires to connect the stations. See also **IEEE 802.3.**

ETX   A control character used in ASCII and EBCDIC data communications to mean end of text.

European Computer Manufacturers Association (ECMA)   Recommends standards for computer components manufactured or used in Europe. Belongs to the International Organization for Standardization (ISO).

Exchange Office   See **Central Office.**

Exposure   The calculated or estimated loss resulting from the occurrence of a threat, as in "The loss from theft could be $42,000 this year." It can be either tangible and therefore measurable in dollars, or intangible and therefore not directly measurable in dollars. You compute a tangible exposure by multiplying the threat's "rate of occurrence" by its "loss per occurrence." You measure an intangible exposure by using a Delphi team and an ordinal risk assessment methodology to arrive at a consensus opinion on the relative risk that threat presents to the organization. See also **Comparison Risk Ranking.**

Extended Binary Coded Decimal Interchange Code   See **EBCDIC.**

Facsimile (FAX)   A system for the transmission of images. The image is scanned at the transmitter, reconstructed at the receiving station, and printed on paper.

FAX   See **Facsimile.**

FCC   See **Federal Communications Commission.**

FCS   See **Frame Check Sequence.**

FDDI   See **Fiber Distributed Data Interface.**

FDM   Frequency division multiplexing. See **Multiplexer.**

FDX   See **Full Duplex.**

Feasibility Study   A study undertaken to determine the possibility or probability of improving the existing system within a reasonable cost. Determines what the problem is and what its causes are, and makes recommendations for solving the problem.

FEC   See **Forward Error Correction.**

Federal Communications Commission (FCC)   A board of seven commissioners appointed by the U.S. President under the Communication Act of 1934, having the power to regulate all interstate and foreign electrical communication systems originating in the United States.

Femtosecond   One quadrillionth of a second (1/1,000,000,000,000,000) or 10^{-15}.

FEP   See **Front End Processor.**

Fiber Distributed Data Interface (FDDI)   A token-ring local area network technology that permits transmission speeds of 100 million bits per second using fiber optic cables (ANSI standard X3T9.5).

Fiber Optic Cable   A transmission medium that uses glass or plastic cable instead of copper wires.

Fiber Optics   A transmission technology in which modulated visible lightwave signals containing information are sent down hair-thin plastic or glass fibers and demodulated back into electrical signals at the other end by a special light-sensitive receiver.

Firmware   A set of software instructions set permanently or semipermanently into a read only memory (ROM). Compare with **Hardware, Shelfware, Software** and **Vaporware.**

Floppy Disk   See **Diskette.**

Flow Control   The capability of the network nodes to manage buffering schemes that allow devices of different data transmission speeds to communicate with each other.

Foreign Exchange Service (FX)   A service that connects a customer's telephone to a remote exchange. This service provides the equivalent of local telephone service to and from the distant exchange.

Forward Channel   A channel in which the direction of data transmission coincides with the direction of the information transfer.

Forward Error Correction (FEC)   A technique that identifies errors at the received station and au-

tomatically corrects those errors without retransmitting the message.

Four-Wire Circuit   A circuit using two pairs of conductors, one pair for the "go" channel and the other pair for the "return" channel. A telephone circuit carries voice signals both ways. In local loops this two-way transmission is achieved over two wires because the waveforms traveling in each direction can be distinguished. In trunk networks, where amplifiers are needed at intervals and multiplexing is common, it is easier to separate the two directions of transmission and effectively use a pair of wires for each direction. At this point it is a four-wire circuit. Contrast with **Two-Wire Circuit.**

Fractional T-1   A portion of a T-1 circuit. A full T-1 allows transmission at 1,544,000 bits per second. A fractional T-1 circuit allows transmission at lower speeds of 384,000, 512,000, or 768,000 bits per second. See also **T-1 Circuit.**

Frame   Generally a group of data bits having an 8-bit flag at each end to indicate the beginning and end of the frame. Frames also contain source addresses, destination addresses, frame type identifiers, and a data message. A frame may encapsulate a packet, or it may carry its data message without the message first being placed in a packet.

Frame Check Sequence (FCS)   Used for error checking in bit-oriented protocols like X.25. FCS uses a 16-bit field with cyclical redundancy checking for error detection with retransmission.

Frequency   The rate at which a current alternates, measured in hertz, kilohertz, megahertz, and so forth. Other units of measure are cycles, kilocycles, or megacycles; hertz and cycles per second are synonymous. See also **Sine Wave.**

Frequency Division Multiplexing   See **Multiplexer.**

Frequency Modulation   See **Modulation, Frequency.**

Front End Processor (FEP)   An auxiliary processor

that is placed between a computer's central processing unit and the transmission facilities. This device normally handles housekeeping functions like circuit management and code translation, which otherwise would interfere with efficient operation of the central processing unit.

FSK Frequency Shift Keying. A modulation technique whereby 0 and 1 are represented by a different frequency and the amplitude does not vary.

Full Duplex (FDX) The capability of transmission in both directions at one time. Contrast with **Half Duplex** and **Simplex.**

FX See **Foreign Exchange Service.**

Gateway A device that connects two dissimilar networks. Allows networks of different vendors to communicate by translating one vendor's protocol into another. See also **Bridge, Router,** and **Brouter.**

Gaussian Noise See **Noise, Gaussian.**

Geosynchronous Orbit A satellite's orbit that is over the equator and traveling in the same direction as the earth's surface, so that the satellite appears to be stationary over a point on the earth.

GHz Gigahertz. One gigahertz is equal to one billion cycles per second in a frequency.

Gigabyte One billion bytes.

GOSIP See **Government Open Systems Interconnection Protocol.**

Government Open Systems Interconnection Protocol (GOSIP) A subset of the OSI seven-layer model protocols that vendors must satisfy when bidding on U.S. government networking Requests for Proposals (RFPs). Its main features relate to E-mail using the X.400 standard and file transfer over T-1 circuits. GOSIP supports IEEE 802.3 (Ethernet) over baseband or broadband, IEEE 802.4 (token bus) over 10 million bits per second broadband or 5 million bits per second baseband, IEEE 802.5

(Token-Ring), and X.25 packet switched networks.

Group 4 Fax The newest and fastest international standard for facsimile machines. It specifies 64,000 bits per second, which can work only on digital channels. It takes six seconds to transmit one page.

Guardband A small bandwidth of frequency that separates two voice grade circuits. Also the frequencies between subchannels in FDM systems that guard against subchannel interference.

Hacker A person who sleuths for passwords to gain illegal access to important computer files. Hackers may rummage through corporate trash cans looking for carelessly discarded printouts.

Half Duplex (HDX) A circuit that permits transmission of a signal in two directions but not at the same time. Contrast with **Full Duplex** and **Simplex.**

Hamming Code A forward error correction (FEC) technique named for its inventor.

Handshaking Exchange of predetermined signals when a connection is established between two data set devices. This is used to establish the circuit and message path.

Hardware The pieces of equipment that are put in place to form a network. Compare with **Firmware, Shelfware, Software,** and **Vaporware.**

HDLC See **High-level Data Link Control.**

HDX See **Half Duplex.**

Hertz (Hz) Same as cycles per second; for example, 3000 hertz is 3000 cycles per second.

High-level Data Link Control (HDLC) A bit-oriented protocol in which control of data links is specified by series of bits rather than by control characters (bytes). Used in ISDN circuits. Matches layer 2 of the OSI model. Approved by the CCITT.

Host Computer In data communications, the mainframe computer that lies at the center of the network. It generally performs the basic centralized data processing functions for which the network was designed. The host used to be where the network communication control functions took place, but today these functions tend to take place in the front end processor or further out in the network. Also called a *central computer*. In a local area network, the server may be the host.

Hotline A service that provides direct connection between customers in various cities using a dedicated circuit.

Hybrid Network A local area network or wide area network with a mixture of topologies and access methods.

Hz Hertz. The number of cycles per second in a frequency. One hertz is equal to one cycle per second.

Idle Character A transmitted character indicating "no information" that does not manifest itself as part of a message at the destination point.

IEEE See **Institute of Electrical and Electronics Engineers.**

IEEE 802.1 The basic IEEE specification for local area networks. It provides the basis for network architecture, network management, and internetworking.

IEEE 802.2 The data link layer (OSI model layer 2) specification for the IEEE 802.3, IEEE 802.4, and IEEE 802.5 physical access methods.

IEEE 802.3 The standard for local area networks using the carrier sense multiple access/collision detection (CSMA/CD) access method. It has become popular because of its use in Ethernet local area networks (Ethernet).

IEEE 802.4 The standard for local area networks using the token-passing bus access method (token bus).

IEEE 802.5 The standard for local area networks using the token-passing ring access method (token ring).

IEEE 802.6 The standard for metropolitan area networks (MANs).

IEEE 802.7 The standard for broadband local area networks.

IEEE 802.8 The standard for local area networks using fiber optic cables.

IEEE 802.9 The standard for local area networks using Integrated Services Digital Networks (ISDNs).

Impedance A measure of the electrical property of resistance; the amount of opposition offered by a circuit to the flow of a carrier wave. In other words, some of the energy is reflected back, which shows as a loss of power when the impedance is mismatched between two cables. Common impedances are 50, 75, 93, and 300 ohms. The resistance, inductance, and capacitance of a transmission circuit combine to give the value of its impedance.

Impulse Noise See **Noise, Impulse.**

In-Band Signaling The transmission signaling information at some frequency or frequencies that lie within a carrier channel normally used for information transmission.

Inductance The amount of stored and released electrical energy. An inductance filter provides filtering action by opposing changes in the electrical current. It helps to average out the carrier wave by keeping it from reaching either its maximum or minimum power values. Capacitors also have this ability.

Information A meaningful aggregation of data. Contrast with **Data.**

Institute of Electrical and Electronics Engineers (IEEE) A professional organization for engineers in the United States. Issues standards and belongs to the American National Standards Institute (ANSI) and the International Organization for Standardization (ISO).

Integrated Services Digital Network See **ISDN.**

Intelligent Terminal Controller A microprocessor-based intelligent device that controls a group of terminals.

INTELSAT The International Telecommunications Satellite Consortium established in 1964 to establish a global communication satellite system.

Interactive Voice Response (IVR) A telephone call receiving unit that permits callers to select the information they want by pressing the appropriate number on their telephone keypad. It enables an organization to offer various options for callers so they can receive specific information automatically.

Interexchange Channel (IXC) A channel or circuit between end offices (central offices).

InterLATA Circuits that cross from one LATA (local access and transport area) into another.

Intermodulation Distortion An analog line impairment whereby two frequencies create a third erroneous frequency, which in turn distorts the data signal representation.

Internet Two networks that are connected together.

Internetworking Connecting several networks together so workstations can address messages to the workstations on each of the other networks.

Interoperability The interconnection of dissimilar networks in a manner that allows them to operate as though they were similar.

IntraLATA Circuits that are totally within one LATA (local access transport area).

Inverse Multiplexer Hardware that takes one high speed transmission and divides it among several transmission channels. See also **Bandwidth-on-Demand.**

ISDN Integrated Services Digital Network. A hierarchy of digital switching and transmission systems. The ISDN provides voice, data, and image in a unified manner. It is synchronized so all digital elements speak the same ''language'' at the same speed. See also **Basic Access Service** and **Primary Access Service.**

ISO International Organization for Standardization, Geneva, Switzerland. The initials ISO stand for its French name. This international standards-making body is best known in data communications for developing the internationally recognized seven-layer network model called the Open Systems Interconnection (OSI) Reference Model. See also **OSI Model.**

IVR See **Interactive Voice Response.**

IXC See **Interexchange Channel.**

Jack The physical connecting device at the interface which mates with a compatible receptacle—a plug. See also **RJ-11** and **RJ-45.**

Jitter Type of analog communication line distortion caused by the variation of a signal from its reference timing positions, which can cause data transmission errors, particularly at high speeds. This variation can be amplitude, time, frequency, or phase.

Jumbo Group Six U.S. master groups frequency division multiplexed together in the Bell System. A jumbo group can carry 3,600 telephone calls on one channel. Compare with **Master Group** and **Supergroup.**

Jumper

1. A small connector that fits over a set of pins on a microcomputer circuit card.

2. A patch cable or wire used to establish a circuit for testing or diagnostics.

K A standard quantity measurement of computer storage. A K is defined loosely as 1,000 bytes. In fact, it is 1,024 bytes, which is the equivalent of two raised to the tenth power.

Kbps Kilobits per second. A data rate equal to 10^3 bps (1000 bps).

Key Management The process of controlling the secret keys used in encryption.

Key Set A telephone instrument designed to provide push-button or switch selection of a specific telephone from several possible incoming circuits.

Key Telephone System (KTS) Key station or key equipment. A KTS has multiline telephone

Customer Premises Equipment that offers limited PBX-type features. It generally has from 2 to 12 trunk lines and from 4 to 40 extensions.

KHz Kilohertz. One kilohertz is equal to 1,000 cycles per second in a frequency.

Kilobits per Second See **Kbps.**

Kilometer A metric measurement equal to 0.621 mile or 3,280.8 feet.

Ku Band The frequency range between 12 and 14 GHz used for satellite communications.

LAN See **Local Area Network.**

Large-Scale Integration See **LSI.**

Laser Light Amplification by Stimulated Emission of Radiation. A device that transmits an extremely narrow and coherent beam of electromagnetic energy in the visible light spectrum. (Coherent means that the separate waves are in phase with one another rather than jumbled as in normal light.)

LATA Local Access Transport Area. One of approximately 200 local telephone service areas in the United States, roughly paralleling major metropolitan areas. (LATA boundaries originally were based on the Standard Metropolitan Statistical Areas—SMSAs—but the Bureau of Census no longer uses the SMSA designation. The LATA boundaries do not necessarily coincide with those of the newer Consolidated Metropolitan Statistical Areas—CMSAs.) The LATA subdivisions were established as a result of the AT&T/Bell divestiture to distinguish local from long distance service. Circuits with both end points within the LATA (intraLATA) generally are the sole responsibility of the local telephone company. Circuits that cross outside the LATA (interLATA) are passed on to an interexchange carrier like AT&T, MCI, or US Sprint.

Leased Circuit A leased communication circuit that goes from your site to some other location. It is a clear, unbroken communication path that is yours to use 24 hours per day, seven days per week. Also called *private circuit* or *dedicated circuit.*

Line A circuit, channel, or link. It carries the data communication signals. An early telephone technology term that may imply a physical connection, such as with a copper wire. Compare with **Channel, Circuit,** and **Link.**

Line Control Codes/Characters The 8-bit characters that control messages. They appear at both the beginning and end of the message to show its beginning and end. They also might appear within the message to show such things as the beginning and end of the text.

Line Loading The total amount of transmission traffic carried by a line or circuit. Usually expressed as a percentage of the total theoretical capacity of that line or circuit. Also may be called *circuit loading.*

Line Protocol A control program used to perform data communication functions over network circuits. Consists of both handshaking and line control functions that move the data between transmit and receive locations.

Link An unbroken circuit path between two points. Sometimes called a *line, circuit,* or *channel.*

Local Area Network (LAN) A network that is located in a small geographic area, such as an office, a building, a complex of buildings, or a campus, and whose communication technology provides a high bandwidth, low cost medium to which many nodes can be connected. These networks typically do not use common carrier circuits, and their circuits do not cross public thoroughfares or property owned by others. LANs are not regulated by the FCC or state PUCs.

Local Exchange Carrier The local telephone company, such as one of the seven Bell Operating Companies (BOCs).

Local Loop The part of a communication circuit between the subscriber's equipment and the equipment in the local central office.

Log

1. A record of everything pertinent to a system function.

2. A collection of messages that provides a history of message traffic.

Logical Sharing The sharing of business applications in which a number of users have access to the same data files.

Logical Unit (LU) In Systems Network Architecture (SNA), a port through which an end user accesses the SNA network to communicate with another end user and through which the end user accesses the functions provided by system services control points (SSCPs). An LU can support at least two sessions—one with a SSCP, and one with another logical unit—and may be capable of supporting many sessions with other logical units.

Logical Unit (LU) Services In Systems Network Architecture (SNA), capabilities in a logical unit to

1. Receive requests from an end user and, in turn, issue requests to the system services control point (SSCP) to perform the requested functions, typically for session initiation.

2. Receive requests from the SSCP, for example, to activate LU-LU sessions via bind session requests.

3. Provide session presentation and other services for LU-LU sessions.

Long Haul Network A network most frequently used to transfer data over distances from several thousand feet to several thousand miles. These networks can use the international telephone network to transport messages over most or part of these distances. Compare with **Wide Area Network.**

Longitudinal Redundancy Check (LRC) A system of error control based on the formation of a block check following preset rules. The check formation rule is applied in the same manner to each character. In a simple case, the LRC is created by forming a parity check on each bit position of all characters in the block. (That is, the first bit of the LRC character cre-

ates odd parity among the 1-bit positions of the characters in the block.)

Loop Current The electrical direct current (dc) from a battery located at the common carrier's end office. It is the presence or absence of this current that allows the automatic switching equipment at the end office to observe (monitor) the telephone set's operating status, such as whether the telephone is off-hook or on-hook.

Loopback Type of diagnostic test in which the transmitted signal is returned to the sending device after passing through a data communication link or network. This test allows a technician or hardware circuit board to compare the returned signal with the transmitted signal to get some sense of what is wrong. Loopbacks often are done by excluding one piece of equipment after another. This allows you to figure out logically what is wrong.

LRC See **Longitudinal Redundancy Check.**

LSI Large-Scale Integration. A type of electronic device comprising many logic elements in one very small package (integrated circuit) to be used for data handling, storage, and processing.

LU See **Logical Unit.**

LU 6.2 In Systems Network Architecture, the set of protocols that makes it possible for applications to communicate directly. It enables **Peer-to-Peer Communications.**

m Milli. The designation for one thousand.

M Mega. The designation for one million as in 3 megabits per second (3 Mbit/s).

M-of-N See **Constant Ratio.**

mA Milliampere. Measurement unit for electric current.

MAC See **Media Access Control.**

Main Distribution Function (MDF) See **Wiring Closet.**

MAN See **Metropolitan Area Network.**

Management Information Base (MIB) The extent of information that can be retrieved from a user microcomputer when using the Simple Network Management Protocol (SNMP) for network management. MIBs are sets of attributes and definitions that pertain to specific network devices.

MAP Manufacturing Automation Protocol. A six-layer protocol model that endorses the IEEE 802.4 token-passing broadband bus local area network designed to transmit at 1, 5, or 10 million bits per second. When MAP is combined with TOP (Technical and Office Protocol), office functions can be integrated. When MAP is combined with CIM (Computer Integrated Manufacturing), manufacturing, design, and business functions can be integrated.

Master Group An assembly of ten Supergroups occupying adjacent bands in the transmission spectrum for simultaneous modulation/demodulation. Compare with **Jumbo Group** and **Supergroup.**

Master Number Hunting A PBX feature that allows a station to seek an open terminal point in a predetermined sequence. In master number hunting, this "station hunting" option is activated by dialing a preset digit.

MAU Either a medium access unit in an Ethernet network or a Multistation Access Unit in an IBM Token-Ring Network. See **Medium Access Unit** and **Multistation Access Unit.**

Mbps A data rate equal to 10^6 bps. Sometimes called megabits per second (1,000,000 bps).

MDF See **Wiring Closet.**

Mean Times See **MTBF, MTTD, MTTF,** and **MTTR.**

Media Access Control (MAC) A protocol that defines how packets are transmitted on a local area network. CSMA/CD, token ring, and token bus are media access methods. See also **CSMA/CD, Token Bus,** and **Token Ring.**

Medium The matter or substance that carries the voice or data transmission. For example, the medium can be copper (wires), glass (fiber optic cables), or air (microwave or satellite).

Medium Access Unit (MAU) A device that connects a microcomputer station to an Ethernet network.

Megabit One million bits.

Megabyte One million bytes.

Mesh Network A network topology in which there is a direct point-to-point connection between every node or station in the network.

Message A communication of information from a source to one or more destinations. A message usually is composed of three parts.

1. A heading, containing a suitable indicator of the beginning of the message together with some of the following information: source, destination, date, time, routing.

2. A body containing the information to be communicated.

3. An ending containing a suitable indicator of the end of the message.

Message Switching An operation in which the entire message being transmitted is switched to the other location without regard to whether the circuits actually are interconnected at the time of your call. This usually involves a message store and forward facility.

Meter A metric measurement equal to 39.37 inches or 3.2808 feet.

Metropolitan Area Network (MAN) A network that encompasses an area of 25 to 50 miles. It usually covers a city-wide area. Because MANs use local area network and fiber optic technologies, transmission speeds can vary from 2 million to 100 million bits per second.

MHz Megahertz. One megahertz is equal to one million cycles per second in a frequency.

MIB See **Management Information Base.**

Microcomputer A complete computer on a microprocessor chip. Also referred to as a PC. It has input, processing, and output capabilities and can support printers, disk storage, and modems. Today it is used as a workstation on networks.

Microprocessor A single or multiple chip set that makes up a microcomputer or is the intelligence contained within a modem, multiplexer, intelligent controller, and so forth. Examples are Intel 80486 and Motorola 68040 chips.

Microsecond One millionth (1/1,000,000) of a second or 10^{-6}.

Milliampere See **mA.**

Millisecond One thousandth (1/1,000) of a second or 10^{-3}.

Minicomputer A computing system with capabilities generally between those of mainframe computers and microcomputers. Often used for specialized tasks.

MIPS One Million Instructions Per Second. Used to describe a computer's processing power.

Mirroring A process in which the database server automatically backs up the disk during each database transaction. During this process, the computer writes on two different hard disks on the same disk channel every time the hard disk is updated. This creates two mirror images of the database data. Disk mirroring can be accomplished only when the database server contains two physical disk drives because the records or data structures are written to both disks simultaneously. Should a problem develop with one disk, the second disk is available instantly with identical information on it. Compare with **Duplexing.**

Mnemonic A group of characters used to assist the human memory. The mnemonic frequently is an acronym.

MNP Microcom Networking Protocol. A proprietary error correcting protocol for modems.

Modem A contraction of the words MOdulator-DEModulator. A modem is a device for performing necessary signal transformation between terminal devices and communication circuits. Modems are used in pairs, one at either end of the communication circuit.

Modem Eliminator A tiny short haul modem used to connect two microcomputers. They can transmit up to 3,000 feet at 9600 bits per second or up to six miles at 1200 bits per second. They get their power through the serial ports. Compare with **Null Modem Cable.**

Modulation, Amplitude The form of modulation in which the amplitude of the carrier is varied in accordance with the instantaneous value of the modulating signal.

Modulation, Frequency A form of modulation in which the frequency of the carrier is varied in accordance with the instantaneous value of the modulating signal.

Modulation, Phase A form of modulation in which the phase of the carrier is varied in accordance with the instantaneous value of the modulating signal.

Modulation, Pulse See **Pulse.**

MTBF Mean Time Between Failures. The statistic developed by vendors to show the reliability of their equipment. It can be an actual calculated figure that generally is more accurate, or it can be a practical (theoretical) figure.

MTTD Mean Time To Diagnose. The time it takes the network testing and problem management staff to diagnose a network problem.

MTTF Mean Time To Fix. The time it takes vendors to remedy a network problem once they arrive on the premises.

MTTR

1. Mean Time To Repair: the combination of Mean Time To Diagnose, Mean Time To Respond, and Mean Time To Fix, indicating the entire length of time it takes to fix a fault in equipment.

2. Mean Time To Respond: the time it takes the vendor to respond when a network problem is reported.

Multidrop (Multipoint) A line or circuit interconnecting several stations/nodes in a sequential fashion.

Multiplexer A device that combines data traffic from several low speed communication circuits onto a single high speed circuit. The two popular types of multiplexing are FDM (frequency division multiplexing) and TDM (time division multiplexing). In FDM, the voice grade link is divided into subchannels, each covering a different frequency range in such a manner that each subchannel can be employed as though it were an individual circuit. In TDM, separate time segments are assigned to each terminal. During these time segments data may be sent without conflicting with data sent from another terminal.

Multiplexing The subdivision of a transmission channel into two or more separate channels. This can be achieved by splitting the frequency range of the channel into narrow frequency bands (*frequency division multiplexing*) or by assigning a given channel successively to several different users at different times (*time division multiplexing*).

Multistation Access Unit (MAU) A multiport connector or concentrator that connects microcomputer stations to an IBM Token-Ring Network.

Multithreading Concurrent processing of more than one message (or similar service requested) by an application program.

MUX Shorthand for multiplexer or multiplexing.

NAK See **Negative Acknowledgment.**

Nanosecond One billionth (1/1,000,000,000) of a second or 10^{-9}.

National Institute of Standards and Technology Formerly the National Bureau of Standards. The agency of the U.S. government responsible for developing information processing standards for the federal government.

NAU See **Network Addressable Unit.**

NCP See **Network Control Program.**

Negative Acknowledgment (NAK) The return signal that reports an error in the message received. The opposite of *ACK,* or acknowledgment.

NETBIOS NETwork Basic Input/Output System. The part of DOS that is the interface between IBM and compatible microcomputers and a network.

NetView IBM's network management program to manage multivendor voice and data networks from the host computer in a Systems Network Architecture environment.

Network

1. A series of points connected by communication channels.

2. The switched telephone network is the network of telephone lines normally used for dialed telephone calls.

3. A private network is a network of communication channels confined to the use of one customer.

Network Addressable Unit (NAU) Components in the path control portion of a Systems Network Architecture network. They are the origin or destination points of information. There are three kinds of host-based network addressable units: logical unit (LU), physical unit (PU), and system services control point (SSCP). Each NAU has a unique network address containing a subarea and an element identifier.

Network Architecture A framework of principles to facilitate the operation, maintenance, and growth of a communication network by isolating the user and the application programs from the details of the network. Protocols and software are packaged together into a usable network architecture system that organizes functions, data formats, and procedures.

Network Control Center (NCC) Any centralized network diagnostic and management control site.

Network Control Program (NCP) The telecommunication access program for front end processors. The NCP controls IBM's Synchronous Data Link Control (SDLC) communications between host computers and remote terminals. It deals with control of the network and manages the allocation, use, and diagnosis of performance of all circuits in the network and the availability of terminals at the remote end of the network. A component of Systems Network Architecture (SNA).

Network Interface Controller   A communication device that allows interconnection of information processing devices to a network.

Network Profile   Every local area network microcomputer has a profile that outlines what resources it has available to other microcomputers in the network and what resources it can use elsewhere in the network.

Network Service   An application available on a network, for example, file storage.

NIST   See **National Institute of Standards and Technology.**

Node   In a description of a network, the point at which the links join input/output devices. The word "node" also has come to mean a switching center in the context of data networks, particularly in the context of packet switching. Also called a *station*.

Noise   The unwanted change in waveform that occurs between two points in a transmission circuit.

Noise, Amplitude   A sudden change in the level of power with differing effects, depending on the type of modulation used by the modem.

Noise, Cross-Talk   Noise resulting from the interchange of signals on two adjacent channels; manifests itself when you hear other people's telephone conversations.

Noise, Echo   The "hollow" or echoing characteristic that is heard on voice grade lines with improper echo suppression.

Noise, Gaussian   Noise that is characterized statistically by a Gaussian, or random, distribution.

Noise, Impulse   Noise caused by individual impulses on the channel.

Noise, Intermodulation   Noise that occurs when signals from two independent lines intermodulate. A new signal forms and falls into a frequency band differing from those of both inputs. The new signal may fall into a frequency band reserved for another signal.

Nonblocking   Describing a switch in which a through traffic path always exists for each attached station. Generically, a switch or PBX switching environment that is designed never to experience a busy condition because of call volume. Contrast with **Blocking.**

Nonprinting Character   A control character that is transmitted as part of the information, but not reproduced on the hard copy.

North American Signal Hierarchy   The signaling format used on T-1 circuits.

NPA   See **Numbering Plan Area.**

NRZ   NonReturn to Zero. A binary encoding and transmission scheme in which 1s and 0s are represented by opposite and alternating high and low voltages, and in which there is no return to a reference (zero) voltage between encoded bits.

NRZI   NonReturn to Zero Inverted. A binary encoding scheme that inverts the signal on a 1 and leaves the signal unchanged for a 0, and in which a change in the voltage state signals a 1 bit and the absence of a change denotes a 0-bit value.

Null Character   A control character that can be inserted into or withdrawn from a sequence of characters without altering the message.

Null Modem Cable   A 6- to 8-foot RS232 cable that makes the two microcomputers connected at each end of the cable think they are talking through modems.

Numbering Plan Area (NPA)   The common carrier's operating area or geographical subdivision. Area code numbers are assigned to each subdivision to facilitate circuit switching.

Octet   A group of eight binary digits operated on as an entity. Also called a *byte*.

Off-Hook   Activation of a telephone set. By extension, a data set automatically answering on a public switched system is said to go "off-hook." The off-hook condition indicates a "busy" condition to incoming calls. The term originated with early telephones that had a "hook" from which the handset was removed when you wanted to start a telephone conversation.

Office, Central or End   The common carrier's switching office closest to the subscriber.

Office, Tandem   A switching office that terminates a tandem trunk circuit.

Office, Toll   A switching office that terminates a toll trunk circuit.

Ohm   A unit of resistance, such that 1 ampere through it produces a potential difference of 1 volt. Ohm's law is applicable to electrical components carrying direct current. It states that the resistance is independent of the current in metallic conductors at a constant temperature and zero magnetic field.

On-Hook   Deactivation of a telephone set. A telephone not in use is "on-hook." The term originated with early telephones that had a "hook" onto which the handset was placed when a telephone conversation ended.

ONA   See **Open Network Architecture.**

Online

1.   Pertaining to equipment or devices under the direct control of a central processing unit.

2.   Pertaining to a user's ability to interact with a computer.

3.   Pertaining to a user's access to a central host computer or a LAN server via a terminal or microcomputer.

Online System   A system in which the input data enters the computer directly from the point of origin or in which output data is transmitted directly to where it is used.

Open Network Architecture (ONA)   The layered protocol model being developed by Bellcore's Open Network Architecture Forum. Its purpose is to promote the interconnection of networks regardless of their hardware or software.

Open Systems Interconnection (OSI) Reference Model   See **OSI Model.**

Open Wire   Communication lines that are not insulated and formed into cables, but mounted on aerial cross arms on utility poles.

Optical Fibers   Hair-thin strands of very pure glass (sometimes plastic) over which light waves travel. They are used as a medium over which information is transmitted.

Ordinal Ranking   The sequencing of network threats or other decision criteria into a series ranked from high to low, as in most risky to least risky.

OSI Model   The seven-layer Open Systems Interconnection (OSI) Reference Model developed by the International Organization for Standardization subcommittee. The OSI model serves as a logical framework of protocols for computer-to-computer communications. Its purpose is to facilitate the interconnection of networks.

Out-of-Band Signaling   A method of signaling which uses a frequency that is within the passband of the transmission facility but outside of a carrier channel normally used for data transmission.

Overhead   Computer time used to keep track of or run the system, as compared with computer time used to process data.

PABX   See **PBX.**

Packet   A group of binary digits, including data and control signals, that is switched as a composite whole. The data, control signals, and error control information are arranged in a specific format. A packet generally is a 128-character block of data.

Packet Assembler/Disassembler   See **PAD.**

Packet Switching   Process whereby messages are broken into finite-size packets that always are accepted by the network. The message packets are forwarded to the other party over a multitude of different circuit paths. At the other end of the circuit, the packets are reassembled into the message, which is then passed on to the receiving terminal.

Packet Switching Network (PSN) A network designed to carry data in the form of packets. The packet and its format are internal to that network. The external interfaces may handle data in different formats, and format conversion may be done by the user's computer.

PAD Packet Assembler/Disassembler. Equipment providing packet assembly and disassembly facilities between asynchronous transmission and the packet switching network.

PAM See **Pulse Amplitude Modulation.**

Parallel Describes the way the internal transfer of binary data takes place within a computer. It may be transmitted as a parallel word, but it is converted to a serial or bit-by-bit data stream for transmission.

Parity Bit A binary bit appended to an array of bits to make the number of 1 bits always be odd or even for an individual character. For example, odd parity may require three 1 bits and even parity may require four 1 bits.

Parity Check Addition of noninformation bits to a message in order to detect any changes in the original bit structure from the time it leaves the sending device to the time it is received.

Parity Checking See **Checking, Parity.**

Passband A fixed frequency range that is contained within a wider frequency band.

Path Control (PC) Network In Systems Network Architecture (SNA), the part that includes the data link control and path control layers.

PBX Private Branch eXchange. Telephone switch located at a customer's site that primarily establishes voice communications over tie lines or circuits as well as between individual users and the switched telephone network.

Typically, also provides switching within a customer site and usually offers numerous other enhanced features, such as least-cost routing and call detail recording; also called PABX for private automatic branch exchange and CBX for computerized branch exchange.

PC Personal Computer. Microcomputers often are referred to as PCs after IBM's early model called a PC. Today it may refer specifically to IBM or compatibles, or generally to any microcomputer. Should not be confused with Path Control (PC) Network.

PCM See **Pulse Code Modulation.**

PCN See **Personal Communication Network.**

PDM See **Pulse Duration Modulation.**

PDN See **Public Data Network.**

Peer A dictionary definition of peer is, "A person who is equal to another in abilities." A peer-to-peer network, therefore, is one in which each microcomputer node has equal abilities. In communications a peer is a node or station that is on the same protocol layer as another.

Peer-to-Peer Communications

1. Communication between two or more processes or programs by which both ends of the session exchange data with equal privilege.

2. Communication between two or more network nodes in which either side can initiate sessions because no primary-secondary relationship exists.

Peer-to-Peer Local Area Network A network in which a microcomputer can serve as both a server and a user. Every microcomputer has access to all the network's resources on an equal basis.

Permanent Virtual Circuit A virtual circuit that resembles a lease line because it can be dedicated to a single user. Its connections are controlled by software.

Permissive Connection Relates to the sending of *nonvoice* information (low speed data and facsimile) over the *voice* communication network. Consequently, the quality of transmission is good as long as the transmission is within the normal voice range of frequencies and conditioning. See also **Programmable Connection** or **RJ-45.**

Personal Communication Network (PCN)   A network using a wireless digital technology that can support both voice and data communications, as well as advanced network capabilities like Signaling System 7 (SS7). Unlike traditional cellular telephone service, PCN is a complete network architecture that replaces the local loop between homes or businesses and the regional BOC end office. Instead of the regional BOC receiving a monthly fee for the telephone service, the PCN operator receives the fee. PCNs compete directly with the regional Bell Operating Companies that control the local loops. If a long distance carrier like AT&T offers PCN service, it can be tied into that common carrier's long distance network.

Phase Modulation   See **Modulation, Phase.**

Photon   The fundamental unit of light and other forms of electromagnetic energy. Photons are to optical fibers what electrons are to copper wires; like electrons, they have a wave motion.

Phreaker   A person who wants to circumvent the telephone system to make free calls.

Physical Sharing   Refers to one microcomputer sharing a device attached to another microcomputer.

Physical Unit (PU)   In Systems Network Architecture (SNA), the component that manages and monitors the resources (such as attached links and adjacent link stations) of a node, as requested by a system services control point (SSCP) via a SSCP-PU session. Each node of a SNA network contains a physical unit.

Physical Unit Control Point (PUCP)   In Systems Network Architecture (SNA), a component that provides a subset of system services control point (SSCP) functions for activating the phys-

ical unit (PU) within its node and its local link resources. Each peripheral node and each subarea node without a SSCP contains a PUCP.

Picosecond   One trillionth (1/1,000,000,000,000) of a second or 10^{-12}.

Pirate   A person who obtains the latest software programs without paying for them. A skilled software pirate is able to break the protection scheme that is designed to prevent copying.

Point of Presence (POP)   Since divestiture, refers to the physical access location within a local access transport area (LATA) of a long distance or interLATA common carrier. The point to which the local telephone company terminates subscribers' circuits for long distance dial-up or leased line communications.

Point to Point   Denoting a channel, circuit, or line that has only two terminals. A link. An example is a single microcomputer connected to a mainframe.

Polling   Any procedure that sequentially queries several terminals in a network.

Polling, Hub Go-Ahead   A type of sequential polling in which the polling device contacts a terminal, that terminal contacts the next terminal, and so on until all the terminals have been contacted.

Polling, Roll Call   Polling accomplished from a prespecified list in a fixed sequence, with polling restarted when the list is completed.

Polynomial Checking   See **Checking, Polynomial.**

POP   See **Point of Presence.**

Port   One of the circuit connection points on a front end processor or local intelligent controller.

Postal Telephone and Telegraph   See **PTT.**

PPM   See **Pulse Position Modulation.**

Preamble   A sequence of encoded bits that is transmitted before each frame to allow synchronization of clocks and other circuitry at other sites on the channel. In the Ethernet specification the preamble is 64 bits.

Primary Access Service In ISDN, twenty-three 64,000 bits per second D channels for data and one 64,000 bits per second B channel for signaling (23 B + D). See also **Basic Access Service.**

Primary Rate See **Primary Access Service.**

Private Automatic Branch Exchange See **PBX.**

Private Branch Exchange See **PBX.**

Private Leased Circuit A leased communication circuit that goes from your premises to some other location. It is a clear unbroken communication path that is yours to use 24 hours per day, seven days per week.

PRMD PRivate Management Domain. The X.400 electronic mail standard defines public and private domains. Public domains are administered by the common carriers, and private domains correspond to corporate electronic mail systems. The part of the mail exchange administered by the private domain is called the private management domain.

Programmable Connection Relates to the sending of data over circuits. See also **Permissive Connection** or **RJ-11.**

Propagation Delay The time necessary for a signal to travel from one point on the circuit to another, such as from a satellite dish up to a satellite or from Los Angeles to New York.

Protocol A formal set of conventions governing the format and control of inputs and outputs between two communicating devices. This includes the rules by which these two devices communicate as well as handshaking and line discipline.

Protocol Converter A hardware device that changes the protocol of one vendor to the protocol of another. For example, if you want to connect an IBM data communication network to a Honeywell data communication network, the protocol converter converts the message formats so they are compatible. It is similar to

a person who translates between French and English for two people who do not speak one another's language.

PSN See **Packet Switching Network.**

PTT Postal Telephone and Telegraph. These are the common carriers owned by governments; the government is the sole or monopoly supplier of communication facilities.

PU See **Physical Unit.**

Public Data Network (PDN) A network established and operated for the specific purpose of providing data transmission services to the public. It can be a public packet switched network or a circuit switched network. Public data networks normally offer value added services for resource sharing at reduced costs and with high reliability. These timesharing networks are available to anyone with a modem.

Public Switched Digital Service (PSDS) A Bell Operating Company dial-up service using full duplex, 56,000 bits per second digital circuits on an end-to-end basis. The circuit switched digital capability known as ACCUNET Switched 56 is AT&T's counterpart.

PUC Public Utility Commission. The state regulatory agency responsible for overseeing intrastate communications. There is one PUC in each of the 50 states.

PUCP See **Physical Unit Control Point.**

Pulse A brief change of current or voltage produced in a circuit to operate a switch or relay or which can be detected by a logic circuit.

Pulse Amplitude Modulation (PAM) Amplitude modulation of a pulse carrier.

Pulse Code Modulation (PCM) Representation of a speech signal sine wave by sampling at a regular rate and converting each sample to a binary number (see Figure 5-21). In PCM, the information signals are sampled at regular intervals and a series of pulses in coded form are transmitted, representing the amplitude of the information signal at that time.

Pulse Duration Modulation (PDM)   Pulse width modulation. A form of pulse modulation in which the durations of pulses are varied.

Pulse Modulation   The modulation of the characteristics of a series of pulses in one of several ways (see Figure 5-20) to represent the information-bearing signal. Typical methods involve modifying the amplitude (PAM), width or duration (PDM), or position (PPM). The most common pulse modulation technique in telephone work is pulse code modulation (PCM).

Pulse Position Modulation (PPM)   A form of pulse modulation in which the positions in time of pulses are varied, without their duration being modified.

QAM, QSAM   Quadrature Amplitude Modulation, Quadrature Sideband Amplitude Modulation. A sophisticated modulation technique that uses variations in signal amplitude, which allows data-encoded symbols to be represented as any of 16 or 32 different states.

QTAM   Queued Telecommunications Access Method. One of IBM's older telecommunication access programs. Replaced by TCAM.

Queue   A line of items.

1. In data communications, there are message input queues, output queues, and various other queues when the network cannot handle all the arriving transactions.

2. In telephony, this feature allows calls to be "held" or delayed at the originating switch while waiting for a trunk to become available.

RAM   Random Access Memory. A type of computer memory where information can be stored and retrieved by the computer in miscellaneous order without disturbing adjacent memory cells. See also **ROM.**

Rate Center   A defined geographic point used by telephone companies in determining distance measurements for interLATA or intra-LATA mileage rates. Basically, this is a central or end office.

RBOC   Regional Bell Operating Company. One of the seven companies created after divestiture of the old Bell system to provide local communications. Includes Ameritech, Bell Atlantic, BellSouth, NYNEX, Pacific Telesis, Southwestern Bell, and US West.

RDC   See **Concentrator.**

Real Time   The entry of information into a network from a terminal that results in the immediate processing of the task.

Reclocking Time   See **Turnaround Time.**

Redundancy   The portion of the total information contained in a message that can be eliminated without loss of essential information.

Reliability   A characteristic of the equipment, software, or network that relates to the integrity of the system against failure. Reliability usually is measured in terms of Mean Time Between Failures (MTBF), the statistical measure of the interval between successive failures of the hardware or software under consideration.

Remote Data Concentrator   See **Concentrator.**

Remote Jack   See **RJ-11** and **RJ-45.**

Remote Job Entry (RJE)   Submission of jobs (that is, computer production tasks) through an input unit (terminal) that has access to a computer through data communication facilities.

Repeater   A device used to boost the strength of a signal. Repeaters are spaced at intervals throughout the length of a communication circuit. Also called an *amplifier.*

REQUEST TO SEND   See **RTS.**

Resistance   The amount of opposition to the flow of the carrier wave or signal moving down the circuit.

Response Time   The time the system takes to react to a given input. If a message is keyed into a terminal by an operator and the reply from the computer arrives and is typed at the same terminal, response time may be defined as the time interval between the operator's pressing the last key and the terminal's typing the first letter of the reply. Response time thus defined includes (1) transmission time to the computer; (2) processing time at the computer, including access time to obtain any file records needed to answer the inquiry; and (3) transmission time back to the terminal.

Retrain Time See **Turnaround Time.**

Reverse Channel A feature of certain modems that allows simultaneous transmission (usually of control or parity information) from the receiver to the transmitter over a half duplex data transmission network. Generally, the reverse channel is a low speed channel ranging from 10 to 50 bits per second.

Ring

1. The hot wire in a telephone circuit.

2. An audible sound used for signaling the recipient of an incoming telephone call.

3. A local area network topology having a logical geometric arrangement in the shape of a ring.

Risk The level or amount of exposure to an item when compared with other items. It is a hazard or chance of loss. Risk is the degree of difference as in, ''What level of risk does one threat have when compared to the other threats?''

Risk Assessment The process by which one identifies threats, uses a methodology to determine the tangible or intangible exposures, and develops a sequenced list of the threats from the one having the highest risk to the one having the lowest risk. The list may be in a sequence based on tangible dollar losses or on intangible criteria such as public embarrassment, likelihood of occurrence, most dangerous, most critical to the organization, and greatest delay. Also called *risk ranking* or *risk analysis.*

RJ-XX Registered Jack or Remote Jack, as in RJ-11 or RJ-45.

RJ-11 A modular telephone plug. It is the plug on your home telephone and is called a per-

missive connection (see Chapter 4, under Line Protectors) by the telephone company. Although it generally is used on two-wire circuits, it can be used on four-wire circuits.

RJ-45 A modular telephone plug similar to the RJ-11 plug, except that it is called a programmable connection and generally is used on four-wire circuits.

RJE See **Remote Job Entry.**

RMON The definitions of what is stored and, therefore, retrievable from a remote user microcomputer when using the Simple Network Management Protocol (SNMP). It is referred to as the RMON MIB (management information base). See also **Management Information Base** and **Simple Network Management Protocol.**

ROM Read Only Memory. A data storage device, the contents of which cannot be altered, except under certain circumstances. Storage in which writing over is prevented. Also, permanent storage. See also **RAM.**

Rotary Hunt An arrangement that allows calls placed to seek an idle circuit in a prearranged multichannel group. If the dialed line is busy, the call finds the next open line to establish a through channel.

Rotary Switching System An automatic telephone switching system that generally has the following features.

1. The selecting mechanisms are rotary switches.

2. The switching pulses are received and stored by controlling mechanisms that govern the subsequent operations necessary to establish a telephone connection.

Router A device that connects two similar networks having the same protocol. It also chooses the best route between two networks when there are multiple paths between them. Compare with **Bridge, Brouter,** and **Gateway.**

RS232 A technical specification published by the Electronic Industries Association that specifies the mechanical and electrical characteristics of the interface for connecting data terminal equipment (DTE) and data circuit terminating equipment (DCE). It defines interface circuit functions and their corresponding connector pin assignments. See also **DB-25.**

RS422   A standard operating in conjunction with RS449 that specifies electrical characteristics for balanced circuits (circuits with their own ground leads).

RS423   A standard operating in conjunction with RS449 that specifies electrical characteristics for unbalanced circuits (circuits using common or shared grounding techniques).

RS449   An Electronic Industries Association standard for data terminal equipment (DTE) and data circuit terminating equipment (DCE) connection which specifies interface requirements for expanded transmission speeds (up to 2 million bits per second), longer cable lengths, and ten additional functions. The physical connection between DTE and DCE is made through a 37-pin connector; a separate 9-pin connector is specified to service secondary channel interchange circuits when used.

RTS   REQUEST TO SEND. A RS232 control signal between a modem and user digital equipment that initiates the data transmission sequence in a communication circuit.

Sag   A sudden decrease of electrical power on a 120-volt electrical power line.

Satellite   See **Geosynchronous Orbit.**

Satellite Microwave Radio   Microwave or beam radio system using geosynchronously orbiting communication satellites.

Satisfice   To choose a particular level of performance for which to strive and for which management is willing to settle.

SC   See **Session Control.**

SDLC   See **Synchronous Data Link Control.**

Serial

1. Pertaining to transmitting bits one at a time and in sequence.

2. Pertaining to the sequential or consecutive occurrence of two or more related activities in a single device or channel.

3. Pertaining to the sequential processing of the individual part of the whole, such as the bits of a character, or the characters of a word using the same facilities for successive parts.

Server   A microcomputer that provides a particular service to the other user or client microcomputers on the local area network. In larger LANs, the server is dedicated to being a server. In a peer-to-peer LAN, the server may be both a server and a user microcomputer. There may be file, database, network, access, modem, facsimile, printer, and gateway servers.

Session   A logical connection between two terminals. This is the part of the message transmission when the two parties are exchanging messages. It takes place after the communication circuit has been set up and is functioning.

Session Control (SC)   In Systems Network Architecture (SNA), one of the components of transmission control. Session control is used to purge data flowing in a session after an unrecoverable error occurs, to resynchronize the data flow after such an error, and to perform cryptographic verification.

Shelfware   A slang term for a computer program that is purchased but never installed. It sits on a shelf unused. Compare with **Firmware, Hardware, Software,** and **Vaporware.**

SIG   Special Interest Group. Many professional organizations have SIGs for members with special interests, and most computer clubs also have SIGs to support users with special needs.

Signal   A signal is something that is sent over a communication circuit. It might be a control signal used by the network to control itself.

Signal-to-Noise Ratio   The ratio, expressed in dB, of the usable signal to the noise signal present.

Signaling Supplying and interpreting the supervisory and address signals needed to perform switching and other operations.

Signaling System 7 (SS7) A signaling protocol that uses destination routing, 8-bit fields, variable length messages, and a maximum message length of 256 bytes of data. In addition, flow control, connectionless services, ISDN capabilities, very fast call setup via high speed circuit-switched connections, the ability to tell who is calling, and remote database interactions are part of SS7.

Simple Network Management Protocol (SNMP) A protocol used in network management for monitoring and configuring network devices. See also **Management Information Base** and **RMON.**

Simplex A circuit capable of transmission in one direction only. Contrast with **Full Duplex** and **Half Duplex.**

Sine Wave A continuous analog waveform of a single frequency having a constant amplitude and phase. See Figure 2-5.

Single Cable A one-cable system in broadband local area networks in which a portion of the bandwidth is allocated for ''send'' signals and a portion for ''receive'' signals, with a guardband in between to provide isolation from interference.

SMDR See **Station Message Detail Recording.**

SMDS Switched multimegabit data service. An alternative to private network data transmission within the LATA areas (intraLATA) in which Bell Operating Companies operate. The aim of the BOCs is to use SMDS for interconnecting local area networks. For example, SMDS allows users to have Ethernet-to-Ethernet or token ring-to-token ring interconnection between two LANs at speeds of T-1 circuits or 1,544,000 bits per second. With SMDS, each corporate regional site requires only one circuit to connect to the BOC end office because messages on that circuit can be switched to the single circuit that goes from the BOC's end office to the organization's headquarters. Prior to SMDS, organizations had six incoming T-1 circuits to the central headquarters if they wanted to connect to six different regional offices.

SMT The station management for the control and management of a fiber optic FDDI network. SMT deals with both the control of local hardware (terminal) and other information about the station parameters and operating conditions. It can do this because information about the MAC (token), the physical layer (OSI model layer 1), and the remote station operation can be passed between stations in the form of a SMT frame.

SN See **Switching Node.**

SNA See **Systems Network Architecture.**

SNA Network In Systems Network Architecture (SNA), the part of a user application network that conforms to the formats and protocols of SNA. It enables transfer of data among end users and provides protocols for controlling the resources of various network configurations. The SNA network consists of network addressable units (NAUs), boundary function components, and the path control network.

SNMP See **Simple Network Management Protocol.**

SNR See **Signal-to-Noise Ratio.**

Software A generic, somewhat slang term for a computer program. Sometimes taken to include documentation and procedures associated with such programs. Compare with **Firmware, Hardware, Shelfware,** and **Vaporware.**

Software Defined Network (SDN) Built on public packet switched networks using virtual circuits instead of the normal physical voice grade circuit. Customer routing information is stored in switch memories so SDNs can operate like lease circuits.

SOH A control character used in ASCII and EBCDIC data communications to indicate start of header or the beginning of the control characters in a data block.

SONET   See **Synchronous Optical Network.**

Special Common Carrier   An organization other than the public telephone companies, registered to sell or lease communication facilities.

Spike   A sudden increase of electrical power on a communication circuit. Spike is a term used in the communication industry. Contrast with **Surge.**

Spread Spectrum   The U.S. military developed spread spectrum through-the-air radio transmission technology primarily to overcome the problem of intentional interference by hostile jamming and secondarily for security. A spread spectrum signal is created by modulating the original transmitted radio frequency (RF) signal with a spreading code that causes "hopping" of the frequency from one frequency to another. By contrast, conventional AM and FM radio uses only one frequency to transmit its signal. Several spread spectrum transmissions can use the same frequency band, provided that each one uses a different spreading code to reduce interference between the multiple transmissions. Only the receiver with the same spreading code as the one used by the transmitter can reassemble the incoming "noise-like" signal into a meaningful message. Some military systems "hop" (change) the frequency thousands of times each second.

The traditional way for multiple users to share the same bandwidth on a through-the-air transmission is to transmit by using a single unique frequency. In spread spectrum, many users can transmit simultaneously over the same bandwidth by using a transmission technique called *code division multiple access* (CDMA). CDMA allows more users to transmit simultaneously over a fixed bandwidth than either time division multiplexing (TDM) or frequency division multiplexing (FDM). Moreover, CDMA tolerates a higher level of interference than either TDM or FDM be-

cause it uses a unique frequency for only a few thousandths of a second before hopping to another frequency. Whereas cellular telephones use a single unique frequency, personal communication networks (PCNs) use spread spectrum because "hopping" allows more simultaneous users to use the same fixed bandwidth than does single frequency assignment.

SQL   Structured Query Language. A language for interrogating, processing, and storing data in a relational database. It is a database management system.

SSCP   System Services Control Point. Part of the Systems Network Architecture (SNA).

SSCP-LU Session   In Systems Network Architecture (SNA), a session between a system services control point (SSCP) and a logical unit (LU); the session enables the LU to request the SSCP to help initiate a LU-LU session.

SSCP-PU Session   In Systems Network Architecture (SNA), a session between a system services control point (SSCP) and a physical unit (PU); SSCP-PU sessions allow SSCPs to send requests to and receive status information from individual nodes to control the network configuration.

SSCP Services   In Systems Network Architecture (SNA), the components within a system services control point (SSCP) that provide configuration, maintenance, management, network, and session services for SSCP-LU, SSCP-PU, and SSCP-SSCP sessions.

SSCP-SSCP Session   In Systems Network Architecture (SNA), a session between the system services control point (SSCP) in one domain and the SSCP in another domain. An SSCP-SSCP session is used to initiate and terminate cross-domain LU-LU sessions.

Start Bit   A bit that precedes the group of bits representing a character. Used to signal the arrival of the character in asynchronous transmission.

Start-Stop (Signaling)   Asynchronous signaling in which each group of code elements corresponding to a character is preceded by a start signal that serves to prepare the receiving mechanism for the reception and registration of the character, and is followed by a stop signal that serves to bring the receiving mechanism to rest in preparation for the reception of the next character. Contrast with **Synchronous Transmission.**

Station   One of the input or output points on a network. Also called a *node*.

Station Message Detail Recording (SMDR)   A private branch exchange (PBX) feature to keep track of telephone call costs so they can be charged to the proper department. Also called *call detail recording (CDR)*.

Station Terminal   The plug supplied by the common carrier into which the modem plugs.

Statistical Multiplexer   Or stat mux or STDM. A time division multiplexer (TDM) that dynamically allocates communication circuit time to each of the various attached terminals, according to whether a terminal is active or inactive at a particular moment. Buffering and queuing functions also are included. See also **Concentrator.**

Stop Bit   A bit that follows the group of bits representing a character. Used to signal the end of a character in asynchronous transmission.

Store and Forward   A data communication technique that accepts messages or transactions, stores them, and then forwards them to the next location or person as addressed in the message header.

STX   A control character used in ASCII and EBCDIC data communications to mean start of text.

Superconductor   A material that conducts electricity without resistance. Expected to be able to transmit data 100 times faster than fiber optics if they can be made to work at room temperature.

Supergroup   A frequency division multiplexer (FDM) carrier multiplexing level containing 60 voice frequency channels. It is the assembly of five 12-channel groups occupying adjacent bands in the spectrum for the purpose of simultaneous modulation and demodulation. Compare with **Jumbo Group** and **Master Group.**

Surge   A sudden increase in voltage on a 120-volt electrical power line. A term used in the electric utilities industry. Contrast with **Spike.**

Switch Hook   The switch on the telephone instrument that activates the circuit when the handset is picked up (off-hook) and breaks the circuit when the handset is placed back onto the telephone instrument (on-hook). Derived from the old wall-mounted, hand-cranked telephones that had a ''hook'' to hold the handset when it was not in use.

Switchboard   Equipment on which switching operations are performed by operators. See also **PBX.**

Switched Circuit   A dial-up circuit in which the communication path is established by dialing. If the entire circuit path is unavailable, you get a busy signal, which prevents completion of the circuit connection.

Switched Multimegabit Data Service   See **SMDS.**

Switched Network   Any network that has switches used for directing messages from the sender to the ultimate recipient.

Switched Network, Circuit Switched   A switched network in which switching is accomplished by disconnecting and reconnecting lines in different configurations to set up a continuous pathway between the sender and the recipient. See also **Circuit Switching.**

Switched Network, Store and Forward   A switched network in which the store and forward principle is used to handle transmission between senders and recipients. See also **Store and Forward.**

Switching Identifying and connecting independent transmission links to form a continuous path from one location to another.

Switching Node (SN) The intelligent interface point where your equipment is connected to a public packet switching network. The switching node is a type of front end, but its primary purpose is packetizing, routing, and scheduling on the packet switching network.

SYN An 8-bit control character that is sent at the beginning of a message block to establish synchronization (timing) between the sender and the receiver.

Synchronize To agree to work together at the same rate or to coincide in time.

Synchronous Data Link Control (SDLC) A protocol for managing synchronous, code-transparent, serial bit-by-bit information transfer over a link connection. Transmission exchanges may be full duplex or half duplex and over switched or nonswitched links. The configurations of the link connection may be point to point, multipoint, or loop. SDLC is the protocol used in IBM's Systems Network Architecture.

Synchronous Optical Network (SONET) The National Exchange Carriers Association standard for optical transmission at gigabits per second speeds. For example, digital signals transmit on T-1 circuits at 1,544,000 bits per second and on T-3 circuits at 44,376,000 bits per second. The slowest SONET OC-1 optical transmission rate of 51,840,000 bits per second is slightly faster than the T-3 rate.

Synchronous Transmission Form of transmission in which data is sent as a fixed-length block or frame.

System Level Control A control that, once implemented, affects *all* applications using the computer, database, or network containing the control.

System Services Control Point (SSCP) Within Systems Network Architecture (SNA), a focal point for managing the configuration, coordinating network operator and problem determination requests, and providing directory support and other session services for end users of the network. Multiple SSCPs, cooperating with one another as peers, can divide the network into domains of control, with each SSCP having a hierarchical control relationship to the physical units and logical units within its own domain. See also **SSCP** entries.

Systems Network Architecture (SNA) The name of IBM's conceptual framework that defines the data communication interaction between computer systems or terminals.

T Carrier A hierarchy of digital circuits designed to carry speech and other signals in digital form. Designated T-1, T-2, T-3, and T-4.

T-1 Circuit A 1,544,000 bits per second digital transmission circuit developed by AT&T.

T-2 Circuit A 6,312,000 bits per second transmission circuit. It is equal to a bundle of four T-1 circuits, or it has four times the bandwidth of a T-1 circuit.

T-3 Circuit A 44,736,000 bits per second transmission circuit. It is equal to a bundle of 28 T-1 circuits. Often referred to as a *45-megabit channel*.

T-4 Circuit A 274,176,000 bits per second transmission circuit. It is equal to a bundle of 178 T-1 circuits and can carry 4,032 simultaneous voice telephone calls.

Tandem Office The high level switching and control facility set up by the local telephone company (common carrier) to which calls originating on the subscriber's local loop are connected from the end office via tandem trunk circuits. Calls made within the purview of the tandem office are outside of the local calling area, but still within the same area code as the end office, and these are referred to as "unit calls." The tandem office is in the middle of the dial-up network hierarchy (see Figure 2-4). Compare with **Central Office** and **Toll Office.**

Tap

1. In baseband, the component or connector that attaches a transceiver to a cable.

2. In broadband, a passive device used to remove a portion of the signal power from the distribution line and deliver it onto the drop line. Also called a *directional tap* or a *multidrop*.

3. In security, unauthorized and illegal access to a network circuit. It involves placing a "tap" or an illegal connection on a communication circuit.

Tariff   The formal schedule of rates and regulations pertaining to the communication services, equipment, and facilities that constitute the contract between the user and the common carrier. Tariffs are filed with the appropriate regulatory agency (FCC or state PUC) for approval and published when approved.

TASI   Time Assisted Speech Interpolation. The process of interleaving two or more voice calls on the same telephone circuit simultaneously.

TCAM   Telecommunications Access Method. One of IBM's telecommunication access software packages. It replaces and extends the older QTAM.

TCP/IP   Transmission Control Protocol/Internet Protocol. Probably the oldest networking standard, developed for ARPANET. It is a reasonably efficient file transfer protocol that permits the sending of large files over sometimes unreliable networks with assurance they will not be corrupted while being transmitted.

TDM   See **Multiplexer.**

Telecommunication Access Programs   The software programs (usually located in the front end processor) that handle all tasks associated with the routing, scheduling, and movement of messages between remote terminal sites and the central host computer.

Telecommunication Monitors   See **Teleprocessing Monitors.**

Telecommunications   A term encompassing voice, data, and image transmissions that are sent over some medium in the form of coded signals.

Telenet   General Telephone and Electronics' (GTE) public packet switching network.

Telephony   A generic term to describe voice communications.

Teleprocessing   Remote access data processing in which a data communication link is used to accomplish a computer-based task.

Teleprocessing Monitors   A set of software programs (usually located in the host computer) that handle the various tasks required for incoming and outgoing messages. For example, the teleprocessing monitor builds the input/ output queues of messages in the host computer and relieves the computer's operating system of many tasks related to the data communication network.

10Base-T   An Ethernet local area network standard (IEEE 802.3) that runs at 10 million bits per second, uses unshielded twisted pair wires, does not specify the distance between nodes, and uses a star topology.

10Base2   An Ethernet local area network standard that runs at 10 million bits per second, uses baseband transmission techniques, and allows 200 meters maximum cable length.

10Base5   An Ethernet local area network standard that runs at 10 million bits per second, uses baseband transmission techniques, and allows 500 meters maximum cable length.

10Broad36   An Ethernet local area network that runs at 10 million bits per second, uses broadband transmission techniques, and allows 3,600 meters maximum cable length.

Terminal Controller   See **Cluster Controller.**

Thick Ethernet   Refers to the original Ethernet specification that uses thick coaxial cable that is both grounded and shielded. The many layers of shielding are of polyvinyl and aluminum, which make the cable wider in diameter than other Ethernet cables. The heavy shielding also makes the cable more expensive and less flexible; therefore, it is impractical for many installations.

Thin Ethernet   Refers to the 10Base2 baseband Ethernet, meaning the version that transmits at 10 million bits per second in baseband at 200 meters maximum. It uses thin coaxial cable. Also called *Cheapernet.*

Threat   A potentially adverse occurrence or unwanted event that could be injurious to the network, the EDP environment, the organization, or a business application. Threats are acts or events the organization wants to prevent from taking place, such as lost data, theft, disasters, virus infections, errors, illegal access, and unauthorized disclosure. In other words, threats are events we do not want to occur.

Throughput   The total amount of useful information that is processed or communicated during a specific time period.

Tie Line   A leased or private dedicated telephone circuit that links two points together without using the switched telephone network. Same as **Point to Point.**

Time Assisted Speech Interpolation   See **TASI.**

Time Division Multiplexing (TDM)   See **Multiplexer.**

Tip

1. The end of the plug that completes a circuit in a manual switchboard. It serves as the positive power source for the station because it is connected directly to the common battery (direct current—dc electricity).

2. In terminal interface processing, a term used by packet switching companies to designate the piece of equipment that accepts data from outlying terminals and reformats it into network language for transmission.

3. The ground wire in a telephone circuit.

Token   The special sequence of characters used to gain access to a token-ring or token-bus network in order to transmit a packet.

Token Bus   A local area network with a bus topology that uses a token-passing approach to network access. In a token-bus LAN, the next logical node or station is not necessarily the next physical node because it uses preassigned priority algorithms. Message requests are not handled in consecutive order by stations. Contrast with **Token Ring.**

Token Passing   A method of allocating network access wherein a terminal can send a message only after it has acquired the network's electronic token.

Token Ring   A local area network with a ring topology that uses a token-passing approach to network access. In a token-ring LAN the next logical station also is the next physical station because the token passes from node to node. Contrast with **Token Bus.**

Toll Office   Where the calls going outside of the area code make their connection to go out. Calls made through a toll office are "long distance calls." Compare with **End Office** and **Tandem Office.**

TOP   Technical and Office Protocol. A model used with the Manufacturing Automation Protocol (MAP) to create a local area network in which both manufacturing and office functions are integrated.

Topology

1. The basic physical or geometric arrangement of the network, for example, a ring, star, or bus layout. The topology is the network's logical arrangement, but it is influenced by the physical connections of its links and nodes. This is in contrast to its configuration, which is the actual or practical layout, including software and hardware constraints. Topologies are the building blocks of a network configuration. Compare with **Configuration.**

2. The electrical topology can be different from the physical topology; for example,

the electrical topology can be a bus with the physical topology a star. The electrical topology is how the signal passes from station to station, whereas the physical topology is how the wiring connects the stations together.

TPA Transient Program Area. The area in random access memory (RAM) where application programs and data are stored in the microcomputer.

Transceiver A device that transmits and/or receives data to or from microcomputer workstations on a local area network. See also **Medium Access Unit, Multistation Access Unit,** or **Communication Interface Unit.**

Transmission Rate of Information Bits See **TRIB.**

Tree A network arrangement in which the stations hang off a common "branch," or data bus, like leaves on the branch of a tree.

TRIB Transmission Rate of Information Bits. A TRIB is the network's throughput. It is the effective rate of data transfer over a communication circuit per unit of time. Usually expressed in bits per second.

Trunk A voice communication channel between switching devices or end offices.

Turnaround Time The time required to reverse the direction of transmission from send to receive or vice versa on a half duplex circuit.

Twisted Pair A pair of wires used in standard telephone wiring. The wires are insulated copper conductors that are twisted around each other. Twisted pairs are placed together in a bundle of thousands of twisted pairs to form cables. They are twisted to reduce interference caused by the other twisted pairs in the same cable bundle. Twisted pair wires go from homes and offices to the telephone company end office. They are shielded if they have an outside wraparound conductor, and they are unshielded if they do not have this outside conductor.

Two-Wire Circuit A circuit formed by two conductors insulated from each other. It is possible to use the two conductors as a one-way transmission path, as a half duplex path, or as a full duplex path with special multiplexing hardware. Compare with **Four-Wire Circuit.**

Tymnet British Telecom's public packet switching network.

UA User Agent. In the X.400 electronic mail standard, the user agent allows a user to create a message, provides a recipient address, and receives messages on behalf of users.

UART See **Universal Asynchronous Receiver and Transmitter.**

Unbalanced The state of impedance on a two-wire circuit when both circuits are not evenly grounded.

Uninterruptible Power Supply (UPS) Provides backup electrical power if the normal electrical power fails or if the voltage drops to unacceptably low levels.

Universal Asynchronous Receiver and Transmitter (UART) A circuit chip that serializes the stream of data bits for the COM1 and COM2 serial ports so they can transmit data. The UART chip handles asynchronous communications. Compare with **Universal Synchronous Asynchronous Receiver and Transmitter (USART).**

Universal Synchronous Asynchronous Receiver and Transmitter (USART) A circuit chip that handles both synchronous and asynchronous communications. It may be incorporated on a serial interface card, which may be an optional accessory for a microcomputer, or it may be built into the microcomputer. Compare with **Universal Asynchronous Receiver and Transmitter.**

Unix A versatile operating system developed at AT&T Bell Laboratories. May be used to run microcomputers, minicomputers, and host mainframes for a wide range of tasks, including multiuser systems and local area networks. Compare with **DOS.**

Unshielded Twisted Pair Wires (UTP) The type of wiring used in 10Base-T Ethernet networks. Same as *twisted pair*.

Upload The process of loading software and data from the nodes of a network (terminals or microcomputers), over the network media, and to the host mainframe computer.

UPS See **Uninterruptible Power Supply.**

USART See **Universal Synchronous Asynchronous Receiver and Transmitter.**

USASCII See **ASCII.**

User Microcomputer The microcomputer on a LAN that uses the resources of the server microcomputer, such as the printer or disk drive. Also called a *client microcomputer*.

UTP See **Unshielded Twisted Pair Wires.**

V.nn The V.*nn* series of Consultative Committee on International Telegraph and Telephone standards relating to the connection of digital equipment to the analog telephone network. Primarily concerned with the modem interface. See the last section of Chapter 9 for a list of the more important V.*nn* standards.

V.32, V.32bis CCITT standards for modem communications. V.32 covers speeds up to 9,600 bits per second, and V.32bis covers speeds up to 14,400 bits per second.

V.42, V.42bis CCITT standards for modem communications. V.42 covers error correction, and V.42bis covers data compression by V.32 modems.

Value Added Common Carrier A corporation that sells services of a value added network. Such a network is built using the communication offerings of traditional common carriers, connected to computers that permit new types of telecommunication tariffs to be offered. The network may be a packet switching or message switching network.

VAN See **Value Added Common Carrier.**

Vaporware A slang term for computer programs or computer program upgrades that are announced to the news media, but that never appear in the marketplace or are so late it appears they will not materialize. Compare with **Firmware, Hardware, Shelfware,** and **Software.**

VDT Video Display Terminal. Compare with **CRT** and **VDU.**

VDU Video Display Unit. Commonly refers to a video monitor that uses a cathode ray tube (CRT), liquid crystal display (LCD), or plasma display for displaying data on its screen. Also called *VDT* (video display terminal).

Vertical Redundancy Checking See **Parity Check.**

Videotex A two-way dialogue through a television set to a central site that offers various services in the home.

Virtual Conceptual or appearing to be, rather than actually being.

Virtual Circuit A temporary transmission path (circuit) in which sequential data packets are routed between two points. It is created by the software in such a way that users think they have a dedicated point-to-point leased circuit.

Virtual Private Network (VPN) A hybrid network that includes both public and private facilities. The user leases a bundle of circuits and configures the VPN on an as-needed basis so that some traffic travels on the private leased network and some travels on the common carrier's public network.

Virtual Storage A computer user may employ a computer as though it has a much larger memory than its real memory. The difference is made up by software rapidly moving pages in and out, to and from a backing store. The apparent memory the user can employ is called *virtual memory*.

Virtual Terminal A terminal defined as a standard on a network that can handle diverse terminals. Signals to and from each nonstandard terminal are converted to equivalent standard terminal signals by an interface computer. The network protocols then operate as though all terminals were the standard ''virtual'' terminals.

Voice Grade A telecommunication link with a bandwidth (about 4 KHz) appropriate to an audio telephone line.

Voice Grade Circuit A term that applies to channels suitable for transmission of speech, digital or analog data, or facsimile, generally with a frequency range of about 300 to 3300 hertz contained within a 4000 hertz channel.

VPN See **Virtual Private Network.**

VRC Vertical Redundancy Check. Same as **Parity Check.**

VTAM Virtual Telecommunications Access Method. One of IBM's more advanced telecommunication access software programs.

WAK Positive acknowledgment but stop sending. Contrast with **ACK** and **NAK.** It stands for Wait-Acknowledge.

Walk Time

1. The time required for the message to travel completely around a ring local area network.

2. The time to switch service from one queue to another when servicing messages.

WAN See **Wide Area Network**

WATS Wide Area Telephone Service. A special bulk rate service that allows direct dial inbound and outbound station-to-station calls. These are the area code numbers that start with 800 and are associated with toll-free dialing. Costs are based on hourly usage per WATS circuit and on distance-based bands, to and from which calls are placed.

Waveguide In microwave communications, a short (10 feet or less) conductive (metallic) tube that carries very high frequency microwave transmissions from the repeater/amplifier on the microwave tower to the dish antenna.

Wide Area Network (WAN) A network spanning a large geographical area. Its nodes can span city, state, or national boundaries. They typically use circuits provided by common carriers. Contrast with **Backbone Network, Local Area Network,** and **Metropolitan Area Network.**

Wideband Circuit The term applied to channels provided by common carriers which can transfer data at speeds from 19,200 to 2 million bits per second (19.2 KHz to 2000 KHz). Basically, any communication circuit that has a bandwidth greater than 4000 hertz.

Wire Center Same as **End Office.**

Wiring Closet Also called a Main Distribution Function (MDF). A central point at which all the circuits in a system begin or end, to allow cross-connection.

Word

1. In communications, a word transmitted over a circuit generally is assumed to be six characters (five plus a space). This hypothetical six-character word sometimes is used for estimating traffic volume when no actual data is available.

2. In computers, the word length depends on the microprocessor chip. It can be from one to four characters. An 8088 chip has a one-character word, an 80286 has a two-character word, and an 80386 or 80486 has a four-character word. One character is equal to eight bits.

Work Group A group of two or more individuals who need to share files and databases. Local area networks sometimes are designed around work groups to provide the sharing of files, programs, databases, or printers, and to promote interaction among the members of a particular work group.

Workstation Input/output equipment at which an operator works. A station in which a user can send data to, or receive data from, a computer for the purpose of performing a job. Usually a powerful microcomputer. Most workstations are much more powerful than the average microcomputer.

X.nn   The X.*nn* series of Consultative Committee on International Telegraph and Telephone standards relating to transmission over public data networks. See the last section of Chapter 9 for a list of the more important X.*nn* standards.

X.3   An international standard for the packet assembly/disassembly (PAD) facility in public packet networks. Approved by the CCITT.

X.25   An international standard for connecting computers to packet switched networks. It is a bit-oriented protocol specifying the structure, content, sequencing, and error handling of messages transmitted over packet switched networks. Approved by the CCITT.

X.75   An international standard for connecting two similar packet switched X.25 networks to one another. Often referred to as a X.75 gateway. Approved by the CCITT.

X.400   An OSI standard that defines how messages are to be encoded for the transmission of electronic mail and graphics between dissimilar computers and terminals. X.400 defines what is in an electronic address and what the electronic envelope should look like. The X.400 standards are a subset of, and conform to, the X.25 standard. Approved by the CCITT.

X.500   An OSI standard that defines where to find the address to put on the electronic envelope of a X.400 transmission. X.500 is the directory of names and addresses similar to the yellow pages of a telephone directory.

INDEX

I-1